MYTH

Myth

A NEW
SYMPOSIUM

EDITED BY

GREGORY SCHREMPP
AND WILLIAM HANSEN

INDIANA
University Press

Bloomington & Indianapolis

This book is a publication of

Indiana University Press
601 North Morton Street
Bloomington, IN 47404-3797 USA

http://iupress.indiana.edu

Telephone orders 800-842-6796
Fax orders 812-855-7931
Orders by e-mail iuporder@indiana.edu

© 2002 by Indiana University Press

The paper used in this publication meets the minimum
requirements of American National Standard for Information
Sciences—Permanence of Paper for Printed Library Materials,
ANSI Z39.48-1984.

Manufactured in the United States of America

Library of Congress Cataloging-in-Publication Data

Myth : a new symposium / edited by Gregory Schrempp and William Hansen.
p. cm.
Includes bibliographical references and index.
ISBN 0-253-34158-2 (alk. paper) — ISBN 0-253-21555-2 (pbk. : alk.
paper)
1. Myth—Congresses. I. Schrempp, Gregory Allen, date II. Hansen,
William F., date
BL312 .M98 2002
291.1'3—dc21
2002002518

1 2 3 4 5 07 06 05 04 03 02

CONTENTS

ACKNOWLEDGMENTS

Many offices and funds at Indiana University, Bloomington, lent support to the Symposium on Myth and to the editing of this volume of papers drawn from it. The editors express their heartfelt thanks to the Office of Summer Sessions and Special Programs, the Office of the Vice President and Chancellor, the College of Arts and Sciences, the Folklore Institute, the Office of Research and the University Graduate School, the Multidisciplinary Ventures and Seminars Fund, the Office of International Programs, the Richard M. Dorson Endowment Fund, and the Department of Folklore and Ethnomusicology. In addition, we are very grateful to Greg Nagy for help along the way.

MYTH

Introduction

GREGORY SCHREMPP

The problems presented by myths and tales will certainly not be finally
solved by this generation. We may be sure that a century from now students
will still be analyzing and trying to reach some kind of syntheses. . . . [I]t
would be interesting to look at all these matters through their eyes and to
see how our theories and ideas appear after a hundred years.

—Stith Thompson

W̲e have not yet traversed the hundred years that Thompson muses
upon in the closing lines of *Myth: A Symposium* (Sebeok 1965), but
we are nearing the halfway point of the journey. Several factors—the im-
pending midpoint, the continuing importance of *Myth: A Symposium* over
these years, and the round of retrospection and speculation prompted by
"millennial fever"—have conspired to suggest the idea of a new symposium
and volume organized in part for inventory-taking, with *Myth: A Symposium* as a point of reference. The present volume represents the fulfillment
of that idea. The earlier volume too bears an unmistakably retrospective
streak, for many of the contributions summarize the results of then long-
running theories and methods—for example, the historical geographic
method (Stith Thompson's "Myth and Folktales"); the myth/ritual school
(Lord Raglan's "Myth and Ritual" and Stanley Hyman's "The Ritual View
of Myth and the Mythic"); and solar mythology (approached with histo-
riographic empathy by Richard M. Dorson in "The Eclipse of Solar Mythology").

 Myth: A Symposium consists of nine essays, presented without additional comment.[1] The present volume, *Myth: A New Symposium,* contains
fifteen contributions organized into six sections, reflecting panels at the
conference that provided the venue for this new exchange of ideas about
myth.[2] Such organizational differences aside, *Myth: A New Symposium* follows its illustrious predecessor in striving for interdisciplinarity within dis-
cernible limits. Owing in part to their shared folkloristic slant,[3] both

collections emphasize close historical and ethnographic approaches and methods. While neither volume can claim to be a scientific sampling of the field or to represent all viable approaches to myth, the fact that the two collections tap into largely coterminous disciplinary traditions suggests that they might be usefully compared as indices of general trends of myth scholarship within these traditions. The comments that follow are offered in this spirit; rather than presenting thumbnail sketches of the various contributions, this introductory statement will draw upon the various contributions, juxtaposing them to those of *Myth: A Symposium*, to offer a more general assessment of the state of myth study.

THE IDEA OF MYTH

Let us begin by noting two basic points of continuity between *Myth: A Symposium* (hereafter *Symposium*) and *Myth: A New Symposium* (hereafter *New Symposium*). The first is the consistent set of criteria adduced in both volumes, though sometimes fretfully or even in dissent,[4] as part of the effort to conceptualize "myth"; myths are recurrently characterized as foundational, primordial, sacred, and theomorphic. Less consistently one finds in both volumes terms such as "fictional," suggesting dissimulation; the issues here are complex and will be considered from different angles in the course of the discussion that follows. Finally, although the concepts of "story" and "narrative" occur repeatedly in *Symposium* and *New Symposium*, both volumes also contain contributions that challenge, explicitly or implicitly, narrative form as necessary to the definition of myth. One encounters, in both volumes, analyses that conceptualize myth as a culture's core ideas or ideology, and that call attention to the variety of media through which these might be expressed. Owing in part to a panel on myth and visual art, articulations of such alternatives are more frequent and explicit in *New Symposium* than in *Symposium*.[5]

A second, quite noticeable continuity between the two volumes is found in eloquent expressions within each of the difficulty, if not futility, of attempting to rigorously uphold distinctions between "myth" and other oral narrative categories like "folktale" and "legend."[6] Yet changes of fashion are also visible. For example, partly because of the popularity of Cassirer in the era of *Symposium*, "myth" seems to have conveyed the idea of a *sui generis* modality of consciousness more readily then than it does now. In the other direction, the most noticeable new (or newly enhanced) connotations of "myth" seem to be those put in circulation by Lévi-Strauss, through his contribution to *Symposium* and his other works. These include a sense of the special efficacy of myth in unifying the disparate and fragmentary— a process which has come to be summarized in Lévi-Strauss's term "bricolage."[7] The conviction that myth embodies such efficacy is reflected in many of the contributions in *New Symposium* and is clearly attributable at least in part to Lévi-Strauss. Vis-à-vis Lévi-Strauss's original formulations—which often focused on dilemmas argued to be intrinsic to particular worldviews—the contradictory circumstances adduced from myth for academic study today are more likely to be those that result specifically from colonial orders or other imposed hegemonic regimes.

PERENNIAL OPPOSITIONS

Myth and Critical Thought, Myth and History

Certain basic contrasts have perennially come to focus in theoretical discourse on myth. Most importantly, we confront an intellectual heritage in which, since the time of Plato, "myth" has been repeatedly cast in opposition to "critical" forms of thought. In the sphere of retrospective discourse, the opposition frequently takes the form of something like a contrast of myth and "critical history" (or even more tersely, "myth" and "history"). While the profound influence of such oppositions is evident throughout both *Symposium* and *New Symposium,* one experiences in the latter an additional theme characteristic of our era: a preoccupation with problematizing such oppositions and probing their motives and ethical consequences.

The difference in this respect between *Symposium* and *New Symposium* is particularly evident in the treatment of the contrast of myth and history. Looking back to *Symposium,* we encounter a number of orientations in which myth is judged to have negligible value for critical history. The tradition of Western critical history of course is regarded as secure; its ideals inspire the intellectual histories by Dorson, Hyman, and others in *Symposium* as well as the attempts to reconstruct the world history of folk narrative (these are discussed in *Symposium* by Thompson). When it comes to myth, however, Raglan (p. 123) is explicit: "Myths as a rule are untrue historically." And one cannot help but note the positive regard in which many contributors to *Symposium* hold functionalist perspectives and Malinowski in particular (e.g., see Bidney, p. 21; Christiansen, p. 65; Raglan, p. 127; Hyman, p. 143).[8] The historical mindlessness of myth is a notorious theme in functionalist approaches to myth; the shaping condition of myth is seen to lie in the utilitarian needs of the present—socially cohesive sentiments, moral models, anxiety-reducing entertainment—rather than in any concern to impartially document the past.[9]

In *Symposium* one also encounters the structuralism of Lévi-Strauss. His new program challenges many of the assumptions of functionalism, but does so within a frame of reference that shares with functionalism, indeed elaborates upon, the analytical privileging of the synchronic over the

4 | GREGORY SCHREMPP

diachronic; functionalism and structuralism together make up a sort of midcentury synchronic interlude in myth study. The attraction of the synchronic no doubt lay partly in the fresh alternative—indeed the escape—this orientation offered by contrast with the older goal of world-historical reconstruction, a goal seen increasingly as onerous and unattainable. Such reconstructionist goals had motivated diffusionist, evolutionist, and degenerationist programs, all of which turned on issues of origins, of both peoples and their stories. Many traces of such ambitions and their intellectual framing devices—Darwinian ur-man, various candidates for ur-civilizations, cultural evolutionism's ur-stage of "savagery" or "mythopoeic" mentality—can still be seen in *Symposium* alongside newer perspectives opened up in the synchronic interlude. Ironically, even scholars inspired by such scenarios of origination were often indisposed to admit a commonality between their project and those projects they analyzed under the rubric of "myth."

When we turn to *New Symposium*, we find two forms of reaction to the polarization of myth and critical history. On one hand, several contributions challenge the polarization, calling attention to evidence of critical purposes and rigorous methods in texts reputedly mythical (e.g., Toelken, Brotherston, Lindow, Sá). These analyses also implicitly indicate that it is difficult to judge the presence or absence of critical purpose when moving between societies that hold different metaphysical presuppositions about the "real." On the other hand, we find a concern with the constructed, agenda-laden, political character of Western historiography, indeed of historiography in general, suffused with the question of whether a myth-free historical consciousness is ever found as an isolate. Fulk (p. 236) comments that myth and history interfuse: "the opposition to myth validates history at the same time that history borrows the tropes of myth to convince us of its authority and verisimilitude."

In some instances, then, the lesson drawn is that such conceptual polarities are too stark, and our definition of myth needs to be reconsidered. In other instances, the stark contrast is allowed to stand conceptually, and the lesson drawn has to do with our applications of it, in particular with the overhasty, prejudicial ways in which this polarity has been apportioned among the world's peoples and intellectual traditions. The presence of potentially contradictory programs of revision, however, only confirms the predicament implied in such polarities.[10]

Literalism and Disinterestedness

Two other themes should be mentioned at this point, both of them foci for important oscillations in myth theory. The first is the long-term issue of whether myth is to be taken as "literal" or "symbolic"; the second, a set of concerns that have centered in recent times around the issue of whether myths are "interested" or "disinterested" formulations.

In regard to the perennial issue of the literal vs. symbolic in myth, one does well to consult Bidney's overview of this antinomy in *Symposium* (the value of which can stand independently of Bidney's own position on this issue). The literal/symbolic issue is perennial in the study of myth precisely because it is inextricable from other basic issues. It is difficult to pass judgment on the issue of historical verisimilitude, for example, without implicitly taking a position in regard to how myth should be read in terms of the congeries of possibilities and alternatives called up by the idea of the "literal."

The positions in *Symposium* on the literal/symbolic antinomy are mixed. Bidney and Thompson, in the opening and closing contributions respectively, pronounce allegiance to literalism in the interpretation of myth. Especially from Bidney's program can one gain insight into the attraction that literalism held for cultural evolutionism; it is much easier to point to the superiority of the scientific description of the world over the mythic if one is allowed to assume in advance that what myths are trying to provide is a literal description. Having noted a widespread interest in Malinowski among contributors to *Symposium,* we should recall that Malinowski discouraged elaborate symbolic interpretations, for myth "is not symbolic, but a direct expression of its subject matter" (1954, 101). On the other hand, Wheelwright's and Lévi-Strauss's contributions to *Symposium* are attentive to figurative processes in mythical thought (see McDowell's appreciative discussion in *New Symposium* of these two contributions).

One can also see the great battle between Müller's "solar mythology" and Tylor's "anthropological" evolutionism, championed by Lang, as a debate between a "literalist" and a "symbolic" perspective on myth. Dorson addresses this battle in *Symposium*. Both Müller and Tylor displayed the nineteenth-century "nature mythology" bent, assuming that the object of myth is the comprehension of nature. Yet below the surface overlap in Tylor and Müller loomed an interpretive abyss: for Müller, mythic analogies were products of an original poetic speech that was rich in metaphors of a kind which later ages no longer comprehended; for Tylor, the same analogies stemmed from erroneous literal associations created by the human sensorium's operating in a condition of primordial ignorance, and out of which humanity would gradually extricate itself through science. Dorson notes the triumph of the anthropological school, but throughout, and as if in search of a rationale, he subtly champions Müller's endeavor.

When we turn to *New Symposium,* the positions, while again mixed, are formulated quite differently from those of *Symposium.* First of all, no general mandates on literalism are proffered in *New Symposium,* a fact which would seem to reflect the turn toward analyses of myth in particular contexts rather than the more explicit generalizing in *Symposium* (this trend will be considered in more detail below). Secondly, the contributors to *New Symposium* generally accept the possibility of a figurative dimension in myth. Hill, for example, tells us about a tradition from Wakuénai society in which "the trickster-creator embodies the principle that nothing people say or do can be interpreted literally or taken at face value but must always be interpreted symbolically" (p. 72), thus heightening the status of figurative discourse.[11] In his discussion of the metaphor of disease in the discourse of American democracy, Ivie uses the term "myth" in part to connote the possibility of metaphor's hardening into literal, uncritical dogma, and he points to the difficulty of discerning the myths we live by. This concern, and this connotation of "myth," are long established in the tradition of political philosophy.[12] Yet in Ivie's fuller perspective, myth is seen to operate on a continuum of figuration and literalization (p. 169). Though literalism and its alternatives no longer form the explicit hub of debate that they did for Greek and early Christian philosophers, such issues are still importantly intertwined in theoretical debates about myth in our era.

A related oscillation relevant to *Symposium* and *New Symposium* has coalesced in more recent times around the polarity of "interested" and "disinterested" knowledge—the latter implying knowledge that grows from "objective" curiosity and is sought for its own sake, and the former implying knowledge that emanates from and is limited by utilitarian activities of life, whether the gathering of sustenance or political strategizing. Malinowski launched his new approach to myth with a diatribe against Müller and other "moonstruck" (1954: 96) proponents of extravagant symbolic readings of myth, charging that they had created a morally debased caricature of human nature: a being wrapped in idle tales, detached from the needs and dangers of life which are the real stimulus to the creation of mythic story and magical charm.

Then came Lévi-Strauss, who launched his own perspective on myth in opposition to Malinowski by reversing the latter's critique of Müller: Malinowski had given us, or reasserted, a pernicious caricature of a "primitive" so steeped in utilitarian pursuits as to be devoid of disinterested speculation about the cosmos (the famous contrast between "good to think" and "good to eat" [Lévi-Strauss 1963, 62, 89]). Some of us will recall that in the early days of structuralism, a return of the pendulum was suggested in a fondness for caricaturing Lévi-Strauss as a latter-day Max Müller. The analogy was prompted in part by Lévi-Strauss's attempt to once again encompass myth theory within linguistic theory, but also by a perceived common exuberance, if not zaniness, that took the form, in both Müller and Lévi-Strauss, of nonobvious myth messages discovered through purportedly rigorous symbolic decodings.

Where are we now on the issue of myth and "disinterested" knowledge? There seem to be gestures toward the "interested" pole in *New Symposium*, reflecting in part a broader waning of enthusiasm, within the humanities at least, for the "disinterested" ideal of knowledge. In *New Symposium* one encounters no inclination to diminish the intellectual sophistication associated with myth; but equally absent is the inclination to align such sophistication with disinterestedness. The change can be traced to a broad-spread contemporary skepticism about the idea of "disinterested" knowledge, no doubt attributable, in part at least, to the widespread influence of Foucault on our present academic worldview (see Fulk's contribution to *New Symposium*, p. 226ff.). Foucault of course arrived at such skepticism by way of critique of structuralist epistemology. As if in resonance with ancient Western debates on the relative virtues of the "active" and the "contemplative" life, support tends to oscillate between "interested" and "disinterested" knowledge in myth theory, even as it is righteously intoned from both sides. In this fashion, reactions against structuralism have often portrayed it as an intricate parlor game comfortably insulated from the moral condition of the world. Sometimes there is the additional implication that intellectual formations, including those we call myths, are revealed as more, not less, intellectually sophisticated when understood as responses to the challenging, sometimes dire, circumstances in which they are created or invoked. In this regard we can particularly note the frequent references to colonial contexts in *New Symposium*, a theme virtually absent in *Symposium*.

CHANGING THEORETICAL CLIMATES

One of the biggest differences in the overall character and "feel" of *Symposium* and *New Symposium* derives from the relative absence from *New Symposium* of the ambitious, world-synthesizing perspectives of the nineteenth century: evolutionism, degenerationism, distributionism, and their immediate descendants, whose influence still lingered in *Symposium*.

These perspectives were perpetuated in *Symposium*, even amidst considerable skepticism toward them, in part because they promised to make the study of myth into a science. The appeal to scientific method, *de rigueur* in nineteenth-century social theory, was given a second wind by the broader social fascination with science that followed World War II.[13] At issue here is not the more general sense of "science" as systematic and rigorous research, but the idea that mythologists should emulate specifically the methods and conceptual apparatus of the natural sciences: looking for underlying building blocks (motifs = atoms), classifying species, and searching out the natural laws of development of their objects of investigation. Two of the most explicitly scientific (in this sense) contributions to *Symposium* are the two "myth/ritual" contributions, those of Raglan and Hyman. The former invokes the "like causes, like effects" formula of nineteenth-century social evolutionism, which Franz Boas had criticized in attacking evolutionism;[14] the latter emphasizes Darwinian evolution, the standard correlations (e.g., of "primitive" ritual with children's games and neurotic behavior) posited in nineteenth-century comparative method, and more recent movements in midcentury neo-evolutionism. The rhetoric of science also permeates Lévi-Strauss's new prolegomenon, from his opening claim that myth study can move from "chaos" to "science" by copying, *mutatis mutandis,* the course by which linguistics has made this transition, to his closing wish that mythology studies will take off in America, where scholars have available more "I.B.M. equipment, etc." than in France.

The world-synthesizing perspective of *Symposium* is manifest also in the contributors' use of mythical allusion and the sort of heroic rhetoric that typically announces the advance of science. Bidney's opening piece depicts an ongoing struggle of scientific reason against irrationality. Dorson, rehearsing late-nineteenth-century debates about myth, tells us how "the giants slew each other" (p. 52). Hyman's presentation of myth/ritualism projects a marvelous confidence in the world-comprehending capacity of this perspective—promising to resolve the riddle of the Sphinx (p. 152)—while leaving the reader to wonder whether there remain any worlds to conquer. Lévi-Strauss closes the announcement of his new paradigm with the quintessential emblem of modern cosmological science: a terse, mathematical formula, in this case one claiming to represent all myths.[15] Thompson's closing statement, though presenting a vision of the future diametrically opposed to the foregoing, is yet similar in its sweep. Skeptical of the world-comparative methods for which he had come to stand, startlingly Boasian in the conclusion that what is missing is the detailed histories of particular stories in specific locales,[16] Thompson's piece nevertheless remains a testament in the grand style, a sort of scholarly *götterdämmerung.*

Thompson's concluding recommendations, in *Symposium,* also provide a point of contact with *New Symposium,* for, in the spirit of those recommendations, most of the contributions to the present volume are focused on close analysis of myth in specific, situated sociohistorical contexts. There is no explicit emulation of the natural sciences (indeed the decoupling seems broadly characteristic of the humanities in our era). The idea of universals in myth is certainly not repudiated, but it is approached rather more gingerly.

Even with the backgrounding of world-synthesizing ambitions, however, the debt of the present generation of mythologists to that of the mid-century cannot be denied. As noted earlier, the influence is most palpably present in the continuing, though diffuse, influence of Lévi-Strauss in our era. Thompson, in voicing the limitations of grand perspectives, cannot bring himself to dismiss them entirely, for "[p]art of the elephant after all was actually like a rope" (*Symposium,* p. 179). In similar spirit, McDowell (*New Symposium,* p. 34) now writes, "Like many other readers of Lévi-Strauss, I find myself skeptical to the bitter end yet constantly wondering whether, after all, he might be on to something important."

On the other hand, the world-synthesizing perspectives of *Symposium* do ultimately rest on methods that tend to neglect detailed sociohistorical contexts and original-language texts. As such they often gloss over aspects of myth that have come to be regarded as critical; two such aspects particularly stand out in the contributions to *New Symposium.*

The first of these is something like agency or a sense of agentive history, as revealed in the details and nuances of particular historical or ethnographic situations. For all of the similarities in the connotation of "myth" in *Symposium* and *New Symposium,* a deep division emerges regarding authorship. In *Symposium* myth remains essentially an anonymous, collective product that develops through abstract processes; to the extent that personal agency is recognized in *Symposium,* it tends to be limited to the eighteenth-century idea of an elite coterie of ideologues foisting self-serving dogma onto gullible masses.[17] Neither the notion of myth as having a collective dimension, nor the possibility of ideologues creating myths for the masses is absent from *New Symposium.*[18] Yet one also notes in *New Symposium* a recurrent concern with individual, active myth-shapers or interpreters, from Joseph Nagy's (p. 133) comments about Tírechán's "acute authorial self-consciousness" in including mythic elements in his seventh-century life of St. Patrick, to the Amazonian storyteller who tells Slater, "See here, the Dolphin is a gringo" (p. 160).[19]

The difference between *Symposium* and *New Symposium* on the issue of agency can also be illustrated in the attention given by contributors in each volume to processes of development and change involving myth in relation to other genres. Considering how much skepticism toward cultural evolutionism was in the air at midcentury, it is interesting to see this doctrine flourishing in miniature, so to speak, in the continuing fascination with the idea of a regular evolution of oral narrative genres—an idea that arises recurrently in *Symposium* (e.g., Raglan, p. 129; Thompson, p. 179; Wheelwright, *passim;* Dorson's perennial fascination with the Chadwicks, p. 41). The majority of contributions in *New Symposium* address processes of genre change, in some cases in the form of the classic issue of euhemerism (see especially Lindow, p. 119ff.). But this topic is now approached on the level of particular cases, as if in accord with Thompson's closing recommendation in *Symposium* that the topic of one form leading into another should be approached as "a local manifestation and not something operating as a world-wide evolution" (p. 179).

The heightened sense of agency in myth creation and use has implications for yet another long-running characterization of myth, one that was given special impetus in the midcentury functionalist era, namely the essentially conservative nature of myth. Departing from *Symposium,* many contributions in *New Symposium* present examples of myth consciously invoked in order to shape, or even induce, change. And yet the assumption of conservatism has not been entirely done away with. Myth still connotes a fundamental testament that uniquely engages mind and emotion, holding together and perpetuating a certain view of the cosmos and way of life. It seems necessary to distinguish different visions of mythic conservatism. At one pole is the notion of mindless masses and mechanistic social functions; at the other a recognition of processes of investing traditional forms with continuously new meaning—"negotiations with mythology," as Leach phrases it in speaking of Roman interpretation of mythological painting (*New Symposium,* p. 184).

Besides agency, the grand methods of *Symposium* also tended to preclude attention to a second concern that is much in evidence in *New Symposium*—specifically matters of style and aesthetic nuance that can be discovered when working in the original languages of myth texts. The methods of world comparativism characteristic of *Symposium* often proceeded by jettisoning at the outset all surface nuance in the quest for abstract, cross-culturally useful units—this is particularly true for Thompson and Lévi-Strauss. One of the consequences in *Symposium* is that myth ends up at best unattached to, and at worst polarized against, poetry or poetics ("poetics" in this instance referring to formal and stylistic features that denote specialized, artistic use of language).

In *Symposium* (pp. 85–86), Lévi-Strauss argues that myth and poetry occupy opposite ends of a continuum defined by how integral poetic form is to their substance as genres—a doctrine highly convenient to his methods, which, though nominally linguistic, rely on "gross constituent units" that are definable largely apart from nuances of style and form.[20] Like Lévi-Strauss, Thompson, in *Symposium,* focuses largely on work in Native American myths. By a very different route, though one influenced by the same disregard for original-language texts, Thompson too ends up polarizing myth and poetry in the context of Native American research, with the conclusion that there are almost no "stories told in poetic form" in this area.

Though certain factors mitigate this comment somewhat,[21] the general drift is quite clear: mythic form stands in contrast to poetic form.[22]

A broader contemporary fascination with the artistry of narrative, and, more specifically, with the possibility of approaching oral narrative as artistic performance has had a noticeable impact on the study of myth, one that is visible in most of the contributions to *New Symposium.* Certainly one of the most noticeable recent movements in the study of Native American narratives is the trend toward presenting Native American texts (whether newly recorded or drawn from older collections) with protocols that signal and convey artistic character and intent—for example in versified, stanzaic, or dramaturgically inspired formats ("acts," "scenes," and so on) (e.g., Hymes 1981;[23] Sherzer and Woodbury 1987; Kroeber 1997). This is sometimes accompanied by a redubbing of "myth," calling it instead "poetry" or "dramatic narrative," for example, as if we are going from a situation of all myth and no poetry to one of all poetry and no myth. Whatever the outcome of this endeavor, it is motivated, at least in part, by reaction to the sort of dichotomizing of the mythic and the poetic exemplified in some of the contributions in *Symposium,* a dichotomization that, in turn, was fostered by mechanistic notions of social functionality and by the favoring of abstracted cross-cultural units and goals over nuanced analysis of native-language texts.

I have drawn upon the contributions that make up *Myth: A New Symposium* to offer some general observations on trends in myth study in the period since *Myth: A Symposium.* As was true of the earlier volume, the current work's greater appeal for many readers will lie in the contributions that most directly engage their particular interests; the range of interests that converge in the idea of myth will remain a source of inspiration to myth scholars. The two concluding contributions (Fulk, Gregory Nagy) focus directly on myth as a concept. Drawing us back to some of the general themes touched on above, both analyses, though from quite different perspectives, offer subtle insights into the historical emergence of the range of definitions and connotations that we have inherited along with the term "myth." As Thompson mused a half-century ago, it would be interesting to know how all these matters will appear another fifty years hence.

NOTES

I am grateful to my coeditor William Hansen for offering detailed commentary on the several drafts of this introduction. Other contributors to this volume also provided useful comments.

1. In addition to those named in the text, *Myth: A Symposium* comprises David Bidney, "Myth, Symbolism, and Truth"; Reidar Th. Christiansen, "Myth, Metaphor, and Simile"; Claude Lévi-Strauss, "The Structural Study of Myth"; Dorothy Eggan, "The Personal Use of Myth in Dreams"; and Philip Wheelwright, "The Semantic Approach to Myth."

Page references in this introduction are to the widely available 1965 edition. Although pagination differs, all passages quoted in this introduction are identical to those occurring in the original 1955 publication (in the *Journal of American Folklore*) and in the first Indiana University Press edition (1958).

2. A Symposium on Myth, May 14–16, 1999, Indiana University, Bloomington. The panels were "Revisiting *Myth: A Symposium*"; "Myth and Ethnography"; "Myth and Historical Texts"; "Myth and the Modern World"; and "Myth and Art." The sixth section of *Myth: A New Symposium* comprises two essays that originated as responses at the conference: Fulk's as a response to the "Myth and Historical Texts" panel, and Gregory Nagy's as concluding remarks to the conference as a whole.

3. *Myth: A Symposium* includes folklorists Reidar Christiansen, Stith Thompson, and Richard Dorson, and was edited by Thomas Sebeok, a Fellow of the Folklore Institute, Indiana University. It was first published in the *Journal of American Folklore*. The conference A Symposium on Myth, from which the contributions to this volume are drawn, was spearheaded by the Folklore Institute and by the Program in Mythology Studies at Indiana University, Bloomington.

4. See especially Hansen's (*New Symposium,* p. 20ff.) criticisms of the "sacred" criterion.

5. In *New Symposium,* Hansen (p. 20) and Glassie (p. 205ff) directly address the place of narrative in the definition of myth; the issue also arises indirectly in a number of other contributions (see, for example, Leach, Ivie, Slater, and Fulk).

In regard to this issue Bidney's and Lévi-Strauss's contributions to *Symposium* are particularly intriguing. Partly because of his survey orientation, Bidney touches on a variety of ways of conceptualizing myth—for example, as belief, ideology, story, a distinct form of thought, or a distinct form of experience. Lévi-Strauss says that the "substance" of myth lies in the "*story* which it tells" (*Symposium,* p. 86), but he then proceeds to analytically reduce the story of Oedipus to a paradigmatic set—a set of irreconcilable propositions—that are diagrammable without reference to narrative progression or unfolding. See McDowell's comments on this point (in *New Symposium,* p. 34).

6. Compare especially Thompson (in *Symposium,* p. 175) and Toelken (in *New Symposium,* p. 89).

7. Lévi-Strauss's was clearly the most innovative contribution in *Symposium* (at least as far as the American audience was concerned). Yet the extent to which Lévi-Strauss's insights were new rather than merely newly phrased is problematic; in both Eggan's and Wheelwright's contributions in *Symposium,* for example, one sees hints of the sorts of processes suggested by "bricolage."

8. Myth/ritualism overlaps with both evolutionism and functionalism, two perspectives that tend to be antithetical. For example, myth/ritualism sometimes posits a sort of universal ur-genre of ritual from which other genres systematically unfold through time—a postulate that fits nicely within cultural evolutionist perspectives. But myth/ritualism could also claim a central tenet of functionalism: the analytical primacy of act over belief (cf. Jarvie 1964).

9. Eggan's contribution to *Symposium* exemplifies the synchronic turn that took place among some of the first generation of Boas's students in parallel with the functionalist revolution. Influenced by the writings of Freud, Ruth Benedict, in *Zuni Mythology* (1935), called attention to the "compensatory" or "projective" function of myth: rather than reflecting a cultural reality, myths present a distorted, wish-fulfilling version of it. In contrast to Boas's early hopes that myth could serve as a source of historical documentary evidence, we encounter in Benedict, indeed in the whole "culture and personality" generation, a con-

viction parallel to that of functionalism: that for the goal of critical history myth is not very useful. Eggan's contribution was written in the midst of a general debate about whether myth "reflects" or "distorts" ethnographic reality, a prominent theoretical issue among American anthropological mythologists of the mid–twentieth century.

10. One encounters similar responses when the opposition is phrased as myth vs. critical thought more generally (rather than as myth vs. history specifically). Ethnographic contributors to *New Symposium* (e.g., Toelken, Brotherston) challenge the strong conceptual polarization of myth and critical thought proffered by Bidney in *Symposium* by demonstrating a critical impulse in traditions and texts of the kind typically labeled "myths" by scholars. Other contributors (e.g., Slater, Ivie) challenge the idea that "myth" is a category relevant only to the analysis of ethnographic "Others."

11. Though *New Symposium* managed to draw out no closet solarists, one cannot fail to note the robust tones in which the figurative, poetic powers of mythic discourse are described by Hill and many other contributors to *New Symposium,* particularly, it seems, the ethnographers. They suggest a kind of answer to Dorson's search for a longer significance for the battle fought by Müller against Tylorian literalism.

12. Schrempp (*New Symposium,* p. 54) considers this usage in his analysis of David Bidney's contribution to *Symposium.*

13. Northrop Frye's widely influential *Anatomy of Criticism* (1957), published at virtually the same time as *Symposium,* offers an impassioned appeal for literary criticism to make itself scientific by emulating the methods of the natural sciences. Frye's work also attests to the saliency of "myth" as a category of literary analysis in midcentury. Thompson (*Symposium,* p. 170) comments on the recent "perversions of the word 'myth' which some of the modern literary critics are employing."

14. Cultural evolutionists, Boas pointed out, often started with cultural forms or artifacts and inferred a cause. Thus they were not following the formula "like causes, like effects" but its reverse, which can be ethnographically disproven (see Boas 1940, 273ff.). Boas presents a number of examples that demonstrate that similar ethnological phenomena have often arisen from different historical causes.

15. It is interesting to juxtapose Lévi-Strauss's and Hyman's contributions to *Symposium.* Opposites—one rooted in evolutionism and ritual action, the other in synchronic and speculative thought—they nevertheless make similar rhetorical moves, invoking key symbols of science augmented with overtures to the myth of Oedipus.

16. Compare Thompson's arguments on this point to those of Boas (1940); the similarities of course may stem from Thompson's immersion in Native American material, much of which was collected and presented by Boas and his students. See also Hansen's (*New Symposium*) discussion of Thompson on issues of origin.

Focusing on a group of German-trained ethnologists working in South America, Sá (*New Symposium*) traces yet another retreat from world-synthesizing theoretical ambition in favor of greater attention to specific indigenous texts and to the ways of understanding the world that they reflect.

17. The notable exception to the general lack of a sense of individual agency in *Symposium* is Eggan's contribution, "The Personal Use of Myth in Dreams." Eggan discusses a particular Hopi individual's synthesis of myths and personal dreams in creating a life strategy. Eggan's piece clearly reflects the influence of the "culture and personality" school of American anthropology, aspects of which would now be seen as quite dated. Yet the piece is interestingly ahead of its time (judged retrospectively, of course) in its recognition of something like individual agency in myth process.

18. Slater's portrayal of contemporary advertisers and media creators in the context of the "myths of the rain forest" has an interesting resonance with the eighteenth-century notion of ideologues using myths to manipulate and control. Ivie discusses the fear of unruly and uncritical masses as a theme in American political discourse.

19. Similar observations might be made about almost every contribution to *New Symposium;* see also, for example, Hill's comments on the interpretive prowess associated with Trickster (p. 73); Ivie's discussions of political performances of the myth of the *demos* (p. 170); Fulk's speculations about Bede's inclusion of pagan traditions in his historical writing (p. 235); Leach's discussion of myth paintings that enter into creative dialogue with texts (p. 188ff.); and the many native exegetical comments in Toelken's and Glassie's essays.

20. In *New Symposium,* both McDowell (p. 34ff.) and Brotherston (p. 141ff.) criticize this aspect of Lévi-Strauss's work.

21. The search for narratives in poetic form was inspired by the ballad. Regarding his own initiation into folk narrative studies, Thompson reports,

> In those days, a half-century ago, there was a general feeling that the balad [*sic*] preceded prose as a form of folk narrative. When I wished to investigate this matter among the North American Indians, a wise professor told me to get hold of a dozen American Indian stories told in poetic form. I searched the literature for weeks and found none, and except for a few extremely simple narrative chants, fifty years of rather close observation has failed to bring any such narrative poems to light. And yet, among these same peoples, not one tribe fails to have a good collection of myths and folktales. (pp. 179–80)

22. Another intriguing instance of the polarization of the mythic and the poetic can be seen in Roland Barthes's influential *Mythologies.* Having aligned myth with ideology, Barthes concludes that

> there is as yet only one possible choice, and this choice can bear only on two equally extreme methods: either to posit a reality which is entirely permeable to history, and ideologize; or, conversely, to posit a reality which is *ultimately* impenetrable, irreducible, and, in this case, poetize. In a word, I do not yet see a synthesis between ideology and poetry. (1995, 158–59)

23. Hymes's *"In Vain I Tried to Tell You"* (1981) combines renewed commitment to artistry and linguistic nuance, on one hand, with the more abstractive formalism against which this new enterprise is sometimes defined, on the other. For while Hymes's analysis is permeated with attention to linguistic/poetic nuance, some of his most important claims are developed through the kind of tabularized gross constituent unit analysis developed by Lévi-Strauss (e.g., 288ff.).

BIBLIOGRAPHY

Barthes, Roland. 1995. *Mythologies.* Translated by Annette Lavers. New York: Hill and Wang.

Benedict, Ruth. 1935. *Zuni Mythology.* 2 vols. New York: Columbia University Press.

Boas, Franz. 1940. "The Limitations of the Comparative Method in Anthropology." In *Race, Language, and Culture,* 270–80. New York: Macmillan.

Frye, Northrop. 1957. *Anatomy of Criticism: Four Essays.* Princeton: Princeton University Press.

Hymes, Dell. 1981. *"In Vain I Tried to Tell You": Essays in Native American Ethnopoetics.* Philadelphia: University of Pennsylvania Press.

Jarvie, I. C. 1964. *The Revolution in Anthropology.* New York: Humanities.

Kroeber, Karl, ed. 1997. *Traditional Literatures of the American Indian: Texts and Interpretations.* 2d edition. Lincoln: University of Nebraska Press.

Lévi-Strauss, Claude. 1963. *Totemism.* Translated by Rodney Needham. Boston: Beacon.

Malinowski, Bronislaw. 1954. "Myth in Primitive Psychology." In *Magic, Science, and Religion, and Other Essays,* 93–148. Garden City, N.Y.: Doubleday.

Sebeok, Thomas A., ed. 1965. *Myth: A Symposium.* Bloomington: Indiana University Press. Originally published in the *Journal of American Folklore* 68 (1955): 379–488.

Sherzer, Joel, and Anthony C. Woodbury. 1987. *Native American Discourse: Poetics and Rhetoric.* Cambridge: Cambridge University Press.

Part I

REVISITING *MYTH:*
A SYMPOSIUM

ONE

Meanings and Boundaries: Reflections on Thompson's "Myth and Folktales"

WILLIAM HANSEN

I n the view of Stith Thompson, writing in 1955, the then-current generation of scholars had not solved the basic problems presented by myths
and folktales. Thompson gives this assessment in his essay "Myth and
Folktales," which stands at the end of the influential collection *Myth: A
Symposium,* edited by Thomas Sebeok.[1] Since Thompson was the only
contributor to have access to the other essays before writing his own, he
alone was able to comment upon the state of opinion represented by the
collection as a whole. He was certain that theories would continue to be
put forth, and that all of the contributors to the volume would eventually
seem old-fashioned; indeed, he wondered how the theories and ideas of his
generation would appear after the passage of a century (1965, 180). Half
of that term has now passed, and I would like to consider two important
problems discussed by Thompson, namely, genre and meaning, in relation
to recent scholarship in mythology.

As Thompson rightly complains, most investigators make little effort to
connect discussions of myth with the texts of actual myths (1965, 170). As
a result it can be difficult to discover what different scholars actually mean
when they employ the term *myth.* When, however, one does know what
different scholars mean by the word, one is also likely to find that they are
talking about different things. Some analytic definitions of myth feature a
particular kind of content as a criterion, whereas others feature a particular
temporal setting or a particular quality or combination of traits. Each criterion has its peculiar difficulty in application. Take content, for example.
Thompson himself distinguishes between strict definitions of myth, which
focus upon the doings of the gods, and broad definitions, which include
stories of human heroes as well (173–74). When, for example, scholars
of Norse mythology speak of myth, they mean stories only of the pagan

gods; although creatures of the so-called lower mythology such as elves and dwarves may be included, heroes are not.[2] But when most classical scholars speak of myth, they have in mind narratives not only of the gods but also of the heroes. To make matters worse, scholars are frequently inconsistent. In "The Structural Study of Myth" Claude Lévi-Strauss declares that "a myth always refers to events alleged to have taken place in time: before the world was created, or during its first stages—anyway, long ago," but then a few pages later he classifies as a myth the story of the Greek hero Oedipus, which is set neither at a time before the world was created nor during its first stages (1965, 84–85, 89–94).

The employment of the term *myth* for various non-narrative phenomena (for example, "value-impregnated beliefs") was also well established by Thompson's day, but he does not mention such usages in his essay, since for Thompson, as for other folklorists, a myth must in any case be narrative in form. The unaddressed question is whether myth is essentially a certain kind of narrative that may or may not serve to express cultural ideology, or essentially cultural ideology that may or may not be expressed in the form of narrative.[3]

Some definitions of myth restrict the application of the term not only to narratives of supernatural beings but specifically to narratives that recount how the world came to have its present form.[4] This constraint is mostly temporal in effect, for mythologies commonly recount a special period of time early in the history of the world when it received its basic physical nature and features. Such a definition creates a problem of classification if it is applied to Old World traditions such as Greek or Norse mythology, in which many stories of the gods have nothing do with the establishment of the cosmos. For example, the ribald story of the love affair of Ares and Aphrodite in Greek tradition (*Odyssey* 8.266–366) does not relate anything about the formation of the world. But if this story is not to be deemed a myth, what is it?

Take another example. A quality frequently included in cross-cultural definitions of myth is sacredness: myths are said to be sacred stories of one kind or another. In his collection *Sacred Narrative: Readings in the Theory of Myth,* Alan Dundes offers this definition: "A myth is a sacred narrative explaining how the world and man came to be in their present form," adding that "the critical adjective *sacred* distinguishes myth from other forms of narrative such as folktales, which are ordinarily secular and fictional" (1984, 1).

The folklorist and anthropologist William Bascom, in a well-known essay on narrative genres that appeared some twenty years before Dundes' book, also associates myths with the quality of sacredness. Discussing the different attitudes that persons have toward different genres of traditional story, he lists "sacred" as the attitude toward myths, and "secular" toward folktales. Legends are in between, varying between sacred and secular. Bascom does not, however, make clear what sacredness means in the case of stories. The first scholar to associate myth and sacredness in print is perhaps the anthropologist Bronislaw Malinowski. In his essay "Myth in Primitive Psychology," which appeared in 1926, Malinowski describes the native genres of oral story among the Trobriand Islanders. He says that stories classified as *liliu,* which he renders "myths," are regarded by the Trobriand Islanders "not merely as true, but as venerable and sacred. They are told during the preparation for rituals, which are performed at different times throughout the year. Their main function is to serve as a justification of the rituals with which they are associated" (1948, 15). Here at least one can see what the author means when he says that myths are sacred, namely, that individual myths are closely linked with corresponding religious rituals.

Nevertheless, an analytic definition of myth as a kind of sacred story is problematic. First of all, sacredness appears to be a secondary characteristic of Trobriand mythic stories. They are not somehow inherently sacred; rather, their venerableness is a derivative quality that depends upon their intimate association with religious ceremony, for which they play the important role of providing a charter. But if these Trobriand narratives are regarded as sacred because of their connection with ritual, what about societies that recount stories of their gods but do not tie their stories closely to rituals? Many, perhaps most, of the stories in Greek mythology that have been called myths have no known connections with solemn ritual, and even in the case of Greek myths that were associated with particular rituals, it is unclear whether the Greeks regarded the myths in question as being especially venerable. The idea of sacredness as a defining quality of myth probably entered scholarly literature from early-twentieth-century ethnography and has come to be repeated somewhat automatically in discussions published by social scientists. Malinowski's definition of myth as sacred story was inspired by the case of a small-scale society in which a certain class of story is closely associated with religious ceremony, but there is insufficient evidence to extend it without further ado to the mythologies of all societies on the assumption that myths are universally associated with rituals and regarded as sacred narratives by their narrators and audiences.

Just how different is myth from other genres of traditional story? Thompson, the great scholar of the folktale, points to several important ways in which myths and folktales are alike. "It is always easier to borrow a myth or a tale than it is to construct one," he observes. "The body of narratives of any particular primitive people is not likely to exceed several hundred, and of these several hundred it is usually possible to find that the great majority are held in common with their neighbors. . . . From this point of view there is no distinction whatever between the ordinary folktale and the myth. They both disseminate, they both take on accretions and are subject to the vicissitudes of memory and forgetting" (1965, 175–76). I add that both are also subject to genre-variance, that is, that what is essentially the same story can be found at one place and time as a myth and at another place or time as a legend or folktale.[5] For many stories that are recounted of gods or heroes in Old World mythologies can be found recounted as folktales elsewhere, narratives that make no claim to being historical, let alone sacred. These commonalities between the genres suggest that scholars overrate the uniqueness of myth. We need a theory of myth that views myth less as a unique and mysterious phenomenon and more as a narrative genre that behaves like and is closely related to other genres of traditional narrative.

Today nothing in Thompson's essay looks more dated than the obsession with origins that he shares with several other scholars in *Myth: A Symposium.* In Thompson's essay a mention of origin is found on nearly every page. For example, "The origins of myths and folktales over the world must be extremely diverse, so that it is not safe to posit any single origin even for those of a particular people" (170). "Nearly all of the writers cited in this paper manifest great interest in origins. Where did myth and folktales come from? How were they invented in the first place?" (175). "But the ultimate origin of nearly all folktales and myths must remain a mystery, just as the origin of language is a mystery" (176). "And in the absence of the facts, I would wish to leave the ultimate origin of any tale or myth with a large question mark rather than with a dubious answer" (176–77). "No three blind men ever investigated the essential nature of the elephant with more surprising results than those who have sought the single answer which would unlock the mystery of the origin and nature of tales and myths" (178). It is so obvious to Thompson that the discovery of origins is the scholar's ultimate goal that he does not question the desirability of the goal, only its feasibility. To discover the origin or early history of a particular myth or folktale is to understand it, to see what it is really about, as it then seemed to Thompson and many other investigators. Never mind what the narrative in question might have meant to later generations who knew nothing of its origin or, for that matter, what it might mean to us.

Of all Thompson's comments on origins, the most striking is that in which he links the meaning of stories with their origins: "On the whole . . . a quest for meanings outside the tale or myth itself is doomed to failure, because we simply do not know the frame of mind of the unknown person in the unknown place and the unknown time and the unknown culture who first contrived the story. The search for the original meaning of any folk story is quite as impossible as the search for the origin of that story. For both quests adequate data are missing" (1965, 178). Thompson conceives of the meaning of a story as being the meaning that occupied the mind of the narrator who first contrived the story. Evidently this original meaning continues to inhere in the story as its true and proper significance, or perhaps the story has other meanings for later transmitters of the story but these meanings are secondary and of no special interest to scholars. Today we would regard such a view as untenable. Or would we?

In an essay published in 1996 the anthropologist Mary Douglas investigates certain myths having to do with cannibalism. Her method is inspired by the work of the nineteenth-century scholar Robertson Smith, whom she believes mythologists have unjustly ignored, with the result that mythologists lack a methodology. Indeed, so far as mythological interpretation is concerned, Douglas claims, more or less anything goes (1996, 33–36). She is particularly partial to Smith's contention that ritual is of primary importance and myth of secondary importance. What was constant in ancient religion, according to Smith, was ritual; myth was of relatively small importance. Different myths might be attached to the same ceremony, so that one had one's choice of which to believe, and no one particularly cared what anyone else believed. Following Smith's lead, Douglas declares she will interpret institutions first and myths afterward. "A myth," she says, "cannot be interpreted without the context in which it is told. Who tells it? To whom? On what occasion? What sort of ceremonial is it used to explain?" (1996, 39).

Somewhat oddly, perhaps, she decides that it is easier to illustrate her myth method with a folktale, in this case the cannibalistic nursery tale of Little Red Riding Hood, since more contextual information is available for this familiar folktale than for the distant myths of cannibalism. For this purpose she examines nineteenth-century French texts of Little Red Riding Hood, which she deems to be the original versions.[6] In French narrations from oral tradition, when the heroine encounters the wolf, he asks her which path she is taking, the way of pins or the way of needles. The girl sometimes answers "pins" and sometimes "needles," so that her particular reply is of no importance. But for nineteenth-century peasant women in some regions of France, pins and needles were symbolic ways of referring to two different stages of female lives, pins referring to girls of courting age, since pins are easy to use and make temporary fastenings, and needles referring to adult women, since needles are difficult to use and make permanent fastenings, in addition to the sexual connotation that the threading of a needle can possess. Douglas believes that when a narrator told this tale and mentioned the way of pins and the way of needles, it signaled to listeners that the tale had to do with sexuality and with the sequence of roles in the lives of girls: the courtship stage of pins, the adult stage of needles, the postsexual role of the grandmother. The meaning of the tale, then, had to do with the play the tale makes with the different roles in the lives of females (1996, 45). The motif of pins and needles and other sexual motifs found in oral texts are omitted in the literary versions of Perrault and Grimm, and Douglas holds that any interpretation that neglects the motif of pins and needles is arbitrary (1996, 43). According to this construction, then, the tale of Little Red Riding Hood is a development of secondary importance that attached itself to the important ceremonies that marked girls' passage through the sequence of their roles in French peasant society, and to the extent that the tale can be said to have a meaning, its meaning lies in the reference it makes to this sequence and its tensions.

It is beside the point here whether this is the essential significance of Little Red Riding Hood as an international tale or only captures certain meanings that the French form of the tale may have had for peasants in nineteenth-century France. What is relevant is that in order to interpret the tale Douglas examines what she regards as its original version and, having offered an interpretation of it, she believes that she has interpreted the tale as a whole.[7] But then what are we to make of all the other versions of Little Red Riding Hood—those from Italian oral tradition, for example, and those found in popular fairytale books?

Take a second example. In his book *Homosexuality in Greek Myth*, published in French in 1984 and in English translation in 1986, the classical scholar Bernard Sergent investigates stories in Greek mythology featuring an erotic relationship between an adult man and a youth. He is particularly interested in the institution of ritualized pederasty, which is attested on Crete in the fourth century B.C. An older man would reveal to the family and friends of a youth that he planned to abduct him. Two or three days later he took the boy away, while the youth's friends and family put up token resistance. The lover, the beloved, and the other persons present at the ritual abduction presently repaired to a place in the countryside selected by the lover, and the party spent two months feasting and hunting. Then they all returned to the city, and the lover gave his beloved certain customary gifts. An abductor had to be of suitable rank in order to be acceptable to the youth's family, and for his part a youth was said to be chosen on the basis, not of good looks, but of manly courage and generally good behavior. Youths who had been so chosen acquired certain civic privileges for the rest of their lives, and for a handsome and well-born youth not to be chosen was a social disgrace, since it implied that he was of poor character. Sergent compares the ancient Cretan institution with the forms of ritualized pederasty encountered by modern ethnographers in Australia and Melanesia. Usually a young man is placed under the tutelage of an older man, who teaches him hunting and other adult male skills. The two enter into a sexual relationship in which the tutor takes the role of the lover and the novice that of the beloved. At the end of a prescribed period their relationship comes to an end; the boy attains to adult status and may marry.

Sergent's thesis is that ritualized, initiatory pederasty was once widespread in Greece and that the evidence for it can be found in Greek mythology. He does not mean merely that the mythology reflects the existence of such an institution but that the myths themselves were an integral part of the institution. "On every page of this book," he writes at the end of his work, "it has been clear that erômenoi ["beloveds"] are pupils, disciples, apprentices. The erastai ["lovers"] are their masters, teachers, and models. . . . The symbolism of initiation is omnipresent. The disciple, the beloved, dies, only to be reborn, explicitly or otherwise, or he performs an exploit that proves his prowess. He then accedes to the status of adult man. He becomes a trained warrior or a king, he marries, and he excels in those areas where his erastes ["lover"] was master" (1986, 268). According to Sergent, then, the myths reflect initiatory pederasty both straightforwardly and symbolically.

Sergent's initial example is the story of the hero Pelops, which Sergent labels a myth. The father of Pelops invites the gods to a feast and, in order to test their omniscience, cooks his son Pelops in a cauldron and serves him up. Most of the gods detect the cannibalistic meal and do not eat, but the goddess Demeter consumes a shoulder. The boy is then resuscitated and outfitted with a shoulder of ivory to replace the one he lost. Sometime later the god Poseidon finds the youthful Pelops attractive and abducts him, taking him to Olympus for his sexual pleasure. Subsequently Pelops's father offends the gods and Pelops is expelled from Olympus. When the youth reaches marriageable age, he learns that a certain king is offering the hand of his daughter to the man who can beat him in a chariot race. Pelops prays to Poseidon, his former lover, asking the god to provide him with equipment for the race. Poseidon lends Pelops his own golden chariot with winged horses, and using these Pelops wins the race and the princess.[8] His story continues, but only this much is of interest in the present connection.

For Sergent the strange episode of the cannibalistic feast and the apparently straightforward episode of the affair with Poseidon are really two forms of the same event, the event being initiatory pederasty. The episode of Poseidon, with its abduction, sexual relationship, and return, gives the ritual sequence literally, whereas the episode of the cannibalistic feast gives the sequence symbolically, as the death of the boy and his rebirth as a man. After the pederastic affair the young hero, aided by the loan of a chariot and horses from his abductor, prepares for the next stage of his life, marriage. Sergent concludes that the entire myth of Pelops is based upon the theme of initiation and that it goes back to a prehistoric Greek institution of ritual pederasty (1986, 58, 64). He concludes, "The complete initiatory sequence, from seclusion of the neophyte to marriage, with mystical death, death cauldron and resurrection cauldron, homosexuality of tutor and pupil, and trial in the form of a race, constitute a coherent, unified whole. Its meaning becomes clear when compared with the known initiatory customs of primitive peoples and the custom known to have been practiced in Crete in historical times" (67). Sergent thus holds that one must interpret the Pelops story according to what it meant to those who originally shaped it. The significance that the story had for them is its true and essential significance, and Sergent's discovery of its ritual origin, as he believes, reveals what that hidden meaning is.[9]

Some fifty years ago Stith Thompson declared his belief that the meanings of a story, apart from that which resided in the text itself, lay in the mind of the unknown person who originally devised it. He despaired of ever catching a glimpse of the mind of that person and therefore of learning the true meaning of a tale, but he did not doubt that the meaning lurked there. Thompson's straightforward and unquestioning association of origins and meanings seems dated now, or at least appears less obviously true, but the view is still being recommended with only slight changes of scenery. Anthropologist Douglas and classicist Sergent share Thompson's belief that the true and essential meaning of a traditional narrative is its original meaning, which for Thompson is the meaning in the mind of the actual creator of the tale and for Douglas and Sergent is the meaning shared by its earliest narrators and consumers. Privileging the original texts and their meanings, or what they suppose are the original texts and meanings, Douglas and Sergent in effect reinvent the myth-ritualist school of interpretation, according to which a particular myth was originally the verbal counterpart of a corresponding ritual, and the two shared a single meaning, since each was a different expression of the same thing.[10] Like Thompson before them, however, Douglas and Sergent leave unaddressed the question of why persons who are ignorant of the original rites and therefore of the meanings of the stories have continued to transmit them. Why do the tale of Little Red Riding Hood and the legend of Pelops still appeal to audiences and readers?

Looking back at Thompson and his colleagues after the passage of fifty years, here is what I see. Their interest in origins and diachrony has largely been replaced by other ways of looking at myth, although a revived myth-ritualism continues to look for the meaning of myths in the minds of their earliest narrators and audiences. The problem of *myth* as a genre term is as confused and confusing as ever, which means that one never quite knows what the different theories of myth are intended by their proponents to apply to. And part of the problem is that we surely overrate the uniqueness of myth, distancing its study unduly from that of the folktale and other traditional narratives.

NOTES

1. Thompson's "Myth and Folktales" is the concluding essay in Sebeok's collection (1965), which was originally published in 1955 in the American Folklore Society's Bibliographical and Special Series.

2. For example, John Lindow (1988, xi) says, "Scandinavian mythology comprises a body of texts, recorded mostly in the thirteenth century in Iceland and dealing with Scandinavian pagan gods."

3. Bidney (1967, 286–326) discusses myth as a form that is usually but not always narrative, citing several scholarly works in which the term is applied to non-narrative cultural ideas. His book appeared originally in 1953, two years before the first publication of Sebeok's *Myth: A Symposium.* Since then this usage has become more common, as for example in Barthes 1972.

4. See for example Dundes' definition, discussed below.

5. For the term see Hansen 1997, 445.

6. Douglas 1996, 40, 43; see also Douglas 1995. Little Red Riding Hood is an international folktale that has been collected in many countries, though the oral versions sometimes show the influence of the well-known literary versions of Perrault and the Grimm brothers. See further Aarne and Thompson 1961, Type 333, *The Glutton (Little Red Riding Hood);* Dundes 1989; Zipes 1993.

7. In contrast, Yvonne Verdier, whose analysis Douglas draws upon for her interpretation of Little Red Riding Hood, emphasizes how much Perrault's late-seventeenth-century literary text (which she terms the popular version) and the nineteenth-century French texts from oral tradition differ in content and meaning (Verdier 1978, 44–45); and Jacopin (1993) elaborates upon this distinction.

8. This is more or less the version of the legend as it is found in Pindar's first *Olympian Ode;* other versions of the story omit the affair with Poseidon. On the story see Hansen 2000.

9. Sergent is vague about the relationship of mythological narratives to the supposed initiatory rituals with which they were connected. This gap in the argument is filled by Georges Dumézil in his preface to Sergent's work. Dumézil (viii–ix) says that the myth may correspond to a rite about which we know little or nothing; or it may be an aetiological myth for a rite that disappeared or changed form, the myth outlasting the practice; or the myth may be a more recent creation that has been composed in imitation of the former two kinds of story. In short, he supposes that most of these stories served as aetiological narratives for rituals of initiatory pederasty. Their original meaning is their true meaning, which is the ritual initiation of a boy into manhood via institutionalized pederasty.

10. For the myth-ritualists see Segal 1998.

BIBLIOGRAPHY

Aarne, Antti, and Stith Thompson. 1961. *The Types of the Folktale: A Classification and Bibliography.* Second revision. FF Communications, no. 184. Helsinki: Academia Scientiarum Fennica.

Barthes, Roland. 1972. *Mythologies*. Translated by Annette Lavers. New York: Hill and Wang.

Bascom, William. 1965. "The Forms of Folklore: Prose Narratives." *Journal of American Folklore* 78:3–20.

Bidney, David. 1967. *Theoretical Anthropology*. 2d edition, augmented. New York: Schocken.

Douglas, Mary. 1995. "Red Riding Hood: An Interpretation from Anthropology." *Folklore* 106:1–7.

————. 1996. "Children Consumed and Child Cannibals: Robertson Smith's Attack on the Science of Mythology." In *Myth and Method*, edited by Laurie L. Patton and Wendy Doniger, 29–51. Charlottesville: University Press of Virginia.

Dundes, Alan, ed. 1984. *Sacred Narrative: Readings in the Theory of Myth*. Berkeley: University of California Press.

————. 1989. *Little Red Riding Hood: A Casebook*. Madison: University of Wisconsin Press.

Hansen, William. 1997. "Homer and the Folktale." In *A New Companion to Homer*, edited by Ian Morris and Barry Powell, 442–62. Leiden: E. J. Brill.

————. 2000. "The Winning of Hippodameia." *Transactions of the American Philological Association* 130:19–40.

Jacopin, Pierre-Yves. 1993. "De l'histoire du *Petit Chaperon Rouge* ou Des transformations d'une histoire de femme." *Ethnologie française* 23:48–65.

Lévi-Strauss, Claude. 1965. "The Structural Study of Myth." In *Myth: A Symposium*, edited by Thomas A. Sebeok, 81–106. Bloomington: Indiana University Press.

Lindow, John. 1988. *Scandinavian Mythology: An Annotated Bibliography*. New York: Garland.

Malinowski, Bronislaw. 1948. "Myth in Primitive Psychology." In *Magic, Science, and Religion and Other Essays*, 93–148. Garden City, N.Y.: Doubleday Anchor.

Sebeok, Thomas A., ed. 1965. *Myth: A Symposium*. Bloomington: Indiana University Press. Originally published in the *Journal of American Folklore* 68 (1955): 379–488.

Segal, Robert A., ed. 1998. *The Myth and Ritual Theory: An Anthology*. Malden, Mass.: Blackwell.

Sergent, Bernard. 1986. *Homosexuality in Greek Myth*. Translated by Arthur Goldhammer, with a preface by Georges Dumézil. Boston: Beacon.

Thompson, Stith. 1965. "Myth and Folktales." In *Myth: A Symposium*, edited by Thomas A. Sebeok, 169–80. Bloomington: Indiana University Press.

Verdier, Yvonne. 1978. "Grands-mères, si vous saviez . . . le Petite Chaperon Rouge dans la tradition orale." *Cahiers de littérature orale* 4:17–55.

Zipes, Jack, ed. 1993. *The Trials and Tribulations of Little Red Riding Hood*. 2nd ed. New York: Routledge.

TWO

From Expressive Language to Mythemes: Meaning in Mythic Narratives

JOHN H. McDOWELL

I t is no secret that there are many ways of thinking about myth, or that myths have multiple layers and levels of meaning. These certainties provoke a number of uncertainties when we attempt to define myth or interpret its meaning. In this essay I will have relatively little to say about the problem of defining myth, but will rather occupy myself with interpretive strategies rooted in the study of language. If we can agree that myth can or must be a story, and that stories are necessarily composed of narrative discourse, then we are well on the way toward recognizing the importance of language as one parameter for assessing the meaning of myth. But our quest will deliver us into some curious paradoxes, when we learn that scholarly programs originating in the study of language can arrive at very different places, and that the very notion of story may be deleted altogether from the enterprise.

In fixing our attention on mythic narrative, we can take a cue from two contributions to Thomas Sebeok's collection of articles *Myth: A Symposium,* published initially as a special issue of the *Journal of American Folklore* in 1955 and subsequently as a paperback anthology by Indiana University Press. Claude Lévi-Strauss's "The Structural Study of Myth" and Philip Wheelwright's "The Semantic Approach to Myth" take their inspiration from modes of inquiry developed by linguists, though the source paradigms are quite different, as is their application to mythic narrative materials. It is nonetheless intriguing to note the almost uncanny ways these two projects intersect, even as they pursue contrasting objectives. I believe that these two luminaries, Wheelwright and Lévi-Strauss, have opened valuable avenues into this tangled domain, avenues that have been traversed to some degree in the ensuing half-century but that have yet to be fully explored. Wheelwright's concept of "expressive language" and Lévi-Strauss's of "mythemes" remain useful as we search out the meanings of mythic narratives. These paradigms, inviting us to view myth as an artistic form of communication on the one hand, and as a parsing of human logic on the other, enhance our appreciation of myth's many meanings.

What words would have passed between Claude Lévi-Strauss and Philip Wheelwright had Sebeok's symposium been actual rather than virtual? We have, on the one hand, Lévi-Strauss, born in Brussels in 1908 and raised in Paris, scion of a family of artists and composers on his father's side, an influential rabbi on his mother's, student and teacher of philosophy, deeply affected by his travels in Brazil and his exile in the United States, already the author of a celebrated monograph on kinship, soon to be appointed to the Chair of Social Anthropology at the Collège de France, where he would remain a fixture for many years. Lévi-Strauss would go on to publish other important work, including the four-volume *Mythologiques,* centered on the mythologies of the South and North American Indian peoples.

On the other hand we have Wheelwright, born in 1901 (and thus seven years Lévi-Strauss's senior) in Elizabeth, New Jersey, educated at Princeton in philosophy and literary studies, professor in turn at NYU, Dartmouth, and the University of California, Riverside, where he had landed a position around the time of Sebeok's virtual symposium on myth. Wheelwright, a member of the American Folklore Society, had just published one of his major works, *The Burning Fountain: A Study in the Language of Symbolism* (1954), and would publish in 1962 his well-known study *Metaphor and Reality.*

Both Lévi-Strauss and Wheelwright were reared in the embrace of philology, where language occupies pride of place, and each man came to see features of language and language analysis as holding the key to the meaning of myth. Philip Wheelwright chose to work within the conventions of philological tradition, grounding his thinking in a discussion of metaphor with roots in the ideas of Max Müller, but reaching toward the illumination provided by contemporary ethnographic accounts. Claude Lévi-Strauss, in contrast, rejected every aspect of the older paradigm in favor of a revolutionary program shaped by his encounter with structural linguistics. Yet his thesis offers, as we shall see, valuable comparativist and functional perspectives on myth, as well as an intriguing vision of myth as a key to human cognition.

WHEELWRIGHT'S EXPRESSIVE LANGUAGE

The argument presented by Philip Wheelwright in *Myth: A Symposium* derives from a basic distinction he makes between what he calls *steno-*

language, "the language of plain sense and exact denotation," and *expressive language,* a language allowing for expression "with maximum fullness." Wheelwright sees these as "two complementary and interpenetrating uses of language," but he clearly regards the latter usage as primarily operative in myth, stating that "expressive language is employed in that wide area which may be designated 'sacred,' and which doubtless includes those forms of story-making that have enough transcendental reference to be properly classified as 'myth'" (1965, 157). We see here Wheelwright's commitment to myth as a form of "story-making," in particular a "sacred" story-making, with "transcendental reference." The distinction between steno-language and expressive language brings to mind ideas of Prague Circle linguists such as Jan Mukařovsky and Bronislav Havránek, later crystallized in Roman Jakobson's distinction between the referential and poetic functions of language (Garvin 1964; Sebeok 1960). But one searches in vain through the footnotes in Wheelwright's books for any reference to this particular body of thought, or to the possibility that Jakobson or his work might connect Wheelwright and Lévi-Strauss.

In any case, Wheelwright focuses his discussion on two basic elements of expressive language, its imagery and its phraseology. The former he captures in the term *diaphor,* coined by Max Müller, which denotes symbolic thinking in which conceptual linkages are forged by innovative, even radical, metaphors. Wheelwright does not accept Müller's thesis that myths arise from "diseased language," that is, language vitiated as names and labels become obscure through the lapse of time, preferring to stipulate a more equitable relationship between language and thought. But he does appear to be comfortable with Müller's "mythopoeic age," a postulated epoch when people habitually thought and expressed themselves through metaphor, formulating what Wheelwright (1965, 156) calls "primary myth."

Wheelwright's discussion of the diaphoric thought process invokes a mythopoeic world, and approaches but then veers away from a key element in Lévi-Strauss's thinking, "the logic of tangible qualities" (Lévi-Strauss 1969). Wheelwright argues that before the familiar process of metaphor we find "a prior semantic movement which operates, often pre-consciously, by bringing raw elements of experience—qualities, capabilities, emotionally-charged suggestibilities, and whatever else—into the specious unity of being represented by a certain symbol" (1965, 159). He hypothesizes that these striking semantic linkages become "gradually formalized into a tribal tradition" and are then played and replayed in the telling of tribal myths. In *Myth: A Symposium* Wheelwright offers two examples of diaphoric thought: the pipe as a manifestation of Wakan Tanka, the Great Spirit of the Lakota Indians, and the scarab, or dung beetle, a powerful symbol of determination and generative potency among the ancient Egyptians. He stresses "the concrete universality, or archetypal character," of diaphoric language (1965, 159).

The other dimension of expressive language that Wheelwright applies to the meaning of myth is what he calls its "sentence" or the process of "sentence-making," by which he intends the verbal constructions housing the diaphoric terms he deems to be typical of myth. Wheelwright helps us grasp his idea of "expressive sentences" by reminding us of those occasions when we add extra vehemence to our utterances in an effort to convey our strong involvement in what we are saying:

> For in regard to all really important affairs where some degree of valuation and emotional commentary enters, we instinctively recognize the inadequacy of strictly logical forms of speech to do justice to our full intended meanings; and we endeavor by tone of voice, facial expression, and gesture, as well as by choice and arrangement of words, to break through the barriers of prescribed definition and express, no doubt inadequately, the more elusive elements in the situation and in our attitude towards it. (1965, 162)

We surmise that expressive sentence-making is a broad and fertile category for Wheelwright, drawing together linguistic, performative, and cognitive dimensions of human speech. What Wheelwright proposes here is nothing less than an artistic rhetoric of verbal performance, assessing the interplay of verbal design, vocal delivery, and personal involvement in the performance of mythic narratives.

Wheelwright's discussion of "sentence-making" provides another moment of false convergence between his project and Levi-Strauss's, when he notes that "expressive sentences tend to function in terms of certain polarities" (1965, 163). On the surface of things, this statement appears to connect with Levi-Strauss's cultivation of opposed or contrary terms in his analysis of myth meanings (1965, 104). But on inspection it becomes clear that these scholars are using the concept of contradiction in very different ways. Wheelwright's polarities have to do with the attitudinal range of expressive language, which encodes, better than other forms of speech, the ambivalence that attaches to the most profound of human experiences. In Levi-Strauss, as we shall see, the notion of opposition is an analytical tool, grounded in human experience but quickly assimilated to the content-less grammar of conceptual forms. This apparent point of contact, like the momentary convergence on the tangible qualities of sensory experience, actually underscores not the proximity of these two projects but the distance that separates them.

LÉVI-STRAUSS'S STRUCTURAL ANALYSIS OF MYTH

Claude Lévi-Strauss, unlike Philip Wheelwright, introduces terms and concepts drawn directly from the linguistics of the period. His focus on language, again unlike Wheelwright's, ultimately leads him away from the actual language of myth and into a different realm altogether, the universal logic of human thinking. For Lévi-Strauss, the methods of structural linguistics offer an escape from the morass (as he might say) of all the old philological questions, and access (he believed) to the clarity of real science. Lévi-Strauss, converted to anthropology through reading Robert Lowie and traveling in Brazil's Matto Grosso, underwent another, equally significant conversion experience some years later in New York City. There, in 1941, he became acquainted with Roman Jakobson, linguist, folklorist, and literary theorist, both men having been cast on America's shores by the turmoil affecting the European continent at the time. Employed on the faculty of the École Libre des Hautes Études, Lévi-Strauss and Jakobson started attending one another's classes (Wiseman and Groves 1998, 86), and Lévi-Strauss, the younger of the two by some twelve years, was struck by the logical precision he saw in Jakobson's treatment of language form and process. These two brilliant refugees became colleagues at the New School for Social Research in the 1940s (Wiseman and Groves 1998).

Roman Jakobson brought into the world of Lévi-Strauss the concepts and methods of structural linguistics, originating in the work of the Swiss linguist Ferdinand de Saussure, and Lévi-Strauss, it is fair to say, never recovered from this moment of mental cross-pollination. The essential premises of structural linguistics—that language is an idealized system of logic, that meaning resides in the relationships among its units, and that language analysis proceeds through binary oppositions—furnished the framework for Lévi-Strauss's reinterpretations of several anthropological domains, including kinship, totemism, primitive thought, and myth. The article included in Sebeok's virtual symposium is Lévi-Strauss's initial and most accessible formulation of his program to apply structural analysis to myth. Later, as I have noted, Lévi-Strauss extends this program in a comprehensive study of myth, the four-volume treatise *Mythologiques* (1964–68), his "mythlogics," working outward from a central myth, of the Bororo of Brazil, to encompass at last a vast corpus of mythology distributed throughout the Americas and beyond, and dipping into a wide spectrum of Western art, literature, and custom for good measure.

Lévi-Strauss's "The Structural Study of Myth" is better known than Wheelwright's "The Semantic Approach to Myth," but it must still be briefly reviewed here. It is hard to say whether Lévi-Strauss's structural program is more remarkable for its ingenuity or its audacity. The audacity is quite breathtaking. Working from what appear to be secure moorings, Lévi-Strauss plunges with suave assurance into a realm of near-total conjecture. Setting forth a program of action grounded in the methods of structural linguistics, he devises interpretations that hurtle off in the direction of whimsy and idiosyncrasy. Yet there is much erudition in this madness, and even more ingenuity. Like many other readers of Lévi-Strauss, I find myself skeptical to the bitter end yet constantly wondering whether, after all, he might be on to something important.

It is easy enough to chart the influence of Lévi-Strauss on a host of followers, some of them prominent scholars in their own right. On this score, we can say he founded, or at the least did much to further, a movement that tended to apply structural analysis to each and every manifestation of human thought and action. We could stand in judgment of his work, finding fault (alongside a phalanx of companions) with its masking of subjectivity in a program dressed to look like objective science. My goal in this essay, however, is to appreciate Lévi-Strauss's ideas, as presented in his essay in Sebeok's anthology. I hope to discover in this work, as we did in Philip Wheelwright's, the kernel of a viable project for assessing the meaning of mythic narratives. In order to accomplish this, I will comment on Lévi-Strauss's notion of myth as a genre, on his technique of paradigmatic analysis, and on the nascent comparativist and functionalist projects subsumed within the structuralist agenda.

Lévi-Strauss argues that myth is unique among the genres on a number of counts. It possesses, he tells us, "a singularity among other linguistic phenomena" as "the part of language where the formula *traduttore, traditore* reaches its lowest truth value" (1965, 85). He asserts that "its substance does not lie in its style, its original music, or its syntax, but in the *story* which it tells" (86). But he doesn't intend *story* in the ordinary sense of narrative plot. Rather, he chooses to disregard this story in favor of an abstract logic embodied in the referents in the tale: the personages, their attributes, and their actions, removed from the narrative flow of the story.

Needless to say, this leap, accomplished so effortlessly in Lévi-Strauss's prose, is highly controversial. For all his dedication to music, Lévi-Strauss denies the original music of mythic narrative in performance, asserting that what is important about myth is the content that can be synopsized. Lévi-Strauss is more interested in references to sensory perception in myth than in myth as a sensuous object in its own right. In one swift gesture, he parts company not only with Philip Wheelwright but also with the many mythographers, myself included, who have come under the spell of mythic narratives performed in the web of living cultures. Many of us would argue that the meaning of myth, whatever it may be, must inhere in the spoken fabric of the narrative, as performed and absorbed in those social settings where myth happens. However, I propose here a slightly different take on the matter; I prefer to say that Lévi-Strauss chooses to pursue a certain perspective on myth. I suppose we can all agree that scholarly projects require this sort of selectivity, and that scholars are not only permitted, but perhaps obliged, to proceed in this fashion.

For Lévi-Strauss, myth is inscrutable, so much so that scholarship on it is "a picture of chaos" (1965, 82) leading to interpretations of its meaning that are either bland or bizarre. He observes that myth at first glance seems to present a world of infinite possibility, yet on inspection it can be seen that the mythic imagination flows through familiar courses:

> With myth, everything becomes possible. But on the other hand, this apparent arbitrariness is belied by the astounding similarity between myths collected in widely different regions. Therefore the problem: if the content of a myth is contingent, how are we going to explain that throughout the world myths do resemble one another so much? (83)

These observations, accurate enough if not particularly novel, suggest to Lévi-Strauss a parallel between the current situation in myth studies and the state of language study before the advent of structural analysis. In order for language study to join the ranks of scientific enterprise, it was necessary to recognize that meaning did not inhere in language elements themselves, but rather in the relationships among these elements. As he writes with regard to phonology, "it is the combination of sounds, not the sounds in themselves, which provides the significant data" (85) These meaning-making sounds are called by Saussure *phonemes*. Later, Lévi-Strauss will label *mythemes* the meaning-making elements in myth (Lévi-Strauss 1985, 144–45).

If this analogy to structural linguistics is apt, to get at the real meaning of myth we must identify the relevant constituent units and the links that bind them into a system. The study of mythology must find what Lévi-Strauss calls the gross constituent units (1965, 86) of myths, gross because they are more expansive than the phonemes and morphemes of linguistic analysis. How do we hit upon these units? Lévi-Strauss recommends a process that is initially mechanical: we analyze the story "into its shortest possible sentences" and write "each sentence on a index card bearing a number corresponding to the unfolding of the story" (87). But we cannot stop there: we must then see how these constituent units relate not to the elements in their immediate narrative environment, but to a set of interpretive codes operating throughout the narrative, and indeed, throughout the corpus of related narratives, and potentially anywhere in the universe of human cognition. What began as a mechanical process, the itemization of story content, becomes a highly imaginative process, the provision of interpretive codes linking story elements into larger paradigms. As Lévi-Strauss has it, "the true constituent units of a myth are not the isolated relations but *bundles of such relations* and it is only as bundles that these relations can be put to use and combined so as to produce a meaning" (87).

Where do we find these thematic containers that give purpose to the mythemes? It is at this stage in the operation, apparently, that a healthy dose of intuition comes into play. But this stage is not entirely random either. It is shaped by a largely implicit functionalism attributing to myth the mission of resolving, or at least deferring or deflecting, points of conceptual tension in the culture. Lévi-Strauss formulates this premise as follows:

> Mythical thought always works from the awareness of oppositions towards their progressive mediation. . . . We need only to assume that two opposite terms with no intermediary always tend to be replaced by two equivalent terms which allow a third one as a mediator. (1965:99)

It is the job of the mythographer to isolate the mythemes in a given myth, to intuit the matrix of conflict they address, and to identify the move toward resolution as opposite terms are replaced with terms admitting of mediation.

In the article we are exploring, Lévi-Strauss discusses in some depth two case studies, what he calls "the Oedipus myth" and the Zuni emergence myth. After the requisite grouping of story elements, the Oedipus myth can be seen to turn on the opposition between "the underrating of blood relations" and "the overrating of blood relations," and ultimately addresses a basic conflict in accounting for the origins of humans:

> The myth has to do with the inability, for a culture which holds the belief that mankind is autochthonous . . . to find a satisfactory transition between this theory and the knowledge that human beings are actually born from the union of man and woman. (1965:91–92)

The Zuni (and by extension the Pueblo peoples in general) are seeking in their emergence myths to resolve (according to this analysis) the fundamental contradiction between life and death by juxtaposing sets of mythemes from the worlds of agriculture and hunting. In these discussions, Lévi-Strauss argues, following a suggestion by Emile Durkheim, that myth is "a logical tool" allowing people to replace an irreconcilable contradiction with terms that can be brought into some form of mediation (Lévi-Strauss 1969, 7).

It is quite a flight of fancy that Lévi-Strauss offers us, as bold as the decision of the bird nester (in a famous myth of the Americas) to venture onto the back of his feathered benefactor. If we take up the offer, we are invited to fly far away from a number of vexing issues, and that is surely part of the seductive power of Lévi-Strauss's ideas. No longer need we search for true or early versions of myths, for in this brave new world of myth analysis all versions are equal, and in fact, interpretations of a myth are merely additional versions of it. Likewise, we no longer need to struggle with the problem of characterizing tribal mentalities, for this approach assures us that primitive thought is no different from civilized thought—the object of thought may be different, but the logic remains continuous. Most importantly, for our purposes, the meaning of myth is now removed from the narrative discourse, which is cast aside as a purely fortuitous vehicle, and relocated in a universal plane of logical process.

MYTH, LANGUAGE, AND THOUGHT

What I have said so far indicates something of the range and scope of ideas presented by these two scholars, both drawn to language analysis as a route to the promised land of understanding myth, but embarked nevertheless on very different missions. I submit that we might admire some features of their programs, and find merit in them, without necessarily buying into the whole project. Both Wheelwright and Lévi-Strauss present inconvenient facets, but setting these aside, I believe that the ideas of each scholar have something of value for us as we continue to search out the holy grail of mythology, the meaning of myth. What I propose to highlight in this last section of the essay are what I see as the most promising threads running through the thought of each of our mythographers, finding expression in a body of valuable scholarship that extends from the day of the symposium to our own and is still capable of inspiring worthwhile thinking about the meaning of myth.

Philip Wheelwright closes his essay with a plea for "a more active liaison between semantics, broadly conceived, and anthropology" (1965, 167), and I believe this plea will help us unlock the mystery of Wheelwright's lasting contributions. Reading through the pages of "The Semantic Approach to Myth," one is struck by Wheelwright's effort to locate and legitimate his philological concerns in the texture of ethnographic fact. In this light, Wheelwright exemplifies a maneuver that in some ways defines modern intellectual history: the attempt to conjoin classical learning with ethnography. Like Francis Barton Gummere, Sir James Frazer, Louise Pound, Stith Thompson, and many others, Wheelwright struggles to bring his literary

theories into focus through contact with firsthand reports from exotic locales. We witness in Wheelwright, as in the others, a telling encounter between European (or Western) erudition and the realities of life as conveyed
in ethnographic descriptions of village and tribal peoples.

Because this encounter, like the symposium on myth, is virtual or mediated, the resulting agenda has the flavor of armchair scholarship. I am not
aware that Wheelwright personally observed or documented a performance
of mythic narrative. In writing of the Plains Indian belief in Wakan Tanka,
he registers some hesitation in using the label "Lakota," imagining that the
source of his information had intended "Dakota" instead. Wheelwright's
hesitation here clearly illustrates the hazards of armchair research. As a consequence, his ideas must remain programmatic rather than deeply grounded in ethnographic context. But we can salvage from this program, I
believe, the outlines of a viable research inquiry into the social aesthetics of
mythic narrative performance.

At the core of this program we find the situated performance of mythic
narratives, much as I have witnessed them among the Kamsá and Ingano in
Colombia's Sibundoy Valley (McDowell 1989, 1994). Wheelwright draws
our attention to this discourse as an instance of expressive language, and he
invites us to take notice of the rhetorical devices, in all relevant expressive
domains, that lend this discourse what he calls "semantic fluidity and plenitude" (1965, 167). This program requires us to attend to facial expression
and gesture, grammatical form, lexical choice, and, of course, the specialized vocabulary of diaphora, as these features converge to create the peculiar efficacy of mythic narrative. It is not difficult to discover in this
program an endorsement for the ethnography of speaking myth, a project
that has advanced significantly from the time of Wheelwright's essay, as is
evident in the work of scholars such as Dell Hymes, Dennis Tedlock, Ellen
Basso, Barre Toelken, Joel Sherzer, Jonathan Hill, Steven Feld, and many
others. My own work in the Sibundoy Valley of Colombia is inspired by
this program.

But Wheelwright's interest in myth as a form of expressive language
does not stop with this ample investigation of mythic narrative discourse.
He has an ulterior motive, which is to describe as closely as possible the attitude toward the sacred held by those who nurture mythic narrative traditions. He presents on this score a most intriguing argument: that the
"genuinely religious believer is one who gives full commitment—not necessarily to the sentences in their literal meanings . . . , but to some half-
guessed, half-hidden truth which the sentences symbolize" (1965, 166). It
is this recognition of the complexity of religious belief that I find especially valuable in Wheelwright's approach. It is his discussion of diaphora, the
active process of symbolization that defines mythical thought, that conveys
Wheelwright to this nuanced treatment of belief.

Diaphora, the formation of radical metaphoric linkages, activates a charged connection between a *vehicle,* the signifier, and a *tenor,* the signified. Wheelwright characterizes the vehicle in diaphora as "usually clear and vivid, although perhaps shocking to everyday standards of probability," and depicts a diaphoric tenor, or referent of the religious metaphor, that "looms darkly behind the scene as something vague, inarticulate, yet firmly intuited and somehow of tremendous, even final, importance and consequentiality." He assesses the patterns of belief attaching to the parts of diaphoric thought:

> To accept the vehicle in its literal aspect exclusively is the way of superstition; to accept its transcendental references (the tenor) exclusively is the way of allegory. The primitively mytho-religious attitude in its most characteristic forms has tended to settle into some kind of fertile tension between these two extremes without yielding too completely to either of them.

Forestalling simplistic notions of primitive belief, Wheelwright argues instead for a rather sophisticated balance between superstition and allegory, partaking to some degree of both. He concludes that "so far as the mythic storyteller is half-consciously aware of the tension his narrative may achieve that tone of serious playfulness which characterizes so charmingly much early myth" (1965, 167).

Dispensing with gratuitous details such as "early" myth and "primitive" thought, we have here a charter for exploring with some delicacy the mental framework of religious belief as conveyed in mythic narratives. Wheelwright offers a contemplative myth-teller, with a refined capacity to shift back and forth between literal and figurative mental frameworks. Although he may not have set out to do so, Wheelwright redeems the cultural "other" (and in the process, he redeems himself and, by extension, the rest of us) as a figure far more complex than the two-dimensional stereotypes of "the savage" or "the primitive" would suggest. Here it seems that Wheelwright's formation in the humanities, with its sensitivity to the coils of human imagination, has usefully tempered the headlong rush of the social sciences to arrive at large-scale generalizations. Wheelwright's doctrine of the "serious playfulness of belief" can readily be abstracted from the discussion of "primary" myth and brought forward as a handle on all ideological systems alleging immanent truth.

What about the ideas of Claude Lévi-Strauss as applied to the meaning of myth? What can we salvage for posterity from the structuralist agenda? I sense an assimilation of Lévi-Strauss's orientation into research and theory on myth. I believe that core ideas, such as "the logic of sensible qualities," the sets of repeating and contrastive elements, and the cultural codes they entail, have quietly found their way into the thinking of most mythogra-

phers writing today. This leaching of ideas into the scholarly agenda is a tribute to the French anthropologist who made mobiles representing mythical
structures and who lived, by his own account, for twenty years with "all these
populations and their myths as if in a fairy tale" (Lévi-Strauss 1995, 132).

If the mechanics and intuitive leaps of structural analysis are set aside
for the moment, we may ask: what of value remains? I see major arenas
where Lévi-Strauss's thinking remains vibrant. The first of these is in the
comparative study of mythology. Alan Dundes argues that "although Lévi-
Strauss's methodology wears the trappings of structuralism, his actual
method is a form, an idiosyncratic form to be sure, of the *comparative
method*" (1997, 41). As a mythographer working in South America, I have
found great value in the compilation of myths from all over the continent
he provides in the *Mythologiques*. Lévi-Strauss established a laboratory in
France for compiling, synopsizing, and translating hundreds of mythic narrative texts, from scores of indigenous communities, collected by dozens of
field researchers. These eight-hundred-plus abbreviated texts (some of
them quite perfunctory), spanning the South and North American continents, receive their M-numbers at the back of each of the four volumes of
the *Mythologiques* and make up the largest available inventory of the mythic narratives of America's native populations.

But is this the extent of it? What are we to make of the structural
method that Lévi-Strauss has applied so assiduously to myth? Is there nothing to be said for the mytheme? It must be conceded that Lévi-Strauss's ex-
cursions across mythologies on the basis of perceived affinities (and
contrasts) lead to interesting and surprising areal mappings, even on occasion signaling something that looks a lot like what he calls "the bedrock of
American mythology" (1978, 255). The lure of Lévi-Strauss shines forth in
a reprise he wrote to Stith Thompson's celebrated study of the Star Husband Tale (1953), and this jousting of rival theories presents an opportunity to assess the merits of structuralist thinking. It is midway through *The
Origin of Table Manners,* volume 3 of the *Mythologiques,* that Lévi-Strauss
launches his structuralist antidote to historic-geographic analysis, in a section called "The Porcupine's Instructions."

Stith Thompson, employing the Finnish or historic-geographic method, assembles a corpus of related narratives from several North American
Indian tribes inhabiting the northern plains and adjacent areas. Using techniques that are familiar to folklorists, he then isolates a basic version of the
tale, and what he calls "the porcupine redaction" found in Arapaho variants.
Thompson concludes that the basic, oldest form of the Star Husband Tale
must have been widely distributed over the northern plains by the eighteenth century, and that the porcupine redaction must have originated
within this zone no later than the 1890s.

Let's focus our attention on the porcupine redaction. I reproduce the outline of the tale, as presented by Lévi-Strauss (1978, 229), omitting the frequencies he provides for each element within the corpus of twenty related myths, from the Arapaho and several other Plains Indian tribes:

> A girl while performing a task follows a porcupine up a tree which stretches to the upper world. The porcupine becomes the moon, the sun, or a star, in the form of a young man. The girl marries him and bears him a son. She is warned not to dig, but disobeys and discovers a sky-hole. By her own efforts or with the help of her husband she descends on a sinew rope, but it is too short. The husband sends down a rock with instructions to kill the wife and spare the son.

Here we have in splendid form the lure and the mystery of myth. The story is engaging, yet it begs for interpretation. What can it have meant to the Plains Indians who told it to one another? What can it mean to us?

Stith Thompson is primarily concerned to position this cluster of myths within the larger setting of the star husband cycle. He views the porcupine redaction as a later, territorially restricted incrustation, but does not tackle the tricky question of the myth's meaning. Lévi-Strauss adopts a friendly stance toward Stith Thompson, calling him "the distinguished American representative" of the Finnish School, thanking him for his meticulous work, without which the present refinement would not be possible (1978, 227). But courtesy does not prevent him from offering a radically different interpretation of the same set of myths, nor does it keep him from leveling a withering attack on the methods and goals of historic-geographic studies. He directs attention to the position of the porcupine in North American mythology, inquiring, "What is its significance? Or rather, what are the myths trying to signify through its agency?" (241).

Lévi-Strauss scolds practitioners of the Finnish method for failing to "raise the question of what constitutes a fact in folklore" (228). This failing, he asserts, causes Thompson to focus on the presence or absence of story details while neglecting the logical relationships evident between the different versions of these myths. He argues that variants of a myth "do not differ from each other in the manner of material objects, whose unequal extensions in space and time are simply to be recorded." Instead, he tells us, myths in this cycle "are dynamically inter-linked, which means that they are in oppositional and correlational relationships with each other" (233). Applying this principle, he rakes additional versions into his net, eventually reaching into South America for distant cognates of a theme he sees as centering on "the wives of the sun and the moon." His mission is not so much to provide a historical account of the myth's origin and movement as to devise "an intelligible synchronic system" (263). Still, as we will see, he is not indifferent to historical permutations.

Following Lévi-Strauss as he searches out the meaning of these myths, we traverse a spectacular cultural field. At the outer edge, we are dealing with instructions provided to young women so that they will acquire the proper life habits. This issue extends beyond the Americas, but themes recurring in this cluster of myths are portrayed as marking the ancient bedrock of American mythology. With regard to the porcupine, we learn much about its cultural importance as the source of quills essential in the beadwork of the Plains Indians, an art practiced by refined women of these tribes. It becomes crucial to uncover the periodicity of the porcupine, whose "quills vary in quantity and quality according to the season" (249), for one semantic component of the myths under consideration is their marking of a temporal code.

It turns out (pursuing this line of reasoning) that the porcupine redaction acquires its meaning through contrast with a set of related myths found among Algonquin tribes and their neighbors centering on the grebe, a duck, who acts as a deceptive suitor to two young women who have escaped their husbands, the sun and the moon. Lévi-Strauss presents diagrams showing that the two clusters, the porcupine redaction and the grebe redaction, systematically reverse all the polarities in the analysis.

I will spare you the full discussion and go directly to its conclusion in an argument that links history and myth interpretation. Lévi-Strauss (1978, 265) displays the two redactions on a map locating the tribes who sustain them. What we contemplate there are two triangular areas whose point of contact lies west of Lake Superior. The grebe redaction occupies a territory that extends from this point east and north across Canada. The territory of the porcupine redaction extends to the west and south across the Great Plains of the United States. This distribution suggests to Lévi-Strauss a rationale for this set of logical oppositions:

> If, as seems to be the case, the Plains Algonquin and their Siouan neighbors came from the northeast, where the porcupine was to be found, they may well, on losing the real animal, have reversed a mythological system which was originally very close to the one retained by the Ojibwa. (271)

The argument rests on this functionalist thesis:

> If the presence of an animal as important as the porcupine . . . is transformed into its absence, then in all those contexts in which it played a part . . . the animal must be projected into a different world. (272–73)

Casting his net widely and asserting structural relations spanning the American continents, Lévi-Strauss proposes a chronology very different from

Thompson's, arguing that "mythic forms common to both hemispheres must have their origin in a very remote past" (271). We are dealing, he claims, "not in decades, but millennia" (233).

So where does this leave us? Some portions of Lévi-Strauss's argument are fairly easy to accept. One equivalence centers on advice received by the young women as they descend from the sky. In one cycle they hear from a meadowlark, a bird that roots about on the forest floor, and in the other from a sequence of creatures marking a gradual approach to the earth (a chickadee, a tree-roaming squirrel, and a ground-roaming squirrel). These and several other junctures in the structural analysis are not difficult to swallow. But what about the correlation alleged between a rheumy old man (who leaks from above) and an incontinent young woman (who leaks from below)? There are numerous junctures that, like this one, require a leap of faith on the reader's part.

It seems we cannot entirely dismiss the fruits of structural analysis, if we accept that it is capable of providing insights into the meaning, purpose, and function of myth. One appealing feature of Lévi-Strauss's program is easily lost in all the mental gyrations, and that is its dedication to a functionalist agenda. In Sebeok's symposium Lévi-Strauss articulates the conviction that myth performs a vital function, that of reconciling or mediating points of conflict within a culture. Myth is presented as a logical tool used by people to resolve, or at least displace, salient contradictions in their cosmologies. In the case of the porcupine redaction, the functionalist argument is grounded in the presence and absence of a vital animal, and explains a systematic reversal in the valencies of mythical elements from one group of tribes to another. Functionalism is not always foregrounded in Lévi-Strauss, but I believe that, on balance, it is the most valuable dimension of his work. The idea that expressive forms might be used to resolve or mediate areas of profound social uneasiness is an idea that is still very much with us.

Wheelwright and Lévi-Strauss offer approaches to myth's meaning that start from a similar point, move off in opposite directions to open contrastive perspectives, yet somehow converge again in staking out a common area of concern. The shared point of origin is the conviction that myth, a form of narrative discourse, can be illuminated through the application of concepts and models drawn from the study of language. But this conviction, we have seen, produces divergent analyses, one leading into the original music of myth, its sensuous medium, the other away from it. Still, it appears that each man is, in the end, concerned with the overarching issue of how people think, each viewing mythic narrative as an especially revealing lens into the process of human thought. Wheelwright, drawn to the social aesthetics of mythic narrative performance, delivers a nuanced model of religious belief, which modulates (in this view) between the poles of super-stition and allegory. Lévi-Strauss, drawn to mythic narrative as an instru-ment of thought, delivers a system of logical operations founded on sensory perception and cultural classifications. The intellectual crux that unites them is a passion for understanding how human beings create and manipu-late symbols: in Wheelwright's account, through diaphoric thought; in Lévi-Strauss's, through the logic of tangible qualities.

My purpose in bringing these two approaches into conversation with one another, in actualizing (through the imagination) the virtual sympo-sium, is to designate one broad arena where the continuing quest for myth's meaning may proceed, an arena defined by myth's necessary com-mitment to mythic narrative. Whether we stick to a social aesthetics of myth or tackle myth's structures of logic, we will do well to explore the piv-otal links between myth, language, and thought. Wheelwright's treatment of expressive language allows us to penetrate the core ambivalence enclos-ing the most charged domains of human imagination. Lévi-Strauss's dissec-tion of mythic narrative offers a unique vantage point on the resolution of deeply rooted conceptual conflicts. These language-based interpretive pro-grams should provide ample inspiration for another generation of mythog-raphers.

BIBLIOGRAPHY

Dundes, Alan. 1997. "Binary Opposition in Myth: The Propp/Lévi-Strauss Debate in Ret-rospect." *Western Folklore* 56:39–50.

Garvin, Paul, ed. and trans. 1964. *A Prague School Reader on Esthetics, Literary Structure, and Style.* Washington, D.C.: Georgetown University Press.

Lévi-Strauss, Claude. 1965. "The Structural Study of Myth." In *Myth: A Symposium,* edit-ed by Thomas A. Sebeok, 81–106. Bloomington: Indiana University Press.

———. 1969. *The Raw and the Cooked: Introduction to a Science of Mythology, Volume 1.* Translated by John and Doreen Weightman. New York: Harper and Row.

———. 1978. *The Origin of Table Manners: Introduction to a Science of Mythology, Vol-ume 3.* Translated by John and Doreen Weightman. New York: Harper and Row.

———. 1985. *The View from Afar.* Translated by Joachim Neugroschel and Phoebe Hoss. New York: Basic.

———. 1995. *Myth and Meaning.* New York: Schocken.

McDowell, John Holmes. 1989. *Sayings of the Ancestors: The Spiritual Life of the Sibundoy Indians.* Lexington: University Press of Kentucky.

———. 1994. *"So Wise Were Our Elders": Mythic Narratives of the Kamsá.* Lexington: Uni-versity Press of Kentucky.

Sebeok, Thomas A., ed. 1965. *Myth: A Symposium.* Bloomington: Indiana University Press. Originally published in the *Journal of American Folklore* 68 (1955): 379–488.

———. 1960. *Style in Language.* Cambridge, Mass.: The Technology Press of the Massa-chusetts Institute of Technology.

Thompson, Stith. 1953. "The Star Husband Tale." *Studia Septentrionalia* 4:93–163. Oslo, Norway.

Wheelwright, Philip. 1965. "The Semantic Approach to Myth." In *Myth: A Symposium,* edited by Thomas A. Sebeok, 154–68. Bloomington: Indiana University Press.

———. 1968. *The Burning Fountain: A Study in the Language of Symbolism.* Revised edition. Bloomington: Indiana University Press. Originally published in 1954.

———. 1962. *Metaphor and Reality.* Bloomington: Indiana University Press.

Wiseman, Boris, and Judy Groves. 1998. *Introducing Lévi-Strauss.* New York: Totem.

THREE

David Bidney and the People of Truth

GREGORY SCHREMPP

E xcept in this sentence, no quotation marks frame the word "truth" in this essay. Or perhaps I should invoke another contemporary formula and say: the concept of truth was not harmed in the writing of this essay. David Bidney would not have liked the implication of the quotation marks; indeed his paper "Myth, Symbolism, and Truth" is directed against perspectives in which, in his view, myth comes out true at the cost of weakening what it means to be true. Bidney's piece in *Myth: A Symposium* is a grand iteration of the twin Enlightenment doctrines of the progress of reason and the displacement of myth by science—doctrines that now appear doubtful if not deeply pernicious to many humanistic scholars. In Bidney's writings on myth, moreover, one encounters terminology that even by the standards of his day is sometimes ethnographically insensitive. Is that why Bidney's essay appears as the opening piece in *Myth: A Symposium*—to have done with it? Bidney's final paragraph says it all:

> Myth must be taken seriously as a cultural force but it must be taken seriously precisely in order that it may be gradually superseded in the interests of the advancement of truth and the growth of human intelligence. Normative, critical, and scientific thought provides the only self-correcting means of combating the diffusion of myth, but it may do so only on condition that we retain a firm and uncompromising faith in the integrity of reason and in the transcultural validity of the scientific enterprise. (1965, 23)

None of the terms are in quotation marks, and this does not augur well for an understanding of Bidney that gives him a place in current approaches to myth.

But among the many motives for historical retrospection is that of checking our own inclination to read the past in terms of present-day formulas. When we read the arguments of past thinkers in terms of their own historical contexts, they often emerge as more complex and less monolithic than they might now appear to us at first glance. I would like to consider some aspects of the context of Bidney's seemingly imperious proclamation, suggesting an expanded sense of what, and whom, he had in mind in opposing myth and truth. In the course of my analysis I will also draw out some dilemmas in the concept of myth that still embroil us, particularly dilemmas posed by the many connotations of the term "myth." Most notoriously, "myth" in some contexts denotes a particular culture's wisdom, while in others—including popular usage—it is synonymous with falsehood. The particular question I will consider is: in Bidney's writings on myth, just who are the people of myth and who are the people of truth? The myth vs. truth opposition has often been aligned with other oppositions—for example, ancient vs. modern, non-Western vs. Western, "primitive" vs. "civilized." Because there is a history of such alignments, the reader could easily read such associations into Bidney's statement. What I want to show is that, at the least, Bidney's sense of who possesses myth and who possesses truth defies any easy dichotomization.[1]

What I will offer is a specific form of contextualization that I was first struck by, improbably, during the Watergate scandal. In particular, a news reporter was criticized for unfairness in quoting without context unflattering comments by Harry Truman about Nixon's moral character. Surprisingly, the context alleged to be missing was not the immediate circumstances of the particular comments or even Truman's full corpus of Nixon comments, but rather the context afforded by Truman's comments about *other* politicians. For what Truman had said about Nixon, his defender argued, was pretty much what Truman said about everybody—and the comments thus told us less about Nixon than about Truman's view of the world. No fan of the Nixon presidency, I do think that this particular point in Nixon's defense was legitimate, and has an insight to offer on the complicated business of historical contextualization. The example offers an interesting spin on the structuralist idea that meaning must be understood as a function of difference: what is a particular speaker saying *differently* about one person or group than about another?[2] To be specific: when one juxtaposes Bidney's commentary on myth with his commentaries on the works of his contemporaries in social science, one finds that the criticisms Bidney levels against myth-tellers are pretty much the same criticisms he levels against his fellow academicians in the social sciences. I would like to explore in more detail the overlap between Bidney's evaluation of myth and his evaluation of the social science of his time, focusing especially on two specific themes. The first has to do with the analytical role of the concept of culture, the second with metaphorical or nonliteral language, the two themes converging in Bidney's critique of anthropologist Alfred Kroeber's theory of culture.

THE ANALYTICAL ROLE OF CULTURE

Of the many social science currents of the mid–twentieth century, Bidney was particularly interested in those that accorded to cultural process a high degree of autonomy from human agency, as though culture ran on its own steam. Bidney was highly skeptical of such currents of thought, seeing them as intellectually indefensible and morally irresponsible.

Bidney's critical writings about the alleged autonomy of culture developed in the context of flourishing mid-twentieth-century debates about the relationship between the various disciplines of social science. Schemes for the organization of academic disciplines are sometimes designed to reflect the hierarchical organization of the natural and social worlds. A potent early-nineteenth-century source of such thinking was Auguste Comte (e.g., see Comte 1975, 87ff.), while during Bidney's era *Toward a General Theory of Action,* edited by Talcott Parsons and Edward Shils (1951), suggested a scheme of this kind for the social sciences. Comte and later Parsons and Shils argue that each supervening level of organization requires its own analytic frame, dedicated to the discovery of the principles of organization at that level.[3] The schema of *Theory of Action* legitimizes three main organizational levels—which happen to correspond to social science disciplines—as relevant to the explanation of human action: psychological, social, and cultural.

Most of Bidney's critical assessments of the social science of his era focus upon junctures between organizational levels of the sort laid out by Parsons and Shils—and specifically upon the paired problems of "emergence" and "reductionism" that occur around such junctures. Bidney's best-known forays are those in which he takes anthropologist Alfred Kroeber to task for positing a cultural "superorganic"—a level of organization in which culture is seen to operate in terms of its own self-contained dynamic. This dynamic is explicable without reference, for example, to the particular "personalities" that appear on the stage at specific times and places. Perhaps following the lead of philosopher G. E. Moore, who called attention to the "naturalistic fallacy" in ethical reasoning, Bidney dubbed Kroeber's error the "culturalistic" fallacy. In the course of Bidney's *Theoretical Anthropology* (1953b) we also hear about the "psychologistic" fallacy, the "ethnologistic" fallacy, and the "sociologistic" fallacy. These tags, and the elaborate analyses that accompany each, challenge the expansionist ambitions of the various social science disciplines—ambitions evident in the inclination of particular disciplines to deny the relevance of the types of factors studied by other disciplines.

Thus, when we look carefully into Bidney's assessment of the social science of his era, one of the things we encounter is an attitude toward science that in fact departs from the seemingly monolithic tone of "Myth, Symbolism, and Truth." The social science that attracted Bidney was variegated; his barbs are aimed precisely at those who reduce all perspectives to one.[4] Bidney was particularly opposed to formulations that left out the personalities—the level of persons as moral agents. I will explore the details of Kroeber's arguments on this issue, and Bidney's criticisms of them, after briefly discussing one other midcentury doctrine that, in Bidney's view, also accorded an unjustified autonomy to the concept of culture—the doctrine of "cultural relativism."

Bidney developed a reputation as a gadfly in regard to "cultural relativism," perhaps the most important anthropological idea of his day. To this doctrine Bidney brought the same charge that he brought to Kroeber's "superorganic": cultural relativism was a defective doctrine because it removed the moral agent from culture (see especially Bidney 1953a). Over against cultural relativism, Bidney espoused the possibility of transcultural truth—a notion which, in our present era, tends to raise the specter of Western culture as global juggernaut. In the realm of the social or moral sciences, such truth was, for Bidney, largely a possibility for the future, not something that anyone now possessed, and it would be based in part on points where the moralities of different cultures converged, which Bidney thought were more numerous than the cultural relativists realized (Bidney 1953a, 694).[5] Bidney saw science not as a monolith but as a way out of monolithism. The defect of cultural relativism in his view was precisely that this doctrine allowed any culture to be monolithic—a closed, self-contained system and ground of its own truth. For Bidney, science was by definition ever-open to critical reassessment; culture as envisioned by cultural relativists did not seem to him to embody a similar openness.[6]

The context that frames Bidney's major discussions of the analytical role of culture and of the doctrine of cultural relativism is the moral and political crises of Western society in the era of World War II—which, I suggest, are the real source for Bidney's views on myth, indeed for his intellectual orientation in general.[7] Closed systems of self-justifying doctrines and analytic schemes that neglect the individual person as moral agent are Bidney's perennial targets; and in regard to these concerns Bidney saw as much to criticize in cultural relativism as in political totalitarianism—indeed, he saw a resemblance between these doctrines. In this context, and owing also in part to his training in philosophy, Bidney's theory of myth emphasized a line of political thought stemming from Plato, in which myth connotes something like the unexamined doctrines that sway social masses. Although there are moments of self-congratulation for things Western, and of dismissal of things non-Western, the image that preponderates in Bidney's writings is neither of these, but rather the moral failure of contemporary Western society.

LITERALISM AND SYMBOLISM
IN MYTH AND SOCIAL SCIENCE

At this point, I turn to a second area of overlap evident in Bidney's attitudes toward myth and social science. This overlap lies in the assessment of the relationship between literal and what, following Bidney, I will call "symbolic" readings (the latter encompassing the range of possible nonliteral readings, e.g., "metaphorical," "allegorical," "figurative"). Bidney's position is summarized in the following passage from "Myth, Symbolism, and Truth":

> Myth has a positive value for the ethnologist and folklorist as a record of man's culture history and as a means of establishing universal patterns of thought. Myth, like great art and dramatic literature, may have profound symbolic or allegorical value for us of the present, not because myth necessarily and intrinsically has such latent, esoteric wisdom, but because the plot or theme suggests to us universal patterns of motivation and conduct. It must not be assumed, however, that the subjective, symbolic value of a myth for us and the actual historical beliefs of its originators are identical. (1965, 22)

This passage and others suggest Bidney's attraction to what I regard as the single most problematic assumption to be found in nineteenth-century theories of myth: the idea that what "others" do in literal error, "we" do as self-aware imagery and artistry.[8] Bidney was familiar with the writings of the nineteenth-century social evolutionist E. B. Tylor, who came to this view while considering the theories of the so-called "solar mythologists" who flourished in the late nineteenth century.[9] Tylor noted that in "civilized" nature poetry and art we encounter the same animistic imagery that is characteristic of ancient mythologies, and concluded that what is now artistic metaphor must have once been literal, and hence erroneous, belief—the product of an archaic age of error. Although Bidney does not go so far as to insist, as did Tylor, that the capacity for "symbolic" reading has only truly developed in more recent epochs, Bidney does believe that the proper methodological stance requires presuming a literal intent in myth unless there is evidence to the contrary. In other words, Bidney follows Tylor in assuming that the mythic mind is inclined to the error of over-literalization.

But when one moves back again to Bidney's evaluation of his contemporary social scientists, it turns out that the ancient creators of solar myths are not the only people Bidney takes to task for literalizing what are really only analogical abstractions. Bidney's writings are part of a broader academic fretting about "reification" and "misplaced concreteness" that characterized midcentury social science theory.[10] Consider a passage from Bidney's "The Concept of 'As If' and Methodological Abstraction," in his *Theoretical Anthropology.* The passage appeared in 1953, when the Bidney/Kroeber debates about the "superorganic" were essentially over.

> [I]t is important that we distinguish between epistemic, methodological levels of abstraction, on the one hand, and metaphysical or ontological levels of reality, on the other. As a methodological device it is frequently useful to abstract certain phenomena for systematic treatment and to ignore the individuals, with their motivations, who were undoubtedly involved. Thus, the historian may consider the history of ideas, of political or social institutions, as a sequence of forms without bothering too much about the individuals who initiated and championed these movements. In this sense there is a certain rhythm in the progression of historical thought; certain configurations emerge and recur which it is possible to demonstrate in the large by abstracting the universal forms from the concrete matter of the personal and social contexts in which they occurred. Natural science has developed greatly as a result of this method of abstraction. Epistemic abstraction as a methodological invention is a fiction of the logical imagination.

Bidney also adds that "the culturalistic fallacy is committed only when one mistakes this epistemic, fictional abstraction for an ontological level of reality or autonomous order of nature," and that "[t]hus, Kroeber, as of 1948, is employing the concept of the 'as if' as a purely methodological pragmatic device" (1953b, 106–107).

What is going on in this passage? First of all, Kroeber, in his original 1917 paper "The Superorganic," had announced the cultural superorganic in full, nonfictional dress, invoking, among other things, the time-honored metaphysical term "substance" to denote the self-contained, autonomous character of culture. Cultural phenomena were to be explained strictly by reference to other cultural phenomena: cultural analysis was never to appeal to biological, psychological, or individual (life-history) factors. Culture became a sort of uncaused cause. Faced with Bidney's attacks, Kroeber capitulated. However, Kroeber retracted not the whole idea of the superorganic, but rather the sense or force—the ontological illocution—with which he had originally proffered it. Kroeber's recantation reads in part,

> I retract, as unwarranted reification, the references . . . to organic and superorganic "substances," entities, or fabrics. While it certainly is often needful to view different kinds of phenomena as of different orders and to deal with them on separate levels of apprehension, there is no need for metaphysically constructing levels of conception or orders of attribute into substantial entities or different kinds of substance. (1952, 23)

The comments by Bidney quoted above, concerning Kroeber and the "as if," can be seen as Bidney invoking something akin to the contrast between literalist and symbolic readings that he discusses in writings about myth, only this time in the context of social science. Kroeber's comment helps to fill out Bidney's specific purpose in the new context. By validating nonliteral—"as if"—usages in social science, Bidney is trying to create a space in which Kroeber, whom Bidney had initially attacked as just plain wrong—or should I say, substantially wrong?—not only escapes this painful state, but is seen as operating within a perspective that has contributed greatly to the development of science. Bidney's admission of nonliteral readings here seems to have the same literal-until-proven-otherwise tone characteristic of his approach to myth; the proof otherwise, in the case of Kroeber, is Kroeber's own statement that literal readings of his theory should be renounced.

Working in part from my memories of Bidney's lectures on this episode, I suggest that the same paragraph can also be seen as an expression of gratitude by Bidney to the great Kroeber, a leading contender for the mantle of Franz Boas, for taking Bidney's philosophical arguments seriously and not only retreating but retreating metaphysically. *Theoretical Anthropology* is dedicated to Kroeber, and passages that follow the one quoted above suggest that Bidney may also have been proposing a new alliance, between himself and Kroeber, arrayed for battle against a third colorful and influential scholar of the same era, Leslie White, a rebellious Boasian. White was still, in Bidney's view, holding out for the ontological and literal formulation of the cultural superorganic. In the context of these and related arguments Bidney several times invokes the term "myth" and its nineteenth-century synonym—"animism" or "animistic thought"—in characterizing the error in his contemporaries' scientific formulations (1953b, 110ff.).

To summarize: for Bidney, one of the problems of the social science of his day was its perennial propensity for myth. Myth for Bidney connoted a universal inclination toward intellectual carelessness and irresponsibility—in this case in the form of a cavalier attitude regarding the "sense" in which a proposition is intended. Bidney was in effect tapping the well-honed philosophical tradition of the critique of myth—thought of, in the legacy of Plato, as uncritical opinion—and deploying this tradition in a critique of social science.

Some of Bidney's arguments were prescient. Certainly, for example, the spirit of his critique of the "superorganic" has something in common with more recent calls for recognizing the role of individual agency within cultural process (e.g., Clifford and Marcus 1986, 15ff). Skepticism toward the robust midcentury forms of cultural relativism also runs deep in our era. While Bidney might not find many takers today for his proposed antidote to cultural relativism (i.e., transcultural science), recognition of universal human values or rights is implicit in much contemporary ethnographic analysis; the minimal distillation seems to be something like the idea of a universal human right to freedom from "hegemonic" regimes. But skepticism is evident particularly in our present-day inclination to hear only half of the idea of cultural relativism that was propounded at midcentury. We hear the part that says that no culture has the moral authority to impose its forms on another culture, while ignoring the part that grounds moral authority in the unique configuration of any particular culture, giving to that configuration a kind of moral autonomy and finality over its adherents. Finally, Bidney also speaks to the reflexive turn of our times, for he was talking about the necessity for a self-critical component in anthropology, which he called "meta-anthropology" well before the "meta" thing became fashionable.

Certainly one source of resistance to Bidney among mythologists is the final nomenclature; there's no denying that for Bidney "myth" is the term that connotes a hegemonic, unreflective, closed spirit, "science" the term that connotes a liberating, critical, and open spirit. Furthermore, Bidney's work, like virtually all anthropological and folkloristic work of his era, affirms problematic distinctions—such as that between "myth" and "science," or "primitive" and "modern"—even when these distinctions are used in arguments that attempt to undercut them; certainly we are not free of such conceptual entanglements today. All of this, and especially the usage of the term "myth," bequeaths to us a terminological situation that many mythologists regard as regrettable—though Bidney did not create it, nor was it laid to rest with him. But if Bidney's use of the term "myth" is treacherous, his use of the term "science" is even more so, for the reader might assume that by it Bidney is referring to those of his contemporaries who identify themselves as the scientific community. While one does find in Bidney a number of loose self-congratulatory references to the scientific spirit of the modern era, they are directed toward science as an ideal; the tone is greatly muted when it comes to specifics, and especially to the social science doctrines of his day. And the ideal of science is accompanied by a caution:

> In scientific thought, there is a tendency to discount narratives of the miraculous and supernatural, but to accept secular myths instead. In our so-called scientific culture we have the secular beliefs of pseudo-science, such as the myths of racial superiority and the stereotypes of racial and national character. (1953b, 325)

Finally, we should keep in mind that Bidney was a philosopher teaching in a department of anthropology—an intersection that provided the perfect

opportunity for opposed connotations of "myth" to collide. In the particular philosophical/political tradition that Bidney represented, "myth" carried
the connotation of unexamined doctrine, often with reference to the political sphere. In the other academic tradition relevant to Bidney's situation—
that of American anthropology—we find some of the same connotations,
but, along with these, other and nearly opposite ones. Specifically, in American anthropology myth often connotes foundational wisdom recorded in
the narratives of particular cultures—and in the case of midcentury anthropology, that of course often meant non-Western cultures. Myth in this
context forms a resource that offers not only an *object* but also a *source* of
comparative critique of Western society. Whether or not it is useful that
such opposed connotations converge in the single term "myth," we have to
ask whether we can ultimately dispense with either of them. On the negative side of their co-presence in one term is the great injustice that is done
when myths of the second sort are automatically assumed to be also (or
merely) myths of the first sort; and Bidney does fall prey at times to just
such—uncritical—elision. On the positive side of the co-presence is the
fact that the two sets of connotations often do belong together, or at least
are impossibly difficult to disentangle. For a certain amount of indoctrina-
tion—an element of faith or axiomatic acceptance—seems to be the price
of admission to whatever wisdom is to be found in any approach to understanding the world.

Bidney's writings, consonant with the spirit of eighteenth- and nineteenth-century evolutionism, do envision a progression of reason that cul-
minates in a point from which the people of truth look back on the people
of myth; but unlike that evolutionism (or at least many versions of it), the
fuller reading of Bidney casts considerable doubt on the notion that anyone
is at, or even well on the way toward, that vantage point. Who then, for Bidney, are the people of truth? The following I think will stand up to a full
reading of Bidney's work. They are people of any time who espouse empirical investigation and critical thought to guide the design of human life, and
who refuse to be cowed by unexamined orthodoxies. They are also the people of one possible (but not inevitable) future of the world—the beneficia-
ries of a humanity that has chosen the course of critical reason in the realm
of human values. Finally, the people of truth are a sort of regulative ideal, a
perennial proclamation of the necessity of "ceaseless vigilance and self-conscious analysis" (1953b, 325–26). It is also possible to say something about
who, in Bidney's view, the people of truth are *not*. They are not people of
ancient civilizations or non-Western peoples who uncritically accept the
doctrinal charters their societies hand to them in religion or mythological
narratives. They are also not the leaders and populace of modern Western
nations in the mid–twentieth century who fell prey to the "sociopolitical

myths of our time" (1953b, 326). And they are not, with a few incipient exceptions, the anthropological bright lights of David Bidney's generation.

NOTES

1. As a graduate student I took several courses from Bidney just before he retired in the mid-1970s. I found him a very colorful and provocative teacher, and my sense of his memorableness was confirmed by comments that followed the presentation, at the "Symposium on Myth," of the original version of this paper.

My focus on the question of just what social dichotomies are created or implied by Bidney's use of the term "myth" is inspired in part by Marcel Detienne's intriguing work *The Creation of Mythology* (1986).

2. Moreover, this contextualizing strategy—i.e., blunting the force of a particular claim by showing that it is merely one instance of a universal claim—strikes me as having a lot in common with one of the analytical strategies that Lévi-Strauss considers in his "The Structural Study of Myth" (1965), which also appears in *Myth: A Symposium*. Lévi-Strauss tries to reveal the structural move through which myths attempt to demonstrate that "cosmology is true" (92). The argument is in part that mythic cosmologies arrange particular defects of the sociological microcosm in parallel with defects of the macrocosm; a local defect is ameliorated by being shown to be an instance of the defective nature of existence in general—the price of existence, one might say. Whether or not Lévi-Strauss's analysis can improve our understanding of Oedipus (a much discussed issue when his piece first appeared), the structure outlined in it is helpful in analyzing Bidney's intellectual orientation. For in Bidney's writings the specific topic of the moment, be it myth, culture, or social science, ends up as instancing his *general* complaint: the uncritical nature of human knowledge and thinking.

3. Comte addressed macro-divisions, such as astronomy and biology, while Parsons and Shils were concerned with establishing the necessary and adequate divisions of social science. In both Comte's era and that of Parsons and Shils, one finds fascinating instances of politicking for the recognition of specific academic disciplines in terms of this type of hierarchical argument. The recognition, for example, of a separate cultural, as opposed to social, level of analysis in Parsons and Shils probably had something to do with the influence of anthropologist Clyde Kluckhohn on their book, in an era in which anthropology was searching for recognition as a necessary discipline.

4. The antireductionism evident in Bidney's analysis of social science disciplines finds a parallel of sorts in his adoption of the skepticism toward animistic thought that is typical of evolutionarily inclined mythologists. For animism is a kind of reductionism, i.e., the extension of properties of animate beings to *all* beings. Bidney tended to be skeptical of closed systems of explanation, whether these were myths, cultures, or social science disciplines.

5. Although Bidney was thoroughly familiar with nineteenth- and twentieth-century ethnographically oriented anthropology, his concern with such universals may also stem from a knowledge, gained through his training in philosophy, of the older anthropology, a field within philosophy, which tended to assume a universal human mental and moral character.

6. The science of society Bidney envisioned would be empirically grounded in the cross-cultural study of society, culture, and values. It would be critical and continually open to reassessment. And it would seek transcultural truths in the realm of political and social values aimed at promoting order and harmony among different societies and around the world.

Can anything else be added? Based on distant memories of Bidney's final courses, I suggest two further points for which I find some corroboration in his written work. First, his science would be rooted in universal human psycho-biological needs and potentials. Bidney considered Malinowski's little-known and posthumously published *A Scientific Theory of Culture* (1944a) to be an important step in this enterprise. Malinowski's work presents an overall schema through which any culture can be analyzed as a response to a specific set of universal human psycho-biological needs.

Secondly, Bidney's science would give a place to both classical scientific determinism and the openness of outcome implied by the idea of "freedom." I specifically recall my frustration in attempting to follow Bidney when he lectured on his metaphysical reconciliation of freedom and determinism, and I am still unable to follow his published arguments on this issue (e.g., in chapter 16 of *Theoretical Anthropology* [1953b]). But it is notoriously difficult to reconcile determinism with humanistic principles such as freedom. Emile Durkheim (1964) faced the problem of reconciling an idealistic if not spiritual vision of society with the demand of scientific method for empirical evidence; he came up with the notion that collective mental states are manifest in observable concrete evidence (e.g., collective symbols such as flags). Malinowski, in another little-known and again posthumously published work, *Freedom and Civilization* (1944b), approaches freedom as a necessary dimension of culture, which can be objectively and comparatively studied anthropologically. He expressly states (3ff.) that this book was prompted by the sociopolitical crisis of World War II. And Bidney (1953a, 695), in discussing the relevance of Malinowski's *Freedom and Civilization* to the idea of a comparative science of values, suggests that it took the international crisis of the war to shake Malinowski's faith in the doctrine of cultural relativism. Another relevant work is Theodosius Dobzhansky's *The Biological Basis of Human Freedom* (1956), which in a very different sense approaches freedom as an empirical phenomenon. For Dobzhansky freedom is empirical in the sense that a high degree of plasticity—a capacity for variation and modification of behavior through learning—is an objective part of the human genetic makeup.

In placing Bidney in the longer tradition of thinkers struggling to reconcile determinism and moral freedom, I choose these three examples—Durkheim, Malinowski, and Dobzhansky—for a specific reason, namely, that as nearly as I can recall (which is more firmly for the first two than for Durkheim), they were central readings in Bidney's courses.

7. For example, the culminating chapters of his *Theoretical Anthropology,* particularly chapters 15 ("Ideology and Power in the Strategy of World Peace") and 16 ("The Problem of Freedom and Authority in Cultural Perspective"), are oriented toward how anthropological knowledge can be used to improve international relations in the postwar epoch.

8. See Bidney 1953b, 323–24. This theme in Tylor is discussed by Tambiah (1990, 50ff.) and by Schrempp (1983).

9. Richard Dorson's contribution to *Myth: A Symposium,* "The Eclipse of Solar Mythology" (1965), provides an interesting commentary on the solar mythology movement and the issues regarding symbolism implicated in it; see also my response to Dorson (Schrempp 1983).

10. The idea of "misplaced concreteness" is associated particularly with philosopher Alfred North Whitehead, who defines it as "neglecting the degree of abstraction involved when an actual entity is considered merely so far as it exemplifies certain categories of thought" (1978, 7–8).

BIBLIOGRAPHY

Bidney, David. 1953a. "The Concept of Value in Modern Anthropology." In *Anthropology Today: An Encyclopedic Inventory,* edited by A. L. Kroeber, 682–99. Chicago: University of Chicago Press.

———. 1953b. *Theoretical Anthropology.* New York: Columbia University Press.

———. 1965. "Myth, Symbolism, and Truth." In *Myth: A Symposium,* edited by Thomas A. Sebeok, 3–24. Bloomington: Indiana University Press.

Clifford, James, and George E. Marcus, eds. 1986. *Writing Culture: The Poetics and Politics of Ethnography.* Berkeley: University of California Press.

Comte, Auguste. 1975. *Auguste Comte and Positivism: The Essential Writings.* Edited and with an introduction by Gertrud Lenzer. New York: Harper and Row.

Detienne, Marcel. 1986. *The Creation of Mythology.* Translated by Margaret Cook. Chicago: University of Chicago Press.

Dobzhansky, Theodosius. 1956. *The Biological Basis of Human Freedom.* New York: Columbia University Press.

Dorson, Richard. 1965. "The Eclipse of Solar Mythology." In *Myth: A Symposium,* edited by Thomas A. Sebeok, 25–63. Bloomington: Indiana University Press.

Durkheim, Emile. 1964. *The Rules of Sociological Method.* Edited by George E. G. Catlin and translated by Sarah A. Solovay and John H. Mueller. New York: The Free Press.

Kroeber, A. L. 1952. *The Nature of Culture.* Chicago: University of Chicago Press.

Lévi-Strauss, Claude. 1965. "The Structural Study of Myth." In *Myth: A Symposium,* edited by Thomas A. Sebeok, 81–106. Bloomington: Indiana University Press.

Malinowski, Bronislaw. 1944a. *A Scientific Theory of Culture, and Other Essays.* Chapel Hill: University of North Carolina Press.

———. 1944b. *Freedom and Civilization.* New York: Roy.

Parsons, Talcott, and Edward A. Shils, eds. 1951. *Toward a General Theory of Action.* Cambridge, Mass.: Harvard University Press.

Schrempp, Gregory. 1983. "The Re-education of Friedrich Max Müller." *Man,* n.s., 18:90–110.

Tambiah, Stanley Jeyaraja. 1990. *Magic, Science, Religion, and the Scope of Rationality.* Cambridge: Cambridge University Press.

Whitehead, Alfred North. 1978. *Process and Reality: An Essay in Cosmology.* Corrected edition, edited by David Ray Griffin and Donald W. Sherburne. New York: The Free Press.

Part II

MYTH AND ETHNOGRAPHY

FOUR

Germans and Indians in South America: Ethnography and the Idea of Text

LÚCIA SÁ

It is not novel to point to the manifold links between late-nineteenth-century German ethnography and the Americas. Among many others, Franz Boas, Karl von den Steinen, Paul Ehrenreich, Curt Unkel Nimuendajú, Theodor Koch-Grünberg, and Konrad Theodor Preuss were all products of that school, and all made their Forschungsreise, or field trips, to the New World in the late nineteenth and early twentieth centuries. Yet key differences developed between them: Boas went on to become the founder of anthropology in the U.S., while his compatriots turned mainly to lowland South America. Boas became identified with academic anthropology in the English-speaking world, and consequently came to be identified as the father of modern anthropology itself, while those Germans who chose South America as their destination and wrote about it in their language remain in the rear of the anthropological pantheon. Even today, their works have scarcely been translated into English or French. Thus, for supposedly general histories of ethnography, they have more or less ceased to exist.

The objective of this article is simply to revisit three of those names, Nimuendajú (1883–1945), Koch-Grünberg (1872–1924), and Preuss (1869–1938), and gauge their achievements, especially with regard to the recording and examination of native texts. In so doing, I hope to begin to fill a certain gap in standard English-language histories of ethnography and anthropology.

Except for Nimuendajú, these Germans were all associated with, if not actual products of, the anthropology program at the University of Berlin, which began in earnest in the mid-1880s. Reflecting the philosophies and ideology of the time, this program was heavily committed to the principles of evolutionary theory, emphasizing origins and ideas about origins. Yet, for all their commitment to a theory recently developed in Europe, these researchers made a point of respecting evidence about origins that was provided by the peoples and societies they went to visit. Koch-Grünberg, Nimuendajú, and Preuss, particularly, valued native texts and the taxonomies and ways of looking at the world that these texts could suggest, which is why I have chosen to concentrate on their work.

Following in the footsteps of Alexander von Humboldt and the Schomburgk brothers, as well as more immediate predecessors like von den Steinen and Paul Ehrenreich, the Germans Nimuendajú, Koch-Grünberg, and Preuss traveled and lived with native peoples in various parts of lowland South America during the first decades of this century, in the rain forest and its immediate environs. Each produced seminal accounts of rain forest cultures that are firmly based on native texts; each worked painstakingly to reproduce, in alphabetic print, major indigenous narratives, chants, and other genres.

Nimuendajú's major work appeared in both German and Guarani in 1914, and was the first publication ever, in a native language, of a full-length lowland South American cosmogony.[1] Its weighty title is *Die Sagen von der Erschaffung und Vernichtung der Welt als Grundlagen der Religion der Apapokuva-Guaraní* (Legends of creation and destruction of the world as basic principles of the religion of the Apapokuva-Guarani; hereafter *Legends*). Curt Unkel, an amateur ethnographer, lived so closely involved with the people he studied and defended—the Apapokuva-Guarani, a group in southwestern Brazil—that he was adopted by them and named Nimuendajú, a name that he made official when he became a Brazilian citizen in 1922. As the leading Brazilian ethnographer Eduardo Viveiros de Castro says, this name has become a legend (Castro 1987). *Legends* reproduces and comments on the Guarani narratives that tell how the earth came into being, and of the Flood. The stories were told to him by the shaman Joguy-rovyjú, and also by Guyrapaijú (described by the ethnologist as "old and conservative") and by the "well traveled" Tupãjú. Nimuendajú's collection brings us into contact with the complex eschatology of the Guarani, with the division of the human spirit into the celestial soul-word and the terrestrial soul-animal. Those texts were also the first published works to provide substantial evidence for the theme of the Guarani migrations in search of *Ivy marã ey*, the "land without ill."

Although Nimuendajú had lived and worked among the Apapokuva-Guarani for several years, for some time he heard no reference at all to their creation narratives. It was only when the Indians decided he was worthy of knowing them that they mentioned their existence to him. Nimuendajú had by then already been adopted by the tribe and was actively involved in defending them, as well as other Guarani groups, in legal battles against neighboring non-native populations and the Brazilian government. He was what we can call a committed ethnographer, and in that guise he took risks and made mistakes. Perhaps the most serious of his errors was convincing a Guarani group who had migrated to the coast in search of the land without ill to go back to the interior. Many died during this return journey, while those who reached the coast remain there to this day (Barbosa and Barbosa 1987, ix). Nimuendajú was the first ethnographer in the history of this discipline in Brazil to "go native," so to speak.

Although he went on to publish many articles on several other Brazilian indigenous groups, the Guarani *Legends* remains his definitive work. In the words of Castro, it "inaugurates contemporary Guarani ethnology, defining the contours of a field in which we still move" (xxii). The culture of the closely related Tupi and Guarani had been studied by outsiders since early colonial times, and several texts by travelers describe their habits, their beliefs, and their society. The Tupi-speaking Tupinambá were the first natives to meet the Portuguese invaders, on the coast of Brazil in 1500, and the first text to describe them was Pero Vaz de Caminha's letter of the "discovery" of the new territory.[2] In their missionary effort, the Jesuits also had recorded a good deal of information about the Tupi and Guarani.[3] But it was only with the publication of *Legends* that native cosmogony was allowed to unfold in and on its own terms, and Nimuendajú's work corrected many misconceptions about Tupi-Guarani religion. It made clear, for example, how Tupã, an entity related to thunder and rain, had been transformed into a monotheistic god by the Jesuits for missionary purposes. It was under this rather than his initial guise that Tupã had been celebrated by the Romantic poets of Brazil and Paraguay. Now that many ethnographies of Tupi and Guarani cultures have been published, Nimuendajú's *Legends* also demonstrates the remarkable coherence between Tupi and Guarani groups as distant as those in Paraguay and those in the Brazilian state of Maranhão, more than two thousand miles to the north.

Legends remains widely read by Indian and non-Indian Guarani speakers in Paraguay and Brazil. The first translation into Portuguese appeared only in 1984, as a result of an understanding between Guarani leaders, indigenous rights groups, and the government of the state of São Paulo, although mimeographed copies of an undated translation by F. W. Sommer had long been circulating among scholars. *Legends* and *Ayvu-Rapyta*, a collection of Mbya-Guarani cosmogonical texts published in 1959 by the Paraguayan León Cadogan under conditions similar to those faced by Nimuendajú, are considered by the Guarani-speaking Paraguayans to be the indigenous sacred texts of greatest significance. A good part of this significance derives precisely from their respect for the integrity of the original texts and the point of view of the narrator, as we can appreciate in the following example:

And he [Ñanderuvuçu] gave the equipment to his son. And he hid again from his son and went to stop the ruin (of the world) and only the Blue Jaguar watches him.

Ñanderyquey is above us (at the zenith). He now watches the Earth and looks after its supporting brace, because, if he leaves, the Earth will fall. Nowadays the Earth is old, our tribe does not want to multiply anymore. We shall see all the dead ones; darkness will fall, the bat will come down, and all of us who are here on Earth will have an end. The Blue Jaguar will come down and devour us. (Nimuendajú 1984, 150, my translation)[4]

Theodor Koch-Grünberg's *Vom Roroima zum Orinoco* (From Roraima to the Orinoco; hereafter *Roraima*) appeared for the first time in 1917. It was the result of the author's four-year journey in northern Amazonia between 1911 and 1914 and his involvement with the Carib-speaking peoples who lived (and continue to live) in the geographically remarkable area that extends westward along the Pacaraima ridge from Roraima, the highest point east of the Andes and a focus of native and Western imagination alike, to the complex headwaters of the Orinoco River, which, defying orthodox hydrography, also flow into the Amazon. *Roraima* was not Koch-Grünberg's first publication about Amazonian Indians. In 1909 he had already published *Zwei Yahre unter der Indianer,* a massive account of his 1903–1905 trip to northwest Amazonia and the culturally rich Rio Negro region. But *Roraima* remains—no one seems to disagree on this—his best work, and in it his ability to handle native texts is more in evidence. It consists of five volumes: a travelogue; a collection of Pemon narratives; ethnographic comments and other texts; photographic images; and a Pemon vocabulary (the latter two published posthumously in 1924). Many of the narratives in the second volume are given in the original language, along with a translation, interlinear or parallel, into German. The texts included in the third volume, the *tarén* (curing formulas) and songs, are also accompanied by interlinear and parallel translations.

The narratives included in the second volume were given to Koch-Grünberg by two principal storytellers. The first was Mayuluaípu (known in Portuguese as José), a Taurepang Pemon Indian with a wide knowledge of different Pemon dialects and a good command of Portuguese. The other was Mõseuaípu, better known by his nickname Akuli (meaning "agouti" or "cutia," a small rodent), a young Arekuna shaman who could not speak a word of Portuguese or any other European language. Using the latest technology of his day, Koch-Grünberg recorded the stories by means of a phonograph. Mayuluaípu would tell his narratives in Portuguese and help the naturalist with cultural information and explanations of relevant native terms. Akuli would narrate in Arekuna and his stories would be translated by Mayuluaípu, who would also add some commentaries of his own. As for the linguistic information given by Mayuluaípu to Koch-Grünberg, it is worth noting that it is still today regarded as a valuable tool for understanding the Pemon languages (Durbin 1985, 333).

The stories by Mayuluaípu and Akuli in volume 2 were told in public, informal performances which took place in the boat or by the campfire, and whose main objective was to keep boredom at bay:

> The days are boring, cool and ugly. Each cloud brings with it a dense light rain. It is the true April weather. But Akuli does not let us get melancholic. . . . Most of the time we squat all together under the big tent, around the fire, and tell each other stories of Piaimá, the evil cannibal, who is finally tricked and killed by a stronger and smarter man (Koch-Grünberg 1917–24, 1:169, my translation)

In volume 3, Koch-Grünberg also gives some details of those performances:

> Little by little the narrator raises his voice, until it reaches a falsetto. All of a sudden he incorporates the character, gesticulating with arms and legs. In quiet tension, the audience listens. For a moment, everything is silent. Then, all of a sudden, a burst of noisy laughter. The joke was strong. The members of the audience spit several times with pleasure. (3:114, my translation)

In order to understand these stories, as well as Koch-Grünberg's complex role as ethnographer, it is most important to bear in mind the structure of the whole five-volume work. For each volume exists as a separate unit at the same time as it interacts with the others. In the travelogue, the "I" is free, theoretically unchained. We are given direct insight into his frustrations, his sense of humor, his favoritisms; nonetheless, the open narrative prose allows Mayuluaípu and Akuli to exist and grow as independent characters. In the course of the journey recounted in the travelogue, we witness the ethnographer's growing friendship with each of them. We learn that Akuli behaves like a trickster, that he is very found of telling stories, jokes, and narratives about his own success with women, and that he is a charming young man; and that Mayuluaípu, more serious, likes to sing songs that he learned from his father and tell shamanic tales (he wants to become a shaman when he returns to the village) and war stories that make Koch-Grünberg compare him to Homer. In fact, volume 2 of *Roraima* is in many senses a result of the admiration that Koch-Grünberg, in volume 1, openly admitted he felt for these two Indians. It is the strong presence of the "I" in the travelogue that allows the voices of the Indians to be more powerful in the second volume. This is so much the case that by volume 3, the native texts exist strongly enough in their own right to make much of the "scientific" commentary seem redundant, or of another order of knowledge.

The opening travelogue also permits us to witness Koch-Grünberg's poor relationship with Manduca, a helper from the neighboring Yekuana people, another Carib group, who are also known as So'to, Majonggong, or Makiritare, and who have been long-standing rivals of the Pemon. Manduca's pride and lack of trust puts the ethnographer off. As David Guss observes in "Keeping It Oral: A Yekuana Ethnology," Koch-Grünberg's harsh attitudes toward the Yekuana contrast vividly with his sympathy for the Pemon:

> In page after page he lacerates the Yekuana in a series of denunciations astounding to the contemporary reader. Showing little of the cultural sensitivity he was to reserve for other tribes (particularly the neighboring Taulipang), he in turn accuses them of moodiness, undependability, rudeness, lack of cleanliness, laziness, obstinacy, dishonesty, and quarrelsomeness. (Guss 1986, 414)

Inquiring into the reasons which would have made Koch-Grünberg so unwilling to accept the Yekuana, Guss arrives at the conclusion that, unlike the Pemon and other tribes, the Yekuana refused "to play Indian," and they repeatedly resisted telling the naturalist their stories.

Guss's account has much to recommend it, not least the fact that he himself has made a major contribution to the modern understanding of the Yekuana through their own texts, in his admirable edition and translation into English of Marc de Civrieux's *Watunna: Mitología Makiritare* (1970). Guss's version appeared in 1980 as *Watunna: An Orinoco Creation Cycle.* Yet Guss overlooks narrative elements present in Koch-Grünberg's travelogue (volume 1) which refer to his Yekuana helper Manduca. The naturalist becomes increasingly irritated with Manduca, to the point of showing a clear contempt for the Indian's description of the Yekuana universe, on one of the rare occasions in which Manduca decides to speak about it:

> The Majonggong also does not want to be left out. He tells us about his tribe's life after death. According to the belief of these Indians, who obviously think of themselves as something extraordinary, the world is a great globe with nine covers, that is, nine skies underneath and above the earth, peopled with various inhabitants of strange shapes and habits, and by spirits and gods, masters and judges of the souls of the dead. (1:169)

This mode of discourse contrasts almost violently with the sensitivity Koch-Grünberg generally shows toward the imaginative tendencies of

Carib cosmogony, and on his own admission it can hardly be thought the result of Manduca's unwillingness to "play Indian." On Koch-Grünberg's own evidence, Manduca is in fact the most helpful of all the Indians who work for him, and at moments he acknowledges as much. Yet he clearly prefers Akuli's poise in telling stories, his "buffonerie" and good humor, and his dramatic talents, to Manduca's pragmatism and pride—even though Akuli, as the naturalist describes him, is not very courageous and can often be a bit lazy and moody as well. Koch-Grünberg's irritation with Manduca is a result of his sympathy for the two Pemon. In other words, he is adopting a Pemon attitude toward the Yekuana, following local rivalry and taking sides within what from an ethnographical point of view is a common Carib culture. If we trace his irritation and his increasing lack of patience with Manduca throughout the narrative, we can easily foresee that his impression of the Yekuana when he finally arrives at their village will be negative; it was already negative before he got there.

As narrators and consultants, Mayuluaípu and Akuli proved so committed to their work that they accepted Koch-Grünberg's request that they deliver the manuscripts of *Roraima* to someone in touch with the outside world. Indeed, they made a long and hazardous journey from Roraima all the way to Manaus in order to hand the manuscripts directly to the German consulate, even though Koch-Grünberg himself had only asked them to leave the papers in the nearest town.

Koch-Grünberg's close attention to the texts, and to the ways in which they were produced, is strongly evident in the second volume. In volume 3, he goes on to give a complete interlinear translation of the curing formulas, including all repetitions and many of the accompanying actions. Another genre transcribed by Koch-Grünberg is what he calls "little innocent songs," usually sung informally at parties and often improvised (3:145). Lyrical and haiku-like, these songs mostly consist of a single stanza plus a refrain, and they generally express a feeling of nostalgia for Roraima. An example:

> kinatoli poítene-pe kómeme-tana azike loloíme
> haí-a ha-ha-ha haí-a
>
> (while the japú stays as a servant, come here Roraima
> haí-a ha-ha-ha haí-a). (3:162)

The japú is a playful, easily domesticated bird, prized by native peoples for its black and yellow feathers, and its working as a servant indicates a time when one is at home, far from the beloved Roraima. By these means, Koch-Grünberg conveyed to his readers not just originals but a whole idea of what literature could mean in Pemon society.

Nimuendajú and Koch-Grünberg both immersed themselves in the cultures and societies they studied, Tupi-Guarani and Carib, and as a result became the transmitters of the major texts of those cultures. For his part, Konrad Theodor Preuss spread himself more, in both a professional and a geographical sense. He worked as an archaeologist as well as an ethnographer, being the first to excavate the ruins of San Agustín (Colombia), and he was active in Mexico as well as South America, collecting narratives from Nahuatl-speakers in Nayarit and Durango (Preuss 1921, 1968), which remain unjustly neglected outside the German-speaking world. This flexibility enabled him to trace deeper Mesoamerican paradigms in the stories he collected in Mexico and to gauge how knowledge of classical Nahuatl could illuminate concepts embedded in them. He was the first outsider with a sensitive ear to enter the well-guarded towns of the Kogi Indians, high in the Sierra of Santa Marta in northern Colombia, beginning a report and transcription of texts which half a century later would be carried forward by the Austrian-Colombian Gerardo Reichel-Dolmatoff (1950–51). He was the first to record at all adequately the cosmogony of the Witoto (Preuss 1921), a linguistically isolated group at the western extreme of the Amazonian rain forest, within what only then were being effectively defined as the national frontiers of Colombia. Preuss's bilingual transcriptions of the Witoto account of how the world came into being establish philosophical dimensions and principles hitherto rarely suspected in rain forest culture, above all the process of conceptualization itself as the corollary to world making, also much in evidence in the Guarani genesis narratives being published at that time by Nimuendajú. The Witoto piece begins,

> A phantasm, nothing else existed in the beginning: the Father touched an illusion, he grasped something mysterious. Nothing existed. Through the agency of a dream our Father Nai-mu-ena kept the mirage to his body, & he pondered long & thought deeply.
>
> Nothing existed, not even a stick to support the vision: our Father attached the illusion to the thread of a dream & kept it by the aid of his breath. He sounded to reach the bottom of the appearance, but there was nothing. Nothing existed.
>
> Then the Father again investigated the bottom of the mystery. He tied the empty illusion to the dream thread & pressed the magical substance upon it. Then by the aid of this dream he held it like a wisp of raw cotton. (Rothenberg 1968, 27)

Preuss was in Colombia when the First World War broke out. Finding himself confined there, he concentrated his energies, as it were, within those national boundaries. Despite great difficulties in getting his work published after the war because of the severe financial punishment the Allies decided to inflict on Germany (and which, much to his credit, Boas, in the U.S., sought to alleviate), Preuss was able to demonstrate several major paradigms in tropical American culture, always thanks to his close involvement with native texts. He brought out, for the first time, key cultural parallels between rain forest peoples like the Witoto and the highland Kogi who, as Chibcha speakers, in other respects look toward Mesoamerica. As an archaeologist, he showed how knowledge of Witoto cosmogony could also help in understanding and interpreting the inscriptions and other iconographic materials that he found during his excavations at San Agustín. In other words, he respected native knowledge and its continuity through time. Indeed, in gathering texts from diverse parts of tropical America and from different historical periods, Preuss acquired the comparative scope later adopted by yet another compatriot: Walter Krickeberg, compiler of the classic anthology of tropical American texts *Märchen der Azteken, Incaperuaner, Maya und Muisca* (1928).[5]

The significance of Nimuendajú's, Koch-Grünberg's, and Preuss's work is indicated by how it has been appreciated by those working, if not in the mainstream, then at the literary edges of ethnography and anthropology. However little known in the English-speaking world they may appear today, each has impinged on the culture of the Americas in other fields of study. In the U.S., Jerome Rothenberg took from Preuss a reworking (as he termed it) of the Witoto creation narrative and featured it in his seminal *Technicians of the Sacred* (1968), making it one of the touchstones of the then emergent school of ethnopoetics, which brought about a rethinking of anthropology's translation and publication practices. Several decades previously, Mário de Andrade had published *Macunaima* (1928), Brazil's first modern novel, after discovering the imaginative wealth of Koch-Grünberg's transcriptions and German translations of Pemon literature. This intertextuality was to be decisive for the future of Latin American literature as a whole. For their part, the texts acquired with so much dedication by Nimuendajú have been definitive for Andrade's indigenist successor Darcy Ribeiro, anthropologist and author of *Maíra* (1976), as they have been for the Paraguayan Roa Bastos, who likewise has moved between anthropology (in *Las culturas condenadas,* 1978) and literature, in his major novel *Yo el supremo* (1974) and in poems written in Guarani that are dedicated to Nimuendajú (*El naranjal ardiente,* 1983).[6]

All of these readings of the Germans' transcription and translation of Indian texts confirm their literary sensitivity, which allowed them to go beyond the evolutionist constraints of their own formation. Nimuendajú, Koch-Grünberg, and Preuss have in common an unusual respect for the native text, drawing from rather than imposing on it larger philosophical and theoretical schemes.

NOTES

1. João Barbosa Rodrigues's *Poranduba Amazonense ou Kochyma Uara Porandub: 1872–1887* (1890) includes the Nheengatu version of several Amazonian stories, but no full-length cosmogony.

2. The letter was followed by Hans Staden's dramatic *Warhaftige Historia und Beschreibung eyner Landtschafft der wilden nacketen grimmigen Menschfresser-Leuthen in der Newenwelt America gelegen* (1557), Pero de Magalhães Gandavo's *História da província de Santa Cruz* and *Tratado da terra do Brasil* (1576), and Gabriel Soares de Sousa's *Tratado descritivo do Brasil em 1587*.

3. See, for instance, Antonio Ruiz de Montoya's *La conquista espiritual* (1639) .

4. Words in square brackets were added by me; words in parentheses were in the original.

5. *Muisca* was Humboldt's term for the Chibcha of Colombia, to whom the Kogi are related.

6. For details on the impact of Koch-Grünberg's and Nimuendajú's collections on the works of Mário de Andrade, Darcy Ribeiro, and Roa Bastos, see Sá 1997.

BIBLIOGRAPHY

Barbosa, Carla Gonçalves Antunha, and Marco Antonio Barbosa. 1987. "Uma Parte da História desta Publicação." In *As lendas de criação e destruição do mundo como fundamentos da religião dos Apapocúva-Guarani*, by Curt Unkel Nimuendajú, translated by Charlotte Emmerich and Eduardo Viveiros de Castro. São Paulo: Hucitec/Edusp.

Castro, Eduardo Viveiros de. 1987. "Nimuendajú e os Guarani." In *As lendas de criação e destruição do mundo como fundamentos da religião dos Apapocúva-Guarani*, by Curt Unkel Nimuendajú, translated by Charlotte Emmerich and Eduardo Viveiros de Castro. São Paulo: Hucitec/Edusp.

Civrieux, Marc de. 1980. *Watunna: An Orinoco Creation Cycle*. Edited and translated by David Guss. San Francisco: North Point. Originally published as *Watunna: Mitología makiritare* (Caracas: Monte Avila, 1970).

Durbin, Marshall. 1985. "A Survey of the Carib Language Family." In *South American Indian Languages: Retrospect and Prospect*, edited by Harriet E. Manelis Klein and Louisa R. Stark, 325–68. Austin: University of Texas Press.

Guss, David. 1986. "Keeping It Oral: A Yekuana Ethnology." *American Ethnologist* 13, no. 3:413–29.

Koch-Grünberg, Theodor. 1917–24. *Vom Roroima zum Orinoco: Ergebnisse einer Reise in Nordbrasilien und Venezuela in den Jahren 1911–1913*. Vols. 1–3. Berlin: Dietrich Reimer.

Nimuendajú, Curt Unkel. 1984. *As lendas de criação e destruição do mundo como fundamentos da religião dos Apapocúva-Guarani*. Translated by Charlotte Emmerich and Eduardo B. Viveiros de Castro. São Paulo: Editora HUCITEC: Editora da Universidade de São Paulo. Originally published as *Die Sagen von der Erschaffung und Vernichtung der Welt als Grundlagen der Religion der Apapokuva-Guaraní,* 1914.

Preuss, Konrad Theodor. 1921. *Die Religion und Mythologie der Uitoto.* Göttingen: Leipzig.

———. 1968. *Nahua—Texte aus San Pedro Jícora in Durango.* Berlin: Mann.

Reichel-Dolmatoff, Gerardo. 1950–51. *Los Kogi: Una tribu de la Sierra Nevada de Santa Marta, Colombia.* 2 vols. Bogotá: Instituto Etnológico Nacional and Editorial Iqueima.

Roa Bastos, Augusto. 1978. *Las culturas condenadas.* Mexico: Siglo Veintiuno.

———. 1983. *El naranjal ardiente: nocturno paraguayo, 1947–1949.* Asunción: Alcandara.

Rothenberg, Jerome. 1968. *Technicians of the Sacred: A Range of Poetries from Africa, America, Asia and Oceania.* Garden City, N.Y.: Doubleday.

Sá, Lúcia. 1997. *Reading the Rain Forest: Indigenous Texts and Their Impact on Brazilian and Spanish American Literatures.* Ph.D. dissertation, Indiana University.

FIVE

"Made From Bone": Trickster Myths, Musicality, and Social Constructions of History in the Venezuelan Amazon

JONATHAN D. HILL

TRICKSTER MYTHS AND HISTORY IN SOUTH AMERICA

Early in my fieldwork with the Arawakan Wakuénai of Venezuela in the 1980s, I became aware that the mythic character of the trickster-creator, called Iñápirríkuli, was a broadly significant principle of strategic interaction that ran through mythic narratives, everyday social life, sacred rituals, and historical memories. Unlike the buffoonish, comical tricksters of better-known North American mythologies (Radin 1956), the trickster-creator in Wakuénai society is an omniscient, powerful being who always anticipates the treachery and deceit of other beings and who skillfully manipulates words and other signs as tools for deceiving and defeating these other beings.[1] More abstractly, the trickster-creator embodies the principle that nothing people say or do can be interpreted literally or taken at face value but must always be interpreted symbolically in relation to knowledge of other texts and contexts that are not part of the immediate situation.

The mythic figure of the trickster-creator in Wakuénai society bears striking resemblance to the West African–derived myths about Esu, or the "signifying monkey" (Gates 1988). "Monkey speaks figuratively, while the Lion reads his discourse literally. For his act of misinterpretation, he suffers grave consequences. This valorization of the figurative is perhaps the most important moral of these poems, although the Monkey's mastery of figuration has made him one of the canonical heroes in the Afro-American mythic tradition" (Gates 1988, 85). Gates's pathbreaking study demonstrates how the trickster's privileging of the tropes forms the cornerstone of an Afro-American theory of language use that informs not only a variety of overtly literary oral and written genres but also many varieties of speech in everyday social life. "Signifyin(g) . . . is the figurative difference between the literal and the metaphorical, between surface and latent meaning" (82).

In the following essay, I will explore South American trickster myths as specific cases of an indigenous theory of meaning construction. Although this indigenous theory is most clearly embodied in expressive activities such as narrative discourses and ritual performances, it is also a pragmatic device that informs everyday social activities in diverse contexts. In both South American and African contexts, the trickster is not merely a symbol but a practical activity of creating a reflexive, interpretive distancing between the acting subject and the immediate situation. Defined in these terms, Amazonian and West African tricksters illustrate Umberto Eco's concept of general semiosic competence, "which permits one to interpret verbal and visual signs, and to draw inferences from them, by merging the information they give with background knowledge" (1990, 204). Amazonian and Afro-American tricksters are semiotic processes of playing with the distinction between literal and tropic meanings. Mythic tricksters open up the conceptual distinction between the interpretation of words and other signs as merely semantic or referential vehicles with very limited social power and their interpretation as fully encyclopaedic symbols carrying a potentially infinite range of knowledges about other signs and the material and social worlds (Sperber 1975; Whitten 1978; Eco 1990).[2]

Defined as a general process of creating reflexive, interpretive distancing through opening up and playing upon the gap between literal-semantic and critical-semiotic levels of interpretation, mythic tricksters encompass a nearly incomprehensible diversity of specific qualities and manifestations. In Gates's words,

> A partial list of these qualities might include individuality, satire, parody, irony, magic, indeterminacy, open-endedness, ambiguity, sexuality, chance, uncertainty, disruption and reconciliation, betrayal and loyalty, closure and disclosure, encasement and rupture. But it is a mistake to focus on one of these qualities as predominant. Esu possesses all of these characteristics, plus a plethora of others which, taken together, only begin to present an idea of the complexity of this classic figure of mediation and of the unity of opposed forces. (1988, 6)

In keeping with Gates's warning, I will not attempt to limit mythic tricksters to any single quality but will instead explore several key dimensions of their ability to interpret, manipulate, and create meanings as a practical activity of strategic social interaction.

Musicality, or more precisely the poetic interplay between semanticity and musicality in natural language (Friedrich 1986), forms the innermost core of mythic tricksters' ability to mediate between sacred and profane orders. Musically performed discourses, as well as instrumentally performed music imbued with verbal meanings, serve both to heighten interpretive possibilities for creating new historical discourses and to constrain the range of possible historical interpretations by grounding the potentially infinite semiosis of words into socially recognized metapragmatic frameworks of interpretation. Understanding these interpretive frameworks as pervasive modes of language use and meaning construction rather than merely as isolated genres of expressive discourse is important for two reasons. First, such interpretive frameworks provide a means for exploring alternative ways in which peoples in non- or paraliterate societies construct histories through the poetics of sound and meaning. And second, studies of such interpretive frameworks demonstrate that what survives over the long run across such massive changes as the "Middle Passage," the "Great Dying," and the Rubber Boom are not specific discourses or genres so much as "an unbroken arc of metaphysical presupposition and a pattern of figuration shared through time and space" (Gates 1988, 6).

ETHNOGRAPHIC CONTEXT

The specific ethnographic examples through which I will explore the linkages among trickster myths, musicality, and social constructions of history come for the most part from my fieldwork with the Arawakan Wakuénai of the Upper Rio Negro region in Venezuela.[3] In earlier publications (Wright and Hill 1986; Hill and Wright 1988), I and my coauthor, Robin Wright, focused on the central role of trickster myths in the way indigenous peoples of the Upper Rio Negro region construct shared understandings of the history of interethnic relations during colonial and more recent times. In 1998, I returned to the Upper Rio Negro for six months of fieldwork dedicated to systematic recording, transcription, and translation of narratives about the mythic trickster (Iñápirríkuli).

Wakuénai narratives about the mythic past outline a complex process of cosmogenesis that began at Hípana, a village on the Aiary River adjacent to the rapids where Iñápirríkuli raised the ancestors' spirits. The world of mythic beginning was miniature in size and chaotic, since cannibalistic animals walked about killing and eating each other. Iñápirríkuli came into this world and began to rid it of dangerous animals by taking vengeance against them. Despite the animals' unceasing attempts to kill the trickster, he repeatedly escaped death through his extraordinary divinatory powers. The space-time of the mythic beginning was a time before spatial distances came into being and when there were not yet any clear distinctions between male and female, human and nonhuman, living and dead beings.

A second set of narratives explains how the miniature world of the mythic beginning was transformed into the life-sized world of rivers and forest inhabited by people, plants, and animals. The central characters of this cycle are Iñápirríkuli, Amáru (the primordial woman), and Kuwái (the primordial human being). Kuwái is an extraordinary being whose body consists of all worldly elements and whose humming and singing, referred to as "the powerful sound that opened up the world" (*kémakani hliméetaka hekwápi*), causes the world to expand and brings into being all living species and natural elements. He teaches humanity the first sacred rituals of initiation, yet at the end of these rituals Iñápirríkuli "kills" Kuwái by pushing him into a bonfire, and the world then shrinks back to its original miniature size. Out of Kuwái's ashes grow the plant materials for making the sacred flutes and trumpets played in initiation rituals and sacred ceremonies today. Amáru and the women steal these instruments from Iñápirríkuli, setting off a long chase in which the world opens up for a second time as the women play Kuwái's instruments in various places. Eventually the men regain the flutes and Kuwái, Amáru, and Iñápirríkuli leave this world to go live in the various celestial regions whence they are invoked in rituals.

A third set of narratives about the human past presupposes the existence of the mythic beginning and its transformation in the primordial human past of Kuwái and Amáru. In this set of narratives, human beings in this world come into contact with powerful spirits from other regions of the cosmos. The narratives are closely related to Wakuénai concepts of illness and death, and their cure or prevention through shamanic ritual. These narratives explain that human beings in this world can cross over into the worlds of the deceased as a result of excessive antisocial behavior. People who do this normally die when they return to the world of the living and tell people about their experiences in other worlds. By contrast, shamans and other ritual specialists routinely cross the boundaries between living and dead without bringing any harm to themselves or others, because they carry out these journeys through the sacred musical language of ritual (*málikai*).

It is difficult to do justice to such a complex figure as the mythic trickster in a single essay. The narrative discourses themselves are quite lengthy, and major themes within the corpus of narratives intermingle in a complex variety of ways with everyday social life, ceremonial exchanges, and sacred rituals. For reasons of space, I can provide only a few glimpses of these intricate narrative discourses and their extratextual meanings. In the following sections, I provide two examples of narrative episodes, one from the early mythic period in which Iñápirríkuli uses critical interpretive powers to survive life-threatening events and the other from a later period of mythic creation. In the latter episode, Iñápirríkuli employs verbal and nonverbal skills to conceal his identity and deceive his rival, the primordial human mother and female (Amáru). From there, I will give brief examples of how people invoke the mythic trickster's critical interpretive prowess in everyday contexts of socializing children and in ritual constructions of a historically expanding world. My hope is that these four brief moments will convey a sense of the experiential and situated meanings of the mythic trickster in Wakuénai social life.

TRICKSTER AS REFLEXIVE, INTERPRETIVE DISTANCING

The trickster's ability to escape death (via drowning, fire, dismemberment, and so on) is common to all genres of Wakuénai narrative discourse and is present at the very beginning of the mythic primordium, when Iñápirríkuli ("Made From Bone") and his two younger brothers, Dzúli and Káali, are made from the bones of their slain father's outer three fingers. In mythic discourse, bones are fragments of the past that become the seeds of contemporary human society and embodiments of the historical coming-into-being of the Wakuénai phratries as living descendants of the mythic ancestors whose musical naming power created nature and society from the sky-world above and whose life-giving powers continue to enliven this world through ritual performances of the sung, chanted, and spoken vocal genre called málikai. Through all of this complex cosmological and ritual process of creation and transformation, the trickster continues to deceive and defeat his rivals. As a model of indigenous subjectivity, the trickster embodies a conception of primordial humanness as an activity of creating a reflexive, interpretive distancing between the acting subject and the immediate situation (which is often depicted as life-threatening or in some way seriously challenging). The trickster always finds a way to cope with difficult situations, not by directly confronting dangerous others but by concealing himself and using his secret knowledge to imagine a way to break out of the present entanglement.[4]

In the earliest period of mythic time (*úupi pérri*), an evil father-in-law figure (Kunájwerri) and his sons repeatedly yet unsuccessfully attempt to kill Iñápirríkuli and his brothers. In one narrative, Kunájwerri tells his wife, who is Iñápirríkuli's father's sister,[5] to send her nephews with him to a new manioc garden that he is preparing to burn.

> *Uupi nawaka, naka nesre.*
> Already they left and arrived there.[6]
> *Lidzeekata najliú napjianikoa dokoli.*
> He [Kunájwerri] made whistles from Cecropia wood for them.
> *Liaku najliú: "Irapawatsa nujliu lipamudzuaka iukandati."*

He said to them, "You are going to dance for me in the middle of the garden."

"Matsiá," pidanaku, "pidukuñeena. Warapatua pisriú," pidanaku.

"Okay," they [Iñápirríkuli and his brothers] said, "light the fire while we dance for you."

Lidukuña likapukua. Likjeedzapita lidukuña. Liwadzaka lidukuña liukeetakawa tidzee.

He went about setting the fire. He walked about rapidly setting the fire. He finished when he had come full circle and encountered the fire.

Likaapa najliú. Karrú kajleka dzujmeena. Matsiá najliúkani.

He looked toward the boys. There was no place for them to survive. They were finished.

Namawadaka narapa. "he-he-he."

They stayed there and danced. "he-he-he." [sound of the whistles]

Tidzee inu naikajle, tsumeetsa.

The fire came toward where the boys were dancing, very close.

"Wasrena wawa."

"Let's go."

Jnete napjianiko jnewita neni.

Then they spit into their whistles.

Napeeku lisruawa jipairiko napjianiko.

They threw their whistles on the ground.

Kamena nakawa.

Already they left.

Jneewawa jipairiko, nanamutuwa awakadalikojle.

They entered in the ground and came out in the forest.

Keenapida nakeeñuakawa jna kojwe até pandza jekuapi.

Thus began the leaf-cutter ants that live to this day.

Kunájwerri ikaapa tidzee liukawa neemakarrumi narapa.

Kunájwerri saw that the fire had reached the place where they were dancing.

"Pandza dekjá. Uupi namawa."

"Now I've got them. They have already burned up."

"Nudíawatsa nukaite rujliú, sru nakuirru, 'nukaiteka iudzatsana. Jnete karrú jneepaka jnua.' Meewatsa nuaku rujliú."

"I will return and say to their aunt, 'I warned them but they didn't pay any attention.' That's what I'll say to her."

"'Kadzu karrú namakawa.' Meewatsa nuaku rujliú."

"'That's how they burned up,' I'll say to her."

Lieema likaapa tidzee. Uupi namakawa.

He stood up to see the fire. Already they were burning up.

"Pandze nawatsa nashada ikakawa."

"Now their guts are going to explode."

Kamena pida likakawa. Jlima pida, "too."
And they burst open. He heard "too."
"Pandza dekjá. Uupi lishada ikawa. Kanakai apadeetsa."
"Now, yes, their guts have burst open. There's one more left."
Kadzu pukudatsan, jlima "too," apada tsenakja. Kametsa neeka.
After a minute he heard "too," once again. That was all.
"Pandza nudíakeena wa."
"Now I will return."
Lidíawa tsumeetsa ñaupo uni.
He returned close to a stream.
Jlima tupikana.
He heard the boys playing there.
Jnete pidaliaku, "Kuaka pandza jna ta? Nawiki nuada?"
Then he said, "Who could this be? Could it be people?"
Lia iñuapitsa. Liuka likaapa, jna katsani.
He went slowly. When he arrived he saw that it was indeed them.
Nakaapa Kunájwerri. "Eh, pidíakeenawa."
They looked at Kunájwerri. "Eh, you've returned."
"Óojon," pidaliaku.
"Yes," he said.
"Uupi wadía pipjeedza. Jamuka wajliú," mepidanaku lisriú.
"We already returned ahead of you. It was very hot for us," they told
   him.
Kerrua pida najliúni.
He became very angry with them.
Nadía nakawa pantirikojle.
They returned and arrived home.

In this episode, Iñápirríkuli anticipates his father-in-law's treacherous plot
and tricks him by leaving the whistles in the middle of the manioc garden.
The sound of the whistles bursting open in the fire fools his adversary into
believing that he has succeeded in killing his three nephews, who have escaped by transforming into leaf-cutter ants and tunneling to safety.

   In the overall corpus of Wakuénai mythic narratives, there is a general
change in the trickster's way of using reflexive, interpretive distancing. In
the first cycle of narratives, about the presocial times of animal-humans,
Iñápirríkuli employs interpretive skills defensively, passively responding to
lethal threats from animal-others. In the twofold cycle of creation myths
about the primordial human beings, he begins to use powers of interpretation and meaning construction in a somewhat more offensive manner, but
still largely in response to other beings' initiatives. Finally, in the third cycle
of narratives, about shamanic space-time, Iñápirríkuli emerges as a fully active interpreter and creator of meanings and is able to use these powers as

offensive weapons in order to mislead, terrorize, and otherwise manipulate adversaries.[7]

The most forceful rendering of Iñápirríkuli's attainment of fully agentive powers of critical interpretation is a myth about the origins of evil omens (*jinimái*). In the opening episode of this myth, the trickster is the target of a murderous plot of seduction and betrayal in which a sister and her two brothers plan to kill him in the forest at night using an extremely lethal combination of witchcraft and sorcery.[8] Iñápirríkuli, blowing tobacco smoke over the sleeping woman to make her unconscious, kills the two brothers with poisoned darts and awakens the woman just in time for her to hear two loud thumps, the sounds of her brothers' bodies falling to the ground from the trees above. Using a series of verbal interpretations attached to sounds, dreams, visions, tactile feelings, and smells, the trickster turns the plot of seduction and betrayal against the woman. He takes complete control of both the creation and the interpretation of signs, and in the process uses these semiotic powers to terrorize the woman, causing her to run in fear back to her father's village.[9] The myth of evil omens compresses the general movement from passive to active use of semiotic interpretation into a single narrative. In a few short episodes, the trickster goes from being the target, or potential victim, of a murderous scheme into a master-poet whose signing overpowers all adversaries.

THE TRICKSTER AS IRONIC MISCOMMUNICATION

Ironic humor forms an important part of the Afro-American literary tradition of Signifying (Gates 1988, 90, 215)[10] and is widely practiced in indigenous South American mythic and historical discourses (Rasnake 1988; Silverblatt 1988). Irony, or the juxtaposition of concepts that are felt to contradict one another, is more socially complex than metaphor and other figures because its interpretation is highly contextual rather than merely formal (Sapir and Crocker 1977). Irony can also be defined as "a self-conscious use of figurative language to call into question its own capacity for distorting reality" (White 1973, 37). Irony is perhaps the trope best suited for expressing the indeterminacy of social orders and the paradoxes that arise in historical conditions of major social change (Hill 1988).

Iñápirríkuli, the trickster-creator of Wakuénai mythology, demonstrates an ability to make use of ironic humor in the second part of the creation myth cycle, when Amáru and the women have stolen the flutes and trumpets of Kuwái and run downstream along the Rio Negro. When the trickster arrives, he greets Amáru in lingua Geral (Yeral), a Tupí-Portuguese lingua franca introduced by Jesuit missionaries in the eighteenth century.

Kamena rúnuka uñaísre.

Already she was coming down to the port.

"Eh, nudaké," pidaruaku, "kjeti pinu?"

"Eh, my grandson," she said, "where are you coming from?"

"Aaa, nunu pukjuete, abo, Kurukwikjite," pidaliaku.

"Aaa, I am coming from downstream, grandmother, from São Gabriel," he said.

Kákukani Ñéngatuliko. Kamena likeeñuéetaka Ñéngatú até pandza jekuapi.

They spoke in lingua Yeral. That is how the Yeral language that is spoken today began.

"Kapjá pikaapa Iñapirríkuli, nudaké?" pidaruaku.

"You haven't seen Iñápirríkuli around here, my grandson?" she asked.

"Karrú pakaapa, abo, karrutsa nuajnédaka Iñapirríkuli," pidaliaku rujliú.

"I have not seen anything, grandmother, I do not even know this Iñápirríkuli," he replied.

"Iñápirríkulipami iájniri jieekuítajni jnua," pidaruaku. "Kadzu karru nuájnika nudáwaka," jniwa pidaruaku.

"That shameless Iñápirríkuli goes around persecuting me," she said. "That's why I go about in hiding."

"Jnua matsiádaru iéemaka nudzákaleliko," pidruaku.

"I live well here in my village," she said.

"Liúkakja waíkajle pandza abó nuíinuákaru mitjani," pidaliaku, "jnua mitja íinuani," pidaliaku.

"If only he were to arrive here today I would kill him," he said. "I'd be sure to kill him."

"Oojontja, nudaké, píinua mitja nudza Iñápirríkuli nukawiña mitja pjiá jorré," pidaruaku lisriú.

"If only it were so, my grandson, if you were to kill Iñápirríkuli, I would pay you plenty," she said.

At this point, Iñápirríkuli asks Amáru if he can stay overnight, and she shows him where he can hang his hammock in a house full of men. The men are obligated to stay in seclusion in a separate house so that they will not be able to see Amáru and the women playing the sacred flutes and trumpets for the first female initiation ritual.

Amáru ia líkajle. Rudée lirawa apada kuya padzáwaru.

Amáru approached him. She brought a gourd full of manioc beer for him to drink.

"Óojon, nudaké, pira padzáwaru," pidaruaku lisriú.

"Here, my grandson, drink some beer," she said to him.

"Joo, abó," pidaliaku. Lira pida tsutsa. Lidieeta rujliú.

"Okay, grandmother," he said. He drank very little, then returned it to her.

Rukaapa pikárrumitsa.
She saw that the gourd was still full.
"Pishenina?" pidaruaku.
"You already drank?" she asked.
"Óojon, abó, nuísrenina."
"Yes, grandmother, I already drank."
"Paaa," pidaruaku, "mairakatsa nuada pjiá, nudaké. Jliá dekjá Iñápir ríkulipami, nudaké, jliá dekjá ira jorré," pidaruaku.
"Paaa," she said, "you drank nothing, my grandson. That shameless Iñápirríkuli, my grandson, he really drinks a lot," she said.
"Karrú dekje jnua," pidaliaku. "Karrú nuíraka kadzu Iñápirríkuli íraka pidza," pidaliaku.
"I do not do that," he replied. "I do not drink like Iñápirríkuli," he said.

In this dialogue, the trickster uses his verbal skills to create a new language, or lingua Geral, as a way of concealing his true identity from Amáru. He also refers to her as "Grandmother" and refuses to take more than a mouthful of manioc beer, convincing Amáru that he is really not the trickster but a polite youngster whose presence (except for his masculine gender) is harmless. Irony gives the trickster a limited ability to control the shape of historical change.

THE TRICKSTER AND POETIC INDETERMINACY IN EVERYDAY SOCIAL LIFE

In mythic narratives, sacred rituals, and public ceremonies, the trickster's reflexive, interpretive distancing receives explicit attention and elaboration. However, the ironic humor and poetic indeterminacy of myth and ritual are not confined solely to sacred discourses and performances but are woven into the fabric of everyday social life.[11] Speech taboos prohibit people who have traveled to distant places or who have participated in unusual events from reporting or describing their experiences. Nor are the returning traveler's family and friends allowed to ask directly for information about these experiences in other places, for to do so would risk the traveler's illness or even death. The traveler's experiences can be learned only through gossip, implicit clues, dream interpretations, and other indirect means of communication. These speech taboos ensure that the trickster's reflexive, interpretive distancing, and especially the significance of places and journeys, are continuously present in everyday social relations.[12]

As might be expected, the trickster's ironic humor and poetic indeterminacy are particularly useful as tools for negotiating situations of potential conflict, such as public criticism of adults or the disciplining of children.

Without evoking the trickster in an explicit sense, a woman can criticize her brother-in-law's laziness as a manioc cultivator by ironically commenting, "He made a really hu-u-u-ge garden for his wife this year." The more she lengthens the vowel, the harder her audience laughs, and the greater the load of irony brought to bear on the lazy brother-in-law.

In the disciplining of children, parents may refer explicitly to the trickster, employing the poetic indeterminacy of everyday things, words, and actions as a means of socialization. In one case, a young boy who was playing with one of the local hunting dogs pulled its tail, and the boy's father yelled at him to stop. Immediately following this outburst, the father calmly told the boy how Iñápirríkuli had created hunting dogs with straight tails to serve as arrows pointing the way for hunters in search of game animals. For the remaining weeks of my stay in the village, the boy never made the same mistake of pulling a hunting dog's tail, and the father never raised his voice to discipline the boy (or any of his other children or grandchildren). In addition to showing how effective the trickster can be as a resource for socializing children, this example illustrates how a seemingly mundane fact of everyday life can become symbolically overdetermined as a mythic and practical sign. Specifically, the father's warning to his son made him reflect upon the trickster's ability to create a semiotic relation (indexicality) between human hunters and game animals via the hunting dog's tail (or "arrow"). The father's speech transformed the hunting dog's tail from a mere thing entering into children's play or the material relations between hunter and hunted into a semiotic relation requiring an ability to interpret signs in relation to mythic and practical knowledge.

MUSICALITY AND HISTORY:
THE TRICKSTER'S LEGACY TO HUMANITY

Through the cycle of mythic narratives about the primordial human mother (Amáru) and child (Kuwái), the trickster's interpretive powers become inextricably bound up with musicality. Language and speech transform into musically dynamic ways of speaking and acting that open up the twin worlds of socialized human beings and collective historical movements. Powerful ritual specialists, or chant-owners, construct this dual opening up of the world through the complex intermingling of semanticity and musicality in the ritually powerful ways of speaking, or málikai. In male and female initiation rituals, the trickster's creation of interpretive distancing is a collective musical process, with the chant-owner's chanted and sung journeys between and across worlds forming the central focus. Women participate in the making of this expanding historical space-time through their drinking songs. Groups of nonspecialist men also play a crucial role in the musical, ritual production of history through collective performances of instrumental music.

These sacred flutes and trumpets come in a variety of shapes and sizes, from short *molítu* flutes up to enormous *dzáwiñapa* ("jaguar-bone") trumpets. All these wind instruments are given anthropomorphic meanings that refer to parts of the body of Kuwái, the primordial human being. The most frequently played flutes, called *waliáduwa*, are made in sets of three, representing the outer three fingers of Kuwái's hand, an intertextual reference to the mythic origin of Iñápirríkuli and his two brothers. When these flutes are played together with pairs of flutes called *máariawa*, the thumb and index finger of Kuwái's hand, the performances constitute a symbolic reassembling of the mythic hand of Kuwái. Other instruments are said to represent Kuwái's arms, legs, and torso, so the men's musical performances are in part a process of constructing the mythic body of the primordial human being.

With one important exception, the sacred flutes and trumpets are also imbued with zoomorphic meanings. The pairs of máariawa flutes, for example, are named after a species of white heron (*máari*), and other instruments are named after agouti (*dápa*), toucan (*dzáate*), and various other forest animal and bird species. These animal names are important as part of the general process of metaphorically transforming groups of men into species of animals, or the construction of naturalized social being. Waliáduwa flutes are an exception to the zoomorphic naming of sacred instruments, for the term *waliáduwa* does not refer to any natural species. *Wali-* is a prefix derived from the word for "new" (*walídali*), and the term *waliáduwa* can be most directly translated as "new-like." In contrast to this semantic interpretation, Wakuénai men say that the term *waliáduwa* means "old woman." The ironic juxtaposition of opposed meanings, "old" and "new," gives concrete expression to the trickster's general significance as an opening of and a play upon the gap between literal-semantic and critical-semiotic levels of interpretation. The juxtaposition of opposing meanings in waliáduwa flutes is highly significant, since the performances are a collective synthesis of male elders and newly initiated men, of the old mythic order of the trickster and the new historical order of human society in which groups of men reassemble Kuwái's hand in order to musically reproduce society. The trickster's ability to manage difficult situations is thus ritually transferred to groups of male flute-players who embody the capacity to coordinate both the passing down of mythic ancestral power from one generation of men to the next and the exchange of female blood kin as a process of creating a shared historical space-time with other peoples.

The simultaneity of change and continuity, or movement and stability, is musically as well as verbally embodied in waliáduwa flute performances.

Because I had been primarily concerned with understanding the intricate semantic and musical dimensions of ritually powerful ways of speaking (málikai) during my doctoral fieldwork in 1980–81, I did not fully grasp the significance of waliáduwa performances until returning to the field in 1984 and 1985. During my first return visit in 1984, the chant-owner in the village which had served as the principal site of my doctoral research in 1980–81 asked me if I would leave a tape recorder and other supplies with his son to help him in learning the sacred songs and chants called málikai. I gladly agreed and asked his son to record performances of ritual music in my absence. The results of this experiment in "ethno-ethnomusicology" were spectacular. The chant-owner's son recorded the entire five-day male initiation ritual in early 1985, from the men's journey out into the forest to cut down palm trees for making the sacred flutes and trumpets of Kuwái all the way through to the final departure of the mythic "hand" of Kuwái from the village at the end of the ritual activities.

In the final waliáduwa performance, the group of male flute-players gradually danced away from the house full of singing, drinking women. The sound of the flutes faded a little as the men reached the port but never missed a beat as they embarked in a canoe. As other men paddled down-stream, the three waliáduwa players continued their slow, unchanging melody, an unbroken arc of musical sound, renewing the historical space-time that had first opened up in the trickster's pursuit of Amáru and the women. Sitting on the village plaza with a group of hung-over, exhausted male companions, the chant-owner's son left the tape recorder running for several minutes, until the faintly audible melody finally vanished in the distance.[13] The reflexive, interpretive distancing of the trickster had reached its ultimate transformation, spreading from the primarily verbal activity of playing with the literal/semiotic distinction, through the verbal and musical activities of song duels and sacred chanting, to the fully musical activity of playing and dancing into being a historical landscape of peoples, natural species, and places, all in perpetual motion and anchored in a continuous flow of musical sound. Iñápirríkuli, like Esu the West African trickster, truly "possesses all of these characteristics, plus a plethora of others which, taken together, only begin to present an idea of the complexity of this classic figure of mediation and of the unity of opposed forces" (Gates 1988, 6).

In this short essay, I hope to have conveyed at least some of the complexity, beauty, and power of the mythic trickster in an indigenous Amazonian society. Many of the specific qualities of Iñápirríkuli, or "Made from Bone," are directly comparable to Afro-American trickster figures descended from the West African trickster, Esu (Gates 1988). My brief overview of an Amazonian trickster is intended to build upon Gates's eloquent argument that the trickster is not merely a symbol of esoteric mythic power but the cornerstone of an indigenous (or vernacular) theory of language use. Although Gates's primary concern is for the multiple ways in which the trickster enters into Afro-American oral and written literature, he does give secondary attention to the importance of Signifying in jazz.[14] My studies of an indigenous Amazonian trickster situate verbal prowess within a broader context of musical discourses and performances. For the Wakuénai (and perhaps also for some Afro-Americans), the interplay of figurative and literal meanings is only one of several levels at which the trickster's interpretive distancing operates. Through musical genres of discourse and performance, the Wakuénai extend the domain of verbal semiotic play into a semi- or nonverbal domain of meaning construction. This higher level of semiotic interpretation, or the creation of felt consubstantiality between language music and mythic meaning (Friedrich 1986), is the basis of historical consciousness in Wakuénai society. In musical discourses and performances, verbal meanings are coupled with patterns of sound and bodily movement in ways that transcend both semantic and figurative interpretations. Ritual performances of málikai, song duels, and sacred flute music are not discourses about or symbols of myth and history; rather, they are social constructions of history.

Understanding mythic tricksters as a general semiotic process rather than merely as isolated discursive forms or symbolic messages allows for interpretation to go beyond the shifting sands of micro-level linguistic and cultural details to a level of broadly significant interpretive frameworks. These underlying theories of meaning construction are grounded in the pragmatics of situated speech and action as well as in more conceptual realms of metaphorical thought, poetic imagination, and critical-semiotic interpretation. By focusing on mythic tricksters as indigenous theories of meaning construction, researchers can balance discursive forms and symbolic meanings without becoming lost in a myriad of linguistic and cultural details. A focus on underlying theories of language use and meaning construction also facilitates comparison across broad cultural and historical differences among indigenous American, Afro-American, and Euro-American peoples.

ACKNOWLEDGMENTS

Funding for six months of fieldwork in the Upper Rio Negro region of Venezuela in 1998 was generously provided by the Office of Research Development at Southern Illinois University Carbondale, the National Endowment for the Humanities, and the Wenner-Gren Foundation for Anthropological Research. I am deeply grateful to the Department of Anthropology at the Venezuelan Scientific Research Institute (IVIC), which granted me the status of Visiting Researcher during my visit. I am especially indebted to my colleague Dra. Silvia Vidal for her logistical support and to my late friend Hernan Camico, whose family served as my local hosts in the Puerto Ayacucho area. Many thanks also to the organizers of the 1999 "Symposium on Myth," William Hansen and Gregory Schrempp, for inviting me to participate and to the anonymous reviewer at Indiana University Press for providing useful comments on an earlier version of this essay. However, the information and interpretations contained in this work are my own responsibility and do not necessarily reflect the views of any of the institutions or persons mentioned above.

NOTES

1. Feldmann noted a similar contrast between African and "New World" (North American) trickster figures, arguing that the African trickster's "amorality is not that of the anomic, presocialized individual, who has not yet matured to a sense of responsibility. Suave, urbane and calculating, the African trickster acts with premeditation, always in control of the situation" (1963, 15). As will become clear below, South American tricksters are more like the African tricksters than like those of North America.

2. Eco distinguishes between semantic and semiotic, or critical, interpretation in the following way: "Semantic interpretation is the result of the process by which an addressee . . . fills up [a text] with a given meaning. . . . Critical interpretation is, on the contrary, a metalinguistic activity—a semiotic approach—which aims at describing and explaining for which formal reasons a given text produces a given response" (Eco 1990, 54). In other words, a semantic approach is concerned mainly with lexical and other signs and their referential meanings, whereas critical, semiotic approaches are concerned with formal meanings, contexts of signification, and the interrelations between form and context.

3. Comparisons with Afro-American mythic tricksters are necessarily briefer, along the lines of suggestions for future comparative research and, hopefully, increased dialogue between specialists in Amazonian ethnology and Afro-American studies.

4. In an extended treatment of trickster heroes created by enslaved Africans in North America, Roberts notes that Br'er Rabbit and other animal tricksters model the trickery and wit needed for survival under conditions of famine, deprivation, and dehumanization (1989, 25ff.). African slaves living in North America "recognized that, like their animal trickster, they were in a contest of an indeterminate duration for both physical and cultural survival, with a limited number of ways of protecting themselves without jeopardizing their own well-being within the system. Therefore, both creatively and in their own lives, they had to rely to a great extent on their own ingenuity to develop endless variations on a single theme: the transcendent power of wit" (38).

5. That Iñápirríkuli's father-in-law is also his father's sister's husband reflects the practice of cross-cousin marriage with the father's sister's daughter. Cross-cousin marriage with the daughter of either the father's sister or the mother's brother is still practiced in some Wakuénai villages today but is increasingly rare.

6. The orthography used in this transcription is one that I developed in collaboration with speakers of the Curricarro dialect of Curripaco living in Venezuela. The letter 'j' is equivalent to the English letter 'h' and is an aspirant that occurs together with 'p', 'n', 'w', and several other consonants.

7. See Urban 1991, 32ff. for a discussion of "agent-" and "patient-centricity" in South American myths. Although Urban argues that "The bias [with respect to agency and patiency] may be actually characteristic of a given culture as a whole" (32), Wakuénai narratives demonstrate that it is important to look for variable levels of agency and patiency within specific cultural settings.

8. Among the Wakuénai, witchcraft consists of an attack upon a person's dream soul, which manifests itself during sleep as a miniature replica of the person's ancestral totem. Sorcery is a distinct practice in which a poison-owner (*májnetímnali*) throws splinters, hairs, or other toxic substances into a victim's food or drink.

9. See Hill 1993, 207ff. for a complete translation and analysis of this extraordinary myth.

10. Gates uses the writings of Juan Latino, a sixteenth-century neo-Latin poet, to demonstrate that the "subtle and witty use of irony is among the most common forms of Signifyin(g)" (1988, 90).

11. See Gates 1988, 80 for a parallel example from the Afro-American tradition of Signifying as "a pervasive mode of language use rather than merely one specific verbal game."

12. These taboos also indirectly support the powers of chant-owners and shamans, since they alone can transcend spatio-temporal boundaries, through their superior knowledge of myth and history and their ability to use song and chant to mediate spatio-temporal relations.

13. Original copies of these tapes are stored at the Archives of Traditional Music at Indiana University (accession number 85–526–F, Jonathan D. Hill, "Initiation Rites of the Wakuénai").

14. "There are so many examples of Signifyin(g) in jazz that one could write a formal history of its development on this basis alone" (Gates 1988, 63). After a discussion of how Jelly Roll Morton "signifies" upon Scott Joplin's "Maple Leaf Rag," Gates reaches the conclusion that "the formal history of solo piano styles in jazz is recapitulated, delightfully, whereby one piano style follows its chronological predecessor in the composition itself, so that boogie-woogie, stride, and blues piano styles—and so on—are represented in one composition as histories of the solo jazz piano, histories of its internal repetition and revision process" (63).

BIBLIOGRAPHY

Eco, Umberto. 1990. *The Limits of Interpretation.* Bloomington: Indiana University Press.

Feldmann, Susan. 1963. *African Myths and Tales.* New York: Dell.

Friedrich, Paul. 1986. *The Language Parallax: Linguistic Relativism and Poetic Indeterminacy.* Austin: University of Texas Press.

Gates, Henry Louis, Jr. 1988. *The Signifying Monkey: A Theory of African-American Literary Criticism.* New York: Oxford University Press.

Hill, Jonathan. 1993. *Keepers of the Sacred Chants: The Poetics of Ritual Power in an Amazonian Society.* Tucson: University of Arizona Press.

———, ed. 1988. *Rethinking History and Myth: Indigenous South American Perspectives on the Past.* Urbana: University of Illinois Press.

Hill, Jonathan, and Robin Wright. 1988. "Time, Narrative, and Ritual: Historical Interpretations from an Amazonian Society." In *Rethinking History and Myth: Indigenous South American Perspectives on the Past,* edited by Jonathan Hill, 78–105. Urbana: University of Illinois Press.

Radin, Paul. 1956. *The Trickster: A Study in American Indian Mythology.* New York: Schocken.

Rasnake, Roger. 1988. "Images of Resistance to Colonial Domination." In *Rethinking History and Myth: Indigenous South American Perspectives on the Past,* edited by Jonathan Hill, 136–56. Urbana: University of Illinois Press.

Roberts, John. 1989. *From Trickster to Badman: The Black Folk Hero in Slavery and Freedom.* Philadelphia: University of Pennsylvania Press.

Sapir, J. David, and J. Christopher Crocker, eds. 1977. *The Social Use of Metaphor: Essays on the Anthropology of Rhetoric.* Philadelphia: University of Pennsylvania Press.

Silverblatt, Irene. 1988. "Political Memories and Colonizing Symbols: Santiago and the Mountain Gods of Colonial Peru." In *Rethinking History and Myth: Indigenous South American Perspectives on the Past,* edited by Jonathan Hill, 174–94. Urbana: University of Illinois Press.

Sperber, Dan. 1975. *Rethinking Symbolism.* Cambridge: Cambridge University Press.

Urban, Greg. 1991. *A Discourse-Centered Approach to Culture: Native South American Myths and Rituals.* Austin: University of Texas Press.

White, Hayden. 1973. *Meta-history: The Historical Imagination in Nineteenth-Century Europe.* Baltimore: Johns Hopkins University Press.

Whitten, Norman. 1978. "Ecological Imagery and Cultural Adaptability: The Canelos Quichua of Eastern Ecuador." *American Anthropologist* 80:836–59.

Wright, Robin, and Jonathan Hill. 1986. "History, Ritual, and Myth: Nineteenth-Century Millenarian Movements in the Northwest Amazon." *Ethnohistory* 33, no. 1: 31–54.

SIX

Native American Reassessment and Reinterpretation of Myths

BARRE TOELKEN

A look back at volume 68 of the *Journal of American Folklore*—that special issue on myth we are more or less celebrating in these essays—confirms the recollection that our colleagues in 1955 were still deeply engaged in discussing what myth *is,* and how it can best be studied and understood. In the intervening years, we have seen a maturation of this field into a forum which more likely considers what myth *does,* what it dramatizes, and how it functions for those who use it. This essay discusses some contemporary examples of the active reconsideration of myths by Native Americans whose stories not only are archived in print or partially preserved in academic discussion, but are still shared in the living culture.

Before proceeding, however, I need to admit a disquietude about the term "myth" itself, for in studying Navajo and other tribal stories over the past forty years, I have not discovered in the narrative materials themselves the academic distinctions suggested by such terms as "tale" (which I would normally define as a fictional traditional narrative), "legend" (which I would call an ongoing narrative believed to represent an actual event, told by a non-eyewitness), and "myth" (which—at its simplest—would be a traditional sacred narrative). For one thing, the Native Americans I have worked with do not see a clear boundary between the sacred and the nonsacred, and are likely to understand these concepts as overlapping or coterminous dimensions. For another thing, many Native stories utilize features of all three of these genres in one narrative (take, for example, the many coyote stories which dramatize sacred and cultural concepts in a patently fictional story which nonetheless dramatizes the origins of real place names or contemporary customs). For this reason, since I am dealing here with Native materials which do not neatly match Euro-American generic preconceptions, my use of the term "myth" will represent a kind of compromise for the sake of our discussion: that is, without attempting a newer or narrower definition (which might be even less useful to us, after all), I will concentrate on narratives which are thought by the Native Americans who tell them to represent large cultural and natural issues, in contradistinction to local reminiscence or mundane entertainment. Even this rather elastic definition will require some equivocation because of the sometimes elliptical and intensely local ways in which Native universals are often expressed.

My field of focus will be selected myths from several western United States Native American tribes, ranging from those who still narrate in their native language (like the Navajo) to those (like the Oregon coastal tribes of the Coos and Coquelle) whose languages were exterminated and who now tell their stories in English. I want to reexamine the idea, once current among scholars, that myth depends upon an essentially conservative and nonrational thought process, a position in part articulated in David Bidney's essay "Myth, Symbolism, and Truth," from that special issue of *JAF*:

> The effectiveness of myth depends in large measure upon ignorance or unconsciousness of its actual motivation. That is why myth tends to recede before the advance of reason and self-conscious reflection. (Bidney 1955, 390)

First of all, I do not see any evidence that myth has receded. More important than that, the assertion that myth (and presumably the related phenomena of its use and discussion) naturally recedes when confronted by reason and reflection asks us to ignore or undervalue the ongoing cultural critique of myth in such rational and self-conscious dialectics as Talmudic discussion. Our problem is, in part, that we are willing to view such things as "liberation theology," Talmudic argument, and "religious studies" as perfectly rational, reasonable, and self-conscious (or at least intellectually aware) efforts to better understand and reinterpret the mythic systems of cultures similar to our own, while we assume that other—especially nonliterate—cultures do not have the capacity, or the interest, or perhaps even the need, to discuss and interpret their own mythic materials. Leaving aside for now the racial arrogance of such an assumption, let me simply observe that, while there was no *written* accumulation of what might be called self-conscious reflection or commentary on their own myths by Native Americans until very recently, there is nonetheless a venerable and continuing Native oral tradition of discussion, critique, reassessment, and reinterpretation that should be instructive to us. Recognizing such a custom requires us to acknowledge the dynamic aspects of myth as seriously as we have accepted its conservative dimensions. More importantly, we will need to adjust our assumptions about the lack of Native intellection, empirical observation, and critical motivation, because—as this essay will at least partly show—a good many myths that may seem superficially to present unlikely scenarios (for example, Coyote's diarrhea becoming a local landmark) turn out to be remarkably memorable dramatizations of real phenomena. This calls for a substantial renovation of our notion of what it is myth actually accomplishes, at least for Native Americans—but perhaps the point is applicable to myth generally. I would start by suggesting a rather simple model, based on the mythic stories I have worked with: while oral histories are usually "about" events which are supposed to have happened, myths are not "about" something but are, rather, complex dramatizations of culturally important issues. To understand a coyote story that ends "that's how Coyote got his yellow eyes" as an account of how coyotes got their yellow eyes is to miss the point, as virtually all Native narrators (when asked) will point out. So, then, what *is* the point? And how do we find out—without reading our own outside assumptions into the picture? One rather basic way is to engage Native narrators in the discussion, and this is what I—and indeed many other scholars—have been attempting to do.

For example, working with Navajos over the past forty-five years, I have been struck by their consistent reference to two totally different narratives concerning their location in the desert Southwest. If we ask, "Where did Navajos come from?" we are usually told either the entirety or a synopsis of the Emergence Myth, in which all living beings emerge onto the surface of the present world after having moved upward from previous levels of existence underneath and within this one (Zolbrod 1984). However, if we ask, "What was this area like when you Navajos first arrived?" we are likely to hear comments like "Oh, when we first came here, we didn't know how to get food, but there were these little people living up in the cliffs who had gardens out on the flat areas below. All we had to do was throw rocks at them and drive them out of the fields. When they'd go up into the cliffs, we could just take whatever vegetables we needed."[1] The first story is easily recognizable as the typical pueblo origin story, and is no doubt modeled on the agricultural metaphor of life in general emerging like plant growth from belowground. Although the dating of the event is still under lively discussion by scholars of the Athabascan cultures, many now believe that the Navajos, originally hunters and fishers from the far northwest (where their many Athabascan cousins still live, in western Canada and interior Alaska), migrated southward, arriving about 500–600 years ago in southwestern deserts which offered them none of their accustomed animal food supply. They survived at first, apparently, by harvesting the gardens of their new pueblo neighbors, but eventually they learned the way of agriculture—including the sacred story which dramatizes its principles—and settled into the area by adopting much of the associated pueblo worldview (including the matrilineal and matrilocal societal structure which privileges female fertility over male hunting as a central feature of cultural reality). For all this may indicate about Navajo syncretism or readiness to adapt, the cultural history of this shift is still vividly archived in the Navajo word for corn, *naadą́ą́*—literally, "enemy food."

Jerrold E. Levy (1998) has argued that the resultant change in mythic perspective was so powerful that the newer system (typified by the text and logic of the Blessingway ceremony) virtually demoted the earlier hunters' shamanic system to the level of shame and embarrassment (as typified by narratives dramatizing the wandering antics of Coyote). I would suggest that the picture is more complicated than that, since animals like the bear, cougar, lynx, and coyote, which would have been common in the far north (and might have been totemic ancestors in addition to sources of food and skins), are still included as central symbols in contemporary Navajo healing ceremonies, and are thought to be still resident in the Navajo world—albeit in the higher elevations of the four sacred mountains. As well, there is an even stronger sense of shamanism, especially with respect to control over death, in the Navajo witchcraft (*yenaaldlooshi*) complex. But Levy's position is certainly valid: a new story, a newer mythic rendering of the Navajo world, dramatizes and celebrates the (relatively) new reality. That this is not a capricious or unique shift of focus is reflected in the fact that the Emergence Myth is adjusted from time to time to accommodate the culturally expanded world in which the Navajos continue to live. Several times over the past few years, I have had the opportunity to speak with *hataałi* (literally, "singers") and hear their versions of the Emergence Myth during appropriate parts of healing rituals. Many of them now include horses, cattle, sheep, and goats among those beings who came up from the lower worlds. When I asked about this apparent anachronism on one occasion, I was told by one very gifted singer, "Of course I know that cows and sheep came here with the Spaniards. I myself never mentioned them in the ceremony until recently. But then I realized that these animals have become a part of us (as you know, we even call sheep 'the mothers of our children'), and I thought, 'how can it be a sacred story if it doesn't include all the important beings in our world?'"[2]

In effect, the Navajos use myth not to "explain" where they came from, but, rather, to narratively claim the world into which they moved, and to adjust that claim as the world has subsequently moved in on them. This would appear to complicate Clifford Geertz's (1963) notion of "agricultural involution," in which cultural change is inhibited by traditional patterns which have become fixed, for although the Navajos have fiercely retained some traditional patterns, they have not been inhibited in changing others (not the least example of which is the almost total abhorrence of fish by elderly Navajos whose northern ancestors specialized in catching and preparing fish). This (perhaps inherent?) ability to adjust and reconstruct mythic constellations is a feature to which we have not paid sufficient attention.

The Kiowa origin myth, which describes people coming out of a world below through a hollow log, presents—among other things—a birth image, a movement from dark to light, from restricted to open space. N. Scott Momaday's reading of the image as the dramatic articulation of the Kiowas' emergence from the forests of the Yellowstone country out onto the open plains could be seen as a modern literary conceit, but it may also be an example of the ways in which Native intellectuals have always seen the myths as richly laden icons of their world and its meanings (Momaday 1969, 16–17). Since the emergence of the Kiowas onto the plains actually did result in the "birth" of a new culture which had not existed before, there is no reason why a contemporary Kiowa like Momaday should not see the story as resonant with the ongoing dynamics of his culture. And it is significant that the story still ends with the detail that someone—a pregnant woman—got stuck in the hollow log; that is, not everyone got out—echoing the accurate information that the Kiowas have relatives who did not come along on their migration (indeed, linguistically related groups like the Tiwa, Tewa, and Towa are well known for long-term habitation in pueblos which use underground chambers—kivas—for ceremonial purposes). We may have a tendency to dismiss such modern Native interpretations of older myths as anachronistic wishful thinking, but if the examples above are even a small indication of what has been transpiring in the cultural interpretations of Native people, I think we should at least entertain the possibility that such revisions are not modern intellectual games but evaluative traditions in themselves.

With this possibility in mind, I have been discussing contemporary attitudes toward myth with a number of Native people in the Pacific Northwest, notably George Wasson (a Coquelle elder), Gordon Bettles (a Klamath cultural leader), Loren Bommelyn (a Tolowa religious leader), and Verbena Green (a Warm Springs elder), in order to get some sense of what the state of mythic conversation is. I found that not only does the ongoing litigation for the re-recognition of terminated tribes make significant use of myths and rituals, but older stories are now used to locate former villages, fishing weirs, and ritual locations. These places can then be studied by archeologists, biologists, and other consultants and colleagues to enable the tribes to reclaim their cultural past. It turns out that tribal anecdotes, myths, and stories, as well as personal recollections of elders' conversations, have been exceedingly accurate about the location of specific sites—even long after the local languages (in the case of the Coos and Coquelles) have been driven out of existence and tribal members dispersed. The tenacity and the accuracy of these narratives is remarkable enough, but along with the "data" carried in the dramatization of such stories come cultural perspectives which are equally noteworthy. For example, when a Coquelle-sponsored dig located a village site previously remembered only in local legend, scientists were able to determine that it had been flooded catastrophically by a tsunami on January 26, 1700, at 9:00 P.M.—the exact computation being made possible by the meticulous earthquake records kept by the Japanese at that time (Hall 2001). After the date and time of day had been established by geologists, the Coquelles were able to describe what had been happening in the village at the moment the wave had struck because they still know the myths and ritual conventions that would have dictated the behaviors of the people at that time of year and that time of day.[3] If the villagers there had indeed followed the seasonal custom of moving inland and tying boats to higher ground, and if they had performed certain rituals which would have necessitated being outdoors, at least some of them might have been able to survive the catastrophe.

Thus, when we hear a serious story being told about a natural phenomenon said to have happened long ago, we are ill advised to discard or devalue it just because it doesn't seem to make sense. Coquelle elder George Wasson, for example, tells the story of a summer in which for more than ten days the sun never came up in the morning.[4] The sky remained dark (and the sky along the Oregon coast can be dark enough even under normal circumstances), the sun appearing rarely and only late in the day, in the south just before sunset. What could such a story mean? Why would anyone pass it on? Why is it told with the gravity of myth? The last of these questions is in some ways the easiest to answer: among the tribes along the Oregon coast, weather phenomena were closely observed and remembered, because they were the key to survival and were considered an indication of whether the world was in order. But that would not account for anyone's telling the story today. On one hand, it is clear to me that Wasson tells this story because he heard it from his father, and thus considers it, in and of itself, an important cultural inheritance. But he also tells it because in recent years he has learned that the Klamaths have a story about the explosion of Mount Mazama about seven thousand years ago, the event which led to the formation of Crater Lake, and he knows enough about the effects of volcanic clouds of ash (everyone in the Northwest does, since the explosion of Mount St. Helens in 1980) to conclude that the Coquelle account of a dark summer is the narrative record of a momentous volcanic explosion. According to University of Oregon vulcanologist William Orr, the ash from the Mazama explosion far exceeded that of the Krakatoa eruption, and would have caused wintry conditions over much of the world.[5] Because of southwesterly coastal winds, it is doubtful that the ashes would have covered the local Oregon coast, but the column of ash immediately eastward of the coast range would have prevented sunlight from coming through until the sun was low in the southwest. Now, whether this story details the particular explosion which formed Crater Lake or one of the many other volcanic events that occurred in the area, the significant point for Wasson is that the story is not as opaque as it might have seemed; for the Coquelle tribe (as for the Klamaths, obviously), it is one more eyewitness account which testifies to aboriginal tenure—not only in North America, but in this particular area, which has been under dispute in the ironic legal arena in which tribes are asked to prove in our courts that they were present before we came along. Stories like this are used routinely today—not always successfully—in the attempt to establish tribal rights and recognition.

The Crater Lake story told among the Klamaths and Modocs is dramatized as a fight between two mountains (the other one is Mount Shasta, also a volcano) over possession of a beautiful young woman, Loha. But in addition to what the myth suggests about the catastrophic results of competitive courtship and illusive beauty, it is also quite articulate about volcanic explosions: mountains shake and crumble, red-hot rocks are thrown in all directions, burning ashes fall everywhere, and fire, described as a river or ocean of flame (lava, no doubt), consumes the nearby forests. Finally, the top of the mountain falls in on the chief of the underworld and next day the tall mountain is gone. The whole account is a startlingly accurate description of the event that formed Crater Lake, and ends by recalling that after the eruption, rain fell for years, filling the crater—a phenomenon which (like accompanying lightning) has been observed in connection with other great eruptions. Coincidence? Or eyewitness account?[6]

Verbena Green, Warm Springs storyteller and cultural resource, has shared with me a number of stories about the formation of the Cascade Mountains, and all of them are dramatized as battles among and between the various mountains, who threw rocks and fire at each other. While those rocks and lava flows are indeed still visible—and are referenced in the stories as testimony to the historicity of the events—we should not hastily conclude that these are only etiological myths which "explain" or account for local landscape features. To be sure, on that level they are striking in their details, which indicate that there must have been eyewitnesses to the eruptions. This in turn has provided a very useful testimony of early presence in the area, meaning that these are mythic documents with political, legal, and economic consequences. But in addition to the accurate geological detail of these stories, there is the cultural construction of the logic behind the plots: the fights between the mountains were caused by petty selfishness, jealousy, arrogant power plays, and ego, and these are the very emotions and attitudes which people in the surrounding tribes believe they are supposed to keep under control. This is to say that the myths are multivalent (as probably all myths are), at once providing a scenario or a rationale for the familiar landscape and dramatizing important cultural values; by connecting landscape and culture in a concrete enactment of the human actions or moods which affect both, such narratives articulate issues of central importance and are thus well worth the renewed attention of Native peoples hoping to stabilize or restore cultural verities and to regain control over stolen land. In these matters, of course, the cultural sense of place remains as important as the physical and legal disposition of the real estate, since the landscape functions as a physical reference to abstract cultural values. The irony is that the legal dispute takes place in the invader's courtroom—arguably not the fairest of venues—and the cultural search often takes place today in the invader's libraries, which house obscure fieldwork projects carried out at the turn of the century by dedicated Euro-Americans (many of them multilingual East Coast scholars of Jewish background who could not bear to let these fascinating languages disappear without scrutiny). Lucky indeed are the tribes who still have some mythic stories in use or in memory, for these cultural documents can be used to guide the interpretation of old field notes, language studies, and collections of narratives.

A simple but impressive case in point is provided by the few stories and rituals still in circulation among the Coos and Coquelle tribes of the southwest Oregon coast. The First Salmon Ceremony celebrated each year by these tribes memorializes the time when salmon first began going upriver. While the assumption behind this ritual might seem questionable at first blush (is it even possible that people were present when the first salmon run occurred?), new researches in coastal geography are showing that there were times in the Pleistocene and Holocene eras when the level of the ocean was much lower than it is now; this, added to the growing evidence of gigantic inland bodies of water which occasionally broke through in floods (like the Great Missoula Floods of about 12,000–15,000 years ago), shows that the rivers and estuary systems of today are relatively recent, and that the salmon migrations have been brought about by the changing environment.[7] It is possible that salmon were originally inland fish (witness the many lakes that still have "land-locked" salmon which have never visited the ocean) who were carried out to sea in the floods described in the myths of virtually all Northwest tribes; and George Wasson notes that there are old stories about what coastal people ate before they had the salmon (mostly *wapato* and skunk cabbage).[8] Since the present coastal water level was more or less stabilized about seven thousand years ago (allowing for river mouths which would accommodate salmon trying to get home), one tantalizing possibility is that the First Salmon Ceremony is indeed the cultural reenactment of an actual event witnessed several thousand years ago. Present-day Coquelles use the ceremony to ritually dramatize the bond of reciprocity they believe exists among humans, salmon, and the aquatic world which supports them both, but in so doing, they may indeed be maintaining an archive of empirical geological observation.

Another story (which echoes a motif found throughout the Northwest, and which might strike us as an entertaining fiction rather than the recollection of an actual event) describes Old Man Coyote dismembering himself after being caught in a hollow tree. The narrative, which Coquelle elder George Wasson and I have discussed elsewhere (Toelken and Wasson 1999), features a hailstorm as well as a field of fully ripe wild strawberries. Since hail would not normally occur in that area when strawberries are ripe, Wasson believes the story is at least in part a dramatization of a year in which a weather anomaly ("el Niño"?) occurred, which the local people may have attributed to the selfish or immoral actions of people inattentive to the requirements of taboo or cultural practice (those features epitomized by Old Man Coyote in Coquelle narratives). Among other things, then, the myth continues to dramatize or enact a world in which the actions of people have a direct relationship to weather and food supply, a much more complex matter than mere strawberries would initially suggest.

In another Coquelle story, Old Man Coyote argues with a small plant about which of them is more powerful, finally triumphing (he thinks) by eating the plant. But the plant continues to argue from inside his belly, and eventually causes such a traumatic case of diarrhea that the resultant pile (now of course fossilized into a rock formation) still indicates the whereabouts of that purgative medicinal plant. Moreover, the story also suggests the proper dosage by dramatizing that a little of this plant goes a long way; and it suggests that in nature small beings are not powerless.[9]

A Coos/Coquelle story of the woman who marries a sea otter (also found among the myths of other coastal tribes) uses the marriage assumptions of these cultures (marriage creates obligations for reciprocation among the larger extended families involved) to dramatize the long-standing right of access to sea otters, fish, and beached whales as symbols of family relationship and interactive responsibility to the food supply (our relatives in the ocean want to supply us with food; we want to supply them with gifts, prayers, stories, and ceremonies). The function of such a myth as a model for assumed relationships to "food resources" is as important today as ever—probably more so since the myth's premises have been challenged by a government concerned with its presumed obligations to commercial and sport fishermen. As well, the model of cooperative interaction with one's relatives in nature also nurtures a cultural—perhaps even spiritual—sense of being at home in this place (Wolgamott 1994b).

Thus far, I have been discussing the kinds of mythic interpretation and reassessment through which the members of a tribe feel they can extend and enrich their sense of themselves and their place by taking a new, or renewed, view of the ideas available to them from their own older oral traditions, from scholarly studies done of their tribes, and from developments in their contemporary situations. More recently I have witnessed a contemporary, even more investigative and philosophical, brand of mythic discussion, and while I have no clear idea how widespread it is, I find it worth a closer look, for—like the other examples discussed here—it challenges the idea of myth as monolithic, and it questions the stereotype of Native Americans as uninterested in analytical discussion. I first became aware of this new level of myth dialogue at a Native American conference at the University of Oregon in 1997, when I found myself listening to a discussion initiated by George Wasson and Loren Bommelyn, a Tolowa religious leader from Smith River Rancheria in northern California. They had invited Dell Hymes and me to lunch to ask what we thought of a certain Lower Umpqua story they had found while searching through old Bureau of American Ethnology publications for coastal materials from the turn of the century. Since neither of these Native leaders is Siuslaw or Lower Umpqua, their interest was not in drawing the text into their cultural domains, but in learning how the brief (but apparently mythic) anecdote might provide a model for understanding their own myths more thoroughly. The story depicts a massive accumulation of ice and snow along the southern Oregon coast, where ice and snow are seldom encountered; they wondered if this text might be another indication that "el Niño years" are referenced and described in coastal myths the way some weather variations are recorded on the "winter count" buffalo robes of the Plains Indians. They were intrigued by the fact that one of the half-dozen speakers of the Lower Umpqua/Siuslaw language still alive at the turn of the century chose this story to tell Leo Frachtenberg. I supply here my own provisional rendering of the interlinear text published by Frachtenberg (Frachtenberg 1922, 627–29; see also Frachtenberg 1914, 76–77) for practical reference. Dell Hymes has been working with this piece as well, and his more linguistically grounded interpretation is certain to uncover still more levels of meaning and nuance in this densely packed narrative.

> Ice was everywhere.
> The ground was covered with snow.
> Everything became cold, everywhere ice.
> How could all the people drink?
> There was only a well to drink from.
> Everyone drank from it.

Although there were many people, they all drank there.
Then ice appears on the water [of the well, presumably].
They didn't know where to go, those inhabitants.
All those people go on top of the ice.
Now then, old people know it, that ancient custom.
Then they shout constantly for that Raccoon,
And also shout constantly for that Coyote.
He is beseeched constantly:
"Raccoon, Raccoon, make it rain everywhere!
Tell this to Coyote!
You two make it rain everywhere!
Poor us! Our bodies are very cold!"
Now then, he is called continually:
"Raccoon, Raccoon, make it rain everywhere!
Coyote, you two make it rain everywhere!"
Then, finally, it starts to rain all over.
All the people believe in this custom.
That's why those two are shouted at continually;
then finally it rains.
Thus it is shouted when that river freezes over.
There it [the story? the ice?] ends; it ends there.
That's the way I know it.

Why do people believe or follow a ritual custom to get rid of ice and snow in an area where snow is rare and rivers never freeze over? And why did the Native speaker find this particular story appropriate or important to tell a visiting linguist?

Bommelyn and Wasson recognized that, in this drama, it is the old people who know the saving custom, and they took that to mean that the exercise of this invocation must have been rare. First conclusion, then: weather events like this occurred so seldom that only the old people had any experience with them. Therefore, old people are valuable, because they are the tribe's only help when odd occasions like this arise. They also concluded that tribes other than their own have narratives which not only record "el Niño years" but dramatize the intimate relationships among the weather, certain animals, and people's ritual practice. In other words, even though we do not have a firm idea about how Raccoon and Coyote functioned in Lower Umpqua myth and ritual, the narrative nonetheless gives us a partial insight into the logic of that tribe's cultural worldview, and this in turn gives us a glimpse of cultural life, as well as the fear of unnatural weather, on the Northwest coast.

Wasson also suggested that the story could recall an even older set of circumstances, that is, occasional and erratic freezing periods connected to the last ice age. Such ancient eyewitness testimony, of course, would establish a very early tenure on the land. In a paper prepared for his tribe's annual publication on Coquelle cultural researches, Wasson points out the existence of plants along the southern Oregon coast which survived the last ice age in a kind of protected pocket. Such plants as myrtlewood, Brewer or "weeping" spruce, *Kalmiopsis leacheana* (a Pleistocene azalea), and Port Orford cedar are found nowhere else in the world except on the southern Oregon coast, and their environment may thus represent a *refugium* where early human migrants would also have been able to establish long-term habitation (Wasson 2001). It is worth mentioning that this area is just south of the lower Umpqua location where Frachtenberg collected the "Invocation for Rain."

Still more can be said about this text. Rain is the common denominator along the Oregon coast (along with wind), and thus the logic of the invocation calls for the restoration of a norm, not simply a cessation of the freezing weather. We can assume, then, not only that Coyote and Raccoon have a strong connection with rain, but that they function as exponents of balance in nature, or as powers who can be persuaded to provide succor, relief, or redemption to people who remember the proper ritual. Was this piece, then, recited as a subtle counter to the Christian messages with which the Native populations were being bombarded? Could it be in itself a metaphor for a people who were feeling "frozen" and powerless, and whose only relief lay with their (by now very few) old-timers and ancient rituals? In any case, it was clear to everyone by the 1920s that there were only a few Native people left at the mouth of the Umpqua River, and so it seems that lurking in this particular performance is the lament, "How will we cope with rare and traumatic events without the old people and the traditions to guide us?" Ongoing Native discussion and speculation about myths like this are testimony to a growing consciousness about the capacity of these old narratives to embody important information and perspectives once feared lost: models of worldview, recollections of settlement, testimonies of early habitation, beliefs about the relationships between humans and the environment, especially the weather (can it be a coincidence that the character called Coyote in some of these tribes shows up as South Wind in the stories of their neighbors?), medicinal information and culturally constructed attitudes about health and healing, and dramatizations of cultural change, to name a few of the most obvious ones.

I am well aware that some readers will consider current Native intellectual interests irrelevant to the question of what the myths "originally" meant. But since we have mostly based our studies on texts generated and published by our culture and its scholars without real collaborative engagement with Natives, I'm not confident we really know what these stories originally "meant" anyway. Perhaps no one does. In any event, since contemporary biblical and religious scholarship continually reexamines and retranslates our own ancient myths, I do not see why we should inhibit or denigrate any other cultural attempts to do the same. And we can only benefit from the perspectives supplied to us by participants in the cultures we study and try to understand. When I asked George Wasson why he was interested in telling and discussing his tribe's myths, he told me that in large part he considers the stories to be, not only narrative expressions, but ongoing critiques of and commentaries about life: "They're like your principles of evolution: they help us understand and cope with the continual changes of earth and nature around us—and especially the changes that have come about since your people started invading us. But beyond all that, these stories let us experience ourselves as a people."

Myth continues to exist because it—like good poetry—engages its audiences in several levels of meaning at one time. And for that reason we are unlikely to come up with a single, simple definition of myth, or a single, simple description of its functions. Nor do we need to. The lively examination and reassessment of myths going on among Native American intellectuals, religious leaders, and writers offers proof that—despite murderous campaigns of cultural annihilation carried out upon them in the past—some Native mythology is alive and well as it moves into a new millennium not of its own making. Indeed, Native people's earnest discussion of their myths, and their parallel reinvigoration of certain rituals, suggests a critical vitality undreamed of by Bidney and others. I think myth persists because reason and philosophical reflection are inadequate to the task of producing a moving dramatization of the deep complexities of natural relationships, moral responsibilities, cultural obligations, and human needs. I suggest that the Native reassessment of myths, like Talmudic discussion, will continue energetically because the myths and their capacity to embody culturally constructed issues will become more intensely meaningful as tribal systems and lands are further threatened and as the relationships between these elements are transformed in the flow of function and history. Moreover, as non-Natives continue to borrow and commodify Native ideas (ranging from "dreamcatchers" to weekend sweatlodge seminars to sacred-pipe healing sessions), Native peoples are becoming even more engaged in enhancing their knowledge of, and extending their control over, their own mythic heritages (Whitt 1995). If we believe in the validity of mythic discussion on more than the academic level, our responsibility is to play a supportive role in the maintenance of the living cultures whose values we so antiseptically discuss in essays like this. In so doing, we will inevitably learn more about the meaning of myth in the modern world.

NOTES

1. Condensed from conversations with Hugh Yellowman in the 1960s and 1970s.

2. Private conversation with Tully Benally, a singer, during a Navajo "sing," 13 December 1993.

3. The exact timing of this flood was reported by a team of scientists at the 1999 annual Coquelle tribal gathering at Coos Bay, Oregon. The Coquelles held a symposium in January 2000 to commemorate the event.

4. The same story is recorded in Frachtenberg 1913, 135.

5. Private communication.

6. A Klamath account of the origin of Crater Lake, recorded by a soldier who collected it from Chief Lalek, is given by Ella Clark in somewhat romanticized language (Clark 1953, 53–55). A Coquelle version is provided by Susan Wasson Wolgamott in Jones and Ramsey 1994, 287.

7. A fascinating account of the Missoula Floods is given by Parfit 1995.

8. A number of other Northwest flood stories, many of them centered in the territory of the Missoula Floods, testify to tribal awareness of the geological marks left by floods, as well as to the fact that there were several inundations which altered the landscape—a bit much for coincidence, one would think (Clark 1953, 12, 31–32, 44–45, 86–88; Clark 1966, 39–40). Vine Deloria, Jr., has discussed other aspects of these floods in *Red Earth, White Lies: Native Americans and the Myth of Scientific Fact* (1995, 207–30).

9. Told to the author by Will Wasson near Sunset Bay State Park, Oregon, in the winter of 1970.

BIBLIOGRAPHY

Bidney, David. 1955. "Myth, Symbolism, and Truth." *Journal of American Folklore* 68: 379–92.

Clark, Ella E. 1953. *Indian Legends of the Pacific Northwest.* Berkeley: University of California Press.

———. 1966. *Indian Legends from the Northern Rockies.* Norman: University of Oklahoma Press.

Deloria, Vine, Jr. 1995. *Red Earth, White Lies: Native Americans and the Myth of Scientific Fact.* New York: Scribner.

Frachtenberg, Leo J. 1913. *Coos Texts.* New York: Columbia University Press.

———. 1914. *Lower Umpqua Texts.* New York: Columbia University Press.

———. 1922. *Siuslawan (Lower Umpqua).* In *Handbook of American Indian Languages,* edited by Franz Boas, part 2, 431–629. Bureau of American Ethnology Bulletin 40. Washington, D.C.: Government Printing Office.

Geertz, Clifford. 1963. *Agricultural Involution: The Process of Ecological Change.* Berkeley: University of California Press.

Hall, Roberta I. 2001. *Nah-so-mah Village, Viewed through Its Fauna.* Corvallis, Oregon: The Coquille Indian Tribe, Sea Grant, and Oregon State University.

Jones, Suzi, and Jarold Ramsey, eds. 1994. *The Stories We Tell: An Anthology of Oregon Folk Literature.* Corvallis: Oregon State University Press.

Levy, Jerrold E. 1998. *In The Beginning: The Navajo Genesis.* Albuquerque: University of New Mexico Press.

Momaday, N. Scott. 1969. *The Way to Rainy Mountain.* Albuquerque: University of New Mexico Press.

Parfit, Michael. 1995. "The Floods That Carved the West." *Smithsonian* 26, no. 1 (April): 48–59.

Toelken, Barre, and George B. Wasson. 1999. "Coyote and the Strawberries: Cultural Drama and Cultural Collaboration." *Oral Tradition* 13, no. 1: 176–99.

Wasson, George. 2001. "Growing Up Human: An Emic Perspective." Ph.D. dissertation, University of Oregon.

———. Forthcoming. *Oral Traditions of the Earliest Humans on the Oregon Coast: A Comparison of Ethnohistorical and Archaeological Records. Proceedings of the Coquelle Tribal Conference, 1999.*

Whitt, Laurie Ann. 1995. "Cultural Imperialism and the Marketing of Native America." *American Indian Culture and Research Journal* 19:1–31.

Wolgamott, Susan Wasson. 1994a. "Coyote Falls in Love and Creates Crater Lake." In *The Stories We Tell: An Anthology of Oregon Folk Literature,* edited by Suzi Jones and Jarold Ramsey, 287. Corvallis: Oregon State University Press.

———. 1994b. "The Girl Who Married a Sea Otter." In *The Stories We Tell: An Anthology of Oregon Folk Literature,* edited by Suzi Jones and Jarold Ramsey, 262–63. Corvallis: Oregon State University Press.

Zolbrod, Paul G. 1984. *Diné Bahane': The Navajo Creation Story.* Albuquerque: University of New Mexico Press.

Part III

MYTH AND
HISTORICAL TEXTS

SEVEN

Myth Read as History:
Odin in Snorri Sturluson's Ynglinga saga

JOHN LINDOW

Scandinavian mythology has long been a well-defined research field. Even though virtually all the texts were recorded two centuries and more after the conversion to Christianity c. 1000 C.E., the corpus of materials clearly presents a world created by the gods and in the end destroyed in a battle between gods and the forces of chaos, only to reemerge anew. The various texts present fairly consistent pictures of the major gods: the duplicitous Odin, master of poetry and magic; the mighty Thor and his hammer; Baldr the innocent, cut down early in life; the one-armed Týr; and so forth. The acts of these gods and their opponents, taken together, make up a clearly articulated social system that has proved amenable to consistent analysis (e.g., Clunies Ross 1994). At the same time, the fact that Christian authors recorded these narratives about pagan gods remains fundamental to any serious study of the field.

The mythology as a system has its own rules of chronology and makes no reference to history as we understand it today or as medieval Christians understood it. However, as early as the time of the first recording of the myths, the gods were also set in a historical context. The most famous such example is in the prologue to the *Edda* of Snorri Sturluson, composed probably c. 1220–30. Snorri's *Edda* contains the clearest and most often read account of the mythology, in the section called *Gylfaginning* (Deluding of Gylfi), which presents the entire sweep from the creation of the cosmos to its end, catalogues and describes the various gods, and recounts a number of myths. *Skáldskaparmál* (Language of poetry), a discourse on poetic diction, is meant by Snorri to follow *Gylfaginning;* it contains numerous lists of the metaphors known as kennings, many of them based on myths, and, toward the beginning of the text, full narratives of some of the most significant myths themselves. That Snorri's *Edda* as a whole was intended as a handbook of poetics—the term *Edda* may well mean "poetics" (Faulkes 1977)—is made certain by the last part of the book, a complex poem called *Háttatal* (Enumeration of meters) exemplifying variations in metrics and diction and equipped with a commentary.

Like many medieval treatises, Snorri's *Edda* was fitted with a prologue, and here the gods are unequivocally made historical. The prologue states that Odin was a historical king who led an emigration from Troy and settled in Sweden. The other *æsir* (the word means "gods" but is often used in the mythology as though it describes a tribe or family grouping) accompany him and are part of this historical immigration into Scandinavia. Snorri was not the inventor of this "myth spun by an errant scholar seeking to interpret another myth" (Lincoln 1999, 78). It had long been the intellectual property of scholars in the north. It figured in the origin narrative produced by Icelandic historians more than a century before Snorri wrote (Heusler 1908), and certainly exemplifies mythic thinking of a sort (Lindow 1997).

Snorri is without question the most famous named author within the entire extraordinary body of medieval Icelandic writing, and his fame rests not only on his *Edda*. Also attributed to him is a vast and masterful compendium of the lives of Norwegian kings, called *Heimskringla* (Orb of the earth) after its opening words. *Heimskringla* is an overtly historical text. It is one of three lengthy compilations of kings' sagas undertaken in the first half of the thirteenth century. The other two are *Morkinskinna* (Rotten codex) and *Fagrskinna* (Handsome codex). *Morkinskinna* covers the kings from around 1035 to the second half of the twelfth century, probably ca. 1177. *Fagrskinna,* which appears to be of Norwegian provenance (but may, even so, have been written by an Icelander), begins far earlier, with the reign of Hálfdan Svarti ("the black") in the ninth century, the father of Haraldr Hárfagri ("fairhair"), who according to tradition first united Norway into a single kingdom. In *Heimskringla,* Snorri goes *Fagrskinna* one better, since he includes a prehistory leading up to Hálfdan Svarti. This prehistory occupies the first saga of the compilation, *Ynglinga saga,* and tells of the kings of Sweden and Norway. Although there has been much discussion of Snorri's possible sources, only one can be identified with certainty, namely the poem *Ynglinga tal* (Enumeration of the Ynglingar), attributed to Þjóðolfr of Hvin, a late-ninth-century skald patronized by several Norwegian monarchs. This poem tells of the manner and place of death of twenty-eight kings, from the early prehistoric kings of Uppsala to Ragnvaldr Heiðumhæri ("the highly honored") Óláfsson of Vestfold.

However, the first three kings of Sweden, according to *Ynglinga saga,* were Odin, Njörðr, and Freyr, all well-known names from the mythology, and they are not to be found in Þjóðolfr's poem. Snorri's sources must have been the same as those he used when writing his *Edda,* which probably preceded *Ynglinga saga* by anything up to a decade. Scholars today often treat the first chapters of *Ynglinga saga* as direct mythological sources, despite their location in a work with an ostensible historical aim. Indeed, *Ynglinga saga* as a whole is often regarded as showing a "mythic" mindset (e.g., Ciklamini 1975), and Aron Gurevich (1971) argued that it embodied a mythic model—a curse leading to killings within a family—that was played out frequently in later sagas in *Heimskringla.* Be that as it may, the early chapters of *Ynglinga saga*—that is, the part of the saga that precedes that based on *Ynglinga tal*—occur at the nexus of myth and history in the medieval north. In my examination of these chapters below, I will analyze Snorri's presentation of Odin, the chief god in the mythological pantheon and in Snorri's euhemerization of it, in light of the tension between myth and history. The analysis will show that Snorri worked far more as a historian than most observers have realized and that he limited his mythography to details that he and his audience would have found historically plausible.

According to the geography of the opening paragraphs of *Ynglinga saga,* a river runs through Sweden the Great or Sweden the Cold (the east of Europe, or Scythia) and separates Asia from Europe; it is properly, Snorri tells us, called Tanais (the Don) but was previously called Tanakvísl or Vanakvísl, where Vanaland or Vanaheimr—the land or world of the *vanir*—was located. To the east of Vanakvísl, the second chapter begins, was Ásaland or Ásaheimr—the land or world of the æsir, whose principal city "they" called Ásgarðr. "They" are presumably the residents of Ásaland or Ásaheimr—Ásíamenn (Asians), as Snorri called them in the prologue to his *Edda,* or æsir (sing. *áss;* the root is *ás-*). We are now firmly within the realm of the mythology, which relates a structural opposition between two groups, the vanir and the æsir, who together make up the community of the gods. Ásgarðr is of course the stronghold of the gods, located at the center of the mythological universe. Nothing Snorri writes here in *Ynglinga saga* explicitly contradicts the mythology, but nothing whatsoever anchors the text in myth, either. This historical Ásgarðr was, according to Snorri, a great place of pagan sacrifice.

Odin appears first in connection with the presentation of Ásgarðr. Snorri describes him as a great and powerful pagan chieftain, victorious in battle and considered charismatic or miraculous by his followers. He laid hands on them before battle and gave them *bjannak.* This hapax legomenon in Norse appears to be related to Celtic words meaning "blessing" and is presumably intended to suggest a pagan parallel to a Christian blessing, distanced from Snorri and his audience by means of the exotic vocabulary. But what Snorri is up to here is an implicit euhemerism. Thus, Snorri writes, his men begin to call on Odin when in tight spots, and in describing this procedure Snorri again plays with vocabulary.

> Svá var ok um hans menn, hvar sem þeir urðu í nauðum staddir á sjá eða á landi, þá kǫlluðu þeir á nafn hans, ok þótti jafnan fá af því fró. Þar þóttusk þeir eiga allt traust, er hann var. (Bjarni Aðalbjarnarson 1941, 1:11; this and other translations are my own)

> Also about his men: wherever they were in narrow straits at sea or on land, they called on his name, and it seemed they always got relief from it. They thought all their consolation was where he was.

The charged nouns in this passage are *fró* and *traust,* which I have rendered "relief" and "consolation" in my translation. The first especially is a fixture of religious literature, as a glance at any dictionary will show. The second has a broad semantic spectrum, but is frequently used of both kings and gods and when used with the adjective "all" often has a religious sense, and in the common expression "Hafði hann allt traust undir guði" [He had all his consolation with God]. Thus here too the mythic and historical realms appear to merge: Odin, known in every other source as a pagan god, was addressed by his followers in something like the way Christians address their god, but also as retainers address their leader.

Next we learn that Odin traveled much. He had two brothers, Vé and Vílir, who ruled the kingdom when he was away. Once, despairing of his return, they divided his inheritance, and both possessed Frigg, Odin's wife, but Odin returned and took her back. This episode, unknown in *Gylfaginning,* has no apparent connection to what precedes or follows in *Ynglinga saga* and might therefore be regarded as mythological material known to Snorri and included because it was not at odds with his historical project. The taking of the inheritance by the two brothers suggests that Odin's marriage to Frigg had produced no legitimate heir, which might also have permitted his brothers' taking her. That aspect of the episode is also known from *Lokasenna,* strophe 26. A seeming parallel, too, is in book 1 of the *Gesta Danorum* of Saxo Grammaticus. There Frigga strips the gold from an elaborate statue of Othinus so as to decorate herself with it and then gives herself to a servant in order to enlist his aid in taking down the statue. In shame Othinus goes into self-imposed exile, and during his exile Mithothyn takes his place. Upon Othinus's return Mithothyn flees to Fyn and is killed by the inhabitants there. The kernel of the parallel lies in Odin's absence, the rule of someone else during it, and his return and reassumption of the kingdom. The absence perhaps foreshadows the travels that will follow and will move Odin and the æsir from Asia to Sweden. It is also worth recalling that, in the emigration to follow in chapter 5 of *Yn-*

glinga saga, Odin leaves Vílir and Vé behind to rule once again over Ásgarðr; this time, however, presumably without the embraces of Frigg. One may suspect a kind of moral amelioration here, the end of double marriages.

The next chapter of *Ynglinga saga* tells of the incorporation of the æsir and vanir into a single group, which is told in *Skáldskaparmál* as part of the story of the origin of the art of poetry and is also alluded to in *Gylfaginning.* Common to Snorri's *Edda* and *Ynglinga saga* is the inconclusive nature of the war between the two groups and the exchanging of hostages in connection with the settlement, although details vary. In *Ynglinga saga* the exchange of hostages is the crux of the settlement, with Njörðr and Freyr joining the æsir and Hœnir and Mímir the vanir. *Gylfaginning* mentions the exchange of Njörðr and Hœnir, but *Skáldskaparmál* is silent altogether on the exchange of hostages. There the settlement takes the form of the mixing of spittle, from which emerges Kvasir, from whom in turn the mead of poetry is fashioned by the dwarfs and ultimately recovered from the giants by Odin. It is perhaps not difficult to see why Snorri left out the mead of poetry in a fully historicized version of these narratives. To the obvious need for verisimilitude, however, we may add a note to the effect that Snorri himself was a poet, and as a Christian he could hardly trace his gift to a mythic liquid. He therefore uses the story in *Ynglinga saga* simply to show how the æsir and vanir, who originally lived on different sides of the Don, were merged into a single group. In this chapter he can also explain in the same way how Freyja, the daughter of Njörðr, came to be a member of the æsir, and he makes it explicit that it was she who brought the magic art of *seiðr* to the æsir. As if to underscore the negative social value of this kind of magic, and perhaps also to suggest a prehistoric ethical amelioration—a natural ethics, as it were—Snorri ends the chapter by recounting that brother-sister marriages had been the norm among the vanir but were banned among the æsir. He does, however, include in this chapter the story of the severed head of Mímir, returned by the vanir to the æsir and preserved by Odin in such a way that it spoke to him and told him many hidden things. Although the story is not found elsewhere, there are many allusions to it, and Snorri was to take it up again soon in *Ynglinga saga.* It was, I would argue, relatively safe within a historical context, partly because it was set in the distant past but perhaps more interestingly because the head was a kind of pagan relic, like the body parts of saints preserved in churches and monasteries throughout Europe and conferring benefits on those who knew how to address them in the proper ways. It therefore could be transferred, as here, from the mythic to the historical realm.

Chapter 5 presents the actual emigration from the Middle East. Most modern readers have a mythological mindset and recall the motivation for this emigration as Odin's prophetic vision that he and his descendants are to prosper in the North, but Snorri also explicitly ties it to the aggressions of Rome. As Bjarni Aðalbjarnarson points out in an acute footnote (1941, 1:14 n. 2), retracing the chronology of *Ynglinga tal* would put Odin at around 100 B.C.E. Snorri's remarks about Roman imperial aggression would thus accord with world history, as it was known in Iceland from such works as *Rómverja saga,* an Icelandic translation of works of Sallust and Lucan, from before 1180, and *Veraldar saga,* a world history probably translated from a now unknown Latin original before 1200. Indeed, the emigration of the æsir from Asia to Sweden was to have its parallel a millennium later in the emigration from Iceland to Norway, again undertaken, according to the Icelandic cultural mythology, to escape the aggressive tax policy of the big-city chieftain Haraldr Hárfagri; Roman leaders such as Pompeius Magnus, Marcus Crassus, and Julius Caesar overwhelmed and took taxes from peoples all around Rome, according to the history known in Iceland as well as the rest of Europe in Snorri's time.

Odin and his followers depart from Tyrkland, presumably Asia Minor. Their itinerary is described: west into Garðaríki (Russia) and then south into Saxland (Saxony). In Saxland Odin establishes several of his previously unmentioned but now apparently numerous sons as rulers, perhaps, some scholars have thought (e.g., Heusler 1908, 50), because Snorri knew of Anglo-Saxon regnal genealogies going back to Odin, perhaps because he knew that the Saxons were pagans whom Charlemagne had converted. From Saxland the way lies north *til sjávar* ("to the sea"), and specifically to the "island" of Óðinsey (literally "Odin's island") "in" (rather than the appropriate "on") Fyn (whither Mithothyn fled in the *Gesta Danorum*). Medieval Icelandic historiography knew of modern Odense both as Óðinsey, as Snorri has it here, and the more etymologically sound Óðinsvé ("Odin's holy place"), as is indicated by the existence of the two forms in *Knýtlinga saga.* If Snorri knew the second form he was careful not to use it.

Just as in *Gylfaginning,* the first stanza in *Ynglinga saga* is from Bragi Boddason the Old's *Ragnarsdrápa,* and just as in *Gylfaginning,* there is a lack of generic conjunction with what follows. This stanza is in *dróttkvætt,* the classic skaldic court meter, and all the other stanzas but one in *Gylfaginning* are from eddic poetry. Similarly, all the rest of the stanzas in *Ynglinga saga,* including not only *Ynglinga tal* but also two stanzas quoted from *Háleygjatal,* are in *kviðuháttr,* an eddic meter. Snorri's use of the stanza about the woman Gefjon in *Gylfaginning* was calculated to achieve certain narrative and mythic results (Lindow 1977; Clunies Ross 1978), but here in *Ynglinga saga* the episode must play a different role. Through Gefjon, Odin was responsible for forming the landscape around Lake Mälar, where he was to settle at Uppsala; she is to get ploughland from King Gylfi, and she goes to Jötunheimar, has children with a giant, and changes them into mighty oxen who plough up land from the Swedish mainland and pull it off to become Sjælland. In *Gylfaginning* there is no indication of Odin's role, and that is the crucial difference, for as the story is told in *Ynglinga saga,* with Gefjon working for Odin and against Gylfi and making use of the giants, the giants become Odin's allies. This is in effect the view of the Church, that gods (whether euhemerized or not), supernatural beings, and demons are all as one, precisely the opposite of the very clear opposition of gods and giants in the mythology. Snorri is also here clearly associating Gefjon's tricking of Gylfi with the more general tricking of him that was the subject of *Gylfaginning* and to which he alludes now in *Ynglinga saga:*

Mart áttusk þeir Óðinn við ok Gylfi í brǫgðum ok sjónhverfingum, ok urðu Æsir jafnan ríkri. (Bjarni Aðalbjarnarson 1941, 1:16)

Odin and Gylfi contested much in tricks and illusions, and the æsir always were the more powerful.

Odin gives Gefjon in marriage to his son Skjöldr. Although Skjöldr figures widely in old Scandinavian historical writing as a son of Odin and the first Danish prehistoric king, Gefjon as his wife does not, and here one senses Snorri knitting together the pieces and making more plausible the connection between Gefjon and Danish prehistory.

Odin himself settles at Sigtúnir (modern Sigtuna), perhaps because Sig- (*sigr* 'victory') functions often as the first component of Odin's bynames (Bjarni Aðalbjarnarson 1941, 16 n. 3). He gives dwellings to five of his *hofgoðar* (temple priests), all presumably in greater Sweden. Four of these places are the mythological dwellings of the gods known from the mythology—Njörðr at Nóatúnir, Heimdallr at Himinbjörg, Thor at Þrúðvangr, and Baldr at Breiðablikk—and these place names alliterate with the names of the gods. Freyr, however, does not get the Álfheimr one would expect from the mythology, but rather the historic seat of the Swedish Yngling kings, Uppsalir (Old Uppsala). Perhaps the connection with elves in the name Álfheimar ("elf abode") seemed unrealistic to Snorri, but we will never know, since Freyr had a long connection with Uppsala in medieval Scandinavian records.

The next chapters summarize Odin's accomplishments or characteristics and make up a rich catalogue of the Odinic mythic dossier. Chapter 6: he appears handsome to his friends and grim to his enemies, for he can change his appearance. He is so eloquent that everything he says appears to be true, and he speaks using the rhymes (*hendingar*) of skaldic poetry. In battle he can render his enemies blind, deaf, and overcome with fear, and their weapons will not bite, and his men can go without armor, wild and strong as animals, and immune to wounds; that is, they are berserks. Chapter 7: he is a shapechanger. His body lies inert while in some other form he travels to other worlds on his or other men's missions. With words he can extinguish fire or still the sea, and he owns a ship, *Skíðblaðnir,* that can be folded up and put away like a piece of cloth. The head of Mímir speaks to him and he sometimes awakens dead men from the earth or sits under hanged men, whence he was called *draugadróttinn* ("lord of ghosts") or *hangadróttinn* ("lord of the hanged"). He has two ravens that he has trained to speak, and they fly about and report back to him. His most powerful accomplishment is seiðr, which enables him to see the future or bring about people's death or misfortune. (Practicing seiðr, which Snorri has already told us was brought by Freyja from the incestuous vanir, exposes a man to charges of *ergi,* ethically charged homosexual behavior or cowardice with an implication of passive homosexuality.) He can locate and obtain buried treasure.

Much of what is catalogued here can be corroborated from other more explicitly mythic sources, and this information can be found in descriptions of Odin in any handbook of Scandinavian or Germanic mythology. It is therefore important to underscore the following point: there is nothing whatsoever that requires Odin to be a deity and much—everything, in fact—that allows him to be a human being, albeit one with control of magic. To begin with his berserks: according to chapter 9 of *Vatnsdœla saga,* one of the sagas of Icelanders, probably from the end of the thirteenth century, Haraldr Hárfagri had berserks on board his ship, who were called Úlfheðnar; they wore wolfskins and defended the prow (Einar Ól. Sveinsson 1939, 24–25). Þorbjörn Hornklofi's *Haraldskvæði* (early tenth century) is in general agreement: Haraldr Hárfagri had a troop of berserks, called *úlfheðnar* (stanzas 20–21). If the almost prehistoric Haraldr had them, why not Odin? They are both proto-kings, Odin of Sweden and Haraldr of Norway.

The main issue, however, appears to be magic. As Snorri describes it, Odin's magic falls into the categories of shapechanging (he can appear to be handsome or terrifying; he can become an animal or fish) and the knowledge and use of magic formulas, explicitly to quench fire and still the sea, implicitly to open the earth to obtain magic treasures and probably also to speak to the head of Mímir and awaken the dead. Recall, for example, that when Odin received the severed head of Mímir, he

> kvað þar yfir galdra ok magnaði svá, at þat mælti við hann ok sagði honum marga leynda hluti. (Bjarni Aðalbjarnarson 1941, 1:13)

> recited magic verse over it and strengthened it in such a way that it told him many hidden things.

Later folk traditions are replete with magic formulas for these and a great many other purposes. The major manifestations of these two accomplishments, shapechanging and control of magical language, appear to be his traveling in changed form on the one hand and his use of seiðr on the other—the famous description of a seiðr ceremony in Viking Greenland from chapter 4 of *Eiríks saga rauða* requires songs called *varðlokur*, which attract the spirits (*náttúrur*). Travel in alternate form and the use of magic and song may be neatly conjoined in the notion of shamanism, even given the recent debate about the utility of such an all-embracing term and the recognition that a universal theory of shamanism has obscured or misrepresented data from all over the world. Indeed, Odin's body's lying inert while his soul is off in the other world on his or the community's behalf might do as a classic definition of shamanism.[1] Shamanism was certainly known in medieval Scandinavia, for it was practiced by the Sami people, with whom the Scandinavians had long had contact. The Norwegian merchant Ohtere (Óttarr), who informed King Alfred about northern geography, will certainly have come into contact with them, but the best Scandinavian record is in Viking Age skaldic poetry, and the best example there is a verse by Sigvatr Þórðarson, which later editors have made into stanza 16 of his *Erfidrápa Óláfs helga*, from the decade after the death of St. Óláfr in the battle of Stikklastaðir in 1030. The entire verse is relevant to this discussion and deserves to be quoted in full.

> Mildr fann gørst, hvé galdrar,
> gramr sjalfr, meginrammir
> fjǫlkunnigra Finna
> fullstórum barg Þóri,
> þás hyrsendir Hundi
> húna gulli búnu,
> slætt réð sízt at bíta,
> sverði laust of herðar. (Bjarni Aðalbjarnarson 1941, 2:383–84; cf.
> Finnur Jónsson 1912–15, B1:261, B2:242–43)

> The generous chieftain himself learned clearly how the very powerful magic formulas (*meginrammir galdrar*) of the magic-controlling Sami (*fjǫlkunnigir Finnar*) protected the vain Þórir, when the giver of gold (*hyrsendir húna*) struck with a gold-chased sword the shoulders of Hundr; dully it bit not at all [alt.: the dull one bit not at all].

First a word on the context. Þórir Hundr, once Óláfr's man but now a retainer of Cnut the Great, was one of the two local chieftains who gathered the army that defeated Óláfr at Stikklastaðir. The verse is retained in Snorri's *Óláfs saga helga* and in the so-called *Separate Saga* of St. Óláfr in the late-fourteenth-century manuscript *Flateyjarbók*. Snorri quotes the stanza in support of an incident at Stikklastaðir, just before Óláfr's death. Þórir Hundr has fought his way up to Óláfr's standard. Snorri tells us in the surrounding prose, both before and after citing the verse, that Óláfr's sword will not bite when he slashes at Þórir. The reason, explained earlier (Bjarni Aðalbjarnarson 1941, chapter 193), is that Þórir has spent two winters trading extensively with the Sami and has had made for himself twelve reindeer skins with such great magic that they are proof against weapons (með svá mikilli fjǫlkynngi, at ekki vápn festi á [Bjarni Aðalbjarnarson 1941, 2:345]). When Óláfr strikes Þórir about the shoulders,

> Sverðit beit ekki, en svá syndisk sem dyst ryki ór hreinbjálbanum . . . ok beit ekki sverð konungs, þar er hreinbjálbinn var fyrir.

> The sword did not bite, and it seemed as if dust flew from the reindeer skin . . . and the king's sword did not bite, where the reindeer skin was in the way.

Odin's ability to cause weapons not to bite, then, was not a motif limited to the mythology but was present in the eyes of the historian Snorri in the last battle of Óláfr Haraldsson the Saint, in the service of a very well known figure in both Scandinavian and English history. In other words, real people could do this kind of thing, and there is no reason to think that Snorri was endowing Odin with anything other than human power.

People who could cause swords not to bite were also known from thirteenth-century records pertaining to Iceland itself. One such person was Þórdís Spákona, of *Kormáks saga*, who arranged first that Kormákr's sword would not bite his opponent Þorvarðr in a duel and then tried to work the same magic on Þorvarðr's sword to protect Kormákr. Worth noting is her cognomen, *spákona* (sorceress), which brings together prophecy and magic, as was the case with Odin. Even more interesting concerning Odin is this statement: "þóttusk margir þar traust mikit eiga, er hon var" [many men thought they had great consolation, where she was] (Einar Ól. Sveinsson 1939, 282). Like Odin, she provided traust, had the gift of prophecy, and could dull swords. The general process of the dulling of the swords is here called *fjölkynngi* ([control of] magic; literally perhaps "multicompetence"), which is precisely an *íþrótt* 'art, accomplishment' of Odin. If a saga from roughly the same time period as *Ynglinga saga*—perhaps a decade or two earlier—can put a woman in western Iceland in the tenth century with these skills, there is no reason why Snorri could not put a man in early Sweden with them.

I return to shamanism. The locus classicus in medieval Scandinavia is in *Historia Norvegiae,* a work composed presumably in Norway before 1211.

In an excursus on the Sami, the unknown author tells of Norwegian merchants visiting the Sami who witness the death of a woman. A magus is called to the scene and begins to manipulate a sieve (perhaps an antecedent of the Sami shaman drum) on which are pictured a whale, a reindeer and sleigh, and a rowboat. After a while his face blackens and his stomach bursts and he dies. A second person learned in the magic arts is summoned, and he revives the dead woman. She reports having seen the first magician in the spirit world in the form of a whale, but adds that another spirit had assumed the shape of a sharp object and pierced the belly of the first one (Storm 1880, 85–86). Here, then, just like the Odin of *Ynglinga saga,* the Sami change shape and travel in the world of the spirits, on other people's business. And, like Odin, they can awaken the dead.

Something similar is indicated by a case in *Vatnsdœla saga.* A seeress named Finna (clearly, in other words, a Sami) has prophesied men's futures in the Norway of Haraldr Hárfagri, among which is included the notion that Ingimundr inn Gamli Þorsteinsson will emigrate to Iceland. Later he employs three Sami men (*Finnar*) to travel to and explore the place where he is meant to settle.

> Hann sendi eptir Finnum, ok kómu norðan þrír. Ingimundr segir, at hann vill kaupa at þeim—"ok vil ek gefa yðr smjǫr ok tin, en þér farið sendiferð mína til Íslands at leita eptir hlut mínum ok segja mér frá landslegi." Þeir svara: "Semsveinum er þat forsending at fara, en fyrir þína áskorun vilju vér prófa. Nú skal oss byrgja eina saman í húsi, ok nefni oss engi maðr,"—ok svá var gǫrt. Ok er liðnar váru þrjár nætr, kom Ingimundr til þeira. Þeir risu þá upp ok vǫrpuðu fast ǫndinni ok mæltu. . . . (Einar Ól. Sveinsson 1939, 34–35)

> He sent for Sami, and three came from the north. Ingimundr says that he wants to make a deal with them: "I will give you butter and tin, and you are to carry out a sending-journey to Iceland to seek out my talisman[2] and tell me about the lay of the land." They answer, "That is a very dangerous journey for Sami[3] to undertake, but because of your earnest request we will try. Now we are to be shut up together in a building, and let no one name us," and this was done. And when three nights had passed, Ingimundr returned to them. They arose and drew deep breaths and said. . . .

It should first be said that this passage takes place in Norway, where there was ample opportunity for contact with the Sami. That Ingimundr apparently understood the rules is indicated by the fact that his return after three days does not disturb the shamans but seems rather to have been expected by them. Perhaps we may conclude that most Norwegians would have known the rules for a Sami shamanic performance, although Ingimundr, it should be noted, may be a somewhat special case, since he is the maternal grandson of Ingimundr the jarl of Gautland, the area of the Swedish mainland lying southeast of Norway and in Norwegian-Icelandic medieval texts regarded as rather exotic.

I repeat: there is nothing in Snorri's description of Odin in *Ynglinga saga* that requires Odin to be anything other than a chieftain living centuries before Snorri did who possessed magic powers, especially those associated with Sami shamanism. Having said this, I allow myself to speculate on Mímir's head. Most of the scholarship on this motif reads it in connection with the well associated with Mímr, and this in turn has led some scholars to see Irish influence (e.g., von Sydow 1920; Ross 1962), which, however, has been convincingly refuted by Jacqueline Simpson (1962–65a, 1962–65b). However, the fact remains that in *Ynglinga saga* there is no mention of the well at all, only of the severed head. Severed heads are hardly a commonplace of shamanism, to be sure, but masks are, and some of the masks that have been preserved look more like entire heads than just faces. Could this be related to Mímir's head?

Be that as it may, in the context of shamanism it is instructive to recall that Odin is not a Scandinavian by birth but an Asian of some sort—he comes from Tyrkland. In the context of ancient Scandinavia, therefore, Snorri is describing an outsider, rather like the Sami.[4] Magic powers are of course often ascribed to out-groups, not least in Scandinavia (Lindow 1995).

The term Snorri uses for Odin's accomplishments, this mastery of magic and shamanism, is *íþróttir* (in the plural), which ordinarily refers to accomplishments, arts, or skills, nearly always those that are learned. Odin's are learned, too, by his followers, whom he teaches.

> En hann kenndi flestar íþróttir sínar blótgoðunum. Váru þeir næst honum um allan fróðleik ok fjǫlkynngi. Margir aðrir námu þó mikit af, ok hefir þaðan af dreifzk fjǫlkynngin víða ok haldizk lengi. (Bjarni Aðalbjarnarson 1941, 1:19–20)

> And he taught most of his accomplishments to his sacrificial priests [*blótgoðar*]. They were second only to him in learning and in magic. However, many others also learned much of it, and thence magic has spread widely and been long maintained.

Snorri clearly attributes to Odin, the historical immigrant from Turkey, the origin within Scandinavia of magic, especially, I would argue, of shamanism—presumably among both the Scandinavians and the Sami. Snorri probably thought that the Scandinavians lost this shamanism when they converted to Christianity but that the Sami maintained it: this kind of magic "has spread widely"—into the mountains of Norway?—"and been long maintained."

This passage goes on:

> En Óðin ok þá hǫfðingja tólf blótuðu menn ok kǫlluðu goð sín ok trúðu á lengi síðan. (Bjarni Aðalbjarnarson 1941, 1:20)

> And men sacrificed to Odin and those twelve chieftains and called them their gods and believed in them for a long time thereafter.

Here again is Snorri's theory of euhemerism,[5] repeated from chapter 2. To this may be compared the less insistent euhemerism of the prologue to Snorri's *Edda:* the æsir leave Tyrkland and travel through Saxony toward Scandinavia.

> En hvar sem þeir fóru yfir lǫnd, þá var ágæti mikit frá þeim sagt, svá at þeir þóttu líkari goðum en mǫnnum. (Normalized from Finnur Jónsson 1931, 5)

> And wherever they traveled through lands, much glory was ascribed to them, for they seemed more like gods than humans.

And later:

> Ok sá tími fylgði ferð þeira, at hvar sem þeir dvǫlðusk í lǫndum, þá var ár ok friðr, ok trúðu allir, at þeir væri þess ráðandi, því at þat sáu ríkis-menn, at þeir váru ólíkir ǫðrum mǫnnum, þeim er þeir hǫfðu sét, at fegrð ok svá at viti. (Normalized from Finnur Jónsson 1931, 6)

> And such good times accompanied their journey, that wherever they tarried in countries, there was peace and prosperity, and everyone believed that they were the cause of it, because powerful men saw that they were unlike other men whom they had seen, with respect to beauty and also to brains.

Following the discussion of Odin's euhemerization in *Ynglinga saga,* Snorri credits to Odin the introduction of funeral cremation and the erection of mounds or memorial stones, "and that custom was long maintained." Here aspects of the visible cultural landscape that diverge from Christianity are given an Odinic origin. Odin also institutes the large public cults of which there were clearly traces in the historic record.

Finally, in chapter 9 of *Ynglinga saga* Odin dies, after a discussion of Njörðr, who is to succeed him as king of the Swedes. Odin dies of old age— no Ragnarǫk here, with the awful wolf tearing at Odin as society and the cosmos dissolve into disorder, just an old and successful king dying and passing on his throne to one of his sons.

Nobody today would take seriously the notion that the opening chapters of *Ynglinga saga* and the presentation of Odin within them are historical in any contemporary sense of the word, and they have in fact been almost exclusively of interest to students of myth and religion. And yet everything Snorri wrote in these chapters—every single word—could and very probably may have been understood as historical by his audience and by Snorri himself. By "historical" I mean two things: fitting in with the medieval Christian sense of the past, and also excluded from a reading that would require any suspension of belief and entry into the realm of the older mythology. This is not to say that Snorri's and other medieval Icelandic historians' thinking was not mythic. It was, but its mythmaking did not call explicitly on the older pagan mythology.

To reiterate my main argument: Snorri intended his portrayal of Odin in *Ynglinga saga* to be historically plausible, by the standards of his day. The chapters of *Ynglinga saga* (6 and 7) most often used by students of myth and religion to describe the Scandinavian or Germanic god Odin contain not one item that cannot be explained as attaching to the shamanism of the Sami people in Scandinavia, which was well known and documented in medieval Norway and Iceland. Snorri made Odin the original importer into Scandinavia of this form of divination and intervention in the spirit world, and he had Odin teach it to his followers, whence it spread widely, to be, in Snorri's view according to my argument, the origin of shamanism and magic practices among the Sami and also, for that matter, among those later Icelanders and Greenlanders who practiced it before their conversion, according to the sagas. Thus Snorri's euhemerism in this instance turns on his imagining a prehistoric world in which shamanism—again, let me stress, a known and documented phenomenon in Norway—did not yet exist. For this reason Odin was regarded as a deity by his followers, and this was the origin of Scandinavian paganism.

This historical understanding of Odin may perhaps also be extended to the Odin of *Gylfaginning*. I have argued above that in *Ynglinga saga*, Snorri showed how belief in the æsir originated in Scandinavia, specifically in Sweden, whither Odin immigrated. In *Ynglinga saga*, Odin teaches his accomplishments and institutes a cult; in *Gylfaginning*, wizards apparently trick Gylfi, a Swedish king, into belief in the æsir (see, for example, Baetke 1950). Snorri in fact alludes to the exchanges between Gylfi and Odin in *Ynglinga saga*, perhaps offering a comment on his earlier work, *Gylfaginning*. Other details in *Ynglinga saga*, too, may permit a more historical understanding of Odin. For example, when Odin's men begin to call on him, we read that they called not on him directly but on his name. One is reminded of the shipwreck of Bishop Guðmundr the Good in September of 1180; in the various redactions of his life, the Icelandic priest Ingimundr and the Norwegian crew rush about striving to remember the highest name of God as the ship is swept into the breakers. As Peter Foote (1981) has shown in elucidating this incident, there were numerous ways to address God in the Judeo-Christian tradition, and I would add that this would accord well with Snorri's intended euhemerization of Odin. However, Snorri had already written, in *Gylfaginning,* of Odin's many names. Thus the later *Ynglinga saga* permits a more historical reading of an aspect of *Gylfaginning.*

Snorri's role as a historian, and his notion of history, have long been subjects of analysis (see, for example, Bagge 1991). While it may make little sense to hold Snorri to our own standards of "critical history," it is plain that he was a very skilled writer with powerful rhetorical skills and a keen social eye. Snorri's sense of history has been less explored as it applies to his mythological (better: mythographic) writings. In this essay I hope to have shown that Snorri's presentation of Odin was essentially that of a historically plausible person. If we read Snorri's intention thus, we may be taking steps toward resolving the apparent contradiction between a Christian and a pagan subject.

My argument also has implications for the long debate on shamanism in Old Scandinavian religion and mythology (see Buchholz 1971 for a summary). Within this debate the picture of Odin has quite naturally been of considerable interest. If I am correct in arguing that Snorri based this picture, in *Ynglinga saga,* on what he knew of or believed about Sami shamanism, the terms of the debate shift. What would be certain is not that *Ynglinga saga* supports a notion of some form of shamanism in old Scandinavian religion, but almost something like the opposite, namely that the greatest historian and mythographer of medieval Scandinavia used Sami shamanism to help create a historical Odin.

NOTES

1. I use the term here only to speak about practices in ancient Scandinavia and might just as easily have used a phrase like "out-of-body divination" or even "George" to refer to it, as I suggested in the discussion following a version of this paper presented as a plenary lecture at the 11th International Saga Conference at the University of Sydney on July 3, 2000 (in response to hectoring from historians of religion about using the term *shamanism*). The terminology I am using here is not meant to take a particular stand regarding the worldwide or even cross-cultural existence of a unified phenomenon. I do, however, accept the notion of shamanisms (Atkinson 1992) and believe that the Sami historical record I discuss here represents one such shamanism.

2. Finna had foretold that a talisman of Ingimundr's, an image of Freyr that had gone missing, would be found in Iceland. This prophecy and the Sami sending-journey are also

found in *Landnámabók* (Book of settlements), which everyone takes to be among the most historical works of medieval Iceland.

    3. In translating *semsveinar* as "Sami" I follow Olsen 1920; see Einar Ól. Sveinsson 1939, 34–35 n. 5.

    4. I do not take up here the issue of kingship arriving from outside the social group, which is also clearly relevant.

    5. As Weber (1993, 223) put it, here the Odin of history became the Odin of mythology.

BIBLIOGRAPHY

Atkinson, Jane Monnig. 1992. "Shamanisms Today." *Annual Review of Anthropology* 21:307–30.

Baetke, Walter. 1950. *Die Götterlehre der* Snorra-Edda. Verhandlungen der sächsischen Akademie der Wissenschaften zu Leipzig, phil.-hist. Kl., 97:3. Berlin: Akademie-Verlag.

Bagge, Sverre. 1991. *Society and Politics in Snorri Sturluson's* Heimskringla. Berkeley and Los Angeles: University of California Press.

Bjarni Aðalbjarnarson, ed. 1941. *Heimskringla.* 3 vols. Íslenzk fornrit, 26–28. Reykjavík: Hið íslenzka fornritafélag.

Buchholz, Peter. 1971. "Shamanism—The Testimony of Old Icelandic Literary Tradition." *Mediaeval Scandinavia* 4:7–20.

Ciklamini, Marlene. 1975. "*Ynglinga saga:* Its Function and Its Appeal." *Mediaeval Scandinavia* 8:86–99.

Clunies Ross, Margaret. 1978. "The Myth of Gefjon and Gylfi and Its Function in *Snorra Edda* and *Heimskringla.*" *Arkiv för nordisk filologi* 93:149–65.

———. 1994. *Prolonged Echos: Old Norse Myths in Medieval Northern Society.* Vol. 1, *The Myths.* Viking Collection 7. Odense: Odense University Press.

Einar Ól. Sveinsson, ed. 1939. *Vatnsdæla saga. Hallfreðar saga. Kormáks saga. Hrómundar þáttr halta. Hrafns þáttr Guðrúnarsonar.* Íslenzk fornrit, 8. Reykjavík: Hið íslenzka fornritafélag.

Faulkes, Anthony. 1977. "Edda." *Gripla* 2:32–39.

Finnur Jónsson. 1912–15. *Den norsk-islandske skjaldedigtning.* 4 vols. Copenhagen and Kristiania: Gyldendal-Nordisk forlag.

———, ed. 1931. *Edda Snorra Sturlusonar: Udgivet efter håndskrifterne.* Copenhagen: Gyldendal-Nordisk forlag.

Foote, Peter. 1981. "Nafn guðs hit hæsta." In *Speculum Norroenum: Norse Studies in Memory of Gabriel Turville-Petre,* ed. Ursula Dronke, Guðrún P. Helgadóttir, Gerd Wolfgang Weber, and Hans Bekker-Nielsen, 139–54. Odense: Odense University Press.

Gurevich, A[ron]. Ya[kovlevich]. 1971. "Saga and History: The Historical Conception of Snorri Sturluson." *Mediaeval Scandinavia* 4:42–53.

Heusler, Andreas. 1908. *Die gelehrte Urgeschichte im altisländischen Schrifttum.* Abhandlungen der königlichen preussischen Akademie der Wissenschaften, phil.-hist. Kl:, Abh. 3. Berlin: Verlag der königlichen preussischen Akademie der Wissenschaften, G. Reimer in commission.

Lincoln, Bruce. 1999. *Theorizing Myth: Narrative, Ideology, and Scholarship.* Chicago: University of Chicago Press.

Lindow, John. 1977. "The Two Skaldic Stanzas in *Gylfaginning:* Notes on Sources and Text History." *Arkiv för nordisk filologi* 92:106–24.

———. 1995. "Supernatural Others and Ethnic Others: A Millennium of World View." *Scandinavian Studies* 67:8–31.

———. 1997. "*Íslendingabók* and Myth." *Scandinavian Studies* 69:454–64.

Olsen, Magnus. 1920. "Semsveinar." *Maal og minne,* 46–48.

Ross, Anne. 1962. "Severed Heads in Wells: An Aspect of the Well." *Scottish Studies* 6:31–48.

Simpson, Jacqueline. 1962–65a. "Mímir: Two Myths or One." *Saga-Book of the Viking Society* 16:41–53.

———. 1962–65b. "A Note on the Folktale Motif of the Heads in the Well." *Saga-Book of the Viking Society* 16:248–50.

Storm, Gustav, ed. 1880. *Monumenta Historica Norvegiae: Latinske kildeskrifter til Norges historie i middelalderen.* Kristiania: A. W. Brøgger.

von Sydow, C. W. 1920. "Iriskt inflytande på nordisk guda-och hjältesaga." *Vetenskaps-societeten i Lund, årsbok* 1920, 19–29.

Weber, Gerd Wolfgang. 1993. "Snorri Sturlusons Verhältnis zu seinen Quellen und sein Mythos-Begriff." In *Snorri Sturluson: Kolloquium anlässlich der 750. Wiederkehr seines Todestages,* edited by Alois Wolf, 193–244. ScriptOralia, 51. Tübingen: G. Narr.

EIGHT

Myth and Legendum in Medieval and Modern Ireland

JOSEPH FALAKY NAGY

The question of genre was certainly on the minds of many of the scholars who contributed to *Myth: A Symposium*. Do we construct a definition of myth that contrasts it with other narrative genres, or is the issue of
generic boundaries a frustrating labyrinth best avoided? Here is what Stith
Thompson had to say about the problem:

> It must be recognized that when we use such European terms as myth, etio-
> logical story, *Märchen, Sage,* or the like, we are merely using these terms as
> points of reference and we must understand that they have only vague ana-
> logues in various countries of the world. . . . Even in the European setting,
> the scholar finds that for most kinds of problems such differentiation is of
> small importance. (1965, 175)

The following study is meant to serve as a contribution from a Celticist
perspective for future considerations of the question of myth and genre, in
that I am examining the way in which mythological themes or story patterns are converted in early Irish literature into the stuff of pious legend,
and tracing the continuation of some of these mythological strands within
the body of legend into the twentieth century. These strands are readily apparent in the repertoire that has been collected from modern Irish storytellers. "Legend" is defined here in the standard folkloristic sense, as a story
that is told or received as a historical proposition, that is, within an ideological framework for understanding the past that approximates our modern
Western notion of "history." But "legend" in this study has other, equally
authentic meanings: it is also a story about a saint (as defined in late-an-
tique and medieval Western Christian tradition), and a narrative that is to
be read or read aloud (historically what the Latin word *legendum* means),
living a literary life that intersects with modes of oral performance, such as

recitation, preaching, and storytelling. As for "myth," as in those mythological themes and story patterns to be examined below, the working definition in this essay, like that of "legend," operates on multiple levels. "Myth" is a collectively shared story about supernaturally powerful beings whose adventures and interactions are set in some primeval time before the "historical time" of legend, although these beings leave profound traces, highlighted in the myth, that are still to be seen in that subsequent "time." (This formulation has much in common with the "practical definition" of the genre begrudgingly given by Thompson [1965, 173].)

Lurking behind this rather orthodox understanding of myth is a much more subversive heuristic model, one that is grounded in the writings of Claude Lévi-Strauss (especially 1965 and 1964–71), although it may sound more poststructuralist than structuralist to those who believe that Jacques Derrida has added substantially to what Lévi-Strauss had already taught us about the structures of human (and particularly mythopoeic) thought. This other "myth" is a metagenre, a rhetorical as well as epistemological strategy that potentially inheres in all storytelling. Myth, according to this understanding, is the narrative manifestation of a collective attempt to cope, at least in the realm of ideas, with an insoluble cultural problem, or an unanswerable cultural question, by means of continually transforming the terms of the problem or question. Myths, in other words, insofar as they tirelessly deal in the business of reformulating the familiar, constitute an open-ended, ever-expanding mythology (that is, a set of "themes" with countless "variations") that probably raises more questions in the minds of its hearers (or readers) than it answers. And while the urge to "mythologize" is shared, and myths are expected by their audience to be phrased in the conventional and stylized terms used within a particular narrative tradition, individual storytellers, whether working in a literary or an oral medium, have plenty of opportunity to apply their own ingenuity, taste, and perspectives to the task of articulating the cultural questions in mythic terms, and of coming up with some tentative answers in narrative form (or, in typical mythopoeic fashion, answering the questions with other questions). As Lévi-Strauss frequently notes, a key question with which all mythologies are destined to grapple has to do with myth itself as it struggles to keep up with the times and respond to the changes that enter into its narrative system, as well as the changes affecting the culture and society whose mythology it is: how in the course of history, and in the proliferation of the mythology itself, does myth maintain its authenticity, its rootedness, and its consistency?

Irish saints, as they are portrayed in the extensive body of literature that has survived from medieval and early modern Ireland and in the many religious legends that have been collected from Irish storytellers in the nineteenth and twentieth centuries, tend to act the way mythical protagonists are supposed to, according to the conventional definition of myth. Saints live in a time when the world as we know it is still under construction, and they assist in that construction by establishing institutions, forming the natural and cultural landscape, and inventing distinguishing characteristics for the humans and other creatures with which they come into contact. I have proposed elsewhere (Nagy 1997) that the extensive lore about saints in Ireland constitutes a mythology in the sense described above, and that a fundamental cultural issue reflexively addressed in this mythology is the question of how to fuse a preexisting narrative repertoire of story patterns and motifs with a newly imported one (biblical and hagiographic), and how to make it all work as an ideologically updated but still traditional narrative system. This web of story—consisting of cycles of tales about particular saints that, like the saints themselves, tend to be interconnected and overlap—is already on display in numerous texts produced in the scriptoria of medieval Irish churches, monasteries, and scribal families, texts that the authors acknowledge to be based on traditions circulating orally among the communities that honor the saint, but which also bear the stamp of literary influence (coming from scriptural and patristic sources as well as other, preexisting saints' lives) and authorial invention. These latter elements, stemming from the epoch-making importation of Christianity, the literate culture it upheld, and the communications technology upon which it relied for its dissemination, interact dynamically with the collective nature and function of these narratives, providing all the more grist for the mythological mill that produces and reproduces a wealth of saints' legends that when compared to one another appear both formulaic—if you've heard one saint's legend, you've heard them all—and variable: each story, and each literary or oral version of a story, reflects a different spin on the shared themes and motifs. The narrative episodes that make up saints' lives, which in their historical evolution have defied any distinction between "learned" and "popular" lore, appear equally at home in medieval Latin or Irish literature and in the repertoires of twentieth-century traditional storytellers.

Tírechán's *Life of Patrick,* a Latin text from the seventh century, is one of the first Irish saints' lives to be produced in Ireland, perhaps the first attempt to recount in literary form the exploits of the patron saint of the Irish, and one of the earliest Irish literary productions to have survived. A celebrated episode in it features Eithne and Fedelm, the two daughters of the pagan king of Ireland, Lóegaire mac Néill, and their encounter with Patrick beside a well (Bieler 1979, 142–44).[1] When the girls, presumably having come to bathe in or to draw from the well, first see the Christian missionary, who happens to be nearby, they do not know who he is, or whether he is of this world or of some (non-Christian) otherworld. At first, says our text, the girls thought Patrick and his retinue were *viros side aut de-*

orum terrenorum aut fantassiam 'people of the *síd* or of the [ranks of] terrestrial gods, or an illusion'. This, by the way, is probably the earliest attestation of the Irish word *síd* 'otherworldly dwelling', a term and concept that are central to the traditional Irish lore of the (non-Christian) supernatural, extending from the Middle Ages to modern times. When Patrick mentions his God to them, they inquire eagerly (breathlessly, even) about this *deus,* asking where he lives, what he looks like, whether he is wealthy and has many children, and *si filiae eius carae et pulchrae sunt hominibus mundi* 'whether his daughters are beloved and deemed beautiful among people of this world'. In response, Patrick, expert missionary that he is, fashions an answer that both hews to the Christian faith and corresponds to the terms set out in the questions asked of him. Capping off his statement of the Christian essentials, Patrick invites the *filiae regis terreni* 'daughters of a terrestrial king' to be mystically married or joined (*conjungere*) to a *rex caelestis* 'celestial king'. The daughters of Lóegaire are eager for this union, responding as if with one voice and one heart (*si ex uno ore unoque corde*) and assenting in faith to all of Patrick's catechetical questions. The enthusiastic neophytes are baptized and veiled, but they remain unsatisfied, wanting to see Christ their spouse (*sponsus*) face to face. Patrick warns that the only way to achieve this union would be for the girls to receive communion and, somehow, die. They gladly assent to this (ultimate) rite of passage, and their souls are thus translated to heaven.

As a *planctus* 'lament' is raised over the princesses' earthly remains, Caplait, the magus or druid who fostered one of them, comes upon the scene, initially distraught but quickly falling under the spell of Patrick's preaching. He now accepts baptism and even tonsure. His brother Mael, hearing of what has happened, is the next to run onto the hagiographic stage, vowing to return his brother to the pagan fold, but he too succumbs to Patrick's words and accepts the tonsorial sign of conversion. In Mael's case Tírechán specifies that before he became a Christian he wore a magical or druidic haircut, the *airbacc giunnae,* and that as a result of what happened, and presumably in reference to the resemblance between the druids and their responses, the most famous of all Irish sayings (*uerbum quod clarius est omnibus uerbis Scoticis*) was coined: *Similis est Caluus contra Caplit,* "Calvus [= *Mael,* 'Shorn'] is like Capl(a)it."

When we examine this seventh-century saintly legend as story, breaking down its elements and attempting to trace some of their possible sources and analogues, comparable scriptural, apocryphal, and hagiographic instances easily come to mind. In the Gospel of John, Christ encounters the Samaritan woman at a well (John 4:3–43), just as Patrick has his meeting with the daughters of Lóegaire *ad fontem qui dicitur Clebach.* In numerous accounts of apostolic and saintly missionary adventure, the man of

God appears to those he meets as a seemingly supernatural being, just as Patrick poses a numinous puzzle to the princesses, who wonder whether he is a denizen of the síd. Moreover the spiritual shepherding of noblewomen who give their all to Christ and the facilitating of their passage from this world to the next are not uncommon features of the saintly vocation as depicted in religious literature written before the Irish hagiographer's time. These are sources that would have been directly or indirectly available to Tírechán or those who preserved and developed this legend, and we as historians of narrative must take these likely sources into account. Also to be weighed in an account of the evolution of our story are the points of similarity between it and other legends attested in early Patrician hagiography: for instance, Muirchú's account of the British maiden Monesan who restlessly seeks God in a godless Britain and is finally brought by her parents to Patrick in Ireland, where, upon being baptized by him, she dies and goes to heaven (Bieler 1979, 98–100). In many respects the story of the daughters of Lóegaire fits into its hagiographic and Patrician setting and can serve as a model of the hagiographer's version of bricolage, the stitching together of elements from scripture or other saints' lives or the recasting of episodes from the life of the saint in question in terms that suggest the life of Christ or other paradigms of Christian behavior. This blatant recycling of and relentless clinging to paradigms are not at all indications of the impoverishment of the hagiographic imagination, as some unsympathetic readers of saints' lives have claimed, but rather the point of the hagiographic exercise—namely, to show how all lives are really but one Christian Life.

And yet we have not accounted for this story about the daughters of Lóegaire mac Néill in full. This legend, like that of Monesan, is theologically curious in that upon being received into the Christian fold the women are dispatched to heaven, in this case at their own insistent request. Moreover, in the pattern of Patrician legend I have dubbed the "family romance" (Nagy 1997, 60–80), the pattern to which these stories testify, the point of Patrick's converting the youth of Ireland despite their parents' opposition is to create a new generation that in turn converts the old and carries Patrick's mission to transform Irish society into the future. The young people in our story, on the other hand, abruptly remove themselves from the human world, having no future in it except as memorialized exemplars.

Another noteworthy aspect of the story as we have it from Tírechán is the prominence of fraternal or sororal pairs. A single daughter of Lóegaire would have sufficed, but two are featured in the story, sisters who, although they are marked as visually distinct both times that they are introduced in the text (*Ethne alba* 'white, fair' and *Fedelm rufa* 'red, ruddy' [Bieler 1979, 138, 142]), in their encounter with Patrick act with one voice and one mind. They are not the only siblings featured in the legend, of course.

Their druidic fosterers Mael and Caplait are brothers, who at first are said to act in concert, bringing an obscuring fog over Mag Aí in order to hide their charges from the approaching Patrick, who has just forded the Shannon River. As they serially encounter Patrick, they turn against one another, only to be reunited finally in the new faith and in the new proverb that emphasizes their similarity. I note in passing that Mael and Caplait are among the very few figures described as magi to survive the encounter with Patrick in the lives featuring this saint. Druids are normally recalcitrant to the end; the only other converted magus to be found in Tírechán's text is Ono or Hono, who accepts Patrick into his home and heart. He is introduced in the company of his brother Ith, also a magus, but Ono is immediately differentiated from him: Ono is the one who welcomes the saint, while Ith's reaction is not described (140). Even in the realm of hagiography, perhaps not all pairs of siblings, druidic or otherwise, ended up seeing eye to eye in connection with the new religion.

Returning to the episode of Lóegaire's daughters, we find yet another, albeit more implicit, allusion to the sibling bond. When brother Mael comes to rescue brother Caplait from Patrick's religion, he speaks harshly to Patrick and to one Mathonus, the latter mentioned nowhere else in Tírechán's text. J. B. Bury's suggestion (discussed in Bieler 1979, 225) is a good one, that this is another name for Benignus, Patrick's successor and constant companion, whose sister Mathona was mentioned by Tírechán just a few lines before. Perhaps this little-used name is introduced into the text here as a way of underscoring the sibling theme. In any event, this episode is relatively populated with references to brothers or sisters who, initial differences notwithstanding, appear almost interchangeable. Looked at within the wider framework of what Tírechán calls the second book of his account (*Incipit* [*liber*] *secundus in regionibus Connacht peractus* [138]), which features Patrick's adventures west of the Shannon among the peoples of the province of Connacht, the encounter with Eithne and Fedelm anticipates Patrick's climactic meeting with the two twin girls who from their mother's womb were calling him to return to Ireland, specifically to the Forest of Fochloth, a summons that Patrick mystically heard (158). (This is obviously a legendary elaboration upon the reference in Patrick's *Confessio* to his hearing the "voice of the Irish," *uox Hiberionacum,* in a dream-vision [Howlett 1994, 66].) These twins, who accept the *pallium* 'veil' from Patrick's hands, as did Lóegaire's daughters, are found at the end of Patrick's odyssey, constituting a sign of vindication and triumph for his mission to recover and rescue the pagan Irish.

Why did Tírechán or his sources cast and ornament this story of Patrick's encounter with the children of Lóegaire in terms of sibling pairs, of sister and sister, brother and brother, or even brother and sister, all as alike as Mael and Caplait? In a hunt for sources we would of course find similar pairs and even actual twins in the Scripture to which hagiographers looked for their inspiration, from Jacob and Esau (Gen. 26:21–26) to the apostle named Thomas, which means "twin" (John 11:16 and elsewhere). But this motif—let us call it dioscuric—is not particularly important in Christian tradition, and especially not in early Christian hagiography. In this case, where we are examining a passage that is veritably studded with ethnographic observations about the pagan Irish—including the use of the term *uiri side* to characterize how Patrick and company were first perceived by the daughters of Lóegaire, an excursion about druidic hairstyles, the recording of what is said to be the most famous proverb of the Irish, and, as we shall see, a brief essay on the burial practices of the pre-Christian Irish—it would be hard to dismiss the presence of the motif of twinning as accidental or unrelated to the uses of this motif in other, more mythological domains of early Irish literature.

This story element—that is, the strategic placing of same- or different-sex pairs of characters who are biologically twins, identical to each other in appearance or action, or given names that are variations of each other—has formed for scholars one of the important bridges between Celtic tradition and its Indo-European cousins. The importance of identical pairs or twins in Indo-European mythologies, pairs such as the Vedic Aśvínā, the Greek Dioskuroi, the Roman Gemini, the Germanic Horsa and Hengist, and the Irish twins of Macha, has been convincingly demonstrated by Donald Ward in his monograph on the Divine Twins (1968; see also Frame 1978, 143–52; Puhvel 1987, 284–90). Ward acknowledges, as do I, that twins are certainly not limited to Indo-European myth, and Lévi-Strauss's work on the role of twins as mediators in native American traditions has taken us far in our understanding of the worldwide fascination with this biological phenomenon and with what the narrative imagination can make of it (Lévi-Strauss 1964–71). I have proposed elsewhere that twins are "good to think with" because they allow for subtle gradations between similarity and difference (Nagy 1997, 199–286). Indo-European twins in particular tend to diverge and converge in their identities. They constitute an answer in specific narrative situations to the very difficult riddle, how can two things be alike yet different?

And so why are twins or twinlike figures introduced into the discourse of religious and cultural conversion that underlies the early lives of Patrick? Perhaps because they provide a vehicle for conveying two very important, interconnected messages in Patrician legend: that the saint's mission to Ireland is a return to the setting of his youth (which he spent in Ireland as a captive), and that the conversion of Ireland is also in key respects a "return," an attempt to bring together divergent members of what the legendary tradition conceptualizes as the same family or the same generation. Twins who look and act alike, speaking with one voice, provide a model of Christianized Ireland as envisioned in hagiography: a model, however, that is rarely achieved in the legends, or even in the ultimate relations among the twinlike figures introduced into saintly narrative, figures between whom some difference must be allowed. In the tale of Lóegaire's daughters, however, the concord is complete, both between the sisters and between their druidic fosterers, not to mention the remarkable concord between saint and magi-turned-tonsured-clerics. The episode ends with Tírechán's allusion to the building of what he describes as a pagan burial mound, *fert* or *ferta,* containing the girls' remains, a monument that he says is called by "us" *relic,* and which was given over into Patrick's control and became the site of a church (Bieler 1979, 144). The harmony between the two princesses, whose lives are coterminous, gives rise to a seamless succession, the druidic *airbacc giunnae* followed by the Christian *tonsura,* the Latin loanword *re(i)lic* taking over from the native *fert,* and the faithful gathered at the church on earth awaiting the realization of the heavenly church.

Arguably this episode from Tírechán employs the dioscuric motif in an even more exclusively Indo-European way. Stig Wikander (1957), Georges Dumézil (1968, 73–89), Ward (1968), and others have identified in Indic, Greek, and Baltic traditions the recurring story pattern of divine or heroic twins rescuing their abducted sister: for instance, Castor and Polydeuces rescuing Helen from Theseus. The fraternal magi, we recall, appear on the scene relentlessly pursuing such an agenda: they envelop Patrick in night and fog in order to protect their fosterlings from his influence; Caplait arrives, albeit too late to rescue the girls from the fate they had wished on themselves; and Mael's mission is to rescue his brother from the new religion. The solitary Patrick, however, thwarts all of these attempts, defeating the dioscuric story pattern and even tweaking its nose in that a lone male redeems a pair of females.

Let us put aside the dioscuric elements in this story and examine another feature that, as I pointed out before, presents something of a paradox as well as questions about the sources the hagiographer was using. The girls approach Patrick, who despite the druid-induced darkness is found by them on their way to the well. They interrogate the saint eagerly, wondering whether he is from another world. Once they are converted, they brook no delay in being united with their *sponsus* Christ, a union that requires their death. In other words, the strong-willed girls' quest, like that of the equally determined Monesan, takes them to Patrick but then separates them from him almost as soon as they meet. They go ahead of him to their eternal reward in heaven, to the home of their *sponsus,* where the saint and his female converts will be reunited in the future. Similarly, the twins said to summon Patrick from their mother's womb approach Patrick instead of being approached by him in the scene where they finally meet: *ecce duae filiae uenierunt ad Patricium*. Bieler has pointed out an analogue to these situations in Brendan legendry, specifically an encounter with a heaven-seeking mermaid in the Latin and Irish lives of this saint (Bieler 1979, 225). The mermaid, who first appears as a gigantic floating corpse, is revived by Brendan, voyaging on the unknown ocean, but chooses to die again upon being baptized and given communion (Plummer 1910, 1:135; 1922, 1:62–63). The motif of the determinedly seeking female who is not long for this world also forms the heart of the Middle Irish tale of the Fosterage of the House of Two Cups (Dobbs 1930), in which the girl hails from the realm of the Túatha Dé Danann—namely the síd, from which the daughters of Lóegaire thought Patrick might be.

It would appear that in these cases we have more than a gendered subtype of the "dialogue with an ancient" scenario that is replayed so often in medieval Irish saints' legends (Nagy 1983). I would argue that all of these females under discussion have something explicitly or implicitly otherworldly about them—an otherworldliness that is transformed from pagan to Christian in the course of their encounter with the saint. The latter figure in turn, or rather the women's perception of him, also undergoes a transformation, from "otherworldly" in a non-Christian sense to "otherworldly" in a Christian sense. In addition to being otherworldly, either in a "coming" or a "going" sense, these women are spectacularly fixed in their intentions, often motivated by what in other Irish literary contexts would be called *grád écmaise* 'love in [or despite] absence', capable of breaking away from not only their roots, their families, and their father (such as the hopelessly heathen Lóegaire), but even him whom they seek out, that is, the saint. In these respects, the daughters of Lóegaire appear to be not-so-distant cousins of the various Mélusine-type figures that are to be found in Celtic storytelling traditions: females from the otherworld married problematically to mortal males. These supernatural women often are depicted as choosing and pursuing their mortal partners aggressively (for instance, Macha in Irish tradition, and Rhiannon in Welsh), although there are also instances in which these females from the otherworld are captured and held in marital captivity.[2] Whether they are willing or unwilling spouses, these supernatural consorts ultimately set their own terms, leaving their male companions upon the violation of a taboo having to do with the boundaries between mortal and immortal or insisting that their mortal lovers be transformed in some dramatic way. In the legend of the daughters of Lóegaire, this traditional story pattern, like that featuring twins and rescue, is both present and pointedly changed: loving Patrick or his God from afar, the girls insist upon their own transformation, not that of the beloved whom they seek, and it is they who propose breaking down the boundary between human and divine in their insistence on seeing the face of their *sponsus* right away.

That mythic elements such as these are present in early Irish saints' legends has long been appreciated by trailblazing scholars such as Charles Plummer and Kathleen Hughes, whose work has done so much to set the literature of early Christian Ireland in its wider religious context.[3] But in Tírechán's text we also detect the presence of another trait endemic to these literary wonder-tales about holy men and women that has received far less attention from scholars in this field: namely, an acute authorial self-consciousness concerning the appropriation of these mythic elements, and a sophisticated awareness of the process of cultural translation that is required for the inclusion to result in a meaningful story (or "myth") for new times. This section of Tírechán's account, starting with the description of the druidic fosterers' bringing about a magical fog that is supposed to hide their charges from the approaching Patrick, is punctuated by a conspicuous reference to a place name: the magi first hear of Patrick when he crosses the Shannon River at a ford our text calls *Vadum Duorum Avium* (Bieler 1979, 138), a Latinizing of the Irish *Snám Dá Én* 'Swim-Two-Birds' (made famous beyond Ireland by Flann O'Brien's novel *At Swim-Two-Birds*). True, Tírechán and other Irish hagiographers of this period did conduct various experiments with fitting Irish personal and place names into their Latin texts, but this constitutes the most ambitious attempt to make the crossing from native toponymy over into Latinate written tradition—appropriately enough, at the point in the hagiographer's account when Patrick himself is crossing over the Shannon River into what will prove to be the setting for his most important adventures: the territory where he lived in youth as a slave of the pagan Irish, and to which he is now returning as the bringer of a new religion and culture. This region beyond the Shannon is also what Tírechán identifies elsewhere in the text as where his own roots lie (134). That such local ties were important to the author is suggested by his name or choice of *nom de plume: tírechán* means "countryman" or "local." For this special return home, or to what was once Patrick's own home-away-from-home, Tírechán constructs this thorough Latinization of a famous Irish place name, in which, however, the influence does not go in just the one direction. Note that the hagiographer allows the gender of the feminine Latin *avis* 'bird' to be overwhelmed by that of the Irish masculine *én* 'bird' (the text reads *duorum,* not the correct *duarum*).

Even more intriguing in this reference than its compromised Latinity is the story that lies behind the "two birds" nominally associated with this shallow stretch of the Shannon River. The bearers of Irish tradition, both medieval and modern, literary and oral, obsessively take delight in pinning stories to particular places and place names, and conversely pinning place names to stories. In the body of tradition recorded in the vernacular a few centuries after Tírechán and known as *dindshenchas* 'place-lore', we find the following story, set in a hazy pre-Christian past, that attempts to explain the name "Swim-Two-Birds" (Gwynn 1911). The woman warrior Eistiu, married to a man named Nár, has a lover named Buide, who along with his foster brother Luan are wont to come in the form of birds to visit her. The metamorphosed Buide and Luan sing birdsongs that put all who hear them to sleep except Eistiu (whose name means "listener"), so that they can enjoy her company unmolested. The suspicious Nár asks his druid to ascertain what is happening between his wife and these birds, and once the druid finds out and tells Nár what the nature of the relationship is, the enraged husband sets out to gain revenge. With a single cast he slays the two birds at the spot beside the Shannon where they used to rendezvous with his wife, who appears on the scene too late to save her lover and subsequently dies of grief, or, in a recorded variant, slays her husband. In memory of this tragic incident, the site in question is named Snám Dá Én.

I propose that Tírechán or the source he is following, by conspicuously alluding to this place and its name, is signaling the relevance of its story to that of the two daughters of the King of Ireland, a tale shortly to be told in his text. The same essential ingredients to be found in that pious legend are already to be found in this onomastic narrative at which we arrive by way of the hagiographer's pointed reference to the place name: the willful love that leads to death, the female with a mind of her own, the encounter with supernatural shapeshifters, twinning, thwarted rescue, and even interfering druids. Of course, there are differences (the twinned protagonists of Swim-Two-Birds are male, not female), but clearly there is an affinity, perhaps even a kinship, between the two narratives, a connection artfully acknowledged by Tírechán, mythographer as well as hagiographer. Here as elsewhere in the laboratory (or should we say archives?) of early Irish *vitae*, the processes whereby pagan is converted to Christian, myth to legend, and oral into written are available for the reader's inspection.

The fusing of narrative genres and the intermixture of tale elements from different strands and chronological layers of tradition continue to characterize the telling of stories about saints down to modern times in Ireland. As they were in the Middle Ages, these processes continue to be both reflective of the creativity and aesthetic choices of the storyteller and also traditionally mandated, since the figure of the saint continues to mediate between collective conceptualizations of cultural past and present. Henry Glassie in *Passing the Time in Ballymenone* (1982) and other folklorists have noted that the Patrick of the modern Irish popular imagination lives on as a culture hero ushering in a new epoch, eminently recognizable as the

Patrick of the seventh-century lives we have been examining, and that some of the legends preserved by Tírechán and Muirchú are still alive and well in the repertoires of Irish storytellers. Among these persistent narratives is that featuring the young pagan female irresistibly drawn to Patrick, but this story, as attested in versions from the Gaelic-speaking parts of Ireland (conveniently assembled in MacNeill 1982, 548–64), tends to be fashioned from the Monesan mold, as opposed to the dioscurically tinged variant upon which this presentation has been focused: that is, there is one girl as opposed to two, and she is the daughter of a distant foreign tyrant or pagan, not a local one. There is, however, a story in the archives of the Irish Folklore Commission, obtained in the nineteen thirties from a Co. Waterford man, Liam Ó Caoimh, that sounds like a fusion of the pious legend and the medieval account of why Swim-Two-Birds is so called. MacNeill summarizes it as follows:

> There was a holy man in France some years ago and he had an only daughter. He thought there was no one in the world holier than himself. She told him one day that she had dreamed of a holier man in Ireland. He asked her if she would like to see this man; she said that she would. He struck her three times with his *cochall draoidheachta* (magic hood), and she flew off as a bird and alighted at St. Patrick's feet. As she arrived, St. Patrick and his companions were walking together just as the sun was about to rise. One of the company saw the bird and pointed it out to Saint Patrick, who hit it with his crozier. She died and Patrick then spoke the *Mairthinn Anna* [an obscure poem, associated with the saint in oral tradition, in which he laments the passing of a pious woman], from which it appears that the girl's name was Anna. (1982, 562)

Poor Anna, winging her way to the saint from whom she expects salvation and a replacement for her father, receives, at the hands of a seemingly thoughtless Patrick, the treatment accorded the thieving birds of the Snám Dá Én story. The possibility of dangerous misidentification and a breakdown in intercultural communication adumbrated at the beginning of Tírechán's telling of the story of the meeting of the two pagan girls with the Christian saint (that is, the girls' mistaking Patrick for an otherworldly visitor) is grimly realized in the twentieth-century Irish storyteller's laconic tale of fatal attraction.[4]

We have seen that in the variants of this story of the girl (or girls) seeking Patrick and a change in life, as attested already in the life of the saint produced by the seventh-century cleric Tírechán and still active in the repertoires of twentieth-century Gaelic storytellers, cultural transformation is phrased in terms of the question "Who gets the girl?" and "myth" in the form of the supernaturally suggestive female is appropriated and given a new lease on life as *legendum,* in the sense of both "saint's legend" and (in the case of the literary saint's life) "that which is to be read." The metafolklore behind the traditional tales examined above celebrates the long-lived project of constructing and perpetuating a mythology of saints and sinners, a project in which the capacity of storytellers both literate and illiterate to innovate within traditional parameters finds its counterpart in the ways that both the saint and his potential devotees are allowed to respond to each other's culturally profound overtures.

NOTES

An earlier version of this paper was presented as the keynote lecture at "Indo-European Mythology and Religion," a conference sponsored by the Royal Irish Academy, Dublin, in October of 1998.

1. Bieler's edition of this Latin text, as well of Muirchú's *Life of Patrick* (see below), is quoted throughout this paper, and his translations form the basis of mine.

2. These and other otherworldly female consorts, who both aggressively pursue and elude their human lovers, are the subjects of the contributions of Bo Almqvist, Proinsias Mac Cana, Brynley F. Roberts, Evelyne Sorlin, and Juliette Wood to Boivin and Mac Cana 1999. On the figure of Rhiannon, there is now Hemming 1998.

3. See, for example, Plummer's survey "Heathen Folk-Lore and Mythology in the Lives of the Celtic Saints" (Plummer 1910, 1:cxxix-clxxxviii) and Hughes's essay on Irish hagiography and its sources (Hughes 1972, 219–47).

4. That there is here, in addition to a struggle between a father and a father figure for the affection of a young girl, an erotic element to the story of "Anna" (an anglicization of Irish *Áine*) is indicated by the other traditions surrounding the *Mairthinn* poem, also "known as *Marbhna Phádraig* or *Marbhna Eithne,* which is part elegy and part charm. Its opening line, *Mise agus Aonghus armghlas* (I and green-armed Aonghus [an otherworldly being who already figures in early Irish literature]) announces the rivalry of pagan and Christian contenders for the soul of the girl, and reflects that of the two mythological rivals who contended for the possession she represented" (MacNeill 1982, 404). A version of the poem is presented in Hyde 1906, 1:352–54, with the same opening line (which, however, is not the line cited as an identifying tag by the storyteller Ó Caoimh). Hyde's informant, Michael Mac Rory of Co. Mayo, gave him the following story behind the poem, an account that construes the mysterious Áine as a martyred defender of her virtue: "'It is said that it was a servant that St. Patrick had, that she was, and she was very pious. And there came in a man one day requesting something to eat. And after his getting it and eating it, he made an attempt to catch hold of her. And after his taking a hold of her she was that pious that she fell into a faint, and she did not come out of that faint until she died. And when St. Patrick came in she was placed above board [laid out], and that was the lamentation he made over her, praising her" (ibid., 353, Hyde's translation of the Irish; also in MacNeill 1982, 563). It is worth noting that the name "Áine" is commonly assigned to otherworldly females in medieval and modern Irish tradition (MacNeill 1982, 30, 151, 186, and elsewhere; O'Rahilly 1946, 286–89). The Áine of the following anecdote, recorded in 1920 from a Co. Galway source, Pádhraic Ó Éighniú, resembles a seductive supernatural paramour, against whom the poem serves as an apotropaic device: "Sonaigh Solmglas, St. Patrick's boy [that is, servant], was in love with Áine Ní Mhóráille. Patrick did not approve of the love

and wished to break it with or without their consent. For that purpose he said the *Marthain Phádhraic,* and since then it has remained on the lips of the people" (MacNeill's translation of the Irish, 1982, 564).

BIBLIOGRAPHY

Bieler, Ludwig, ed. and trans. 1979. *The Patrician Texts in the Book of Armagh.* Dublin: Dublin Institute for Advanced Studies.

Boivin, Jeanne-Marie, and Proinsias Mac Cana, eds. 1999. *Mélusines continentales et insulaires. Actes du colloque international tenu les 27 et 28 mars 1997 à l'Université Paris XII et au Collège des Irlandais.* Paris: Editions Champion.

Dobbs, M. E., ed. and trans. 1930. "Altromh Tighi Da Medar." *Zeitschrift für celtische Philologie* 18:189–230.

Dumézil, Georges. 1968. *Mythe et épopée.* Vol. 1. Paris: Gallimard.

Frame, Douglas. 1978. *The Myth of Return in Early Greek Epic.* New Haven: Yale University Press.

Glassie, Henry. 1982. *Passing the Time in Ballymenone: Culture and History of an Ulster Community.* Philadelphia: University of Pennsylvania Press.

Gwynn, E. J. 1911. "Snám Dá Én." *Ériu* 5:219–25.

Hemming, Jessica. 1998. "Reflections on Rhiannon and the Horse Episodes in *Pwyll.*" *Western Folklore* 57:19–40.

Howlett, D. R., ed. and trans. 1994. *Liber Epistolarum Sancti Patricii Episcopi: The Book of the Letters of Saint Patrick the Bishop.* Blackrock, Ireland: Four Courts.

Hughes, Kathleen. 1972. *Early Christian Ireland: Introduction to the Sources.* Ithaca: Cornell University Press.

Hyde, Douglas, ed. and trans. 1906. *The Religious Songs of Connacht.* 2 vols. London and Dublin: T. F. Unwin and M. H. Gill and Son.

Lévi-Strauss, Claude. 1965. "The Structural Study of Myth." In *Myth: A Symposium,* ed. Thomas A. Sebeok, 81–106. Bloomington: Indiana University Press.

———. 1964–71. *Mythologiques.* 4 vols. Paris: Plon.

MacNeill, Máire. 1982. *The Festival of Lughnasa: A Study of the Survival of the Celtic Festival of the Beginning of Harvest.* Dublin: Comhairle Bhéaloideas Éireann. Originally published in 1962.

Nagy, Joseph Falaky. 1983. "Close Encounters of the Traditional Kind in Medieval Irish Literature." In *Celtic Folklore and Christianity: Studies in Memory of William W. Heist,* edited by Patrick K. Ford, 129–49. Santa Barbara and Los Angeles: McNally and Luftin, and the UCLA Center for the Study of Comparative Folklore and Mythology.

———. 1997. *Conversing with Angels and Ancients: The Literary Myths of Medieval Ireland.* Ithaca: Cornell University Press.

O'Rahilly, Thomas F. 1946. *Early Irish History and Mythology.* Dublin: Dublin Institute for Advanced Studies.

Plummer, Charles, ed. 1910. *Vitae Sanctorum Hiberniae.* 2 vols. Oxford: Clarendon.

———, ed. and trans. 1922. *Bethada Náem nÉrenn: Lives of Irish Saints.* 2 vols. Oxford: Clarendon.

Puhvel, Jaan. 1987. *Comparative Mythology.* Baltimore: Johns Hopkins University Press.

Sebeok, Thomas A., ed. 1965. *Myth: A Symposium.* Bloomington: Indiana University Press. Originally published in the *Journal of American Folklore* 68 (1955): 379–488.

Thompson, Stith. 1965. "Myth and Folktales." In *Myth: A Symposium,* edited by Thomas A. Sebeok, 169–80. Bloomington: Indiana University Press.

Ward, Donald J. 1968. *The Divine Twins: An Indo-European Myth in Germanic Tradition.* Berkeley and Los Angeles: University of California Press.

Wikander, Stig. 1957. "Nakula et Sahadeva." *Orientalia Suecana* 6:66–96.

NINE

The West and the People with Myth

GORDON BROTHERSTON

I n his classic statement *Europe and the People without History* (1984), Eric Wolf showed how ideology had followed in the footsteps of Western imperialism, robbing the objects of that imperialism, especially in Latin America and East Asia, of their own history. He noted how awareness of this phenomenon remained scarce in Western institutions of knowledge, since mainstream anthropology had preferred to study societies in isolation from each other and as somehow "timeless," while for its part history had continued to be very picky about what it would accept as valid evidence, preferring the documents of the colonizers every time. Wolf recommended, therefore, that the two disciplines should become more sensitive to each other's aims and practices, with a view to remedying, at least at the intellectual or academic level, some of the damage done to the world by Western imperialism.

This argument becomes the more persuasive when we introduce the concept central to this symposium, myth, while attending to how the narratives and chronologies of the "people without history" have been effectively silenced by imperialism, a concept Wolf's work does not explore. From the very first moment it entered the lexicon of the Western academy, "myth" has been fraught with the ideology of global domination. Myth may imply a cosmogony immeasurably more responsive than the biblical Genesis to the facts of terrestrial nature and the sky; it may chart terrain more authoritatively than any ordnance map; it may propose social and kinship models both practical and subtle; and it may record history with decidedly less murderous bias than the chronicles of the triumphant West: yet by definition it was born to be banished from the domain of true knowledge.

According to the *Shorter Oxford English Dictionary,* the English word *myth* is not old at all, and its use became widespread only a century and a half ago, along with the swift expansion at that time of British imperialism itself. And *myth* entered this language only to have its Greek pedigree sadly debased, being made to serve as the synonym of *false, fictitious, unprovable* in the new scientistic lingo of the day. It is no coincidence that the term *scientist* itself entered the language at more or less the same moment (1830, 1840). At the time, the inherent untruth of myth had everything to do with the emergence of the particular sciences which used it most, as Max Müller's 1861–64 *Lectures on the Science of Language* reminds us (Detienne 1981, 9). In other words, from the start it was caught in a basically evolutionary model of knowledge, where it denoted an early or primitive state of affairs which necessarily had to be superseded. Even in the mid–twentieth century, when Thomas Sebeok's *Myth: A Symposium* (1965) appeared here in Bloomington, that old scientism was far from dead. How else to hear David Bidney's highly quotable opinion, in that volume, that " [m]yth must be taken seriously as a cultural force but it must be taken seriously precisely in order that it may be gradually superseded in the interests of the advancement of truth and the growth of human intelligence" (Bidney 1965, 23)?

Meanwhile, myth has still been (or again come to be) considered a latent force, rather than just a state of mind to be superseded. Such is the message, for example, of Jungian and Freudian psychology, Ernst Cassirer's ventures into language and politics and his notion of the "myth of state" (1949), and Roland Barthes's *Mythologies* (1957), which has been described as "the classic exposition of the ways in which ideology is naturalized in the discourses, images and myths of twentieth-century society" (Belsey 1980, 103). More recently (1998), Bourdieu has declared his own resistance to "the new myths of our time." As a result, it has been easier to intuit how, in modern society, political and historical information might become intelligible to the larger public precisely when (and perhaps only when) it slotted into a carefully constructed and enabling mythic frame, the case of the U.S. being in this sense notorious. In his contribution to the Bloomington volume, "The Structural Study of Myth," Claude Lévi-Strauss completely rejected Bidney's scientism when anticipating the epoch-making arguments he would later develop in the four sizeable volumes of *Mythologiques* (1964–71):

> Prevalent attempts to explain alleged differences between the so-called "primitive" mind and scientific thought have resorted to qualitative differences between the working processes of the mind in both cases while assuming that the objects to which they were applying themselves remained very much the same. If our interpretation is correct, we are led toward a completely different view, namely, that the kind of logic which is used by mythical thought is as rigorous as that of modern science, and that the dif-

ference lies not in the quality of the intellectual process, but in the nature of the things to which it is applied. (Lévi-Strauss 1965, 105–106)

Liberating in its day, Lévi-Strauss's structuralism led to entirely new perceptions of myth, particularly of what we could hope to learn from the myths of the Americas, where he did his main fieldwork. Yet his championing of the scope and intellectual nature of myth in turn soon became the object of fundamental critique, notably in Edmund Leach's *Claude Lévi-Strauss* (1970) and Jacques Derrida's highly philosophical *De la grammatologie* (1967). Derrida deconstructs the phonocentrism inherent in Lévi-Strauss's approach, and its categorical reliance on a notion of "orality" which is both formally opposed to "writing" and socially derivative of Rousseau's romantic communalism.

For our immediate purposes here, in considering myth and historical texts, we need to focus on the particular concept of writing and script within the far-ranging and complex debates surrounding the structuralists and their successors. Writing, after all, remains the prerequisite for Western notions of history. In this respect, Lévi-Strauss's notions of writing may indeed be exposed as not just restrictive but positively self-contradictory. This is certainly the case with what he has to say in his early essay on the Nambikwara "writing lesson," where he combines Montaigne's sixteenth-century view of the Tupi-Guarani as a "world so new and infantine it has yet to learn its ABC" with the functionalism developed by the Africanist Jack Goody in *Literacy in Traditional Societies* (1968); and in his report in *Mythologiques* on how Muyusu brought script to the Mundurucu, "désireux d'enseigner l'écriture aux hommes" (Lévi-Strauss 1964–71, 1:331), where, without noticing or at least referring to the conundrum, he points to the great importance that the supposedly "oral" societies of tropical America attach to the ability to record and conserve, in script-like media, their experience of the past and of the surrounding world.

Yet more serious is what Lévi-Strauss's structuralism did to the notion of the *text* of a myth. He began his *Myth: A Symposium* paper with an epigraph from Franz Boas: "It would seem that mythological worlds have been built up only to be shattered again, and that new worlds were built from the fragments." Whatever else this dictum may be thought to refer to, as far as Lévi-Strauss's own project goes it is he who does the shattering and the rebuilding when presenting and explaining myth to his reader. His method required him to work with "myth units," each a potted summary in French of what in practice could be very different orders and types of sources, all the way from a passing observation made by a European traveler to the authorized narrative of a native American scholar writing in his or her own language. Only with this kind of flagrant disrespect for the idea and the fact of native texts could he manage to reveal (or construct) the finer and all-encompassing logic that he saw in myth. Having once celebrated the unrivaled cultural achievement of tropical America in the "cumulative history" of the planet (Lévi-Strauss 1952), he went on effectively to rid that achievement of its geographical and material significance and, above all, to cancel the idea that it has been (and still is being) brilliantly recorded in texts authored by native societies all over the American continent. He came to want myth to have its own ontology and to function unimpeded by the "external" constraints of history or cosmogony.

Hence his reluctance to engage with the American classics, and with extended native texts that are highly articulated in their own terms. Lévi-Strauss's method prevents the reader from becoming aware of the full scope and argument of such texts, of how they correlate whole levels or strata of time, inserting human and political history into the larger scheme of cosmogony in the style of *Diné bahane, Inomaca tonatiuh* (also known as "Legend of the suns"), *Watunna, Jurupary, Ayvu rapyta, Runa yndio* (the Quechua text from Huarochirí), and the "American bible" *Popol vuh* (written in Rigoberta Menchu's language, Maya-Quiché).[1]

In order to engage with the question of myth and the historical text, in this sense, we may turn to two tropical American tales of the journey to a homeland, whose nature has been much discussed in recent scholarship. One tells how the Aztecs traveled southeast from the island Aztlan in order to set up their future capital, Tenochtitlan, today's Mexico City. The other follows the Carib trail along the Pacaraima ridge, westward from Roraima to Marahuaka, the home of the Yekuana or Soto. For all their apparently mythic qualities, they have in common the affirmation of material history and territory; to this extent, they would seem to resist the tendency demonstrated in Eggan's key article "From History to Myth: A Hopi Example" (1967).

The migration from Aztlan was first recorded in Aztec books. These books, *amoxtli,* are part of the Mesoamerican corpus, most of which was burned by European invaders; they use a type of script, *tlacuilolli,* which along with other American recording systems has been underexamined and undertheorized in Western philosophy. The oldest examples are to be found in inscriptions of the first millennium B.C.; already at these early dates, phonetically specific varieties of this script had been developed by the Zapotec, Olmec, Maya, and others.

Classic Aztec migration accounts belong to the specific genre of annals (*xiuhtlapoualli* 'year-count'); they adhere therefore to the simple but key reading principle of moving forward through time, according to the years of the Mesoamerican calendar. These annals record much (Meso)american history, locating it in landscape and material fact. They weave a vast and many-threaded text, telling a story which politically begins with the first city, lowland Tula, and includes the Classic cities of Oaxaca, the Chichimec migrations from the northwest said to have begun in the seventh century A.D., and, finally, the Aztec arrival from Aztlan.

The sheer time-depth and scale of this scheme have caused problems for some, who find it ideologically unsettling to have to acknowledge such conscious antiquity in the "New" World; this despite all that is now independently known, from archaeology, about the several millennia of Mesoamerican experience. U.S. archaeologists (even today and even at I.U.) continue to refer to all preinvasion America as "prehistoric": Linda Schele and David Freidel more aptly proclaimed Mesoamerican calendrical records to be "American history" (Schele and Freidel 1990). It is also true that, as a genre, these records have a counterpart throughout North America, in the year counts and winter counts of the Pima, Kiowa, Dakota, and several other nations, some of which cast back to periods well before Columbus, using calendrical conventions that are directly comparable with those of Mesoamerica.

In this Aztec case, the migration story spans the period from the twelfth century (the departure from the island Aztlan) to the founding of Tenochtitlan on another island in the Basin of Mexico in 1325. It validates rights to the new homeland, surrounded on the lake shores by city-states that had been settled by others long before. It also explains the choice of hour and season (midnight at the winter solstice) for the politically decisive New Fire ceremony and hence Mexica-Aztec usage within the Mesoamerican calendar system.

Some Western scholars have had difficulty locating Aztlan, find the "island-to-island" symmetry (Carrasco 1991) suspiciously neat, and see discrepancies in the course and the detailed timing of the journey, and therefore have wished to consign the migration story to myth in the (bad) old sense of the term. Indeed, the whole migration has been dismissed as bogus—either a mere back-projection from the position of imperial strength later enjoyed by the Mexica or the invention of a past by a tribal group that had none, no adventure to speak of, prior to their rise to power. Thus certain U.S. archaeologists, citing a thin slice of ceramic and stratigraphic data, say the Aztecs never arrived from anywhere at all and made the whole story up. According to them, no self-respecting student of the past should waste even a minute considering the "mythical" accounts of foundation given in native texts like these.

Yet the native accounts of the journey from Aztlan are strongly consistent (Brotherston 1995, 45–61), and to deny their historicity altogether must imply a certain arrogance toward the worth of native annals generally. The sequence of main events summarized above, falling as it does between the twelfth and fourteenth centuries A.D., finds important cross-references in other highland texts: though the dates that plot the migration itself show a certain slippage, the Cuauhtitlan Annals and the Nahua historian Chimalpahin support the Mexica texts with respect to the departure from Aztlan and the start of the imperial reigns. Chimalpahin adds the telling detail that upon first arriving in the highland Basin of Mexico, the Aztecs were shocked by Popocatepetl's erupting, a sight familiar enough to longer-term residents. Again, the roadside vegetation of tuna-cactus and mesquite shown in the Aztlan Annals indicates Mexico's northern deserts while the overall direction of the journey, from northwest to southeast, is similarly consistent and can be plotted on a modern map.

In this example, our "scientific" preference effectually turns native history into myth, invalidating an antecedent which Mexicans and, not least, Chicanos continue to draw on today. In U.S. archaeology conferences of the last decade, the same arrogance led to open warfare against those ready to accept as valid evidence about the Maya people what is said in hieroglyphic texts written by them that were then being deciphered (by us) for the first time.

Notable for learned works on myth in the structuralist tradition, Alfredo López Austin has also had his doubts about the historicity of the journey from Aztlan, yet for reasons having more to do with the tinier details of its chronology (1985). He notes how, according to the version told in the Mexicanus and Azcatitlan Annals, on the eve of Huitzilopochtli's celestial birth and of the first "official" New Fire ceremony in the year 1195, one night was said to have lasted for three nights. This is an astronomical impossibility, he says; therefore the Aztec story must be deemed a "myth" on these grounds alone.

Now, if we look more closely, we see that the same native annals also inform us a) that the precise timing of the New Ceremony was made according to the position of a constellation (the Pleiades) at midnight at the winter solstice; b) that the years of the calendar were those of the sun; and c) that the Aztecs set up their political system and succession of emperors at Tenochtitlan at the New Fire ceremony of 1403 (four fifty-two-year calendar cycles later). In astronomical terms, the "mythical" three days is exactly the amount of time which accumulates over these calendrical 208 years when we take into account the difference that exists between the sidereal year of the sun with respect to the Pleiades (or any other constellation along its path; 365.256 days) and the solar year of the sun with respect to either solstice or either equinox (365.242 days). The phenomenon, known as the precession of the equinoxes, has been correlated with the myth and early phases of the history of the Old World, albeit sporadically (Santillana and von Dechend 1970; Yourgrau and Breck 1977).

In other words, far from lurching into the misty realms of myth, the Aztec annals could be pointing to a more precise measuring of the nature and passage of time than Western historians are used to. (Western historians, for example, customarily number years "B.C.", perhaps at times unaware that astronomers do it differently.) Here, our science fails even in its own limited terms and refuses, as the first Christian missionaries in Mexico once did, to imagine that the "other" (to use Todorov's [1982] entirely loaded term) could know more than we do and could calibrate history accordingly.

The story of the other journey, which the Caribs made from Roraima, is told in a text first published in 1970 by the French-Venezuelan anthropologist Marc de Civrieux. It has been translated into English by David Guss, under the title *Watunna: An Orinoco Creation Cycle* (Civrieux 1980). The text of *Watunna* results from close collaboration with its Carib authors and indeed reflexively offers clues to its composition and performance. In so doing, it confounds the structuralist binary between orality and script by indicating how the sacred chants through which it is conserved, in its core form, may have a script-like function even within speech. It is a major work in itself, and it also establishes multiple points of historical reference for other, briefer or less articulated Carib texts from the region.

A true American classic, *Watunna* has a vast cosmogonical scope. It is closely akin to such rain forest texts as *Jurupary* and the Desana cosmogony recounted by Umasin Panlon (1995), and its geological and zoological logic further compares with that of the Mesoamerican scheme of world ages recounted in the *Popol vuh* and *Inomaca tonatiuh,* the "Suns" which end in catastrophes of flood and eclipse. It similarly links local flora, notably palms, to the stars, and implies a similar understanding of the evolution which runs from fish and saurian to bird and monkey, here adapted to local fauna, notably the anaconda version of the plumed serpent motif found throughout tropical America.[2] In *Watunna,* the transition into human history is also comparable, insofar as it is characterized by the first agriculture: in this case, the bringing of plant cuttings and seeds along the Pacaraima ridge from what Schomburgk called the "botanical El Dorado" of Roraima (Sá 1997, 26). This event corresponds to settling in the homeland defined by the mountain Marahuaka, the western twin of Roraima, at the headwaters of the Orinoco. *Watunna* specifically names and recognizes these peaks, along with the Casiquiare canal that links the Orinoco and the Amazon in an extraordinary hydrography. Hence, this Carib text had the answer all along to the enigma that defeated Humboldt and Western science generally up till the Franco-Venezuelan Orinoco expedition of 1950 (of which Civrieux was a member). There follows a detailed log of encounters with others, Indian neighbors and then Western invaders (Dutch, Spanish, English, Venezuelan), which is distinguished by its native priorities and point of view, in the sense that these have been defined in the volume edited by Jonathan Hill, *Rethinking History and Myth: Indigenous South American Perspectives on the Past* (1988).

The hinge of the text, the journey from Roraima to Marahuaka, bridges and links the domains of cosmogony and human history; and for this reason it actively serves to defend the political interests of the Soto at the deepest level, along with their right to a homeland, one which is being increasingly invaded by the disease-bearing conquistadors of today. In this sense, it fits generically into the concept of legal title (*título*), which when respected has greatly enhanced understanding of the literary-historical strategies deployed in many, perhaps most, native American classics written in the alphabet, beginning with the sixteenth-century *Popol vuh* of the Maya-Quiché.[3] In other words, recognizing the territorial claim embedded in *Watunna* is inseparable from adequately reading the text as literature, a possibility that is little enhanced if the narrative is considered strictly mythical.

In general, this dimension of the American classics recalls work done already at the start of the nineteenth century by Karl Otwin Müller, who strove to reconstruct the historical context and physical landscape of the major myths of the Old World (Detienne 1981, 125–26), an initiative that culminated in the recuperation of the supposedly immaterial Troy, through Schliemann's archaeological excavations. In America, victim of a cultural and historical dispossession that has no parallel on the planet, this order of restitution and a proper appreciation of what "foundation myth" can signify are obviously going to have a far more immediate and urgent political resonance.

As a dispossessed continent, America has been a favorite playground for mythologists. Its original inhabitants have been perceived *par excellence* as the scriptless "other" and the "people with myth." Yet, carefully read in the texts these same people have in fact authored, the wealth of American myth suggests, rather, that mainstream Western theory on the subject suffers from severe, even perverse, limitations. This is true with regard to the deeper history of creation and the many centuries it is taking the West, caught in the dogmas of the Bible and then its own universally imposed science, to catch up intellectually with American cosmogony. And it explains why respected academics can go on referring with impunity to "prehistoric" America when in fact they should be asking, "Who, in 1492, entered whose history?"

NOTES

1. See, respectively, Zolbrod 1984; Bierhorst 1992; Civrieux 1980 and 1992; Hugh-Jones 1979, Reichel-Dolmatoff 1996, and Medeiros in press; Bareiro Saguier 1980; Arguedas 1966 and Urioste 1983; Edmonson 1971 and Tedlock 1985. Brotherston 1992 offers a general commentary.

2. For example, *Watunna's* Huiio strongly resembles the *Popol vuh's* Gucumatz, a parallel that can have escaped notice only because of the fragmentation of our scholarship; cf. Brotherston 1992.

3. Among the first to focus on this legal dimension of the American classics was Georges Raynaud, whose French translations of the *Popol vuh* and the *Annals of the Cakchiquels* were turned into Spanish by his one-time pupil in Paris, Miguel Angel Asturias (Asturias and Mendoza 1927); see also Edmonson 1971 and Carmack 1973.

BIBLIOGRAPHY

Arguedas, José María. 1966. *Dioses y hombres de Huarochirí: Narración quechua recogida por Francisco de Avila.* Lima: Museo Nacional de Historia y el Instituto de Estudios Peruanos.

Asturias, Miguel Angel, and J. M. González de Mendoza. 1927. *Los dioses, los héroes, y los hombres de Guatemala antigua o El libro de consejo Popol vuh de los indios Quichés.* Paris: Editorial París-Américana.

Bareiro Saguier, Rubén. 1980. *Literatura guaraní del Paraguay.* Caracas: Monte Ávila.

Barthes, Roland. 1957. *Mythologies.* Paris: Seuil.

Belsey, Catherine. 1980. *Critical Practice.* London: Methuen.

Bidney, David. 1965. "Myth, Symbolism, and Truth." In *Myth: A Symposium,* edited by Thomas A. Sebeok, 3–24. Bloomington: Indiana University Press.

Bierhorst, John. 1974. *Four Masterworks of American Indian Literature.* New York: Farrar Strauss.

———. 1992. *History and Mythology of the Aztecs (Codex Chimalpopoca).* Albuquerque: University of Arizona Press.

Bourdieu, Pierre. 1998. *Acts of Resistance: Against the New Myths of Our Time.* Translated by Richard Nice. Cambridge: Polity.

Brotherston, Gordon. 1992. *Book of the Fourth World: Reading the Native Americas through Their Literature.* Cambridge: Cambridge University Press.

———. 1995. *Painted Books from Mexico: Codices in UK Collections and the World They Represent.* London: British Museum Press for the Trustees of the British Museum.

Carmack, Robert. 1973. *Quichean Civilization: The Ethnohistorical, Ethnographic, and Archaeological Sources.* Berkeley and Los Angeles: University of California Press.

Carrasco, David, ed. 1991. *To Change Place: Aztec Ceremonial Landscapes.* Niwot: University Press of Colorado.

Cassirer, Ernst. 1949. *Vom Mythus des Staates.* Zürich: Artemis.

Civrieux, Marc de. 1980. *Watunna: An Orinoco Creation Cycle.* Edited and translated by David Guss. San Francisco: North Point.

———. 1992. *Watunna: Cosmología maquiritare.* 2d edition. Caracas: Monte Ávila.

148 | GORDON BROTHERSTON

Derrida, Jacques. 1967. *De la grammatologie*. Paris: Minuit.

Detienne, Marcel. 1981. *L'invention de la mythologie*. Paris: Gallimard.

Edmonson, Munro S. 1971. *The Book of Counsel: The Popol vuh of the Quiché Maya of Guatemala*. New Orleans: Middle American Research Institute, Tulane University.

Eggan, Fred. 1967. "From History to Myth: A Hopi Example." In *Studies in Southwestern Linguistics,* edited by Dell Hymes, 33–53. The Hague: Mouton.

Goody, Jack. 1968. *Literacy in Traditional Societies*. Cambridge: Cambridge University Press.

Hill, Jonathan D., ed. 1988. *Rethinking History and Myth: Indigenous South American Perspectives on the Past*. Urbana: University of Illinois Press.

Hugh-Jones, Stephen. 1979. *The Palm and the Pleiades: Initiation and Cosmology in Northwest Amazonia*. Cambridge: Cambridge University Press.

Leach, Edmund. 1970. *Claude Lévi-Strauss*. New York: Viking; London: Fontana.

Lévi-Strauss, Claude. 1952. *Race et histoire*. Paris: Gonthier.

———. 1964–71. *Mythologiques*. 4 vols. Paris: Seuil.

———. 1965. "The Structural Study of Myth." In *Myth: A Symposium,* edited by Thomas A. Sebeok, 81–106. Bloomington: Indiana University Press.

López Austin, Alfredo. 1985. "El texto Sahaguntino sobre los mexicas." *Anales de Antropología* (UNAM) 22:287–336.

Medeiros, Sérgio, ed. In press. *A leggenda do Jurupari de Stradelli*. São Paulo: Perspectiva.

Reichel-Dolmatoff, Gerardo. 1996. *Yurupari: Studies of an Amazonian Foundation Myth*. Cambridge, Mass.: Harvard University Press.

Sá, Lúcia. 1997. *Reading the Rain Forest: Indigenous Texts and Their Impact on Brazilian and Spanish American Literature*. Ph.D. dissertation, Indiana University.

Santillana, Giorgio de, and Hertha von Dechend. 1970. *Hamlet's Mill: An Essay on Myth and the Frame of Time*. London: Macmillan.

Schele, Linda, and David Freidel. 1990. *A Forest of Kings: The Untold Story of the Ancient Maya*. New York: Morrow.

Sebeok, Thomas. 1965. *Myth: A Symposium*. Bloomington: Indiana University Press. Originally published in the *Journal of American Folklore* 68 (1955): 379–488.

Tedlock, Dennis. 1985. *The Popol Vuh: The Definitive Edition of the Mayan Book of the Dawn of Life and the Glories of Gods and Kings*. New York: Simon and Schuster.

Todorov, Tzvetan. 1982. *La conquête de l'Amérique: La question de l'autre*. Paris: Seuil.

Umusin Panlon. 1995. *Antes o mundo não existia: Mitologia dos antigos Desana-Kehíripõrã*. 2d edition. São João Batista do Rio Tiquié: UNIRT/São Gabriel da Cachoeira: FOIRN.

Urioste, George L. 1983. *Hijos de Pariya Qaqa: La tradición oral de Waru Chiri*. 2 vols. Syracuse, N.Y.: Maxwell School of Citizenship and Public Affairs.

Wolf, Eric. 1984. *Europe and the People without History*. Berkeley and Los Angeles: University of California Press.

Yourgrau, Wolfgang, and Allen D. Breck. 1977. *Cosmology, History, and Theology*. London: Plenum.

Zolbrod, Paul G. 1984. *Diné Bahane: The Navajo Creation Story*. Albuquerque: University of New Mexico Press.

Part IV

MYTH AND THE
MODERN WORLD

TEN

Myths of the Rain Forest/ The Rain Forest as Myth

CANDACE SLATER

S econd Eden," "Lost Paradise," "Green Hell," "Living Laboratory"—characterizations of the Amazon vary over time. Although today the term "rain forest" has become a virtual synonym for Amazonia, the idea of the region as a fragile, though exuberant, treasure trove of bio-diversity is relatively new. What is not new is the broader notion of the Amazon as the epitome of nature and, as such, the polar opposite of civilization, science, and technology.

The Amazon that we see in newspaper headlines, on television, and on Mistic fruit drink bottles is, above all, a primeval realm. The handful of "Stone Age" Indians and tree-loving rubber tappers who make an appearance in the great majority of these portrayals live close to nature, are rich in "ancestral knowledge," and possess a wealth of narratives that go back to the beginnings of time. It is easy to see these "natural" peoples' stories of shape-changing snakes and dolphins, of birds that talk to humans and humans who turn into jaguars, as mythic in a more or less traditional scholarly sense. By this, I mean that these tales appear "*primordial* in the sense of transpiring in an initial phase; *foundational,* in describing formative moments when the world was acquiring its present shape; and *counter-factual* in featuring actors and actions that confound the conventions of routine experience" (McDowell 1998, 80). I also mean that these tales are likely to address deep-rooted tensions by obfuscating or circumventing conflicts while defining or reaffirming humans' particular place within the world.[1]

My argument in the first part of this paper is that many accounts of the rain forest by and for outsiders reveal elements every bit as "mythic" in their own way as traditional creation stories. These accounts include the descriptions of an emerald wonderland that enliven containers of Rainforest Crunch ice cream and the appeals to save a virgin nature emblazoned on

Sierra Club calendars or World Wildlife Fund posters. The primordial, foundational, and counter-factual qualities of these portrayals suggest that, despite its geographic and biological reality, today's Amazon Rain Forest is as much a mythic entity as the conquistadors' gleaming El Dorado or the women warriors of antiquity who gave their name to the great river.

WAXING MYTHIC

To illustrate my point, I offer what initially looks to be an improbable example—namely an ad for a car polish marketed by Simoniz and manufactured in part from the Brazilian carnauba palm.[2] At first glance, the use of rain forest imagery in such an advertisement is surprising because car wax, with its pragmatic, Machine Age associations, seems so remote from the jaguars, river-bottom cities, and shapechanging anacondas that appear in native myths as well as in present-day folk narratives told by *caboclos* and *mestizos*.[3] The lack of the sort of clear beginning, middle, and end which figure in many scholars' definitions of myth also makes the ad seem an odd choice.[4] In addition, the ad's heavy reliance on graphic images (an Amazonian Indian and a sleek black bottle of car polish) is foreign to traditional definitions of myth. Finally, the ad is surprising because much of its force lies in its conscious, gentle parody of elements associated with traditional myths.

Designed to cover two full pages but distributed as well in several more compact versions (one occupying a page, another no more than a single column), the ad appeared in a variety of niche-market magazines including *Sports Illustrated, Rolling Stone, Car and Driver,* and *Home Mechanix,* as well as several in-flight airline publications, during the spring of 1995. In the two-page version, the entire left half of the ad pictures a highly ornamented "Chief Tunabi" who stares out at the reader as he stands before a backdrop of leaves. The right half of the ad depicts a sleek black bottle of Simoniz Advanced Total Car Finish, the bright yellow half-sun on its label set in a red band that echoes the band of red paint which accents Tunabi's dark eyes. Grainy in a way that recalls bark or raw silk, with its much-touted "natural imperfections," the pale background provides a contrast for the streamlined, high-tech bottle, above which a quotation from the chief appears. "I bring carnauba wax from the Amazon to new Simoniz. May it make your car's finish the envy of your village," Tunabi declares.

A double line of type beneath the bottle identifies its contents as "easy-to-use wax and polish mysteriously unified in one." The text goes on to promise a "transcendent total finish" on each and every car. "No dust or streak demons," it announces. "Magically beads rain." An irregular turquoise border with an artisanal-looking geometrical design runs down and

10.1 Chief Tunabi (Simoniz ad). Simoniz is a registered trademark of
Simoniz USA, Inc.

across the outer margin of each of the two pages, drawing chief and bottle
into a common graphic universe. The red-brown, earth-tone highlights of
the border create further links between the two. The fine print in the
right-hand corner below and outside the border offers the assurance that
"the harvest of carnauba wax does not damage the Brazilian carnauba
palm."

At first glance, the ad appears to be no more than a good-humored
spoof aimed at drawing attention to the exotic extra in this "advanced total
car finish." While few Amazonian native peoples would find either Tunabi's
"folkloric" sentiments or his apparent ingenuousness (in his reference to
our "village") funny, the ad's creators clearly intend the references to dust
and streak demons and to the magic beading of the rain to be tongue-in-
cheek. It is precisely the disjuncture between the prosaic, anticlimactic
quality of car wax and the awe-inspiring grandeur of a mythic universe
conjured up through terms such as "mysterious" and "transcendent" that
makes the ad appealing. The conversion of normally fear-inspiring supernatural beings who hold sway over elemental forces (rain, wind, fire) into
clearly fictive dust and streak demons insures that Tunabi's claims need not
be taken figuratively.

The ad thus capitalizes on the expectations surrounding "real" myths in order to appeal to car owners in an industrial or postindustrial society. At the same time, however, it draws its force in part from that unfettered abundance for which the Amazon rain forest has become a virtual synonym. The red and black face paint, the bead earrings, and the brilliant blue feather aureole around Tunabi's head suggest natural riches. So does the luxuriant tangle of seed necklaces around his neck. The thick ornamental bands around each upper arm and the heavy pectoral of what looks like silver-coated feathers further emphasize both the exotic beauty and the abundant economic possibilities of the leafy treasure trove that Tunabi represents.

The high visibility of "Save the Rain Forest" campaigns suggests that while Tunabi himself may be a tongue-in-cheek creation, this larger world of nature remains a serious matter for many of the present-day readers who are the targets of the ad. As a result, at the same time that the ad sets out to make the viewer chuckle all the way to the cash register, it also plays on profound hopes and fears. The underlying fragility of the rain forest, which finds expression in both the seed-adorned Tunabi and the palm fronds that caress his shoulder, is also part of the ad's appeal.

The aura of authenticity paradoxically invoked by an ersatz Indian ("*genuine* quality," asserts the label on the sleek black bottle) links the Simoniz piece to other ads for rain forest products. When, for instance, the label on the clear glass jug of R. W. Knudsen Family Rain Forest Punch pictures a macaw and a toucan popping up from a green bed of bird-of-paradise and hibiscus flowers as pink as the juice in the container, it plays on a similar blend of authenticity and exoticism.[5] "Exclusively fruit juice sweetened," this beverage concocted from grape juice and various more exotic-sounding fruits culled "from *our* tropical Rain Forests" contains "no preservatives, artificial flavors or colors. *No artificial anything!*" [my italics]. Just as the car polish's "rich" finish and "enduring" protection evoke a world in which things are somehow truer, more immediate, and more vivid, so the universe of the punch bottle is one of unadulterated goodness.

Rain Forest Punch has a revealing history.[6] In the late 1980s, Knudsen marketed three separate juices from exotic tropical fruits—guanabana, calmansi, and cupuassu. These were identified on bottle labels as products of the rain forests of the Philippines, Malaysia, and the Brazilian Amazon.[7] Part of the profits from their sale (1%) was slated for donation to rain forest preservation projects, and the promotional material for the juices sent to potential vendors underscored not just their "exotic flavors" and "tropical personality," but also their socially responsible quality. ("The R. W. Knudsen Family is helping indigenous peoples fund the preservation of their homelands.")[8]

Probably because they sounded *too* exotic and were therefore too hard for consumers to remember, the triad of tropical juices was not commercially successful. However, when Knudsen introduced a single Rain Forest Punch in 1991, it gained considerably wider market acceptance. Although the punch never made the list of the company's top twenty sellers, it did manage to survive for nine years—a more than respectable shelf life in an industry where products may last no more than a season or two.[9] While today all mention of the rain forest has disappeared, Knudsen now markets a group of "tropical blends" that promise "a taste of the exotic" as they transport purchasers "with one sip to a foreign isle."[10]

While the new juices are described as "one-of-a-kind worldly" (the foreign isle is presumably not uncomfortably distant), Rain Forest Punch is more explicitly tied to the biblical Eden.[11] While neither the Simoniz nor the Knudsen texts refer explicitly to Adam and Eve or to the Garden, the story of Genesis lies close beneath the surface of both. Hints of this original paradise unite the sleek black bottle with the intentionally chunky and "un-fancy," though fully recyclable, juice bottle. Tunabi can bring carnauba wax to the global village because he continues to reside in a universe in which the magic bond between human beings and plants and animals persists unbroken. Even while the chief himself is no superhuman entity, the nature of which he is both extension and intermediary confounds the conventions of routine experience by leading the car wax user back into a world that is at once more elemental and infinitely more mysterious. As a result, the ad suggests the potential resolution of a series of conflicts and contradictions at the very heart of today's rain forest.

The first of the tensions to which it speaks is the perceived gulf between the world of nature and the world of technology. The visual correspondences between the two halves of the ad reinforce the possibility of harmonious commerce in all senses between two very different worlds. Just as the half-sun on the glossy, aerodynamic bottle with its promise of "*advanced* total car finish" provides a graphic echo of the forest's dappled leaves, so the gold medal on the bottle finds echoes in the wreath of silver around the chief's neck. The earth-toned frame that encircles the two halves of the ad emphasizes the theme of shared riches, bringing the human and nonhuman actors into a common universe which transforms the factory-manufactured car wax into a more organic entity.

In bringing together nature and technology in a "mysterious union" of easy-to-use wax and polish, the ad eases the potential friction between consumption and resource conservation. The wax that confers a "transcendent total finish" upon the family station wagon can do so without damage to a single palm tree. As a result, Tunabi can offer up the crimson bounty of the forest at no apparent cost to either plants or people.

The promise of a cost-free development contained within the fine print that appears outside the ad's border (and, thus, beyond the realm of fantasy) is thoroughly mythic in its cloaking of a number of essential contradictions. The idea that the car wax purchaser is actively protecting, not just his own chassis, but the world's rain forests neatly circumvents the assault on the environment represented by freeways, carbon dioxide emissions, and an entire commuter culture with its miles of fast-food restaurants and chain stores offering discount automobile supplies. Thus, at the same time that the ad promises protection from acid rain and highway grime, it plays on far larger hopes and fears about the effects of a commodity-intensive way of life upon Tunabi's world. The idea that the wax has no negative environmental impact allows consumers to continue driving off into a smog-ringed sunset without any worries about the clouds of exhaust that their Hondas, Fords, and Fiats are spewing into the air.

If the implicit story that the ad tells has primordial and foundational elements, it is also counter-factual in several senses. Not just larger than life, Tunabi is a full-fledged fiction. The pleased aplomb with which he puts "his" palm trees at the disposal of the global village contrasts sharply with the actions of actual Amazonian Indian groups such as the Yanomami and Kayapó.[12] Although the Yanomami's desire to live apart contrasts with the Kayapó's astute manipulations of (and, often, active dealings with) loggers and miners, both find themselves locked in an ongoing struggle with exploitative outsiders. Their reluctance to cheerfully hand over the forest's riches to a world beyond their borders presents a striking contrast to Tunabi's nonchalant largesse. By covering over the real price native peoples pay for the rain forest commercial ventures spearheaded by multinational enterprises, the ad once more assuages readers' feelings of unease or guilt.

In the end, of course, no one really expects Tunabi to act like a flesh-and-blood Indian. Because, however, the ad accords such a central place to the carnauba palm, it does come as a surprise to learn that this tree is native, not to rain forests, but rather to the very driest areas of the Brazilian northeast. Indeed, the glossy coating on its fronds is the palm tree's way of conserving moisture in a climate subject to catastrophic droughts. As a result, it would take a true magician to bring Amazonian carnauba wax to new Simoniz, and its assumed presence within the rain forest is an outright fallacy or "myth" in the word's most common and colloquial sense.[13]

The story, however, does not end here. It is precisely those droughts to which the palm has so well adapted that drove scores of desperate peasants from the northeast to the Amazon to try their fortunes in the Rubber Boom. The few carnauba palms which do grow in the Amazon today are almost all found in the home gardens which these northeastern transplants established during the second half of the nineteenth and the early twentieth centuries.[14] The carnauba is thus a living reminder of the sorts of deeply rooted processes and impulses that remain inseparable from the representations that we label "myths."

THE ENCANTE AS ANOTHER SORT OF MYTHIC SPACE

Similar, even while distinctive, mythic impulses show up in a large group of Amazonian folk stories that I have been studying since 1988. Rooted in far older, still surviving indigenous narratives of aquatic seducers, which most scholars would be quick to label myths, the Encantado stories are about enchanted places (Encantes) and enchanted beings (the Encantados).[15] Recounted by the Spanish- and Portuguese-speakers who presently account for some 97 percent of the Amazonian population of twenty-three million, these stories reflect the Amazon's rich ethnic background in their additional borrowings from African and European sources.[16]

Paralleling these various borrowings, the Encantado stories also reveal a mixture of different genres, including legend, memorate, oral history, and folktale. While some storytellers are convinced of the truth of the events in question, others express doubt ("I don't know if these things really happened, but everybody tells the story") or even outright disbelief ("It's a very pretty story, but, of course, it isn't true"). If one compares the following piece of an indigenous narrative with a typical Encantado story, some of these differences are immediately clear. In the first example, recorded among the Shipibo people of the Peruvian Amazon, two nephews who suspect that their aunt is having sex with a dolphin resolve to spy on the sleeping woman.

> They arrived at the bank and when they were hidden—well-hidden—the sound of the dolphin was heard. The dolphin came to the canoe landing. It was very quiet for a while as he approached. Some moments later the dolphin climbed out of the water. He emerged and began to approach the woman. When he was very, very close the woman began to sleep—*hëën*. When the dolphin reached her, he entered her. The two nephews then began to approach the copulating couple. The dolphin carried an *iscohina* around his dorsal fin. He wore it thus on his back as he entered the woman's mosquito netting. When he was leaving it afterward, one of the two nephews began to shoot arrows at him with his bow. The dolphin fell to the ground impaled. He struggled to raise himself on his ventral fins and crawled with great difficulty toward the lake. The other nephew then shot him with an arrow when he was very near to the port. Then he gave the dolphin a blow with his *macana*. The wounded dolphin managed nonetheless to crawl into the water and escape. (Roe 1982, 51–52)[17]

In the second story, which I taped on a boat bound for the city of Itaituba in the eastern portion of the Brazilian Amazon, a dolphin also has sex with a human woman. Here, however, the dolphin is an enchanted being, an Encantado, which transforms itself into a man in order to have intercourse. The storyteller in this case is a young caboclo with a checkered tote bag full of T-shirts, movie magazines, and a plaster Virgin, who is headed for a stint in the gold mines of the Tapajós River. His breezy tone, as well as his comments about contemporary occurrences, immediately set the tale apart from its indigenous counterpart.

> Now then, these Dolphins [I capitalize the word in order to indicate an Encantado] are completely shameless. They go to country dances and pick up the prettiest girls. So then, there was one named Juliano, who whenever there could be a party in Água Fria, Aréia Branca, he would go there to dance. He'd show his pockets full of dollars and all of the girls would ditch their boyfriends in order to dance with him. Afterwards, he'd jump into the prettiest girl's hammock and remain there all night till dawn. Except that once, he decided to mess with a girl named Mariane. And her boyfriend suspected that he must be a Dolphin because of the hat [that enchanted dolphins use to hide their blowholes] and he went after him. He gave him such a beating that he never again appeared here. At least, that's what they say. But look, after people began arriving here in every corner, there are far fewer Encantados in any case. I think that they can't stand the noise of the machines that cut down the forest in order to build houses, and they probably don't like the heat. Because where there is no forest, it gets really hot.[18]

The obvious divergences in vocabulary, in tone, and in historical positioning between the indigenous narrative and its Encantado counterpart make it easy to see the one as more "mythic" than the other. And yet, while there is no doubt that the first is "primordial," "foundational," and "counterfactual" in very different ways than is the second, both reveal elements that might fit this three-part definition. Moreover, the Encantado stories address deep-seated tensions and seek to define the human relationship to nature every bit as much as do their indigenous counterparts.

While, for instance, the events in the indigenous myth unfold in a time different from the present, the Encantado stories reveal their own sense of "before" and "after." Many storytellers refer to a time before Christianity "fixed," or imposed limits on, a protean universe in which the birds and animals still conversed regularly with human beings.[19] "The Encante comes from the beginning of time. It is the chaos upon which Christ imposed order," explains one young fisherman in a green T-shirt stamped with the smiling face of a local politician.[20] "Cobra Norato [an enchanted anaconda about whom stories abound] set that evil sister of his beneath the altar stone of the Óbidos cathedral but she is still there—all one has to do is move the stone in order to see her monstrous, serpent head," a young woman who is dangling a chubby baby over a washtub full of soapy water affirms with something between horror and triumphant glee.[21]

For some storytellers then, the "time before" is that era preceding the arrival of the Catholic priests who stop rocks from turning into fish or birds by dousing them with holy water. For others, however, this time is the epoch before widespread deforestation. "The Encante is disappearing because the Encantados don't like to live in the city," says a woman who has lived in the same tiny village for all but one of her forty-seven years. "They need trees, they need clean water with no motor boats to give them headaches. So then, they get mad and they gather up all their fish and animals and head off for another place where there are trees and peace and they can hear themselves think straight."[22]

Some Encantado stories are readily recognizable creation stories. A number of present-day Amazonians explain the so-called "meeting of the waters" in which one "black" and one "white" river flow beside each other before gradually fusing as an ongoing struggle between a "good" and a "bad" snake. "One is a good snake, of whom we humans are the children," explains one young, very sunburned fisherman on the Araguaia River, "but the other is a bad snake who enjoys destruction."[23]

However, even when the stories deal directly with origins, the tellers often turn out to be less interested in how things first came into being than in why they are the way they are today. Thus, the fisherman goes on to explain that "those people who today destroy the forest and pollute the waters so that others can no longer hunt or fish, they are helping the bad snake." In contrast, "the children of the good snake remain heirs to a whole city full of golden roofs and crystal sidewalks that lies there, enchanted for the moment, at the river bottom." The foundational quality of these stories is thus, once again, present-oriented. While the storytellers may begin with a reference to a remote past, their real concern is present-day environmental destruction and its social costs.

A deep preoccupation with this destruction, and with the other sorts of cultural, political, and economic transformations presently sweeping the Amazon, pervades even those Encantado stories which make little or no mention of a remote past. Even the teller who appears to reject the literal truth of the Encantados may use these larger-than-life entities to comment on ongoing changes. One man, a rubber tapper whose blue eyes suggest remote Dutch ancestry,[24] laughs and shakes his head from side to side when I ask if there are really enchanted dolphins. Nonetheless, he is quick to make use of the enchanted beings in describing an all-too-real injustice.

See here, the Dolphin is a gringo. He loves to take everything that belongs to other people, and afterwards, the little bit of money that he leaves in payment turns into seaweed. Look, it's my thinking that the Dolphin isn't even a dolphin. He's a shark, he's all those people who only know how to rob. And how people let these shameless ones keep on robbing, ah, that's the true mystery of the Encante. Because I don't know from where the Dolphin came or where he hangs out, but I do know that injustice is as old as the beginning of the world.[25]

Once more very different from myths that recount the beginning of the world in a specialized, if not sacred, language, the Encantado stories nonetheless address deep-seated tensions in their own way. Although the narratives reveal real differences among individuals, their tellers, as a group, tend to be overwhelmingly concerned with the relationship between human beings and nature.

Affirmations of the continuing fluidity of the boundaries between the river and the earth, the Encantado stories underscore the alien quality of what looks most familiar. The fact that the enchanted beings are able to assume the guise not just of humans in general, but of a spouse, a friend, a parent, brings home the deceptive nature of appearances. It also confirms the precariousness of fixed definitions in which, as one seventy-year-old woman whose hair is still jet-black says scornfully, "X is always X and Y is always Y." At the same time, the unceasing transformation that is the hallmark of the Encantados suggests the continuing mystery of a world under assault from without. No mere remnants of the past, the stories serve as a dynamic forum for debates about the interface between human and nonhuman nature. If the Dolphin is a gringo, he is also a kind of latter-day, thoroughly Amazonian trickster who laughs at the technology that denies his existence.[26] The speaker below is the same dark-haired older woman, who pauses in the midst of shucking corn to underscore the truth of the Encantados' ever-shifting river-bottom city.

They say that the Encantados don't exist. But that's exactly what they want people to think. The Dolphin, the Anaconda, they like it when outsiders say that it's all a lie, they like it when they say that the Encante is just ignorant talk. It's in this way that they can continue to live in peace. Because if outsiders thought that there was a city of gold beneath the water, they'd dredge the entire river in order to find those riches. So, it's for this reason that the Encante keeps on disappearing. Because if it were to remain here in plain view, no one would have a moment's peace, of that you can be sure.[27]

My point here, as in the preceding section about the Simoniz ad, is not that the actual representations in question are "myths" in any sort of strict literary or formulaic sense. In the end, I am considerably less concerned with pinpointing the particular generic properties of either the Simoniz ad or the Encantado stories—neither of which is "myth" according to traditional definitions—than I am with highlighting the mythic dimensions of the Rain Forest and the Encante which these examples simultaneously reinforce and help to create. The Rain Forest will initially strike most outsiders as a biological and geographic reality, while the Encante will appear to be a blatant fiction. In the end, however, both serve as a nexus of powerful and decidedly contradictory ideas about the human relationship to a particular sort of nonhuman nature.

The understanding that the Rain Forest [the capital letters indicate the iconic entity as opposed to multiple rain forests] and the Encante are, on some level, explanations of how human beings relate to nature highlights that shared heritage which makes the Amazon far more than a treasure trove of flora and fauna. This intertwining symbolic legacy permits us to reenvision our own assumptions about nature in portrayals as apparently flippant as the ad for car wax or as self-consciously serious as the calls to save the world's rain forests that appear on posters, magazine announcements, and television screens.

The realization that other people have other ways of describing the world, which we are quick to set apart as "mythic," has profound implications for policy. If, for instance, we can identify our own desire for an unspoiled natural paradise in posters of a rain forest inhabited by birds, tall trees, and a handful of "Stone Age" natives, we will be more able to see (and, thus, to respond to in a more effective, less uniform manner) the rich variety of people, as well as plants and animals, that exist within the Amazon. By leading us into the dense and tangled heart of our own most cherished assumptions, the reconsideration of how and why myth works can help us to see Amazonia—and all of nature—in a new light.

NOTES

The first half of this essay draws on material from my book *Entangled Edens* (2001).

1. I am thinking here of Wm. Blake Tyrrell's assertion that "[m]yths tend to deal with sources of conflict and tension in the social order and human condition. Their function is to elicit responses to their explanations in the minds and emotions of their receptors in order to obfuscate, circumvent, or mediate those conflicts and tensions" (Tyrrell 1984, xiv).

2. The ad for Simoniz car polish ran for several months in the spring of 1995. According to the STP Group Product Manager, the image of "Chief Tunabi" was not used for retail displays. (Letter from David R. Berlin, 19 July 1995)

3. "Caboclo" is used loosely to refer to persons of mixed ethnic heritage—a designation that fits approximately 97 percent of Amazonia's present population of twenty-three million.

4. See, for instance, Philip Wheelwright's "The Semantic Approach to Myth," in which the author underscores both "the narrative character" and "the transcendent referent" of myth (1958, 95). In identifying myth as a particular sort of narrative, Wheelwright is by no means alone.

5. I take the text that follows from a bottle of R. W. Knudsen Family Rain Forest Punch, which the label describes as "an exotic juice beverage from tropical fruit purees and fruit concentrate."

6. I thank Diane Contreras of Knudsen Juices' customer relations department for this information. Unfortunately, when I later requested permission to reproduce the Rain Forest Punch label and some of the graphics from the publicity material, Smuckers Corporation refused.

7. "Guanabana grows in tropical forests around the world; but ours comes from the Philippines, where indigenous tribes are threatened by encroachments into their homelands" ("Questions and Answers about Tropical Rain Forest Juices," an information sheet provided by Knudsen Juices).

8. The money actually went to organizations such as Cultural Survival, which the promotional material described as "a non-profit, charitable organization dedicated to helping tribal peoples and ethnic minorities protect their human rights and land rights, and utilize their resources in a sustainable manner."

9. While the average life cycle of a product was once about five years, it can now be as short as six weeks. In 1983, 5,700 new products were introduced to American consumers; that number had risen to 21,000 only twelve years later.

10. I take these descriptions from the R. W. Knudsen Web site: <http://www.knudsen-juices.com/products/tropical.html> (accessed 23 October 2001). In addition to its "tropical blends," the company offers a variety of other lines, including "organic fruit juices," "sports beverages," "aseptic juices," "celebratory beverages," and "single strength juices." Interestingly enough, the chief ingredients in the "tropical blends" are the not-so-exotic (and indeed, in some cases, not-so-tropical) pineapple, coconut, mango, peach, papaya, guava, and strawberry.

11. See Slater 1995.

12. For an overview of the problems faced by these quite different native peoples, see Rabben 1998.

13. For a description of the carnauba palm, see Henderson, Galeano, and Bernal 1995, 60–61. The authors identify the carnauba's habitat as "low-lying areas, especially along river or lake margins that are liable to seasonal flooding followed by seasonal or prolonged drought." A photograph appears as plate 8. The carnauba is not even mentioned in Henderson's *The Palms of the Amazon* (1995). For more on the carnauba, see Leite 1975, 143–45.

14. I thank Nigel J. H. Smith for this information, and for a firsthand description of carnauba palms located around Monte Alegre in the Brazilian Amazon.

15. For a fuller discussion of these stories, see Slater 1994 and 2001. For an earlier study that provides an excellent basis for comparison, see Galvão 1955. Maués 1990 and Smith 1996 are also worth attention.

16. The figure of twenty-three million includes the less densely forested area called "Legal Amazonia" in Brazil. Without Legal Amazonia, the Amazon is home to slightly more than seventeen million persons, spread out over nine different nations. Some scholars do not include Suriname and French Guiana in their definitions of the Amazon, thereby reducing the total Amazonian population by approximately half a million.

17. The myth is one of various contemporary Shipibo narratives that appear in Roe 1982. Roe identifies the *iscohina* as an archaic form of Shipibo ceremonial costume in which a man dressed in a *tari* (cotton poncho) dangled a bunch of four *isco* tail feathers attached to a glass-beaded necklace suspended over his back. The *isco* (*paucar* in jungle Spanish), Roe notes, is a starling-sized bird, with a black body and brilliant yellow tail feathers. The *macana* is a kind of club.

18. The teller of this tale was a twenty-three-year-old man who had been born in the interior of Oriximiná on the Trombetas River. He was single and had worked as a plumber's assistant; he had had one year of high school, "but the honest truth, ma'am, is that neither myself nor any of my friends were much for books."

> Ora, esses botos são completamente safados. Vão lá nas festas e pegam as moças mais bonitas. Aí tinha um por aqui chamado Juliano, que sempre que tinha festa em Água Fria, Aréia Branca, esses lugares, ia lá dançar. Mostrava os bolsos cheios e de dólar e todas as meninas largaram os namorados para dançar com ele. Depois, ia para a rede da mais bonita, ficava a noite inteira até o sol raiar. Só que uma vez inventou mexer com uma menina por nome de Mariane. E o namorado desconfiou que fosse boto por causa do chapéu, e ia atrás. Deu uma surra nele que nunca mais apareceu por estas bandas. Bom, assim dizem. Mas veja bem, depois que começou chegar gente por tudo que é lado, tem muito menos Encantado de todo jeito. Acho que não aguentam o barulho daquelas máquinas que derrubam a mata para botar casa, não deve gostar também do grande calor. Pois onde não tem mata, faz um calor danado.

All quotations from Amazonian informants are taken from my tapes and fieldnotes made in various parts of the Brazilian Amazon between 1988 and 1999. The translations are my own.

19. See Guss 1985 for various other examples of interspecies communication.

20. This was a single, twenty-two-year-old man from Boa Vista who had also worked as a gold miner. He had had five years of grade school, "but honest, ma'am, it hasn't helped me."

21. This was a twenty-year-old woman, born in the interior of Juruti Velho and living in Parintins. Married ("but my husband has another"), she crocheted fringe for hammocks, and had had four years of grade school.

22. She had been born in Terra Preta. Married, she kept house and helped her husband farm; she had had no formal schooling, "but my mother taught all of us children a thing or two."

23. This was a married twenty-five-year-old man, born in the interior of Araguainha. He had had "little" schooling.

24. A large number of Amazonian rubber tappers originally came from the northeast, an area controlled in the 1600s by the Dutch, who intermarried with the local population. Many of those said to be their descendants have blue eyes and blond or reddish hair. To be sure, there were various other European settlers in the northeast as well as in the Amazon. The idea, if not biological reality, of Dutch ancestry nonetheless remains strong among some segments of the population.

25. This was told by a forty-two-year-old woman, born in the interior of Marantão. Married, she normally worked at odd jobs and had had four years of formal schooling.

> Veja bem, o Boto, ele é um gringo. Adora levar tudo que é dos outros e depois o pouco de grana que deixou em pagamento vira algas. Olhe, eu penso assim, que o Boto nem é boto. É tubarão, é todo aquele pessoal que não sabe outra coisa for a de roubar. Como o povo deixa estes safados ficarem roubando, ah, isso é o verdadeiro mistério do Encante. Pois não sei de onde o Boto veio ou onde anda, mas sei que a injustiça vem do começo do mundo.

26. For more on the Dolphin as a gringo, see Slater 1994, 202–32.

27. The story was told by a woman about sixty-five years old. Born in the Juruá region, she had lived in Parintins for the past seven years. She was widowed and supported by her children, and had had two years of schooling.

> Dizem que os Encantados não existem. Mas é assim que eles mesmo querem. O Boto, a Cobra Grande, gostam que os de fora digam que é tudo mentira,

acham bom quando eles dizem que o Encante é só fala do povinho. Assim que eles podem continuar a viver em paz. Porque se o pessoal de fora achasse que tivesse uma cidade de ouro por debaixo d'água, iam secar o rio inteiro até encontrar aquela riqueza. Então por isso, que o Encante sempre some. Pois se ficasse por aqui na vista de todo mundo, ninguém tinha sossego, pode confiar.

BIBLIOGRAPHY

Galvão, Eduardo Enéas. 1955. *Santos e visagens: Um estudo da vida religiosa de Itá.* São Paulo: Companhia Editora Nacional.

Guss, David M., ed. 1985. *The Language of the Birds: Tales, Texts, and Poems of Interspecies Communication.* San Francisco: North Point.

Henderson, Andrew. 1995. *The Palms of the Amazon.* Oxford: Oxford University Press.

Henderson, Andrew, Gloria Galeano, and Rodrigo Bernal. 1995. *The Palms of the Americas.* Princeton, N.J.: Princeton University Press.

Leite, Fernando Barboza. 1975. *Tipos e aspectos do Brasil: Excertos da Revista Brasileira de Geografia.* 10th revised edition. Rio de Janeiro: Departamento de Documentação e Geográfica e Cartográfica.

Maués, Raymundo Heraldo. 1990. *A ilha encantada: Medicina e xamanismo numa comunidade de pescadores.* Belém: Universidade Federal do Pará.

McDowell, John. 1998. "What Is Myth?" *Folklore Forum* 29, no. 2: 75–89.

Rabben, Linda. 1998. *Unnatural Selection: The Yanomami, the Kayapó, and the Onslaught of Civilisation.* Seattle: University of Washington Press.

Roe, Peter G. 1982. *The Cosmic Zygote: Cosmology in the Amazon Basin.* New Brunswick, N.J.: Rutgers University Press.

Slater, Candace. 1994. *Dance of the Dolphin: Transformation and Disenchantment in the Amazonian Imagination.* Chicago: University of Chicago Press.

———. 1995. "Amazonia as Edenic Narrative." In *Uncommon Ground: Towards a New Perspective in Environmentalism,* edited by William Cronon, Jr., 114–31. New York: W. W. Norton.

———. 2001. *Entangled Edens: Visions of the Amazon.* Berkeley and Los Angeles: University of California Press.

Smith, Nigel J. H. 1996. *The Enchanted Amazon Rain Forest: Stories from a Vanishing World.* Gainesville: University of Florida Press.

Tyrrell, Wm. Blake. 1984. *Amazons: A Study in Athenian Mythmaking.* Baltimore: Johns Hopkins University Press.

Wheelwright, Philip. 1958. "The Semantic Approach to Myth." In *Myth: A Symposium,* edited by Thomas A. Sebeok, 95–103. Bloomington: Indiana University Press.

ELEVEN

Distempered Demos:
Myth, Metaphor, and U.S. Political Culture

ROBERT L. IVIE

T he story of "democracy" as a symbol of national purpose is ironic in its capacity to alienate citizens from civic life and to set the United States at odds with the rest of the world. It displaces political power from the people to a ruling elite by portraying the demos as a primitive Other, not unlike the pagan outside the polity. Instead of promoting participatory politics domestically and internationally, it evokes potent rituals of republican fear to diminish the voice of the people while magnifying the threat of social disorder and global chaos. Such is the irony that reveals the significance of myth to a rhetorical republic, the trope that exposes opposing forms of power talk in a liberal democracy where liberalism struggles to contain democracy's unruly impulse without entirely dissociating itself from the legitimizing ethos of self-rule.[1] Since the very recognition of this irony would be an incentive to restore power to the people, mythic discourse continues to mask liberalism's dominance over democracy. Thus my goal is to explore the mythic function of the metaphor of disease as it has contributed to the degrading image of a distempered demos in U.S. political culture.

ROBUST DEMOCRACY IN ANCIENT ATHENS

In order to establish a useful point of comparison, I turn now briefly to the polis of ancient Athens, where a robust democratic culture emerged from the productive tensions among rhetoric, the demos, and the elite. I concur in Josiah Ober's judgment that the "Athenian example has a good deal to tell the modern world about the nature and potential of democracy as a form of social and political organization." As he observes, the demos "was master of Athens" when rhetoric "was a key form of democratic discourse" that mediated between ordinary and elite citizens well enough to allow for "direct democratic decision making" (Ober 1989, 9, 8, 338, 35). The contrast with U.S. political culture, where the masses are disciplined and rhetoric distrusted, is both remarkable and intriguing. Unlike democracy today, which is an insignia of good government but attenuated in actual practice, Athenian democracy was vigorously practiced during the fifth and fourth centuries B.C. even though condemned by philosophers in its own time.[2]

Although it restricted the franchise to freeborn males, Athenian democracy was direct rather than representative and thus lacked an "entrenched governing elite." Officials were typically selected by lot, given short terms and limited duties, and held accountable to judicial review by large panels of citizens. The Athenian Assembly, which comprised all citizens, met often and regularly to deliberate and vote on matters of state. A Council of five hundred citizens chosen by lot set the Assembly's agenda. Egalitarianism was an ingrained principle of Athenian politics, requiring elites to become reconciled with the masses in order to sustain social stability. "Along with drama in the theater and gossip in the streets," Ober notes, "public oratory, in the courts and the Assembly, was the most important form of ongoing verbal communication between ordinary and elite Athenians" (1989, 7, 31–32, 45). Orators, especially Athenian upper-class political orators who served as leaders of the people, were known as rhetors.

Although philosophers condemned rhetoric's centrality to Athenian democracy and criticized demagogues for appealing to emotion and prejudice, the Athenian citizen was neither perfectly logical nor simply irrational. "The successful orator," Ober argues, "was one who could consistently and seamlessly combine ideas drawn from mass ideology with moral principles and pragmatism in presenting a workable policy, a defense of his policy, or an attack on the policy of an opponent." Thus, the relationship of rhetor to demos was fraught with ambiguity and rich in complexity. Ordinary citizens were suspicious of the demagogue's powers of persuasion but expected from him entertaining oratory that instructed and influenced them on issues of public policy. Moreover, Athenian culture generally celebrated the intelligence of citizens and the wisdom of their collective decisions. The elite training and talent of the rhetor coexisted with an egalitarian faith in the general competency of the demos. The political orator in the Athenian democratic polity was expected to express the will of the people, to provide sound advice, and even to assume a leadership role when circumstances warranted. The role of rhetors as elite political leaders was to articulate "real alternatives on important issues" to assist the mass of citizens in making real political decisions (Ober 1989, 124, 178, 189–90, 314, 337). In this way, ancient Greeks achieved a discourse of democracy that assumed citizens were capable of ruling themselves.[3]

DISEASED DEMOCRACY IN
EIGHTEENTH-CENTURY AMERICA

Not so in eighteenth-century America, where democracy was reduced to a subordinate position in the constitutional design of the early republic, and a citizen among the masses was demoted from decision maker to bystander. During these formative years, a mythos of the demented demos was firmly established in U.S. political culture, so that the revered fiction of "the people" no longer referred to the assembled populace but instead to their representatives, elected and appointed from the political elite. By means of the metaphor of disease, the discourse of democracy was degraded so that it no longer presumed citizens capable of self-rule. As Alexander Hamilton declared at the constitutional convention of 1787, "The voice of the people has been said to be the voice of God; and however generally this maxim has been quoted and believed, it is not true in fact. The people are turbulent and changing; they seldom judge or determine right" (Farrand 1966, 1:299). Why? Because, as James Madison declared in Federalist 10, they lacked "a republican remedy for the diseases most incident" to popular government. "The instability, injustice, and confusion introduced into the public councils have, in truth," he continued, "been the mortal diseases under which popular councils have everywhere perished." Accordingly, Madison postulated in Federalist 55, "[h]ad every Athenian citizen been a Socrates, every Athenian assembly would still have been a mob" (Kramnick 1987, 128, 122, 336).

What was this republican remedy Madison concocted for the disease of popular government? To overcome the threat of anarchy that he perceived in the weak and overly democratic governments of certain states operating under the Articles of Confederation,[4] Madison proposed a "proper cure": the substitution of representative or republican government for the troubled regime of "pure democracy" or citizen self-rule, which could "admit of no cure for the mischiefs of faction." This strategy of "guarding against the confusion of a multitude" by "the delegation of the government . . . to a small number of citizens elected by the rest" would "refine and enlarge the public views by passing them through the medium of a chosen body of citizens, whose wisdom may best discern the true interest of their country." The "public voice, pronounced by the representatives of the people," Madison surmised, would prove to be "more consonant to the public good than if pronounced by the people themselves" (Federalist 10 in Kramnick 1987, 122, 126, 127). Democracy, according to Richard Matthews (1995, 51, 55), was to Madison "a fool's illusion"; cool reason could only be exercised by individuals in isolation because people assembled in groups stirred hot passions that overrode reason and justice. Thus, as a safeguard against this "infection of violent passions," Madison observed in Federalist 63 that the "true distinction" between the pure democracies of ancient Greece and the proposed republic of the United States "lies *in the total exclusion of the people in their collective capacity*" from any share in government (Kramnick 1987, 373; emphasis in original).

Metaphor and the Myth of Reason

Curiously, Madison never addressed the question of why even an assembly of citizens as wise as Socrates would succumb to "the confusion and intemperance of a multitude." He merely presumed that "in all very numerous assemblies, of whatever characters composed, passion never fails to wrest the scepter from reason" (Federalist 55 in Kramnick 1987, 336). Thus, as Matthews notes about the man who promoted an "empire of reason," one of the main premises of his "entire theoretical edifice rests on an unchallenged philosophic assumption not grounded in reason." One is left wondering, then, on what insight this pessimistic view of humanity was based, especially when Madison's good friend Thomas Jefferson "conceived of citizenship as an ennobling activity" instead of a tyranny of popular passions, which Madison identified as the mortal affliction of prior republics (Matthews 1995, 23, 66, 240, 243).

Perhaps an answer to this question is suggested by Madison's personal fixation on disease. This man, who was the principal architect of the nation-building federal Constitution, also was a secret epileptic and perpetual hypochondriac who dressed in black and anticipated death throughout much of his adulthood. He lived to the age of eighty-five but thought of himself by age twenty-one as too "infirm" to "expect a long or healthy life" (Matthews 1995, 4). Throughout adulthood, according to his biographer Robert Rutland (1990, 20, 105–106), Madison regularly complained of "high fevers, diarrhea, or seizures." Another biographer, Irving Brant (1941, 106–107), has diagnosed Madison as suffering from the psychic trauma of hysterical epilepsy rather than any organic form of the disease. Thus, as Matthews (1995, 5) observes, it should not be too surprising that Madison relied on medical imagery throughout his public writing to characterize a "sick and fatal republic."

If Madison's deity was Reason, his devil was Disease. Perhaps his greatest fear was letting a distempered demos loose in the delicately balanced republic he had so carefully designed to slow the inevitable, long-term decay of political order and to preserve the property rights and power of the elite minority against the tyranny of an irrational majority. "If men were angels," he wrote, "no government would be necessary" (Federalist 51 in

Kramnick 1987, 319). In mass, they become demonic creatures infected by Passion when Reason should rule. Clearly, it seems to me, Madison was witness to a great struggle of mythic proportions in which storied deities such as Reason, Disease, and Passion were implicated in the founding of a nation and the constitution of a political cosmos. Madison's Calvinist universe must ultimately fail, but he called upon Reason to postpone the inevitable decay (Matthews 1995, 244).

The mythos of the distempered demos is of particular interest for what it illustrates about the mythic function of Madison's disease metaphor and thus, more generally, the relationship of myth to metaphor in a context of cultural critique. If we wish not only to describe and account for myth but also to engage and transform problematic appropriations of myth in political culture, then metaphor serves both as an indicator of myth's otherwise invisible and reified presence and as a heuristic for critical reinterpretation and rhetorical reconstruction. This is not to say that metaphor is an instrument for transcending myth or a bridge from primitive irrationalism to enlightened rationality, but instead to acknowledge that myth in one form or another is a necessary presence in political culture and the origin of any rationale or rationality. Reason is grounded in perspective and culture. To modify a mythic formation is to revise a cultural logic, and metaphor is our most tangible access to mythic thought in its present iterations and potential applications. Myth and metaphor, operating on a continuum of figurative and literal expression, cycle from fiction to ideology and back again according to their use.

As the locus of creativity and innovation and an indispensable cultural resource for apprehending the unknown (Arden King, cited in Black 1973, 542), myth operates in the realm of metaphor. Pursuing this theme, Turbayne (1970, 19, 59) suggests that myth consists of "extended or sustained metaphors" that can be "taken literally" as the "correct" or "best explanation of the facts" in an otherwise incoherent and disorienting existence. Metaphors, as condensed analogies, articulate relations that establish basic structures of reality from which we can reason practically about contingencies of human existence (Perelman and Olbrechts-Tyteca 1969, 398–405). Thus, Northrop Frye (1990, 7) argues that myth and metaphor are inseparable. In each, similarities are expressed as identities and essences (Cassirer 1955: 67), but always with the possibility of reconfiguring them to redescribe reality. In Nietzsche's famous words, truth is but a

> movable host of metaphors, metonymies, and anthropomorphisms: in short, a sum of human relations which have been poetically and rhetorically intensified, transferred, and embellished, and which, after long usage, seem to a people to be fixed, canonical, and binding. Truths are illusions which we

have forgotten are illusions; they are metaphors that have become worn out
and have been drained of sensuous force, coins which have lost their em-
bossing and are now considered as metal and no longer as coins. (1979, 84)

Nietzsche's overman, whom we might associate with cultural critique and
renovation, overcomes truth's blinders not just to debunk a reified metaphor but to renew the mythic quest itself, for the conventionalized metaphors to which we have become accustomed are those that are presently
taken literally and therefore mistaken for reality but remain subject to delit-
eralization and novel applications that would restore their figurative force.
As metaphor functions mythically to rearticulate relations of meaning, it
thereby exercises a human will to power by reordering political relations. It
is the source of cultural stability and decay in its literalized presence, and
for Nietzsche it is also the site of meaning's fluidity and thus the essence of
eternal flux, human creativity, and cultural revitalization (Cantor 1982, 72,
75–77).

Accordingly, Stephen Daniel (1990, 10, 12, 4, 6) treats metaphors as
myths in miniature or, following Giambattista Vico, as abbreviated myths,
arguing that just as "complexes of metaphors . . . constitute myths,"
metaphors "serve as the elements of change within myth." This creative
function, this act of genesis, which presents "a world that only becomes
meaningful in virtue of the account given in the mythic expression," exists
only in the telling and retelling of the myth. Experience, through the ritual
of performing a myth, is organized "in ways that validate claims, establish
values, and identify problems." Thus metaphors, such as Madison's metaphor of disease, fulfill the mythic function of inventing a universe of meaning and interpretation, of providing the presuppositions of any thought
about political community and the origins of any understanding of the
people and their capacity for self-governance, indeed, of generating the existence of such a world and even the possibility of its being known. Each expression of such a metaphor recreates a mythic world and, in each unique or
variant performance, the possibility and even risk of realigning that reality.
Rationality, including Madison's deity of Reason, does not exist as the rationale behind the myth but instead is itself established in the performance
of a myth.[5] There is no origin of meaning beyond metaphor performing its
mythic function. It is the irreducibly arbitrary antecedent of historical understandings as well as of new or emerging interpretations. As such, Daniel
(1990, 33) concludes, metaphor and myth, in "their irresolvably creative
character," are "the indicators of the aboriginal character of a pattern of
thought."

Moreover, when myth determines worldviews, as William Doty (1996,
449, 452, 451) explains, myth and ideology become synonymous. Even as

myth "taps into the imaginative human propensities" it remains "a component of rational discourse," and when it is interpreted literally it produces normative prescriptions. The metaphoric and mythic side of culture brings the connotative and analogical dimensions of meaning into play with their denotative and logical extensions to produce serious and authoritative stories that Bruce Lincoln (1989, 24, 25) compares to "charters, models, templates, and blueprints"—mythic acts that evoke "the sentiments out of which society is actively constructed."

Yet, even in this reified or literalized state as social charters and political blueprints, mythic metaphors are seldom, if ever, completely unrecognizable or inaccessible for purposes of reconfiguring relations of meaning and power. At the surface of a narrative text or performance one can usually identify a number of figurative terms and readily mark them as metaphorical vehicles. Once attention is initially drawn in this way to these particular vehicles as figurative vestiges of myths that have been reified into conceptual language, other conventionalized terms throughout the text or performance begin to reveal their figurative origins. With each repeated observation, the operation of the myth itself comes increasingly into view through the clusters of previously literalized metaphors by which it was constituted into a conceptual system and model for aligning political relations (Ivie 1997b, 73–74; 1997a, 104–107).

"Disease," the case in point, is a charter or model of a distempered people that deconstructed the democratic discourse of citizen self-rule and constituted in its place an unthinking, irrational mob whose emotions are preyed upon by demagogues, a common herd that lacks sufficient virtue to consider the good of the community. Madison's oft-repeated metaphors, with which he ritualistically rehearsed throughout the Federalist papers this legitimizing story for a republican constitution of representative, or weak, democracy, included references to a "proper cure" for "dangerous vice," "confusion," "mortal diseases," and the "impulse of passion" to "convulse a society," to "curing the mischiefs of faction," a "remedy" for being "inflamed with mutual animosity," "the confusion of a multitude," "rage," and "malady," an "antidote for the diseases of faction," "alarming symptoms," "the most dark and degrading pictures which display the infirmities and depravities of the human character," "the pestilential influence of party animosities [which is] the disease most incident to deliberative bodies and most apt to contaminate their proceedings," "a patient who finds his disorder daily growing worse," that which would "inflame the passions of the unthinking," the "miseries springing from [America's] internal jealousies," and "a defense to the people against their own temporary errors and delusions" and "the infection of violent passions."

Others performed similar metaphorical rituals. Hamilton referred, in his contributions to the Federalist papers, to "a torrent of angry and malignant passions," "domestic factions and convulsions," popular assemblies "subject to the impulses of rage, resentment, jealousy, avarice, and of other irregular and violent propensities," faction as the "poison in the deliberations of all bodies of men," and even "the contagion of some violent popular paroxysm." Not surprisingly, less famous participants in the public debate over the Constitution regularly performed the myth of the distempered and incompetent demos as well, lacing their discourse with images of "the folly and blindness of the people," "haranguing the Rabble," the public becoming "dupes" to "those who wish to influence [their] passions," the threat of "popular rage," and, ultimately, the danger of "fits of passion" and "paroxisms" (Bailyn 1993, 13, 15, 33, 132, 133).

With these sentiments, a nation was constituted in the 1780s that, as Gordon Wood (1969, 595) observes, was a peculiar kind of democracy—a democratic republic or representative democracy in which representation was grafted upon democracy. The principle of representation was the "pivot," in Madison's view, on which the American system moved, the redemptive source of rationality that the ancient Athenians had lacked (Federalist 63 in Kramnick 1987, 372). All officials in every branch of the government, not just the elected representatives in the House, became agents of, and thus substitutes for, the people, thus taking "the people out of the government altogether." Representation was the "healing principle" that would arrest the "decay and eventual death of the republican body politic" by allowing "the natural aristocracy" to "assert itself and dominate" a government that operated in the name of the people as if it were the people. These nation-builders believed they had broken the cycle of history by telling the story of a people who "could diagnose the ills of its society and work out a peaceable process of cure," the story of "a constitutional antidote 'wholly popular' and 'strictly republican' for the ancient diseases" of a purely democratic polity. This story produced a Constitution which "was intrinsically an aristocratic document designed to check the democratic tendencies of the period" with "an elitist theory of democracy" (Wood 1969, 599, 606, 613, 614, 513, 517). The people, who could not be trusted to govern themselves because of their infirmities and intemperate passions, were reinvented as a national sovereignty transcending local government and dispersed throughout the federal authority. In short, Madison's mythic metaphor of a distempered demos legitimized the invention of a sovereign people who were disembodied and removed from self-rule through the fiction of representation, all of which was designed, as Edmund Morgan (1988, 267, 282, 286) concludes, "to secure popular consent to a governing aristocracy." Wood (1969, 562) concurs that this achievement, "using the most popular and democratic rhetoric available to explain and justify [an] aristocratic system," produced "a distinctly American political theory" that impoverished "later American political thought."

Madison's metaphor of disease, a truncated myth of the public's political incompetence, told a very different tale of Athenian direct democracy than Josiah Ober's more nuanced version of a robust citizenry assembled in ancient Greece to make genuine decisions on important issues by deliberating actual alternatives advanced in public oratory. Madison's performance of the myth of the demos altered its meaning and valence by varying its metaphoric expression. Demagogues were transformed from upper-class political orators who instructed, advised, and led the deliberations of the assembled citizenry into deceitful and fractious manipulators of popular prejudice. Madison's demagogue made "ignorance . . . the dupe of cunning, and passion the slave of sophistry and declamation"; the people, forever "subject to the infection of violent passions," could only be "misled by the artful misrepresentations of interested men." Accordingly, in Madison's mythic account, the people of Athens were incompetent to reason or judge the truth. They might have escaped their "bitter anguish" only by living in a republic instead of a "turbulent democracy," a republic guided by a principle of representation that removed the demos from the seat of power in order to protect the multitude from "the tyranny of their own passions" and the nation from "the violence of faction." Through the metaphor of disease, Madison derived the notion that men were not angels—a mythic creation for apprehending the unknown—and therefore that the people must be controlled by government rather than allowed to govern themselves (Federalist 58, 63, 14, 10, and 51 in Kramnick 1987, 351, 371, 141, 371, 122, 319–20). Thus he invoked the Enlightenment god of Reason as his ultimate constitutional authority.

Jefferson's Dormant Mythos

A different story of the people might have been told if Thomas Jefferson had been invited to participate in the formative deliberations of the Constitutional convention of 1787 instead of remaining in Paris as minister to France, for Jefferson's more favorable inclinations toward democracy were premised on a metaphor of life rather than death. Moreover, Jefferson seemed more in touch with the mythic rhythm of political life than Madison, whose mechanistic and instrumental Reason shrouded the myths he lived by in a veil of literal truth. In Jefferson's view, as he wrote to Charles Thompson in September 1787, "[t]he moment a person forms a theory his imagination sees in every object only the traits which favor that theory" (quoted in Matthews 1984, 1). Where Madison had a liberal faith in the private individual, as Matthews (1984, 18) points out, Jefferson was convinced that "man was a social, harmonious, cooperative, and just creature who, under the appropriate socioeconomic conditions, could happily live in a community that did not need the presence of the Leviathan," that indeed humans require one another's presence to make life meaningful and that sharing the tragedy endemic to social life promotes healing (Matthews 1995, 241). Similarly, Jefferson's mythic sensibility was reflected in arguments constructed self-consciously on first principles, which he labeled "self-evident," and on his commitment to the "moral sense" of man's heart, rather than the reason of his head, as the means of living in tranquility (Matthews 1984, 20; 1995, 239). As Matthews (1984, 43) notes, the pastoral Jefferson relied on a "figurative, mythopoetic language [eschewing "the sparse, arid, and analytic language of political economy"] to capture more adequately his image of a democratic society."

One witnesses these Jeffersonian qualities in the creation myth of the People who, as he proclaims in the Declaration of Independence, assume "the separate and equal station to which the laws of nature and of nature's God entitle them" and declare certain "truths to be self-evident: that all men are created equal; that they are endowed by their Creator with certain unalienable rights," including "life, liberty, and the pursuit of happiness," and that governments, "deriving their just powers from the consent of the governed," are "instituted among men" and also "abolished" by "the people" as necessary to secure their rights. The ideology evoked by this positive image of democratic revolution was averse to Madison's Constitutional taming of the demos. Jefferson instead advocated a system of participatory ward politics, dividing counties into units small enough for citizens to act in person on matters related exclusively to them, and embraced the idea of a revolution every generation to renew the people's commitment to the laws by which they are governed (Matthews 1984, 81).

This mythic cycle of rebirth and renewal every twenty years was an expression of faith in the resilience of the people and the perpetuity of the nation. Garry Wills's recovery of Jefferson as essentially a man of the Enlightenment, which is intended to counter Lincoln's romantic appropriation of the Declaration of Independence, only underscores key differences between Madison's mythic constitution of death and Jefferson's mythic declaration of life. Lincoln's mythic version, Wills argues, created "the cult of the Declaration as a mystical founding document," which, among other negative consequences, encouraged a belief in America's "extraordinary birth, outside the processes of time," and "led us to think of ourselves as a nation apart, with a special destiny, the hope of all those outside America's shores" (1978, xix). Wills counters Lincoln by reconnecting Jefferson to the Enlightenment context in which his contemporaries, including Madison, operated, but not without capturing Jefferson's difference and uniqueness. Even as a man who preferred to do things by the numbers, for instance, Jefferson expressed himself in the mythical rhythm of life, decay, and rebirth, which is the spirit in which his observations of nature and mathematical operations were conducted. In Wills's words, "Since living men should not be bound by the will of the dead, no contract's term should be extended for more than nineteen (or in the rounded number, twenty) years. This is the numerical path Jefferson trod to some of his most famous and revered statements—e.g., that 'the earth belongs in usufruct to the living'" (1978, 124). Just as Jefferson felt deprived of a chance to participate in the drafting of the Constitution, he believed the continuing health of the republic required faith in a radical, revolutionary ethic that Madison, who imagined a fundamentally sick nation, was sure could lead only to anarchy. Where Madison's view amounted to "the rule of the dead from beyond the grave," Jefferson himself, as he told John Adams, found "the dreams of the future better than the history of the past" (Matthews 1984, 85; 1995, 244, 259, 262).

My purpose is not to account for why Madison's fictive image of the people prevailed over Jefferson's effort to rehearse an old story of direct, radical democracy, although such an account would be a worthy and interesting study of the contextual, or intertextual, dynamics of myth-making in U.S. political culture. The fact is that Jefferson's was a lone voice among the founders in expressing so much faith in the demos (Matthews 1984, 81). Nor could the arguments of the anti-Federalists in his day break the spell of republicanism. Even today, Jefferson's image of participatory politics as a democratic balance to Madison's liberalism remains largely dormant and well outside of conventional wisdom within an American commercial republic. The standard, self-sustaining image is of the people as an unthinking mob, violent and destructive, whose emotions are preyed upon by demagogues and who lack sufficient virtue to consider the good of the community. Madison's republican remedy instantiated a mostly rich ruling class as the people, a governing elite anguishing episodically over outbreaks of popular politics and the decline in standards of public discourse, as when Andrew Jackson assumed the presidency in 1828—a governing elite that deftly advanced the business model of expert democracy in the guise of direct democracy at the turn of the century and that today rallies under the flag of deliberative democracy.

This tradition of a fearful, elitist discourse of democratic distemper summoned by present-day proponents of rational deliberation aims to tame the popular passions aroused by the rhetorical republic. Deliberative democracy, according to the likes of James Fishkin (1991, 1, also Bessett 1994), is a rational antidote for such demagoguery, a way to "reconcile" democracy and deliberation. The aim of this movement is to preserve the

integrity of representative or liberal democracy against the threat of an un-
enlightened and unreflective mass public exercising direct authority, or at
least being appealed to directly by the president over the heads of Congress
in this age of mass communication. Thus passion remains the infirmity of
the people, enslaving them to the cunning of contemporary sophistry.
When policy serves rhetoric instead of reason, according to this mythic
construction, it infects the majority with a tyrannizing passion to trample
the rights of the minority elite. This frightful image of a rhetorical republic
persists as an ungovernable assemblage of destructive forces.[6]

INVISIBLE MYTH

As I say, my purpose is not to explain how or why this debilitating image
of the public persists but instead to call attention to its mythic function.
Whether the mythos of the demented demos is rehearsed in the scholarly
works of political theorists and philosophers decrying the poor state of
public deliberation, calling for a reasonable and rational democratic practice, and wishing for the return of a vibrant civil society, or takes the form
of popular culture on daily television talk shows and news programs that
repeatedly dramatize in so many different ways the standard story of an ignorant, distracted, and fickle public, such ritualized performances sustain
an arbitrary but conventional fiction of the people that discourages any experimentation with participatory politics, for who would want their fate
determined by rogues and fools? It is not difficult to discern the implications of this way of thinking. Clearly, one should wish for a more vibrant
public sphere and a reinvigorated civil society but recognize, given the
choice between angels and devils, that a liberal democracy which contains
the irrational impulses of everyday citizens is the only realistic option. To
engage the people directly is to risk political dysfunction and social disorder. The domestic Other has to be controlled—transformed and embodied
symbolically as a governing elite—rather than addressed and asked to decide on matters of public policy, no less than the foreign Other has to be
disciplined by the financial, moral, and military superiority of the United
States in its capacity as the only remaining superpower and sole essential
nation. "Realistically," that is, the United States must remain as fearful of
the world at large as it has always been of the unruly domestic multitude.[7]

That much is clear so long as this particular myth remains literalized in
U.S. political culture. The difficulty of seeing reality as myth, of discerning
the myths we live by, is compounded by the distinction we routinely make
between history and fiction. The stories we tell about ourselves from within a culture are taken as historical fact; the stories we observe at a distance in
exotic cultures and report as outsiders are deemed figurative and fictional

musings about the mysteries of "life, death, divinity, and existence" (Baldick 1990, 143; Black 1973, 542). This latter group consists of "crucial 'framing stories' that are *treated* as 'true' by the people who tell them" in order to "provide justification for a social structure" through appeals to "a great hero [who] can conquer evil." Such myths occur "outside of normal historical time" and "outside of the normal world" while relying heavily on archetypal language (Rowland 1990, 103–104). Primary myths interpreted literally and internalized as ideology remain invisible to us even as they determine our own worldview, our ethics, and our sense of the rational. For how can children of the Enlightenment recognize themselves as "Odysseus, sacker of cities, the sceptre in his hand, and by his side flashing-eyed Athene, in the likeness of a herald" as they, too, rise to speak to the multitude (*Iliad* 2:280–85)? What reveals our own history as myth even as we invoke the god of Reason to dispel the curse of mass hysteria? The answer I offer is that these myths are condensed in key metaphors, such as our standard association of the public with vehicles of disease, and that the stories they tell can reveal more clearly to us the arbitrary origins of our most basic beliefs and values. The better we come to understand the myths we live by, the greater our opportunity of awakening from the republican nightmare of demented demons everywhere.

NOTES

1. For a discussion of liberalism and democracy as opposing forms of power talk, see Hanson 1985, 13–15.

2. For a recent and thorough treatment of Athenian democracy, see Hansen 1999.

3. On the linguistic assumption of citizens' competency for self-rule, see Hanson and Marcus 1993, 3, and Barber 1993. For further discussion of the role of the orator and citizenship in the Athenian democracy, see Yunis 1996 and Poulakos 1997.

4. See Matthews 1995, 48–49.

5. On this point, see Daniel 1990, 10.

6. For a critical review of this literature on the rhetorical republic, see Ivie 1996, 157–66.

7. The theoretical and normative literature on deliberative democracy, which problematically features rational deliberation as the salvation of an unruly democracy, is critiqued by Mouffe (2000). Also see Ivie on "Democratic Deliberation in a Rhetorical Republic" (1998, 491–505). For a treatment of how America's continuing fear of the demos works its will ironically in the post–Cold War foreign policy of democratization, see Ivie 2000 and 2001.

BIBLIOGRAPHY

Bailyn, Bernard, ed. 1993. *The Debate on the Constitution.* New York: The Library of America. Distributed by Viking.

Baldick, Chris. 1990. *The Concise Oxford Dictionary of Literary Terms.* New York: Oxford University Press.

Barber, Benjamin. 1993. "Reductionist Political Science and Democracy." In *Reconsidering the Democratic Public,* edited by George E. Marcus and Russell L. Hanson, 65–72. University Park: Pennsylvania State University Press.

Bessett, Joseph M. 1994. *The Mild Voice of Reason: Deliberative Democracy and American National Government.* Chicago: University of Chicago Press.

Black, Mary B. 1973. "Belief Systems." In *Handbook of Social and Cultural Anthropology,* edited by John J. Honigmann, 509–77. Chicago: Rand McNally College Publishing Company.

Brant, Irving. 1941. *James Madison.* Indianapolis: Bobbs-Merrill.

Cantor, Paul. 1982. "Friedrich Nietzsche: The Use and Abuse of Metaphor." In *Metaphor: Problems and Perspectives,* edited by David S. Miall, 71–88. Atlantic Highlands, N.J.: Humanities.

Cassirer, Ernst. 1955. *The Philosophy of Symbolic Forms: Mythical Thought.* Translated by Ralph Manheim. New Haven, Conn.: Yale University Press.

Daniel, Stephen H. 1990. *Myth and Modern Philosophy.* Philadelphia: Temple University Press.

Doty, William G. 1996. "Myth." In *Encyclopedia of Rhetoric and Composition: Communication from Ancient Times to the Information Age,* edited by Theresa Enos, 449–52. New York: Garland.

Farrand, Max, ed. 1966. *The Records of the Federal Convention of 1787.* Revised edition, 4 vols. New Haven, Conn.: Yale University Press.

Fishkin, James S. 1991. *Democracy and Deliberation: New Directions for Democratic Reform.* New Haven, Conn.: Yale University Press.

Frye, Northrop. 1990. "The Koine of Myth: Myth as a Universally Intelligible Language." In *Myth and Metaphor: Selected Essays, 1974–1988,* edited by Robert D. Denham, 3–17. Charlottesville: University Press of Virginia.

Hansen, Mogens Herman. 1999. *The Athenian Democracy in the Age of Demosthenes: Structure, Principles, and Ideology.* Translated by J. A. Crook. Revised edition. Norman: University of Oklahoma Press, 1999.

Hanson, Russell L. 1985. *The Democratic Imagination in America: Conversations with Our Past.* Princeton, N.J.: Princeton University Press.

Hanson, Russell L., and George E. Marcus. 1993. "Introduction: The Practice of Democratic Theory." In *Reconsidering the Democratic Public,* edited by George E. Marcus and Russell L. Hanson, 1–32. University Park: Pennsylvania State University Press.

Ivie, Robert L. 1996. "Tragic Fear and the Rhetorical Presidency: Combating Evil in the Persian Gulf." In *Beyond the Rhetorical Presidency,* edited by Martin J. Medhurst, 153–78. College Station: Texas A&M University Press.

———. 1997a. "Metaphor and the Rhetorical Invention of Cold War 'Idealists'." In *Cold War Rhetoric: Strategy, Metaphor, and Ideology,* by Martin J. Medhurst et al., revised edition, 103–27. East Lansing: Michigan State University Press.

———. 1997b. "Cold War Motives and the Rhetorical Metaphor: A Framework of Criticism." In *Cold War Rhetoric: Strategy, Metaphor, and Ideology,* by Martin J. Medhurst, et al., revised edition, 71–79. East Lansing: Michigan State University Press.

———. 1998. "Democratic Deliberation in a Rhetorical Republic." *Quarterly Journal of Speech* 84:491–505.

———. 2000. "A New Democratic World Order?" In *Critical Reflections on the Cold War: Linking Rhetoric and History,* edited by Martin J. Medhurst and H. W. Brands, 247–65. College Station: Texas A&M University Press.

————. 2001. "Democratizing for Peace." *Rhetoric and Public Affairs* 4:309–22.

Kramnick, Isaac, ed. 1987. *The Federalist Papers.* New York: Penguin.

Lincoln, Bruce. 1989. *Discourse and the Construction of Society: Comparative Studies of Myth, Ritual, and Classification.* New York: Oxford University Press.

Matthews, Richard K. 1984. *The Radical Politics of Thomas Jefferson: A Revisionist View.* Lawrence: University Press of Kansas.

————. 1995. *If Men Were Angels: James Madison and the Heartless Empire of Reason.* Lawrence: University Press of Kansas.

Morgan, Edmund S. 1988. *Inventing the People: The Rise of Popular Sovereignty in England and America.* New York: W. W. Norton.

Mouffe, Chantal. 2000. *The Democratic Paradox.* London: Verso.

Nietzsche, Friedrich. 1979. "On the Truth and Lies in a Nonmoral Sense." In *Philosophy and Truth: Selections from Nietzsche's Notebooks of the Early 1870's,* edited and translated by Daniel Breazeale, 79–97. Amherst, N.Y.: Humanity.

Ober, Josiah. 1989. *Mass and Elite in Democratic Athens: Rhetoric, Ideology, and the Power of the People.* Princeton, N.J.: Princeton University Press.

Perelman, Chaim, and Lucie Olbrechts-Tyteca. 1969. *The New Rhetoric: A Treatise on Argumentation.* Translated by John Wilkinson and Purcell Weaver. Notre Dame, Ind.: University of Notre Dame Press.

Poulakos, Takis. 1997. *Speaking for the Polis: Isocrates' Rhetorical Education.* Columbia: University of South Carolina Press.

Rowland, Robert C. 1990. "On Mythic Criticism." *Communication Studies* 41:101–16.

Rutland, Robert A. 1990. *The Presidency of James Madison.* Lawrence: University Press of Kansas, 1990.

Turbayne, Colin Murray. 1970. *The Myth of Metaphor.* Revised edition. Columbia: University of South Carolina Press.

Wills, Garry. 1978. *Inventing America: Jefferson's Declaration of Independence.* Garden City, N.Y.: Doubleday.

Wood, Gordon S. 1969. *The Creation of the American Republic, 1776–1787.* New York: W. W. Norton.

Yunis, Harvey. 1996. *Taming Democracy: Models of Political Rhetoric in Classical Athens.* Ithaca, N.Y.: Cornell University Press.

Part V

MYTH AND VISUAL ART

TWELVE

Imitation or Reconstruction: How Did Roman Viewers Experience Mythological Painting?

ELEANOR W. LEACH

From time to time in Ovid's *Metamorphoses,* persons who are asked to tell stories rehearse a list of possible subjects in the process of making a decision (*Met.* 4; 8). The invitation to speak about any aspect of mythology in ancient art poses a similar challenge of decision making, since mythology was virtually the most favored subject for representation in Greek and Roman artistic culture, but the topic I shall discuss here, Roman viewers' response to mythological painting, is in keeping with a conference focused upon functions of mythology in context. Behind the question of my title there lies, of course, a methodological question: "How does a classicist go about investigating the viewer's response to, or evaluation of, mythological painting?" In exploring some links between verbal and visual texts with a dimension of social relevance, I hope to cast some light upon the larger question: how Romans in general viewed mythology, which had a certain remoteness about it as a commodity imported from a foreign culture, but with which they also enjoyed a certain intimacy, since it was an element of everyday life.

Roman mythological paintings, as we know them, form part of the environment of everyday life because they are painted directly on walls with a kind of fresco technique. The vast majority of extant examples are those preserved by the catastrophic eruption of Mount Vesuvius in A.D. 79, which buried cities and villas in the territory of Campania. Naturally they represent only a small survival from a once incalculably large corpus of ancient mythological paintings, some of which were painted on movable tablets that could be carried from place to place. A few of these paintings decorate such public buildings as a market place or a temple of Isis, but the greater number by far are in domestic contexts. Because of this domestic location we can focus our questions upon the owner of the house and the guests who are the hypothetical audience for his pictures. Are these pictures purely aesthetic objects valued for the qualities of their artistry? Are they economic goods with investment value? Are they status symbols or spatial fillers? Did their subjects matter at all?

Roman negotiations with mythology are constructed within cultural frameworks. The framework of my first example is actually double; it is a picture within a picture. I will begin with a passage in St. Augustine's *Confessions* (1.16) that frames a mythological picture within a context of late Roman rhetorical education, an institution that the good bishop melodramatically calls the "river of human custom" "that rolls the sons of Eve into a great and fearful sea." Augustine is talking about the way in which he and other students first encountered stories about gods and heroes in the early stages of the studies that prepared them for rhetorical practice. As Augustine speaks of Jupiter "both thundering and committing adulteries" we hear clear echoes of Plato's voice proclaiming against the false impressions of deities given by Homer and Hesiod, but Augustine adds a graphic flourish to this familiar topic when he incorporates lines from Terence's comedy *Eunuchus,* one of the texts he read in school:

> At quem deum! (Inquit) qui templa caeli summo
>   sonitu concutit
> ego homuncio id non facerem? Ego vero illud
>   Feci ac libens.[1]

> "But what a god" (says he), "the one who shakes the precincts of the sky with consummate sound! Shouldn't I, little man that I am, do likewise? Indeed I did that and even gladly." [This and all other translations are my own.]

Augustine cites this passage to illustrate how students learn rhetoric by imitating literary models. Models may have elegant diction, but their pagan content is corruptive. The passage itself concerns imitation of a physical rather than a literary kind, as a young man who has just ravished a virgin justifies his sexual aggression by a celestial example. Claiming to have taken his inspiration from a picture of Zeus descending in a golden shower for the rape of Danae, he boasts how he has made out like the god. Not only does Augustine quote directly the young man's response to the painting, but also he incorporates directly the words that describe the picture in Terence's text:

> Ita ergo non cognosceremus verba haec, imbrem et aureum et gremium et fucum et templa caeli et alia verba, quae in eo loco scripta sunt, nisi Teren-

tius induceret nequam adulescentem, proponentem sibi Jovem ad exemplum stupri, dum spectat tabulam quandam pictam in pariete, ubi inerat pictura haec, Iovem quo pacto Danae misisse aiunt in gremium quondam imbrem aureum, fucum factum mulieri?

So therefore should we never have understood the words rain and golden and lap and painted and precincts of the sky and the other words that are written in this place unless Terence had brought in this wastrel youth proposing to himself Jove as an example of lust while he looked at a certain painted tablet on the wall in which there was painted these things the way in which they say that Jupiter once sent a golden rain shower into the lap of Danae, a painted deed of deception?

What Augustine omits, of course, in abstracting this passage from its place in the comedy is the humorousness of the situation in which the young lover makes his boast. Like Jupiter, he has entered a house in disguise, scarcely by transforming himself into a golden shower, but rather by borrowing the clothes of an aged eunuch—hence the play's title—which his elder brother had intended as a gift for the courtesan Thais, in whose house the girl of his fancy is living as a guest. Thais knows something that the lover does not know: that the girl is, in fact, a well-born virgin, whom she is planning to reunite with her lost brother, now living in Athens. When her citizen status becomes known, the lover will marry the girl, but that is beside the point here. Knowing nothing of the girl's origins, the young man contrives a plan of access; he borrows the clothes of an old eunuch sent to Thais by her admirer, his elder brother. The audience is in on the trick. Being assigned in this safe-seeming costume to attend in the girl's chamber, he watches her toilet and observes the painted image on the wall (*Eunuchus* 583–89):

> Dum adparatur, virgo in conclavi sedet
> suspectans tabulam quandam pictam: ibi inerat pictura haec,
> Iovem
> quo pacto Danaae misisse aiunt quondam in gremium imbrem
> aureum.
> egomet quoque id spectare coepi, et quia consimilem luserat
> iam olim ille ludum, impendio magis animu' gaudebat mihi
> deum sese in hominem convortisse atque in alienas tegulas
> venisse clanculum per inpluvium fucum factum mulieri.

While she was being dressed, the virgin sat in the chamber looking at a certain scene painted on a tablet in which was represented the way in which they say that Jove once dropped a rain of gold into the lap of Danae. I also began looking at it and since he had already

once staged a similar deception it pleased my mind all the more
that the god had transformed himself and had come stealing over
foreign roof-tiles through the impluvium to work his deception on
the woman.

The passage could not serve the moralist's purpose more aptly, since it involves not only a double tier of imitations but also a double deception. Because parents are paying good money for their sons to learn their language
lessons from such examples, the myth, with its rain, gold, lap, etc., constitutes the very paradigm of deception paid out in coinage. "Could we not
have understood these words otherwise?" Augustine asks. "See in which
way the young man roused himself to desire as if by a celestial teacher? Not
only are the words more easily learned through this shame," as he goes on
to say, "but through these words debauchery itself is the more confidently
perpetrated."

What should we think of the moral that Augustine imposes upon Terence, that mythological paintings are enemies of virtue? We can actually
find a classical poet, the elegist Propertius, making a similar point in a poem
that seems likely to constitute an intertextual play upon Terence, since it
begins with the House of Thais (2.6.1–4):

> Non ita complebant Ephyraeae Laidos aedis,
>   ad cuius iacuit Graecia tota fores;
> turba Menandreae fuerat nec Thaidos olim
>   tanta, in qua populus lusit Ericthonius.

> Not as full was the house of Corinthian Lais at whose door all Greece
> used to camp, nor was ever upon a time such a crowd for Menander's
> Thais where the populace of Ericthonius played.

Propertius's poet-lover uses this comparison to criticize the comings and
goings of men in and out of his mistress's house. She calls them "kissing
cousins"; he doubts the kinship. Culture itself promotes wantonness, he
goes on to say. He arraigns the whole history of Greek and Roman myth as
a panorama of erotic derelictions and laments the custom of painting these
on walls (2.6.27–32):

> quae manus obscenas depinxit prima tabellas
>   et posuit casta turpia visa domo,
> illa puellarum ingenuos corrupit ocellos
>   nequitiaeque suae noluit esse rudis.
> A gemat, in terris ista qui protulit arte
>   turpia sub tacita condita laetitia!

Notably, it is not even a house of ill fame in which the images are painted, but a *casta domo,* a family household in which the eyes of young women are naive. Here again myths pose the peril of corruptive lessons. The innocent young women who view these paintings might be equated with the virgin of Terence's play. Yet perhaps the lurking *laetitia* subverts the poet's ostensible moral with a hint that fallen innocence has its pleasurable compensations.

What kind of reality, if any, underlies these condemnations of mythological painting? As evidence for the currency of mythological paintings in domestic contexts they are valuable, but do they tell us anything about the paintings themselves? Are their images really so suggestive? Conceivably Roman readers might understand a brothel to be decorated with erotic pictures, which is certainly the case in the Pompeian *Lupanar,* but such sexually graphic representations as occur in this place are on rather a lower genre plane and do not represent Danae or any other mythological personage.[2] The Elder Pliny, whose *Natural History* is our fullest source for information on painters, subjects, and locations, does cite a few notorious instances of spectators' conceiving crushes on beautiful nude heroines in paintings, but implies that these are irregular and indecorous.[3] As for the manner in which Danae as a subject is represented, Pliny mentions her name twice. A painter named Artemon (35.139) painted her amidst wondering pirates. Presumably this refers to her fortunes after the rape, when her angry father has put her and the infant Perseus adrift in a chest. In another place Pliny speaks of a picture of Danae displayed in the Temple of Augustus in Rome, perhaps placed there by Tiberius Caesar. Possibly—the syntax is very ambiguous—it was the work of Athenian Nicias the younger, a painter of the early third century B.C. who painted women with especial care. Neither of these can be Terence's Danae, since the first is of the wrong subject while the second came to Rome long after Terence's lifetime.

Turning, however, to Pompeii, we can see that Danae, while not the most popular subject for representation, occurs with a certain frequency. Schefold's index of subjects in Pompeian painting lists nine images of her. Eight of these are pictured in Salomon Reinach's useful *Repertoire of Greek and Roman Painting* (1970, 10–11).[4] Two examples corroborate Pliny's notice of Danae and the chest, while the others in one form or another portray the golden rain much as described by Terence and Augustine. Figure 12.1, still to be seen in the Casa della Regina Margherita, shows Jupiter present in human form simultaneously with the shower of gold. On the basis of facial expressions we might even consider this a lascivious picture, although the two figures show no real communication, Danae gazing with wonder or desire at the golden shower itself while holding out her garment to capture it, and Jupiter looking complicitously at the viewer as if to share his knowledge of the metamorphic deception in progress. Such glances toward the spectator are often used in painting to reveal erotic intentions (Leach 1988, 397–98).[5] Figure 12.2—no longer extant—includes an Eros, pouring out the gold, as well as Jupiter. As a figure signifying desire, Eros is a very common appearance in Roman paintings. Almost identical with the figures of Danae and Eros in the right half of this composition is figure 12.3, taken from a room in the Casa della Caccia Antiqua and now stored in the Naples Museum. Although Jupiter does not appear bodily in this panel, his *numen* is metonymically represented in the right-hand corner by his thunderbolt, a two-sided weapon complete with hand grip. The golden shower is dispersed by Cupid. Other versions from which Jupiter is absent represent simply the golden shower, and from these one can see that Danae has her own iconographical sign; she always extends her himation to receive it. By this gesture we can identify her even out of context, among figures in a frieze zone which may well be intended to mimic statuary. The seated figure in the Casa di Arianna (figure 12.4) is positioned above a picture panel showing Perseus courting Andromeda. Yet all these are quite decorous paintings with fully clothed heroines, and insofar as they could be thought to approximate the example described in the *Eunuchus,* I submit that neither Augustine, nor Terence's young protagonist, nor any other everyday viewer would be able to connect the components of the paintings to make a mythological story line that would infuse them with erotic suggestivity unless he or she already knew the myth.

Response to the painting involves verbalization; verbalization, in turn, makes the painting a signifier that points in whatever contextual direction the spectator wants it to, which is to say that the myths to which Propertius refers in painting as containing immoral messages for the corruption of chaste girls function in precisely the same manner as the mythological allusions with which he interweaves his poetry (Williams 1982, 162–73; Gaisser 1977, 381–91; Lyne 1980; Leach 1988, 409–40). In poetry the function of mythological allusion is to engage readers with the text by forcing them to supply the relevant connections that determine meaning. When Propertius himself mentions Danae, he focuses upon the bronze tower with which her father was said to have surrounded her, and leaves the "golden rain" for the reader to supply (*Elegies* 2.32.59–60):

> nec minus aerato Danae circumdata muro
> non potuit magno casta negare Iovi.

No less able was chaste Danae, enclosed within a wall of bronze, to refuse great Jove.

Horace, whose *Ode* 3.16 begins with two stanzas on Danae, is scarcely more explicit. The maiden "would have been safe from noctural adulteries"

12.1 Jupiter and Danaë. Pompeii, Casa della Regina Margherita. Author's photo.

12.2 Line drawing of Jupiter, Danaë, and an Eros. Pompeii. After Reinach 1922, p. 10, fig. 7.

12.3 Line drawing of Danaë with an Eros and Jupiter's thunderbolt. Pompeii, Casa della Caccia antica. After Reinach 1922, p. 11, fig. 1.

12.4 Seated Danaë in the frieze zone on the right. Pompeii, Casa di Arianna. Author's photo.

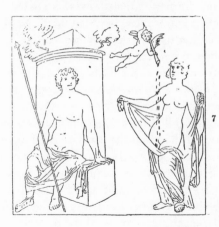

had not Venus and Jupiter mocked her guard and "opened safe passage with the deity converted into a price."

Allusion not representation is also the mode of communication employed by the visual images. If indeed you wish to imitate mythological *exempla* you must first fill out their outlines, and this filling out is the action by which the spectator comes to participate in the myth. For this reason, especially, understanding readers' contributions to reading or reception has been particularly useful in understanding how Romans may have responded to mythology in pictures.[6] The texts that concern painting and show us spectators in the act of viewing suggest that reading pictures is a complex process, similar to the process of understanding literary allusion, which involves supplying indeterminacies or animating the subject through a rehearsal of its narrative.

How and where might this process work? To pursue this question we must look further into the Roman culture of mythology and consider from what sources painters might have derived the ideas for their compositions and how viewers might come by the information that allows them to enter a room and read its myths or recognize connections between them. Naturally, as St. Augustine indicates, the first source is elementary education, where, as not only he but many other writers tell us, young students have their first encounters with literature en route to the study of rhetoric. Before this they may well have heard stories read or related in the nursery,[7] but the association of myths with rhetoric as an area of elite education constructs myth as a status symbol and the ability to recognize it as a mark of class. Suppose, however, that the viewers have not the usual establishment education? The classic dramatization of such a deficiency occurs within Petronius's first-century novelistic narrative *Satyricon,* where an aspirant to culture, a wealthy freedman named Trimalchio, attempts to exhibit his conversance with mythical story lines before his dinner guests and gets them all wrong. Attempting to play host, Trimalchio has followed the upper-class custom of bringing in a troupe of performers, whom he calls *Homeristae,* to entertain his guests. While they allegedly read from Homer in Greek, Trimalchio keeps them company by reading from a Latin book. Here is what he reads:

> Diomedes and Ganymedes were two brothers. Helen was their sister. Agamemnon carried her off and substituted a deer of Diana. So now Homer says how much the Trojans and Tarentines fought with each other and he gave his daughter Iphigenia to Achilles as his wife. For which reason Ajax is behaving like a madman and will soon reveal the argument. (59.4)

At this moment the performance of this Trojan War reaches its climax with a pantomime as a cooked calf is carried in on a dish, followed by an

Ajax waving his sword, who immediately reveals himself as the carver and proceeds to distribute pieces of veal among the guests. Amusing as this slap-stick scene may be in itself, we may find it all the funnier if we see it not as mockery of a freedman, but rather as a parody of upper-class dining room entertainment (Jones 1991). What kind of book could Trimalchio have been reading? One of the popular compendia of mythology, perhaps, but whatever it was it cannot have contained the scrambled details of Trimal-chio's recitation.[8] The easy solution is to suppose that Trimalchio cannot read at all but is merely reciting from imperfect memory.[9] All the same, his pantomime reveals at least a degree of mythological knowledge, since some of it—the madness of Ajax—derives from Sophocles' tragedy. However wrong he may get the preliminaries, we can see that his performance builds to a purposeful climax; it is a reverse imitation, making myth into a partici-pating picture. But the theatrical nature of Trimalchio's pageant should re-mind us that for real everyday Romans who lacked an elite education there is a very accessible source of mythological knowledge in theatrical perfor-mances. This source of knowledge, I suggest, lies behind a particular form of mythological painting in which the viewer's participation is of consum-mate importance. It is called continuous narrative,[10] because it purportedly tells a story, but as will be seen it cannot realize its narrative potential unless the viewer is prepared to do his part. However, any spectator who has wit-nessed the plays in the theater is equipped to interrelate the stages of the ac-tion depicted and rehearse the plot in his mind.

My first example is the familiar myth of the young hunter Actaeon, whom the goddess Diana transformed into a deer to be chased and killed by his own hunting dogs (figures 12.5 and 12.6). There are different ver-sions of Actaeon's culpability, but the one that took hold in Hellenistic lit-erature was that he had come upon the goddess bathing naked, and this is the way that the story is represented in Campanian painting. One such painting includes multiple figures of both Actaeon and Diana, a repetition that invites the viewer to rehearse the story by recreating the interaction of the goddess and her victim from first glimpse to final catastrophe. Is he guilty or innocent of deliberate voyeurism? Ovid's version of the narrative in the *Metamorphoses* asks this question with strong implications of divine cruelty (3.253–55):

> rumor in ambiguo est: aliis violentior aequo
> visa dea est, alii laudant dignamque severa
> virginitate vocant; pars invenit utraque causas.

> Reports buzz about indecisively; to some persons the goddess seems more violent than is just; some praise her and call her act appropriate to her unyielding virginity; a part finds arguments for both sides.

12.5 Continuous narrative representing the myth of Actaeon and Diana. Pompeii, Casa del Frutteto. Deutsches Archäologisches Institut, Rome (DAI). Neg. 64.9951.

12.6 Line drawing of a continuous narrative of Actaeon and Diana. Pompeii, Casa di Epidio Sabino. Deutsches Archäologisches Institut, Rome (DAI). Neg. W346.

12.7 Theatrical relief plaque
with masks of Polyphemus
and Galatea (from Nemi).
Museo nazionale romano,
Palazzo Massimo alle Terme.
Author's photo.

12.8 Polyphemus serenading
Galatea. Pompeii, Casa del
Sacerdote Amando. Author's
photo.

12.9 Continuous narrative representing the punishment of Dirce. Pompeii, Casa di Giulio Polibio. Istituto Centrale per il Catalogo e la Documentazione (ICCD), Neg. 45603.

Different versions of the painting, showing Actaeon confronting the goddess with different attitudes, may invite the viewer to ask the same questions Ovid poses to his readers as he recreates the myth.

That Actaeon was enacted by mime performance in the theater is attested by a very early reference in Varro's Menippean satire *Synephebus* 513 to stage dancers playing the voracious dogs,[11] but the next myths I shall show have even better documented affiliations, both visual and literary, with the stage. A painting in the Metropolitan Museum of Art depicts the Cyclops Polyphemus, that one-eyed monster who terrorized the crew of Odysseus, but the Polyphemus we see here has been cast in a new and most paradoxical role that appealed to the Hellenistic craving for novelty. He is in love and serenading his fantasy mistress, the sea-nymph Galatea, who may be listening or may be only a figment of the lover's besotted imagination. While the painting foregrounds this unusual turn of the myth, it retains in the background the figure of the savage Polyphemus stoning Odysseus's ship to indicate that the transformation wrought by love is neither complete nor permanent (von Blanckenhagen and Alexander 1990; Leach 1988). This new, romanticized version of Polyphemus had its origins in a dithyramb—which was actually satirical—and was adapted by Theocritus in a charming pastoral idyll. We know that Polyphemus and Galatea were performed as a theatrical entertainment on the evidence of a theatrical plaque from Nemi that shows masks for the two figures, the nymph and the Cyclops with his pipe (figure 12.7). But in addition the crag and the cave shown in the painting in figure 12.8, and the crag in the pendant painting of Perseus and Andromeda, are standard elements of theatrical staging, as will appear in my next example.

The association between these rocky settings and the stage is most apparent in a continuous narrative painting of Dirce and Antiope (figure 12.9). With four actual stages of action, this is the fullest example of continuous narrative that we know. Although this story line is probably less familiar than that of Actaeon or Perseus to modern readers, it was well known in the ancient world through several dramatic incarnations, including one by Euripides and a Latin adaptation by Pacuvius that was perennially popular on the Roman stage.[12] Ennius also would seem to have written a version, since the mythographer Hyginus ascribes this epitomized plot in a nutshell to his authorship (*Fabulae* VIII):

> Antiope was the daughter of King Nyctaeus in Boetia. Attracted by the beauty of her form, Jupiter made her pregnant. When her father wanted to punish her for her debauchery, Antiope escaped and arrived by chance in the very same place where Epaphus of Sicyon was staying. He married her and took her home. Nyctaeus took this badly and, as he was dying, he commanded by his will that his brother Lycus, to whom he was leaving his kingdom, should not let Antiope go unpunished. So upon his death Lycus came to Sicyon; having killed Epaphus, he led Antiope in chains to Cithaeron, where she brought forth twins which a shepherd subsequently reared and named Zethus and Amphion. Antiope was given to Lycus's wife Dirce to be

crucified; seizing an opportunity she took flight and arrived where her sons were, of whom Zethus, thinking her a runaway, would not receive her. Into this very place came Dirce performing Bacchic ritual for Liber; there she was dragging the rediscovered Antiope to her death, but the young men, having been informed by their tutelary shepherd that she was their mother, quickly pursued and snatched Antiope away and bound Dirce to the bull by her hair. When they were on the point of killing Lycus, Mercury forbade it, but at the same time ordered Lycus to yield up the kingdom to Amphion.

To which I must add that fragments of the Euripidean drama make clear that the penultimate scene, in which Mercury hinders the vengeful murder of King Lycus, transpires within a stage property, a roll-on cavern (Leach 1988, 333–39). In the final scene Mercury teaches Amphion how to summon stones with his lyre to build the walls of Thebes.

The four stages of action shown here can be seen in correspondence with a sequence of scenes from the drama. A man, either the shepherd or one of Antiope's sons, appears in the upper left corner. In the center is the identification scene by the shrine of Dionysus; the old herdsman, pointing, instructs Antiope's twins to lay hold of Dirce. At the lower left is Dirce tied to the bull, and at last Amphion's magical building of Thebes. Of these scenes, the dragging of Dirce could not have been shown on stage and must have been reported by a messenger, but it becomes the signature image of the myth, persisting even when continuous narrative itself has virtually disappeared as an artistic style. Beyond this, the fact that such paintings are deployed in rooms most likely to have been used for dining suggests that they functioned as conversation pieces.

In reviewing these paintings I have merely hypothesized how a viewer might interact with the painted image on the basis of likely sources of knowledge. But in some literary sources that write a spectator's reaction into description, we can see pictures serving more explicitly as scripts for vicarious experience. First, in the narrative contexts of the Greek novel, we find detailed verbalizations of visual texts operating as scripts for a viewer's response. Achilles Tatius's novel *Leucippe and Clitophon* contains three detailed descriptive passages. The story begins with the storyteller's own viewing, in the Phoenician city of Sidon, of a seductively life-like painting of Jupiter's abduction of Europa in the guise of a bull. His description is a very orderly one, prefaced by an overview of the subject, whose setting encompasses both land and sea:

The sea was Phoenicia's; the land was Sidon. On the land were represented a meadow and a chorus of maidens, on the sea swam a bull, and on his back was seated a beautiful maiden, sailing on the bull towards Crete. (Reardon 1989, 234)

Subsequently the narrator moves our eye over the painting, area by area, describing the luxuriant flowering of the meadow, the attitudes and emotions of the maidens who are Europa's companions, the color and temper of the sea, the bull with its passenger, and finally the figure of Eros guiding the bull.

The composition depicts a moment different from that of our most common Pompeian portrayals of Europa, which either foreshadow the abduction or else show the bull already swimming in the sea.[13] However, some records of lost representations containing both land and sea match this description, which is so full and precise in detail that the viewer might almost reproduce the composition from it. The moment is frozen in time, as we can see by the fleeting expressions and characters caught in mid-utterance. The narrator is also concerned to let us know how very life-like the painting is, and herein lies its seductive element, for the same careful description given to every inch of the landscape also comprehends every contour of Europa's body as she clings to the back of the bull. Rather than fearful, she seems confident and satisfied with her unexpected adventure.

That this painting should be displayed in Sidon is appropriate, since the city is Europa's place of origin. It could even be taken as a claim to control other lands. The narrator calls it a votive, which suggests that its subject has some relationship to an experience of its sponsor. While the novelist never addresses that issue, the response of his narrator is immediate and personal. He gives his attention to the figure of Eros because of his own interest in passion:

> Though the entire picture was worthy of admiration, I devoted my special attention to the figure of Eros leading the bull for I have long been fascinated by passion, and I exclaimed "To think that a child can have such power over land and sea!" (177)

To this quasi-objective response, however, is added that of a second viewer, hitherto unnoticed by the narrator, who corroborates the narrator's observation concerning Love's power. This is Clitophon, the narrator-elect, who views the image retrospectively as the paradigm of those sorrows Eros has visited upon him. These sorrows, of course, will make up the substance of the novel, whose plot is based upon multiple abductions which the painting foreshadows. The real foreshadowing, however, is done by the details that bring the story to life, which, if studied closely, will show Europa as a participant in her own abduction. Shadi Bartsch's contextualized reading of the passage (1989, 44) highlights the discrepancy between Clitophon's subjective response to Eros and the triumphant role that the narrator has indicated, but the reader will soon discover that the narrator has scarcely misjudged the image's aesthetics of erotic mimesis. The Eros signifying Zeus's pleasure within the picture also gives pleasure to the reader, in inverse proportion to the woes he brings to Clitophon. The more times that this protagonist suffers when his Leucippe is exposed at the very brink of sexual abuse, the more exciting the romance. What the picture really foreshadows is the titillation that the novel as a whole will offer to its reader.

Can we take this description out of its novelistic context and apply it to the common Roman expectations of art? Clitophon's response to the "Rape of Europa" embodies a kind of oblique notion of mimesis. Although we might place it a degree higher on the scale of responses than Augustine's direct and vulgarized imitation, still the use of painting to foreshadow experience can only be a literary, not a practical, function of art. Imagine how confusing it would be to walk through a picture gallery if we had to believe that every painting had some hidden bearing upon our lives. In fact the very mistakes that these novelistic characters fall into may suggest that the real aim of interpreting pictures is to see properly and to control one's responses to art. So let us look behind all these graphic descriptions to the literary creator's point of view. The art of describing a painting is a branch of rhetoric in which a teacher should excel. I will conclude with some examples of this art as practiced for its own sake from the two books called *Imagines* or *Eikones* by a professional rhetorician named Philostratus, who belonged to the second Sophistic movement of the second century A.D.

The setting is a large house in Naples whose owner has brought together a large number of pictures by various artists—all unnamed—and displayed them in galleries on a series of terraces facing the sea. A collection of such magnitude might well be thought to belong to the public sphere instead of the private, although in fact there are Pompeian houses with as many, but the mode of display transcends the boundary between the spheres in any case. The speaker is a guest in the mansion, a visiting teacher of rhetoric who has come to Naples at the time of the games as a spectator, not a performer. In fact he is a rival to the official festivity, because he is giving private demonstrations for a group of young men who frequent the house. For several days he has been thinking that he should compose some disquisitions in praise of the pictures. On the particular day in question he does just that, in response to the urging of the ten-year-old son of his host. The audience he addresses comprises the young men who come to hear him. They are disciples of rhetoric, eager, as our speaker puts it, "for words." His purpose, he says, is to "describe examples of painting in the form of addresses which we have composed for the young, that by this means they may learn to appreciate paintings and to appreciate what is esteemed in them" (*Imagines* 295K). That is, his descriptions, rather than a mere display of encomiastic rhetoric, are paradigms of verbal interaction that must take place between the viewer and the visual subject.

A Homeric picture provides the basis for the first description, which takes the form of an active lesson in the process of looking. The subject is a rather remarkable one: the descent of Hephaestus in fire to thwart Achilles in battling the River Scamander. Addressing the boy, who at age ten must surely be well versed in Homeric studies, the speaker shows him how to correct naive admiration by observing the differences between image and literary text. Does he not see how the picture is based upon Homer, or is he simply caught up in the visual image, "lost in wonder how fire can live in the water"? Look away from the picture, recall Homer, then look back at the image and compare.

The picture of Polyphemus serenading Galatea (*Imagines* 2.18) is also constructed from literary references, but now they are concealed rather than being exposed as an interpretive guide that can penetrate beneath appearances to reveal the underlying psychology of the image. The rhetor epitomizes the content of Polyphemus's courtship song. He knows it, of course, from Theocritus's eleventh idyll, which we can tell from the fact that the opening lines of the song are cited obliquely from this poem, but visual signs could not have told us for certain of this appropriation. From Theocritus also comes the rhetor's understanding of Polyphemus's lack of self-knowledge; he does not see the external ugliness that we as spectators of the painting perceive. Galatea, however, we see with a lover's eyes. Here "wonder," expelled from the earlier example, is a permissible response to painting because it commends artistic skill. Galatea's eyes are a wonder because they look over far distances to the limits of the sea (2.18.4: βλέπουσι γὰρ ὑπερόριόν τι καὶ συναπιὸν τῷ μήκει τοῦ πελάγους).

The painting of Amphion building Theban walls to music contains technical information concerning the accuracy with which the painter has constructed the lyre. If the viewer does not already from these details hear its sound he will soon do so, because the painting itself enacts the power of music. In this composition Amphion has been separated from his literary context as the focal center. As he hears the description the viewer will begin to experience the singer's power by hearing the music himself. A visual sign, the slight showing of the teeth, tells us that Amphion is singing here. What he sings is a song of earth, which animates the stones. Finally, we will hear the very rhythm of the song in the positioning of the singer's hands on the instrument and in the beat with which he keeps time. And how do we see the stones themselves? They are building the wall in three stages.

Did these paintings really exist? Although the speaker never names the artists, he claims that the variety of the collection represents the best available talents, selected with the most discriminating judgment. On this basis art historians have hotly debated the issue, which is naturally important if one wants to consider the descriptions as evidence for real compositional types. Very few of them, however, coincide with known topics, and of these almost none have the same postures.[14] In Philostratus's Perseus and Andromeda, for instance, Eros is unfastening the maiden's fetters and leading her from her crag while an exhausted Perseus rests nearby. In the most common Roman compositions, which show Perseus himself releasing Andromeda, there is no sign of Eros.[15] But what the images tell us about their subjects is much less important than what they can tell us about the culture of viewing.

In his introduction, Philostratus claims that painting can produce truth. He asserts that painters contribute as much as poets to our knowledge of the deeds and appearance of heroes. His descriptions place particular emphasis upon color, which not only brings out distinctions of light and shade but also provides means for the expression of emotions and the elaboration of ambience. Color, which figures in rhetorical theory as the final articulation of shades of meaning, here supplies a tool for perception as re-experiencing. He also knows that emotional response can be a by-product of this contact, but his aim in rehearsing the experiences of the paintings is to control such responses by teaching students to pay attention to the appropriate details. In this respect painting is not merely a topic of conversation, but actually a preparation for the mastery of listeners' responses that an orator studies to achieve. And this is, after all, the lesson that Augustine and his fellow students were supposed to be learning—and that Augustine clearly did learn, as demonstrated by the eloquence of his condemnation of pagan art.

NOTES

1. Augustine's text is altered from Terence's original by the insertion of "(inquit)" and by a change in a case ending so that Terence's *summa*, modifying *templa*, becomes *summo*, modifying *sonitu*.

2. Pliny (*Natural History* 35.72) speaks of a painter whose work includes *minoribus tabellis libidines*, a species of painting apparently inferior to his chief works. Such inferior paintings were, of course, frequent. Myerowitz 1992 discusses erotic painting in houses; Jacobelli 1995 (83–102) gives a comprehensive discussion of the topic as background for her argument that the pornographic pictures in the Suburban Baths are to be seen as a sophisticated joke.

3. For example, at 35.17–18 he mentions Caligula, whose passion for images of Atalanta and Helen painted at Lanuvium was so excessive that he wished to cut the paintings from the wall.

4. A compendium of all Greek and Roman representations of the myth is available in *Lexicon Iconographicum Mythologiae Classicae*, vol. 2, 326–27.

5. One example is a Pompeian painting that shows Jupiter, disguised as a bull, courting Europa.

6. For more extended discussion see Leach 1988; Bryson 1994, 255; Elsner 1995.

7. Strabo *Geography* 1.2.8 speaks of the enjoyment and enlightenment that children derive from myths.

8. The Bulfinch of Augustan Rome was a writer named Julius Hyginus, the librarian in the Palatine Libraries, whose compendium of plots in a nutshell was surely intended as a cultural initiation for persons lacking elite education.

9. This apparently is Slater's opinion (1990, 71–72), although he later (158) remarks that we should give credit to the incident for its literary status.

10. What precedents it might have we don't know, but its flourishing period in Pompeii is rather short, extending only from the late Augustan age to the early Julio-Claudian, and its execution depended upon the skills of a particular kind of painter or painters adept at creating elegant landscapes.

11. Varro also refers to the myth as a fable in his agricultural treatise *De Re Rustica* 2.9.10.

12. Testimonies to the popularity of this play are numerous throughout the history of Latin literature. Among the most significant tributes is that of Cicero in *De Finibus* 1.4.2 as he defends the value of Roman literature for Roman audiences:

> Quis enim tam inimicus paene nomini Romano est qui Enni Medeam aut Antiopam Pacuvi spernat aut reicat, quod se isdem Euripidis fabulis delectari dicat?

> Who is there so nearly hostile to a Roman name that he scorns or casts aside the Medea of Ennius or Pacuvius's Antiope, because he says that he gets his pleasure from these same dramas in Euripides?

Propertius's short narrative in *Elegies* (3.15) covers the whole story.

13. Wattel-de Croizant 1986 surveys the repertoire.

14. For the argument in favor see Lehmann 1941, but also the critique in Bryson 1994.

15. For the iconographical history of this topic see Phillips 1968.

BIBLIOGRAPHY

Bartsch, Shadi. 1989. *Decoding the Ancient Novel: The Reader and the Role of Description in Heliodorus and Achilles Tatius.* Princeton, N.J.: Princeton University Press.

Blanckenhagen, Peter H. von, and Christine Alexander. 1990. *The Augustan Villa at Boscotrecase.* With contributions by Joan R. Mertens and Christel Faltermeier. 2d edition; originally published as *The Paintings from Boscotrecase* (Heidelberg: F. H. Kerle, 1962). Mainz am Rhein: P. von Zabern.

Bryson, Norman. 1994. "Philostratus and the Imaginary Museum." In *Art and Text in Ancient Greek Culture,* ed. Simon Goldhill and Robin Osborne, 255–83. Cambridge: Cambridge University Press.

Elsner, Jas. 1995. *Art and the Roman Viewer: The Transformation of Art from the Pagan World to Christianity.* Cambridge: Cambridge University Press.

Gaisser, Julia. 1977. "Mythological *Exempla* in Propertius 1.2 and 1.15." *American Journal of Philology* 98:381–91.

Jacobelli, Luciana. 1995. *Le pitture erotiche delle terme suburbane di Pompei.* Soprintendenza archaeologica di Pompei 10. Rome: "L'Erma" di Bretschneider.

Jones, Christopher R. 1991. "Dinner Theater." In *Dining in a Classical Context,* edited by William J. Slater, 185–98. Ann Arbor: University of Michigan Press.

Leach, E. W. 1981. "Metamorphoses of the Acteon Myth in Campanian Painting." *Mitteilungen des Deutschen Archaeologischen Instituts, Römische Abteilung* 88:307–28; pls. 131–41.

———. 1986. "The Punishment of Dirce: A Newly Discovered Continuous Narrative in the Casa di Giulio Polibio and Its Significance within the Visual Tradition." *Mitteilungen des Deutschen Archaeologischen Instituts, Römische Abteilung* 93:118–38; color pl. 1; pls. 49–59.

———. 1988. *The Rhetoric of Space: Literary and Artistic Representations of Landscape in Republican and Augustan Rome.* Princeton, N.J.: Princeton University Press.

Lehmann, Karl. 1941. "The *Imagines* of the Elder Philostratus." *Art Bulletin* 23:16–44.

Lyne, R. O. A. M. 1980. *The Latin Love Poets from Catullus to Horace.* Oxford: Oxford University Press.

Myerowitz, Molly. 1992. "The Domestication of Desire: Ovid's *Parva Tabella* and the Theater of Love." In *Pornography and Representation in Greece and Rome,* edited by Amy Richlin, 131–57. Oxford: Oxford University Press.

Phillips, Kyle M. 1968. "Perseus and Andromeda." *American Journal of Archaeology* 72: 1–24; pls. 1–20.

Philostratus. 1931. *Imagines.* Translated by Arthur Fairbanks. New York: G. P. Putnam's Sons.

Reardon, B. P., ed. 1989. *Collected Ancient Greek Novels.* Berkeley and Los Angeles: University of California Press.

Reinach, Saloman. [1922] 1970. *Répertoire de peintures grecques et romaines.* Rome: "L'Erma" di Bretschneider.

Schefold, Karl. 1957. *Die Wände Pompejis; topographisches Verzeichnis der Bildmotive.* Berlin: W. de Gruyter.

Slater, Niall W. 1990. *Reading Petronius.* Baltimore: Johns Hopkins University Press.

Wattel-de Croizant, O. 1986. "L'emblème de l'enlèvement d'Europe à Prèneste (Barberini-Oldenberg) ou l'histoire d'une mosaïque oublié du temple de la Fortune." *Mélanges de l'École française de Rome, Antiquité* 98:491–564.

Williams, Gordon. 1982. *Figures of Thought in Roman Poetry.* New Haven, Conn.: Yale University Press.

THIRTEEN

Mud and Mythic Vision: Hindu Sculpture in Modern Bangladesh

HENRY GLASSIE

To study myth is to enter a cultural system that interconnects cosmological knowledge, affecting action, and a desire for consequence. Art, the sensate dimension of affecting action, offers the conspicuous, courteous entry to mythic systems. The study of myth will expand through exploration of the inchoate, the occluded, and the occult, while a theory emerges to account for how and why the cosmological is communicated, but the study will make its start in art: in music and dance, in ritual, in painting and sculpture, in story. For the analyst in whose tradition the word was in the beginning, it is natural to fix upon the verbal, to think first of narrative, to commence study with stories of the sacred, called myths.

In Ballymenone, the Irish community where I spent a decade in study, the word "myth" was not used, nor was the word "legend," but the tellers of tale—they were called historians—spoke a variety of legend that was mythic in function, that lay between knowledge and desire. They named the genre by topic: stories of the saints.[1] Variable in detail, the stories were alike in plot. A holy man or woman comes to this place, the place where we live, and leaves upon it a sign of power.

I presented Peter Flanagan with the results of my simple-minded structural analysis of the stories that he, Hugh Nolan, and Michael Boyle had told me, commenting that Saint Febor caused the Sillees River to twist, and Saint Naile lifted a spring of silvery water to the surface at Kinawley, and Saint Patrick discovered a medicinal herb on Inishmore, but the stories, while different, all followed one narrative line. He said, surely: all the stories have one meaning. All testify to the existence of God.

Ballymenone's stories of the saints are set in the time of the beginning, the early Christian era when the world was still new, mutable and malleable. Earlier times excited the ancient saints themselves, but they hold no interest for Ballymenone's historians. Their tale begins with the Christian dawn, when the saints put the finishing touches on creation and brought the Good News to the people of Ireland, burdening them with awareness, obliging them to righteous conduct. The stories entail the cosmological, enfolding the proposition of mediation. God's infinite power is transferred to the earthly realm and emplaced by virtuous men and women. And then the stories point forward, conditioning the actions of people yet unborn. Since, as Peter Flanagan argued, the stories all mean that God exists, explaining local phenomena as signs of divine power, they comfort the soul, countering doubt and urging people to accept God's great commandment, which Peter repeated: "Love your neighbor as yourself, and in that you shall live." Given to gossip, fistfights, and lawsuits, split by religious and political persuasion into Catholic and Protestant factions, the neighbors were hard to love, but love is God's commandment, Peter said, and then he continued catechistically. "And who is your neighbor?" All mankind, is the answer. Chartering society, the stories of the saints establish life's sacred foundation and charge people to build upon it a universal social order governed by love. Hate abounds, but the story artfully told helps the mind hold steady on God so that some peace may be found amid the travail, and eternal life in Heaven will follow.

Such stories of the beginning, sacred at the base and designed to influence conduct, condition the vision of myth that bookish people transport from place to place during cross-cultural analysis. When I shifted my attention from Christian Ireland to Muslim Turkey, I could still read the texts set before me. The texts—discrete, composite units—were woven of wool or painted on clay, not made up of words; they were abstract, geometric, and not directly representational, but, reiterating the revelation of the Holy Koran, they delighted the senses in order to instruct the mind and lead the human actor through a life of peace to an eternity of joy in a garden with streams flowing by. The highest of the arts, in the estimation of the artists, was calligraphy. Submitting to the discipline of tradition, the calligrapher integrates distinct letters into compositions that display, on paper in frames, the word of God that was selected from the Holy Koran, elegantly written, and that is set now before people to guide their lives.[2]

When, after a decade of study in Turkey, I pressed further east and came into the company of Hindu artists in Bangladesh, I found the word to be displaced, deposed. There was no single fundamental book, no Bible or Koran. I discovered images, not narratives, at the heart of the mythic system. It is my purpose in this paper to describe the operation of a system in which the familiar is reversed, in which the image is central, ritual forms the prime context, and stories are cast in an ancillary, illustrative role. The sculpture of the Western cathedral illustrates a story. The story of Hindu

Bangladesh illustrates a sculpture. It serves to clarify the image so that it can be shaped and worshiped properly, but the basic information is transmitted through image making, from sculptor to sculptor. Stories are often rationalized extrapolations from the appearance of the image, and of the three expressive components in the mythic system—icon, ritual, and narrative— the narrative, the myth, is of the least importance. It would be clumsy, maybe wrong, to enter this system through tales. Sculpture shows the way.[3]

For clarity's sake, I must make two points before proceeding. First, though I restrict myself to what I learned from the Hindu sculptors in modern Bangladesh, I believe the principles are transportable, just as the principles derived from traditions that focus on the word have proved transportable. I leave to my colleagues in classics the question of what implications the situation among modern Hindus may hold for ancient Greece, but I am certain that mythic systems centered by icons, rather than narratives, are not peculiar to Hinduism alone. I have found something comparable in the domestic worship of Japanese Buddhists, and I gather from his brilliant trilogy on art that Robert Plant Armstrong was, before his death, working toward similar conclusions with regard to the Yoruba people of West Africa (Armstrong 1971, 1975, 1981).

My second preliminary point is this: from my reading, and more from my fieldwork in South India, I know that what I am describing is not the Hindu system, but the Hindu system as it has developed in the environment of eastern Bengal, the territory of the People's Republic of Bangladesh. Here, for eight centuries, two great religions have coexisted in a turbulent state of conflict and compromise. Radically different in theology, they have shaped radically different artistic traditions: Islam is aniconic, while Hinduism is iconic in the extreme. And yet each religion contains a mystical strain that offers opportunities for synthetic creation. The *bhakti* strand of Hinduism and the Sufi strand of Islam have intertwined in devotional practice and in a tradition of mystical song that, mature in Mughal times, flourishes still. Today's bards, whether Hindu, Muslim, or Baul, ratify the contract of love between the Creator and the creature, and they provide an interpretive resource that counters divisive orthodoxies.[4]

Beauty and complexity have drawn me again and again to Bangladesh over the last fourteen years. The student of art must find exciting the place where the world's most different traditions have abraded and effervesced in long contact, where Hindus, members of a diminishing minority, have adjusted, just as Muslims have adjusted, during centuries of interaction. In song, the Muslim bard will invoke the goddess Saraswati as muse, and use Krishna and his lover, Radha, as the embodiment of the Sufi principle of love. Krishna, avatar of Vishnu and the focus of Vaishnavite worship, is called the third incarnation of time. Fourth was the Bengali mystic Chaitanya Dev, called Gauranga, whose devotion fused with Sufism in the sixteenth century, reconciling the irreconcilable and opening the option for synthesis that my friends, the artists, seize upon in discussion of their work. To put it simply, the Hindu image of Bangladesh resembles Hindu images from other places, but the interpretations developed by the artists reflect an old accommodation to the presence of Islam.

The touch and recoil of Hinduism and Islam have shaped one feature of the environment. Another is physical. Surrounding life with heat and damp, suffusing life with a sweet melancholy, the physical environment provides the palpable ground of the mythic system. In a way that should entertain Claude Lévi-Strauss, our greatest mythographer and a man who has done time on the delta of Bengal, the mythic and the geological converge. The moist earth is the nature that art transforms into culture.

From the world's tallest mountains, great rivers run to the sea. Their silt has built the world's widest delta, vast and flat and free of stones. The delta's earth is dug up and borne in headloads to form the mounds that lift the villages above the flood. It is planted with rice so that people may eat. It is shaped and baked into vessels so that water can be carried, food can be cooked, and people can get through another hard day.

In Bangladesh, the nation of the delta, there are 680 villages given to making pottery, something like half a million people who use clay to make art because clay is what there is. Under the topsoil spreads a layer of pale, sandy clay, and beneath that lies a deeper layer of clay, which is black and sticky. The potters dampen and mix the two, treading and kneading the earth into a smooth new substance from which they make useful pots and useful statues.

The nation is predominantly Muslim, but the potters are mostly Hindus who bear the same surname—Pal—indicating their membership in the craft-caste of the workers in clay. The Pals divide into two *gotras*, one native, the other intrusive. Formerly the gotras were strictly endogamous, but the old restrictions have relaxed, and today division is made by craft. They use the same clay blend, but, as the potters put it, some Pals make *kalshis*, others make *murtis*.

The kalshi is a spherical jar. Capable of containing water, large and light to ease the labor of the woman who carries it, the kalshi is the most difficult of the potters' creations, the pride of their repertory, but potters who make kalshis make utilitarian vessels of all kinds. Women and men use different techniques to make identical kalshis, and they use different techniques when collaborating to make *patils*, bowls for cooking. Smoothed, slipped, then fired to ruddy buff or silvery black, their vessels go to market. Through commercial exchange, Hindu products pass to Muslim consumers, unifying society in the honorable ethic of utility.

In the villages I know, one household out of ten contains men who make murtis, images of the deities for worship. Few of them can survive by making only sculpture. In the slack season, they make lesser things, but in the *puja* season, the time of public worship stretching from late summer to early winter, they are busy filling commissions for murtis. They are all men, I am told, for the same reason that the priests in the temples are all men.

Work begins with a prayer. Repeating a mantra of praise to the deity, the potter receives a direct revelation of the divine. Then, much as the artist of realism works to materialize an image that registered on the retina, the maker of murtis works to materialize an image that God placed before the mind's eye. It is dramatically different in South India, where the potters tell me their goal is to craft an image in line with the canonical, classical tradition. In Bangladesh, the act is mystical. Prayer brings the divine gift of an image. It might be conventional, but it might be unique, and the task is to maintain the spirit of prayer while arranging materials from the earth to match a vision that, unmediated by tradition, came straight from God.

God is omnipresent and without form. Called Bhagaban, called Allah, God appears in the mind in the form of a particular deity. The deities each have a shape and a mission. This is Bengal; the chief deity is Devi, the Goddess, manifest as Durga in power and Kali in rage. Her missions are spread among her children: Saraswati, the goddess of wisdom; Lakshmi, the goddess of wealth; Kartik, the dapper god of war; and Ganesh, the Lord of Beginnings, with his opulent paunch and white elephant's head. To further a particular mission of God on earth, the artist fashions a particular form, shaping it of rice straw on an armature of sticks and then coating the straw with clay. In sculpting the body of a goddess, the embodiment of God, the artist models with his hands, applies molded components, and pushes toward beauty.

The aesthetic of the murti is oriented to the transcendent. Watching the artists at work, I saw how every motion was pitched toward unnatural perfection. Steady hands, trained to repetition in common work, figured pieces into neat patterns. The eye extracted nature's implicit orders, the mind refined them geometrically, and the murti was shaped into singing symmetry. Finally, nature's roughness was erased by smooth, dampened layers of fine clay.

Smooth on its surface, abstracted toward the geometric in form, idealized in appearance—exhibiting the qualities commonly found in what is called folk art—the image is not a failed attempt to depict a woman of the world. This is a goddess. Perfect in fecund youth, complete in her beauty, she does not belong to this world.

That is what I could learn by watching and talking with the artists, with Manindra Chandra Pal and Sumanta Pal in Kagajipara, with Babu Lal Pal in Khamarpara, with Lal Chand Pal in Rayer Bazar. Now I will deepen the account by accepting the direction of Haripada Pal. Born in Norpara, trained by his grandfather Niroda Prasad Pal, Haripada left the village for the city of Dhaka when he was a teenager. Having learned all he could there, he went west to Calcutta and east to Tripura, working to bring his gift to maturity. He learned from great masters, and he was trained in esoteric interpretation by a saintly ascetic, Surendra Chandra Sarkar. Haripada can always take things to another level, and I count his explanation of the meaning of his work, which I recorded in his shop in Dhaka and set into print, as a high point of my professional life.[5]

Haripada Pal teaches that the slow process of modeling the clay to smooth, geometrical perfection is an aesthetic act and an act of devotion. Nature, he says, is marbled with God. In the clay he works, there is God, the seed of creation that springs to life with prayer. In Haripada's body, there is a drop of God, the soul that enables all action. As he patiently massages the clay, pressing into its softness, it yields to his touch and symmetries take shape, while the power in his body ejaculates through the tips of his fingers to fuse with the seed of creation in the clay, effecting a reunion of the divine, and impregnating the image with sacred power, power that is one with the dampness in the clay of the murti and with the dampness in the body of its creator. Haripada Pal says that he is not rich, but he is lucky, because in his daily work he unites with God, and his work is worship. His murti is a prayer, damp with power, and it is a splendid realization of his skill as a working artist.

The utilitarian vessel is fired to become useful in the quotidian sphere. The murti is not fired. The potter of South India fires his image of the god to purify it, but Haripada Pal says that fire kills the power that abides in the damp interior of the murti. A fired image, he says, might be decorative, you could put it in a museum, but it is of no use during worship. The murti is double: its interior is for power, its exterior is for beauty.

Once it is dry enough, the dark murti is sanded and covered with a coat of thickened white paint that seals the surface and provides a base for the application of luminous color. Bright paint completes the aesthetic program: smooth and bright, ideal in shape, the murti departs from the rough, dull world and stands ready for service.

On the day set in scripture, the murti is elevated on a stage beneath a pleated canopy. There is a murti at the temple, commissioned by its executive committee, and there are others along the street, above the street, in shops and homes, commissioned by workingmen's associations, social clubs, and wealthy men.

In other places, the priest completes the icon, painting the pupils of the eyes, awakening it to life and making it—literally, as in Catholic commu-

13.1 Babu Lal Pal with his image of Radha and Krishna. Khamarpara, Shimulia, Bangladesh. 1996.

nion—the deity. But in Bangladesh, the potter does all the painting, and the murti is not the deity. According to the potter Amulya Chandra Pal, Hindus do not pray to the murti, but through it, just as Muslims do not pray to the mihrab in the mosque, but through it to God.

The murti is not God. It is a receptacle for God's power in the form of a particular deity. It is a prayer that in its beauty says, Behold, this is how perfect thou art in our eyes. As the artist called the goddess into his mind with a prayer of praise, now at the appointed hour the priest calls the goddess into the clay with a prayer and, complimented by the beauty of the image prepared to receive her, she descends. Garlanded as a revered guest should be, she is held in place with entertainment. Flattered by litanies of praise, delighted with dancing lights, throbbing drums, and the sweet smell of incense, she will remain so long as the entertainment continues.

Her devotees, women on one side, men on the other, crowd forward to see, to take *darshan,* connecting eye to eye with the potter's image. The large eyes in the large head, the deep color and sparkling ornament, pull the people forward. Contact is visual. Their eyes meet, then the water in the body of the devotee connects with the water in the clay of the murti, then the soul in the devotee connects with the goddess in the statue. Visual connection has become physical; the unity of God with God that occurred in the sculptor's work is repeated in the puja. Communication becomes possible. The devotee asks for worldly favors: from Saraswati, good grades in school; from Lakshmi, an increase in pay. The request is accompanied by promises, and the deal is sealed with gifts. The goddess is given flowers. The devotee takes *prasad,* sweet cakes and fruit, palpable, consumable signs of blessings to be received, of promises made, of a contract struck.

So long as the people come and go, looking with love and offering words of praise, so long as the incense smokes and the drums beat, so long as the puja continues, that long the goddess remains. The rule differs for each deity, but normally after a week in the case of Durga, a day in the case of her daughter Saraswati, worship ends. It is silent. The goddess has gone. The statue is empty, no more than a pretty, glittery shell, a husk, bereft of power. Its work is done. Then—at the end of the puja in the case of Durga, after a year in the case of Saraswati—the statue is fed and lifted onto a truck. The engine erupts, and the truck wheels into the parade, joining the crowd and the brass bands. The murti lurches along, following others in a jubilant, carnivalesque procession to the riverside. Carried onto a wooden boat, the statue sways above the water in clouds of incense. In the middle of the channel, boys lift the image, turn in a circle, and, to the ululation of the women, throw it overboard. One boy follows, diving after the murti in its descent, retrieving holy water to bless those who have come to witness the end. The water is smooth and black. The statue is gone. Unfired clay decays into the

13.2 Haripada Pal with his image of Balarama. Shankharibazar, Dhaka, Bangladesh. 1995.

water, becoming the silt out of which the kalshis and murtis of the future will be created. The cycles continue, the rivers go on flowing.

Haripada Pal says that some people find it strange that he would work for a month to create a statue that will exist for only a few days, but, he says, once the deity has abandoned the murti, it is of no more value than the body after the soul has flown. Some bury the body, others burn it, and the empty murti, too, must be eliminated. Now it is worthless, but it was once the seat of the deity, so it is treated with respect. It is immersed with ceremony, sacrificed in running water. Next year he will make another. His livelihood and his devotion depend on an endless series of renewals.

That is the story of the murti. It incarnates the cosmological proposition of reincarnation. Soil, borne by the water, is shaped into a beautiful body that is ornamented to receive the spirit, the damp breath of God, and then, after the spirit has left, it returns to the water from which it came.

Like a myth, the murti is an artful configuration of cosmological knowledge, designed to have positive consequences in human life. The murti is shaped ritually, then located in a ritual where people use it to make requests that make life in the world tolerable. The murti is a powerful tool. The divine power in the clay and the divine power in the artist's body fuse in labor and linger in the moist core of the statue so that it can serve as a device for communication between the worlds, this and the other. Haripada Pal calls the murti a mediator. It brings people into connection with God. It is a tool of the sacred, like a prayer, and its beauty is essential to its work. Symmetrical, smooth, and bright, it attracts the goddess, and it attracts her devotees, so that its power can work for their mutual benefit. The goddess wants devotees. The devotees want blessings. The potter brings them together through a thing shaped magnificently out of sticks and straw and mud.

For the potter, for Haripada Pal, there is pleasure to be taken from the service he provides, a service that brings the Hindu community into union, but the effort he expends in creation, in his struggle to make the statue beautiful, outstrips any social function and runs beyond any payment he might receive in the form of gratitude, prestige, or cash. The exquisite beauty of his murti is the honorable response to his gift from God, the blessing of talent, which certainly brings him money and respect but, more importantly, allows him to spend each day in rapt concentration, away from the world in union with God. He makes the murti to represent the fullness of his talent in its beauty, hoping to so please God with his dedication that, upon his death, he will not be returned to this miserable place, where it is hard to keep the mind balanced. Instead, he hopes to be released from the cycles of reincarnation and launched into a timeless state of perpetual bliss.

Mud to mud: through creation and use in ritual, where the potter's work mediates between the worlds, connecting the universe together, the story of the murti—the devotional focus of Hindus in Bangladesh—can be told without recourse to any narrative made of words. So let me turn back in a search for the place of myth in this mythic system.

Identification is necessary to the system's functioning. The artist must craft an image that the devotee can identify, so that the proper deity can be venerated properly to bring blessings. But the coherent aesthetic of the murti works against identification. Shaped to one visual taste, made to be beautiful, the deities resemble one another. The face is a smooth oval, like an egg, divided symmetrically by a straight, sharp nose, and featuring wide almond eyes set beneath arched brows. It is the same for male and female figures, and when the artist is working hastily to a modest commission, instead of modeling by hand, he will save time and effort by using the same mold for the faces of different deities. Even the bodies, while subtly different for each gender and distinguished by costume, adhere to a similarly full and curvaceous ideal. Coats of paint clarify identification, but do not completely resolve the matter.

Saraswati is conventionally white and slimmer than her sister Lakshmi, but, in recent years, university students, devotees of Saraswati and patrons of the potters, have requested innovations in color and form. Discussions with patrons precede the work and figure in the prayers that bring the artists their visions. A wish to please his customers and serve his community complicates the artist's task as he bears down in concentration, fulfilling the inner urge to excellence and striving, above all, to please God. Many of the artists resist—Manindra Chandra Pal does so adamantly—refusing to accommodate their patrons' requests, but others have complied, and images of Saraswati, gold in hue, like Durga or Lakshmi or Radha, or blue like Krishna or Kali, and as plump as a Bangladeshi movie star, have appeared on the altars at Dhaka University during Saraswati Puja.

Context is not sufficient. The image installed for worship at Saraswati Puja will be Saraswati, but the murtis in the temples make a mixed crowd. The books are right when they say that Hinduism divides into three great cults, one for Devi, one for Shiva, and one for Vishnu, but they are wrong if they imply rigid distinctions. Temples are dedicated to one cult or the other, but in practice, in their display of images, they tend to cross boundaries and assemble power toward union. At the core, and repetitively on the facade of the massive Sri Minakshi Sundaresvara Temple in Madurai, Tamil Nadu, a perfect union is represented in an image of Vishnu presenting his sister Minakshi—Parvati, Devi in her wifely embodiment—to Shiva in marriage. In Bangladesh, a mingled exhibit is the norm. On Shankharibazar in Dhaka, the temple to Kali—Devi in wrath—displays a monumental, formidable murti of the goddess by Haripada Pal. Then, on one of the side walls, he sculpted an image in relief of Shiva, and on the other a beautiful image of Krishna, the eighth avatar of Vishnu. A few blocks north, in Tanti Bazar, the temple dedicated to Krishna offers statues of Radha and Krishna, of their incarnations as Gauranga and Nitai, and it holds the trident and bull of Shiva. Dhaka's great temple, Dhakeswari, is dedicated to Durga; the inner room containing her image is flanked by rooms that house images of Lord Shiva in the form of the phallic, black Linga. In a little temple on a rooftop in downtown Dhaka, I find not only an assembly of Hindu gods but also a lithograph of the Christ of the Sacred Heart and calligraphed Koranic inscriptions.

The mix of images vexes the foreign observer who wishes to classify and categorize, but it suits the Hindu desire to add power to power, creating a superabundance that overflows in wonder, eradicating distinctions and gesturing toward the single, all-encompassing power of God. The crowd of powerful images on the altar presents no problem to the worshiper, for God's unified, incomprehensible power is made accessible to devotion through its division into missions distributed among the deities. To a particular deity, easily identifiable in the crowd, the devotee addresses a specific concern.

It is not the full, rounded body, nor even the ritual setting, that assures identification. The deities are differentiated by signs, by clear, nonverbal labels. Each deity has a *vahana,* a vehicle and symbol in animal form. The lovely woman with a swan is Saraswati, not to be confused with the lovely woman with an owl, Lakshmi, or the lovely woman on a donkey, Sitala, the goddess of smallpox. Saraswati is further distinguished by the stringed instrument, the *vina,* that she plays or displays.

Swan and vina: it is Saraswati, at a glance and from a distance, even if she is fat and yellow like Lakshmi. The presence of the attributes suffices to direct worship properly. No matter how abstract or poorly crafted, once recognized, the murti becomes useful. More than identification is unnecessary, but deeper knowledge enriches the experience, just as a beautifully crafted image does.

Many people told me that Saraswati, the goddess of wisdom, is accompanied by a swan because the swan is wise, capable of separating milk and water that have been mixed together. It is like the ability to separate the wheat from the chaff. Wisdom divides the useful from the useless; its mode is analytic, its task is Cartesian: to break units into their constituent parts. Most people knew the reason for the swan, but my requests for an explanation of the vina brought blank looks. Saraswati, the goddess of wisdom, also rules the realm of music; music is part of wisdom. That is what I was told, and it seemed to meet the needs of almost everyone. Then I encoun-

13.3 Saraswati. Saraswati Puja, Dhakeswari Mandir, Dhaka, Bangladesh.
1987.

tered esoteric knowledge. In the beginning, I was told, there was a single sound, *om,* which Saraswati shattered into musical notes and arranged into scales. Music became possible. The separate strings of the vina, each tuned to one note, can be sounded into integrated patterns. Unity is broken down so it can be recombined into new unities, useful to humankind. The vina is like the swan. Its capacity to discriminate, to divide wholes into parts, symbolizes wisdom itself, the sphere of Saraswati.

The information that accompanies the murti is like the illustration that accompanies a narrative. It amplifies and deepens, but it is not necessary. Without the illustration, the narrative can be read. Without expansive information, the murti is identifiable. It is enough to read the visible attributes and proceed with prayer. Further, in the context of my argument, it is important to add that this information about Saraswati was never, in my hearing, shaped into a coherent narrative.

But other images do summon stories in their explanation. Ganesh can be identified by his vahana, the rat. The small, skittery rat contrasts with the large, ponderous elephant whose head the god wears. The contrast, like the god's soft body, contributes to the affection in which he is held. A god of the second generation, perpetually a child, a consumer of sweets, Ganesh inspires love. I recall a little boy in a museum smiling brightly, throwing his arms around a precious ancient statue of the god and giving him a tight hug, despite the cold bronze, the harsh light, the tall pedestal, the wordy label, and the amused, uniformed guard. As a creature who scampers past every trap and barrier, the rat fits Ganesh in his role as the god who removes all obstacles, opening the path for human action. But what identifies Ganesh, and calls for explanation, is the elephant's head. The story is generally known. Shiva, the wild ascetic, would not answer Parvati's desire for a child, so she formed one out of the scrapings of her flesh, and set him to guard the door while she bathed. He blocked Lord Shiva's entry. In fury, Shiva cut off his head. Then, to restore the dead boy to life, he replaced the missing head with one cut from a passing elephant. Ganesh stands as an instance of life overcoming death, as the embodiment of reincarnation, as the god of new beginnings.

We will never know whether the statue was created out of the story, or the story out of the statue. What we can know is that the information that glosses the image has taken narrative form, and that the image does not illustrate the story. Ganesh stands or sits, looking forward, lifting weapons in his hands. His image obliterates narrative logic. He stands guard as he did before he was beheaded; the elephant's head is in place as it was after Shiva's rash act. The image does not illustrate the story; rather, the story illustrates the image. If it is stripped away, the image remains comprehensible—timeless, potent, loveable. Known by his elephant's head, Ganesh is guardian of

13.4 Durga by Sankar Dhar. Dhakeswari Mandir, Dhaka, Bangladesh. 1996.

portals, remover of obstacles, the Lord of Beginnings, who is invoked in prayer at the commencement of action.

Durga is different. Her image incorporates action. It depicts the climactic episode of a myth. Threatened by the Buffalo Demon, the deities pooled their virtues in the creation of a superhero, a goddess as beautiful and powerful as all of them combined. Durga represents power in plenitude. The number of arms is one index of power: Saraswati has two, Ganesh has four, Kali and Vishnu also have four, but Durga has ten. All of her hands hold weapons. Her posture is erect, undisturbed. Her beautiful golden face is placid, about to smile. A silver spear angles down, bringing death to the Demon, who writhes and rages in his ultimate, doomed human form. The severed head of the buffalo, slain previously, glances up to watch his final defeat. In the image of Durga, there is narration. Myth and murti have met.

Nirad C. Chaudhuri was a wonderfully independent writer on Indian themes. His book on Hinduism (1979) is the only one that tallies with my experience in Bangladesh, the place where he was born. Chaudhuri found it disturbing that devotees would respond with love to the violent, bloody image of Durga (Chaudhuri 1994, 72–84; 1979, 70, 186). He was looking with a literal eye. Like Durga's vahana, the lion on which she stands, the action displayed by her image is an attribute, an elaborate sign. The devotee looks beyond the details to see the goddess, who gazes out of the scene with serene unconcern. A story surrounds her, a lion snarls beneath her. Durga stands still in the fullness of power, beautiful, calm, eternal, worthy of love.

What is most necessary, truly essential to this system, is not knowledge but love. In the creation of love, the murti is central. It attracts by beauty and works by power, unifying the worlds by making devotion possible. Stories, when present, serve an adjunct, supportive, explanatory function. They are to the murti as art-historical discourse is to a great painting: entertaining, enlightening, but ultimately dispensable. Sculpture, I repeat, is central to this mythic system. Its dynamic is bodily—visual and physical. Its mood is emotional more than intellectual. Its effect is aesthetic, mystical, and transcendent—beyond words.

Since that conclusion might continue to seem unconvincing to those of my colleagues who feel most at ease with texts formed of words (though the word *text* was borrowed from the world of handwork, where it designated a weaving together, a textile), I will try again with a last example.

During a talk at a scholarly conference, I once showed a slide of the murti of Kali that Haripada Pal had created for the temple on Shankharibazar. The learned people in my audience asked if I had reversed the slide, for it showed Kali holding a sword in her right hand, when it should be in her left. The slide was right, I replied. The artist must be wrong, they said, and they construed his error to be evidence of the degeneration of Hinduism in the Muslim nation of Bangladesh. I took their complaint to Haripada. He said, quite correctly, that there are many things that American professors do not know. Haripada knows of 108 different images of Kali. They differ in color: some are blue, some are black. Some are clothed, some are naked. Some are beautiful, others are not. Yes, in most of them, he said, the sword is in one of her two left hands, but in a few, the sword is in one of her right hands. Then he told me the myth that explains the issue.

Beautiful Kali set out to destroy the evil in the world. Wielding the sword in her left hand, in the midst of her violent success, she forgot the difference between good and evil. She began to destroy everything. In terror, the people went to Lord Shiva, beseeching him to do something. Shiva positioned himself in her path and fell asleep. Continuing on her wild course, Kali stepped on him. Her foot knew Shiva's flesh. Her tongue shot out and lolled in shocked embarrassment and sudden understanding. Recognizing the wrong she had done by putting her foot on her husband's body, she remembered her duty to him. Particular understanding became general. The sword switched from her left hand to her right as a sign of her understanding of the wrong she had done to the world and of her recognition of the duty she owed to humankind.

In the image, Kali is caught in the flash of awareness. Her tongue hangs to signal her ability to distinguish right from wrong. With the sword in her

13.5 Shamakali by
Haripada Pal. Shama Puja,
Shankharibazar, Dhaka,
Bangladesh. 1998.

13.6 Rakshakali by Haripada Pal. Shankharibazar Kali Mandir, Dhaka,
Bangladesh. 1995.

left hand, she is Shamakali, strong and enraged. With a sword in each hand, in the midst of transition, or in her right hand only, a split instant later in mythic time, she is Rakshakali, strong and benign.

We sat on the floor of his close, humid shop, holding hands, and Haripada Pal told me the myth. While speaking he did not make a breakthrough into performance. He shared information with me to explain the images he makes. The information chanced to take narrative form, but Haripada delivered it conversationally, just as he would have done if no tale were involved.

My point is not that myths are not told in Bangladesh. I recorded a deeply moving myth from Amulya Chandra Pal, potter and poet, in the village of Kagajipara.[6] In Amulya's story, King Karna, called charitable and the best of the world's warriors in the *Mahabharata*, kills and cooks his son; then, having passed God's terrible test, he has his son restored to him. "What a wonder," Amulya concluded; "never have I seen a dead son come to life." Amulya is a father who has seen three sons die.

Like a murti, Amulya's myth, transcribed and translated in my book on Bangladesh, was founded upon the proposition of reincarnation and created for presence in a religious setting. As befits Bengal, it shifted a tale known widely in the subcontinent toward accommodation with the myth, shared by Muslims, Jews, and Christians, of Abraham's willingness to sacrifice his son at the command of God. And also as befits Bengal, a place justly renowned for the quantity and quality of its poetry, Amulya Chandra Pal shaped his narrative into a poem, a kind of ballad called a *pala*.

As he would do in sculpting the statue of a deity, Amulya made his myth as beautiful as possible, and that meant that it was shaped as a poem and presented as a song. To others whose Bengali is better than mine, I leave investigation of the possibility that, in Bangladesh, when a myth is truly performed it will be a song in a ritual—like a murti in beauty and context—and I return to the run of my argument.

The mythic system I am describing is not the only one in Bangladesh; most Bangladeshis are Muslims, people of the word. I am describing it because it is an example of a kind of system that, being found as well in other places, could help balance the philological obsession of our effort. In this system oral narrative is present, but peripheral. Haripada Pal knew the tale that explained the image that baffled the American experts. But he felt no urge to develop it poetically into an affecting presence, a work of art. His artistic performance involves manipulating clay, not words, though he is gifted in speech as well as sculpture. His story was only part of a vast resource of esoteric knowledge that helps him create images. Most important in his creative act, however, is not knowledge, but the mystical connection he makes to God, the passionate love for God that drives him toward beauty, that might carry him to eternal bliss in a place without facts or logic or words.

The people for whom Haripada Pal creates know far less than he does. For them it is enough to know that when Kali has the sword in her left hand, she is Shamakali, to whom one prays for deliverance from the demons of the world, the muggers and terrorists who make life miserable, and with the sword in her right hand, she is Rakshakali, to whom one prays in order to receive the blessings of God.

NOTES

1. Generically legends, functionally myths, Irish stories of the saints are treated in Glassie 1982, 159–80, 626–65.

2. Turkish works of art, mythic in purpose, are described in Glassie 1993, 109–42, 836–48.

3. Hindu sculpture in Bangladesh, created by the Pals, is presented in Glassie 1997, 128–67, 185–95, 216–23, 313–66, and Glassie 1999, 19–34.

4. Historical support for this argument is available, obliquely, in Banu 1992, Chakravarti 1985, Eaton 1996, Kennedy 1993, McDaniel 1989, and Roy 1983.

5. For Haripada Pal, see Glassie 1997, chapter 6.

6. Amulya Chandra Pal's ballad is translated, quoted, and interpreted in Glassie 1997, 108–15. The story, adjusted to the Bengali context (see Glassie 1997, 465 for a preliminary, inept effort at historical analysis), belongs to a narrative complex spread widely in India, for which see Shulman 1993.

BIBLIOGRAPHY

Armstrong, Robert Plant. 1971. *The Affecting Presence: An Essay in Humanistic Anthropology.* Urbana: University of Illinois Press.

———. 1975. *Wellspring: On the Myth and Source of Culture.* Berkeley and Los Angeles: University of California Press.

———. 1981. *The Powers of Presence: Consciousness, Myth, and Affecting Presence.* Philadelphia: University of Pennsylvania Press.

Banu, U. A. B. Razia Akter. 1992. *Islam in Bangladesh.* Leiden: E. J. Brill.

Chakravarti, Ramakanta. 1985. *Vaisnavism in Bengal, 1486–1900.* Calcutta: Sanskrit Pustak Bhandar.

Chaudhuri, Nirad C. 1979. *Hinduism: A Religion to Live By.* New York: Oxford University Press.

———. 1994. *The Autobiography of an Unknown Indian.* Bombay: Jaico Publishing House.

Eaton, Richard M. 1996. *The Rise of Islam and the Bengal Frontier, 1204–1760.* Berkeley and Los Angeles: University of California Press.

Glassie, Henry. 1982. *Passing the Time in Ballymenone: Culture and History of an Ulster Community.* Philadelphia: University of Pennsylvania Press.

———. 1993. *Turkish Traditional Art Today.* Bloomington: Indiana University Press.

———. 1997. *Art and Life in Bangladesh.* Bloomington: Indiana University Press.

———. 1999. *The Potter's Art.* Bloomington: Indiana University Press.

Kennedy, Melville T. 1993. *The Chaitanya Movement: A Study of Vaishnavism in Bengal.* New Delhi: Munshiram Manoharlal.

McDaniel, June. 1989. *The Madness of the Saints: Ecstatic Religion in Bengal.* Chicago: University of Chicago Press.

Roy, Asim. 1983. *The Islamic Syncretistic Tradition in Bengal.* Princeton, N.J.: Princeton University Press.

Shulman, David. 1993. *The Hungry God: Hindu Tales of Filicide and Devotion.* Chicago: University of Chicago Press.

Part VI

MYTH AS CONCEPT

FOURTEEN

Myth in Historical Perspective: The Case of Pagan Deities in the Anglo-Saxon Royal Genealogies

R. D. FULK

The Symposium on Myth was an occasion for appraising mythology as an academic project, for taking stock of an exceptionally interdisciplinary realm at a time of intense interest in interdisciplinary ventures. Mythology is an especially pliable area of study, one that has been continually remade over the course of its history as an academic endeavor. It began as a branch of classical studies and came to inform and be informed by the methodologies of a series of new disciplines as they arose, including folklore studies, anthropology, and literary hermeneutics, especially of the structuralist variety. The history of mythological studies thus is in many ways a history of major academic trends of the past century and a half. This was, then, one of the sorts of history that particularly interested me when I was asked to comment on the panel titled "Myth and Historical Texts," even though the session papers were devoted to exploring history in another sense of the word—history as a narrative of the actual rather than the imaginary past. The point of the juxtaposition of myth and history seems self-evident: locked in a Saussurean embrace, the two terms define each other, so that if we know what history is we are sure to have a better grasp of the meaning of mythology. But of course the opposition has already shaped what myth can mean in this context, drawing our attention away from certain other possibilities, such as myth as the narrative expression of ritual, or of the unconscious. This is not to say that there is no value in the comparison, but to say that it is limited from the outset. Comparing mythology with history might at first seem an unpromising way of getting at its meaning, since presently there could hardly be a more contested issue than how to define history. But it is the very indeterminacy of the question that makes the comparison valuable. Historians of late have been particularly concerned with questions of subjectivity and interestedness: who writes histories, from which perspective, for what sort of audience, and with what political objectives in mind? If the comparison with history accomplishes anything, it should lead us to confront more directly these same questions in regard to mythology. Thus a consideration of history in the sense of a narrative of actual events does lead us back to history in the sense I first mentioned, the history of academic practices in regard to mythology.

For the purpose of tracing that history, some recent models of historiography, particularly some that follow in the footsteps of Foucault, invite lexicology to the task by insisting that the deed must be cousin to the word—that intellectual history is inseparable from the bland facts of language. Concepts cannot exist independent of the discourse that contains them or the terminology that designates them, and thus there was, for example, no homosexuality before the nineteenth century, no intellectualism, no class struggle; for that matter, no lexicology. Nomenclature thus becomes an essential element of the study of historical modes of thought. This is obviously quite a different matter from making etymology the final arbiter of meaning, an error explained by William Hansen elsewhere in this volume. The purpose of tracing the development of terminology is not to let past meanings determine present ones, but to highlight the differences and reveal the contingencies of our own epistemological categories, revealing them to be time- and culture-bound rather than transcendent verities. Viewed from this perspective, myth turns out to be a peculiar beast. As Gordon Brotherston points out in another chapter of this volume, *myth* is not an English word of great antiquity. On the evidence of the citations in the *OED,* there was no such word in use in English before 1830. That is a surprising gap, given what a useful term *myth* is. How, for example, did English speakers manage to do without the term during the later sixteenth century, when poetry was all Ovid and Olympians? That the *OED* has not simply missed significantly earlier attestations is demonstrated well enough by the history of the form *mythos,* which was first used in English nearly a century earlier. The word retains its Greek inflection—in fact, its first attestation, in 1753, is a Greek plural, *mythoi*—and that is a clear sign that the word was not yet naturalized in English, and thus that we should not expect to find the inflectionless form until some time after this. That the word *myth* was still recognized as a neologism in the nineteenth century is further shown by the continued use of *mythos* and the Latinized *mythus* to refer to familiar classical Greek and Roman myths as late as the middle of the nineteenth century. It is also shown by the instability of the pronunciation of *myth:* those etymology-conscious Hellenists who first borrowed the word into English, Oxbridge scholars who knew their Homeric meter, gave the word the vowel of *bite* rather than of *bit.* This scholarly pronunciation was replaced in everyday speech by the present one over the course of the nineteenth century, in tandem with the word's slow naturalization.

The semantics of the word have also changed over the years, though not in the way one might have expected. Although Homeric *mûthos* refers neutrally to oral discourse (compare the derivative verb *mūthéomai,* which means simply "to speak"), from the time of Pindar (d. ca. 438 B.C.E.) the word has some pejorative connotations, denoting the fabulous, as opposed to the historical *lógos.* When they were first borrowed into English the words *mythos* and *myth* brought with them these same negative connotations, as when in 1803 George S. Faber, in his *Dissertation on the Mysteries of the Cabiri,* wrote, "I cannot but be persuaded that the poem of Homer at least is a mere mythos" (*OED*). The academic, folkloric significance of the word is actually a later development, the result of a semantic shift occasioned by the rising fortunes of mythology as an academic subject. We might have expected a longer history for the term in English, given the longevity of its counterpart *history.* Both *history* and its derivative *story* (via Old French *estoire*) originally were fairly neutral with respect to truth value, designating both true and false narratives. But under the influence of the new humanistic learning, in the fifteenth century *history* took on its Latin connotation of true narrative, and the more elevated meaning of this word drove down the fortunes of *story,* so that by the sixteenth century we find reference to "frivolous stories." *History,* incidentally, had an antonym from the very start, *fable,* with all the deprecating connotations of Latin *fabula,* and so the need for a word meaning "myth" was not so pressing in the Middle Ages.

But another reason, it turns out, that the word *myth* was not required in English before the nineteenth century is that there was already a word with precisely this meaning: *mythology.* It is already to be found early in the fourteenth century, when it could designate a mythological story, a meaning that *mūthología* had already in Greek, and hence also *mythologie* in French. It is not until much later that *mythology* takes on its two present meanings, referring to a body of myths (first attested 1781) and to the study of myths (1836). This last development was taking place at about the same time as the introduction of the word *myth,* which it helps to explain. The rise of nineteenth-century science accustomed Englishmen to thinking of words ending in *-ology* as designating academic discourses, and so *mythology* also had to have this meaning; the subject of mythology then naturally ought to be *myth,* and the meaning of the word *myth* was duly altered to fit the circumstances.[1] The word *myth* has subsequently acquired one other meaning, a meaning in use for at least half a century, though it is not yet recognized by the *OED:* since the word *mythology* is ambiguous, referring to either a body of or the study of myths, *myth* can now disambiguate the reference by assuming the latter meaning—as in "A Symposium on Myth."

The most illuminating point to emerge from the history of the word is that all of these changes are the result of the attitudes of academics. The popular meaning of *myth*, "a fiction," is in fact one of its earliest meanings in English and goes back to Attic usage, while the more academic meanings of the word are later developments, one of them fairly recent. The prejudices of academics, however, dictate that the popular meaning should be viewed as a corruption, and that is why in most dictionaries the meaning "an untruth," though it is actually older, is listed last. In the history of this word we see the history of the discipline: the word appears just as mythology is being formed as an academic subject, and some of the earliest instances are to be found in the writings of those who first framed the subject, including Thomas Keightley and Max Müller. When the word was borrowed into English it must have had a particularly scholarly ring to it, not just because of its Greek derivation, but also because there was already a serviceable word in English for an untrue narrative. It must also have seemed avant-garde, given what an intellectual stir the new field of mythology was raising in the middle of the nineteenth century. This aura of the new was lost by the middle of the twentieth century, and so the adaptation of *myth* to mean "mythology" in some contexts about that time—as in *Myth: A Symposium*—is harder to explain. We can only speculate, but one possibility is that structural anthropologists, intent on making mythology their methodological proving ground, sought to insulate their new approaches from the taint of outmodedness by substituting *myth* for *mythology*, lending the former a jaunty new feel to suit its new theoretical underpinnings.

The history of these words also sheds light on the founding myths of the field of mythology. Even though anthropological methods perhaps offer the best hope of transcending our presentism and our ethnocentrism, mythology, even when viewed as a branch of anthropology, would seem by its very conception to be deeply implicated in a history of maintaining illusions about our own culture as well as about ancient and non-Eurocentric ones. Gordon Brotherston's essay in this volume serves as an insistent reminder of how mythology has at times been used to validate our own culture at the expense of others'. The opposition between myth and history that privileges the literacy of European cultures was built into mythology at the time it was constituted as an academic subject: we have seen how the dismissive implications of the word *myth* preceded the word's appropriation as a scholarly term. Moreover, since the history of the term reveals that most of its meanings derive from academic usage, the responsibility for the prejudicial classification of other people's history as mythology is not diffused vaguely throughout Western culture, as we might like to think, but rests squarely on the shoulders of academics.

Still, the attitudes that have engendered the opposition between history and myth certainly have a longer genealogy than the English words themselves. British imperialism may have particularly welcomed such ideas, but undoubtedly they were inherited, with the words, from the Greeks and Romans, who themselves were notoriously convinced of their own cultural superiority, and who used these terms, or similar ones, with many of the same connotations we do. The distinction is to be found elsewhere, too. In his essay in this volume John Lindow shows very convincingly that Snorri Sturluson also distinguished firmly between myth and history. Though some scholars treat *Ynglinga saga* as a mythological source, Snorri apparently meant just the opposite by it. Because we have his earlier edda for comparison, it is particularly easy to see how he excluded from *Heimskringla* material pertaining to Óðinn that must have seemed to him particularly unhistorical. Though the story of how Gefjun ploughed up the island of Sjælland from the mainland of Sweden is obviously fantastic, there is nothing told about Óðinn himself that is intrinsically implausible from a thirteenth-century point of view. This is made all the clearer now that Lindow has shown that the forms of magic associated with Óðinn are precisely the forms that thirteenth-century Norsemen believed really existed, since they associated them in particular with the contemporary Sámi. Euhemerization is itself a historicizing strategy, clearly demonstrating Snorri's intention to differentiate historical and mythic elements of Óðinn's reign. By contrast, Snorri expressly discounts any claim that the material of his *Edda* is true, since he says in *Skáldskaparmál,* "Eigi skulu kristnir menn trúa á heiðin goð ok eigi á sannindi þessar sagnar annan veg en svá sem hér finsk í upphafi bókar" [Christians must not believe in pagan gods, nor in the truth of this tale in any way other than the one found at the beginning of this book] (Faulkes 1982b, xviii), and he is referring here to the prologue of *Gylfaginning,* where he offers a euhemeristic account of the Vanir and the Æsir that robs them of any claim to deity.

Although the distinction between myth and history seems sometimes arbitrarily imposed and often politically charged, it is nonetheless a useful distinction, and one obviously recognized in widely different times and places. There could be no clearer sign of the utility and significance of the difference than its political consequences. To this point I have been concerned primarily with the politics of mythologizing in modern times; but if one hopes to avoid the solipsism of fitting all mythologies to the procrustean bed of modern Western conceptions, it is worthwhile to try to understand the political contexts of mythologies in other times and places as well. The particular instance I would like to examine is the use of mythical elements in the so-called Anglian collection of Anglo-Saxon royal genealogies, since I think they expose some of the fault lines where these tectonic

plates of myth and history rub against each other. This is unusual ground
for the study of myth because this is a nondiscursive genre, offering only
lines of descent emptied of their narrative content. What could be a more
effective historicizing strategy than to dispose of the myths themselves?
Only the names remain to summon up the untold stories. The Old English
royal genealogies have been the subject of some brilliant studies, particularly those of Kenneth Sisam (1953) and David N. Dumville (1976, 1977),
and what I have to say is no more than a footnote to their findings.

The later genealogies of the West Saxon kings illustrate with particular
clarity the political uses of such royal pedigrees. They contain a series of
recognizable blocks of accretions that show how, piece by piece, the kings'
pedigrees were extended back in time to incorporate the names of gods,
Scandinavian monarchs of heroic legend, and biblical figures as far back as
Adam, or God himself. It is by now a scholarly commonplace that such
genealogies have a bald political purpose. The familiarity of heroic and biblical names lends verisimilitude to the entire production, which in turn
confers upon a monarch all the authority that longevity of lineage can afford. A king who can trace his ancestry through a royal line back to Adam
obviously has a greater claim to the right to rule than a king who came to
the throne by dint of arms.[2] This view may be traced to Alcuin himself,
who, in a letter dated 757, explicitly links length of lineage to royal vigor:
"Et vix aliquis modo, quod sine lacrymis non dicam, ex antiqua regum
prosapia invenitur, et tanto incertiores sunt orginis, quanto minores sunt
fortitudinis" [And hardly anyone, though I cannot say it without tears, is to
be found from the ancient lineage of kings, and the less secure they are of
origin, the less is their fortitude].[3]

But even the earliest of the Anglo-Saxon genealogies all show fabrica-
tions in the names from the most distant past. In an extraordinary fragment
of a Mercian book which, very unusually for an Anglo-Saxon manuscript,
is closely datable to the period 805–12, following various episcopal lists
there is a set of royal genealogies for the monarchs of five kingdoms,
Northumbria (including the subkingdoms of Deira and Bernicia), Mercia,
Lindsey, Kent, and East Anglia. Versions of these pedigrees are found in
some later manuscripts, as well.[4] These diverse materials are referred to as
the "Anglian collection" of royal genealogies and regnal lists. Nearly all of
the five royal lines in this Vespasian manuscript begin with Frealaf and his
son Woden. Sisam argues that the archetype was Mercian and was compiled
late in the reign of Offa, who ruled from 757 to 796. But Dumville offers
cogent reasons for thinking the original collection is of Northumbrian
provenience, and thus he assigns the archetype to the reign of the last
Northumbrian monarch named, Alhred, who ruled from 765 to 774, or to
the first reign of his twice-enthroned successor, Æthelred, from 774 to 779.

Yet even if the archetype from which the Anglian collection derives should be dated to this period, there is some reason to regard the second half of the eighth century as merely the date at which preexisting genealogical materials were assembled rather than the date of their fabrication. One earlier genealogy, the pedigree of the Kentish king Æthelberht, the first Anglo-Saxon king to embrace Christianity, is given in two parts in Bede's *Historia ecclesiastica gentis Anglorum,* a work completed in the year 731. Bede traces the king's ancestry back four generations to Hengest, said to be the first Anglo-Saxon invader of Britain (II, 5); and in an earlier passage Hengest's line is traced back four generations to Woden, "de cuius stirpe," Bede says, "multarum provinciarum regium genus originem duxit" [from whose stock the line of kings of many provinces has derived its origin] (I, 15). Though it is the only one he offers, this apparently was not the only English royal pedigree Bede knew; he made use as well of genealogies or regnal lists for Essex and Northumbria (Dumville 1977, 97, 100), and possibly Mercia (Thornton 1999). Thus it seems probable that Bede is referring to English royal lines derived from Woden rather than Continental ones. Early Continental sources, after all, in surviving copies do sometimes claim divine descent for kings, though Woden is never actually mentioned, at least by that name: in Jordanes's *Getica* the pedigree of the Visigothic ruling Amali, drawn from the lost Gothic history of Cassiodorus, starts from Gapt, called a *semideus* (on whom see below); the Lombards, according to the prologue to the mid-seventh-century *Edict* of Rothari, traced the descent of the great Alboin from Gausus, whose name reflects the same stem as Gapt's;[5] and one Frankish genealogy derives the various Germanic tribes from Ermenius, Ingo, and Escio, corresponding to the three eponymous grandsons of the god Tuisto in Tacitus (*Germania* 2), the second to be identified with Old Icelandic *Ingvi,* son of Óðinn (sometimes treated as identical with Freyr) and progenitor of the Swedish royal line of Ynglingar, according to *Snorra edda.*[6]

Bede's genealogy of Æthelberht is in fact clearly an earlier version than that represented in the Anglian collection, since, as mentioned above, the latter begins not with Woden but with Frealaf, and in one case, the Lindsey line, Frealaf's ancestry is traced back four more generations, through Frioðulf, Finn, and God(u)ulf, to Geot. This Frealaf is a figure unknown to any mythological tradition, and one whose dithematic name suggests a legendary rather than a mythological background.[7] Woden, being the *Alfaðr,* 'All-father', as Snorri calls him, ought not to have any father; and in any case some other genealogies of Anglo-Saxon kings show that Frealaf is extraneous here: the pedigrees given in the Harleian recension of the *Historia Brittonum,* a bricolage of materials of various antiquity assembled in 829–30, agree with Bede in beginning the line with Woden rather than Frealaf, and so does the pedigree of Cerdic in the West Saxon Regnal Table and most of the pedigrees of the West Saxon kings in the various versions of the Anglo-Saxon Chronicle (Sisam 1953, 293, 295, 298). It may well be that some, or even most, of these pedigrees are modeled on one or two originals: Sisam (1953, 302–305) and Dumville (1977, 78–81) argue that the West Saxon and Kentish pedigrees are based on those of Bernicia and Deira, respectively, and Dumville further urges that we think of Woden as a marker placed in all the Anglian pedigrees as a way of reinforcing the boundaries of a political unit, the Anglian kingdoms, which in the eighth century had overlordship of the South (hence the inclusion of Southern material). Still, the derivation of the East Saxon royal line from Seaxneat rather than Woden in an unrelated text in a fragment of a different manuscript suggests that if these divine derivations do have political significance they are part of a very old tradition dividing the Angles from the Saxons, since Seaxneat's name is cognate with that of Saxnot, a figure known to have been worshiped by the Continental Saxons.[8]

The mythological content of the Anglian collection is not limited to the name Woden. *Gēot*, the name of the progenitor of the royal line of Lindsey in the Vespasian manuscript, is an archaic or Northumbrian dialect spelling of *Gēat*, the Old English equivalent of *Gapt* and *Gausus* in the Gothic and Langobardic genealogies mentioned above. Jordanes calls Gapt one of the *ansis*, a word that he equates with *semidei*, and which is cognate with Old Icelandic *Æsir*, the name of Óðinn's family of gods. The Old English equivalent is **Ēs*, which is found only in the genitive plural *Ēsa* in a metrical charm, though the singular *Ōs-* (Old Icelandic *Ás-*, Old High German *Ans-*) is common in personal names. *Gautr*, the Old Icelandic cognate of *Gēat*, is a name that Óðinn applies to himself in *Grímnismál* (54:6) in the elder edda—though scholars have perhaps been hasty to assume that the connection is very old.[9] The Anglo-Saxons certainly understood Geat to be of divine origin, as shown by the genealogy of Hengest and Horsa, the progenitors of the Kentish royal line, in the *Historia Brittonum*, a genealogy of course derived from an English source. There we are told that Geat, "ut aiunt, filius fuit dei, non ueri nec omnipotentis Dei . . . sed alicuius ex idolis eorum quem, ab ipso daemoni caecati, more gentili pro deo colebant" [as they say, was a son of a god, not actually of Almighty God . . . but of one of their idols which, blinded by the same demon, they worshiped for a god in the manner of pagans] (Dumville 1985, 82–83). More to the point, in the later ninth century in his life of Alfred the Great the Welsh priest Asser provided a genealogy for the West Saxon kings that also included Geat in the line of descent, and the text identifies this as the same Geat whom "iamdudum pagani pro deo venerabantur" [for a long time the pagans venerated as a god] (Stevenson 1959, 3). One of Woden's sons, Waðolgeot in the Mercian line, is probably an avatar of this same Geat. In Old English the word *waðol* appears just once, but the meaning "wandering" is determinable from the Old High German cognate *wadal;* and though *Waðol-* is not an actual name element in Old English, *Wadal-* is attested several times on the Continent (Förstemann 1900, 1439). Thus the name *Waðolgeat* would appear to derive either from archaic heroic legend or from a Continental source.

The name of another of Woden's sons, Beldaeg in the Bernician line, has perhaps been contaminated by proximity to the name of another of Woden's sons, Wegdaeg, who appears in the parallel Deiran line.[10] This sort of confusion is especially plausible if, as Sisam has argued, the genealogies in the Vespasian manuscript derive from a compilation in tabular form, with parallel columns in which the two names would have stood next to each other. In any case, Beldaeg would appear to correspond (as the preface to *Snorra edda* asserts and the *Chronicle of Æthelweard* implies) to Baldr, Óðinn's son in Norse myth, whose death at the hands of his brother Hǫðr powerfully shook the foundations of the Æsir's and Vanir's world and prompted Óðinn's vain attempt to bring his son back from Hel.[11] The myth of Baldr's death is historicized in *Beowulf,* where Herebeald, the second element of whose name is cognate with Old Icelandic *Baldr,* is killed by his brother Hæthcyn, the first element of whose name is cognate with Old Icelandic *Hǫðr.* Like Óðinn in Norse tradition, Herebeald and Hæthcyn's father Hrethel is deeply affected by this killing. Eventually he dies of grief. One wonders whether the *Beowulf* poet was not in fact aware of the mythological connection between Hrethel and Woden in this context, since Hrethel's sorrow reminds the poet of the lamentation of a father for his hanged son; hanging is a form of death closely associated with Óðinn in Norse myth.

The other sons of Woden do not seem to be relatable to Norse mythology (one is in fact "Caser," i.e., *Caesar,* the Old English word for emperor), though in this and later Anglo-Saxon royal genealogies there are some other names familiar from myth and heroic legend. But this brief examination of the chief mythological figures in the Anglian collection is sufficient background to a consideration of the conditions under which myth and history collided in these texts. How is it that the names of gods appear in these lists? Though there are notable exceptions, earlier scholarship tended to view these genealogies as windows on a remote past, as reliable reflections of ancient oral tradition. This was the view, for example, of such influential scholars as H. M. Chadwick (1924, 252) and Raymond Chambers (1959, 316–17, originally published 1921). As recently as 1960, Karl Hauck (119 n. 69) expressed astonishment at the suggestion that such *Götterstammbäume* should have been fabricated after the conversion to Christianity. More recent work on these genealogies is more skeptical about their antiquity, taking as axiomatic their design for political ends and thus their continual alteration to suit the changing political situation. The work of Sisam and Dumville in particular is masterful and makes it painfully clear how credulous earlier views were.

Yet even if belief in the reliability of the genealogies was naïve, it was predicated on some reasonable observations that have perhaps given us too little pause ever since. Anglo-Saxon churchmen regarded pagan gods as devils—one Old English word for heathen worship is *dēofolgield*, literally "devil-tribute"—and since for most of the Anglo-Saxon period literacy was with rare exceptions the province exclusively of ecclesiastics, it is difficult to believe that they would have been complicit in the construction of genealogies that traced the descent of Christian monarchs from devils.[12] Recent scholarship has not ignored this problem; nor has it dealt adequately with it. When the matter has been broached it has been framed as a question about Bede: how could this most orthodox and discerning of historians have derived the line of Æthelberht from Woden without betraying a hint of skepticism or moral repugnance? Harrison (1976) would account for this peculiarity by assuming that Woden was regarded not as a god but as an ancient, mortal hero. This explanation seems unsatisfactory, since there is good evidence that Woden, by *interpretatio Romana*, was widely regarded as the equivalent of Mercury and was known to have been worshiped by pagans, as for instance Æthelweard tells us (Campbell 1962, 9, 18), and as the poet of the collection of maxims in the Exeter Book clearly knew.[13] North (1997, 116–17) supposes that Bede sanitized Woden for Christian use by associating him typologically with Jacob, since Bede (*Hist. eccl.* I, 34) once compares Æthelfrith of Northumbria (a descendant of Woden, according to the Anglian royal genealogies) to Jacob's descendant Saul. John (1992) would dispose of the problem altogether, arguing that Æthelberht's genealogy is an interpolation in Bede's text. Miller (1975, 254 n. 1) offers a solution with the argument that Bede "does not take Woden as more than a means of defining royalty." Dumville agrees, reasoning that "he is a convention, and *his* inclusion at least is not intended to be taken literally in any reading of the genealogy" (1977, 79). But even if this explanation is regarded as plausible, it accounts only for Bede's genealogy of Æthelberht, and not for any other of the Anglo-Saxon genealogies in which Woden appears. Moreover, this view attributes to Bede a carelessness in distinguishing the literal and the symbolic that seems to me uncharacteristic of the *Historia ecclesiastica*. Such a view seems rather a consequence of the way Bede in modern scholarship is routinely viewed as our contemporary, a man unlike other Anglo-Saxons, a scholar with the principles of a modern historian and therefore one who does not necessarily himself believe the things he tells us.[14] Davis (1992, 25–26) thus rejects the explanations of Miller and Dumville on the grounds that they attribute excessive cynicism to Bede; and yet his own position, that Bede simply had not yet made up his mind about whether Woden was a "convenient political fiction," a genuine ancestor later deified, or a devil, brings us no closer to understanding why Bede bothered to include such unorthodox material at all.

This is the real significance of my point about mythological figures in the genealogies. In this context the exact process by which they found their way there is not so important, and in any case it may never be known to us. We can speculate about it: my suspicion is that one or more Anglo-Saxon royal houses maintained such a descent before the arrival of the missionaries from Rome and Ireland, and after the Conversion, rather than contradict the claims of a ruling family and falsify oral tradition, churchmen kept the pagan gods' names in the pedigrees and regarded them as euhemerizations. Indeed, the need not to falsify tradition explains why euhemerization, rather than outright denial of the existence of pagan deities, was standard practice in the early Middle Ages.[15] Moisl (1981, 217–18) has rendered such a view plausible with persuasive evidence that divine descent was a belief of long standing among the ancient Germanic peoples, evidence starting with Tacitus's remarks on the descent of all the Germanic tribes from the god Tuisto. But regardless of the precise mechanism, it should be apparent that just as in ancient times the gods may have served an ideological function in the pedigrees (reinforcing royal authority) and were permitted to remain there on another ideological basis (euhemerization as Church policy for dealing with pagan belief), so, too, our attempts to explain their presence are predicated on ideological principles that have little to do with the Anglo-Saxon age but are responses to the intellectual tenor of more recent times. This is particularly clear in regard to scholarship of the nineteenth century, which sought in (and interpreted into) early Germanic records evidence of the pagan origins that Romanticism so desperately needed to find there in its quest for originary primitivism.[16] But it is also true of more recent scholarship, even that which serves to expose the credulousness of the Victorian age. When we attribute to Bede an ironic detachment with respect to Woden and assume that Old English genealogists scarcely hesitated to falsify received traditions in the pursuit of political objectives, we are attempting to mold the Anglo-Saxon period in our own image, as well as to make our understanding of these texts conform ideologically to current academic orthodoxies. Moreover, the preoccupation of current Anglo-Saxon scholarship with exposing the errors of Romanticism is not a value-free quest for truth but the product of historical forces, of, as Shippey (1993) has pointed out, twentieth-century politics, particularly in the form of the reaction to German nationalism.

This brings us back to where we began, with the inconstant fortunes of mythological studies and the mutable ideologies on which they depend. If, as I suggested at the outset, there are intimate connections between the two meanings of *myth* and *history*—between the history of the profession and the professional treatment of myth by historians—probably the central issue they have in common is the utility of myth. The line between myth and history gets continually redrawn in order to ensure the value of myth in the historical present. It gets redrawn in part because the tension between the two cannot be resolved conclusively, since the opposition to myth validates history at the same time that history borrows the tropes of myth to convince us of its authority and verisimilitude, as demonstrated elegantly by Joseph Nagy in this volume. Just as Bede and the Anglo-Saxon genealogists found myth useful to their purposes and thus historicized it, so modern historians also find it useful and, rather than marking it off as irrelevant to historical study, assimilate it and draw on it as evidence—in this case, of Bede's modern-seeming professionalism. If this is not exactly an answer to the questions posed at the outset—who writes myths, from which perspective, for what sort of audience, and with what political objectives in mind?—it is because these questions, it can now be seen, assume that myths have a particular point of origin, when they might more profitably be viewed as components of a mythological intertext. The concept of utility suggests that we should think of myths as stages in developing processes, processes governed by changing historical conditions. And those conditions exert as profound an influence over the development of myth as of the study of myth—that is, over the development of *myth* in both academic senses of the word.

NOTES

1. This process was very likely aided by the consideration that Greek *mûthos* is sometimes found with a meaning approximating this one, e.g., in Herodotus and in Attic prose.

2. See, among many others, Wallace-Hadrill 1971, 112–13 and Taviani-Carozzi 1993, 370.

3. Alcuin, letter to the clergy and nobles of Kent, in Haddan and Stubbs 1871, 3:510; also in Dümmler 1895, 192. See also Chaney 1960, 201 and Wormald 1978, 57. For further evidence of such Anglo-Saxon attitudes see Loyn 1984, 15.

4. The material is assembled in Dumville 1976, 30–37.

5. It is generally agreed that the stem is **Gaut-*: see Helm 1938, Birkhan 1965, and Wolfram 1977, 90–92.

6. For Gapt, see Mommsen 1882, 76, 142–43; for Gausus, see Beyerle 1947, 4; and for the Frankish material see Kurth 1968, 521. Moisl (1981, 223–26) offers other, less secure evidence for Northern gods in the Frankish succession, and Hauck (1978, 68–69) in the Saxon one.

7. Davis (1992, 28–29) suggests rather that Frealaf is the English equivalent of Old Icelandic Freyr, or his son, and this is not implausible, especially given Freyr's association with Ingvi.

8. The source of our knowledge about Saxnot is a passage from the ninth-century Old Saxon "Abrenunciatio and Credo," a baptismal formula of renunciation: "Forsachistu diabolae? . . . End allum dioboles uuercum? respondeat end ec forsacho allum dioboles uuercum and uuordum, Thunaer ende Uuoden ende Saxnote ende allem them unholdum the hira genotas sint" [Do you renounce the devil? . . . And all the devil's works? Let him/her respond, And also I renounce all the devil's works and words, Thuner [Þórr] and Woden and Seaxneat and all those fiends who are their associates]. For the East Saxon genealogy, see Dumville 1986, 31–32; for the Old Saxon text, Gallée 1894, 248.

9. There is a tendency in scholarship on these names to assume that Woden is the original, and that he attracted other names to himself. But the name *Woden* is in origin an epithet, "crazed," and it is possible that Gaut is the older deity.

10. Uegdaeg (to give the manuscript spelling) is otherwise unknown, but the element -*daeg* is also found in the name *Suebdaeg*, which, as the author of the preface to *Snorra edda* noticed, resembles the name *Svipdagr*, a figure with strong mythological connections, especially with the name *Gautr*, in both the elder edda and *Ynglinga saga*. But de Vries (1970, 233, §488) regards *Beldaeg* as the more original form of the name, and Old Icelandic *Baldr*, ultimately, as a corruption of it.

11. The preface to *Snorra edda*, drawing on the Old Icelandic *Langfeðgatal* in providing English names and their perceived Icelandic equivalents, is explicit: "Beldegg, er vér kǫllum Baldr" [Beldegg, whom we call Baldr] (Faulkes 1982b, 5). Æthelweard, on the other hand, merely substitutes *Balder* (probably a Norse form, as North [1997, 124] argues) for the name *Beldaeg* that the sources for his West Saxon genealogy adopted from the Bernician one (as argued by Sisam 1953, 302–305). For Æthelweard's pedigree of Æthelwulf see Campbell 1962, 33.

12. Johnson (1995) argues that euhemerization and demonization may or may not be coincident in Anglo-Saxon attitudes toward the old pagan divinities, but the problem remains that we do not expect regard of any sort for pagan deities among Anglo-Saxon churchmen. Still, Johnson's evidence effectively counters the impression given by Faulkes (1982a, 110) that euhemerization and demonization are opposing strategies.

13. Lines 132–34: "Wōden worhte wēos, wuldor alwalda, / rūme roderas; þæt is rīce god, / sylf sōðcyning, sāwla nergend" [Woden made idols, [but] the all-wielder [made] glory, the broad skies; that is a powerful god, the true king himself, savior of souls] (Krapp and Dobbie 1936, 161). That Woden was not regarded as an ordinary hero is further suggested by his association with magic, both in Old Icelandic and in a metrical charm called the *Nine Herbs Charm*, in which we are told, "Wyrm cōm snīcan, tōslāt hē man; / ðā genām Wōden viiii wuldortānas, / slōh ðā þā næddran, þæt hēo on viiii tōflēah" [A serpent came crawling, it tore apart a man; then Woden took nine glory-twigs [that is, nine herbs], struck then the serpent, so that it burst into nine pieces] (Dobbie 1942, 119–20).

14. Wormald (1978, 32–33), for example, warns against this common view of Bede.

15. For Anglo-Saxon examples of euhemerizing strategies see the letter of Daniel, bishop of Winchester, to Boniface, datable to 722–32, in Whitelock 1979, 795; Æthelweard's remarks on Woden's deification by barbarians (Campbell 1962, 9, 18); and Ælfric's sermon on false gods (Pope 1967–68, 2:681–86). Faulkes (1982a, 109–10) traces the development of this practice in early Christian writers.

16. The most familiar of many demonstrations of this point are the studies by Stanley (1975) and Frantzen (1990).

BIBLIOGRAPHY

Beyerle, F., ed. 1947. *Die Gesetze der Langobarden.* Weimar: H. Bohlaus Nachf.

Birkhan, Helmut. 1965. "Gapt und Gaut." *Archiv für deutsches Altertum* 94:1–17.

Campbell, A., ed. and trans. 1962. *The Chronicle of Æthelweard.* London: Nelson.

Chadwick, H. Munro. 1924. *The Origin of the English Nation.* Cambridge: Cambridge University Press.

Chambers, R. W. 1959. *Beowulf: An Introduction to the Study of the Poem, with a Discussion of the Stories of Offa and Finn.* 3d edition, revised by C. L. Wrenn. Cambridge: Cambridge University Press.

Chaney, William A. 1960. "Paganism to Christianity in Anglo-Saxon England." *Harvard Theological Review* 53:197–217.

Davis, Craig R. 1992. "Cultural Assimilation in the Anglo-Saxon Royal Genealogies." *Anglo-Saxon England* 21:23–36.

de Vries, Jan. 1970. *Altgermanische Religionsgeschichte.* 2d edition. 2 vols. Berlin: de Gruyter. Original edition, Grundriss der germanischen Philologie 12, 1956–57.

Dobbie, Elliott Van Kirk, ed. 1942. *The Anglo-Saxon Minor Poems.* The Anglo-Saxon Poetic Records, 6. New York: Columbia University Press.

Dümmler, Ernst, ed. 1895. *Epistolae Karolini Aevi.* Vol. 2. Monumenta Germaniae Historica, Epistolae, 4. Berlin: Weidmann.

Dumville, David N. 1976. "The Anglian Collection of Royal Genealogies and Regnal Lists." *Anglo-Saxon England* 5:23–50.

———. 1977. "Kingship, Genealogies, and Regnal Lists." In *Early Medieval Kingship,* edited by P. H. Sawyer and I. N. Wood, 72–104. Leeds: School of History, University of Leeds.

———. 1986. "The West Saxon Regnal List: Manuscripts and Texts." *Anglia* 104:1–32.

———, ed. 1985. *The Historia Brittonum, 3: The "Vatican" Recension.* Cambridge: D. S. Brewer.

Faulkes, Anthony. 1982a. "Descent from the Gods." *Mediaeval Scandinavia* 11:92–125.

———, ed. 1982b. *Snorri Sturluson, Edda: Prologue and Gylfaginning.* Oxford: Clarendon.

Förstemann, Ernst. 1900. *Altdeutsches Namenbuch, 1: Personnennamen.* 2d edition. Bonn: P. Hanstein.

Frantzen, Allen J. 1990. *Desire for Origins: New Language, Old English, and Teaching the Tradition.* New Brunswick, N.J.: Rutgers University Press.

Gallée, J. H., ed. 1894. *Old-Saxon Texts.* Leiden: E. J. Brill.

Haddan, Arthur W., and William Stubbs, eds. 1871. *Councils and Ecclesiastical Documents Relating to Great Britain and Ireland.* 3 vols. Oxford: Clarendon.

Harrison, Kenneth. 1976. "Woden." In *Famulus Christi: Essays in Commemoration of the Thirteenth Centenary of the Birth of the Venerable Bede,* edited by Gerald Bonner, 351–56. London: Society for Promotion of Christian Knowledge.

Hauck, Karl. 1960. "Die geschichtliche Bedeutung der germanischen Auffassung von Königtum und Adel." In *Rapports du onzième congrès international des sciences historiques, Stockholm, 21–28 août 1960,* 96–120. Göteborg: Almqvist & Wiksell.

———. 1978. "The Literature of House and Kindred Associated with Medieval Noble Families, Illustrated from Eleventh- and Twelfth-Century Satires on the Nobility." In *The Medieval Nobility,* edited by Timothy Reuter, 61–85. Amsterdam: North-Holland.

Helm, Karl. 1938. "Gaut." *Beiträge zur Geschichte der deutschen Sprache und Literatur* 62:27–30.

John, Eric. 1992. "The Point of Woden." *Anglo-Saxon Studies in Archaeology and History* 5:127–34.

Johnson, David F. 1995. "Euhemerisation versus Demonisation: The Pagan Gods and Ælfric's *De falsis diis.*" In *Pagans and Christians: The Interplay between Christian Latin and Traditional Germanic Cultures in Early Medieval Europe,* edited by T. Hofstra et al., 35–69. Groningen: E. Forsten.

Krapp, George Philip, and Elliott Van Kirk Dobbie, eds. 1936. *The Exeter Book.* The Anglo-Saxon Poetic Records, 3. New York: Columbia University Press.

Kurth, Godefroid. 1968. *Histoire poétique des Mérovingiens.* Genève: Slatkine Reprints. Original edition, Paris: A. Picard, 1893.

Loyn, Henry R. 1984. *The Governance of Anglo-Saxon England, 500–1087.* Stanford: Stanford University Press.

Miller, M. 1975. "Bede's Use of Gildas." *English Historical Review* 90:241–61.

Moisl, Hermann. 1981. "Anglo-Saxon Royal Genealogies and Germanic Oral Tradition." *Journal of Medieval History* 7:215–48.

Mommsen, Theodor, ed. 1882. *Iordanis Romana et Getica.* Monumenta Germaniae Historica, Auct. Antiqq. 5, pt. 1. Berlin: Weidmann.

North, Richard. 1997. *Heathen Gods in Old English Literature.* Cambridge Studies in Anglo-Saxon England, 22. Cambridge: Cambridge University Press.

Pope, John C., ed. 1967–68. *Homilies of Ælfric: A Supplementary Collection.* 2 vols. Early English Text Society o.s. 259–60. London: Oxford University Press.

Shippey, T. A. 1993. "Recent Writing on Old English." *Æstel* 1:111–34.

Sisam, Kenneth. 1953. "Anglo-Saxon Royal Genealogies." *Proceedings of the British Academy* 39:287–348.

Stanley, E. G. 1975. *The Search for Anglo-Saxon Paganism.* Cambridge: D. S. Brewer. Reprint of articles from *Notes & Queries,* 1964–65. Also reprinted in Stanley's *Imagining the Anglo-Saxon Past* (Cambridge: D. S. Brewer, 2000), 1–110.

Stevenson, William Henry, ed. 1959. Asser's *Life of King Alfred.* New impression. Oxford: Clarendon.

Taviani-Carozzi, Huguette. 1993. "De l'histoire au mythe: La généalogie royale anglo-saxonne." *Cahiers de civilisation médiévale* 36:355–73.

Thornton, David E. 1999. "Regnal Lists." In *The Blackwell Encyclopaedia of Anglo-Saxon England,* edited by Michael Lapidge et al., 388–89. Oxford: Blackwell.

Wallace-Hadrill, J. M. 1971. *Early Germanic Kingship in England and on the Continent.* Oxford: Clarendon.

Whitelock, Dorothy, ed. and trans. 1979. *English Historical Documents c. 500–1042.* 2d edition. London: Eyre Methuen.

Wolfram, H. 1977. "Theogonie, Ethnogenese, und ein kompromittierter Großvater im Stammbaum Theoderichs des Großen." In *Festschrift für Helmut Beumann,* edited by K. Jäschke and R. Wenskus, 80–92. Sigmaringen: Thorbecke.

Wormald, Patrick. 1978. "Bede, *Beowulf,* and the Conversion of the Anglo-Saxon Aristocracy." In *Bede and Anglo-Saxon England,* edited by Robert T. Farrell, 32–95. British Archaeological Reports, 46. Oxford: British Archeological Reports.

FIFTEEN

Can Myth Be Saved?

GREGORY NAGY

The meaning of *myth* in academic language continues to resist any definition that is uniform, universally valid.[1] I propose here to consider three historical reasons for this resistance. Once considered, these reasons will leave us as far removed as ever from any uniform definition. Instead, we may achieve something more important, namely, a brief overview of the word *myth* and its meanings. Such an overview will lead in another, altogether different, direction: far from requiring a definition of uniformity, myth needs to be explained to the fullest possible extent of its multiformity. Through an understanding of this multiformity, the idea of myth may yet be saved.

Of the three historical reasons for the lack of a uniform academic definition of the word *myth*, the first and most important is the cumulative empirical evidence gathered by anthropologists and folklorists. This evidence indicates a vast variety of different attitudes in different societies (or even in any given single society) concerning the inherent truth or reality of what may be called myth. At one extreme are small-scale traditional societies whose members view the equivalent of myth as something definitively true, definitively real. A case in point are the Yukuna of the Colombian Amazon, whose myths are as definitive as they themselves: the Yukuna word *yukuna* can be translated not only as "Yukuna people" but also as "myths" (Jacopin 1981, 360). For the Yukuna, what is at stake in their understanding of myth is their very identity. At another extreme are larger-scale traditional societies such as the Navajo: in their Coyote narratives, for example, it is near-impossible for researchers to distinguish between what is "myth" and what is "story," since "generic distinctions are far less relevant than those textural keys which allow the listeners to gain access to the important levels of meaning" (Toelken 1976, 158).

A second reason for the lack of a uniform definition of *myth* in academic language derives from a simple fact of its usage in everyday language: so long as a myth is generally understood to be a story about something that is not real, not true, we may safely predict that no single academic definition will ever prevail.[2] Even though the members of a given society may think that their myths concern what is real or true, such thinking cannot be equated with the kind of thinking we associate with empiricism and rationalism. To the extent that the academic world resists any such equation, myth becomes a foil for truth in such pairings as *myth and science, myth and history,* or even *myth and reason.*[3] Granted, if myth is examined by researchers such as anthropologists or folklorists, unbelieving outsiders who are looking in, as it were, on the thinking of the insiders, then the myth may indeed become a reality—but only to the extent that it serves as an object of study. That is, myth becomes a structure suitable for structural analysis. Still, the actual content of the myth can remain unreal and untrue for the researcher. Even if some aspect of a myth's meaning were to be proved to correspond in some way to empirically and rationally verifiable truth, such a truth would still be considered merely a "kernel of truth," to be highlighted against a background of untruth.

Such a perspective brings us to a third reason for the failure of academic consensus about the meaning of *myth:* the meaning of the ancient Greek word *muthos* was already destabilized in the fifth and fourth centuries B.C.E., the historical context from which it was borrowed into modern usages (by "modern" here I mean, simply, "not ancient"), and this destabilization was even expressed poetically by visualizing *muthoi* (plural) as a background of untruth that served to highlight *alêtheia* 'truth' in the foreground (Nagy 1994, 65–68). In other words, the ancient Greek idea of *muthos* anticipates—and even inspires—the modern idea of *myth* as the opposite of the real and the true. There is a striking illustration in the words of the fifth-century B.C.E. poet Pindar. Here is my working translation of the relevant wording, in Pindar, *Olympian* 1.27–29:

> Indeed there are many wondrous things. And the words that men tell, myths [*muthoi*] embellished by varied falsehoods, beyond wording that is true [*alêthês*], are deceptive.

In Pindar's poetics, "*muthoi* 'myths' stand for an undifferentiated outer core consisting of local myths, where various versions from various locales may potentially contradict each other, while *alêtheia* 'truth' stands for a differentiated inner core of exclusive pan-Hellenic myths that tend to avoid the conflicts of the local versions" (Nagy 1994, 66).

The etymology of *alêtheia* is important to understanding how myths were differentiated into multiple, destabilized versions. The word reveals a mentality of absolutization: it combines a negativizing prefix *a-* 'non-' with the root *lêth-* 'forget', which is the opposite of the root *mnê-* 'remember, recall'. The negation of *lêth-* absolutizes the idea of remembering. In other words, the "unforgettable" truth of *alêtheia* becomes something that must be remembered absolutely: *mnê-* is now the absolutizing idea of total recall (Nagy 1996a, 122–27, 151–52). Moreover, the positive idea of *mnê-* implies narration: it means not just "remember" but "narrate from memory." Once that idea is absolutized, the root *mnê-* can now mean "recover the essence of being by way of narration" (Nagy 1996a, 126, following Vernant 1985, 108–36). In earlier or "archaic" Greek cultural terms, the ultimate narrator is the poet as master of truth, of *alêtheia*, while in later or "classical" terms that mastery defaults from the poet to the philosopher (Detienne 1996, 9–27).

There is no need to postulate that the word *alêtheia* was some kind of rationalistic invention meant to counter the irrationalities of *muthos*. The idea is contradicted by the earliest attested phases of "archaic" Greek culture, as reflected in Homeric poetry. Here we see that the word *muthos* itself was explicitly connected with narrating from memory (Martin 1989, 44), and that such narration was viewed as the rhetorical act of recollection (Martin 1989, 80; Nagy 1996a, 122). In Homeric poetry, *muthos* 'myth' and *alêtheia* 'truth' still coexist as complementary ideas (Nagy 1996a, 122). Thus the absolutist truth-value of *alêtheia* 'truth' is inherent also in the earliest attested uses of *muthos* 'myth'. The difference is that *muthos* became destabilized in the process of being replaced by *alêtheia* and other rival terms for the absolute.

The destabilization of the ancient word *muthos* is comparable to the instability of the modern word *myth*. Edmund Leach has this to say about the word *myth*: "From the viewpoint of a social anthropologist like myself, myth loses all meaning when it is taken out of context." He argues that "myth is 'true' for those who use it, but we cannot infer the nature of that truth simply from reading the text; we have to know the context to which the text refers" (Leach 1982, 6–7).

It is useful to heed Leach's warning about the danger of reading myth as text. The common assumption that myth is a text—even if we use "text" merely as a metaphor—threatens to flatten our conceptualization of myth: it removes the dimension of myth-*performance* (Jacopin 1988, 132). Further, such an assumption makes the dimension of myth-*composition* seem static rather than dynamic. In terms of the opposition of *parole* and *langue*, as formulated by Ferdinand de Saussure in the field of linguistics (Saussure 1972 [1916]; Ducrot and Todorov 1979, 118–20), myth is really a matter of *parole* as well as *langue* (Jacopin 1985, 6–7). A persistent problem with thinking of myth merely as a text is that we risk losing the sense of reality conveyed by the myth in its own social context: "it has become customary to think that one understands myth when one finds out what is its subject matter—as if knowing the data of a discipline is equivalent to the knowledge of the discipline itself." A textual view of myth leads to confusion about its relationship with oral poetry, obscuring the terminology connected with "ethnopoetics" (Jacopin 1988, 132). From the standpoint of anthropological and folkloristic work on oral traditions, it is clear that the cognitive processes of oral poetry, as of myth, are independent of the concept of a text, whether we view "text" merely as a metaphor for a composition or as some concrete realization of writing as a technology (Nagy 1994, 8; Lord 1995, 105 n. 26).

Once we view myth as performance, we can see that myth itself is a form of ritual: rather than think of myth and ritual separately and only contrastively, we can see them as a continuum in which myth is a verbal aspect of ritual while ritual is a notional aspect of myth (Nagy 1989, xi; 1994, 30–33). The "reality" to which myth refers matches the "reality" to which all related nonverbal rituals refer, so that ritual is "the best proof of myth" (Jacopin 1988, 137). I would go so far as to say that the referential world of any given myth-ritual continuum is not the "real world" as we know it but the system or structure or syntax (or whatever metaphor we choose) that we see in the myth-ritual continuum itself.

May we say, then, that myth in turn is "the best proof of ritual"? Here we must reckon with a basic problem: in any society, myth may become destabilized over time, for reasons ranging from structural breakdowns to any number of historical contingencies. But the point is, myth cannot "prove" ritual—once it is destabilized. And yet, ritual may turn out to be one of the possible causes of destabilization in myth. A case in point is the Greek *muthos:* its eventual destabilization—in actual function as well as in meaning—can be explained in terms of its fundamental relationship to ritual (Nagy 1996a, 128).

The question can be posed in historical terms: why did the word *muthos,* in juxtaposition with words like *alêthea* 'true things' and *alêtheia* 'truth', eventually became marginalized to designate unreliable speech? The answer has to do with a historical trend specific to the ancient Greeks: we see in their history a tendency to avoid, in pan-Hellenic traditions of poetry, explicit references to details of local traditional *myth* as it relates to local traditional *ritual* (Nagy 1994, 52–81).

The meaning of the word *muthos* reenacts the relationship between myth and ritual, word and action, in ancient Greek society. For an understanding of this basic relationship, it is useful to apply the Prague School's distinction between marked and unmarked speech (Waugh 1982; cf. Nagy 1996a, 119). This distinction is most evident in the least complex or smallest-scale societies, where marked speech is reserved for contexts of ritual and myth, while "everyday" language is unmarked (Nagy 1994, 31–32; cf. Ben-Amos 1976). Likewise *muthos,* the prototype of the word *myth,* had in its earlier phases meant the "special speech" of myth and ritual as opposed to "everyday" speech (Nagy 1982). A related concept is conveyed by the ancient Greek word *muô,* meaning "I have my eyes closed" or "I have my mouth closed" in everyday situations, but "I see in a special way" or "I say in a special way" in ritual. The idea of special visualization and verbalization is also evident in two derivatives of *muô: mustês* 'one who is initiated' and *mustêrion* 'that into which one is initiated'. A third derivative, it has been argued, is the word *muthos* itself, which can be understood as meaning, ultimately, "a special way of seeing and saying things" (Nagy 1994, 31–32, 66–67).

As Richard Martin (1989) has shown, *muthos* in the language of Homeric poetry designates not only the ritualized speech-acts of characters who are "quoted" by that poetry but also the speech-act of poetry itself. In this sense, then, the *muthos* of Homeric poetry can be understood as a notional totality embracing all ritual speech-acts. The idea of myth, as conveyed by *muthos,* implies ritual in the very performance of myth.

The notional totality of *muthos* in Homeric poetry is comparable with that of myth as observed in small-scale societies. Edmund Leach offers this formulation:

> The various stories [i.e., the myths of a given small-scale society] form a *corpus.* They lock in together to form a single theological-cosmological-[juridical] whole. Stories from one part of the corpus presuppose a knowledge of stories from all other parts. There is implicit cross-reference from one part to another. It is an unavoidable feature of storytelling that events are made to happen one after another, but in cross-reference, such sequence is ignored. It is as if the whole corpus referred to a single instant of time, namely, the present moment. (Leach 1982, 5)

As a corpus, myth must be viewed not only "vertically," along a paradigmatic (metaphoric) axis of selection, but also "horizontally," along a syntagmatic (metonymic) axis of combination.

The sequencing inherent in the syntagmatic axis is often neglected in the study of myth (Jacopin 1988, 151). The principle of sequencing in the interplay of myth and ritual requires a mentality that is chronological and even logical:

> According to Jacopin, the myth has both a syntagmatic and a paradigmatic axis, and the "logic" of episodic transition along the syntagmatic axis is a fundamental aspect of mythical performance. The logic is *metonymic:* the relation of one episode to the next is like that of one stanza to the next in a nursery rhyme such as "The House that Jack Built." With a kind of perfect

economy, each element generated in one episode of the myth is preserved, assumed, and subsumed in the next episode, which then bases all its elements on the existence in sequence of the elements generated in the previous ones, such that the last episode, logically if not explicitly, incorporates the whole sequence. Each episode of the myth is something like a hollow wooden doll that can be taken apart to reveal a smaller doll within; that smaller doll, in turn, contains another even smaller doll, and so forth. In the same way each episode in a myth can reveal its metonymic relationship to previous ones by recapitulating them, and such recapitulation is a narrative tendency, if not a constant, of mythical performance. (Muellner 1996, 53–54, following Jacopin 1988)

The strong sense of sequencing in myth explains why Aristotle in his *Poetics* still uses the word *muthos* to designate the "plot" of any narration in poetry—whether it be drama or epic or any other form of poetry. For Aristotle, poetry has become the prime medium of myth, though he would say it differently, as if *muthos* 'plot' were a prime aspect of poetry. Although *muthos* has become destabilized as a truth-value, as we see most glaringly from a reading of Scroll 10 of Plato's *Republic*, it retains for Aristotle its vitality as a functioning aspect of a corpus. Granted, this corpus is for Aristotle not the same thing as a myth in the sense of Leach's anthropological definition: rather, it is a body of poetry, which is the heir to the performed *muthos* of earlier ages. For Aristotle, the reality of this *muthos* is the plot of the narration.

And yet, even if we take *muthos* merely in the sense of "plot," we can still see in its contents the evidence for earlier workings of *muthos* in the sense of myth as "reality in context." On questions of myth and "reality," especially as conveyed by traditional poetry, I find it most useful to refer to the seminal observations of Albert Lord (Lord 1970, 29–30). In my own work on archaic Greek poetry, I rely on his observations as I consider the debate over whether the Homeric heroes ever existed in "real life" (Nagy 1999, 71). Following Lord, I offer this discussion of the relationship between archaic Greek poetic form and content:

This relationship reveals the tradition that shapes both the poet and the poetry, and for me it is the poetic tradition itself that serves as the primary empirical evidence at my disposal. For others, however, what the poet says about anything counts as raw data, serving as the basis for a "scientific" reconstruction of the poet and the poet's world, as also for any educated second-guessing about the poet's reasons for saying what is said in the poetry. The second-guessing can then lead to various opinions about what we are or are not permitted to believe about the poet's testimony—all in accordance with our own privileged sense of verisimilitude. It is as if the poet's words existed in a vacuum, just waiting to be discovered as direct information about the past, for the exclusive use of future generations. I prefer instead to treat the poetic tradition itself as the primary evidence, as manifested mainly in the language of the surviving texts. (Nagy 1994, 4)

The eventual specialization of *muthos* as "myth" in this destabilized sense of the word was caused, I conclude, by the breakdown of the symbiosis of myth and ritual in the archaic and classical periods of ancient Greece. We can find analogous patterns of differentiation in other historical situations where we see a transition from smaller-scale to more complex societies.

Even in the ancient Greek traditions of philosophical thinking, where the "word" as *logos* 'logic' displaces the "word" as *muthos* 'myth', we can find a sense of nostalgia for a mythologized earlier phase of *muthos* as the conveyor of a stabilized universe. In Plato's *Republic,* for example, *muthos* becomes discredited and is thus banned from the ideal state—only to be allowed by Socrates to stage a stealthy return through the back door, provided it proves itself "useful" in serving what is truly ideal. The Myth of Er, Plato's own recreation of such a saving myth at the conclusion of the *Republic,* becomes in the end linked with the salvation of myth itself. Plato has Socrates himself saying at the end of the *Republic* (10.621b8-c1), with reference to this Myth of Er, *kai ho muthos esôthê* 'and the myth was saved'.

Similarly, the ultimate model of rationalism in "Western" thinking, Aristotle himself, professes his personal sense that myth (as most clearly manifested in the "plots" of tragedies and epics) is something to be saved and even cherished. As he becomes ever more solitary and lonely with the passage of time, he says he becomes ever more fond of *muthos* (Aristotle fr. 668 Rose, via Demetrius 144: *hosôi gar autitês kai monôtês eimi, philomuthoteros gegona*).

Such a holistic sense of *muthos,* as the saving integration of one's own personality, reflects the former integrity of the word—and of the idea—at a time when myth and ritual were still a continuum. The recovery of such an integral idea of myth, through a study of all its multiformities, may yet turn out to be its salvation.

<hr />

NOTES

1. See Gregory Schrempp's introduction to this volume.
2. Several of the contributors to this volume make this point, in a variety of ways.
3. See Schrempp's introduction, especially notes 5 and 10.

BIBLIOGRAPHY

Austin, J. L. 1962. *How to Do Things with Words.* Oxford: Oxford University Press.

Bakker, Egbert. 1993. "Activation and Preservation: The Interdependence of Text and Performance in an Oral Tradition." *Oral Tradition* 8:5–20.

Bauman, Richard. 1977. *Verbal Art as Performance.* Rowley, Mass.: Newbury House.

———. 1986. *Story, Performance, and Event: Contextual Studies of Oral Narrative.* Cambridge: Cambridge University Press.

Bausinger, Hermann. 1980. *Formen der "Volkspoesie."* 2d ed. Berlin: E. Schmidt.

Ben-Amos, Dan. 1976. "Analytical Categories and Ethnic Genres." In *Folklore Genres,* edited by Dan Ben-Amos, 215–42. Austin: University of Texas Press.

Detienne, Marcel. 1981. *L'invention de la mythologie.* Paris: Gallimard.

———. 1996. *The Masters of Truth in Archaic Greece.* 3d edition. Translated by Janet Lloyd. New York: Zone.

———, ed. 1988. *Les savoirs de l'écriture: En Grèce ancienne.* Lille: Presses universitaires de Lille.

Ducrot, Oswald, and Todorov, Tzvetan. 1979. *Encyclopedic Dictionary of the Sciences of Language.* Translated by Catherine Porter. Baltimore: Johns Hopkins University Press, 1979.

Jacopin, Pierre-Yves. 1981. "La parole générative de la mythologie des Indiens Yukuna." Ph.D. dissertation, University of Neuchâtel.

———. 1985. "Mythe et technique: Exemple des Indiens Yukuna." *Techniques et Culture* 6:1–29.

———. 1988. "On the Syntactic Structure of Myth, or the Yukuna Invention of Speech." *Cultural Anthropology* 3:131–59.

Leach, E. R. 1982. Critical introduction to *Myth,* by M. I. Steblin-Kamenskii, 1–20. Ann Arbor: Karoma.

Lord, Albert Bates. 1970. "Tradition and the Oral Poet: Homer, Huso, and Avdo Medjedovic." In *Problemi Attuali di Scienze e di Cultura,* vol. 139, Atti del Convegno Internazionale sul Tema 'La poesia epica e la sua formazione' [Accademia dei Lincei, Rome], 13–28, plus discussion at pp. 29–30. Rome: Accademia nazionale dei Lincei.

———. 1991. *Epic Singers and Oral Tradition.* Ithaca, N.Y.: Cornell University Press.

———. 1995. *The Singer Resumes the Tale.* Edited by Mary Louise Lord. Ithaca, N.Y.: Cornell University Press.

———. 2000. *The Singer of Tales.* 2d edition. Edited and with a new introduction by Stephen Mitchell and Gregory Nagy. Cambridge, Mass.: Harvard University Press.

Malinowski, Bronislaw. 1926. *Myth in Primitive Psychology.* London: K. Paul, Trench, Trubner and Co.

Martin, Richard. P. 1989. *The Language of Heroes: Speech and Performance in the Iliad.* Ithaca, N.Y.: Cornell University Press.

Muellner, Leonard. 1996. *The Anger of Achilles: Mênis in the Iliad.* Ithaca, N.Y.: Cornell University Press.

Nagy, Gregory. 1982. Review of *L'invention de la mythologie,* by Marcel Detienne. *Annales: Economies, Sociétés, Civilisations* 37:778–80.

———. 1989. Foreword to *The Language of Heroes: Speech and Performance in the Iliad,* by Richard P. Martin, ix–xi. Ithaca, N.Y.: Cornell University Press.

———. 1990. *Greek Mythology and Poetics.* Ithaca, N.Y.: Cornell University Press. Revised paperback version 1992.

———. 1994. *Pindar's Homer: The Lyric Possession of an Epic Past.* Revised edition. Baltimore: Johns Hopkins University Press.

———. 1996a. *Homeric Questions.* Austin: University of Texas Press.

———. 1996b. *Poetry as Performance: Homer and Beyond.* Cambridge: Cambridge University Press.

———. 1999. *The Best of the Achaeans: Concepts of the Hero in Archaic Greek Poetry.* 2d edition. Baltimore: Johns Hopkins University Press.

Saussure, Ferdinand de. 1972 [1916]. *Cours de linguistique générale.* Critical edition edited by Tullio de Mauro. Paris: Payot. Original edition edited by Charles Bally and Albert Sechehaye, with the collaboration of Albert Riedlinger, Paris: Payot.

Searle, J. R. 1979. *Speech Acts: An Essay in the Philosophy of Language.* Cambridge: Cambridge University Press.

Tambiah, S. J. 1981. "A Performative Approach to Ritual." *Proceedings of the British Academy, London* 65:113–69.

———. 1985. *Culture, Thought, and Social Action: An Anthropological Perspective.* Cambridge, Mass.: Harvard University Press.

Toelken, Barre. 1976. "The 'Pretty Languages' of Yellowman: Genre, Mode, and Texture in Navaho Coyote Narratives." In *Folklore Genres,* edited by Dan Ben-Amos, 145–70. Austin: University of Texas Press.

Vernant, Jean-Pierre. 1985. *Mythe et pensée chez les Grecs: Études de psychologie historique.* 2d edition, revised and augmented. Paris: La Découverte. The English-language version, *Myth and Thought among the Greeks* (London: Routledge and Kegan Paul, 1983), is based on the 1st edition (Paris, 1965), and needs to be updated.

Waugh, Linda R. 1982. "Marked and Unmarked: A Choice between Unequals in Semiotic Structure." *Semiotica* 38:299–318.

CONTRIBUTORS

Gordon Brotherston is Research Professor in the Department of Literature, University of Essex, and Visiting Professor at Stanford University. He is the author of *Book of the Fourth World: Reading the Native Americas through Their Literature* (1992; published also as *La América indígena en su literatura: Los libros del Cuarto Mundo* [1997]), *Painted Books from Mexico: Codices in UK Collections and the World They Represent* (1995), and more than ten other volumes. He has received awards from the British Academy, CONA-CYT, CNPq, and Rotary International, as well as from the Guggenheim, Alexander von Humboldt, Nuffied, Astor, and several other foundations.

R. D. Fulk is Chancellor's Professor of English at Indiana University, Bloomington. He is the author of *The Origins of Indo-European Quantitative Ablaut* (1986), *A History of Old English Meter* (1992), and, with Christopher M. Cain, *A History of Old English Literature* (forthcoming). He has also edited *Interpretations of Beowulf: A Critical Anthology* (1991) and prepared a new edition of *Eight Old English Poems,* edited by John C. Pope (2001).

Henry Glassie is College Professor of Folklore at Indiana University. He is the author of *Pattern in the Material Folk Culture of the Eastern United States* (1969), *Folk Housing in Middle Virginia: A Structural Analysis of Historic Artifacts* (1975), *All Silver and No Brass: An Irish Christmas Mumming* (1975), *Passing the Time in Ballymenone: Culture and History of an Ulster Community* (1982), *Irish Folktales* (1985), *The Spirit of Folk Art* (1989), *Turkish Traditional Art Today* (1993), *Art and Life in Bangladesh* (1997), and *Material Culture* (1999).

William Hansen is Professor and Chair of Classical Studies, Professor of Folklore, and Co-director of the Program in Mythology Studies at Indiana University, Bloomington. His books include *The Conference Sequence: Patterned Narration and Narrative Inconsistency in the Odyssey* (1972), *Saxo Grammaticus and the Life of Hamlet: A Translation, History, and Commentary* (1983), *Phlegon of Tralles' Book of Marvels* (1996), *Anthology of Ancient Greek Popular Literature* (ed., 1998), and *Ariadne's Thread: A Guide to International Tales Found in Classical Literature* (2002).

Jonathan D. Hill is Professor and Chair of Anthropology at Southern Illinois University, Carbondale. He did fieldwork with the Arawak-speaking peoples of the Venezuelan Rio Negro in the 1980s and 1990s. He edited *Rethinking History and Myth: Indigenous South American Perspectives on the Past* (1988) and *Keepers of the Sacred Chants: The Poetics of Ritual Power in an Amazonian Society* (1993) and is currently editor of the journal *Identities: Global Studies in Culture and Power.*

Robert L. Ivie is Professor and Chair of Communication and Culture at Indiana University, Bloomington. His work on rhetoric and public culture reflects his interest in metaphor, myth, the rhetorical construction of democracy, and a critique of war within U.S. political culture. He is coauthor of *Congress Declares War: Rhetoric, Leadership, and Partisanship in the Early Republic* (with Ronald L. Hatzenbuehler, 1983) and *Cold War Rhetoric: Strategy, Metaphor, and Ideology* (with Martin J. Medhurst et al., 1990, revised 1997). His current project is a study of democracy as it is articulated in the American experience to constitute a republic of fear.

Eleanor W. Leach is Ruth N. Halls Professor of Classical Studies at Indiana University, Bloomington. Her interests include areas of intersection between Roman literary texts and visual art, as exemplified by her book *The Rhetoric of Space: Literary and Artistic Representations of Landscape in Republican and Augustan Rome* (1988). Her other publications include articles on iconography in wall-painting and self-representation in Latin authors, including Cicero and Pliny.

John Lindow is Professor of Scandinavian at the University of California, Berkeley. He has published numerous books and articles in the fields of Old Norse–Icelandic literature and culture, Scandinavian mythology, and folklore. A recent book dealing with myth is *Death and Vengeance among the Gods: Baldr in Scandinavian Mythology* (1997).

John H. McDowell is Professor and Chair of Folklore and Ethnomusicology at Indiana University, Bloomington. He is the author of several books and articles dealing with verbal art performances in Latin America, including *"So Wise Were Our Elders": Mythic Narratives of the Kamsá* (1994) and *Sayings of the Ancestors: The Spiritual Life of the Sibundoy Indians* (1989). His most recent monograph is *Poetry and Violence: The Ballad Tradition of Mexico's Costa Chica* (2000), which contains an audio CD of field recordings.

Gregory Nagy is Francis Jones Professor of Classical Greek Literature and Professor of Comparative Literature at Harvard University, and Director of the Harvard Center for Hellenic Studies in Washington, D.C. He is a past president of the American Philological Association. His special research interests are archaic Greek literature and oral poetics, and his books include *Comparative Studies in Greek and Indic Meter* (1974), *The Best of the Achaeans: Concepts of the Hero in Archaic Greek Poetry* (1979, revised 1999), *Pindar's Homer: The Lyric Possession of an Epic Past* (1990, revised 1994), *Greek Mythology and Poetics* (1990), *Poetry as Performance: Homer and Beyond* (1996), and *Homeric Questions* (1996).

Joseph Falaky Nagy is Professor of English at the University of California, Los Angeles. He is the editor of the new journal *Yearbook of the Celtic Studies Association of North America* and the author of *Conversing with Angels and Ancients: The Literary Myths of Medieval Ireland* (1997), *The Wisdom of the Outlaw: The Boyhood Deeds of Finn in Gaelic Narrative Tradition* (1985), and various studies of Celtic and Indo-European mythology.

Lúcia Sá is Assistant Professor of Brazilian Literature at Stanford University. She is the author of *Reading the Rain Forest: Indigenous Texts and Their Impact on Brazilian and Spanish American Literatures* (forthcoming) and has published several articles on subjects related to Brazilian and Spanish-American cultures.

Gregory Schrempp is Associate Professor of Folklore and Ethnomusicology and Co-director of the Program in Mythology Studies at Indiana University, Bloomington. He is the author of *Magical Arrows: The Maori, the Greeks, and the Folklore of the Universe* (1992) and numerous articles on myth and on the history of anthropological thought.

Candace Slater is Marian E. Koshland Distinguished Professor in the Humanities at the University of California, Berkeley, where she teaches courses on oral traditions as well as on Brazilian literature and culture in the Department of Spanish and Portuguese. She is the director of the Townsend Center for the Humanities and the author of six books, the most recent being *Entangled Edens: Visions of the Amazon* (2001).

Barre Toelken is Professor of English at Utah State University, where he has been director of the Folklore Program since 1985. He is a past president of the American Folklore Society, former editor of the *Journal of American Folklore,* and current editor of *Western Folklore*. His books include *The Dynamics of Folklore* (1979, revised 1996), *Morning Dew and Roses: Nuance, Metaphor, and Meaning in Folksongs* (1995), and *Native American Oral Traditions: Collaboration and Interpretation* (ed., with Larry Evers, 2001).

INDEX

Page numbers in *italics* refer to illustrations.

WILLA CATHER IN PERSON

Portrait of Willa Cather by Leon Gordon appeared
in *Good Housekeeping*, September 1931

Selected and edited
by L. Brent Bohlke

Willa Cather
in Person

☞ *Interviews,*

☞ *Speeches,*

☞ *and Letters*

University of Nebraska Press: Lincoln and London

The paper in this book meets the minimum require-
ments of American National Standard for Information
Sciences–Permanence of Paper for Printed Library
Materials, ANSI Z39.48-1984.

Library of Congress Cataloging-in-Publication Data
Cather, Willa, 1873-1947.
Willa Cather in person.
1. Cather, Willa, 1873-1947 – Interviews.
2. Cather, Willa, 1873-1947 – Correspondence.
3. Novelists, American – 20th century – Inter-
views. 4. Novelists, American – 20th century –
Correspondence. 5. Fiction – Authorship.
I. Bohlke, L. Brent, 1942-   II. Title.
PS3505.A86Z477   1987   813'.52 [B]   86-19161
ISBN 0-8032-1184-8 (alk. paper)

Acknowledgments for the use of copyrighted
material appear on pages xv–xvii.

For my mother and in memory of my father

Contents

ILLUSTRATIONS

Preface

Willa Cather, referring to the development of the singer Thea Kronborg in *The Song of the Lark,* thought that "the play of blind chance" and "fortunate accidents" determine our way. Bernice Slote, in many ways the parent of this book, recognized as much in her introduction to *The Kingdom of Art.* This book, like Slote's, was the result of one of those accidents. A fellow student and I shared an office in the Department of English at the University of Nebraska–Lincoln while we were both working on our graduate degrees. When my friend had finished his degree and was moving on, he gave me a copy of James B. Meriwether and Michael Millgate's *Lion in the Garden,* a collection of interviews with William Faulkner from 1926 to 1962, with a simple note: "For you if you need it." As I continued work on my dissertation on Cather and religion, that book gave me an idea. I began noting references to Cather's interviews. I was surprised. There were far more of them than I had expected. As I pursued references in other works, scoured indexes, and followed up oblique mentions in her correspondence, I discovered not only interviews but articles about her speeches and additional published letters.

The image I had received from my initial studies of Cather was that of an artist who grew increasingly reclusive—one who disliked social discourse and intercourse more and more as she grew older. I soon discovered that in reality, Cather remained a public figure, but a more discriminating one in her middle and later years. She was not a personality of the age of mass media, yet she was receptive to public notice for most of her life.

I had seen virtually all of her extant correspondence in the course of my dissertation research, and the woman I had found there was wise, witty, and warm. Yet the restriction in her will concerning the publication of her correspondence led me to believe that there was one side of her person that she was ready to let the public know and another that she reserved for her family and friends.

What I finally discovered about her was more openness than I had originally assumed. She granted interviews with considerable regularity until her final illness. She gave speeches quite frequently; during the twenties she seemed almost compelled to do so. She also responded to articles and essays in papers and journals by writing letters to the editor, which were, in turn, published. She did not hide from public notice; instead, she continued to court it, only more judiciously.

Although the items in this collection are not well-polished, finely edited, thoughtfully written works to compare with her other published writings, they are, nevertheless, Cather's. The words are hers. And they give us, perhaps, a more intimate and impromptu glimpse of the artist whose major public appearances were always studied, refined, elegant. They allow us to see the spontaneous wit, the gregarious warmth, the bluff side of the ebullient woman behind the canon. This book is in no way an exposé; it is a genesis—a beginning—an attempt to better understand the author.

The contents are arranged generically—interviews, speeches, letters—and chronologically within each section. The first two sections contain accounts by others of her oral presentations; the third comes just a bit closer to her other works in being written by her own hand. There has been no attempt to eliminate the repetition among the various items. Cather's repetitions give us an insight to the themes and subjects that were continually important to her; the repetitions of the interviewers and reporters show us what the public was continually interested in. On some occasions the variations in the repetitions show us how memory—or the expression of it—changed.

In acknowledging the help I have received in the preparation of *Willa Cather in Person,* my first and deepest gratitude is to the late Bernice Slote, who first interested me in Cather, and the late Virginia Faulkner, who sustained and enriched that interest. From both of them I learned the value of scholarship and relentless editing. I also thank Willis Regier, my former officemate, who is responsible for this book and has waited for it patiently. I thank the Nebraska State Historical Society, in particular the staff in the Microfilm Collection, for their assistance and forbearance. The Interlibrary Loan Service of Love Library at the University of Nebraska–Lincoln has been indispensable in the pursuit of microfilms, no one more than Shirley Rockel. Professor James Woodress has been kind enough to read my typescript and point out a number of errors. Professor Margaret O'Connor has been generous in allowing me to use an interview that she discovered. Helen Cather Southwick, Vi Borton, Ann Billesback, Mildred Bennett, and Susan Rosowski have all been of great assistance in a number of ways. Jean Preston, the curator of manuscripts at Princeton University, has been most helpful, as have numerous other librarians and curators. The people of the Church of St. John the Evangelist in Barrytown, New York, have been patient as their rector pursued such arcane adventures, and so have the staff and students at Bard College. To them I extend my gratitude.

My mother and my late father have given me parental urging and encouragement. My parents-in-law provided me space, time, and other help in completing the manuscript. Most of all I thank my wife, Beverly, who has said at times, complimentarily, "I don't see how you get it done," when in reality she does; it is by neglecting her and my daughters. For her prompting, her patience, and her understanding, I am eternally grateful.

I acknowledge with thanks the courtesies extended by the following publishers who have granted permission to reprint these works:

"The Vision of a Successful Fiction Writer," by Ethel M. Hockett, reprinted by permission of the *Lincoln Star*.

"Willa Sibert Cather: To Our Notion the Foremost American Woman Novelist," by Henry Blackman Sell, copyright Field Enterprises, Inc. Reprinted with permission.

"A Talk with Miss Cather," reprinted by permission of the *Red Cloud Chief*.

"Willa Cather, Famous Nebraska Novelist, Says Pioneer Mother Held Greatest Appreciation of Art—Raps Women Who Devote Themselves to Culture Clubs," by Eleanor Hinman, reprinted by permission of the *Lincoln Star*.

"How Willa Cather Found Herself," by Eva Mahoney, reprinted with permission of the *Omaha World-Herald*.

"Fiction Recalls Violinist Lost in War: An Interview with Willa Cather," copyright I. H. T. Corporation. Reprinted by permission.

"The Editor's Column," reprinted by permission of the *Red Cloud Chief*.

"First Meeting with Willa Cather," and "Another Glimpse of Willa Cather," by Burton Rascoe, reprinted from *A Bookman's Daybook* by Burton Rascoe, by permission of Liveright Publishing Corporation. Copyright 1929 by Horace Liveright, Inc. Copyright renewed by Hazel Luke Rascoe, 1956.

"Willa Cather," excerpt from *We Were Interrupted,* by Burton Rascoe. Copyright 1947 by Burton Rascoe. Reprinted by permission of Doubleday and Company, Inc.

"Restlessness Such as Ours Does Not Make for Beauty," by Rose C. Feld. Copyright 1924 by the New York Times Company. Reprinted by permission.

"Glimpses of Interesting Americans, II—Willa Sibert Cather," by Walter Tittle. Copyright Current History Inc. Reprinted by permission.

"Readers and Writers," reprinted by permission of the Journal-Star Printing Company.

"Willa Cather," by John Chapin Mosher, reprinted from *The Writer* magazine. Copyright 1926 by The Writer, Inc.

"Literature Leads to High Place for Red Cloud Woman Nominated to Write Long-Awaited Great American Novel," reprinted by permission of the *Hastings Daily Tribune.*

Famous Nebraska Authoress Visits New Superior Hospital," reprinted by permission of the *Superior Express.*

"Profiles: American Classic," originally published in the *New Yorker,* 8 August 1931. Reprinted by permission of Ruth Limmer, literary executor, Estate of Louise Bogan.

"Willa Cather: Civilized and Very American," by Stephen Vincent and Rosemary Benet, reprinted by special arrangement with Brandt and Brandt, Literary Agents, Inc.

"Willa Cather—Novelist," by Arthur G. Staples. Copyright 1926 by Bowdoin College. Reprinted by permission of the President and Trustees, Bowdoin College.

Willa Cather, "On the Novel," speech broadcast by NBC Radio to Friends of Princeton University Library, 4 May 1933. Published with permission of Princeton University Library, Whitney Darrow Collection, Box 1, folder 1, and Charles E. Cather, Trustee: Under the Will of Willa Cather.

The frontispiece by Leon Gordon is reprinted from *Good Housekeeping,* September 1931.

The illustration on page xxxi by Bertrand Zadig is reprinted from *Critical Woodcuts* by Stuart Sherman with the permission of Charles Scribner's Sons.

The illustration on page xxxii is reprinted from the *Pittsburg Press,* 28 March 1897.

The illustration on page 74 by William Auerbach-Levy is reprinted from the *New York World,* 19 April 1925.

The illustration on page 82 by Walter Tittle is from *The Century* magazine, July 1925. Copyright Current History Inc. Reprinted by permission.

The illustration on page 93 by John Chapin Mosher is from *The Writer* magazine, November 1926. Copyright 1926 by The Writer, Inc. Reprinted by permission.

The illustration on page 128 is reprinted from the *Nebraska Alumnus,* April 1936.

"The Program of the Institute of Modern Literature," on page 153, copyright 1926 by Bowdoin College, is reprinted by permission of the President and Trustees of Bowdoin College.

A Note on the Editing

The material included in this collection comes from a number of newspapers, journals, and periodicals, all of whose editorial principles differed. Hence, they have been kept as close as possible to the original printed versions without perpetuating obvious typographical errors and garbled sentences. For most such writing during this period there was no primary text that was proofread by the interviewer, the reporter, or the subject. On rare occasions Willa Cather might have seen the text before printing, but it is highly unlikely. Printing errors did occur, as would mishearing by interviewers—especially in the days before mechanical recording devices. Consequently, one is dependent upon the printed text as it appeared, even though it may contain glaring errors.

The interviews, speeches, and letters in this collection have been lightly edited, primarily to remove obvious typographical errors and their resulting confusions. Misspelled words have been corrected. Proper names that have changed over time in usage have been allowed to stand as originally printed, making for some degree of inconsistency. The most notable example is *Pittsburg,* an early variant spelling of *Pittsburgh.* Punctuation has been largely retained, unless it would result in confusion. Just as punctuation and usage are often individual matters in Willa Cather's writing, so they would be in her speech. There has been no attempt to regularize them or make them consistent, except as noted above. All titles and quotations and punctuation in introductory material by others have been regularized only for clarification.

The one exception to all the rules of editing is the 1921 interview in the *Omaha Bee.* The original of that interview is so badly edited that it may well represent the cause for Cather's disgust with the press—or at least part of it. In order to convey the outrageous nature of much that was printed in that era, the article remains exactly as printed in the newspaper, along with the consistent misspelling of Cather's name.

ALS   Autographed letter signed.

BLYU   Beinecke Rare Book and Manuscript Library, Yale University, New Haven, Connecticut.

FLPU   Firestone Library, Princeton University, Princeton, New Jersey.

GH   *Good Housekeeping.*

HLSM   Huntington Library, San Marino, California

JPM   J. P. Morgan Library, New York, New York.

KA   *The Kingdom of Art: Willa Cather's First Principles and Critical Statements, 1893–1896,* ed. with two essays and a commentary by Bernice Slote. Lincoln: University of Nebraska Press, 1966.

NLC   Newberry Library, Chicago, Illinois.

NSHS   Nebraska State Historical Society, Lincoln, Nebraska.

NSJ   *Nebraska State Journal,* Lincoln, Nebraska.

NYT   *New York Times.*

OW-H   *Omaha World-Herald*

TLS   Typed letter signed.

WCL   *Willa Cather Living,* by Edith Lewis. New York: Alfred Knopf, 1953.

WCPM Willa Cather Pioneer Memorial, Red Cloud, Nebraska.

Introduction

Willa Cather courted and enjoyed public notice, yet she loved anonymity and seclusion. She was enamored of the notice of the press and deeply resentful of the intrusions the press made upon her time and energies. She sought fame but disliked attention. This civil war in Cather's personality is but another of the intriguing aspects of her talent, and it relates to a number of the characters in her fiction. Thea Kronborg, Godfrey St. Peter, Clement Sebastian, and others seek fame but are not pleased when it arrives. The public notice that Cather sought as a youth became more and more detrimental to her work as a mature artist. It was not necessarily that the pleasure of fame lessened, but that she felt such fame became a kind of thief, stealing time she wanted to devote to other endeavors— time that became steadily more precious. Aware of so much still to be done, she often said, "The end is nothing; the road is all."

Willa Cather's first press notices came early in her life. As a child in Red Cloud she was first written up for her performance in a church school program in 1885: "The Sunday School concert at the Baptist church Sunday Eve was of the usual high standard—Miss Willie Cather electrified the audience with her elocutionary powers." Later that year she was again the subject of journalistic praise: "The recitation by Miss Willa Cather was particularly noticeable on account of its delivery which showed the little miss to be the possessor of extraordinary self-control and talent."[1] Willa Cather was then eleven years old. She was to go on using both that talent—and that self-control—and to be involved in and with the press for the next sixty years, sometimes willingly, sometimes not.

The story of Cather's childhood and early education has often been told, frequently (and with greater or lesser veracity) by Cather herself. Bernice Slote has noted that

as her college friend Louise Pound was fond of saying in later years, there was a good deal of myth about Willa Cather. The standard biographical sketch begins with the untutored western girl running wild on her pony and talking to old Bohemian women on the Nebraska Divide, and continues with the abrupt transformation of the undergradute amateur writer to the Eastern editor to the serene novelist for whom books almost wrote themselves.[2]

Cather loved to talk of her childhood on the Nebraska prairie, and even a brief perusal of the interviews she granted gives ample evidence that Cather was a consummate creator of fiction—even if that fiction was about herself. Originating in certain of her early interviews, the romantic vision of the young Virginia lass transplanted to the Midwest and riding recklessly across the Nebraska plains caught the imaginative penchant of a number of reporters. The image was used again and again until it would seem that even Cather herself began to believe it.

Following her childhood notices, the next factual account of importance in the media came with Cather's commencement address on graduation from high school in Red Cloud. The reporter for the *Red Cloud Chief* noted that her speech was a "masterpiece of oratory," and that "her line of thought was well carved out and a great surprise to her many friends."[3]

Cather indicated in her commencement oration that she had her sights set on a career in medicine. However, as she herself said many times, the publication of one of her student essays, without her knowledge, had a profound effect on her life. Seeing her essay on Thomas Carlyle in the *Nebraska State Journal* was an electrifying experience—so much so that it changed her career plans: "That was the beginning of many troubles for me. Up to that time I had planned to specialize in science; I thought I would like to study medicine. But what youthful vanity can be unaffected by the sight of itself in print! It was a kind of hypnotic effect."[4] From that time Cather began her love/hate relation with the press, the very instrument in many ways responsible for her career. Her achievements for the rest of her life were to be noticed by the press. Though that notice occasionally became burdensome, it was her livelihood—her future. Without it, Cather's career would have dwindled; with it, Cather became irked.

Cather became an accomplished journalist during her college years. Bernice Slote has pointed out the weight of her criticism in drama, music, and literary circles.[5] Following her graduation from the university in 1895 she spent another year in the activity that had helped put her through college—writing for two Lincoln newspapers, the *Journal* and the *Courier*. After that year in Red Cloud and Lincoln, she went to work for a periodical in Pittsburgh, the *Home Monthly*—in June 1896. As the managing editor she got more than she had bargained for; she later admitted to having written most of several complete issues.[6] She soon caught the public eye in Pittsburgh, and the *Pittsburgh Press* called her "a thoroughly up-to-date woman . . . among the pioneers in woman's advancement."[7]

The publication of *April Twilights* in 1903 brought her first national recognition from the press. *Poet-lore* magazine spoke of Cather's "ranch period" and added that she "did not go to school at all." The article went on to say that "for two years the child ran wild, playing with the little herd girls, and visiting the Danes and Norwegians who had settled there as farmers."[8] The legend was born. But as recent biographical studies have shown, Cather had as many contacts with artistic and cultured people in Red Cloud during her formative years as she did with the immigrant farmers. Her education may have been unorthodox, but it was broad. Mildred Bennett observes that "Willa was by no means the untutored roughneck run in off the prairie that she later implied she had been."[9]

In 1900 Cather wrote to her old mentor, Will Owen Jones of the *Nebraska State Journal*, that she had several things coming out in print and that it caused her to find the world a good place in which to live.[10] She was pleased to be noticed, and at this point in her life she needed an audience. Writing from Red Cloud in 1912 to her friend Zoë Akins, she said that part of what made living in rural Nebraska so hard was that none of her stunts, except for riding bareback, could make any "effects." Her poetry could get absolutely no response from a cow.[11]

But at home she was a celebrity. In May 1903 the *Nebraska State Journal* ran the following column, entitled "People You Know":

New York, May 8.—(Special Correspondence.)—Miss Willa Cather of Pittsburg, who is so well known to the Nebraska readers of the Journal and to the people of Lincoln, was in the city this week. She was summoned by the McClure people who have of late taken a lively interest in her literary work. It is said that an arrangement has been made for the publication of some of her stories in the magazine. To be taken up by Mr. McClure is counted a decided recognition, and Miss Cather's friends will understand that this means that she has "arrived."[12]

One week later the *Journal* reviewed *April Twilights* glowingly as "the harbinger of many future achievements of her facile pen.'' The reviewer also commented on a piece accompanying the publisher's announcement: ''A very interesting sketch of her life on a ranch in southwestern Nebraska and after in Red Cloud where she ran wild some years before beginning her school education that was completed at the state university.''[13]

She was soon at work in New York for *McClure's*. Her first major assignment was a revision of a biography of Mary Baker Eddy, submitted by one Georgine Milmine. Her new position, and especially the time spent in Boston working on the biography, brought her into contact with many of the famous people whom she admired, but it may well mark the beginnings of her doubts about the press and about journalism as a career. She discovered that most of the manuscript about Mrs. Eddy had not been documented; much of it was doctored and it was filled with errors. Her revision turned into a complete rewrite of the book; none of Mrs. Milmine's words remained, yet Cather denied her authorship of the book for the rest of her life.[14]

It was during her time at *McClure's* that Cather decided to dedicate her talent to writing fiction. In the meantime, she also wrote many nonfiction articles and reviews, most of which have been collected in *The World and the Parish*.[15] Her next notice in the national press came in 1908. *The Bookman* had an interview concerning her first volume of short stories, *The Troll Garden*. Even though she was getting favorable press coverage, there were indications that her world was about to change. The administrative structure of *McClure's* had been insecure since before her arrival and the days of the magazine were numbered. Although Cather stayed on after a reorganization that put McClure's son-in-law, Cameron MacKenzie, in charge, she soon decided to leave the world of journalism.

Before she left the magazine, the publication of her first novel, *Alexander's Bridge,* made her ''public property.'' Her interview in the *New York Evening Sun* on 25 May 1912 marked her entrance into the world of a celebrity. She was to be courted and squired by the press until near the end of her active career. Her opinions were sought; her techniques were queried; her advice was envied. Gradually she came to resent most of these intrusions because they kept her from doing the work she most wanted to do—writing.

Cather's sense of not having enough time increased as she grew older. Time and again she declined invitations to luncheons and requests to serve in various capacities for conferences, workshops and meetings.[16] When she had to move from her Bank Street apartment, the disruption was most disturbing to her because it took time from her writing. She wrote to her friend Mary Austin that it was a broken-up, wasted interlude that gave her no fun. Just then life was all messed-up for her, and she found only occasional intervals when she could manage to make things move smoothly and snatch a bit of work out of the temporary calm.[17] Later she wrote to Austin that her old friend Ferris Greenslet was trying to force her to write a biography of Amy Lowell. She felt that would be about as likely as her writing a history of the Chinese empire; it had about as much appeal — and would have no more if the entire Lowell estate were offered to her. Money was of little importance to her, but her own life and liberty — and time — were of extreme value.[18] If she allowed her energies to be scattered, she got all mixed-up, Cather wrote. She even began hating life and believing everything to be a dreary chore. She felt that a person in that state was of no use to anyone, so it was better to be unobliging in order to remain pleasant. When her unfinished commitments began weighing upon her she detected a meek and apologetic tone sneaking into her stories. Hence, she became careful about taking on any extraneous obligations.[19]

Part of her reluctance to respond to public invitations was due to her feeling that she had been taken advantage of on a number of occasions. Too many journalists approached her on false pretenses. On one occasion, she befriended a writer, a Russian refugee, whom she thought to be both gentlemanly and scholarly, only to find when she arrived on the West Coast that he had mimeographed her letter to him and distributed it to all the booksellers there.[20] She was also annoyed by the inaccuracies perpetrated by the press (though she had falsified much information about herself, including her birthdate), and she spent an inordinate amount of time trying to correct the falsehoods she did not like.[21] When Dorothy Canfield Fisher, her long-time friend, was writing about her for the *New York Herald-Tribune,* she sent a draft of her article to Cather, who approved of its lack of legend.[22]

By the mid-thirties, when Cather was working on *Lucy Gayheart,* she felt completely besieged by the movies, attorneys, investment representatives, and relatives — all of whom were concerned about her financial state. That seems to have mattered little to her in comparison to her art.[23] It was all primarily a disturbance to her creative effort. She finally resorted to having her telephone shut off during her working hours and having her secretary write formal letters in place of the personal responses she would rather have made.[24] Hollywood's attempt to get the rights to *My Ántonia* was the last straw. It seemed to her that there was a conspiracy afoot involving both man and God to keep her from the work she loved.[25]

Her experience with the press — perhaps both as a member of it and a victim of it—led her to believe finally that one should never express one's opinions publicly. The ordeal she underwent after expressing her opinions about Sarah Orne Jewett in *Not Under Forty* convinced her that one should keep one's credo—one's articles of faith—entirely to oneself. It was important to be silent about one's own opinions—and about one's friends.[26]

In the late twenties and thirties she declined more and more invitations to receive honorary degrees and to lecture.[27] In fact, she didn't even want to be held responsible for the public utterances she had made as recently as ten years before. She felt her opinions were constantly changing and that to speak publicly was to freeze things.[28] She didn't mince words:

> In this country a writer has to hide and lie and almost steal in order to get time to work in—and peace of mind to work with. Besides, lecturing is very dangerous for writers. If we lecture, we get a little more owlish and self-satisfied all the time. We hate it at first, if we are decently modest, but in the end we fall in love with the sound of our own voice. There is something insidious about it, destructive to one's finer feelings.[29]

She told Henry Seidel Canby that the habit of public speaking—even in "forums"—had nothing but a bad effect on authors and on humanity in general. They all ought to stay home and write something interesting.[30] Furthermore, she said, "I've seen people's reality quite destroyed by the habit of putting on a rostrum front. It's especially destructive to writers, even so much worse than alcohol, takes their edge off."[31]

Even though she continued to grant interviews at fairly regular intervals until her health failed in the last six or seven years of her life, she gained the reputation of being reclusive, but as she told Dorothy Canfield Fisher, she limited her interviews only to save herself for the people she really cared about.[32] Her friend Mrs. Louis Crofts, wife of the publisher of Appleton, Century, and Crofts, says, "She was no recluse; she was a very private person. There's a big difference."[33]

It is perhaps ironic that the press, to which Cather had devoted at least fifteen years of her career and from which she had learned much of her craft, became her enemy in later years. Journalism was once her medium, her ally, but she came to have little sympathy for journalists. At the beginning of her career, Willa Cather from Nebraska loved the entrée that journalism gave her to the famous—Stephen Crane, Rudyard Kipling, Anthony Hope Hawkins, Sarah Orne Jewett, Ethelbert Nevin, Olive Fremstad. After her career was established and she was famous herself, Willa Cather from Park Avenue was annoyed with young journalists who were constantly seeking her. She did not grant them the same generous access that she had once been accorded. She did give interviews to those whose talent and seriousness were known to her, and they always found her to be polite, charming, and endearing.

In the last twenty years Cather suffered from the loss of her intimate audience. The frequency with which she sent press notices and articles about herself to her parents, family, and friends indicates the importance of that group of close associates for her. But both of her parents were dead by 1931. Zoë Akins's husband was killed in an automobile accident in 1932. Her brother Douglass and her dear friend Isabelle McClung died in 1938. Roscoe, her closest brother, suffered a heart attack in 1941 and died four years later. She wrote Zoë that after one's forty-fifth birthday death seemed to rain all around one and that after fifty it became a veritable thunderstorm.[34] Just as the young poet could get no response from the cows, the mature author could not get from strangers and public notice her desired and needed response. Like Marian Forrester in *A Lost Lady,* she felt that she was continuing to act in a play after most of the characters were dead.[35]

Although as a youth she had sought fame, Willa Cather was never comfortable with it. She was embarrassed about having a Park Avenue address. She disliked being recognized in public.[36] She never registered at the Shattuck Inn, her favorite vacation spot in Jaffrey, New Hampshire. She always went into the hospital under Edith Lewis's name.[37] She preferred to be known to the public by her works alone. She had admired this separation of public and private life in Eleonora Duse many years before:

> The woman lives among us, in our own time, in our own land, yet we know as little of her as we know of Shakespeare. We know where she was born, whom she married, and that she has a child, but more than that we know not. In this age of microscopic scrutiny and X rays to have maintained such absolute privacy is little short of genius itself. . . . Duse has kept her personality entirely free, her relations with her public are of the most self-respecting and platonic character. . . . If the insatiable curiosity of the public were granted, if it were permitted to inspect every detail of this woman's daily life it would be none the wiser and very much bored for its pains.[38]

She was puzzled when Sir James Barrie requested an autographed copy of one of her books. She said the signature that mattered was on every page of the book.[39]

xxviii Introduction

Fanny Butcher, a friend for almost forty years, may have summed up best the enigma of Cather's public and private life:

A public figure through her own efforts, she steadfastly refused to play the public figure, but lived a sedulously quiet life with her close friend and companion Edith Lewis in a Park Avenue apartment. Now and then she would be seen at concerts or theatre, and now and then she would entertain a few such guests as Sigrid Undset, Yehudi Menuhin, or Thornton Wilder, but most of the time she kept her distance from the world, and expected the world to keep its distance in return.[40]

NOTES

1. *Webster County Argus,* 14 May 1885, p. 3, col. 4; 11 June 1885, p. 3., col. 5.

2. Bernice Slote, "Writer in Nebraska," in KA, p. 3.

3. "Annual Commencement Exercises of the Red Cloud Public Schools," *Red Cloud Chief,* 13 June 1891, p. 5, cols. 3–5. Cather's commencement address, though referred to by many biographers and critics and frequently quoted in part, has been reprinted in full for the first time in the "Speeches" section of this book.

4. "Congratulations from Willa Cather," NSJ, 24 July 1927, Sec. F., p. 6, col. 2. The letter is reprinted in full in the "Letters" section.

5. See KA.

6. Willa Cather, ALS to Mrs. C. H. Gere, 13 July n.d. (probably 1896) and ALS to Mariel Gere, 4 August 1896, Gere Family Collection, NSHS.

7. *Pittsburg Press,* 28 March 1897, p. 11, col. 6. Cather marked the article and sent it home to her parents. The original is now in the Willa Cather Pioneer Memorial Collection. The article is reprinted in full in the "Interviews" section of this book.

8. "Glimpses of Present Day Poets: Willa Sibert Cather," *Poet-lore,* Winter number, 1903, p. 113.

9. Mildred R. Bennett, Introduction to *Willa Cather's Collected Short Fiction, 1892–1912,* ed. Virginia Faulkner (Lincoln: University of Nebraska Press, 1965), p. xv.

10. Willa Cather, ALS to Will Owen Jones, 29 September 1900, Cather Collection, Clifton Waller Barrett Library, University of Virginia, Charlottesville, Virginia.

11. Willa Cather, ALS to Zoë Akins, 21 October 1912, Cather Collection, HLSM.

12. NSJ, 11 May 1903, p. 6, col. 2.

13. Ibid., 18 May 1903, p. 4, col. 6.

14. Cather admitted the extent of her involvement only once. See Willa Cather, TLS to Edwin H. Anderson, 24 November 1922, Anderson Papers, Manuscripts and Archives Division, New York Public Library, New York. For complete discussion see L.

Brent Bohlke, "Willa Cather and *The Life of Mary Baker G. Eddy,*" *American Literature* 54 (1982): 288–94.

15. Willa Cather, *The World and the Parish: Willa Cather's Articles and Reviews, 1893–1902,* selected and ed. with a commentary by William M. Curtin, 2 vols. (Lincoln: University of Nebraska Press, 1970).

16. See, for example, Willa Cather, ALS to Mr. Harold Goddard, 10 August 1922, Baker Library, Dartmouth College; Willa Cather, TLS to Norman Foerster, 16 April 1936 and 13 February 1939, University of Nebraska–Lincoln, Archives. The Cather Collection at the American Academy in New York consists mainly of letters from Cather declining requests for luncheons, dinners and speaking engagements. There are twenty-six such letters in the collection, dating from June 1928 to November 1946.

17. Willa Cather, ALS to Mary Austin, 9 November 1927, HLSM.

18. Willa Cather, ALS to Mary Austin, 9 May 1928, HLSM.

19. Willa Cather, TLS to Helen McAfee, 7 February 1924, BLYU.

20. Willa Cather, TLS to Thomas S. Jones, 11 November 1931, Cather Collection, Butler Library, Columbia University, New York, New York.

21. See, for example, Willa Cather, TLS to Head of the English Department, Mount Saint Mary's College, Emmitsburg, Maryland, 7 February 1940, Clifton Waller Barrett Library, University of Virginia; Willa Cather, TLS to Miss Hoyer, n.d., 1941, Yale University; Willa Cather, TLS to Cyril Clemens, 27 January 1934, University of Virginia.

22. Willa Cather, ALS to Dorothy Canfield Fisher, n.d., 1933, Fisher Collection, Guy W. Bailey Library, University of Vermont, Burlington.

23. Willa Cather, ALS to Zoë Akins, 2 January 1934, HLSM.

24. Willa Cather, TLS to Bishop George Allen Beecher, 13 February 1934, Beecher Collection, Nebraska State Historical Society; and Willa Cather, ALS to Carrie Sherwood, 25 November 1935, WCPM Collection, Red Cloud, Nebraska.

25. Willa Cather, ALS to Zoe Akins, n.d., 1937, HLSM.

26. Willa Cather, ALS to Zoë Akins, 28 October 1937, HLSM. Cather's ideas about literature as an escape generated much press reaction in the mid-thirties.

27. See, for example, Willa Cather, TLS to Norman Foerster, 13 February 1939, University of Nebraska–Lincoln, Archives; and Willa Cather, TLS to Allan Nevins, 18 March 1939, Butler Library, Columbia University.

28. Willa Cather, ALS to Frederick Paul Keppel, 16 February 1940, Butler Library, Columbia University.

29. "Readers and Writers," unsigned interview in NSJ, 5 September1926, p. 4C, col. 8. The interview is reprinted in full in the "Interviews" section of this book.

30. Willa Cather, TLS to Henry Seidel Canby, 2 March 1938, BLYU.

31. "Readers and Writers," p. 4.

32. Willa Cather, ALS to Dorothy Canfield Fisher, n.d., 1933, University of Vermont.

33. Personal interview with the writer, 28 January 1985.

34. Willa Cather, ALS to Zoë Akins, 21 November 1932, HLSM, Willa Cather turned fifty in 1923.

35. Willa Cather, ALS to Dorothy Canfield Fisher, 30 September 1930, University of Vermont.

36. "The Gossip Shop," in *The Bookman*, October 1925, p. 231.

37. Elizabeth Yates, "Required Reading," *New Hampshire Profiles* (December 1955): 18. See also Sarah Bloom, TLS to Mabel Luhan, 28 July 1942, BLYU.

38. Willa Cather, NSJ, 22 March 1896, p. 9. Reprinted in KA, p. 154.

39. Willa Cather, TLS to William Lyon Phelps, 29 May 1943, BLYU.

40. Fanny Butcher, "Three Long Short Stories by Willa Cather," *Chicago Daily Tribune*, 12 October 1948, p. 3.

"Willa Cather," by Bertrand Zadig, from Stuart
Sherman's *Critical Woodcuts* (1926)

Willa Cather as "A Woman Editor" appeared
in the *Pittsburg Press*, 28 March 1897

Interviews

1897–1940

1897: PITTSBURGH

Willa Cather arrived in Pittsburgh on 3 July 1896 and went to work as an assistant editor for the Home Monthly. *The story of her precocious advancement and assumption of authority at the new magazine has often been told. In less than eight months in her new position her public notice was sufficient for her to be included in a feature story in the* Pittsburg Press *entitled "Pittsburg's Pioneers in Woman's Progress." The author, Jeannette Barbour, points out a number of women involved in untraditional professions and occupations in Pittsburgh. She chronicles in detail twenty-one women and their vocations. While not traditional interviews in form, the material gathered on each of the women involved an interview situation. Fairly realistic line drawings are included for one of the women architects, an embalmer, a physician, a dentist, and a woman real estate dealer; but cartoons are employed for the woman sign painter, a second woman dentist, and "Allegheny's woman watchmaker," as well as the Gibson Girl cartoon of "A Woman Editor." In addition to the cartoon of Cather the cover design on the February issues of the* Home Monthly *illustrates the story.*

Even in this first, early interview, Cather's talent for fiction is evident. That same talent, expressed on other occasions, often makes her interviews less than reliable sources of information. There were five newspapers published in Red Cloud at the time of Cather's graduation from high school. There is no other record of her father's foreclosure or of her three months of newspaper work. Her active work on the Nebraska State Journal *and the* Lincoln Courier *was considerably less involved than is implied. It is interesting to note, however, that the age given for her move from Virginia to Nebraska is one year older*

than she actually was — yet an age that was to move progressively downward in
future interviews, a movement hinted at in the last paragraph of the interview,
where Cather's age is lowered by one year. None of this negates the insightful
comment of the interviewer that Willa Cather is just beginning "a career worth
watching."

Cather tore out the cartoon and the first two and one half sentences of the
article, marked it with two large cross-hatches (a favorite method of hers), and
sent it to her family in Red Cloud (WCPM Collection). ☞

A WOMAN EDITOR

by Jeanette Barbour

Miss Willa Cather, the editor of the *Home Monthly,* is not Pittsburger, but she is carrying on her editorial work here and is such a thoroughly up-to-date woman she certainly should be mentioned among the pioneers in woman's advancement. Miss Cather was originally a Virginian, and lived at Winchester, Virginia, until she was a child of ten, when she went west with her family to Red Cloud, Nebraska, a small ranch town. When she was a girl of fifteen her father foreclosed a mortgage on the only newspaper in the town, and as he was not a newspaper man, he left the paper in charge of his daughter until he could get someone else to conduct it. This was not very easily managed, and so for three months little Miss Willa was both editor and business manager of the paper, and what is more, insisted in drawing the salaries for both positions.

She had just finished the course at the neighboring high school, and after devoting the summer to the paper she entered the state University of Nebraska in the fall, using for her education the money she had earned in her newspaper work. This was, of course, totally insufficient to see her through, and in her junior and senior years she held the position of dramatic editor on the *Nebraska State Journal.* During the summer she did special work for other western papers. She graduated from the University in 1895, and was engaged in active work on the *Nebraska State Journal* and the *Courier* until last July, when she came to Pittsburg as editor of the *Home Monthly.* This magazine is published in the East End, but next month will be moved to the seventh floor of the Heeren building, Penn avenue.

Miss Cather is just beginning her career, but she is doing it with the true progressive western spirit, that fears neither responsibility nor work, and it will be a career worth watching. To go off, when one is but twenty-one, into an entirely new part of the country and undertake to establish and edit a new magazine requires plenty of "grit"—a quality as valuable in a business woman as in a business man.

Pittsburg Press, 28 March 1897.

1903: NEW YORK

The publication of April Twilights *gave Willa Cather national notice for the first time. The book was reviewed by the* New York Times, *the* Critic, *the* Dial, *the* Boston Evening Transcript, *the* Bookman, *and other nationally known publications. One of the more laudatory reviews, "Glimpses of Present Day Poets," appeared in* Poet-lore. *It included a photo of the author and reprinted in full the three poems said to be her favorites. Bernice Slote has pointed out that publicity was probably involved somewhere in the review since Badger Books, publishers of* April Twilights, *were printed by Gorham Press, the publisher of* Poet-lore. *Slote says that "because Willa Cather was certainly consulted about the article, it does have some valuable information on the poems" and Cather's opinions of them (*AT *1903, pp. xix, 54). The review also gives us the first picture of Cather as a child running "wild" with "the little herd girls" and may be the first time that 1876 was given as her birthdate (she was born in 1873). Cather's early reading list was confirmed by Edith Lewis fifty years later (*WCL, *p. 14).* ☞

GLIMPSES OF PRESENT-DAY POETS: WILLA SIBERT CATHER

Miss Willa Sibert Cather, whose delightful volume of poems, entitled *April Twilights,* was recently published, was born near Winchester, Virginia, in 1876. When she was ten years old, the family moved to a ranch in Southwestern Nebraska, and for two years the child ran wild playing with the little herd girls and visiting the Danes and Norwegians, who had settled there as farmers.

During the ranch period and for some time after, Miss Cather did not go to school at all, and her only reading was an old copy of Ben Johnson's plays, a Shakespeare, a Byron, and *The Pilgrim's Progress,* which latter she said she read through eight times in one winter. The first two years of her course at the University of Nebraska, where she graduated in 1895, were spent in the hardest kind of study, but then she discovered herself and began to write a little. She edited a creditable college magazine, and did remarkably discriminating dramatic criticism for the *Nebraska State Journal.* Later she wrote for the Lincoln *Courier,* and in 1896, she came to Pittsburg, where she was for several years on the staff of the *Leader,* doing clever dramatic and literary criticism in addition to her regular work.

Miss Cather's first story, "Eric Hermanson's Soul," a study of the effect of western climatic conditions on the Scandanavian temperament, was translated into German and republished by *The Dresden Critic,* Eugene Von Sempskey.

All of the verse published in Miss Cather's volume, *April Twilights,* has been done within the last five years. Her early effort was all toward prose, her verse always being incidental and usually accidental. "Grandmither Think not I Forget," the best poem of the collection, was never retouched after the first writing.

Miss Cather has contributed prose and verse to various American periodicals. Her latest story, "A Death in the Desert," published in *Scribners,* shows that her feeling for western atmosphere has in no-wise diminished. She has also completed a series of short stories, all of which are studies of artist life.

The following poems are Miss Cather's favorites: "Grandmither, Think not I Forget," "Mills of Montmartre," and "The Hawthorn Tree."

Poet-lore, Winter 1903.

1905: NEW YORK

The publication of Willa Cather's book, The Troll Garden, *was the next occasion on which she was put in a public spotlight. She was also at the beginning of a new career at McClure's, a career brought about largely by the stories in her second book. The reviewer is less concerned with biographical detail than with the author's method of creating fiction, particularly in the instance of "Paul's Case." The article, accompanied by a picture of Miss Cather, is the first to quote her directly. ☞*

MISS CATHER

Miss Willa S. Cather, whose book *The Troll Garden* has caused a good deal of discussion, began her literary career, like many authors, at an early age. When eight or nine years old, according to a man who knew her as a child in Virginia, she not only wrote a play, but arranged and supervised its performance with remarkable effect. Shortly after that period her family took her to Nebraska, where she lived for a while a healthful, quite unliterary life, spending most of her time in the open on horseback. Graduating at the University of Nebraska, she became correspondent for several newspapers, wrote, and in 1903 published, a volume of verse called *April Twilights,* and then took to writing the stories which have now been gathered in book form. In Pittsburg, where Miss Cather is living there was a foundation of fact for the incident around which she built her story of "Paul's Case." Two boys employed by a firm that managed a large estate ran away with two thousand dollars. They were found at the Auditorium Hotel in Chicago about ten days later, their money gone, and they were brought home. The papers were full of the affair for a time, but as one of the boys was a minister's son, and as the money was refunded, the firm did not prosecute. This story, of all the stories in the book, comes nearest to being based on actual occurrences; so that Miss Cather's psychology is all the more a remarkable attainment. There may be deduced a certain endorsement of her accuracy from the fact that concerning these accounts of hers of abnormal artistic personalities she receives in her mail a regular succession of such outpourings as have caused her to exclaim, "I never knew before there were so many madmen at large." Miss Cather herself is a hard-headed, clear-visioned, straight-forward young woman.

"Chronicle and Comment," *Bookman,* July 1905.

1912: NEW YORK

Alexander's Bridge, Cather's first novel, brought about her first authentic interview in a weekly feature of the New York Sun *entitled "Literary News, Views, and Criticism." Cather clipped the interview, marked it with heavy black lines, and sent it home to her family (WCPM Collection). It is one of the rare instances when she talked at any length about the book. Unsigned, the interview would seem to indicate that Miss Cather dominated after the opening sentence, to the extent of repeating the interviewer's questions. Her later interviews clearly show, however, a different style. "Certainly," "Not at all," and "Certainly not," are the far more characteristic, terse responses that she made to questions.*

This interview was drawn upon heavily but not identified by Grant M. Overton in his chapter on Cather in the first edition of The Women Who Make Our Novels *(New York: Moffat, Yard and Company, 1918).* ☞

EXPLAINING HER NOVEL
Alexander's Bridge Has Nothing to Do with Whist

Willa S. Cather has been kept busy denying that her novel *Alexander's Bridge,* which was recently published by Houghton Mifflin Company, has anything to do with whist. "The only kind of bridge in the story," she says, "is a cantilever bridge. No, it isn't an industrial novel either. It does not give any more information about bridge building than it does about whist. In fact it doesn't give information about anything. Do I believe in the industrial novel that does give information? Certainly, but that is one kind of a story; this is another.

"This is not the story of a bridge and how it was built, but of a man who built bridges. The bridge builder with whom this story is concerned began life a pagan, a crude force, with little respect for anything but youth and work and power. He married a woman of much more discriminating taste and much more clearly defined standards. He admires and believes in the social order of which she is really a part, though he has been only a participant. Just so long as his ever-kindling energy exhibits itself only in his work everything goes well; but he runs the risk of encountering new emotional as well as new intellectual stimuli.

"Is Alexander himself meant to be a portrait of a noted New York architect? Not at all. He was not suggested by any one person. He simply has some of the characteristics which I have noticed in a dozen architects, engineers and inventors.

"Is the actress in the story meant to be much like Hilda Trevelyan? Certainly not. Miss Trevelyan is a different sort of person. I tried, however, to give the actress in this story certain qualities which I have found oftener in English actresses than in our own."

New York Sun, 25 May 1912.

1913: PHILADELPHIA

Cather felt that in many important ways her career as an author really began with the publication of O Pioneers!. *The book was received favorably and with considerable excitement by many reviewers, who saw in it several things that were quite new, including its location and its immigrant cast of characters. It also resulted in her first full-length interview, in the* Philadelphia Record, *by an interviewer signed only as "F. H." As Bernice Slote has often noted, this first interview is of great importance since it was used for many years following by reviewers and even by other interviewers as a source of biographical information (KA, p. 445). Of some subjects, Cather would never again speak publicly with such candor and comprehensive detail: her arrival in Nebraska, her first attempts at writing, her debt to Sarah Orne Jewett. In other subjects the beginnings of a life-long continuity can be observed: the necessity of honesty, of writing from one's own experience, the importance of simplification.*

O Pioneers! had been reviewed in the Record *the previous day, 9 August 1913, by P. A. Kinsley, who called it a "story of abundant merit," and went on to say, "We hope Miss Cather will not neglect to till the promising field for fiction she is among the first, if not actually the first, to disclose."* ☞

WILLA CATHER TALKS OF WORK

Miss Willa Sibert Cather, whose new novel, *O Pioneers!* has just placed her in the foremost rank of American novelists, began to do newspaper work on the *Nebraska State Journal* while she was still an undergraduate in the University at Lincoln. From Lincoln Miss Cather came East as far as Pittsburgh, to go on the regular staff of the *Daily Leader*.

Leaving the newspaper life, while still very young, Miss Cather then accepted a position to teach, first Latin and afterward English, in the Pittsburgh High School. It was during this time that she wrote the verse and short stories which secured her the post of associate editor of *McClure's Magazine* and took her finally to New York.

Miss Cather's new novel, *O Pioneers!* is of special interest to Philadelphians—this magnificently grave and simple and poetic picture of early days on the uplands of Nebraska—if only for the strong influence of Whitman which the writing shows. There is the wise, clean-earthed philosophy of Whitman in the selection of the book's theme, too, and Miss Cather quotes her title direct from our superb white-bearded old lover of the world.

Though Miss Cather no longer spends all her time in the McClure Publications offices, on Fourth Avenue (she was managing editor of *McClure's Magazine* for four years), she is still connected with that publishing house; and I was eager to have her opinion of modern short-story writing in the United States.

"My own favorite American writers? said Miss Cather. "Well, I've never changed in that respect much since I was a girl at school. There were great ones I liked best then and still like—Mark Twain, Henry James and Sarah Orne Jewett.''

"You must have read a lot of work by new people while you were editor of *McClure's?*" I suggested.

"Yes," smiled Miss Cather, "I suppose I read a good many thousand stories, some good and some bad."

"And what seemed to you to be the trouble with most of the mediocre ones?"

"Simply this," replied Miss Cather unhesitatingly, "that the writer had not felt them strongly enough before he wrote them. Like everything else in the world, this is a question of—how far. No one person knows much more about writing than another. I expect that when people think they know anything about it, then their case is hopeless. But in my course of reading thousands of stories, I was strengthened in the conclusion that I had come to before; that nothing was really worth while that did not cut pretty deep, and that the main thing always was to be honest.

"So many of the stories that come into magazines are a combination of the genuine and the fake. A writer has really a story to tell, and he has evidently tried to make it fit the outline of some story that he admires, or that he believes has been successful. You can not always tell just where a writer stops being himself and begins to attitudinize in a story, but when you finish it, you have a feeling that he has been trying to fool himself. I think a writer ought to get into his copy as he really is, in his everyday clothes. His readers are thrown with him in a personal relation, just as if they were traveling with him; and if he is not sincere, there is no possibility of any sort of comradeship.

"I think many story writers try to multiply their ideas instead of trying to simplify them; that is, they often try to make a story out of every idea they have, to get returns on every situation that suggests itself. And, as a result, their work is entertaining, journalistic and thin. Whether it is a pianist, or a singer, or a writer, art ought to simplify—that seems to me to be the whole process. Millet did hundreds of sketches of peasants sowing grain, some of them very complicated, but when he came to paint 'The Sower,' the composition is so simple that it seems inevitable. It was probably the hundred sketches that went before that made the picture what it finally became—a process of simplifying all the time—of sacrificing many things that were in themselves interesting and pleasing, and all the time getting closer to the one thing—It.

"Of course I am talking now about the kind of writing that interests me most—I take it that is what you want me to do. There is *The Three Guardsmen* kind, which is, perhaps, quite as fine in its way, where the whole zest of the thing is the rapid multiplication of fancies and devices. That kind of writing, at its best, is like fencing and dancing, the games that live forever. But the other kind, the kind that I am talking about, is pretty well summed up in a letter of Miss Sarah Orne Jewett's, that I found among some of her papers in South Berwick after her death:

" 'Ah, it is things like that, which haunt the mind for years, and at last write themselves down, that belong, whether little or great, to literature.'

"It is that kind of honesty, that earnest endeavor to tell truly the thing that haunts the mind, that I love in Miss Jewett's own work. Reading her books from the beginning one finds that often she tried a character or a theme over and over, first in one story and then in another, before she at last realized it completely on the page. That wonderful story, 'Martha's Lady,' for instance, was hinted at and felt for in several of her earlier stories. And so was the old woman in 'The Queen's Twin.'

"I dedicated my novel *O Pioneers!* to Miss Jewett because I had talked over some of the characters in it with her one day at Manchester, and in this book I tried to tell the story of the people as truthfully and simply as if I were telling it to her by word of mouth."

"How did you come to write about that flat part of the prairie west, Miss Cather, which not many people find interesting?"

"I happen to be interested in the Scandinavian and Bohemian pioneers of Nebraska," said the young novelist, "because I lived among them when I was a child. When I was eight years old, my father moved from the Shenandoah Valley in Virginia to that Western country. My grandfather and grandmother had moved to Nebraska eight years before we left Virginia; they were among the real pioneers.

"But it was still wild enough and bleak enough when we got there. My grandfather's homestead was about eighteen miles from Red Cloud—a little town on the Burlington, named after the old Indian chief who used to come hunting in that country, and who buried his daughter on the top of one of the river bluffs south of the town. Her grave had been looted for her rich furs and beadwork long before my family went West, but we children used to find arrowheads there and some of the bones of her pony that had been strangled above her grave."

"What was the country like when you got there?"

"I shall never forget my introduction to it. We drove out from Red Cloud to my grandfather's homestead one day in April. I was sitting on the hay in the bottom of a Studebaker wagon, holding on to the side of the wagon box to steady myself—the roads were mostly faint trails over the bunch grass in those days. The land was open range and there was almost no fencing. As we drove further and further out into the country, I felt a good deal as if we had come to the end of everything—it was a kind of erasure of personality.

"I would not know how much a child's life is bound up in the woods and hills and meadows around it, if I had not been jerked away from all these and thrown out into a country as bare as a piece of sheet iron. I had heard my father say you had to show grit in a new country, and I would have got on pretty well during that ride if it had not been for the larks. Every now and then one flew up and sang a few splendid notes and dropped down into the grass again. That reminded me of something—I don't know what, but my one purpose in life just then was not to cry, and every time they did it, I thought I should go under.

"For the first week or two on the homestead I had that kind of contraction of the stomach which comes from homesickness. I didn't like canned things anyhow, and I made an agreement with myself that I would not eat much until I got back to Virginia and could get some fresh mutton. I think the first thing that interested me after I got to the homestead was a heavy hickory cane with a steel tip which my grandmother always carried with her when she went to the garden to kill rattlesnakes. She had killed a good many snakes with it, and that seemed to argue that life might not be so flat as it looked there.

"We had very few American neighbors—they were mostly Swedes and Danes, Norwegians and Bohemians. I liked them from the first and they made up for what I missed in the country. I particularly liked the old women, they understood my homesickness and were kind to me. I had met 'traveled' people in Virginia and in Washington, but these old women on the farms were the first people who ever gave me the real feeling of an older world across the sea. Even when they spoke very little English, the old women somehow managed to tell me a great many stories about the old country. They talk more freely to a child than to grown people, and I always felt as if every word they said to me counted for twenty.

"I have never found any intellectual excitement any more intense than I used to feel when I spent a morning with one of those old women at her baking or butter making. I used to ride home in the most unreasonable state of excitement; I always felt as if they told me so much more than they said—as if I had actually got inside another person's skin. If one begins that early, it is the story of the maneating tiger over again—no other adventure ever carries one quite so far.''

"Some of your early short stories were about these people, were they not?''

"Yes, but most of them were poor. It is always hard to write about the things that are near to your heart, from a kind of instinct of self-protection you distort them and disguise them. Those stories were so poor that they discouraged me. I decided that I wouldn't write any more about the country and people for which I had such personal feeling.

"Then I had the good fortune to meet Sarah Orne Jewett, who had read all of my early stories and had very clear and definite opinions about them and about where my work fell short. She said, 'Write it as it is, don't try to make it like this or that. You can't do it in anybody else's way—you will have to make a way of your own. If the way happens to be new, don't let that frighten you. Don't try to write the kind of short story that this or that magazine wants— write the truth, and let them take it or leave it.'

"I was not at all sure, however, that my feeling about the Western country and my Scandinavian friends was the truth—I thought perhaps that going among them so young I had a romantic personal feeling about them. I thought that Americans in general must see only the humorous side of the Scandinavian—the side often presented in vaudeville dialect sketches—because nobody had ever tried to write about the Swedish settlers seriously.

"What has pleased me most in the cordial reception the West has given this new book of mine, is that the reviewers in all those Western States say the thing seems to them true to the country and the people. That is a great satisfaction. The reviews have concerned themselves a good deal more with the subject matter of the story than with my way of telling it, and I am glad of that. I care a lot more about the country and the people than I care about my own way of writing or anybody else's way of writing.''

F. H.   Special Correspondence of the *Philadelphia Record,* 10 August 1913.

1915: LINCOLN

Willa Cather's career was followed closely by people in Nebraska, particularly in Lincoln. The Lincoln papers had a more than passing interest in her future

*because of their personal connections with her. Her new positions were noted
by her old friend Will Owen Jones in his column, and her books were reviewed—not always sympathetically, because of what was considered an unflattering portrayal of the Midwest in some of them. Celia Harris called "The
Bohemian Girl" a "rare, troubling" story with an effect that was "beautiful
but disturbing," and went on to note that even in* O Pioneers! *"the native Americans have not a single significant representative"* (NSJ, *3 August 1913*).

*With the publication of her third novel, Willa Cather was finally inter-
viewed by a paper in the city where she began her journalistic career. While
visiting in Lincoln in mid-October 1915, on her way back to New York from Red
Cloud, she was interviewed by Ethel M. Hockett for the* Lincoln Sunday Star.
*The interview was run on page one of the "News and Editorial Section,"
covering all seven columns of the bottom third of the page and including a
photo of the author with the caption "Willa Sibert Cather, from Nebraska, one
of America's foremost novelists and magazine writers."* ☞

THE VISION OF A SUCCESSFUL FICTION WRITER

by Ethel M. Hockett

For the benefit of the many young people who have literary ambitions and to
whom the pinnacle of success attained by this Nebraska novelist appears as the
most desirable thing to be gained in the world, Miss [Willa] Cather was persuaded to give the time from her busy hours in Lincoln of living over school
days with old acquaintances, to give a number of valuable suggestions from her
rich fund of experiences.

"The business of writing is a personal problem and must be worked out in
an individual way," said Miss Cather. "A great many people ambitious to
write, fall by the wayside, but if they are the discourageable kind it is better that
they drop out. No beginner knows what he has to go through with or he would
never begin.

"When I was in college and immediately after graduation, I did newspaper
work. I found that newspaper writing did a great deal of good for me in working
off the purple flurry of my early writing. Every young writer has to work off the
'fine writing' stage. It was a painful period in which I overcame my florid, exaggerated, foamy-at-the-mouth, adjective-spree period. I knew even then it

was a crime to write like I did, but I had to get the adjectives and the youthful fervor worked off.

"I believe every young writer must write whole books of extravagant language to get it out. It is agony to be smothered in your own florescence, and to be forced to dump great carloads of your posies out in the road before you find one posy that will fit in the right place. But it must be done, just as a great singer must sacrifice so many lovely lyrical things in herself to be a great interpreter."

Miss Cather is pre-eminently qualified to give advice to young writers, not only from her own experiences in traveling the road which led her to literary success, but because she has had opportunities to study the writings of others from the viewpoint of a buyer.

After she had worked on Lincoln newspapers, one of which was edited by Mrs. Sarah Harris Dorris whom she visited last week, Miss Cather went to Pittsburgh where she worked on a newspaper for several years. She tired of newspaper work and became the head of the English department in the Allegheny high school in Pittsburgh where she remained three years. It was while teaching that she wrote the verses which appeared in the book *April Twilights,* and the short stories which made up the book *The Troll Garden.* These stories and verses were published by McClure's, most of them appearing in the *McClure's* magazine. A year after their publication, Mr. McClure went to Pittsburgh and offered Miss Cather a position on his magazine which she accepted. Exceptional opportunities were shortly afterward afforded Miss Cather, as Miss Ida Tarbell, Mr. Philipps, Mr. Baker and several other prominent writers, left *McClure's* and bought the *American* magazine. Within two years, therefore, Miss Cather was managing editor of *McClure's.* She held that position for six years. Although life as managing editor was stimulating, affording Miss Cather opportunity for travel abroad and in this country, she could do no creative work, so left in order to produce the stories pent up in her mind. She says the material used in her stories was all collected before she was twenty years old.

"Aside from the fact that my duties occupied much of my time, when you are buying other writers' stuff, it simply isn't the graceful thing to do to do any writing yourself," she said.

Leaving *McClure's,* Miss Cather moved to a suburb of New York and wrote *Alexander's Bridge* and *The Bohemian Girl.* She went to Arizona for the summer and returned to New York to write *O Pioneers!*

Miss Cather's books all have western settings, in Nebraska, Colorado and

Arizona, and she spends part of each year in the west reviewing the early impressions and stories which go to make up her books.

"No one without a good ear can write good fiction," was a surprising statement made by Miss Cather. "It is an essential to good writing to be sensitive to the beauty of language and speech, and to be able to catch the tone, phrase, length of syllables, enunciation, etc., of persons of all types that cross a writer's path. The successful writer must also be sensitive to accomplishment in others.

"Writers have such hard times if they just have rules and theories. Things that make for integrity in writing are quite as unnameable as the things that make the difference between an artist and a near-artist in music. And it is the longest distance in the world between the artist and the near-artist.

"It is up to the writer and no one else. He must spend thousands of uncounted hours at work. He must strive untiringly while others eat and sleep and play. Some people are more gifted than others, but it takes brains in the most gifted to make a success. Writing has to be gone at like any other trade. One trouble is that people aren't honest with themselves; they are awfully unfrank about sizing themselves up. They have such queer ways of keeping half-done things stored by and inconsistently saying to themselves that they will finish them after a while, and never admitting they shrink from that work because they are not qualified for it.

"One trouble with young writers is that they imitate too much, often unconsciously," said Miss Cather. "Ninety-nine out of every hundred stories received by magazines are imitations of some former success. This is a natural mistake for young people to make. The girl or boy of 24 or 25 is not strong enough to digest experiences in the raw, therefore they take them pre-digested from things they read. That is why young writing does not as a rule amount to much. These young writers can sometimes give cries of pain and of rapture and even the cry from a baby sometimes moves.

"Young writers must care vitally, fiercely, absurdly about the trickery and the arrangement of words, the beauty and power of phrases. But they must go on and on until they get more out of life itself than out of anything written. When a writer reaches the stage where a tramp on a rail pile in Arizona fills him with as many thrills as the greatest novel ever written, he has well begun on his career.

"William Jones once expressed this idea well when he told me great minds like Balzac or Shakespeare got thousands and thousands more of distinct impressions and mental pictures in every single day of life than the average man got in all his life.

"I can remember when Kipling's *Jungle Tales* meant more to me than a tragic wreck or big fire in the city. But I passed through that stage. If I hadn't again grasped the thrills of life, I would have been too literary and academic to ever write anything worth while.

"There are a great many young people who like good literature and go to work on a magazine or newspaper with the idea of reforming it and showing it what to print. It is all right to have ideas, but they should be kept locked up, for the beginner should do the things in his employer's way. If his ideas are worth anything, they will come out untarnished; if they are not, they will get mixed up with crooked things and he will be disillusioned and soured.

"I have seen a great many western girls and boys come to New York and make a living around magazines and newspapers, and many rise to very good positions. They must be wide awake, adaptable and not afraid to work. A beginner can learn a lot about magazine requirements and style by proof-reading, or doing other jobs other than writing the leading editorials. Every magazine has its individual style.

"Most people have the idea that magazines are like universities—existing to pass on the merits of productions. They think if stories and articles are accepted, it is an honor, and if they are refused, it is a disgrace. They do not realize the magazine is in the business of buying and selling.

"The truth is that many good stories are turned down every day in a magazine office. If the editor has twenty-five children's stories in the safe and a twenty-sixth good children's story comes in with one poor adventure story, he must buy the poor adventure story and return the good children's story. It is just like being overstocked in anything else. The magazine editor must have variety, and it is sometimes maddening the way the stories come in in flocks of like kinds.

"The young writer must learn to deal with subjects he really knows about. No matter how commonplace a subject may be, if it is one with which the author is thoroughly familiar it makes a much better story than the purely imaginational.

"Imagination, which is a quality writers must have, does not mean the ability to weave pretty stories out of nothing. In the right sense, imagination is a response to what is going on—a sensitiveness to which outside things appeal. It is a composition of sympathy and observation."

Miss Cather makes the comparison between learning to write and learning to play the piano. If there is no talent to begin with, the struggler can never become an artist. But no matter what talent there is, the writer must spend hours and years of practice in writing just as the musician must drudge at his scales.

Miss Cather laughed merrily as she said that her old friends in Lincoln insist on dragging up what she pleased to call her "shady past," and reminding her of her rhetorical and reformative flights of her youth. It was recalled by one friend that she led the last cane rush in the university, that she wore her hair cropped short and a stiff hat and that the boys among whom she was very popular, called her "Billy." Miss Cather graduated from the University of Nebraska in 1895.

Lincoln Daily Star, 24 October 1915.

1919: CHICAGO

Henry Blackman Sell (1889–1974) was literary editor of the Chicago Daily News *from 1916 to 1920. He then went on to edit* Harper's Bazaar *(1920–26), served in the Roosevelt administration during World War II, was editor of* Town and Country *magazine (1949–72), and returned to* Harper's *until his death in 1974. While at* Harper's *he made the decision in 1925 to publish Anita Loos's* Gentlemen Prefer Blondes *in six installments, which began its crazy success story.*

In Chicago he was a part of the literary scene that brought the Windy City to the forefront and included such people as Carl Sandburg, Floyd Dell, Ben Hecht, Burton Rascoe, Edgar Lee Masters, Sherwood Anderson, and others. The literary pages of the Chicago Tribune *and* Daily News *rivaled their New York counterparts.*

*Sell visited New York and interviewed Cather at her apartment for his "A Page about Books and the People Who Write Them." He was certainly one of the first to call Cather the "Foremost American Woman Novelist." Although Sell says he learned about "her opinions on the Cather method of novel writing," his article focuses more upon her life and personality. It does show, however, that she had already formed the opinion about Alexander's Bridge which she expressed in the 1922 preface to the new edition of her first novel. Cather tore out the entire top half of the page containing the article and sent it to her parents (*WCPM *Collection).*

A large portion of Sell's article was reprinted as a part of an article entitled

"A Freedom in Her Book: Willa Cather's Life on a Nebraska Ranch May Be the Reason," which appeared in the Kansas City Times *on 18 March 1919.* ☞

WILLA SIBERT CATHER
To Our Notion the Foremost American Woman Novelist   *by Henry Blackman Sell*

My Ántonia . . . is not only the best done by Miss Cather, but also one of the best that any American has ever done, east or west, early or late. It is simple; it is honest; it is intelligent; it is moving. The means that appear in it are means perfectly adapted to its end. Its people are unquestionably real. Its background is brilliantly vivid. It has form, grace, good literary manners. In a word, it is a capital piece of writing. . . . There is, in the ordinary sense, no plot. There is no hero. There is, save as a momentary flash, no love affair. There is no hortatory purpose, no show of theory, no visible aim to improve the world. The whole enchantment is achieved by the simplest of all possible devices. . . . Here a glimpse, there a turn of phrase, and suddenly the thing stands out, suddenly it is as real as real can be — and withal moving, arresting, beautiful, with a strange and charming beauty. . . . I commend the book to your attention, and the author no less.

—H. L. Mencken in the current *Smart Set.*

" . . . and the author no less."
Prompted by this unusual enthusiasm of the wary Mencken, I called on Miss Cather the other day in New York, and gathered there some interesting facts about her life and her opinions on the Cather method of novel writing.

Willa Sibert Cather (pronounced to rhyme with rather, if you please) is, from handshake to simple gown, honest. Her bright, plump face shines with determined sincerity. Her clear, mellow voice gives instant assurance of a square deal. As we took off our wraps in a little side room my companion whispered, "Isn't she a regular fellow? Couldn't you go to her with your troubles!"

Miss Cather's rooms are walled with books. Her chairs have an enviable quality of sittableness. Comfort, sincerity, good homely taste, a warm open fire on a cold morning, comradeship, and a decent pride in work done and in the doing are the impressions taken from a half hour in the second floor apartment, front, at 5 Bank Street. Even the address hath a substantial sound.

Willa Sibert Cather is a Virginian, an American for several generations.

For the benefit of those who like to go 'way, 'way back, be it known that the Cathers came from Ireland and the Siberts from Alsace. When little Willa was nine years old her father heard the call of the big west, and left Virginia for a Nebraska ranch. No "gentleman's farm" was his ranch, but a tract in the thinly populated part of the state where the acreage of cultivated land was a mere kitchen garden beside the vast stretches of raw prairie. A sprinkling of Americans there were in this district, but most of the "near" neighbors were Scandinavians and ten or twelve miles away there was an entire township settled by Bohemians. Winter and summer, rain and shine, found the future novelist on her pony, riding and visiting the neighbors. Miss Cather feels that those youthful visits to the foreigners, her long talks, as she played and worked with them, were the greatest influence of her literary life. There she learned to know and understand the people of *My Ántonia* (Ann-ton-ee-ah—stress the e—as in the Bohemian). There she learned how hard life can be. There she learned what heroism is.

Miss Cather graduated from the University of Nebraska at the age of nineteen, took a position on the *Pittsburgh Leader* (where she was telegraph editor and dramatic critic for some years). Later she gave up journalism to head a high school English department. While teaching she published a book of verse and a book of short stories. This work attracted the attention of the editor of *McClure's* magazine, and for four years she was a member of the McClure staff.

Alexander's Bridge, her first novel, was published in 1912. An interesting first novel, but conventional. I hazard a guess that Miss Cather would survive the shock if she should receive word that her publisher's janitor had stolen the plates of *Alexander's Bridge* and escaped to darkest Africa or some other inaccessible place. But it did bring her to the attention of a knowing writer, Sarah Orne Jewett, who gave her the following excellent advice:

"Write it as it is, don't try to make it like this or that. You can't do it in anybody's else way—you will have to make it your own. If the way happens to be new, don't let that frighten you. Don't try to write the kind of stories that this or that magazine wants—write the truth and let them take it or leave it."

O Pioneers! was the result of Miss Jewett's urging, and there began the upward career of our foremost American woman novelist. Miss Cather's next novel was *The Song of the Lark,* a long, fine piece of writing. Her latest, *My Ántonia,* is one of the two or three outstanding novels of the last year. It is a

story of the west, and the strange people among whom she lived in her childhood. As to its particular qualities, I suggest that you read again the brief of H.
L. Mencken's opinion, printed above, and then get the book. To read one of
Miss Cather's books is to read three and gain many pleasant hours. Her writing
has that indefinable quality that we call "charm."

Chicago Daily News, 12 March 1919.

1921: NEW YORK

The Bookman *was one of the first periodicals to give Cather national exposure.
In 1905 the brief article/interview entitled* "Miss Cather" *had appeared in the
July issue. In 1921 it was again the first magazine of any national prominence
to interview Cather after the successful publication of* My Ántonia *and* Youth
*and the Bright Medusa. The interview is a familiar one, and various portions of
it have been quoted on numerous occasions. In it the newly recognized author
talks about her dependence upon memory, her early attempts at writing, her
sources, her work habits, and something about the effect she is trying to
achieve in her writing. The interviewer, who has obviously done some home-
work, brings her career up to date by providing other, supplementary material.*

*Archer Latrobe Carroll (1894–), joined the Century Company as a
member of the editorial staff following his graduation from Harvard University
in 1918. In 1920 he became a staff writer for the Foreign Press Service. From
1924 to 1934 he was on the editorial staff of* Liberty *magazine and then began
his career as a free-lance writer. With his wife, Ruth Robinson Carroll, he has
written a number of successful children's books, including the award-winning*
Peanut *(1953) and* Digby the Only Dog *(1955).* ☞

WILLA SIBERT CATHER

by Latrobe Carroll

On the Nebraska prairie some years ago, a little girl rode about on her pony,
among settlements of Scandinavians and Bohemians, listening to their conversation, fascinated by their personalities. She was Willa Sibert Cather, who,
as a woman, was to give in her novels the story of their struggle with the soil.
Ever since those early years, she has been studying people, until she is today
one of that small group of American writers who tell of life with beauty and

entire earnestness. She has won the praise of those critics whose standards are highest, whose condemnation of insincerity and distortion is severest. Listen to Randolph Bourne: "She has outgrown provincialism and can now be reckoned among those who are richly interpreting youth all over the world." And to H. L. Mencken: "There is no other American author of her sex, now in view, whose future promises so much."

Miss Cather's reputation is of recent growth. Though her first novel, "Alexander's Bridge", was published in 1912, she remained comparatively unknown until about five years ago. Then critics realized that every successive book of hers had shown an advance, and began to look forward with interest to her future work. She is, however, still unknown to large sections of the American reading public.

Not long ago, she sat in her New York apartment in Greenwich Village, and talked to me about her books. She seems just the one to have written them. She is sincere, vigorous, self-controlled. There is no flippancy about her. She has not made herself the heroine of any of her novels, but she is akin to her own heroines. In "The Song of the Lark", one of the characters remarks that Thea Kronborg, the central figure, "doesn't sigh every time the wind blows". Miss Cather herself is that sort. She has a mental sturdiness.

She spoke of the beginnings of her impulse to write.

"When I was about nine," she said, "father took me from our place near Winchester, Virginia, to a ranch in Nebraska. Few of our neighbors were Americans—most of them were Danes, Swedes, Norwegians, and Bohemians. I grew fond of some of these immigrants—particularly the old women, who used to tell me of their home country. I used to think them underrated, and wanted to explain them to their neighbors. Their stories used to go round and round in my head at night. This was, with me, the initial impulse. I didn't know any writing people. I had an enthusiasm for a kind of country and a kind of people, rather than ambition.

"I've always had a habit of remembering mannerisms, turns of speech," she explained. "The phraseology of those people stuck in my mind. If I had made notes, or should make them now, the material collected would be dead. No, it's memory—the memory that goes with the vocation. When I sit down to write, turns of phrase I've forgotten for years come back like white ink before fire. I think that most of the basic material a writer works with is acquired before the age of fifteen. That's the important period: when one's not writing. Those years determine whether one's work will be poor and thin or rich and fine."

After a high school preparation, Miss Cather entered the University of Nebraska. She said, of this time:

"Back in the files of the college magazine, there were once several of my perfectly honest but very clumsy attempts to give the story of some of the Scandinavian and Bohemian settlers who lived not far from my father's farm. In these sketches, I simply tried to tell about the people, without much regard for style. These early stories were bald, clumsy, and emotional. As I got toward my senior year, I began to admire, for the first time, writing for writing's sake. In those days, no one seemed so wonderful as Henry James; for me, he was the perfect writer."

When Willa Cather graduated at nineteen, her instructors and friends expected her to become a "writer" in a few months, and achieve popular success. But they were disappointed. For almost nine years she wrote little besides a volume of verse, the experimental "April Twilights", and a dozen stories for magazines. Most of these stories she now dismisses as "affected" and "bad".

"It wasn't that I didn't want to write," she said of this period. "But I was too interested in trying to find out something about the world and about people. I worked on the Pittsburg 'Leader', taught English in the Allegheny High School, went abroad for long periods, and traveled in the west. I couldn't have got as much out of those nine years if I'd been writing."

In 1905 there was published a collection of her stories, "The Troll Garden". Largely by reason of these, she was offered a position on "McClure's Magazine", of which she was managing editor from 1908 until 1912.

"I took a salaried position," she said, "because I didn't want to write directly to sell. I didn't want to compromise. Not that the magazine demands were wrong. But they were definite. I had a delightful sense of freedom when I'd saved up enough to take a house in Cherry Valley, New York, and could begin work on my first novel, 'Alexander's Bridge'.

"In 'Alexander's Bridge' I was still more preoccupied with trying to write well than with anything else. It takes a great deal of experience to become natural. People grow in honesty as they grow in anything else. A painter or writer must learn to distinguish what is his *own* from that which he admires. I never abandoned trying to make a compromise between the kind of matter that my experience had given me and the manner of writing which I admired, until I began my second novel, 'O Pioneers!' And from the first chapter, I decided not to 'write' at all—simply to give myself up to the pleasure of recapturing in memory people and places I had believed forgotten. This was what my friend

Sarah Orne Jewett had advised me to do. She said to me that if my life had lain in a part of the world that was without a literature, and I couldn't tell about it truthfully in the form I most admired, I'd have to make a kind of writing that would tell it, no matter what I lost in the process."

"O Pioneers!" placed Miss Cather definitely among the writers who count. It is an epic of the early struggles of Swedish and Bohemian settlers in Nebraska—a book of beauty and power. In taking for a title the name of one of Walt Whitman's poems, the author drew attention to his influence upon the mood of her narrative.

In "The Song of the Lark", Willa Cather chose a less impressionistic method. It is longer than "O Pioneers!", less concentrated, resembling more closely the conventional psychological novel. It is the story of Thea Kronborg, a Swedish-American singer, who wrenches herself away from an environment antagonistic to art, and becomes an opera "star". Critics took widely divergent attitudes toward the book. To many, it has not the same *aliveness* as "O Pioneers!" Randolph Bourne found it a digression into a field for which Miss Cather was not really fitted, either by her style, or her enthusiasm. But Edward Everett Hale discovered in it "a sense of something less common than life: namely, art as it exists in life—a very curious and elusive thing, but so beautiful, when one gets it, that one forgets all else."

Miss Cather's most recent novel, "My Antonia", is a fuller evocation of the "old, old west" than was "O Pioneers!" The descriptions of the western prairie, brief, poignant, lift us from our easy chairs and set us down on those high plains. The book is ruthless, poetical, tremendously alive. It is the finest thing Miss Cather has written. H. L. Mencken laid it down with the conviction that it is the best piece of fiction done by any woman in America. The portrayal of Antonia is masterly.

"She was a Bohemian girl," Miss Cather said, "who was good to me when I was a child. I saw a great deal of her from the time I was eight until I was twelve. She was big-hearted and essentially romantic."

Willa Cather's foreigners are true to type. August Brunius, after noting that the Swede, as presented by writers outside his own country, usually seems absurd to a Swedish reader, goes on to say that in "O Pioneers!" and "The Song of the Lark", Swedes are presented with true insight and art. Small wonder that all Miss Cather's books have been translated into the Scandinavian and are to be translated into French.

Her latest volume, "Youth and the Bright Medusa", is a collection of eight short stories. Simply and vividly told, they are studies of the artistic temperament. In them, there is none of the usual sentimentalizing about the artist. They are widely recognized as work of distinction. An anonymous critic in "The Nation" slyly remarks that the collection "represents the triumph of mind over Nebraska".

Willa Cather's best work is satisfying because it is sincere. In her books, there is none of the sweet reek that pervades the pages of so many "lady novelists". Love, to her, is "not a simple state, like measles". Her treatment of sex is without either squeamishness or sensuality. She loves the west, and the arts, particularly music, and she has sought to express feelings and convictions on these subjects. She tried, failed, and kept on trying until she succeeded. For example, we have her word for it that at college she attempted to tell about immigrants in rough sketches. She drew them more skillfully in "The Bohemian Girl", a short story which appeared in "McClure's Magazine" in 1912. Then came "O Pioneers!", a work of art. In "My Antonia", she reached what she had been advancing toward for many years. Similarly in her exploration of the minds and emotions of artists, she has striven to tell the truth—the truth stripped of sentimentality. She experimented in "The Troll Garden", succeeded partially in "Youth and the Bright Medusa", grasped fully what she had sought in "The Song of the Lark". It would, of course, be unfair to speak of the books and stories that led up to this novel and to "My Antonia" as preliminary studies, for there is too much in them not touched upon in the two later novels. But there is a certain summing up, in these books, of two subjects which have interested Miss Cather profoundly: the life of foreigners in the west, and the mind and heart of the artist. Of the books, the author herself said: "I think 'My Antonia' is the most successfully done. 'The Song of the Lark' was the most interesting to write."

"I work from two and a half to three hours a day," Miss Cather went on to say. "I don't hold myself to longer hours; if I did, I wouldn't gain by it. The only reason I write is because it interests me more than any other activity I've ever found. I like riding, going to operas and concerts, travel in the west; but on the whole writing interests me more than anything else. If I made a chore of it, my enthusiasm would die. I make it an adventure every day. I get more entertainment from it than any I could buy, except the privilege of hearing a few great musicians and singers. To listen to them interests me as much as a good morning's work.

"For me, the morning is the best time to write. During the other hours of the day I attend to my housekeeping, take walks in Central Park, go to concerts, and see something of my friends. I try to keep myself fit, fresh: one has to be in as good form to write as to sing. When not working, I shut work from my mind.''

At present Miss Cather is writing a new novel—she says of it:

''What I always want to do is to make the 'writing' count for less and less and the people for more. In this new novel I'm trying to cut out all analysis, observation, description, even the picture-making quality, in order to make things and people tell their own story simply by juxtaposition, without any persuasion or explanation on my part.

''Just as if I put here on the table a green vase, and beside it a yellow orange. Now, those two things affect each other. Side by side, they produce a reaction which neither of them will produce alone. Why should I try to say anything clever, or by any colorful rhetoric detract attention from those two objects, the relation they have to each other and the effect they have upon each other? I want the reader to see the orange and the vase—beyond that, *I* am out of it. Mere cleverness must go. I'd like the writing to be so lost in the object, that it doesn't exist for the reader—except for the reader who knows how difficult it is to lose writing in the object. One must choose one's audience, and the audience I try to write for is the one interested in the effect the green vase brings out in the orange, and the orange in the green vase.''

Miss Cather has never sought publicity, or quick success. It took her three years to write "The Song of the Lark", and three to write "My Antonia". Of the two paths of art—give the public what it wants, or make your work so fine that the public will want it—she has consistently chosen the path of fine work. She is moving unhurriedly toward a richer self-expression.

Bookman, 3 May 1921.

1921: RED CLOUD

Cather had begun working on One of Ours *in 1918. Her progress on the novel was slow and difficult. By the spring of 1921, she was writing friends about the trouble she was having in finishing the book. In January of that year the Writers' Club of New York had designated Cather one of the six great American novelists, along with Theodore Dreiser, Edith Wharton, James Branch Cabell, Booth Tarkington, and Gertrude Atherton. In April, Sinclair Lewis in a speech to the Omaha Society of Fine Arts said that Cather was "a greater author than he dared hope to ever be." He went on to call her one of the "biggest things Nebraska has produced" and concluded, "Willa Sibert Cather is greater than*

General Pershing; she is incomparably greater than William Jennings Bryan. She is Nebraska's foremost citizen because through her stories she has made the outside world know Nebraska as no one else has done'' (Argus, *14 April 1921). Mr. Cather sent a newspaper clipping about the speech to his daughter. Willa Cather must have seen another account of the speech, for on the day it appeared in the* Argus *she wrote Sinclair Lewis thanking him for his kind remarks. She was happy that he had read her books and liked them, but she was even more touched that he told her own people. She felt he probably did more to get Nebraskans to read her books than her own books could do. The respect of other young writers like Lewis meant more to her than almost anything else in the writing business (JPM).*

Also in April, Cather went to Toronto to stay with Jan and Isabelle Hambourg for a few months. Working steadily there, she completed One of Ours *and sent it off to Knopf. In September she visited Red Cloud for the first time in three years. The* Nebraska State Journal *of 24 September 1921 reported that she had written to her old friend, Dr. Julius Tyndale, about the relief she felt in having finished this new work. "Now," she was quoted, "I am going to lie in the hammock for a few weeks." Elsewhere in that same issue, the* Journal *quotes the telegram sent to Cather by Knopf after he had read the manuscript.*

Cather was at a new peak in public recognition and fame, but she must certainly have felt not only relief but a kind of freedom as well, for she stayed on in Nebraska for over three months. During that time she delivered an unusual number of public speeches and granted interviews to almost every major paper in the state. It was an unprecedented and unrepeated flash of visibility, during which she spoke out on many issues, some of which were rather controversial (see "Speeches" section).

The famous Nebraska author often described the conflicting emotions she had concerning her home state, and that conflict is apparent in the interviews and speeches of this period. She is by turns sentimental, nostalgic, critical, and ridiculing.

In September 1921, Cather stopped by the office of W. D. Edson, editor and publisher of the Webster County Argus, *for a chat. The resulting article is not a formal interview, but it is a well-ordered summary of the conversation, presented in indirect discourse. The tone is conciliatory and would seem to express an authentic fondness for her hometown. The audience for whom she was speaking was not the usual one, and no doubt this accounts for the absence of the more exciting and exaggerated tales that appear in other interviews. The readers of this page would* know. *They would remember.*

The article was reprinted in the Nebraska State Journal *on 9 October 1921 and reprinted in* Resources for American Literary Study *(Spring 1979).* ☞

A TALK WITH MISS CATHER

It always gives us much pleasure when some reader of the *Argus* here on a visit calls at the office for a friendly chat because of the feeling that those who read the paper and those who are charged with its preparation belong to one big family. Naturally we were especially pleased when last Friday Miss Willa Cather, whose address is New York City, but who is at home in Red Cloud, New York, London, Paris, or any other city on earth in which she happens to be, called at this office for that reason. Miss Cather is enjoying a several weeks' visit with her parents, Mr. and Mrs. C. F. Cather.

While her work has called her to other scenes Miss Cather told us that there is not any place in this world that is more interesting to her than Red Cloud. She came here from Virginia with her parents when a child, and here grew to womanhood, graduating from the local high school. During part of her course she wrote school items for the *Argus,* which may have been her first contributions to the public press. In those days she was often called upon to stay in her father's office while he was at the court house making abstracts or was out of the city on other business. She had her own desk in the office, and here she did much studying and writing. But the matter which she deems of greatest importance in this connection was the acquaintances formed with the leaders in the life of the community who, calling to transact business with her father, remained to visit with her, telling her of personal affairs in the way that grownups will disclose to a child matters which they would not discuss with a mature person. Often she accompanied Dr. Damerall or Dr. McKeeby on their long trips into the country, and listened with childish admiration as they talked on a variety of subjects from their personal experiences. There were no trained nurses here in those days, so sometimes she was called upon to assist them with surgical operations. In the best homes of the city she was always a welcome visitor. Red Cloud had many men and women of exceptional ability. Miss Cather looks back to her association with these as one of the brightest and most helpful periods of her life.

But the time came when it was necessary that she leave her home and friends. Greater opportunities in other places called her. Times were hard in Nebraska. Her father had acquired large holdings of land, but these were not producing enough revenue to pay the taxes. She could not be contented to stay here and depend upon her parents for support. But the thought of leaving her family and friends who meant so much to her was almost too much, and she confessed during her visit the other day that at one time she was actually on the point of giving up, when some words of timely counsel from Mr. and Mrs. O. C. Case gave her new courage and led her to go on with her plans for self improvement.

The interest which has been felt by Red Cloud people in *My Ántonia,* many of the scenes of which are laid in this city, led us to turn the conversation to that subject. Three characters of the story, Miss Cather said, were intended as comparatively faithful pictures of citizens of Red Cloud about 1888 or 1889. These were the author's grandparents, whose characteristics made a deep impression upon her youthful mind when she first came here from Virginia, and Mrs. J. L. Miner—the Mrs. Harling of the book, in whose home she was a frequent guest. In the first draft of the story the picture of Mrs. Harling was of a very different character. While the manuscript was being revised by the author, news came to her of Mrs. Miner's death. So profound an impression did this make upon her, and so active were the memories of old times brought to mind by the news that she made changes in some parts of the book in honor of her friend of early days.

Another character in the book, she informed us, was in part a picture of a former Red Cloud man, and in part of a man she had known in the east. For some reason, she said, this treatment of a character is a very natural one for an author to give. We inquired if these were not because the life of the average person is so commonplace that a faithful delineation of him alone would not make interesting reading. Miss Cather wholly disagreed with this view. She contended that the average person has just as interesting emotions and experiences as public personages. She knew Red Cloud people whose experiences were no less intense and thrilling than those of the public personages with whom she was well acquainted. She found people here just as interesting as those she met in London and Paris, although in a different way. She summed up the matter by saying that if a person is wide awake and not self-centered he can see those interesting things in the life of those about him.

My Ántonia has been translated into a number of different languages, and has had a very large sale. Miss Cather is very familiar with the French tongue, and was able to revise the manuscript after the translator had completed his work in that language. This gentleman was a very scholarly man and in the main did excellent work, but he was a little handicapped by never having lived in the prairie states. Miss Cather found that when he came to the word "gopher" at various places in the book he had used the French word meaning "mole." This might have passed among the French readers had it not been for a passage where the gophers were spoken of as playing about in the sun.

Miss Cather writes of Nebraska, not from any sense of duty, but because her early life was so bound up with this commonwealth that this part of the world is of greatest interest to her. She has just completed a new book, some of the scenes of which are laid in this part of the state. That it is bound to be one of her greatest successes is indicated by a telegram received from her publisher, after reading the last installment of the manuscript.

Just finished the book. Congratulations. It is masterly, a perfectly gorgeous novel, far ahead of anything you have ever yet done, and far ahead of anything I have read in a very long while. With it your position should be secure forever. I shall be proud to have my name associated with it.

Webster County Argus, 29 September 1921.

1921: OMAHA

Cather ended her lengthy stay in Red Cloud on 27 October 1921, her departure being noted in true small town fashion in the Argus *that day: "Miss Willa Cather, Mrs. W. A. Sherwood, and Mrs. Irene Weisz were passengers to Omaha this morning." Her companions were her childhood friends, the Miner sisters. They stayed at the Fontenelle Hotel, where Cather was scheduled to speak on Saturday, 29 October. On Friday evening she was visited by interviewers from the* World-Herald, *the* Daily News, *and the* Bee, *and three interviews were published the next day, a fourth a little later. Though short, the interviews contain interesting statements with remarkably little overlapping.*

The World-Herald *interviewer deals most with* One of Ours, *the novel Cather had just completed, and her early journalistic work in Lincoln and points out that she had only been in Omaha once before this occasion.* ☞

WILLA CATHER WILL SPEAK TO FINE ARTS SOCIETY TODAY

Willa Sibert Cather, Nebraskan, whose pen has given Nebraska prairies a place in literature along with the far west of Bret Harte and the New England of a dozen writers of that region, is in Omaha to speak before an Omaha audience for the first time. Not unusual for one so close to Nebraska's heart to be in the state's metropolis one might say, but this is her second visit to the city in her life.

Miss Cather is to speak before the Omaha Fine Arts society at the Fontenelle at four o'clock today.

Refreshed after a visit to the home of her parents, Mr. and Mrs. C. F. Cather at Red Cloud, Nebraska, Miss Cather is returning to New York to prepare her latest novel for the publishers. Except to state that the title of the new work is *One of Ours,* and that it is the story of a Nebraska boy presented in an entirely new way, the woman novelist is silent regarding it.

"It's a secret, and it's something new," she said at the Fontenelle last night. And when the writer of *My Ántonia, O Pioneers!,* and *The Song of the Lark,* not to mention a score or more of other writings equally read, declares "it's a secret," no one is going to know much about "it." She did say, however, that she intends working over eight pounds of page-proof of the novel, which will consume most of the winter.

Miss Cather spoke lightly of her success as a writer. Graduating from the University of Nebraska when nineteen, she went to Pittsburg, Pa., to the *Pittsburg Leader.* She taught in the Allegheny high school, soon joining the staff of *McClure's* magazine, where she rose to be managing editor. Holding that position until 1912, she resigned and entered the independent work which has since brought her to the fore among writers of the country. Nearly all of her work has been done in the east.

"I really had to work to go through college," she declared. "I was dramatic critic on the Lincoln *State Journal,* receiving one dollar a night for my work. On Sundays I had four columns of trash in the paper. I got four dollars for this. It was just trash, too, for what could a kid of nineteen write?" Her previous visit to Omaha was made when she was engaged in this work. She came to see Sarah Bernhardt.

"What are you to speak on before the arts society today?" Miss Cather was asked.

"Oh, on the 'Standardization of Literature and Art,' " she laughed. "I was too lazy to make up a good title for it. That won't be it exactly, but it will be something like that."

OW-H, 29 October 1921.

The interviewer from the Omaha Daily News *was more interested in Cather's*

childhood experience than her current work. There seems to be some confu-
sion, either on the part of the interviewer or Irene Miner Weisz, about whether
the make-believe town was Sandy Point or Stony Point. Other sources agree on
the former, but the town was fictionalized as Speckleville in Cather's 1898
short story, "The Way of the World." ☞

TO LIVE INTENSELY IS CREED OF WILLA S. CATHER, AUTHORESS

To live intensely — that has been the creed of Willa Sibert Cather from the days
when, a born feminist, she was mayoress of the play-town of "Sandy Point" in
a Red Cloud, Nebraska backyard, to the present, when she had achieved recognition as one of America's foremost novelists.

Miss Cather is to speak before the Fine Arts society at the Hotel Fontenelle
ballroom at four p.m.

"Tremendous output, tremendous reserve, that's the secret of success in
any vocation," said Miss Cather.

Superbly does Miss Cather live her creed. Splendid strength, well-
controlled, shone from her clear blue eyes, as with the help of her friend, Mrs.
Irene Weisz, she resurrected the little girl Willa Cather, the livest live-wire in
Red Cloud, over the dinner table at the Hotel Fontenelle Friday night.

"There's no question about it, Willa started her literary career in 'Stony
Point,'" said Mrs. Weisz. "She was editor of our play-paper, 'The Stony Point
News,' as well as the mayoress."

"But, I didn't want to be an author. I wanted to be a surgeon!" protested
Miss Cather. "Thank goodness, I had a youth uncorrupted by literary ambitions. I mean it! I think it's too bad for a child to feel that it must be a writer, for
then, instead of looking at life naturally, it is hunting for cheap effects.

"I have never ceased to be thankful that I loved those people out in Republican Valley for themselves first, not because I could get 'copy' out of them,"
she said.

"How I loved the long, rambling buggy rides we used to take," exclaimed
Miss Cather. "We went over the same roads this summer. I could tell who lived
at every place and all about the ailments of his family. The old country doctor
and I used to talk over his cases. I was determined then to be a surgeon."

"When you go back to them," said her friend, "you're the same Willa
Cather who was mayoress of 'Sandy Point.' Do you remember of buying my
vote with a sack of candy?"

"My only plunge into politics," laughed Miss Cather.

Of her books, Miss Cather enjoyed writing *The Song of the Lark* most. She wants her public to judge her by her new book, *One of Ours;* she considers it her best.

Miss Cather denied living in Greenwich village. "The village doesn't exist," she said. "How could it in these times when the last cellar is empty?"

Miss Willa Cather will be honor guest of the dinner this evening given by the League of Women Voters at the Brandeis tearoom. One hundred and fifty reservations have been made. Mrs. Rose Berry of Berkeley, California, general federation chairman of Fine Arts, will be present.

Omaha Daily News, 29 October 1921.

The Omaha Bee *interview, aiming at a certain comprehensiveness, covers more biography. It is also filled with errors. In editing this particular piece, titles have been regularized, but otherwise the interview is reprinted just as it appeared. Some of the mistakes may have been the typesetter's, but some are obviously the interviewer's. Not only is Cather's name consistently misspelled but the dates of her graduation and employment with "McClure" magazine are in error. "The Bohemian Girl" is cited as a book. Cather's plans, which she may not have made clear, were to go to Lincoln before returning to New York, rather than fleeing from the stage, as implied in the article. It may well have been this type of error and misinformation, which occurs frequently in her interviews but rarely in such concentration, that led Cather to be more niggardly in granting them.* ☞

LURE OF NEBRASKA IRRESISTIBLE, SAYS NOTED AUTHORESS

Willa Cathers, one of the foremost American women writers of the modern school, will have it distinctly understood that she is not an eastern, western, northern or southern writer, but first and foremost a Nebraskan.

When questioned as to why she considered herself a Nebraskan after so many years abroad and in the east, she replied, "Because my father and mother still live in Nebraska. They have lived here for 30 odd years, and because I came to Nebraska when I was 8 and lived here until I finished college at 19, and the years from 8 to 15 are the formative period of a writer's life, when he unconsciously gathers basic material."

"He may acquire a great many interesting and vivid impressions in his mature years, she continued, but his thematic material, he acquires under 15 years of age. Other writers will tell you this.''

''Lord Dunsany once told me that he believed he had never used any basic material he had acquired after his 15th year.''

Willa Cathers, when 8 years old, came with his father and mother from Winchester, Va., where she was born, to what she described as one of the most picturesque places of the country, to Nebraska, near Red Cloud, in the southern part of the state.

''This country was mostly wild pasture and as naked as the back of your hand,'' said the author. ''I was little and homesick and lonely and my mother was homesick and nobody paid any attention to us. So the country and I had it out together and by the end of the first autumn, that shaggy grass country had gripped me with a passion I have never been able to shake. It has been the happiness and the curse of my life.''

Miss Cathers has taken an apartment in Paris with some friends, but she is skeptical about remaining there, for as she recalled Paris last autumn, when the leaves were turning yellow on the cottonwoods along the boulevards, she said she would sit by the Seine and feel weepy and homesick for the Republican valley. ''I always come back to Nebraska,'' she concluded.

Willa Cathers graduated from the University of Nebraska in 1905 with a B. A. degree. The following year she went east and held the position of telegraph editor on the *Pittsburgh Leader* for three years.

In 1908 she accepted a position as managing editor of the *McClure* magazine and remained in that position until 1912.

''Those four years were used in preparing myself to write the sort of book I had always wanted to, for during this time I did but little writing,'' said Miss Cathers. She was abroad much of the time while connected with the McClure magazine.

In 1912 Miss Cathers resigned to take up a home in Cherry Valley, N. Y. ''I moved there to write without molestation and in the way I had been preparing myself for,'' she said.

During this period her books, *Alexander's Bridge* and ''Bohemian Girl'' appeared serially in *McClures*. Then followed *O Pioneers!, The Song of the Lark, Youth and the Bright Medusa,* and *My Ántonia*. The latter book is said by many to be the most brilliant of her literary efforts. It is written with the Bohemian settlement near her home in Red Cloud, as the background.

Willa Cathers' latest work, to be published some time next summer, has just been completed while she visited at her home in Red Cloud. The title is *One of Ours*.

Miss Cathers will lecture before the Omaha Society of Fine Arts this after-noon at 4, in the ballroom of the Hotel Fontenelle.

She will leave immediately after for Chicago and the east where she will make final plans for the publication of her latest work. She plans to leave for Europe early in the spring.

Omaha Bee, 29 October 1921.

A longer World-Herald *interview by Eva Mahoney was published three weeks after the others that resulted from Cather's visit to Omaha; meanwhile, Cather had gone to Lincoln. This interview stresses the importance of friendship for Willa Cather. It traces Cather's meteoric rise in the literary world and re-counts, again, the shifting emphasis in her fiction.*

Eva Mahoney, a native of Omaha, joined the staff of the World-Herald *in 1917. For many years she edited the "Mary Lane" column, advice for the love-lorn, and went on to have responsibilities in women's news, general news, and feature writing. She retired to Tucson in 1954, where she died in 1968.*

Miss Mahoney recalled the effect of Sinclair Lewis's speech (see "1921— Red Cloud") and uses a great deal of Dorothy Canfield Fisher's Yale Review *article. The interview is well known and often quoted.* ☞

HOW WILLA CATHER FOUND HERSELF
After Ten Years of Practice at Following Henry James' Style,
She Finally Wrote Her Own Nebraska in Her Own Way. *by Eva Mahoney*

When one starts out to write about Willa Sibert Cather, distinguished Nebraska novelist, he must approach his subject with simplicity and sincerity. If he does not he will sin not only against the canons of art but against Miss Cather's high-est ideals, for sincerity and simplicity are the fundamental characteristics of this gifted writer and of the art of literature as she so beautifully interprets it.

Miss Cather spent several days in Omaha late in October at which time she spoke before the Omaha Society of Fine Arts and the Nebraska League of Women Voters. She has been going through Omaha from New York City on her way to her home in Red Cloud, Neb., for the last twenty years but she never stopped off here. She is going to stop off every time from now on, she says, because she renewed some old friendships and made some new ones while here. And Miss Cather is just that homey sort of a person who loves her friends—not social acquaintances—but friends. That's why she has been coming back each year to Nebraska to visit her father and mother and her friends—to see the people and the things with which she is familiar.

And that fact more than any one thing accounts for the success that has come to Miss Cather as a writer. She tells about people and things with which she is familiar.

She did not always do this. For more than ten years after her graduation from the University of Nebraska at the age of 19, she wrote about things that she knew only superficially, she says. And success evaded her. Then her pen poised for an interval and when it dropped again to paper it did so to record the story of life in Nebraska as lived by those sturdy pioneer farmers near Saline and Webster and Franklin counties. She had known these people from childhood, and she had heard stories of their early struggles by word of mouth, and so she wrote about them.

The voices of those Scandinavian and Bohemian farmers had heretofore remained mute in the literature of this nation. Their joys and their sorrows; their loves and their hates; their failures and their successes no one had put into words. But they found their spokesman at last in *O Pioneers!*, and well they had been repaid for their long silence. They had been immortalized. Critics of two continents proclaimed Miss Cather a superb artist and assigned *O Pioneers!* to its rightful place among the great literatures of the world.

The critics had spoken. They were unanimous in their praise, but Miss Cather waited a bit breathlessly to hear from her reading public. And then her reading public spoke and in no uncertain terms. Letters poured in from the Danes, Swedes, Germans, and Bohemians from all over the state, letters of praise and gratitude that a great artist had portrayed their lives truthfully and lovingly.

And then Willa Cather knew that she had come into her own—that she had done a new sort of thing in American literature. She had treated a new subject in a language that her subject gave her. Years before Miss Cather's good friend and critic, the late Sarah Orne Jewett, the writer, divining the Nebraska woman's mental conflict, had said: "What you really care for is new material that has never been used. Don't write about other things. If you have to create a new medium, have the courage to do it."

Miss Cather had the courage to do just this thing. The result is that many critics proclaim her the foremost woman novelist in America today. Some critics do not qualify their statement but say unreservedly that she is the foremost novelist in America.

O Pioneers! was not Miss Cather's first novel, but it was her first one that made the world sit up and take notice. Her first book was a collection of stories, *The Troll Garden*. In 1912, she published her first novel, *Alexander's Bridge*. Before this she had written a volume of light verse, *April Twilights,* and many stories for magazines. In fact, back in the files of the college magazine of the University of Nebraska can be found honest but cumbersome efforts on Miss Cather's part to tell in story something of the lives of those early settlers who had lived near her father's farm near Red Cloud. Amateurish though these stories were, perhaps they pointed the way to the heights toward which Miss Cather was traveling, her friends say.

The Song of the Lark was published next. Critics accorded it high praise but were less of one opinion regarding its merit. Miss Cather, herself, cares less for it than for any of her books, although she admits frankly that she enjoyed writing it.

Then came *My Ántonia,* conceded by many to be her masterpiece. She had been three years writing this book as she had in writing *The Song of the Lark.* When H. L. Mencken, most caustic of American critics, read *My Ántonia,* he declared it to be the best piece of fiction done by any woman in America.

"Ántonia was a Bohemian girl who had been kind to me when I was a child," says Miss Cather simply in speaking about this striking character in fiction.

Miss Cather's latest book, *Youth and the Bright Medusa,* is a collection of short stories, some of them rewritten from an earlier period.

Nebraska people, except those about whom she has actually written, have been backward in coming to a full realization that a literary genius was taking the trouble to write about their state. It is a bit humiliating to admit, but such is the case. The great centers of the United States and other countries had paid their highest tribute to Miss Cather long before this state awakened to its great opportunity to proclaim its own prophet.

It is true the University of Nebraska translated into Czech *O Pioneers!* at the time it was published, but the recognition did not spread much further. While Nebraska was dilatory, the remainder of the world was not. *O Pioneers!* was serialized in a daily paper in Norway; conservative Scandinavian critics wrote in high praise of the book; now all Miss Cather's books have been translated into the Scandinavian and *My Ántonia* has been translated in Prague, Czecho-Slovakia. All her books are now being translated into French, and Miss Cather goes to Paris next summer to aid in this work of translation.

And so the world is proclaiming Miss Cather's literary triumph. Yet it took Sinclair Lewis, that big, boyish, jubilant author of *Main Street,* who came lecturing here last winter, to tell Omaha people very emphatically just how great a writer Willa Cather is.

"Miss Cather is Nebraska's foremost citizen," declared Sinclair in his positive way. "The United States knows Nebraska because of Willa Cather's books."

It was not until Sinclair Lewis issued his militant proclamation that Miss Cather's own father, C. F. Cather of Red Cloud, knew just how brilliant a daughter he had given to the world. At that time he wrote a loving little letter to his daughter in New York and in it paid a tribute to her genius, a bit awkwardly put, for full realization had come to the father with rather startling force.

"Father is a very modest man, and he wants me to be modest," said Miss Cather when in Omaha recently, and the phrase had in it nothing of affectation, for success has left Miss Cather without affectation, modest and unspoiled, just as her father would have her. And then it was that all the rest of the Cather family rejoiced, and as Miss Cather is one of seven children, "all living and hale and hearty," as she says, the rejoicing was widespread.

This sketch about Miss Cather's success sounds quite simple in the telling. She seems to have moved unimpeded along the path to achievement. Actually this is far from the truth. With her as with most people, success represents a terrific struggle. It represents years of youthful uncertainty and mental chaos when she was learning her technique and learning also the ways of the world in this country and abroad. Studying and working and striving to express herself, Miss Cather wrote for magazines, did newspaper work on the Pittsburg *Leader*, taught English in an Allegheny high school, was editor of *McClure's* magazine, and in other ways served the hard apprenticeship that precedes a great literary triumph.

When she tells about those years there comes into her voice an occasional break—that is the only sign of emotion, for Miss Cather has about her nothing of foolish sentimentality, although she has a penetrating warmth of genuine sentiment. But she wants it known that she has had a good time during those years of struggle; that she was happy in her travels, her love of music, her friends, her work—but happiness in her actual achievement was long deferred.

"A book is made with one's own flesh and blood of years. It is cremated youth. It is all yours—no one gave it to you," said Miss Cather when speaking of her work in Omaha, and the quiet solemnity of a beautifully modulated voice, the sensitive play of emotion on her delicately chiseled face gave force to her words and made one realize just how much more than mere craftsmanship goes into the making of a great book.

Miss Cather tells about those years of tireless effort as follows:

"When I left the University of Nebraska after graduating and went to New York City, I wanted to write after the best style of Henry James—the foremost mind that ever applied itself to literature in America. I was dazzled. I was trying to work in a sophisticated medium and write about highly developed people whom I knew only superficially.

"It was during the six years when I was editor of *McClure's* magazine that I came to have a definite idea about writing. In reading manuscripts submitted to me, I found that 95 per cent of them were written for the sake of the writer— never for the sake of the material. The writer wanted to express his clever ideas, his wit, his observations. Almost never did I find a manuscript that was written because a writer loved his subject so much he had to write about it.

"Usually," she added, "when I did get such a manuscript it was so crude it was ineffective. Then I realized that one must have two things—strong enough to mate together without either killing the other—else one had better change his job. I learned that a man must have a technique and a birthright to write—I do not know how else to express it. He must know his subject with an understanding that passes understanding—like the babe knows its own mother's breast."

It was through this critical analysis of story writing that Miss Cather finally found herself. "I had been trying to sing a song that did not lie in my voice," Miss Cather declared.

"There I was on the Atlantic coast among dear and helpful friends and surrounded by the great masters and teachers with all their tradition of learning and culture, and yet I was always being pulled back into Nebraska," she continued. "Whenever I crossed the Missouri river coming into Nebraska the very smell of the soil tore me to pieces. I could not decide which was the real and which the fake 'me.' I almost decided to settle down on a quarter section of land and let my writing go. My deepest affection was not for the other people and the other places I had been writing about. I loved the country where I had been a kid, where they still called me 'Willie' Cather.

"I knew every farm, every tree, every field in the region around my home, and they all called out to me," she added earnestly. "My deepest feelings were rooted in this country because one's strongest emotions and one's most vivid mental pictures are acquired before one is 15. I had searched for books telling about the beauty of the country I loved, its romance, and heroism and strength and courage of its people that had been plowed into the very furrows of its soil, and I did not find them. And so I wrote *O Pioneers!*."

And in the writing of this book and the other books that followed, Willa Cather saw all those early years had been in preparation for her rightful task. Out of her experience with complex people and complex things had come a great work of literature about simple people and simple things.

This, too, Sarah Orne Jewett had epitomized for Miss Cather when she said to her: ''You have to know the world so well before you know the parish,'' and so after coming to know the world, Miss Cather went back home and wrote about the parish.

Another literary friend, Dorothy Canfield Fisher, has recently written in the *Yale Review* in unreserved praise of Miss Cather's work. Strangely enough Miss Cather and Mrs. Fisher were schoolmates at the University of Nebraska, and now both are writers of national distinction. Mrs. Fisher wrote as follows:

''There is no writer living in whose excellence Americans feel a warmer, prouder pleasure than we all feel in the success of Willa Cather. I do not mean by success the wide recognition given her, although that is delightful to see. I mean what must give much more satisfaction to Miss Cather, herself, her real inner success, her real excellence, her firm, steady upward growth and expansion into tranquil and assured power. It is as heartening and inspiring a spectacle as the rich, healthful growth and flowering into splendor of a plant in our gardens, for she is a plant of our own American garden to her last fiber.

''Here is an American to whom European culture (and she has always had plenty of that) is but food to be absorbed and transformed into a new product, quite different, unique, inimitable, with a harmonious perfection of its own. I cannot imagine any excercise which would be of more use to a young writer than to take the last story in her new volume, *Youth and the Bright Medusa* (what an inspired title!), and compare it line by line with the original version which was published in the January number of *Scribner's* in 1903. The whole story of Miss Cather's development is there, and an uninformed writer would learn more by pondering on the changes made by Miss Cather in her own story after eighteen years of growth and work than by listening to many lectures from the professors of literature.

''So often writers, even very clever ones, spoil their earlier work when they try to alter it, have not the firm mastery of their craft to know how to smooth out the crudeness without rooting out the life, are so startled by the changes in their own taste that they do not know where to begin. Miss Cather, conscious, firm-willed artist that she is, has known just where to lay her finger on the false passages and how to lift them without destroying the life of the story.''

In her New York home, Miss Cather works but three hours a day—hours of perfect joy and happiness, she describes them. She finds that at the end of two or three hours she has exhausted her best efforts. She spends the remainder of the day with her friends, or taking a walk in Central park, or listening to good music or busying herself with housework and forgets about her work. She believes that a writer should keep in as good physical condition as a singer, and so she regulates her life on a simple, normal schedule. She writes easily and seldom tears a paragraph or a page to pieces. She sometimes revises, but she does not fuss over her writing. "I let life flow along the pages," says this consummate artist.

Miss Cather has just completed a new book, *One of Ours*. It is now in proof form. She worked three years on this book, and she considers it her best effort.

"The hero is just a red-headed prairie boy," said Miss Cather. "I always felt it was presumptuous and silly for a woman to write about a male character, but by a chain of circumstances I came to know that boy better than I know myself. I have cut out all descriptive work in this book—the thing I do best. I have cut out all picture making because that boy does not see pictures. It was hard to cease to do the thing that I do best, but we all have to pay the price for everything we accomplish, and because I was willing to pay so much to write about this boy, I felt that I had a right to do so."

Lucky prairie boy! To have Willa Cather to write about him.

OW-H, 27 November 1921.

1921: LINCOLN

Following her two appearances in Omaha, Cather made plans to spend some time in Lincoln. The Lincoln Star proclaimed in a headline on Sunday, 30 October: "Nebraska Woman Who Achieves Fame in Literary World, Visits Her Old Home." The article went on to say that Cather would "arrive in Lincoln Monday to be the guest for a few days of Mr. and Mrs. Max Westerman." On Tuesday she was interviewed by a reporter for the Journal and by Eleanor Hinman for the Star. The Journal interview appeared on Wednesday, 2 November, and the Star interview on the following Sunday, 6 November.

The Journal interview covers several of the topics that Cather had been speaking on recently in Hastings and Omaha: the cottonwoods, imitation of the east, and the interest of ordinary places and ordinary people. She also talks for the first time at some length about the simple mechanical details of her writing process. ☞

MISS CATHER IN LINCOLN

Miss Willa Cather is giving only two days to Lincoln, which was her home during the years of her university course. Many old time friends and others who would have liked to meet one of the country's most distinguished novelists have been disappointed at her inability to accept offers of such hospitality. In chatting Tuesday with a friend of her school days, Miss Cather expressed deep appreciation of her native prairies and their people. She expressed the wish that women's organizations would study trees, flowers and other beauties of the state instead of turning back to Botticelli and early art.

"I often recall what Sarah Orne Jewett said to me many years ago," said Miss Cather. "Miss Jewett said a knowledge of the world was needed in order to understand the parish. When in big cities or other lands, I have sometimes found types and conditions which particularly interested me, and then after returning to Nebraska, discovered the same types right at home, only I had not recognized their special value until seen thru another environment."

Miss Cather is particularly interested in saving the cottonwoods planted by the pioneers out in the state. "The pioneers feel that the cottonwoods are bound up with their lives," said Miss Cather. "Yet everywhere the tall rugged trees are being cut down. Cottonwoods are out of date. The soft maple is the thing. I gave a talk at Hastings not long ago and made a plea for the preservation of the native trees. You should have seen the number of old people who stayed to talk to me and all spoke of how it hurt when one of the big trees they loved was felled.

"A flat country like Nebraska needs great forking trees like cottonwood or poplar. The poplar gets winter killed in Nebraska, but it also does that in Lombardy. The cottonwood is the only tree of beautiful form that grows easily and naturally in this state without any care. Farmers say the cottonwood draws moisture from the fields. I am not asking them to plant more, but to let stand those great trees that are dear to the pioneers. Their faculty of drawing moisture makes the cottonwoods needed in low places along the roads to take up water which would otherwise form a slough. On high barren pasture land, where nothing else will grow, the cottonwood will thrive. Just as great indifference is shown to the groves of ash and native elms. The farmers will not take the trouble to thin them. The soft maples, which have been planted in many districts to replace the hardier trees, live at the most only about thirty-five years.

"The French people appreciate the beauty of the cottonwood. Great rows are seen along the Seine in Paris. These are of the cotton-bearing variety, too, and in the spring all Paris is aflutter with cotton and no one seems to mind. The spreading roots of these trees draw up the too great moisture along the river banks.''

Miss Cather was asked to tell just what was meant about aping the east in the published report of her after dinner speech before the league for women voters at Omaha. She said she had found in a number of Nebraska cities visited a foolish adherence to the supposed fashions and customs of large cities like Chicago and New York. "It is not necessary," she said, "for a stout woman to wear an absurdly short skirt, or a large hat because that is supposed to be the style, any more than it is necessary to plant the same kind of trees as everybody else."

Miss Cather came to Lincoln Monday from Omaha and has since been the guest of Mr. and Mrs. Max Westermann. She will leave for New York at 4:30 Wednesday afternoon. She has been in the state for two months, most of the time with her parents at Red Cloud, where she completed the manuscript of a new novel to be entitled, *One of Ours*. The first part of this story is laid in Nebraska. Miss Cather expects to give much of the winter months to proof reading and final polishing of the work. The novel will not emerge from the publisher until next fall. Miss Cather has already arranged to go to Paris next autumn as soon as this book is entirely off her hands. She will take an apartment there with friends, for which she will carry over some of her possessions, but will retain her apartment in New York.

"I shall never live abroad permanently," said Miss Cather. "I do not want to. But for a number of reasons it is easier to work in Paris than in New York. There are fewer interruptions and the comforts of life, such as good food and service, are obtained with less effort."

Miss Cather told of her method of working. Each morning she devotes two and a half hours to literary labor. Last winter these working hours were so interrupted by telephone calls that she had her telephone removed. The full plan of a story is distinct in her mind before beginning to write. The first draft is in long hand. She then rewrites by typewriter. This copy is again revised and re-typed by Miss Cather, and again revised before being turned over to a professional typist. The last copy is subject to many corrections and changes and is then ready for the printer. On the proof sheets much elimination and condensation takes place. All of which shows that Miss Cather's vigorous, terse style, keen sense of fine meanings in words, and gripping characterization have not been gained without labor.

Lincoln State Journal, 2 November 1921.

Eleanor Hinman's interview with Willa Cather while she was in Lincoln is the longest to date in her career. It is an important interview in that the author speaks of a number of subjects that appear frequently in her fiction. The presentation gives the impression of a plain, down-to-earth, friendly person who is open and energetic. She reiterates the importance of her childhood experiences and tells, for the first time, the details of the conception of My Ántonia. *The relationship of her characters to actual people is described a bit differently than it was in her visit with the editor of the* Argus, *but this is the version she repeated on later occasions. It is perhaps her discussion of "beauty" that is most illuminating while it draws her back to her speech themes. Her idea of finding art in ordinary work, in cooking, in raising children, in life itself, is found in* My Ántonia, Death Comes for the Archbishop, Shadows on the Rock, *"Neighbor Rosicky," and other works, and her comments here aid in an understanding of that theme in her fiction.*

Cather also speaks in this interview about her opinion of career women. It is one of the few places where she spoke publicly about that issue.

The interviewer was apparently confused about Cather's schedule. She had come to Lincoln from Omaha after her lecture. ☞

WILLA CATHER,

Famous Nebraska Novelist, Says Pioneer Mother
Held Greatest Appreciation of Art—Raps Women
Who Devote Themselves to Culture Clubs   *by Eleanor Hinman*

"The old-fashioned farmer's wife is nearer to the type of the true artist and the prima donna than is the culture enthusiast," declared Miss Willa Cather, author of *The Song of the Lark, O Pioneers!, My Ántonia, Youth and the Bright Medusa,"* who has earned the title of one of the foremost American novelists by her stories of prima donnas and pioneers. She was emphasizing that the two are not so far apart in type as most people seem to imagine.

Miss Cather had elected to take her interview out-of-doors in the autumnal sunshine, walking. The fact is characteristic. She is an outdoor person, not far different in type from the pioneers and prima donnas whom she exalts.

She walks with the gait of one who has been used to the saddle. Her complexion is firm with an outdoor wholesomeness. The red in her cheeks is the red that comes from the bite of the wind. Her voice is deep, rich, and full of color; she speaks with her whole body, like a singer.

"Downright" is the word that comes most often to the mind in thinking of her. Whatever she does is done with every fibre. There is no pretense in her, and no conventionality. In conversation she is more stimulating than captivating. She has ideas and is not afraid to express them. Her mind scintillates and sends rays of light down many avenues of thought.

When the interviewer was admitted to her, she was pasting press clippings on a huge sheet of brown wrapping paper, as whole-heartedly as though it were the most important action of her life.

"This way you get them all together," she explained, "and you can see who it is that really likes you, who that really hates you, and who that actually hates you but pretends to like you. I don't mind the ones that hate me; I don't doubt they have good reasons; but I despise the ones that pretend."

When she had finished, she went to her room and almost immediately came out of it again, putting on her hat and coat as she came down the stairs, and going out without a glance at the mirror. She dresses well, yet she is clearly one of the women to whom the chief requirement of clothes is that they should be clean and comfortable.

Although she is very fond of walking, it is evidently strictly subordinate in her mind to conversation. The stroll was perpetually slowing down to a crawl and stopping short at some point which required emphasis. She has a characteristic gesture to bring out a cardinal point; it commences as though it would be a hearty clap upon the shoulder of the person whom she is addressing, but it checks itself and ends without even a touch.

I had intended to interview her on how she gathers the material for her writings; but walking leads to discursiveness and it would be hard to assemble the whole interview under any more definite topic than that bugbear of authors, "an author's views on art." But the longer Miss Cather talks, the more one is filled with the conviction that life is a fascinating business and one's own experience more fascinating than one had ever suspected it of being. Some persons have this gift of infusing their own abundant vitality into the speaker, as Roosevelt is said to have done.

"I don't gather the material for my stories," declared Miss Cather. "All my stories have been written with material that was gathered—no, God save us! not gathered but absorbed—before I was fifteen years old. Other authors tell me it is the same way with them. Sarah Orne Jewett insisted to me that she has used nothing in all her short stories which she did not remember before she was eight years old.

"People will tell you that I come west to get ideas for a new novel, or material for a new novel, as though a novel could be conceived by running around with a pencil and [paper] and jotting down phrases and suggestions. I don't even come west for local color.

"I could not say, however, that I don't come west for Inspiration. I do get freshened up by coming out here. I like to go back to my home town, Red Cloud, and get out among the folk who like me for myself, who don't know and don't care a thing about my books, and who treat me just as they did before I published any of them. It makes me feel just like a kid!'' cried Willa Cather, writer of finely polished prose.

"The ideas for all my novels have come from things that happened around Red Cloud when I was a child. I was all over the country then, on foot, on horseback and in our farm wagons. My nose went poking into nearly everything. It happened that my mind was constructed for the particular purpose of absorbing impressions and retaining them. I always intended to write, and there were certain persons I studied. I seldom had much idea of the plot or the other characters, but I used my eyes and my ears."

Miss Cather described in detail the way in which the book *My Ántonia* took form in her mind. This is the most recent of her novels; its scene is laid in Nebraska, and it is evidently a favorite of hers.

"One of the people who interested me most as a child was the Bohemian hired girl of one of our neighbors, who was so good to me. She was one of the truest artists I ever knew in the keenness and sensitiveness of her enjoyment, in her love of people and in her willingness to take pains. I did not realize all this as a child, but Annie fascinated me, and I always had it in mind to write a story about her.

"But from what point of view should I write it up? I might give her a lover and write from his standpoint. However, I thought my Ántonia deserved something better than the *Saturday Evening Post* sort of stuff in her book. Finally I concluded that I would write from the point of a detached observer, because that was what I had always been.

"Then, I noticed that much of what I knew about Annie came from the talks I had with young men. She had a fascination for them, and they used to be with her whenever they could. They had to manage it on the sly, because she was only a hired girl. But they respected and admired her, and she meant a good deal to some of them. So I decided to make my observer a young man.

"There was the material in that book for a lurid melodrama. But I decided that in writing it I would dwell very lightly upon those things that a novelist would ordinarily emphasize and make up my story of the little, every-day happenings and occurrences that form the greatest part of everyone's life and happiness.

"After all, it is the little things that really matter most, the unfinished things, the things that never quite come to birth. Sometimes a man's wedding day is the happiest day in his life; but usually he likes most of all to look back upon some quite simple, quite uneventful day when nothing in particular happened but all the world seemed touched with gold. Sometimes it is a man's wife who sums up to him his ideal of all a woman can be; but how often it is some girl whom he scarcely knows, whose beauty and kindliness have caught at his imagination without cloying it!"

It was many years after the conception of the story that it was written. This story of Nebraska was finally brought to birth in the White Mountains. And Miss Cather's latest novel, which will be published next fall, and which alone of all her prairie stories deals with the Nebraska of the present, was written largely on the Mediterranean coast in southern France, where its author has been during the past spring and summer.

It is often related that Miss Cather draws the greater part of her characters from the life, that they are actual portraits of individual people. This statement she absolutely denies.

"I have never drawn but one portrait of an actual person. That was the mother of the neighbor family, in *My Ántonia*. She was the mother of my childhood chums in Red Cloud. I used her so for this reason: While I was getting under way with the book in the White Mountains, I received the word of her death. One clings to one's friends so—I don't know why it was—but the resolve came over me that I would put her into that book as nearly drawn from the life as I could do it. I had not seen her for years.

"I have always been so glad that I did so, because her daughters were so deeply touched. When the book was published it recalled to them little traits of hers that they had not remembered of themselves—as, for example, that when she was vexed she used to dig her heels into the floor as she walked and go clump! clump! clump! across the floor. They cannot speak of the book without weeping.

"All my other characters are drawn from life, but they are all composites of three or four persons. I do not quite understand it, but certain persons seem to coalesce naturally when one is working up a story. I believe most authors shrink from actual portrait painting. It seems so cold-blooded, so heartless, so indecent almost, to present an actual person in that intimate fashion, stripping his very soul.''

Although Miss Cather's greatest novels all deal with Nebraska, and although it has been her work which has first put Nebraska upon the literary map, this seems to have been more a matter of necessity with her than of choice. For when she was asked to give her reflections about Nebraska as a storehouse of literary or artistic material, her answer was not altogether conciliatory.

"Of course Nebraska is a storehouse of literary material. Everywhere is a storehouse of literary material. If a true artist was born in a pigpen and raised in a sty, he would still find plenty of inspiration for his work. The only need is the eye to see.

"Generally speaking, the older and more established the civilization, the better a subject it is for art. In an old community there has been time for associations to gather and for interesting types to develop. People do not feel that they all must be exactly alike.

"At present in the west there seems to be an idea that we all must be like somebody else, as much as if we had all been cast in the same mold. We wear exactly similar clothes, drive the same make of car, live in the same part of town, in the same style of house. It's deadly! Not long ago one of my dear friends said to me that she was about to move.

"'Oh,' I cried, 'how can you leave this beautiful old house!'

"'Well,' she said, 'I don't really want to go, but all our friends have moved to the other end of town, and we have lived in this house for forty years.'

"What better reason can you want for staying in a house than that you have lived there for forty years?

"New things are always ugly. New clothes are always ugly. A prima donna will never wear a new gown upon the stage. She wears it first around her apartment until it shapes itself to her figure; or if she hasn't time to do that, she hires an understudy to wear it. A house can never be beautiful until it has been lived in for a long time. An old house built and furnished in miserable taste is more beautiful than a new house built and furnished in correct taste. The beauty lies in the associations that cluster around it, the way in which the house has fitted itself to the people.

"This rage for newness and conventionality is one of the things which I deplore in the present-day Nebraska. The second is the prevalence of a superficial culture. These women who run about from one culture club to another studying Italian art out of a textbook and an encyclopedia and believing that they are learning something about it by memorizing a string of facts, are fatal to the spirit of art. The nigger boy who plays by ear on his fiddle airs from *Traviata* without knowing what he is playing, or why he likes it, has more real understanding of Italian art than these esthetic creatures with a head and a larynx, and no organs that they get any use of, who reel you off the life of Leonardo da Vinci.

"Art is a matter of enjoyment through the five senses. Unless you can see the beauty all around you everywhere, and enjoy it, you can never comprehend art. Take the cottonwood, for example, the most beautiful tree on the plains. The people of Paris go crazy about them. They have planted long boulevards with them. They hold one of their fetes when the cotton begins to fly; they call it 'summer snow.' But people of Red Cloud and Hastings chop them down.

"Take our Nebraska wild flowers. There is no place in the world that has more beautiful ones. But they have no common names. In England, in any European country, they would all have beautiful names like eglantine, primrose, and celandine. As a child I gave them all names of my own. I used to gather great armfuls of them and sit and cry over them. They were so lovely, and no one seemed to care for them at all! There is one book that I would rather have produced than all my novels. That is the Clemens botany dealing with the wild flowers of the west.

"But why am I taking so many examples from one sense? Esthetic appreciation begins with the enjoyment of the morning bath. It should include all the activities of life. There is real art in cooking a roast just right, so that it is brown and dripping and odorous and 'saignant.'

"The farmer's wife who raises a large family and cooks for them and makes their clothes and keeps house and on the side runs a truck garden and a chicken farm and a canning establishment, and thoroughly enjoys doing it all, and doing it well, contributes more to art than all the culture clubs. Often you find such a woman with all the appreciation of the beautiful bodies of her children, of the order and harmony of her kitchen, of the real creative joy of all her activities, which marks the great artist.

"Most of the women artists I have known—the prima donnas, novelists, poets, sculptors—have been women of this same type. The very best cooks I have ever known have been prima donnas. When I visited them the way to their hearts was the same as to the hearts of the pioneer rancher's wife in my childhood—I must eat a great deal, and enjoy it.

"Many people seem to think that art is a luxury to be imported and tacked on to life. Art springs out of the very stuff that life is made of. Most of our young authors start to write a story and make a few observations from nature to add local color. The results are invariably false and hollow. Art must spring out of the fullness and the richness of life."

This glorification of the old-fashioned housewife came very naturally from Willa Cather, chronicler of women with careers. What does Miss Cather think of the present movement of women into business and the arts?

"It cannot help but be good," was her reply. "It at least keeps the woman interested in something real.

"As for the choice between a woman's home and her career, is there any reason why she cannot have both? In France the business is regarded as a family affair. It is taken for granted that Madame will be the business partner of her husband; his bookkeeper, cashier or whatever she fits best. Yet the French women are famous housekeepers and their children do not suffer for lack of care.

"The situation is similar if the woman's business is art. Her family life will be a help rather than a hinderance to her; and if she has a quarter of the vitality of her prototype on the farm she will be able to fulfill the claims of both."

Miss Cather, however, deplores heartily the drift of the present generation away from the land.

"All the farmer's sons and daughters seem to want to get into the professions where they think they may find a soft place. 'I'm sure not going to work the way the old man did,' seems to be the slogan of today. Soon only the Swedes and Germans will be left to uphold the prosperity of the country."

She contrasts the university of the present with that in the lean days of the nineties, "when," as she says, "the ghosts walked in this country." She came to Lincoln, a child barely in her teens, with her own way to make absolutely. She lived on thirty dollars a month, worked until 1 or 2 o'clock every night, ate no breakfast in the morning by way of saving time and money, never really had enough to eat, and carried full college work. "And many of the girls I was with were much worse off than I." Yet the large majority of the famous alumni of the university date from precisely this period of hard work and little cash.

In making her way into the literary world she never had, she declares, half the hardships that she endured in this battle for an education. Her first book of short stories, to be sure, was a bitter disappointment. Few people bought it, and her Nebraska friends could find no words bad enough for it. "They wanted me to write propaganda for the commercial club," she explained.

"An author is seldom sensitive except about his first volume. Any criticism of that hurts. Not criticism of its style—that only spurs one on to improve it. But the root-and-branch kind of attack is hard to forget. Nearly all very young authors write sad stories and very many of them write their first stories in revolt against everything. Humor, kindliness, tolerance come later."

Some of the stories from this unsuccessful volume, *The Troll Garden,* were reprinted in *Youth and the Bright Medusa,* the recent volume which has had a wide success.

Miss Cather spent Monday, Tuesday, and Wednesday with Mrs. Max Westerman, going from here to Omaha to deliver a lecture before the fine arts club.

Lincoln Sunday Star, 6 November 1921.

1922: NEW YORK

Although Willa Cather frequently claimed to have drawn only one of her characters from memory—in detail—her interviews and other remarks are continually turning up other characters who were modeled upon people whom she had known or met at various times in her life. The use of David Hochstein as a model for David Gerhardt in One of Ours *is another of these examples.*

David Hochstein was born in Rochester, New York, on 16 February 1892. He studied the violin initially in New York and later with Leopold Auer in Petrograd and Otakar Sevcik in Vienna. He received a scholarship and a first prize of a thousand crowns from the Austrian government. After his debut as a violinist in Vienna in 1911, he toured England and then was heard widely in the United States, appearing at Carnegie and Aeolian Halls and the Metropolitan Opera House and touring with Amoto and Frieda Hampel, well-known musicians of the day. When he was called to military service, Hochstein canceled his schedule of concerts and tours, which brought him an estimated $20,000 in 1918 alone. First stationed at Camp Upton, Long Island, where he was headmaster of the 306th Infantry, he organized an orchestra, which he directed, and continued his musical interest. On 10 March 1918, he reported to the New York Times *that,*

It has done me good in many ways. Physically—well, I feel like a different person. It is partly the outdoor life and the exercise—though I have always tried to take exercise and keep fit—but it has been even more, I think, the regular hours for sleep and the fact that it has been possible, really, to sleep in those hours. But it isn't only that; I'm better physically. There are other things that are just as important. I have learned the value of odd minutes, for one thing. I think what has impressed me more than any other single thing here is that no time is wasted. The odds and ends aren't thrown away;

they all fit in. And we are all learning that out here. It is bound to make a difference to us afterward. (NYT, 10 March 1918, sec. 7, p. 5, col. 1)

Hochsteins' enthusiasm echoes that of Gerhardt and Claude Wheeler. Unfortunately, Hochstein's reaction to the news item that appeared in the New York Times *on the following day was never recorded for posterity. On 11 March 1919, the* Times *reported that Hochstein's violin, a Stradivarius valued at over $25,000 had been ruined—"smashed to bits"—in a car accident at Mineola on the previous day:*

> The troupe left the train at Mineola, and Hochstein, crowded into a small auto bus, which was to take them to Rockville Centre. They had gone only a short distance when the front wheels of the car collapsed under the weight, and the windshield was smashed as it crashed into a telegraph pole.
>
> Everyone in the car was shaken up, but the Depot Brigade Quartet began to sing, and the rest of the party recovered their composure and hurried off to find another car. A limousine was borrowed from a nearby estate, and the journey to Rockville Centre was finished in good time. Shortly before the matinee commenced Sergeant Hochstein called to his accompanist, Private Max Glazer, to rehearse one or two numbers with him. When Sergeant Hochstein opened the soft leather case which held his violin he found the instrument in pieces. When the accident occurred, Charles Wayland Towne, amusement director of the YMCA, who was in charge of the troupe, called out to Hochstein: "Is the Strad all right, David?" And Hochstein, finding the case apparently unscathed, replied that it was safe.
>
> Hochstein was stunned when he saw the instrument broken. He closed the case on the fragments, and took the first train to New York on his way to Rochester, where he will leave the broken instrument. He intends bringing a less valuable instrument back to camp with him for use in future concerts.
>
> The violin was valued by Hochstein at $25,000, and he carried $10,000 insurance on it. It is believed here that if he goes to France he may arrange for the purchase in Europe of a Stradivarius for the amount which the Insurance company will give him. Hochstein used his violin for the last time during a recital by Miss Margaret Wilson, daughter of the President, on Friday night in the YMCA Auditorium here. (NYT, 11 March 1918, p. 7, col. 3)

By 9 December 1918, the Times *was running an article which proclaimed that Hochstein's friends were searching for any news concerning his where-abouts. His former managers, the Music League of America, or his mother were to be notified by anyone who had any news. He had gone overseas in April and had requested transfer to active service at the front. He was then promoted to first lieutenant with the 60th Infantry.*

> *He was with his company during the summer drive at Verdun and on October 8, when his regiment was in "rest billets," he played a concert in the city of Nancy. The day after that concert he wrote a letter to the Music League enclosing the notices of the concert and saying that his regiment would return to the front the following day. Since that time no word has been received from him either by his family or his managers, and their cables and telegrams have brought no reply. (*NYT*, 9 December 1918, p. 11, col. 2)*

Word of his death in the Argonne Forest was finally reported in the New York Times *on 28 January 1919 (p. 9, col. 4). Willa Cather recalls him in the following interview three years later. Incidentally, she speaks erroneously of the trout quintet as having two cellos. It is scored for cello, string bass, violin, viola, and piano.* ☞

FICTION RECALLS VIOLINIST LOST IN WAR   An Interview with Willa Cather

David Hochstein was killed in the Argonne on November 10, 1918. He was a well known violinist, and echoes of regret for the cutting off of this recognized talent are still heard; reminiscences of the young artist by musicians and intimate friends have been published and so have poems composed in a strain of gentle sorrow. A stanza of one of the best known copy of verses inscribed to his memory is here given:

> O the fire of your violin melted us then,
> Till we granted your saying was sooth;
> That a man of the fiddle was not least of men
> When he fought as he sung for the truth!

And a character in a recently published novel seemed to embody the lost musician. The author, Miss Willa Cather, in her "David Gerhardt," by the circumstances of his enlistment in the A. E. F., his war experiences, and his death, appeared to have had David Hochstein in mind. Admirers of the violinist asked the novelist if this were true, and she replies in the interview that follows. It may be added that the words of the following explanation are Miss Cather's own:

"Yes," Miss Cather said, "I think that character must have been done from David Hochstein. It's not a portrait; it's not even an impressionistic sketch of him, for I met him in all just three times. But if I hadn't met him those three times Claude Wheeler's friend and fellow officer would certainly have been another person. He wouldn't have been a David Gerhardt; he probably wouldn't have been a violinist."

"You say you didn't know Hochstein well?"

"Not at all. But he was the sort of person to whom you gave your whole attention. One knew him as well as one could under the circumstances. The first time I met him as at Harold Bauer's apartment in the Wellington Hotel, one afternoon in the winter of 1916. A group of musicians had met together to play things they liked. Hochstein was among them. I had not heard him before, but when I asked who he was, Jan Hambourg told me he was a very gifted young American violinist. They played a lot of chamber music that afternoon, Schubert's *Death and the Maiden* among other things, but what I particularly remember was their beautiful playing of Schubert's *Die Forelle* (The Trout), a quintet not often played in public because it requires two cellos. That afternoon Boris Hambourg took one cello part, Maurice Dambois the other. Thibaud played first violin, Hochstein second, and I think Monteux, now conductor of the Boston Symphony Orchestra, was at the piano. I was very much interested in Hochstein from the moment they began to play, and in that quintet I thought his playing simply splendid. I had the feeling that he was playing at the top of his form and that he cared particularly for that composition. Thibaud had been playing a lot of Mozart and was tired.

"As I say, I had never heard Hochstein before, and I felt that he was a very poetic violinist and that he had the *stimmung* of that particular composition on that occasion more than any of the other players. He was enjoying himself thoroughly. To this day I cannot be sure whether his eyes were really yellow-brown or whether that color simply stays in my mind as a connotation — the yellow-brown of trout streams in sunlight. He was sitting by a window in a strong glow of afternoon sun that made his hair distinctly auburn. He looked very handsome — very young and fresh among the older men; he was then, I believe, about 24. His face and the shape of his head were distinctly intellectual, not at all the Toscha-Mischa kind. There is a certain drawing of Father Damien, one that used to hang in the rooms of college girls, which might stand as a portrait of Hochstein. The resemblance was quite remarkable. A friend of mine took him into a picture shop on Fifth Avenue one day to prove to him how like him this picture was. When he was confronted with the drawing he blushed and didn't seem to like it.

"After the music was over the musicians settled down to talk. Hochstein didn't care to talk apparently. He said he must be going and put on his hat and overcoat. We went down in the elevator together and up to Carnegie Hall, where I took my bus. We were talking about the Schubert things they had been playing. I found that, as I had suspected, he was a very thoughtful young man; that he had a great many ideas and opinions and rather kept them to himself. He was reticent, but what he had to say was extremely interesting; and you didn't feel that he had said it all before to a great many people. He hadn't, in short, yet acquired the professional manner which an artist must have to save his soul, but which is, after all, more attractive in the breach than in the observance. His manner in conversation with a stranger, even with his friends, was cordial but not effusive—distinctly not effusive.

"I did not meet Hochstein again until after America had gone into the war and his number had been drawn for military service. There was, of course, warm discussion among his friends and fellow artists as to whether he ought not to get exemption from military duty. He was very low in mind about the matter. He hated the idea of giving up his work and going into the service; and he hated the idea of being a quitter. From the beginning of the war his sympathies had not been entirely pro-Ally. He had got his musical training in Germany and admired many things about German civilization. Moreover, he hadn't the kind of mind that easily takes sides, that adopts opinions and says, 'These opinions are right, and are the only right ones, because they are mine.' Hochstein was a nephew of Emma Goldman. He was a Socialist and had read and thought a great deal about economics and systems of government. His father, I believe, was a student. I got the impression that Hochstein himself had given a good deal of time to the study of philosophy. He knew too much about history to draw rash and comforting conclusions. He didn't believe that any war could end war; he didn't believe that this one was going to make the world safe for democracy, or that it had much to do with democracy whatever. He couldn't see any Utopia ahead. He didn't believe that the war was going to get the world anywhere, no matter how it came out. But he didn't like to see himself getting exemption. That picture didn't attract him. That role looked undignified to him. However, he applied for exemption. The Local Board looked into his case, found he was the only support of his widowed mother, and granted his discharge. After he got his discharge he was unhappy. He presented himself again before the Board, told them he had made arrangements for his mother during his absence and wished to enter the service. The chariman of the Board wrote that they were 'struck by his manly bearing and fine appearance,' and well might they be! He was too proud not to fight—too proud, at any rate, to accept the only alternative.

"I met Hochstein again after he had been in camp a few weeks, and he was a much discouraged young man. The drill, the wooden discipline, the apparent waste of time, the boredom, were very hard for him to bear. He terribly missed the companionship of men with his own interests. He said his mind felt heavy, as if it were going to sleep, as if he were drugged. And he couldn't but feel it was all for nothing. He was giving up everything to adopt a course of action which was mostly the deadliest kind of inaction and which led nowhere. He didn't talk about it a great deal, but he looked older; his face seemed frozen in a kind of bitter resignation. I couldn't believe it was the same countenance, so full of romantic feeling and delicate humor, that I had watched that afternoon when he was playing the Trout quintette. It was soldiers of his kind, who hadn't any simple, joyful faith or any feeling of being out for a lark, who gave up most, certainly.

"About three months after this I saw Hochstein for the third and last time. I had in the meantime heard from some of his friends that David was feeling very differently about everything that pertained to his military duties; that he had become quite reconciled to his life in camp. He looked, indeed, very different. He was not dejected; he bore himself as if he liked his uniform. Something keen and penetrating and confident had come back into his face. When he talked there was a glow of enthusiasm in his eyes. When I came upon the scene he was talking. Yes, he was saying, he wouldn't have missed it. The life at camp was a deadly grind at first, but now he wouldn't have missed it. He had found something there that he had vaguely felt the lack of all his life.

"Some one asked him if it was the exercise, the regularity, the lack of any personal responsibility. 'Oh, it's everything,' he said. 'It's difficult to explain.' He went on a little further. I don't remember just what he said; but those of us who were with him understood clearly that what he liked, what he got something out of, was his relation to other young men. He didn't mention the war, didn't seem to be dwelling on the larger issues of it. His whole attention now seemed fixed upon his company and what was going on at Camp Upton. We asked him if he wasn't bored. No, not at all now; the men were splendid.

"Splendid, no doubt, but not very stimulating, probably, and all a good deal alike. Hochstein laughed and shook his head. 'No, they're not alike. The men are all right, fine fellows. I'm learning a great deal.' Didn't he miss the kind of food and comfort and personal freedom he had always been used to, we asked him, and the company of other artists? At first, he said, but not now. 'For me there's something in that life, just as it is; something I've always wanted.'

"Really, Hochstein said very little more that day than that he particularly liked the young men he was with in camp; that they were a kind he hadn't known well before and he wouldn't have missed knowing them; and that he was 'getting something he had always wanted.' He didn't say what that something was, perhaps he couldn't have said. He was not loquacious, but by a few words he could indicate a great deal. His friends felt absolutely reassured about him. He had never looked handsomer, never seemed easier in his mind or more easily pleased and amused. He announced his intention of going to Hickses to get a large, possibly several large, ice cream sodas before he started for camp. He persuaded Mrs. Jan Hambourg to go with him in search of their refreshment.

"In the winter of 1917, I think it was on a holiday of some kind, the Hambourgs telephoned me that Hochstein would be in from camp to march in the parade on Fifth avenue and that, as he expected to sail soon, it would probably be the last chance to see him before he went. It was a very stormy day; heavy slush under foot and snow falling in big wet flakes. I stood at the window and deliberated for some time, but I decided it would be dreary to stand on Fifth avenue waiting for a parade and that probably there was small chance of picking out one man on foot among so many marching men, all uniformed alike. Late in the afternoon Jan Hambourg and his wife came in for tea and said I had made a mistake not to go; the men had looked splendid, marching in the snow, and when the band came down the avenue they had recognized Hochstein at once; he was playing a slide trombone! Jan caught his attention in some way, and he smiled and waved to them. That was their last glimpse of him. He sailed soon after.

"The next autumn the news came that Hochstein had been blown to pieces by a shell in the Argonne Forest. On the night of the 14th of October Hochstein and a fellow officer had brought a small wagon train of hot food over almost impassable roads, under shell fire, up to men who were to make an important attack in the morning. The next day, Hochstein, in command of the headquarters runners, was killed during the action.

"Letters to his mother, some of which were published, show how seriously he took his military duties. Soon after he got his commission he wrote her:

" 'You don't know (I don't yet) what it means to be a platoon commander. It means having the lives of fifty-eight others in your control. And they must be cared for. It isn't just commanding. I never before (even after ten months in the army) realized what it did mean. I have no military ambition, but I know how few can lead; and I know that I would rather lead than be led.

" 'The first of October will mark a year service for me, and I will be granted my commission as Second Lieutenant on that date.

" 'I shall at last have a raincoat that shuts out rain. I shall have many material comforts I never before had in the service but much added responsibility. I shall write you, however, soon again. The future is unknown and many things may happen.'

"Again he writes his mother:

" 'When you have seen and met men who have been through the inferno many times, every belief you ever held is either destroyed or tempered more strongly, and I have had many to destroy—in whose place I find newer, better, and stronger ones. Every one finds his belief, his religion—here I have found mine. I adhere to no creed, no more than my father did, nor to any particular kind of God, but, dear mother, I *believe*. I have faith. I know that for all these heroic souls gone to the beyond there is some future. There is much that is materialistic about the war—too much. But those who died, be it recklessly or by the most unexpected exploding shell, have a compensation more than a mere title of hero or a posthumous service cross. You don't try to explain it—but you know it in France.'

"Any one who knew Hochstein would know that these were not conventional platitudes reeled off to soothe his mother. From a very thoughtful young man, critical by habit, a doubter of governments and religions and schools of thought, such statements mean something. They mean that something very revolutionary had happened in Hochstein's mind; I would give a good deal to know what it was!

"In the days when I met David Hochstein I was not writing *One of Ours*. I was busy writing *My Ántonia,* and this latest book of mine was no more in my thoughts than it is in yours. An event which touched my own life rather closely, and which came later, produced the book. Afterward, in 1920, when I was deep in this story, I wanted my red-headed soldier from a prairie farm to 'get some of his back,' as the phrase is, through a fine friendship; so many splendid friendships grew up between young men during the war. I wanted him, in daily life, at last to have to do with someone he could admire. I had the good fortune to know a great many fine young soldiers, some of them very well, so I had a wide latitude of choice.

"But when I came to that part of the story, it was the figure of Hochstein, whom I had known so little, that walked into my study and stood beside my desk. I had not known him well, but neither would Claude Wheeler know him very well; the farmer boy hadn't the background, the sophistication to get very far with a man like Hochstein. But there was a common ground on which they could know and respect each other—the ground on which Hochstein had met and admired his fellow soldiers at Camp Upton. And Claude would sense the other side of David and respect it. Hochstein's comrades sensed it. Lately several of them, non-commissioned officers, have taken a good deal of trouble to look me up and arrange an interview, merely to ask me whether Hochstein 'amounted to much' as a violinist. In each case these were men who knew nothing and cared nothing about music, and they apparently knew no musicians to consult. But they seemed to need this fact to complete their memory of him, to pull their mental picture of him together, though it was merely as a soldier that they had admired him.''

New York Herald, 24 December 1922, sec. 8, p. 4, cols. 1–4; p. 12, cols. 3–4.
Reprinted in the *Commercial Advertiser*, 3 September 1923, p. 2, cols. 1–4; p. 3, col. 1.

1923: PARIS

When Willa Cather was awarded the Pulitzer Prize for One of Ours *in 1923, she was only the fourth novelist so honored since the inception of the prizes in 1918. Ernest Poole was the first recipient in 1918, Edith Wharton in 1921, Booth Tarkington in 1919 and 1922, and no award was given in 1920. The awards were announced on 13 May 1923. Cather's citation was "for the American novel published during the year which shall best present the wholesome atmosphere of American life, and the highest standard of American manners and manhood." The cash stipend was $1,000. Many objected to the award— some because they felt the novel was not good and others because they felt the citation missed much of the point of what Miss Cather was trying to do in the book. The* New York Times, *however, defended Cather's prize in a spirited editorial on 15 May 1923, saying, "In the first place,* One of Ours *is admirably written, in English always lucid." That, alone, put it in a class by itself among books of the day. Second, Cather seemed to realize that World War I had some objective, a notion the* Times *felt that many other authors missed. "She knows as well as any of them that war has 'horrors,' and doubtless she hates it as much as any of them; certainly she does not laud it as among the more commendable of human activities. But she is as little of a pacifist as of a militarist; she is a sane woman who understands that there are worse things than war"* (NYT, *15 May 1923, p. 18, col. 5).*

As the interview in the World *makes clear, Cather was in France when the awards were announced. Some twelve years later, in 1935, when her good friend Zoë Akins received the Pulitzer Prize in drama for her adaptation of Wharton's* The Old Maid, *Cather wrote to Zoë, confessing her own true reactions. She told Zoë that to have refused the Pulitzer would have exhibited the poorest taste in the world (she might well have had Sinclair Lewis in mind, since he did just that in 1926). Nevertheless, Cather acknowledged that the Pulitzer was more annoying than it was pleasant. She gave thanks to the Lord that she had been in France at the time hers was announced. Her best advice to Zoë was to avoid becoming flustered by it, and in time she was sure Zoë would be able to laugh about the whole matter (*ALS, *10 May 1935,* HLSM). ☞*

TODAY'S NOVELS GIVE MUCH HOPE TO MISS CATHER

Paris, May 20. — Delighted at the news her novel *One of Ours,* won the Pulitzer prize, Miss Willa Cather confessed to *The World* correspondent this afternoon that she is also much surprised, as she had never thought of her book in connection with such an award.

Miss Cather has just started another novel, but she good-humoredly declined to say anything about its nature or setting, declaring:

"I never tell even intimate friends anything whatever about my work until it is finished. I find that if I talk about a novel on which I am at work it has a disturbing influence on me and I lose my grip on the story."

Miss Cather is living with friends, Mr. and Mrs. Jan Hambourg, in the quiet suburb Ville Davray, and expects to remain in Europe a year. Although much better in health, she is still suffering slightly from the effects of her illnesses in New York last winter. Speaking of the literature of today, she told *The World* correspondent she sees much promise and hope in the new movement in America, despite its little absurdities.

"The new American novel," she explained, "is better than the old-fashioned conventional one, with its plot always the same, its accent always on the same incidents. With its unvarying, carefully dosed ingredients, the old-fashioned American novel was like a chemist's prescription.

"I certainly prefer the modern novelist, even if he does become a little ridiculous when he carries too far the process of chopping up his character on the Freudian psycho-analytical plan. Imagine what Hamlet would have been if Shakespeare had applied Freudian principles to his work.

"So long as a novelist works selfishly for the pleasure of creating character and situation corresponding to his own illusions, ideals and intuitions, he will always produce something worth while and natural. Directly he takes himself too seriously and begins for the alleged benefit of humanity an elaborate dissection of complexes, he evolves a book that is more ridiculous and tiresome than the most conventional cold cream girl novel of yesterday."

Miss Cather was diffident on political matters, but said she is convinced a nation like France, with "wonderful qualities of concentration," is bound to pull through the present crisis. She sees some inconsistency in Parliament, but expresses the opinion "bad Governments come and go without altering the direction of a people's progress. The sanity of people always brings things right."

New York World, 21 May 1923.

1923: RED CLOUD

One of the activities occupying Cather during her stay in France was sitting for a portrait. A group of citizens in Omaha had conducted a fund-raising campaign in order to honor the Nebraska writer and wanted to commission a portrait to hang in the Omaha Public Library. The request for the portrait came to her at almost the same time as she received the news of winning the Pulitzer. She chose Léon Bakst, a painter best known for his set designs. The following article explains how that choice took place. Although not an actual interview, the information is pertinent. Or, as the article itself states, "this information has come indirectly, but it is doubtless authentic."

The painting was never exactly popular, and its merit has often been debated. Carrie Miner Sherwood was said to have admired the plant in the background. ☞

THE EDITOR'S COLUMN

Much interest is shown, not only in Nebraska, but also in the east, in the portrait of Miss Willa Cather, which is being painted by Bakst, the famous Russian artist. The picture is eventually to be placed in the Omaha public library, but eastern friends have requested that it be exhibited there before being permanently located in Omaha. Before long, all Red Cloud poeple who visit Omaha will expect to call at the library and see the portrait before returning home, and many from other parts of the state will make similar pilgrimages.

An interesting account of how Bakst came to paint the portrait was told me by a friend of Miss Cather. It seems that after the Omaha friends had arranged to have the likeness painted, but had not secured an artist, Miss Cather met Bakst at a social affair, and in course of conversation mentioned the plans of her Omaha friends. Bakst suggested that he might do the work. Miss Cather replied that to engage so celebrated an artist would probably require a higher price than her friends would desire to pay. Bakst replied that he would do the work for half the usual fee. It seems that he was then doing entirely different work, and desired to paint one portrait by way of change, also that he was moved by Miss Cather's notable achievements in the world of letters.

Miss Cather had expected to find the sittings rather tedious, but she writes that they are proving quite enjoyable. The artist entertains her as he works by telling Russian folk tales, which not only interests her, but doubtless furnishes material which will later be incorporated into her stories. Bakst speaks very excellent French, and Miss Cather is using this opportunity to perfect her present very good knowledge of that language. He requests that she always address him in English in order that he may learn more of that tongue.

It is also stated that Miss Cather is becoming a little homesick for the prairies of her home state, and will be back with her old friends once more soon. All of this information has come indirectly, but it is doubtless authentic, and will be interesting to *Argus* readers.

Ten copies of Miss Cather's new book, *The Lost Lady*, were placed on sale at the Cotting store yesterday, and by night several were gone and one or two more were engaged. Mr. Cotting did not lay in a large supply, thinking that perhaps the demand would not be so great on account of the story having been published in the *Century*. He has ordered additional copies, however, and plans to supply all customers.

Webster County Argus, 13 September 1923, p. 2, col. 3.

1923: OMAHA

Not only were Willa Cather's hometown newspapers interested in the progress of her career in the early twenties; other Nebraska papers followed her avidly, as well. Although the exact source for the information contained in her letters home is never identified, one can assume that her parents and family were interviewed often. The portrait commissioned for the Omaha Public Library naturally generated a certain amount of interest in that city, as the following article makes plain. Like the preceding entry, this one is not technically an interview but does give some indirect information about Cather's plans, her physical health, the portrait, and the public reaction to her latest novel. ☞

WILLA CATHER PLANS TO VISIT NEBRASKA THIS FALL

Red Cloud, Neb. Oct. 12—Miss Willa Cather has written to her parents, Mr. & Mrs. C. F. Cather of Red Cloud, that she expects to leave France for home early in November. She plans to spend a short time in New York, and will probably be in Red Cloud early in December to remain until after the holidays. Her letters indicate that she is eager to be in Nebraska again.

An attack of neuritis in her right shoulder has considerably lessened the pleasure of her stay in France, and has interfered with her work. She is now experiencing some relief from this, and expects to continue her sittings for the painting that is being made by Bakst, who plans to lay aside his other work in order to be able to finish the painting before Miss Cather sails.

Miss Cather's book, *One of Ours,* is to be published in French soon. It is being read in English by some of the French people, and is winning much appreciation from them. Miss Cather writes that it is interesting when riding on the trains to hear the book and its author discussed in French, which she understands very well, the persons conversing little thinking that the author whom they are discussing is on the same train. The book is now in its sixtieth thousand and selling better than ever.

Miss Cather writes that her friends have suggested a special program when the portrait is placed in the Omaha library, and are considering having her mother, Mrs. C. F. Cather of Red Cloud, to unveil the picture. If this is pleasing to Mrs. Cather, it will be very satisfactory to her distinguished daughter. However, it is quite likely that plans will not be completed until Miss Cather arrives home.

OW-H, 13 October 1923.

1924: NEW YORK

Burton Rascoe (1892–1957) began his journalistic career at the age of sixteen, working in Oklahoma on the Shawnee Herald. *In 1911 he moved to Chicago and spent two years at the University of Chicago before becoming the literary and dramatic editor for the* Chicago Tribune. *He left Chicago in 1921 for New York City and the associate editorship of* McCall's, *and in less than two years became the literary editor of the* New York Tribune *at the age of twenty-nine.*

He quickly became known around the city and in journalistic circles for his boundless enthusiasm and energy. The Bookman *referred to his "affable arrogance" in pursuit of his work. At the* Tribune *he reviewed a book a day and was also responsible for a weekend literary supplement. The latter became so successful within a few months that it was turned into a special tabloid insert, "Book News and Reviews." Rascoe's best-known contribution was his column "A Bookman's Daybook," in which he told almost every day about what he read, whom he met, what they had said to him, and what he had said to them. It involved a great deal of name-dropping and anticipated Walter Winchell's gossip, making the literary world appear exciting to his readers. He lost his position after the* Herald *and the* Tribune *merged in 1924 and was succeeded by Stuart P. Sherman. Rascoe went on to write a syndicated column, "The Daybook of a New Yorker," which appeared in over four hundred daily papers between 1924 and 1928. He was at various times associated, most often as literary editor, with the* Bookman, Arts and Decorations *magazine,* Vanity Fair, Plain Talk, *the* New York Sun, Esquire, Newsweek, *the* American Mercury, *and the* New York World-Telegram. *He went on to become a best-selling author with his* Titans of Literature *(1932) and several other books.*

The first two of the following three impressions initially appeared in Rascoe's column in the Herald-Tribune *in February 1924, shortly before his departure from that paper, and were reprinted in his anthology entitled* A Bookman's Daybook. *Many of the subjects are familiar: Cather's interest in good food, her outspoken opinions, and her fondness of tennis. This third interview is a recounting of the first meeting from* Arts and Decorations. *It, too, was later reprinted—in Rascoe's* We Were Interrupted. *The discrepancies in date probably reflect faulty memory. Rascoe is more detailed in recounting the subjects, which include, besides the previously mentioned familiar ones, Ellen Terry, Cather's recent portrait, and some unusually harsh words about Sarah Orne Jewett.* ☞

FIRST MEETING WITH WILLA CATHER

Tuesday, February 19

I met Miss Willa Cather for the first time to-day at lunch with Thomas Beer. She impressed me at once as a remarkable woman, in a way I had so far from expected that I was sometime in orientating myself to her personality and so getting my ease. She is full-blooded, vigorous, substantial, sure of herself, matter-of-fact, businesslike, and somehow I had expected her to be reticent, uncommunicative, rather sweet and softish. She looks as though she might conduct a great law practice or a successful dairy farm, superintend a telephone exchange or run a magazine with equal efficiency, ideas and energy.

The first thing I heard her say concerned matters of a practical nature. She said that she refused to autograph books sent to her for the quite legitimate reason that lately her publisher is bringing out limited autographed editions of her work, and for her to autograph books sent to her would cut in on his business. One bookseller had had the nerve, she said, to send her twenty-five books to autograph for sale, but she sent them back with promptitude and gave him a bit of her mind. She is fond of the table and she discourses with gusto on food; she knows where the best meals are to be had in Paris, London and New York; she taxies uptown frequently from Bank Street to eat at a restaurant where the food is so good that she told Beer, who had never been there: "Young man, the next time I see you I want you to have been at Voisin's"; she sent back her chicken pie, reminding the waiter curtly that it was insufficient in sauce and that it is not to be eaten dry. She is free from the usual inhibitions to comfortable and easy discourse; she uses good, colloquial and pungent words. I could have embraced her with joy and admiration when she exclaimed, the moment a certain academic critic's name was mentioned, "Oh, that muttonhead!" That is, in my opinion, precisely what he is, and no one had ever said it before. She is brief, decisive and sharp in her criticism of writers and of people. When Beer said he had been called to task for not mentioning Octave Thanet in his book and said he had not read her, Miss Cather replied, "There's no reason why you should; she was a carpenter. Her stories are well-nailed, uninteresting goods boxes."

New York Herald-Tribune, 19 February 1924.

Reprinted in *A Bookman's Daybook* (1929).

ANOTHER GLIMPSE OF WILLA CATHER

Friday, February 22.

Hazel joined me at the office, and we went to Miss Willa Cather's for tea. Over her fireplace I observed with interest a large framed engraving of George Sand, with a small cutting, portraying Sand in a top hat, sliced from a periodical and stuck in the corner; and this I found significant. Miss Cather talked mostly of

Suzanne Lenglen, the tennis champion, whom she greatly admires, and said that, though she is not, in the American sense, a good sport and does not take even the promise of defeat easily, she is a magnetic and enchanting figure, playing not at all on beef and muscle, but on nerves.

I asked her if it was permissible to talk about her books, when I found that she and Hazel had been discussing ''The Song of the Lark,'' and when she said there was no objection, I asked her if I was right, so far as her own artistic intention was concerned, in saying that the story of ''The Lost Lady'' had to do entirely with Mrs. Forrester and not with the disillusion of the young chap who fell in love with her. She said, of course, it was; that in order to portray Mrs. Forrester it was necessary to show her as she was reflected in the minds of a number of men; the young man who was disillusioned was no more necessary to the portrait than the butcher boy who brought the flowers at the time of Forrester's death, but he was more directly connected with Mrs. Forrester's career than the butcher boy, and therefore he figured more importantly in the story.

New York Herald-Tribune, 22 February 1924.
Reprinted in *A Bookman's Daybook* (1929).

WILLA CATHER

I met Miss Willa Cather in March 1924; she had returned from a year's residence in France, during which time she had written that beautiful little masterpiece, *A Lost Lady*. At an evening with Ernest Boyd, Thomas Beer had told me that he was having Miss Cather to lunch on a Tuesday and invited me to join them. I suffered some delay in getting away from the house, and Beer and Miss Cather were waiting for me on the much too prominently placed settle at the Crillon, which faces the dining-room doorway — a restaurant appointment having the advantage of throwing you into immediate contact with the person you are seeking, but having the disadvantage of forcing the person who has to wait to remain on display like an object in a shop-window.

My tardiness ruffled the composure I had been at some pains in attaining at the prospect of meeting the woman whom I consider to be the finest artist of her sex now writing in English. I was not put any the more readily at my ease by my discovery that she was amazingly unlike my conception of her as a person. I had somehow expected her to be wistful — though if I had troubled to recall her biography I should have known that no woman could have once been a telegraph editor of a daily newspaper and later managing editor of a magazine and still be wistful precisely. Miss Cather is quite the reverse of that; she is alert, alive, quick-witted, vigorous-minded, and assertive, not at all dreamy, preoccupied, self-isolated, or diffident.

I believe the first thing I noticed about her was the forceful masculinity of her hands; they are strong hands without the so-called artist taper—which, by the way, I have observed very few artists possess.

Her features are bluntly decisive in line; her eyes are pale blue and set wide apart, with eyebrows high enough to give her ordinarily a look of challenge and appraisal; her mouth is ample, with full, flexible lips whose movements are as expressive an accompaniment of her speech as are the gestures of a Latin; and her nose is a nose, not a tracery.

All the pictures I have seen of her amount almost to libels, for they portray a faintly sullen expression about her mouth, and such an expression she is not guilty of, I believe, ever. Hers is a mouth capable of sternness, severity, stubbornness, perhaps, but not sullenness.

I like the way she sits, relaxed without slumping, free, easy, assured, without tension. She wears her hair parted slightly to the right of the middle and drawn up in a loose knot in the back. She has the extraordinary courage to wear at the same time salmon and green, and she does it with complete success. I can now very easily imagine that she has sat for Leon Bakst's most successful portrait; whereas I had wondered why the women of Omaha had chosen that artistic Tartar barbarian, of all painters, for the honor of doing her likeness as a memorial to her as Nebraska's eminent novelist, there is probably no portraitist who would be more understanding and appreciative of the strength and subtleties of her character and handsomeness.

I was not surprised to hear her expatiate with the keenest admiration upon the character and personality of a woman who is pretty much her own direct opposite—Ellen Terry, a talented, capricious, intensely feminine woman who has pirouetted gracefully and radiantly over the surfaces of life, learning nothing of its sordidness apparently (if we are to judge from her memoirs) which she might not have learned as a charming, imitative, ingenuous child in the nursery.

Histrionism and mimicry, playing at life and finding it enchantingly colorful, an escape into an imaginative world where drabness and time-serving are forgotten in the illusion of adventure—these are the things which attract Miss Cather to the singers and actresses who figure so prominently in her stories. And because she has emotional understanding as well as intelligence, sympathy as well as insight, her stories have warmth and poetry in them. They touch both the heart and the intellect. Mrs. Forrester, the heroine of *A Lost Lady,* is one of the few women in fiction whose author has endeavored to convey the idea of a heroine who is irresistible, and whom you *know,* you *feel* to be charming, radiant, attractive, and beautiful—not through any description but because of the effect, carefully observed, that she is depicted as having upon men. Miss Cather knows her decorative women of electric energy and she knows the other sorts too.

Her conversation is staccato; she chops her spoken sentences out incisively, in short, neat links. In this respect she reminds me somewhat of that other dynamo of creative zeal, Miss Amy Lowell. It is impossible to register and recall as a continued or amplified discourse any topic she touches on, because she disposes of any topic that interests her with expedition and economy of words.

One remembers only the high points—"One of those women with round chins. Women with round chins have terrible tempers . . . Sarah Orne Jewett was too much cuddled by her family. They'd have kept her in cotton wool and smothered her if they'd had entirely their own way about it. She was a very uneven writer. A good portion of her work is not worth preserving. The rest, a small balance—enough to make two volumes—is important. She was a voice. She spoke for a slight but influential section of the American people. She was clearly a voice, an authentic voice. . . . Suzanne Lenglen plays perfect tennis, entirely on her nerves, not on beef and muscle. She has no American conception of sportsmanship: she goes in simply to win and if she loses her confidence in herself for a moment before a match, she goes into hysterics and refuses to play. She is a superb player, though, when she has control of herself. . . ."

Miss Cather is interested in good food; she is proud of her cook; she walks a great deal for the exercise; she is fascinated by the spectacle of life; she is a capable businesswoman, or at least gives the impression of so being; and she is without sentimentality, prudery, or false values of any sort. She uses such good, sanguine words as "muttonhead," "cub," "scamp," and "ninny" with delightful colloquial effectiveness.

She provokes in me the belief that she early formed a just and reasonable estimate of her gifts and decided to cultivate them pretty much to the exclusion of everything else. She was, I believe, intelligently aware of her genius and had the will to bring it to fruition. On the strength of her work she has already accomplished I think that she is more secure to posterity than Mrs. Edith Wharton, whose great lack as a writer is that of human warmth.

Arts and Decorations, April 1924.
Reprinted from *We Were Interrupted* (1947).

*Willa Cather's vigor and assertive mind, which had been noted by Burton Ras-
coe, become more and more evident in the mid-twenties. Where the previous
interest had been in her work habits, her personal theories about her own art,
and her background, she was now solicited for (or volunteered) her opinions
about all kinds of topics. She certainly seems none too reticent in expressing
her feelings about American culture and civilization, the current state of art,
French culture, and a number of other things. Her only interview in the* New
York Times, *occurred at the end of 1924, and, no doubt, it was a kind of high
water mark of Cather's popularity and the public's interest.*

*This interview sparked more response than any she had granted to date.
The* Bookman *took issue with her opinions and was still referring to the interview nine months later. In March 1925, John Farrar, the editor, wrote concerning Cather's opinions:*

> *Art, she sees largely in repose; beauty, she finds, must come from a civi-
> lization more like that of France than our own. No beauty in restlessness,
> she says—and she forgets all the restless, sensitive, striving beauty of
> youth. No beauty in machinery? She forgets the etchings of Pennell and the
> poetry of Carl Sandburg. If she means art, the technique of art, she is
> perhaps right in her feeling that America is not contemplative enough. We
> could not in this period have produced Anatole France; but we did pro-
> duce, as she admits, Whitman. She forgets, too, the beauty of revolt, the
> beauty of struggle, the beauty of the very rugged unformed state she
> abhors. That our standards of success are warped we cannot deny; but the
> avarice of the French is no prettier a characteristic than our money mad-
> ness, and the striving of the present generations, Miss Cather, is building
> up wealth for the leisure of those quietly cultured souls you so miss in this
> welter of "cinema" and "radio" publics. You regret, too, the days long
> past when these new readers did not exist and only a fine, intelligent public
> greeted the best books. This, you say, Miss Cather, is not intended to be a
> snobbish attitude. You will not deny that it is, at least, aristocratic! (4–5)*

*In September of the same year, Farrar was still making references in his col-
umn to Cather's December interview and her opinion that art "was the privilege of aristocracies."*

*Rose Caroline Feld (1895–1981), was born in Rumania and came to the
United States in 1898. After graduating from the New York Training School for
Teachers, she entered a career in journalism. She was a member of the staff of
the* New York Times *from 1916 to 1922 and then became a free-lance contribu-*

tor to several national magazines and the book sections of the Times *and the* Herald-Tribune. *She had published her first book,* Humanizing Industry, *in 1920, and went on to write* Heritage *(1928),* Sophie Halenczik, American *(1943), and other books.* ☞

"RESTLESSNESS SUCH AS OURS DOES NOT MAKE FOR BEAUTY"

by Rose C. Feld

Tea with Willa Sibert Cather is a rank failure. The fault is entirely hers. You get so highly interested in what she had to say and how she says it that you ask for cream when you prefer lemon and let the butter on your hot toast grow cold and smeary. It is vastly more important to you to watch her eyes and lips which betray her when she seems to be giving voice to a serious concept, but is really poking fun at the world—or at your own foolish question. For Willa Sibert Cather has a rare good sense, homespun sense, if you will—and that is rare enough—which she drives home with a well-wrought mallet of humor.

It started with the question of books and the overwhelming quantities which the American public of today is buying. What exactly was the explanation of that? Did it mean that we were becoming a more cultured people, a more artistic people? Miss Cather was suffering from neuritis that day. It was difficult to understand, therefore, whether the twinge that crossed her face was caused by the pain we gave her or that of her temporary illness.

"Don't confuse reading with culture or art," she said, when her face cleared. There was laughter in her blue eyes. "Not in this country, at any rate. So many books are sold today because of the economic condition of this country, not the cultural. We have a great prosperous middle class, in cities, in suburbs, in small towns, on farms, to whom the expediture of $2 for a book imposes no suffering. What's more, they have to read it. They want a book which will fill up commuting boredom every morning and evening; they want a book to read mornings after breakfast when the maid takes care of the apartment housework; they want a book to keep in the automobile while they're waiting for tardy friends or relatives; they want fillers-in, in a word, something to take off the edge of boredom and empty leisure. Publishers, who are, after all, business men, recognize the demand and pour forth their supply. It's good sense; it's good psychology. It's the same thing that is responsible for the success of the cinema. It is, as a matter of fact, the cinema public for whom this reading material is published. But it has no more to do with culture than with anarchy or philosophy. You might with equal reason ask whether we are becoming a more cultured people because so many more of us are buying chiffoniers and bureaus and mirrors and toilet sets. Forty or fifty years ago these things were not to be found in the average home. Forty or fifty years ago we couldn't afford them, and today we can. As a result, every home has an increased modicum of comfort and luxury. But, carrying the thought a step further, every home has not increased in beauty.

"Not so long ago I was speaking to William Dean Howells about this subject of book reading and book publication. He said something which was of interest to me and which may be of interest to you. Forty years ago, he maintained, we were in the midst of a great literary period. Then, only good books were published, only cultivated people read. The others didn't read at all, or if they did it was the newspapers, the almanac, and the Bible on Sundays. This public doesn't exist today any more than the cinema public existed then. Fine books were written for fine people. Fine books are still written for fine people. Sometimes the others read them, too, and if they can stand it, it doesn't hurt them."

Her lips twitched in a smile she tried to suppress. She shook her head at a wayward thought.

"That discrimination is not a snobbish one," she went on. "Don't think that. By the fine reader I don't necessarily mean the man or woman with a cultivated background, an academic, or a wealthy background. I mean the person with quickness and richness of mentality, fineness of spirituality. You found it often in a carpenter or a blacksmith who went to his few books for recreation and inspiration. The son of a long line of college presidents may be nothing but a dolt and idiot in spite of the fact that he knows how to enter a room properly or to take off a lady's wraps. It's the shape of the head that's of importance; it's the something that's in it that can bring an ardor and an honesty to a masterpiece and make it over until it becomes a personal possession.

"I am not making generalities, I hope. I hate generalities. There's no sense to them. They're superficial; they're easy. People in talking of art and art appreciation make the generality, for instance, that all singers come out of the mud. Mud has nothing to do with it, just as being a carpenter has nothing to do with the accident of a good mind. Art requires a vast amount of character. It's a whole lot more than talent. It demonstrates itself in relationships the artist thinks important. I am not speaking of morality. It means great, good sense, as well as the gift of expression. The singer who is born in the mud doesn't arrive unless he's very good; there are so many obstacles which he must surmount. It requires a very little effort for a person with a mediocre voice and a deep, lined purse to get a hearing; it requires unusual ability for the poor man. When the latter arrives, it is because he has proved his genius. Mud had nothing to do with it; it only made his progress more difficult.

"Because of this vast amount of writing and reading, there are many among us who make the mistake of thinking we are an artistic people. Talking about it won't make us that. We can build excellent bridges; we can put up beautiful office buildings, factories; in time, it may be, we shall be known for the architecture which our peculiar industrial progress has fostered here, but literary art, painting, sculpture, no. We haven't yet acquired the good sense of discrimination possessed by the French, for instance. They have a great purity of tradition; they all but murder originality, and yet they worship it. The taste of the nation is represented by the Academy; it is a corrective rod which the young artist ever dreads. He revolts against it, but he cannot free himself from it. He cannot pull the wool over the eyes of the academy by saying his is a new movement, an original movement, a breaking away from the old. His work is judged on its merits, and if it isn't good, he gets spanked. Here in America, on the other hand, every little glimmer of color calls itself art; every youth that misuses a brush calls himself an artist, and an adoring group of admirers flatter and gush over him. It's rather pathetic.

"Read the life of Manet and Monet, both great artists, great masters. The French people had to be sure of their genius before it would acclaim them. Death almost took them before acknowledgment of their power was given them. It is good sense, deliberation, and an eagerness for the beautiful that keeps up the fine front of French art. That is true of her literature as well as of her painting.

"France is sensitive; we are not. It may be that our youth has something to do with it, and yet I don't know whether that is it. It's our prosperity, our judging success in terms of dollars. Life not only gives us wages for our toil but a bonus besides. It makes for nice, easy family life but not for art. The French people, on the other hand, have had no bonus. Their minds have been formed by rubbing up cruelly with the inescapable realities of life; they've played a close game, wresting their wages from a miserly master. Mrs. Wharton expressed it very well in a recent article when she said that the Frenchman elected to live at home and use his wits to make his condition happy. He don't want an easier land. He chose France, above all, as the home of his family and his children after them. There you are.

"The Frenchman doesn't talk nonsense about art, about self-expression; he is too greatly occupied with building the things that make his home. His house, his garden, his vineyards, these are the things that fill his mind. He creates something beautiful, something lasting. And what happens? When a French painter wants to paint a picture he makes a copy of a garden, a home, a village. The art in them inspires his brush. And twenty, thirty, forty years later you'll come to see the original of that picture, and you'll find it, changed only by the mellowness of time.

"Restlessness such as ours, success such as ours, striving such as ours, do not make for beauty. Other things must come first: good cookery; cottages that are homes, not playthings; gardens; repose. These are first-rate things, and out of first-rate stuff is art made. It is possible that machinery has finished us as far as this is concerned. Nobody stays at home any more; nobody makes anything beautiful any more. Quick transportation is the death of art. We can't keep still because it is so easy to move about.

"Yet it isn't always a question of one country being artistic and another not. The world goes through periods or waves of art. Between these periods come great resting places. We may be resting right now. Older countries have their wealth of former years to fall back upon. We haven't. But, like older countries, we have a few individuals who have caught the flame of former years and are carrying the torch into the next period. Whistler was one of these; Whitman was another."

Miss Cather poured some tea into a cup and diluted it with the cream we asked for but didn't want. We let it stand on the arm of the chair and proceeded with a question that her words had awakened.

"If we have no tradition of years behind us, the people who come to live here have. Are they contributing anything to the artistic expression of the country?"

Again that twinge crossed her face. This time it was plain that the question had started it.

"Contribute? What shall they contribute? They are not peddlers with something to sell; they are not gypsies. They have come here to live in the sense that they lived in the Old World, and if they were let alone their lives might turn into the beautiful ways of their homeland. But they are not let alone. Social workers, missionaries—call them what you will—go after them, hound them pursue them and devote their days and nights toward the great task of turning them into stupid replicas of smug American citizens. This passion for

Americanizing everything and everybody is a deadly disease with us. We do it the way we build houses. Speed, uniformity, dispatch, nothing else matters.

"It wasn't so years ago. When I was a child, all our neighbors were foreigners. Nobody paid any attention to them outside of the attention they wanted. We let them alone. Work was assigned them, and they made good houseworkers and splendid craftsmen. They furnished their houses as they had in the countries from which they came. Beauty was there and charm. Nobody investigated them; nobody regarded them as laboratory specimens. Everybody had a sort of protective air toward them, but nobody interfered with them. A 'foreigner' was a person foreign to our manners or custom of living, not possible prey for reform. Nobody ever cheated a foreigner. A man lost everything in the esteem of the community when he was discovered in a crime of false barter. It was very much better that way. I hate this poking into personal affairs by social workers, and I know the people hate it, too. Yet settlement work is a mark of progress, our progress. That's that. I know there's much to be said for it, but nevertheless, I hate it.''

We spoke about *My Ántonia,* Miss Cather's story about the immigrant family of Czechs.

"Is *My Ántonia* a good book because it is the story of the soil?'' we asked. She shook her head.

"No, no, decidedly no. There is no formula; there is no reason. It was a story of people I knew. I expressed a mood, the core of which was like a folksong, a thing Grieg could have written. That it was powerfully tied to the soil had nothing to do with it. Ántonia was tied to the soil. But I might have written the tale of a Czech baker in Chicago, and it would have been the same. It was nice to have her in the country; it was more simple to handle, but Chicago could have told the same story. It would have been smearier, joltier, noisier, less sugar and more sand, but still a story that had as its purpose the desire to express the quality of these people. No, the country has nothing to do with it; the city has nothing to do with it; nothing contributes consciously. The thing worth while is always unplanned. Any art that is a result of preconcerted plans is a dead baby.''

Miss Cather is now writing a new novel which will come out next Autumn. "There will be no theories, no panaceas, no generalizations. It will be a story about people in a prosperous provincial city in the Middle West. Nothing new or strange, you see.''

New York Times Book Review, 21 December 1924, p. 11, cols. 1–5.

1925: NEW YORK

Willa Cather agreed to "teach" writing just once—in 1922 at the School of English at Breadloaf, the summer conference at Middlebury, Vermont. A correspondent from the Bookman *visited the conference and wrote, "Willa Cather was there, and we would have given a good deal to hear her five lectures on writing. She was also working on a novelette, and they had given her a delightful cabin, with a view of the mountains, in which to write of a morning" (September 1922, 127). Later she refused many invitations to teach there again or to be a part of other writing conferences. In her correspondence with friends she indicated that she had accepted the invitation in 1922 during a weak moment and later regretted it. She makes plain her feeling about the indifference of such efforts to teach writing in this interview three years later. It is another well-known article and contains the famous quotation from Michelet, the French historian: "The end is nothing; the road is all." She goes on to talk about that "road" at considerable length and reveals that her original name for Neil in* A Lost Lady *was Duncan, giving the novel another Shakespearean connection besides the epigraph. She also rejects an overidentification with the Midwest, but in so doing she uses a most agricultural—and midwestern—analogy to explain her reasons.*

Flora Merrill, the interviewer, was a native New Yorker and a free-lance journalist and author. She went on to write Flush of Wimpole Street *and* Broadway *(1933) and* Kippy of the Cavendish *(1934), both books about dogs.* ☞

A SHORT STORY COURSE CAN ONLY DELAY,
It Cannot Kill an Artist, Says Willa Cather

by Flora Merrill

In Willa Cather's quick movements and rapidity of speech there is a faint suggestion of Minnie Maddern Fiske, a gentler, less vibrant Mrs. Fiske. And there is something of the actress's manner in the way she greets one at the door. It becomes a special moment, and one knows one is in her hands for good or bad.

Miss Cather lives in an old-fashioned apartment house in Greenwich Village. During an hour's conversation she sat in a low chair, her chin resting on one hand, and analyzed her own methods and writing in general in a comprehensive, original manner. Her replies came in paragraphs rather than single

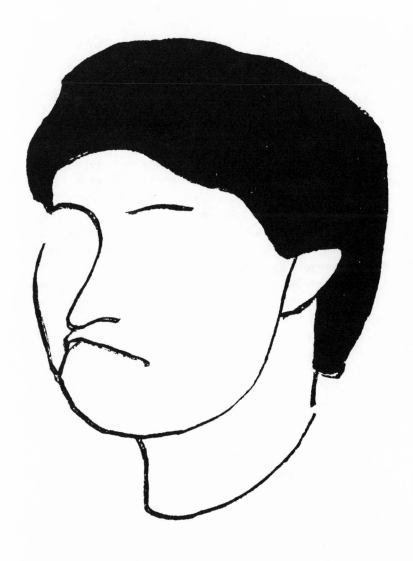

"Can't Be Caricatured," it was said of Willa Cather, the subject
of William Auerbach-Levy in the *New York World*, 19 April 1925

sentences, with a homely, informal quality. They were her opinions, and, whether one agreed with them or not, one found them provocative.

While of a seemingly positive nature, Miss Cather permits one to take her ideas or leave them. Your agreeing with her is a matter of indifference. One meets in the woman the same calm, intelligent, and worldly outlook evidenced in the manner in which she handles sex in her books. Partly because she avoids all womanish skimming of surfaces and writes realistically, her work had been characterized as having a manlike quality. One cannot imagine that she herself could be carried away by her own daring and frankness. Both in the written work and in person she evidences a quiet courage, sanity and balance of mind.

She wore a very lovely orange blouse embroidered in gold and had flung around her shoulders a bright green chiffon scarf, both of which were in contrast to the sidecombs in her hair. Beauty lies in her eyes and in her smile. She candidly admits she presents a problem to the caricaturist. Upon the assurance of one that he needed but half an hour in which to sketch her she suffered his presence for three afternoons. Another worked feverishly while she lunched at the Algonquin, but all the results, she insisted, looked like Gilbert K. Chesterton without his mustache. Consequently, photographs or nothing is her dictum.

The driving force behind Willa Cather's story-telling has not been the need of money, nor the thrill of seeing her words in print. Writing has been purely a source of pleasure to her. In earning a living she employed other methods. She writes because it is the most interesting activity of which she knows. Yet there have been long periods in her career, one lasting six years, when she did none. In fact, she devotes only five months of each year to creative work and spends the rest vacationing in Europe or the West.

"Writing does entail labor, certainly," she admitted, "but to me it has always been a joy, like golf or tennis. Playing tennis for one who loves it isn't work. A player's footwork may be bad and he may have been indifferently taught, but his joy in working a mediocre game into good tennis is a delight.

"I don't mean to say there isn't a struggle in writing, but it is an activity which stimulates you just as playing on a violin excites the violinist. There are always a lot of people who have a little vocation—I like that word better than talent—and then there are people with a very great vocation for the violin, such as Heifetz, whose career has meant a great power for work. The six years I spent on *McClure's* Magazine in an editorial capacity I call work. It meant responsibilities and duties. I did no writing then, but I was abroad much of the time meeting interesting English authors.

"I quit editorial work because it afforded me no time in which to write. The more you pursue your hobby, the more the other things drop out. The reason I didn't like my newspaper experience as telegraph editor and dramatic critic on the *Pittsburgh Daily Leader* was because it gave me so little time for the things I wanted to do; while teaching English at Allegheny High School gave me work I liked, I wasn't much older than some of the students, so we studied together.

"When I was in college," she reminisced, "I admired certain writers and read the masters of style, who gave me great pleasure. Those ideas have changed. All students imitate, and I began by imitating Henry James. He was the most interesting American who was writing at that time, and I strove laboriously to pattern after him. All students began imitating those they admire, and it is a perfectly right form of education. It takes a long time to get out from under the traditions which hamper a young writer. It is a recognized fact that young painters should imitate the work of great masters, but people overlook the fact that it is an equally good plan for young writers. Later you find your own style. It is dangerous, however, to try to be 'original' too early.

"I can't remember a time when I particularly wanted to get into print," she continued. "My early newspaper work soon took away that thrill. When I am in New York I work nearly every day, writing first in longhand and typing the second and third copies. Then the manuscript goes to my typist, and on her sheets I make the last corrections before it is sent to the publisher. When people ask me if it has been a hard or easy road I always answer with the quotation, 'The end is nothing, the road is all.'

"The cups mean nothing to the tennis champions," said Miss Cather.

"I keep referring to tennis because it is the most sportsmanlike sport we have. It is the one game you can't play for money. That is what I mean when I say my writing has been a pleasure. I have never faced the typewriter with the thought that one more chore had to be done.

"Next to writing I love best to prowl around the Western country, seeing little towns and how the people live in them. To me, the real West begins with the Missouri. Colorado, Nebraska, Arizona, New Mexico, and Nevada do not seem like separate states to me, but are linked together in my mind like one big country.

"In my writing, however, I do not want to become too identified with that region. There is little of the West in *The Professor's House*, the book I am working on now. Using one setting all the time is very like planting a field with corn season after season. I believe in rotation of crops. If the public ties me down to the cornfield too much I'm afraid I'll leave that scene entirely. However, I suppose I'd sneak back, perhaps under a different name. I love the West so much."

Concerning schools and courses of short-story writing, Miss Cather had this to say:

"They can only teach those patterns which have proved successful. If one is going to do new business the patterns cannot help, though one does not deliberately go out to do that. *My Ántonia,* for instance, is just the other side of the rug, the pattern that is supposed not to count in a story. In it there is no love affair, no courtship, no marriage, no broken heart, no struggle for success. I knew I'd ruin my material if I put it in the usual fictional pattern. I just used it the way I thought absolutely true. *A Lost Lady* was a woman I loved very much in my childhood. Now the problem was to get her, not like a standardized heroine in fiction, but as she really was, and not to care about anything else in the story except that one character. And there is nothing but that portrait. Everything else is subordinate.

"I didn't try to make a character study, but just a portrait like a thin miniature painted on ivory. A character study of Mrs. Forrester would have been very, very different. I wasn't interested in her character when I was little, but in her lovely hair and her laugh which made me happy clear down to my toes. Neither is 'Niel' a character study. In fact, he isn't a character at all; he is just a peephole into that world. I am amused when people tell me he is a lovely character, when in reality he is only a point of view.

"*A Lost Lady* was written in five months, but I worked with some fervor. I discarded ever so many drafts, and in the beginning wrote it in the first person, speaking as by the boy himself. The question was, by what medium could I present her the most vividly, and that, of course, meant the most truly. There was no fun in it unless I could get her just as I remembered her and produce the effect she had on me and the many others who knew her. I had to succeed in this. Otherwise, I would have been cheating, and there would have been no more fun in that than there is in cheating at solitaire.

"Your memories are like the colors in paints, but you must arrange them, and it is a hard job to do a portrait in ink without getting too much description. I am amazed that I was as successful as I was in making people who knew the actual model for Mrs. Forrester feel that it was very like her.

"Oh, yes, the real character died. It never occurred to me to write the story until she had, and there are no children who could be hurt.

"In that book I again tried the indirect method. I had to have something for Marian Forrester's charm to work on, and so I created Duncan—I mean 'Niel.'

I called the boy Duncan in the beginning. You can't talk about beauty for pages and pages. You have to have something for it to hit, and the boy answered that purpose. Now, a youngster beginning to write would get too fussed up over the story. He would have to have a certain love theme, and in his telling the bank failure in Denver would be made a great deal of, and so it would end in being a conventional novel.

"I like best of my books the one that all the high-brow critics knock," Miss Cather confessed. "In my opinion, *One of Ours* has more of value in it than any one of the others. I don't think it has as few faults perhaps as *My Ántonia* or *A Lost Lady*, but any story of youth, struggle, and defeat can't be as smooth in outline and perfect in form as just a portrait. When you have an inarticulate young man butting his way through the world you can't pay that much attention to form.

"Sometimes the discords and errors in drawing are necessary for the important effect. You must have the thing that is most precious to you even if you have saved it at the cost of a number of conventional things. You can't get a delicate face laughing at you out of a miniature, which I hope I got in *A Lost Lady*, and also have a lot of Western atmosphere and a dramatic bank failure. I like a book where you do one thing.

"You must work out your own fashion," she mused, "work it out from under the old patterns. Without doubt the schools develop good mechanical writers, and if a born artist happens to take the course it won't do him any harm. In my opinion, you can't kill an artist any more than you can make one. Take, for instance, the talented violinists who have played in cabarets. While the experience may delay a career, it does not necessarily destroy talent.

"Such commonplace things as health and character are essential for a successful career. By health I mean a stamina and vitality which permits one to sense and feel life. The most talented youth won't get on very well if he tries to eat all the dinners people give him and drink all the cocktails that he doesn't have to pay for. I knew the writer about whom Mr. Dreiser wrote in *Twelve Men* who dies from prolonging the wining and dining system to the bitter end. If a young man is beginning to write pretty well and a lot of people want to dine, wine, and lunch him and he eats and drinks himself to death, he lacks character."

Regarding the respective importance of style and ideas in writing, Miss Cather had this to say:

"Style is how you write, and you write well when you are interested. A writer's own interest in a story is the essential thing. If there is a flash of warmth in him it is repeated in the reader. The emotion is bigger than style.

"I don't think there is anything in ideas. When a young writer tells you he has an idea for a story he means he has had an emotion that he wants to pass on. An artist has an emotion, and the first thing that he wants to do with it is to find some form to put it in, a design. It reacts on him exactly as food makes a hungry person want to eat. It may tease him for years until he gets the right form for the emotion.

"Now the writer of little talent is all the time on the lookout for what he calls an idea, a situation and combination which will enable him to produce a story that will interest the reader. I am not speaking disparagingly of this kind of writing, for even the elder Dumas employed this method. The situation counts greatly for the writer who makes his stories out of the ideas he picks up, but very little for the one who writes from his personal experience and emotions.

"The type of writer we have been talking about has a brain like Limbo, full of ghosts, for which he has always tried to find bodies. *A Lost Lady* was a beautiful ghost in my mind for twenty years before it came together as a possible subject for presentation. All the lovely emotions that one has had some day appear with bodies, and it isn't as if one found ideas suddenly. Before this the memories of these experiences and emotions have been like perfumes. It is the difference between a remembered face and having that friend one day come in through the door. She is really no more yours then than she has been right along in your memory.

"Of course, there are mechanical difficulties for all writers. Every presentation has its own obstacles. To me, the one important thing is never to kill the figure that you care for for the sake of atmosphere, well balanced structure, or neat presentation. If you gave me a thousand dollars for every structural fault in *My Ántonia* you'd make me very rich. I know they are there, and made them knowingly, but that was the way I could best get my squint at her. With those faults I did better than if I had brought them together into a more perfect structure. Sometimes too much symmetry kills things."

When asked whether in her opinion the tremendous influx of writers was a help to culture, or detrimental to it, Miss Cather said:

"I like horses better than automobiles, and I think fewer and better books would be a great improvement. I think it a great misfortune for every one to have the chance to write—to have a chance to read, for that matter: A little culture makes lazy handiwork, and handiwork is a beautiful education in itself, and something real. Good carpentry, good weaving, all the handicrafts were much sounder forms of education than what the people are getting now.

"One sad feature of modern education is that the hand is so little trained among the people who have to earn their daily bread, and the head so superficially and poorly educated. The one education which amounts to anything is learning how to do something well, whether it is to make a bookcase or write a book. If I could get a carpenter to make me some good bookcases I would have as much respect for him as I have for the people whose books I want to put on them. Making something well is the principal end of education. I wish we could go back, but I am afraid we are only going to become more and more mechanical."

New York World, 19 April 1925, sec. 3, pp. 1, 6, cols. 1–5, 4–5.

Reprinted in *NSJ*, 25 April 1925, p. 11, cols. 1–5.

Walter Tittle, (1883–1966) was born in Springfield, Ohio, and studied art in New York. For many years he contributed illustrations, cartoons, and articles to Harper's, Scribner's, Century, Life, *and other magazines. A well-known and popular portrait painter, his subjects included such personages as George Bernard Shaw, Joseph Conrad, G. K. Chesterton, Arnold Bennett, Charlie Chaplin, Mary Pickford, Douglas Fairbanks, Rear Admiral Richard E. Byrd, Havelock Ellis, Walter de la Mare, and Presidents Taft, Wilson, Coolidge, and Franklin Roosevelt. He frequently wrote about his subjects, as well, a practice that culminated in his book* Roosevelt as an Artist Saw Him *(1948).*

In 1925, Tittle did a series for Century *magazine entitled "Glimpses of Interesting Americans," in which he both interviewed and drew his subjects. The July issue concerned literary Americans—William Allen White, Ring Lardner, Will Rogers, and Willa Cather. The interview is somewhat refreshing in that it does not become overinvolved in complicated literary theory but pursues other aspects of Cather's life and personality—travel, food, and art. Cather's description of Swinburne is curiously reminiscent of her later description of Clement Sebastian's accompanist, Mockford, in* Lucy Gayheart. *Her identification with the Midwest seems almost in direct opposition to the disclaimer she had given in the* World *interview only a few months earlier.* ☞

GLIMPSES OF INTERESTING AMERICANS
Willa Sibert Cather

by Walter Tittle, Drawing by the Author

Penetrating westward from Washington Square one crosses an area devoted, in recent years, to an industry that may be described by the name that this locality bore when it was a settlement separate from New York. Greenwich Village is now a business, carried on in the spot where the little town of that name once stood. One does not need to be old to remember when its streets were quiet, at least when evening fell; but now it is the haunt of Bohemianism, Incorporated, where from humble beginnings that were more sincere have risen myriad dance-halls, taxi-stands, tea-shops, theaters, and cabarets with *couvert* charges and like ostentations that promise soon to rival Broadway. Persevere still farther west, and one is rewarded. This modern commerce has not yet obliterated all of the former charm. The crooked streets again resume their quiet, and an Old World touch is contributed by occasional lingering architectural fragments of Georgian flavor. In this pleasant back-water I found the dwelling of Willa Sibert Cather.

In response to my ring came Miss Cather herself, with a friendly smile, and a cordial greeting that seemed particularly hospitable because of its unmistakable flavor of my own Middle West. Her fine blue eyes revealed in their possessor the precious gift of humor, and contrasted pleasantly in their color with her dark lashes and strongly marked brows. Her straight, almost black, glistening hair, growing very low on her forehead, was caught back with effective simplicity from a parting just off the middle, and the harmony of it with her slightly olive skin and a colorful shawl or scarf made a picture that cried for a full palette rather than black and white.

No sooner were we settled, with pose and lighting selected, than tea appeared, bringing with it vivid memories of the importance of this unfailing comfort and promoter of sociability in England. I remarked on the great degree to which social life in that country hinges on this daily function, and discovered that for her the association bore recollections as pleasant as my own. A further pursuit of the subject revealed friends and acquaintances in common, yielding material for a considerable comparison of notes and much entertaining reminiscence. Included in this was an interesting word-portrait of Swinburne, whom she had met by chance at the British Museum with Sir Sidney Colvin. She pictured him as being far removed in reality from Watts's rather sugary portrait of him—a dwarf with a large head and abnormally tiny hands and feet. His

"Willa Cather," by Walter Tittle, from *The Century* magazine, July 1925

stringy blond hair stayed horribly young when he was old, giving an uncanny effect that one could see repeated in the mummy room of the museum where they met. His manner betrayed a self-conscious timidity that seemed to indicate a pitiful sensitiveness to his physical deficiencies.

We found so much to admire and love in this land of generous hospitality, charming people, fascinating tradition, and antiquity that I am sure that even a native of the place could forgive us for the detail that we found least to our liking. A vital detail it was—the national cuisine. I related my actual physical suffering as a result of the heavy Gargantuan diet that possibly is demanded by their drastic climate, regretting that, in a land I love so well, it is so difficult for me to find viands with which my digestive equipment can successfully cope. On three separate occasions I had suffered prolonged tortures as a result of the struggle to adapt myself to the too monotonous and carnivorous cuisine. Twice the services of a physician were required, and I was able to aver that this was not because of over-indulgence!

"Why is it that a people so progressive in other things neglect the development of an art so tremendously important?" I asked. "They insist on fresh air for their lungs; surely an attractive and well balanced diet for their stomachs is just as vital. In France a department of culinary art has recently been added to their Salon, along with painting and sculpture. In that country of supposedly rich food no gastronomic ills exist for me."

Her response to my remarks took the form of a discourse on cooking that was so able and thorough, amplifying so systematically and intelligently numerous phases of the subject, that I record a few of her remarks.

"Preparation of food is one of the most important things in life, and the reason the Anglo-Saxon has so little sense of it compared with the Frenchman is due to the fact that in all matters of art and taste the French are older, more sensitive, backed by traditions of greater purity and age and are instinctively connoisseurs in the art of living, a gift that the English and Americans have not yet received. Our native American dishes are better than the English ones, but, among other shortcomings, cream and sugar seem to be the universal panacea here for rescuing almost any dish from failure. If in doubt, add sugar and smother with cream! The French, who build a menu as an artistic and scientific composition of perfect balance, look with horror at our indulgence in butter at the same time we eat soup, duplicating the fats, or at the consumption of fried potatoes with meat. Many similar incongruities exist in our combinations of food that are to them not only an unmusical discord against the sense of taste, but a scientific affront against digestion as well. They prefer to enjoy their vegetables as separate courses, resenting the confusion of flavors and odors that result from our method of eating meat, vegetables, and often salad, at the same time. Their use of wines and liquors is in marked contrast to ours. They do not start a meal with an *apéritif* so violent that the senses are dulled, following in haphazard fashion with wines that have no place in the beautifully balanced scheme of their repast. French restaurant cuisine in America never was as good as the best that Paris offers, but its late woeful decadence is due largely to prohibition. Not only is the chef denied the wines that were so imperative to him as ingredients in his creations, but the restaurants cannot afford to serve such excellent viands, with increased costs due to the war, and the profit from sale of wines and liquors as beverages denied them. This has taken the heart out of the really good chefs who had pride in their product; they depart, giving polite excuses for returning to France. They must go back because of the death of some relative, or to comfort their old parents in their declining years; they have inherited a little house perhaps, anything to get away. I had an excellent French cook who made life a joy, but I lost her. An expensive and extravagant negro followed who did very well when she kept to the dishes she knew, but no matter how often I objected, there was always cream in the soup. Sugar and cream and butter were the invariable solutions to any doubtful problem.

"I can easily comprehend your difficulty with English food. A friend of mine had the same experience, her troubles vanishing, like yours, as soon as she arrived in Paris. The things that any sensitive person eats must attract the palate and the eye in order to fulfil successfully their function. Is cooking important? Few things in life are more so! My mind and stomach are one! I think and work with whatever it is that digests."

"Aren't you tempted to desert your native land and live abroad? It is easy for writers to go where they choose, their necessary impedimenta being small."

"No, I cannot do my work abroad. I hate to leave France or England when I am there, but I cannot produce my kind of work away from the American idiom. It touches springs of memory, awaking past experience and knowledge necessary to my work. I write only of the Mid-Western American life that I know thoroughly, and I must be here, where the stream of that life flowing over me touches springs that release early-caught and assimilated impressions. I cannot create my kind of thing without American speech around me and incidents that cause memories to rise from the subconscious. This is probably not true of all writers, but it is of me. I stayed for a time at Ville d'Avray, and loved the life there so much that I could hardly tear myself away; but I was so busy drinking in the beauty of the place that I could not work. Those wonderful French skies! They fascinated me. They are so different from the usual hard, bright skies of New York. I went from there to Paris, hoping to achieve a working state of mind, but again it proved impossible. The Seine absorbed my thoughts. I could look at it for hours as it reflected every mood of the ever-changing skies, and the colorful life surging around me was utterly distracting as well.

"The American language works on my mind like light on a photographic plate, or on a pack of them, creeping in at the edges. In Paris, whatever it is that makes one work got used up from day to day. New York has no such effect upon me. I come here for seclusion from my family and friends for five or six months of the year, and do all of my actual writing in that period. Then I return to my family in Nebraska, Colorado, and New Mexico with no thought of work. This is a period of relaxation, absorption, and refreshment at the fountain-head of the life I write about. Then I return again to my task, systematically. I work as a pianist practises, who does his daily stint just as he takes his bath or breakfast. This enables me to achieve a great deal in a comparatively short period. Of course I don't publish everything that I write. Sometimes the Lord gives us grace to tear up and destroy."

A portrait on the wall of George Sand by Couture, done in the lithographic medium that I was employing, turned our talk to artists of the brush and pencil. The Impressionists take a high place in Miss Cather's predilections, Manet standing out, for her, above them all. Among contemporary Frenchmen the powerful Forain spells for her only horror and brutality. I was amazed at her accurate memory of the pictures in the Commondo collection in the Louvre. Each canvas seemed indelibly stamped upon her memory; my own was put to shame even though these rooms were a favorite haunt of mine. I should have been warned by this when later we argued about the authorship of a picture that I have known for twenty years, a work of Tintoretto, the original of which I had seen in the Doge's Palace rather recently in the same room with some paintings of Veronese. Being a bit less robust in treatment than the former master's usual manner, I attributed it to the latter, persisting despite Miss Cather's objection. A wager was the outcome of the argument, payment proceeding promptly to my antagonist when a book on Tintoretto had heaped upon me chagrin for my fickle memory.

Century Magazine, July 1925.

1925: CLEVELAND

In 1925, after finishing the manuscript of The Professor's House, *Cather fulfilled speaking engagements at Bowdoin College, the University of Chicago, and the Women's City Club in Cleveland. Her schedule that year alone reveals the falsification of her claim to have given only one lecture previously, to say nothing of her whirlwind speaking tour in 1921 (see "Speeches" section). She had visited Red Cloud; gone back to New York; gone to Jaffrey, New Hampshire; returned to New York; then lectured in Chicago on 17 November, accompanied by her friend Irene Miner Weisz; and stopped in Cleveland en route back to New York.*

This interview, apparently done shortly after Cather arrived at her hotel, reveals both the warm and the bristling sides of Cather's personality. The lost invitation referred to was undoubtedly part of the trunk of mail that once fell to the bottom of the Grand Canyon. However, in describing the incident to Mary Ellen Chase, Cather called it the "happiest moment of my whole life" ("Five Literary Portraits," Massachusetts Review, Spring 1962).

Cather's fondness for good cooking has been documented many times and is apparent in her fiction. She wrote to Julian Street that she had studied French cookery for fifteen years under her cook and that she learned the art of it more thoroughly than she had ever learned anything else. The only problem with such proficiency was that if she wanted something really good, she had to go into the kitchen and make it herself (ALS, 9 November 1939, Julian Street Papers, FLPU). Her comments here make unsurprising Rebecca West's later declaration that a gathering of distinguished epicures and gourmets in London had reached the verdict that Willa Cather was "one of the two best women cooks in the world." The other was, ironically enough, the anarchist Emma Goldman, the aunt of David Hochstein (NYT, 19 March 1933).

As happens frequently in her interviews, Cather's claims to have "studied medicine" at the University of Nebraska are a bit of a distortion. ☞

PRIZE NOVELIST FINDS WRITING AND EATING KIN

by Allene Sumner

Because a letter was lost in the bottom of one of the great chasms in the canyon country of which Willa Cather writes, the authoress, considered by some critics the greatest woman writer, was in Cleveland Friday to speak for the first time here.

The letter was from the Woman's City Club, asking Miss Cather to lecture before that organization this winter.

"It's only the second lecture I have ever made in my life," explained Miss Cather at the Statler Friday. "But since the letter was lost and unanswered so many months, it seemed rude not to atone some way."

She speaks at the Women's City Club Friday evening.

This woman writer, who won the Pulitzer prize for her novel *One of Ours,* is an elusive creature, shunning publicity and "fussing" of any sort.

Only sleuthing revealed her at her hotel, and not even officials of the club appeared to know when their lecturer would arrive, and where she would be.

"I figure," said Miss Cather when cornered, "that if there's anything at all interesting about a writer it comes out in her books."

Her sentences are crisp and almost terse. One feels almost a constant antagonism between Miss Cather and the world, until one realizes that perhaps it is merely the mantle of self-defense against the probings of a curious world.

Critics have said that Willa Cather is not yet used to her fame; that "it just happened," and she does not consider herself a great authoress at all, but only one of the seven brothers and sisters out west who came east part of the time to write about the west.

Miss Cather's austere face warms when speaking of her family. "My home is out there with them," she says. "I just come east about five months out of the year to get away from the folks I love, and work."

"And are you working on a new novel now?" I asked Miss Cather.

"Yes."

"When will we have it?"

A period of ominous silence. Then, flushed with a slight peeve, Miss Cather brusquely exploded. "Say, even my publishers don't dare ask me that! I get my books out when I can, and not before."

"And its title, please?"

"I never give out titles or any information about my books until they are ready," she replied.

But she will talk about cooking and life in Greenwich Village before it became Bohemia, Inc.

Miss Cather is forty-nine. She took her little suite in the bizarre village before it was that—when it was just a gentle spot of old Georgian red brick homes with brass knockers, filled with folks who liked quiet and rest and mellow living.

"I still insist that I am in that sort of a village," said Miss Cather. "The rest just flows over my head." Yes, she likes to cook, and her greatest worry is finding good cooks!

"My mind and my stomach are one," she laughed. "I think and work with whatever it is that digests. I think the preparation of foods the most important thing in life. And America is too young a nation to realize it. It makes musical discords in the cooking realm."

One recalls Ántonia in Miss Cather's *My Ántonia* who didn't "want to die and stop cooking."

Miss Cather never meant to be a writer. She studied medicine at the University of Nebraska, where she graduated and was side-tracked into the teaching of English when English profs praised her themes.

She was a reporter and dramatic critic in Pittsburgh for several years, and in between assignments wrote her *April Twilights,* poems which filled her first published book in 1903.

She claims that every bit of her material was gathered before she was twenty when, as a child, she rode her pony over the "Great Divide" after mail, and played in the canyon country, and the wide prairies.

"I never have had any intellectual excitement more intense than spending a morning with a pioneer woman at butter making and hearing her talk," says Miss Cather. "It was 'agettin under her skin that always set me thinking."

The authoress says she must get back to this fountainhead of her work and replenish her being at least once a year. This fountainhead is Nebraska and points west, "the hinterlands with the yokels," of our more sophisticated writers. "I just cannot write when outside of America," she says. "I must have the American speech around me, touching the springs of memory. America works on my mind like light on a photographic plate."

"I seem to be the sort of person who really is a reporter in fiction. I can only write about what I have seen and felt and been close to. I must write things as they are. Sarah Orne Jewett told me always to do that."

She is a shy woman, claiming that "what I am shows in my books. I don't like to talk." She breezed into Cleveland Friday morning in a bright green and gray fur coat with gold and black velvet toque, and bright green bag to match. But she's no Bohemian!

Cleveland Press, 20 November 1925.

1926: NEW YORK

In 1924, Willa Cather agreed to four interviews in nationally known publications. That was equal to the number of such interviews she was to grant in the next four years. In 1925 she granted two interviews and began making evident her distaste for the entire process. In 1936 or 1937 she wrote to a Mr. Byron expressing regret over some of her early careless interviews and saying that she had since learned it was unwise to grant interviews at all (TLS, BLYU). She was beginning to be more protective of her privacy and more selfish with her time. "The Gossip Shop," a regular column of the Bookman, *showed that growing tendency in Cather in the issue of October 1925:*

> *From Denver comes news that Willa Cather spent the first two weeks of August there incognito. She was gathering some authentic tradition about the region for her new novel of Mexico and, being absorbed in her work, was desirous of no attention or publicity. It became necessary, however, for her to make herself known to the employees of the Denver Public Library, and Librarian Malcolm Wyer gave her a private tea at which the entire library staff was present. It can never be said that women cannot keep secrets—at least for a time—for these fifty women, respecting Miss Cather's wishes, said nothing of the secret entrusted to them and the press was never apprized of celebrity in their midst. Miss Cather visited Pueblo and Colorado Springs with the same good fortune. No one spotted her. It is reported that she has succumbed to one of those new cretonne jackets, that she is lovely and gracious, that she cannot mix women's clubs with hard work. (231)*

That desire for seclusion in order to pursue her work becomes more and more pronounced in her correspondence and her declinations of public appearances. The Cather collection of the American Academy of Arts and Letters in New York City has as its greatest bulk twenty-four refusals from Cather in response to requests to appear on programs or serve on various boards or panels, all dating from 1928.

This short interview, obviously wrested from her in an inescapable moment, reveals her impatience with the press, her wit, and much about her personality. It also explains, in part, her feelings about authors and public appearances. As printed here, it is taken from the Nebraska State Journal. *It seems obvious that the interview originally appeared somewhere else, prob-*

ably a New York paper, but no source is indicated by the Journal, *and the original appearance has not been located.* ☞

READERS AND WRITERS

Interviewed at the Grand Central station, where she was waiting for a train one hot July day, Willa Cather said:

"Yes, I'm getting out of town—it's rather evident. No, not west this time. I have just come back from three months in New Mexico. Now, I'm going up into New England."

"What part of New England?"

"Oh, several places! Mr. Knopf and Mr. Reynolds will always have my address if you should wish to reach me about something important. Seriously, I'm going away to work and don't want to be bothered."

"But this is vacation time."

"I've just had a long vacation in New Mexico. I need a rest from resting."

"Are you beginning a new novel?"

"No, I'm in the middle of one."

"When will it be published?"

"The book? About a year from now. The serial publication will begin sometime this winter. I want to finish the manuscript by the middle of February and get abroad in the early spring."

"I suppose, Miss Cather, it's no use to ask you for the title. You told me several years ago that you never announced the title of a new book until it was completed."

"Did I tell you that? Well, this time I'll make an exception. I don't like to get into a rut about anything. I call this book *Death Comes for the Archbishop*."

"And the scene?"

"Oh, that remains to be seen! My train is called."

"One general question on the way down, please. What do you consider the greatest obstacle American writers have to overcome?"

"Well, what do other writers tell you?"

"Some say commercialism, and some say prohibition."

"I don't exactly agree with either. I should say it was the lecture bug. In this country a writer has to hide and lie and almost steal in order to get time to work in—and peace of mind to work with. Besides, lecturing is very dangerous for writers. If we lecture, we get a little more owlish and self-satisfied all the time. We hate it at first, if we are decently modest, but in the end we fall in love with the sound of our own voice. There is something insidious about it, destructive to one's finer feelings. All human beings, apparently, like to speak in public. The timid man becomes bold, the man who has never had an opinion about anything becomes chock full of them the moment he faces an audience. A woman, alas becomes even fuller! Really, I've seen people's reality quite destroyed by the habit of putting on a rostrum front. It's especially destructive to writers, even so much worse than alcohol, takes their edge off.''

"But why, why?''

"Certainly, I can't tell you now. He's calling 'all aboard.' Try it out yourself; go lecture to a Sunday school or a class of helpless infants anywhere, and you'll see how puffed-up and important you begin to feel. You'll want to do it right over again. But don't! Goodbye.''

NSJ, 5 September 1926.

The theme of fame and its demands is again taken up in this 1926 interview from The Writer *magazine. The tone of interview has a curious backward look about it. The content is much closer to those early pieces when Cather was not well known. The subject is her early days on the prairie, the small towns, family, immigrants—all the topics that constituted her first public appearances. Gone are the opinions about present-day American culture and art, except for the contrast between the East and the Midwest. Instead, we learn that she goes to Rin-Tin-Tin movies.*

Part of this shift could well be the responsibility of the interviewer, but it also corresponds to a backward vision that appears in her letters at this time in her life. The changes she observed in New York City were unsettling to her, and she talked often of moving someplace else—back to Nebraska, or even to San Francisco. She had recently completed the writing of My Mortal Enemy, *a book that also possibly reflects her unrest in this period.*

John Chapin Mosher (1892–1942) was a free-lance writer and author of short stories. He was born and died in New York City. ☞

WILLA CATHER

by John Chapin Mosher

Fame has no glamour for Willa Cather, for she has known its way and workings for twenty years, to be sure only recently as a possession of her own, but for years before that she was in a position to learn its mechanism in the cases of other people. When she came to McClure's Magazine the zest for "human interest" articles, the passion for the inside story of the celebrated, had begun, and she saw the machinery by which the great are revealed to the world, and by what strategies many of them contrive to keep before the public eye. It is a disillusioning and distasteful performance, and she knew at once that never, if she should become a public figure, would she have anything of it. Since *My Ántonia* this resolution has been no abstract remote problem.

It is her aim now to live as she has lived for many years, and not be battered with invitations and callers, autograph seekers and celebrity hunters. Before her work received its great acclaim she had succeeded in living as she wished. In New York that is a triumph, worthy in itself of a Pulitzer prize. Out of the enormous mêlée of the city she picked and chose, as though, when she came there first from the prairies, she had known all about the city, and what was for her, and what was trash.

That apartment of hers in an old street near Washington Square bears witness to the discrimination of her life, and to the substantial standards by which it has been guided. The photographs and paintings on the walls are of people and places which have enriched her life, and the many shelves of books (Tolstoy, Conrad, Merimee, Proust) are those which she has most enjoyed.

Here she sees the people she wants to see—tries to, at least, and here in the mornings she works. No friend would dream of calling upon Miss Cather in the mornings. That she writes only two or three hours a day is one detail of her career that the young and aspiring may ponder on. The rest of the time she devotes to operas and concerts, long walks in Washington Square; has a few people in to tea or to dinner. There is no doubt too that there is something in the rumor that she has been remarked at the movies, during a performance of Rin-tin-tin.

This is her New York life, and it isn't very exciting to her, or very significant. For the music she lives here, and of course for the demands of her business. But her heart is far west on the Nebraska plains, with the Bohemians, Danes, Czechs, the pioneers. They are the real people to her, and this trim tailored world of critics and clever urban people is just a bit fatuous in her eyes.

"Willa Cather" appeared in *The Writer*, November 1926

She is distinctly not one of those artists who has had to revolt against the narrow confines of the home. That struggle of the artist in provincial America does not touch the story of her career. She stands an embarrassing refutation of the whole theory.

Certainly no environment would seem less promising to the literary career than Red Cloud, Nebraska, except that it was the scene of Willa Cather's early days there, blessedly untouched by the blight of suburban "culture." She was nine years old when she was brought there to her grandmother's house from Winchester, Virginia. The neighbors were Danes, Swedes, Norwegians, Bohemians. On Sundays she went sometimes to the Norwegian church, with a sermon in Norwegian, sometimes to a Danish, or a Swedish, or a French Catholic, or Czech, or German Lutheran. There was a Czech theatre. — And New York considers itself cosmopolitan.

"It is in that great cosmopolitan country known as the Middle West that we may hope to see the hard molds of American provincialism broken up."

She graduated from the University of Nebraska at nineteen, and for about nine years did little writing except a few stories for magazines, some of which were later collected in *The Troll Garden,* and one or two included in *Youth and the Bright Medusa.* It was a period of jobs, a job on the Pittsburgh Leader, teaching English in the Allegheny High School, saving up for trips abroad, and for travel in the west. Then came the story, "Paul's Case," which so interested S. S. McClure that he invited her to join his staff on McClure's Magazine. The New York phase began.

In her editorial capacity she met prima donnas, actors and actresses, journalists, the artists and celebrities of the city. She was a girl in her twenties with a background of a ranch and a schoolhouse. She was in the heart of the best New York has to give, and serenely and with assurance she knew her way in this world, and knew that, compared with that Nebraska life, this was only glitter, and trifling.

Not that she was blind to its power. Those early stories, *Youth and the Bright Medusa,* show the spell of the great personalities she met then. But with her keener eye she saw too the struggle that a great singer, say, must undergo. Her interest in such people was not romantic, but akin to that knowledge she had of the struggle to survive on the western plains. It was the effort their ambition and their genius forced upon them that was significant to her, rather than their beauty and romance.

She was four years with McClure's, and then with enough money saved up, she rented a house in Cherry Valley, New York, and spent a summer writing her first novel, *Alexander's Bridge.* That novel was swayed a little by the life she had just been leading, the New York contribution. All her following achievement was to prove how little that really meant to her. "When I began to remember," she has said, "I began to write." There came then *O Pioneers!* and *The Song of the Lark,* and the west had claimed her back for its own forever.

Now her portrait by Bakst hangs in Omaha. *My Antonia* is translated into French and Czech, and all her books are translated into Swedish. She is the first citizen of Nebraska, and it is her first country. When she first left Red Cloud, she cried in complete misery, and on every possible occasion she makes her way back there. The town is no longer pioneer; it has its garages and moving picture "Bijoux," and very possibly its "New York Store," which would be a heresy indeed. But its roots are her own. She can remember her grandmother's house, when first the turf dwellings were being replaced with clapboard structures, and she remembers those mornings when she rode on horse-back twelve miles for the mail.

"From east to west, this plain measures five hundred miles; in appearance it resembles the wheatlands of Russia, which fed the continent of Europe for so many years. Like little Russia, it is watered by slow-flowing, muddy rivers, which run full in the spring, often cutting into the farm-lands along their banks; but by midsummer they die low and slumber, their current split by glistening white sandbars half overgrown with scrub willows."

When she speaks of this country it is with great longing and homesickness for it. Her small sitting-room may be crowded with critics, artists, editors, each caught in the strait-jacket that the New York intelligensia is, and the argot of the New York intelligensia fills the place. But if the West is brought up for discussion, Willa Cather will dominate the room, and it is a strange spell she casts with her accurate and ardent speech.

What she does is almost unkind. She manages so easily to shake the conviction of all these people that New York is the only place in America in which to live. She instills a cruel dubiety as to the value of the Manhattan program. Is it possible that there is a life more vivid on the Nebraskan plain than this one of first nights and special performances, that the Avenue is dull and dingy compared with the wheat fields? Is it possible that those stolid toiling men and women on the plains have a surer wisdom than these traveled and urban people?

It is perhaps fortunate that the New York habit has so strong a hold on its victims. Otherwise we might have the picture of a caravan of covered wagons filled with literary and artistic people, critics and columnists, with maids and managers, trouping out to the great prairies. Fortunate, that is, for Nebraska.

The Writer, November 1926, 527–30.

1927: HASTINGS

Almost immediately upon Cather's completion of Death Comes for the Archbishop, *her life underwent a radical disruption. She was forced to move in the summer of 1927 because the construction of a new subway called for the demolition of her Bank Street apartment. She then went to Wyoming to visit her brother Roscoe but was called to Red Cloud suddenly in August when her father suffered a heart attack. It was during this brief stay that Cather was approached by an interviewer from the* Hastings Daily Tribune, *somewhat insensitively, given the circumstances of her visit. She obviously refused to be quoted, so that what the writer put together might best be described as a rather creative non-interview.*

Her planned trip to Italy was later canceled because of her father's health. She spent a brief time in New Hampshire, returned to Red Cloud for Christmas, and was called back there in March 1928 for his funeral.

*Her interest in Italy and its politics increased over the years, and by 1938 her correspondence with Sinclair Lewis expresses great alarm at what Mussolini had done to a once lovely country. She also felt that Stalin had duped Russia and the world (*TLS, *14 January 1938,* BLYU).

Despite the inopportune timing and the obstacles involved, the article expresses the affection and pride held by Nebraskans for "their" author. ☞

LITERATURE LEADS TO HIGH PLACE

for Red Cloud Woman Nominated to Write Long-Awaited Great American Novel

It is legitimate enough for any Nebraskan to have curiosity in regard to what literature has done for Miss Willa Cather. There have been opportunities to observe the reaction of many other Nebraskans to success of varying degrees in many lines, and they are all interesting enough. But in literature or that much of it as is encompassed by novels, it is impossible to recall another from Nebraska who occupies quite the position Miss Cather does.

This is probably the conclusion, whether based upon the reader's own judgment of the novels or upon the reviews and criticisms he has read.

"According to standards that are intelligible to me," comments a reviewer in the *Manchester Guardian* (England), "Miss Willa Cather is more likely to write the Great American Novel than Mr. Sinclair Lewis or Mr. Theodore Dreiser."

Miss Cather is a Red Cloud, Nebraska, woman, but all the reviews one sees assume it is common knowledge that her rank is among the foremost who write English. Why, then should one not be curious as to what Miss Cather thinks of life in general? For that would point the answer as to what the production of literature has done for her.

But Miss Cather will not tell what she thinks for publication in newspapers, and for reasons that are sound enough when she states them. Ask her something of her thought of Nebraska and her reply that she has already told it in her writings is answer enough, for one recalls the many minute descriptions of the land, the seasons, the crops, and the people, and that all the descriptions are with fondness, warmth, and appreciation. They are answer enough.

Moreover, here was Miss Cather in Red Cloud recently. And she was here last year, and the year before—every year. Just a ten days' call this time to visit her parents.

To write, then, of Nebraska, in a way that makes reviewers nominate the author as a possible writer of the long-awaited Great American novel, still leaves Miss Cather a lover of Nebraska, and concerned enough about parents to make a long journey for a visit. It is encouraging to know that this is true, and it is, although Miss Cather said nothing about it.

Miss Cather spent the summer in the Big Horn Mountains of Wyoming, passing through Hastings enroute about six weeks ago. The time was devoted to sections of Wyoming that the author had not visited before. The visit to Red Cloud was a run down from Wyoming, and then Miss Cather went to Denver to join a party of friends for the return to New York. Late this month she will sail for Italy on the *Berengaria*.

It is quite evident that Miss Cather is looking forward with zest to Italy. And in this, it is easy to believe, her visitor may observe one of the things that literature has done for her—sharpened curiosity about the causes of great movements.

What changes has Mussolini brought about in Italy?—Miss Cather would see, and understand, if possible. She has heard that waiters in Italy no longer accept a tip. If preferred, they refuse, explaining that now they receive ten per cent as the regular thing.

That in itself is a small matter, but Miss Cather would see if it is but one of the signs of widespread and permanent change in the general Italian status. In her novels she frequently portrays changes and their causes in Nebraska. Literature, apparently, has given her similar interest in motives and results wherever they may be.

As the editor of *McClure's Magazine*, Miss Cather's duties took her yearly to England, and the visits brought contact with writers of the day and took her to places of literary and historical note. That has been the experience to be sure of many others, but the point that interests a Nebraskan is that in this instance it is the experience of a Nebraska woman, one whose childhood days were spent in the smaller town environment, which many regard as circumscribing and an obstacle to achievement.

But in Miss Cather's case it appears that the environment was the very stimulus that awakened appreciation to the point of enabling her to make literary valuations that are striking and convincing.

Once only did it occur to her that life in Europe would be pleasanter than here. With a house to live in where time had mellowed the landscape, and centuries of life had made traditions, she settled down in an atmosphere that apparently offered everything that could be desired.

But it would not do. It was impossible to go to any point where a house was not in view. The great open stretches could not be found, and without the open stretches, best typified by the prairie, there was something wanting in the landscape that was every whit as much something wanting as a missing item in a necessary diet. So Miss Cather returned to the land where the open stretches can be found.

But the author only wants the realization that these places are available and is very conscious that one must have contact with fellow workers of similar taste to be stimulated to best activity and to maintain requisite standards. Thus one finds in Miss Cather a warm appreciation for both cities and the country.

Her latest novel will be published in September. It will be the product of six months' work and her lifetime of observation and preparation. Six months of constructive work is allotted to each year, but one infers that each waking moment is one of preparation, direct or indirect.

But though the work that Miss Cather has done makes her distinct, one of the familiar figures among the generally known writers of English, the everyday Nebraskan finds her conversation easy and delightful, though well considered and extremely human.

The mention of war may cause her to recall the effects of the revolution in Russia. She may sketch a little picture of Russian princesses and of women of the nobility practically destitute in Paris plying their needles for a livelihood. Or it may be that she will tell of Russian men of rank, in a similar plight, who were observed driving a line of taxies in the French capital.

It may be that she will allude to some charming place of interest in England and remind you that if you go prowling around Chester it will pay you next time not to overlook Ludlow, only a short distance off.

Miss Cather's ever lively interest in these things is strictly a human interest, just like yours, and you will forget for a time that you are in the presence of a creator of imaginary worlds and peoples.

But you did have a curiosity to know what literature had done for Willa Cather, and after you have left her you feel convinced that it has developed her interest in people and things.

The *Berengaria*, for instance. Miss Cather will not take passage in the big Cunarder because it is palatial or because it happens to be going at the time she wishes to leave, no; she remembers that once before when she crossed the Atlantic on that boat the passengers were notably of good spirit and congenial. The boat is then associated in her mind with pleasant voyage companionship. So she selects the *Berengaria*.

And it is literature that gives Miss Cather the trip to Italy, as it has given others. Not a gift to be despised—a sojourn in Europe with opened eyes to see and with carefully erected standards to judge.

Conversation and magazines are filled with discussions of the present day girl and woman, discussions that condemn, that exalt, that are sanguine, and are hopeless. One reads that Miss Cather wore bobbed hair long before it was the vogue and would like to know what she thinks of the drift of womanhood.

But though she does not speak Miss Cather herself seems to answer the question. She is an assuring presence and seems in no fear that the world will come crashing around her feet. Allusions here and there enable one to assume with a fair degree of certainty that she recalls that woman has always been Poppaea, Sappho, and Cleopatra, as well as Ruth, the Madonna, and Susan B. Anthony. Perhaps there is a period when the skirt is shorter. But what of it? There is a limit, and when one limit has been reached, the trend will be toward the other.

The calm assurance of Miss Cather some way suggests her faith that the nature of woman is essentially little different from the woman of all history and literature.

Take it all in all, the average Nebraskan will be very pleased with what literature has done for Miss Cather. One bears a faint recollection of orange and a white hat, an easy posture, independence, resolution, but all yielding, versatile conversation that shows sympathy and breadth of vision. The conclusion will be warranted that if literature call, really call, there need be no hesitancy in following the call, regardless of where one may be when it comes.

Hastings Daily Tribune, 27 August 1927, p. 5, cols. 1–4.

1928: SUPERIOR

The life of Evelyn Brodstone parallels in many ways that of Willa Cather. Born in Wisconsin in 1875, she moved with her parents and her brother Louis to a farm near Superior, Nebraska, in 1878. After graduating from the Superior High School, she was employed briefly at a local milling company. While taking a business course in Burlington, Iowa, she visited friends in Chicago and answered a "stenographer wanted" advertisement placed in the Chicago paper by Vestey Brothers, a British-based international meat-packing firm. She got the job and left Superior in 1895. From her position as a $45 a month stenographer in the Chicago offices of the firm she was promoted to auditor, then manager of the American branch, and finally to traveling auditor for the entire firm. She became famous as the world's highest paid woman executive, reputedly earning a salary in excess of $250,000 a year.

She took an active part in expanding the business and building new packing houses. During World War I she was in charge of the Vestey interests in South America and Australia, and on one occasion she visited the uncharted interior of Australia with only a native guide, becoming the first white woman to enter the area. She purchased six million acres of land there for cattle raising and visited Russia, China, and Africa to establish new business for the company.

At the age of forty-nine in 1924, she married her employer, Lord William Vestey of Kingswood, London, and became Lady Vestey. Although she traveled widely and was known around the world, she always remained fond of her hometown of Superior. She visited there often, frequently to see her mother until the latter's death in 1924 and her brother Louis until his death in 1936. She brought with her many artifacts, several of which are now in the Nuckolls County Museum. She sent gifts to the local children at Christmas, established a scholarship fund for students, donated money and land for a children's playground and a bird sanctuary, and purchased land for a home for the elderly. After her mother's death she and her brother donated to the community the

Brodstone Memorial Hospital, which was later renamed the Nuckolls County Hospital.

She continued to reside in London, and the beginning years of the Second World War caused her much grief. When a number of passenger ships of the Vestey Blue Star Line, of which she was an executive officer, were torpedoed and sunk, many of her friends and longtime employees were lost. Her husband, Lord Vestey, died in December 1940. The following 23 May, Evelyn Brodstone, Lady Vestey, affectionately known as the "Cinderella Lady" of Superior, died near London as she was attempting to find refuge from the Nazi bombs.

The Brodstone family of Superior had quite early become friends with the Miner family of Red Cloud, and it was through her friends, the Miner girls, that Willa Cather first met Evelyn Brodstone and her mother and brother. She visited the family with the Miners during her high school and early college years and maintained some contact with Evelyn after that, but as Cather admits in this interview, she had not been in Superior between 1893 and 1928. When the Brodstone Hospital was constructed, Willa Cather was asked to write the inscription for the dedicatory tablet in memory of Lady Vestey's mother, Matilda Emelia Larson Brodstone (see "Letters" section). When Louis Brodstone died in 1936, Cather wrote a letter of condolence to Mary Miner Creighton saying that he would be greatly missed, that he was a great fellow with a kind heart, but that like Peter Pan, he had never quite grown up. She thought that he was probably happier because of that (ALS, 6 December 1936, NLC). ☞

FAMOUS NEBRASKA AUTHORESS VISITS NEW SUPERIOR HOSPITAL

Accompanied by two of her intimate friends, Mrs. Creighton and Mrs. W. A. Sherwood, Miss Willa Cather, noted Nebraska Authoress motored down from Red Cloud Wednesday afternoon and inspected the new hospital donated to the people of Superior and vicinity by her old friends The Lady Evelyn Vestey and Lewis T. Brodstone. The ladies also visited a short time in the home of Mr. Brodstone. Enroute home the party stopped at the plant of the Superior Floral Company where the proprietor, Victor Ryhd, universally known as the "Rose King of Nebraska," presented the famed writer with a bouquet of beautiful roses.

The visit of Miss Cather had not been given publicity and only a few of her

Superior friends were at the hospital to greet her. Several other friends, not knowing of her contemplated visit, were in Lincoln Wednesday, for which fact they were much disappointed upon their return to the city when they learned of Miss Cather's visit.

Conducted through the hospital "from cellar to garret" by the Superintendent, Miss Grandy, and the staff surgeon, Dr. McMahon, Miss Cather found much in the institution over which to enthuse. She remarked particularly over the beautiful steel furniture, saying that she had never realized that furniture of such beauty, color and warmth could be constructed out of such a cold and repelling substance as steel. The window drapes, the beautiful furniture in reception rooms and parlors and the many attractive pictures also called forth exclamations of pleasure from her. Visiting the operating room she stated that her experiences in such places would not permit her to enthuse very much over them, but that she thought it was as pleasant as a room of its kind possibly could be.

Miss Cather has a right to feel an air of proprietorship over the hospital for it was she who wrote the inscription for the dedicatory bronze tablet which is to appear at the doorway of the hospital. It was much regretted by the management of the hospital that this tablet, as well as the accompanying picture of Mrs. Brodstone were not in their places. The tablet and the bronze frame of the picture are in the hands of a bronze manufacturing company in the east and their manufacture and delivery have been unavoidably delayed.

Miss Cather, who, for the past several years, has maintained a residence in New York where the bulk of her writing has been done, returned to the home of her parents in Red Cloud early in the winter to attend their wedding anniversary. Later she was again recalled to Red Cloud by the serious illness of her father, and, upon his improvement remained in Red Cloud to spend the holidays in her old home. It is the longest visit she has paid Red Cloud in many years and her pleasure in her home stay has been equalled only by the pleasure of her family and friends in her extended visit. It was her first visit to Superior since 1893.

The distinguished authoress, during her Red Cloud visit has decided to surrender her New York apartment, at least temporarily, and will make an extended tour of the Pacific Southwest, the scene of several of her novels. She expects also, to make a tour of Europe before returning to New York.

It is not difficult to understand, after meeting her, why Miss Cather is so popular and beloved by her friends and acquaintances. Despite her literary successes her personal charm is augmented by her democracy, and her easy and gracious commonness. In her presence one realizes that the greatest source of the charm in her delightful novels and sketches lies in her pleasant and versatile personality.

After spending fourteen years in industrial surgery in the mining centers of America, Dr. McMahon has become convinced of the large and almost undeveloped field of romance and novelty in the life of the American miner. To Miss Cather he spoke of this field and stated that he felt that no American Author was better equipped to enter this field than herself. "But Doctor," she said, "I know nothing of this life. A novel is not the result of a mere interest and the realization that in a field lies the basis for a novel. One must live the life, without thought of a novel until suddenly in its living there comes to a person the understanding that here is a story worth writing down." "I can easily understand that about your epics on Nebraska," returned the doctor, "but what of your tales of the southwest, as *Death Comes to the Archbishop?* "Doctor," replied Miss Cather, "I spent a large part of fifteen years in the southwest, living the life of the southwestern people. I have ridden thousands of miles on ranch ponies, and the experiences I have related in the stories to which you refer are not based upon fancies or upon reading of that territory and those people, but upon my own life and experiences there."

There is little doubt that many of the experiences mentioned by Miss Cather were undergone without the present realization that in them lay the basis for a great novel. But later, in connection with other related events she has woven them into her novels with dexterity and effect. And who knows but that in her future and greater novels—for each of her novels seems successively finer than those that have come before—there will some time be a place for the authoress' visit to the beautiful House of Mercy donated to Superior by her girlhood friends?

Superior Express, 12 January 1928.

1928: RED CLOUD

Present-Day American Literature *was founded in 1928 by Julius Temple House at New River State College in Montgomery, West Virginia (now West Virginia Tech). House, a professor of English at the school, was a native of Wayne, Nebraska, which led to a continuing personal interest, reflected in his journal, in Nebraska authors. Comprehensive coverage was frequently given to John G. Neihardt, who by 1929 was listed on the masthead as a sponsor of the journal.*

Among the associate editors was Orin Stepanek of the University of Nebraska, Lyle Dowling of Madison, Nebraska, and J. G. W. Lewis of Wayne, Nebraska. Neihardt was a frequent contributor, as were Hartley Burr Alexander, who had been a student at the University of Nebraska while Cather was there, Walter Lippman, Sara Teasdale, Edna St. Vincent Millay, Mary Austin, Witter Bynner, Walter de la Mare, Elizabeth Shepley Sergeant, Robert Lowell, and other young authors whose names were to become better known with time. The subjects included Neihardt, E. A. Robinson, Sinclair Lewis, e. e. cummings, contemporary American writers of every stripe, certain political and philosophical articles, and frequent items about Cather. The journal was conceived as a quarterly but was published monthly from 1928 to May 1932. In October 1932 it became a quarterly and ceased publication in August 1933, when the editor went to Europe.

Another contributor to the magazine was first identified only as "J.F., initials of a young woman who lives in Red Cloud, Nebraska." In later articles, her full name is given—Jo Frisbie. Ms. Frisbie, born and raised in Red Cloud, met Willa Cather, and has long served on the Board of Governors of the Willa Cather Pioneer Memorial. She now lives in Omaha.

The personal tone of the interview is charming, as is the famous author's apparent modesty when in her hometown. Although the meeting occurred in December 1927, the article was not published until the following July. ☞

WILLA CATHER AND RED CLOUD

by J. F.

"Red Cloud?" people query in that mildly disinterested tone that they reserve for polite conversation. Then, before one has time to explain, their eyes brighten and they add quickly: "Oh yes, isn't that Willa Cather's home town?" Their interest is no longer merely polite: "Tell us about her. What sort of a person she is and what Red Cloud thinks of her."

If one is in a hurry, one can truthfully say: "Red Cloud is proud of her" and let the matter drop; but few people from Red Cloud are in a hurry when Miss Cather's name comes up. Besides, it is not a question that should be answered in one short sentence. The answer involves too many things: her kindness toward all her old friends here; the cordial manner with which she always greets anyone from Red Cloud; and the graciousness of the woman herself.

Once an actress from Denver was spending the winter in New York. She tried to arrange a meeting with Miss Cather but was unsuccessful. Finally, in desperation, she sent in her card with a note saying that her father was Tom P of Red Cloud. She gained a reception immediately. "Why didn't you tell me before that you were Tom P's daughter?" demanded Miss Cather as soon as she saw her.

Her kindness, it is true, is not always understood. One year when she was spending the holidays at Red Cloud she went in to Cotting's Drugstore. A farmer was buying a book for a Christmas present. Miss Cather noticed that he had decided on *One of Ours*. With her customary thoughtfulness, although she did not know the man, she approached him and said: "Would you like to have me autograph it for you?" He looked a bit puzzled and, seeing that he did not know her, replied haughtily: "No I don't want nobody writin' in my books."

In spite of the four miles of paving of which Red Cloud boasts, it is quite possible for two people to be in town at the same time without seeing each other. Although Willa Cather has been in Red Cloud many times, I never had the privilege of meeting her until last winter during the Christmas holidays. It was with great delight that we looked forward to tea at the Cather home on Thursday afternoon. Even though husbands and grandmothers had to be drafted into service to help take care of the children, none of us wanted to miss the opportunity.

To appreciate an account of the afternoon one must know something of the Cather family. Although they have lived in Red Cloud for many years, they came originally from Virginia, and they have never lost that quality that the story-books call "true Southern hospitality". Miss Willa's mother and two sisters were there. One sister is the wife of a Red Cloud banker and the other has the reputation of being one of the best teachers that ever taught English in the High School at Lincoln.

Papers and magazines have a way—a most distressing way—of collecting old pictures of celebrities and publishing them. I am afraid that my impression of Miss Cather had been somewhat influenced by these old prints. At least I was wholly unprepared for the nicely dressed, cordial hostess who greeted us. She is about medium height with a slight tendency toward plumpness. Her hair is dark and fluffy. She does it very simply and becomingly. That afternoon she wore a two piece tan crepe dress trimmed in brown. Her pumps were black with one strap and her hose were that color of sand which is fast becoming conventional. If I had not gone to the trouble consciously to examine her dress, it would have gone unnoticed. It was far too becoming to be conspicuous. When you talk to her you notice her vigor and herself, not her clothes.

Two things particularly took my attention during the afternoon's conversation. One was her extreme alertness. The other was the care with which she chose her words. One felt that when she asked: "Is the water hot for tea?" she was certain that those were the very best words to use in making her inquiry. At first her deliberate manner bothered me, but, as soon as I realized what she was doing, it became pure delight to listen. She talks as she writes, clearly and unaffectedly.

Something had detained the niece who was to help serve, and as I was sitting near she asked me to help. Of course I was delighted. She sat at the big square table in the diningroom to pour. It was covered with a long white cloth and the usual tea accessories. Tea with Willa Cather is not a foolish affectation; it is a ceremony. She used a very special technique in preparing it for her guests.

"Go in and ask each lady," she directed, "how she likes her tea. Then tell me and I'll fix it for her. It will save passing all these things"—pointing to the usual cream, sugar, and lemon.

Mrs. Foe wanted only one lump and no cream. Miss Cather put in the lump and then held another over the top of the cup speculatively.

"One hardly seems enough," she said in her deliberate way, "These are such small lumps, and yet I don't want it too sweet." The steam poured up out of the cup, and I expected to see the lump melt and disappear while she was considering, but she decided: "I'll put the extra lump on the side of the saucer. Then she can put it in if she needs it."

Now and then she would peer into the teapot anxiously lest the tea steep too long. Once, when it looked a little too dark, she poured some out in a bowl at her left, explaining as she did so: "I'll just pour a little of this out so there will be room for more water. This bowl is what the English call a 'slop-bol'—a most inelegant name!"

It was the week after Christmas, and she showed us many things her friends had sent her. Part of the candy she served came from friends in California. The cake she brought around for us to see before she cut it had come from a friend who was teaching in an eastern college. She showed us a wreath of a particular kind of evergreen that another friend had sent from California.

"He sends me one every year," she said. "I hang it on the candelabra in my apartment in New York. Each one lasts two years; so I always have two. Now when I go back to New York I'll put this one up and take down the one he sent two years ago."

After tea was over, she called our attention to the group of figures on the table in front of the window. They were figures about six inches high of the

Christ Child, Mary, Joseph, the Wisemen, the shepherds, and the gifts they had brought. They were arranged on a thick carpet of pine needles. The child and its parents were at the top of several tiny steps, and the others were in the various stages of coming up. She lit the six or eight candles that were stationed among the figures, just at dusk. She spoke of the madonna:

"I have two Marys, one French, and one German. It was hard to decide which to use. The French mother is charming but she looks a little affected. I finally chose the German one. The French mother might love her child, but I felt sure that the German mother would take better care of it."

The only gentleman at the party that afternoon was her small nephew, a child somewhere in the neighborhood of kindergarten age who had come to spend the week with his grandparents. He was very proud of the fact that he had tea every afternoon with his Aunt Willa. She explained that he was fascinated by the little figures in the window. One thing had troubled him, however; he saw that the shepherds had brought gifts, but that, while there were plenty of oxen among them, there were no cows. He was sure that such a tiny child should have milk. He persuaded someone to take him to the tencent store at the first possible moment so that he could purchase a cow. He brought it to his auntie one afternoon when she was in the bath tub. He stationed himself just outside the door with the package and a pair of scissors so she could open it as soon as she came out. The afternoon we were there the cow was occupying a prominent place in the procession. Miss Cather seemed more proud of it than of the figures that had come from Italy and France.

As I was walking home that evening it suddenly occurred to me that during the whole afternoon no mention had been made of any of Willa Cather's books, or of herself as a literary lady.

Present-Day American Literature 1, no. 3 (July 1928).

1931: SAN FRANCISCO

The year 1928 began badly for Willa Cather with the death of her father in March. Following the funeral, Mrs. Cather, who was deeply shaken, apparently more so than those around her had expected, was convinced by her son Douglass to accompany him to California for a rest. She was never to return to Red Cloud. In December, shortly after returning to New York from Quebec and Grand Manan, Cather received word that her mother had suffered a stroke. She dropped her writing on Shadows on the Rock *and made plans to go to Cali-*

fornia to aid in arranging for her care. For the next two and a half years, all during her mother's illness, her writing was disrupted. In that time she made three more trips to Quebec and one to France to do research on her novel and made three separate painful trips to California. Her final trip occurred just after she had completed the page proofs for Shadows on the Rock *and received the gold medal of the American Academy of Arts and Letters for* Death Comes for the Archbishop. *When she arrived, Mrs. Cather was in a worsened condition, paralyzed on one side and practically speechless. She spent most of her time sitting by her mother's side. While there she visited Zoë Akins as often as possible and received an honorary degree from the University of California in March. That degree spurred a two-part interview in the* San Francisco Chronicle, *which appeared on the twenty-third and twenty-ninth of March, 1931. The interviewer, Harold Small, was either mistaken or exaggerating in claiming that it had been six years since her last interview. She had granted interviews in Nebraska less than three years before and had been interviewed by* The Writer *shortly before that.* ☞

WILLA CATHER TELLS "SECRET" NOVEL'S TITLE

by Harold Small

Willa Cather, whom many critics name as the foremost living American novelist, is about to spring a surprise on the readers, reviewers, admirers, and analysts of her books.

She has written a novel different from any of her others, and she won't utter a word about it except to say that its title will be *Shadows on the Rock*. She is informed by her publisher that he expects to bring it out in August.

"A book should speak for itself." That was all she would say about *Shadows on the Rock* yesterday in the first interview she has permitted in six years.

The University of California, following the academic custom of granting the honorary degree of doctor of laws in recognition of abilities and achievements that have nothing to do with law, has just honored Miss Cather in that way for her novels.

This has been given an impetus to speculation about what her next novel would be like; but she leaves the wonderers to their own guesses just as she did three years ago when she surprised everyone with *Death Comes for the Archbishop*.

The novelist was ready and willing yesterday to say some new things about that book. It amused her that many readers and reviewers had been puzzled by *Death Comes to the Archbishop* until she had written, months after the book was published, a brief explanation of her reasons for writing it in the way she did—more like a chronicle than a novel—"not to use an incident for all there is in it, but to touch and pass on."

Why, I suggested, hadn't she published that explanation with the book as a preface that would have set her readers on the right track from the start?

She smiled a rebuke. "They found out what it was before they were done with it, didn't they?" she said.

"Well, some of them still think it was pretty nearly simon-pure biography."

"That won't hurt them," she observed. "I think I was accurate where accuracy was needed.

"But, do you know, I had no idea of writing about those pioneer priests in the Southwest until one night I was reading the letters that Father Macheboeuf wrote to his sister.

"Then, before morning, the story was in my mind. The way of it was on the white wall of that hotel room in Santa Fe, as if it were all in order and color there, projected by a sort of magic lantern.

"In the large, it was ready, and I wrote it just so. But I did make a slip in a minor matter. I never should have said that the painting—the masterpiece that had strayed from the Old World to far New Mexico—was a painting by El Greco. Why, I had dozens of letters from readers of the novel, and they were sure they had found that 'missing El Greco' in their attics.

"They would ask me what art dealer they should send it to, and some of them thought their fortunes were made. The next time I mention a painting, I'll invent a name for the artist.

"It was a painting, by the way, that made the first scene of that story for me. A French painter, Vibert, once did a precise piece of work in the manner of his day, called 'The Missionary's Return.'

"It showed a gorgeously furnished room with cardinals, in scarlet, sitting at ease with their wine, and speaking to them, telling of the hardships and glories of missionary work in some far part of the world, a pioneer priest, his garments dull and worn, but his face all alight."

San Francisco Chronicle, 23 March 1931, p. 19.

WILLA CATHER RAPS "SINCERITY HERESY"

by Harold Small

"Sincerity." Willa Cather bristles at the word, not as it stands, but as chatterers about modern writing make use of it as a battle cry. She will have no truck with the heresy that sincerity and art are strangers, that writing is sincere only when it is in the rough, undisciplined, uncouth.

This distinguished novelist who has just been paying one of her rare visits to San Francisco has a high respect for her profession, and a low opinion of writers who don't respect their work.

"What do you think," I asked her, "about all this sincerity talk?"

She answered in parables.

"Suppose," she said, "a man comes up to you and you rise to greet him. He is your friend. You know him. You respect him. You have a genuine affection for him. Do you rush at him, paw him, pound his back and roar at him? No. The sincerity of feeling between you and your friend requires and fixes a form, a way of greeting each other, that isn't a slapstick show. Very likely you won't need more than a word in a quiet voice, nor any gesture more than a simple handshake.

"Art is form; and sincerity fixes form, naturally and in a way that expresses and earns respect.

"Suppose again that we are watching a country dance. The boys and girls are having a good time. They are behaving decently to each other because they respect each other. They are sincere in their good behavior. But now a young bully breaks into the fun. He is a boorish fellow; he doesn't know how to behave. What does he do? He starts rough-housing. He is provoked by his discomfort in the presence of these others who are enjoying each other. He wants to attract attention, and his only way of showing off is to raise a ruction."

This, I thought, must be a parable for those writers who mistake for "scribbler's itch," which may not be troublesome to anyone but themselves, a more virulent and obnoxious malady, the itch for making a public sensation.

"There are discriminations to make, of course," Miss Cather went on. "The arts can not stand still; if they mark time, they die. There must be experimenting, if that is the right word for it. I have done two books now—*Death Comes for the Archbishop* and a new one not yet published, *Shadows on the Rock*—that are different from anything that I wrote earlier and from each other. It hasn't seemed to me this was experimenting, though each time the form fixed itself and seemed right.

"Some of the modern painters, centers of much controversy, have been sincere enough. They have wished to paint the effects of light in a new way. What they have painted doesn't mean that they are putting Rembrandt in the wrong; it means that they see the effects of light in a different way from his way.

"But what shall we say about those writers who cut and shuffle prose and call it poetry? Or string out any words that come into their heads and call it prose? Is there any definite and demanding sincerity in this? Sincerity demands form. It is some other impulse that runs to formlessness."

Miss Cather works in a way from impulse. "What I write," she said, "results from a personal explosional experience. All of a sudden, the idea for a story is in my head. It is in the ink bottle when I start to write. But I don't start until the idea has found its own pattern and fixed its proper tone. And it does that; some of the things that I first consider important fade into insignificance, while others that I first glimpse as minor things, grow until they show that they are the important things. It seems a natural process. I tried to put into *Death Comes for the Archbishop* what I thought was the best chapter I had written for that story, but it didn't fit. I left it out. A novel should be like a symphony, developed from one theme, one dominating tone. That chapter was out of tone."

There is a tone, by the way, to Miss Cather's name.

> Some make Cather
> Rhyme with bather;
> She would rather
> They said Cather.

But correctly, the first part of the name is just like "Cath" in "Catholic."

That recalls an example of her writing from impulse. Miss Cather is not a Catholic. She never intended, she said, to write about the pioneer Catholic priests of New Mexico. "Being a Catholic must be a sort of technique, like being an engineer, and I don't know anything about the life of an engineer, and would hesitate to write about that. But when I read Father Macheboeuf's letters, that very night I had the idea for my story of *Death Comes for the Archbishop*.

"I hope the readers of that story have enjoyed reading it as much as I enjoyed writing it. I like my stories to be read because people like them. I didn't want to be 'assigned reading' for university classes, a duty, a target for information vampires. Why should anyone try to teach contemporary literature, anyway? Stories are to be read. 'Sincerity' again. The sincerity of feeling that is possible between a writer and a reader is one of the finest things I know."

San Francisco Chronicle, 29 March 1931, sec. D, p. 5.

1931: NEW YORK

In June 1931, Princeton University granted its first honorary degree to a woman — Willa Cather. "Although the list of notables so honored included Colonel Charles A. Lindbergh, Frank B. Kellogg, and Newton D. Baker, the conferring of the degree of Doctor of Letters upon Willa Cather, the novelist, seemed to attract the greatest attention from those present," reported the New York Times *on 17 June (p. 3, col. 1). The citation read:*

> *Willa Cather, since her graduation in liberal arts from the University of Nebraska, successively journalist, editor, and novelist. In all her work she disclosed power to create a suitable atmosphere of time and place and nowhere more than in the great early novels of pioneer life on the frontier — the land of opportunity and the school of character, built on hardships endured and overcome. In these earliest novels she first disclosed an art distinguished by an inexorable sense of truth and a quality of exquisite rightness in her limpid English prose, a prose which disdains the tricks of clever epigram and superficial ornament and reveals in every phrase the fine flavor of literary distinction.*

The degree sparked a flurry of interest in Cather, but the author herself was most interested in being on the platform with Lindbergh, whom she admired greatly. One result of the honor was Cather's only interview in the New Yorker. *Louise Bogan, (1897–1970), almost fifteen years Cather's junior, was a writer of great promise at the time she interviewed the recipient of the honorary doctorate. Bogan, a native of Maine, had attended the Mount Saint Mary's Academy in New Hampshire, the Girls' Latin School in Boston, and Boston University. She had been the winner of the John Reed Memorial Prize, awarded by* Poetry — A Magazine of Verse *in 1930 for her previous publication of two volumes of verse,* Body of This Death *in 1923 and* Dark Summer *in 1929. She later went on to win numerous prizes and grants, and was the recipient of honorary doctorates from Western College for Women and Colby College. She frequently contributed verse and criticism to the* New Republic,

New Yorker, *the* Nation, *and* Poetry. *She was the poetry editor of the* New Yorker *until her death in 1970.*

The interview emphasizes Cather's role as a woman novelist and as a midwestern writer, but it also brings out her "plainness," her "down-to-earth" quality. Although the interview employs few direct quotes, it is, perhaps, the first to capture the entire scope of Cather's career to this point. Bogan's perception is such that she attains a number of insights that were not to be shared by others until after Cather's death. The result is a critical interview that, besides soliciting Cather's opinions, delivers a number of mature, well-thought-out opinions of Cather as an author.

The "mind over Nebraska" tag refers to a controversial review by T. K. Whipple that appeared in the Literary Review *on 8 December 1923, and was quoted from the* Nation's *review of* Youth and the Bright Medusa. ☞

PROFILES: AMERICAN CLASSIC

by Louise Bogan

When, on June 16 of this year, Princeton University awarded a degree of Doctor of Letters to Willa Cather, it awarded an honorary degree to a woman for the first time in its history. Princeton University may well have experienced, on that day, the excitement and perturbation which naturally follow after any break with tradition. Miss Cather, make no mistake, took the whole thing as a matter of course. She is no stranger to the degree of Litt. D. The Universities of Michigan, Nebraska, Columbia, and Yale have eagerly taken her, before this, under their honorary wings. Miss Cather would not be surprised at anything now. For she well knows that she has accomplished, in the last decade or so, a miracle which should cause any university now extant to forget and forgive her sex. When all the rewards were going to writers of fiction who compromised with their talents and their material in order to amuse or soothe an American business culture, she, as one of her most intelligent critics has said, used her powers not in mimicking reality but in practicing fiction as one of the fine arts. She knows that she represents, to use another critical tag, "the triumph of mind over Nebraska."

She would be the first person to admit her limitations. She has admitted them, in each successive novel, by working more and more closely within them, by letting what she could not do alone. She is not a profound or subtle psychologist. Madame Colette's minute dissections of intimate personal relationships are not in her line. She lacks the broad canvas of Sigrid Undset. But she is a writer who can conjure up from the look of a place and the actions of people a narrative as solid as a house, written in prose as surely counterpointed as music. She produced, in *My Ántonia,* an undoubted American masterpiece, which will be read when most contemporary novels are as outdated as the publishers' blurbs on their jackets.

If you think of the author of a contemporary masterpiece as a person as solid as his own work, uncompromising, natural, and heartily in life, Miss Cather will fit your picture. She is the antithesis of the romantic artist at odds with himself and the world—that, it may be, supposititious figure who raises himself from the pillow where lamentable habits have put him to write a few immortal words before the miasma again sets in. Her life has been free from turmoil; she is at home in her country and her society. She has not needed to expatriate herself in order to do her work, and she is as scornful of expatriate writers as she is of literary cliques and cabals. Although she now divides her time between California, where her mother lives, and a hotel in New York, she formerly lived, as much as possible, in one spot. She rooted herself in an apartment in Bank Street, in New York City, for almost ten years. Here she saw her friends, at parties and dinners always slightly tinged with formality. She refused to encourage proselytes and adorers; she picked her intimates with care. For most of the year she sat down to her desk every morning and worked at writing. Writing was her job; she accepted it as part of a natural day, as one accepts bath and breakfast. She saw few strangers and gave few interviews. She saw New York change from horizontal vistas of brownstone stoops, from gaslight and horse-cars, into a city presenting itself vertically to the eye. But Carnegie Hall remained in the same place, though Mouquin's disappeared, the Crillon and the Brevoort could be trusted to serve good food; the values of good prose persisted as always. She went each year, for rest and refreshment, to Santa Fe or Quebec. Taos and Santa Fe she has known well since 1912, long before the days of motorbuses and nationally advertised Indian Detours. Several of her books have used Southwestern material, notably *Death Comes for the Archbishop,* which drew extensively on Southwestern legend and history. Her new novel, *Shadows on the Rock,* is about Quebec. She does not like to call it an historical novel, although its time is the seventeenth century and Count Frontenac is one of its characters.

She likes the French Canadians because they have remained practically unchanged for over two hundred years, Quebec because it is built to last, and because its buildings show the influence of French architects of France's best period. Its inhabitants like good food and simple pleasures. They are almost indestructible in their racial traits, and Miss Cather admires indestructible qualities in human character.

"Quebec never would have changed at all," she says, "if the American drunks had left it alone."

It is difficult to realize, after a glance at the Willa Cather who has shaken herself free from any influence which might hamper her work or her career, the indisputable fact that her career got off, in her first two books of prose, to a bad start. She stepped, in *The Troll Garden,* a volume of short stories, and *Alexander's Bridge,* a novel, not out onto the Nebraskan prairie but into the artist's studio and the drawing-room. This mis-step, when one considers the state of American fiction at the time (the years 1905 to 1912), was only natural. Henry James, in his steady progress through tapestried and marble halls, had lugged American fiction after him. His disciple, Mrs. Wharton, save for one lapse, in 1911, when she published *Ethan Frome,* had carried on the genteel tradition. O. Henry, it is true, had reported on people in hall-bedrooms and corner saloons, with some success. His influence, however, with the young who cared for beautiful prose was negligible. Young Willa Sibert Cather wanted to write beautiful prose about temperamental, ambitious, enchanting people. She now admits that this ambition was a grave mistake. Her talents had no real scope in the drawing-rooms of New York and London.

She walked into London drawing-rooms by way of Pittsburgh. Directly after her graduation, in 1895, from the University of Nebraska, at the age of twenty, she came east, to work for two years as telegraph editor on the Pittsburgh *Leader.* A friend who knew her ambition and her desire for Eastern experience got her the job. She left the newspaper to teach English literature in the Allegheny High School in the same city. She was not much older than her pupils; she remembers them as nice, intelligent children.

In Pittsburgh a new life began for the young Nebraskan. She met, for the first time, people with money and taste, who entertained actors and musicians. Pittsburgh was one of the first stops on the road; plays arrived there fresh from the New York stage. Singers and members of the theatrical profession were more generous with their time and talents, more grateful for hospitality, in the provinces than they were likely to be in New York itself. Public entertainers in those days were not carried away by the ambition to look and act like everyone else. They never could be mistaken for other people. Miss Cather was no more afraid of hero-worship then than she is now. She wrote down her new and exotic acquaintances. She crowded everything in. The early stories are full of furniture, salon pictures, literary conversation, phrases in foreign languages, glittering clothes, sweeping opera cloaks, bouquets, and gold slippers. The Western plains appear briefly now and then, but the characters hasten to leave them as quickly as possible. Trains whistle in and out of the action; people go back, but almost immediately escape again.

After nine years of Pittsburgh Miss Cather's career took another turn, in an upward direction. The *Cosmopolitan* (then a periodical of great seriousness), *Lippincott's, Scribner's,* and finally *McClure's* had accepted her stories. *McClure's Magazine* was far more enterprising in its editorial policies than any of the others. S. S. McClure, after his triumph in the field of newspaper syndicates, was an expert at drawing native and imported literary talent into his pages. He had published Anthony Hope, Stevenson, Kipling, and Conan Doyle. He had taken Ida M. Tarbell away from historical essays on the paving of Paris to an historical summing-up of the Standard Oil Company. Willa Sibert Cather could write as good stories as any young disciple of James. She could be trusted to know a good story when she saw it. In 1906, S. S. McClure hired her as a member of the staff of his magazine.

Miss Cather worked in New York as managing editor of *McClure's* from 1908 to 1912. She and McClure were sympathetic; they both were simple, ambitious, and straightforward. Every summer she accompanied the McClures to London, to assist in the magazine's author-seining expeditions. She went everywhere and met everyone: the older generation of authors and critics, in the persons of Edmund Gosse, Sidney Colvin, and the Meynells, and the newer generations: Chesterton, Leonard Merrick, Wells, and Galsworthy. She enjoyed everything, old and new. "I wasn't out to spy on life," she says of these days. "I was out to live it."

While she worked on *McClure's,* she published practically nothing. Samuel McClure's autobiography came out in 1912; it bears the acknowledgement: "I am indebted to the cooperation of Miss Willa Sibert Cather for the very existence of this book." *Alexander's Bridge,* that artistic stepchild, appeared the same year. "In *Alexander's Bridge* I was still more preoccupied with trying to write well than with anything else," she has since explained. "A painter or writer must learn to distinguish what is his *own* from what he admires. I never abandoned trying to compromise between the kind of matter which my experience had given me, and the kind of writing I admired, until I began my second novel, *O Pioneers!.*

Miss Cather was not a young writer, as such things go, when she wrote

O Pioneers!. She was thirty-eight. But at that age she found herself so certainly that she never again has needed to fumble about. From then on, in five succeeding books, she remembered Nebraska, where she had spent her youth. She was born in Virginia, outside Winchester, where her forebears had lived as farmers for three generations. When she was nine her father went west and settled in south-central Nebraska, near Red Cloud. The section had previously been peopled, soon after the opening of the Union Pacific and Burlington Railways, in the late sixties, by Norwegians, Swedes, Russians, and Czechs. Much of the country was still raw prairie. Young Willa rejected a regular primary education; until the time when she entered the high school in Red Cloud, her education went on at home. She rode about and made friends with her neighbors. She learned all there was to know about the prairie, including how to kill rattlesnakes and how prairie dogs built their towns. The neighbors, although immigrants living a hard life in difficult surroundings, were of a high type, especially the Czechs and Norwegians. They were musical; their cooking, at its best, compared well with the best culinary art of Prague or Vienna. They planted trees and gardens in the bare little towns, and dreary saloons, under their influence, blossomed out into beer gardens. They were worth bringing to mind. But Miss Cather was surprised when Ferris Greenslet, of the Houghton Mifflin Company, accepted *O Pioneers!*. Her first novel had opened with a description of a gentleman on his way to a tea party on Beacon Hill. Her second, in its first sentence, disclosed a Nebraska town in a high gale of wind. For Miss Cather, the wind was at last blowing in the right direction.

William Heinemann, who brought out *O Pioneers!* in England, rejected her next book, *The Song of the Lark,* on the ground that "the full-blooded method, which tells everything about everybody" was the wrong one for Miss Cather to use. She took his words to heart. She now considers the higher processes of art to be the process of simplification. To her, the first law of writing is to be yourself and to be natural.

One can see at a glance that she herself has always been that rare accident of Nature, a perfectly natural person. She speaks, without the shadow of a doubt, in the accent she acquired as a child. Her voice is deep and resonant. Her dresses are bright in color; she likes brilliant embroidery, boldly designed materials, and exotic strings of beads. She is of medium height and of the build best described as stocky. She stands and moves solidly. She sits with an air of permanence, as though the chair were, and had always been, her home. She smokes a cigarette as though she really liked the taste of ignited tobacco and rice paper. Her eyes are fine; gray-blue and set well apart. She has a thorough smile. Her face, when she detects some affectation in another's words or actions, can lose every atom of warmth and become hostile and set. It is impossible to imagine her strong hands in a deprecatory gesture. The remarks, "Oh well" and "What does it matter?" have never, in all probability, passed her lips. She admires big careers and ambitious, strong characters, especially if they are the careers and characters of women. The most fortunate and most exciting of human beings, to her mind, is a singer with a pure, big voice and unerring musical taste. She also understands men and women who are her direct opposite: delicate, capricious figures full of charm, but with no staying powers or will to endure. She knows that these last, the world being what it is, usually come to a bad end. She has nothing but contempt for people who refuse, because of indolence or indifference, to get the best they can out of life.

She does not like to work away from America, although some of *A Lost Lady* was written in Europe. In Paris she misses clear American skies, becomes absorbed in watching the changing soft colors of the Seine, and gets nothing done. She delights in the turns and sound of colloquial American speech. In literature she admires the power and breadth of the Russians even more than the delicacy and form of the French. Pushkin, Gogol, Turgenev, and Tolstoi receive her praise; she does not mention Dostoevsky and considers Chekhov too despairing and bloodless to be of the first rank. No one can convince her that sociological reasons can explain the appearance of great writers in certain places at certain times. Greatness, to her mind, is up to the individual; the culture into which he is born can be of little help and less hinderance to the complete, freely functioning artist. She would not give a penny for any literature that present-day Russia can produce. "Liberty," she says with a snap of her eyes, "sheds too much light."

She does not believe that the critical faculty, applied to literature, can really find out how the thing goes. "Anyone," she remarks, "who ever has experienced the delight of living with people and in places which are beautiful and which he loves, throughout the long months required to get them down on paper, would never waste a minute drawing up lists of rules or tracing down reasons why."

Her later novels approach more and more closely to the ideal she has set herself; human character and setting put down almost without accent, keyed to the quietest level, denuded of everything but essentials. This ideal she has herself termed "the novel *demeuble*." *Death Comes for the Archbishop* was an example of this style, and, it may be added, her greatest financial success; it went into four times as many printings as any of her earlier books. In contemporary writing, pure style and no nonsense are her demands. She is willing to be stirred by the work of young writers, if they can write in a way of which she can approve. She read *The Bridge of San Luis Rey* against her own prejudices (she thought that the wrong people had admired it), and has prayed for the fortunate continuance of Thornton Wilder's talent ever since. She likes W. R. Burnett's *Little Caesar,* because it is direct—because it sounds as if it might have been written by Little Caesar.

The ladies of Omaha commissioned Bakst, when he was in America, to paint her portrait. They made an extremely appropriate choice. For, Bakst gained a subject who, in spite of her Irish-Alsatian ancestry, her American up-bringing, has a strain of Tartar in her temperament. She has come through in spite of everything—unsubordinated by her material, her early sentimentality, false starts, and bad choices. Her integrity cannot be sufficiently remembered with awards, whether they be Pulitzer Prizes, medals of the American Academy, or honorary degrees. She has made herself complete mistress of her talent. Her foot is on her native heath, and her name is Willa Cather.

New Yorker, 8 August 1931.

In September 1930, Good Housekeeping *magazine announced a solemn and self-proclaimed "grand" task: "a search for the twelve greatest living American women" (84). The magazine asked its readers to consider thoughtfully the women they considered great and to assist in answering their challenge "for the mass mind," whatever that creature might be. The readers were to mark a ballot enclosed in the magazine, listing the twelve native-born or naturalized women they considered great. Their first choice was to be on line one; the other eleven could be in any order. They were to accompany their ballot with a letter of two hundred words or less giving the reasons for their selection. The ballots were to run in the September through December issues. As an incentive to nominators, there was a total of $5,000 offered in prizes, ranging from a $500 first prize to one hundred sixth prizes of $10 each. The contest was to close in December, and the January issue would announce the first of the twelve winners, based on the tabulations of votes and the decisions of the judges, since "this investigation [was] not in any sense a popularity contest." One test of greatness took into account how high the nominee would be held in the esteem of the world in fifty or a hundred years.*

The panel of judges included Dr. Henry Van Dyke, noted clergyman and writer; Newton D. Baker, secretary of war during the Wilson administration; Otto H. Kahn, banker, president of the Metropolitan Opera and director of the American Federation of Arts; Booth Tarkington, the novelist; and Bruce Barton, editor and journalist.

Each announcement of one of the twelve winners was to be accompanied by an interview with the subject and a "full-page portrait in four colors, painted by special commission, of the first women in Good Housekeeping's *Gallery of Great Women." In October, progress on the search was reported, along with the information that "For the painting of these portraits* Good Housekeeping *has commissioned Leon Gordon, a brilliant young artist whose canvasses have given him a place of genuine importance in contemporary American art." In November, the issue announced the three hundred "frontrunners," and talked briefly of the letters of support that had been coming in. In December, it was announced that the list of nominations was nearing seven hundred. The January issue announced the first winner: Cecelia Beaux. The following months' winners included: Jane Addams, Grace Abbot, Martha Berry, Carrie Chapman Catt, Grace Coolidge, Minnie Maddern Fiske, Helen Keller, Dr. Florence Rena Sabin, Ernestine Schumann-Heink, and Dr. Mary E. Woolley.*

*The September issue announced Willa Cather as one of the twelve honorees. The painting was a lovely and interesting one—quite different from any done before, in particular from the Bakst portrait hanging in the Omaha Public Library. It showed Willa Cather as the "Virginia lady" Bernice Slote always said she wanted to be (see frontispiece). Following the announcements in the magazine, the portraits were exhibited at the Milch Galleries (*NYT, *24 November 1931, p. 22; col. 6). The artist, Leon Gordon (1889–1943), went on to paint Will Rogers, President Coolidge, Winston Churchill, John L. Lewis, and Helen Keller. He went to Florida to paint the parents of Congressman Claude Pepper and died of a heart attack in his hotel room in Tallahassee on the last day of 1943. Although Gordon had tried to sell the collection of portraits, and his heirs later tried to do the same, his studio was destroyed by fire in 1956, along with the originals of the entire* Good Housekeeping *commission.*

Cather's interviewer for the Good Housekeeping *article was Alice Booth (Hartwell). She was an associate editor of* Good Housekeeping *at the time of the interview. Born in Bloomington, Indiana, she had been educated at Indiana University and Columbia University. Her* Anthology of Mother Stories *had appeared in 1928, and another anthology,* The Best Stories in Good Housekeeping, *appeared in 1931. Her articles appeared frequently in* Good Housekeeping, Cosmopolitan, House Beautiful, Parents, McCall's, *the* New York Tribune, *and other publications. Booth's interview again brings out Cather's down-to-earth quality.* ☞

America's Twelve Greatest Women

WILLA CATHER Who Believes There is

Nothing in the World Finer to Write About Than Life,

Just as It Is, and People, Just as They Are   by Alice Booth

It was a winter day when I first met Willa Cather—a keen, still day of icy cold. Her high suite in a Fifth Avenue hotel looked on eastern skies, pale blue with fleecy clouds. All the windows had been opened, and the air in the room fairly stung with the February chill.

Wrapped in a long coat of velvet, worn to the shade and sheen of antique amber, Miss Cater tramped up and down, as we talked about people—and books—and life. Occasionally she flung out a fine, strong hand, groping for a word—and when it came it was never a foreign word, never a high-flown word, never a complicated word—but just the exactly right word.

Her great collar of tawny fox framed a face extraordinary in its honesty and in its intelligence. So often honest people are inclined to take things for granted and not observe accurately the motives of others. One feels that Miss Cather would never be deceived about another's honesty. Her eyes are as keen as they are truthful. And her every word, every intonation, was marked by simplicity and complete lack of pretense or affectation.

The woman who had written "One of Ours," the Pulitzer Prize novel of 1922, "Death Comes for the Archbishop," that superb word-painting which I believe will go down in history as long as books will last, "The Professor's House," "My Ántonia," a dozen others; who had been honored with degrees conferred upon her by the University of Nebraska, the University of Michigan, the University of California, Columbia, Princeton, and Yale; who had been acclaimed as the greatest living American novelist by the most distinguished critics of our time—that woman stood here before me. And I knew that always and always I would read her books with the memory of that crystal-clear, shadowless winter day in my mind, and the icy pure breath of that winter cold in my nostrils. . . .

I think it was Amelia Barr who said that the most successful way to develop an author was to change his environment just when he was at the impressionable age. And she cited a long list of notable writers who had had this experience. Willa Cather's name might well head that list. At the age of eight, her family left Virginia, a state bound in tradition, lapped in bonds of history and custom, and went to Nebraska, where there was no tradition and no custom, and an alien race, strange to our soil, was just beginning to make history. The child Willa left a state where grandfathers were everything, for a state where only the survival of the race, so that there might be grandchildren, counted.

She learned to know these people engaged in a superb war with nature—Bohemians, Danes, Norwegians, Russians—and something in her responded to their simplicity and their courage and their pathos. She made friends with the old men and the old women bending their backs in toil to smooth the way for the coming generation. She made friends with the children transplanted to this new world and beginning to learn of it and for it. And something of the great fields and the wide skies and the character and temperament of the people became part of her soul-stuff, so that she could never quite get away from them.

Instead of going to school, she spent her days riding about the country on her pony, making friends with these people who seemed an integral part of the country itself, like the mountains, like the trees; and in the evening she learned to know the English classics by reading them aloud to her two grandmothers. High school in the little town of Red Cloud was her first formal education.

When she went away to college she was homesick, and, reaching back to the grain country in memory she began to write for the college paper little sketches of the people she had known—descriptions, stories. When she came East to Pittsburgh to teach, she continued to write of the country and the people which had been a part of her girlhood, although the love of music, which has also been a factor of her life, had already influenced the beginning of what was to be a book of stories involving musicians.

For several years she taught, enthusiastically, joying in the vivid contact with youth, and the eager response to learning she met with in her pupils. And then opportunity came.

She had sent stories to *McClure's Magazine,* then at the peak of its power and position, and Mr. McClure offered to publish some of them and to give her a position as assistant editor on his magazine.

Before she left for New York City, Willa Cather did something that proves for all time her ability to see herself with the same honesty with which she sees other people—she took the completed manuscript of a finished book, and tore it to pieces and threw it in the waste basket.

"It wasn't good enough," she said simply.

But would any of the rest of us have had the faith in our own judgment to make that decision—and the ruthlessness to execute sentence on our own work!

As an editor Willa Cather found her writing slowed up—almost impossible. A book of short stories came out soon after she began her editorship—but for five years no book was listed from her pen. She resolved inexorably to set aside a portion of her earnings, so that she might stop all work but writing.

In those days on a magazine, dozens of people came to her asking advice— what to write and how to write it—ignorant of the fact that the person who really has something to write usually asks advice from no one. Willa Cather, I imagine, never asked anyone what to write, or how to write it.

"Unless you have something in you so fierce," she used to tell them, "that it simply pours itself out in a torrent, heedless of rules or bounds—then do not bother to write anything at all. Why should you? The time for revision is after a thing is on paper—not before."

She knew—this girl who had torn up a book written in spite of herself— that genius—true genius—can not be restrained, can not be commanded; only a cool critical judgment can take up the work of ordering and assorting an irresistible outpouring of the creative soul.

Finally the day came when she left her desk—that desk where she had met so many noteworthy people—that desk where she had edited so many of their books—for the life upon which she had fixed all the forces of her strong character.

A friend of Miss Cather's told me that once she had asked her:

"In setting aside a sum of money to live on until your writing began to pay, how accurately did you calculate? Was it too much or too little or just enough?"

And Miss Cather answered, "Oh, it was far too much—much more than was necessary!"

From the beginning Willa Cather was a name that editors and critics knew and watched. With "My Ántonia" it became a name that every one knew.

Those earlier books of hers, she told me, were just a little different from her later ones—the old man she used later in "My Ántonia," for instance.

"In those days," she said, "I was afraid that people, just as they were, were not quite good enough. I felt I had to trim them up, to 'prettify' them. I had just heard Bernhardt, and the magic of her voice was still in my ears—and so I made my old man a violinist—a good violinist, who had once played an obligato with a great singer, when she came to the little theatre in which he was first violin in the orchestra. I made that a frill for him . . . and did not realize that old *Shimerda,* just as he was, was good enough for anybody. He was not a violinist. He was just a fiddler—and not even a very good fiddler. He did not need to be. He was enough just as he was.''

And so in her later books Willa Cather has portrayed people—just as they are. And the success of her method was acknowledged when in 1922 ''One of Ours'' received the Pulitzer Prize. This story of an inarticulate youth of the Nebraska corn lands, whose whole nature was released, converted, by the Great War, which acted as a solvent, is an amazing piece of writing, the wonder consisting in just how Miss Cather gets her effects withot seeming to get them.

Technically speaking, all her appeal is direct. Her characters act before you, as they would on a stage, and you are left to draw your own conclusions about them, while the usual method of a novelist is to qualify them with adjectives calculated to inspire you with the author's idea of them. Never, for instance, does Miss Cather use the adjectives ''sweet,'' ''noble,'' ''charming,'' ''delightful,'' and others of their ilk. She never seeks to influence you in your opinion. To you the principal male actor in a novel of hers may be a hero or a villain, according as you make up your mind about him. She gives you the character merely. Take him or leave him, on what he says, on what he does.

I read ''A Lost Lady'' as it was published serially in the old *Century Magazine* and I remember well my waiting from month to month, and the picture of Mrs. Forrester as it grew before my eyes. I shared with Niel the shock of complete disillusionment when he came to leave wild-roses at his lovely lady's window—and discovered that she was indeed a lost lady, after all. To this day she is as vivid to me as some of the old neighbors I knew then but have never seen since . . . an unforgettable portrait of an unforgettable woman. And I knew at once that here was a book, and here was a writer, that were amazing, new, strange, vital, and of extraordinary power.

Sometimes Miss Cather's books are constructed on a technical problem—like ''The Professor's House.'' That book is a singular mixture of the manner of ''One of Ours,'' and of ''Death Comes for the Archbishop,'' which followed it. From the stark realism of the upper room where the sewing machine and the stuffed dress-body held sway, to the golden sunshine of the enchanted mesa where the two boys dug for treasure is all the distance between the corn fields of Nebraska and the mellow, sun-kissed walls of the Archbishop's cathedral.

''The Professor's House'' was constructed on an old Italian form, Miss Cather told me—the *roman* in the *nouvelle*—a full novel-length book in which the story is interrupted by a long personal narrative. And also her conception was influenced by those Dutch pictures which show a trick lighting and double scene—one in particular which she remembered, cast in a dull, grayed interior—and showing through an open window a sunlit wharf with fishing boats ready to set off for all the magic ports of the seven seas—brighter and more alluring for the very grayness of medium surrounding that open window into all the possibilities and all the promise of a rainbow future.

Cleverly, subtly, "The Professor's House" duplicates this effect—for surely never was sunshine so golden as that on the enchanted mesa the Professor could visualize only across the plateau of a dingy, roll-top desk crowded with all the minutiæ of a thoroughly dulled and detailed existence.

"Death Comes for the Archbishop" wrote itself, Miss Cather told me. Completely visioned, it went from day to day with miraculous swiftness. Six months—and the thing was done. Six months for that piece of peerless prose, rippling into exquisite rhythms of color and sound.

"It wrote itself," she said, "and in only six months."

Yet few people who do not write know the labor those six months cost. Day after day Miss Cather works all morning long. And work, to an author, does not mean the slow, industrious, idle performance of a task—but work like the work of a runner trying to break a speed record—work like sending so many words a minute over a telegraph wire—fingers racing, chasing, in frenzied effort with pen or pencil or typewriter to keep up with an idea that now stops dead and will not start—and now travels faster than any force can keep up with.

Writing is a driving, grueling effort. After a long morning of it—for a morning is the limit of a high-tension, high-pressure job—Miss Cather is exhausted, mentally and physically, and must sleep before she can go on with life.

After the writing is done, there is revision, endless revision. Most of Miss Cather's work is done by hand in the first draft, completely rewritten by hand in the second draft, and then typed. Hers is no novel-a-week method. A book a year, by the hardest kind of hard work, is about the peak of her output.

"Death Comes for the Archbishop" will always be my favorite, I suppose, if only for its lovely singing sentences and its purple shadows and its mellow sunlight. Next comes "A Lost Lady," with its matchless portrait of a woman who "always had the power of suggesting things lovelier than herself."

But Miss Cather's latest novel, "Shadows on the Rock," strikes out in a new direction and in a new manner. Cast late in the 17th century, when Quebec was making a desperate stand against all the forces of this new continent, it has both the simplicity and the understanding of "One of Ours." Some of the black cold of the Nebraska prairies has gone into those winter nights when the frost pressed close, lke an enemy, and the light and color of France seemed like a dream that would never come true. Some of the house-pride and cozy comfort of those peasant women, working to create a tiny oasis of well-remembered cheer on the bleak prairies of the Northern grain fields, must have animated these new descriptions of little *Cécile,* doing in faith and love the tasks her mother taught her, which would always keep alive the French tradition of good living.

Softly, gently, effortlessly, Miss Cather paints her picture. Never once is there a straining after effect, never once a glaring color. It is like a tiny, warm picture of a tiny, warm house. It is like an old ballad, sung without accompaniment, before the fire on a winter evening.

But it is more than that, too. It is a promise and a wonderment for the future. For here is a woman who has written in her life fourteen books—books in which not only the subject matter, but the style and technique, have varied. No one knows what she will do next. Perhaps she herself does not know. More than any other writer that I have ever heard of, she has avoided imprisonment in any one environment, in any one set of characters, in any one method, even in any one way of writing. Her mind, as well as her manner, is capable of infinite variation.

So that of her next book we can only wonder. . . . Will it be another "Lost Lady" or another "One of Ours" or another "Archbishop" or something completely new and different?

One thing about it we can promise ourselves—that it will be a piece of superb workmanship, a book over which no pains have been spared, a book which is as good as Willa Cather can make it . . . or it will be no book at all.

GH (September 1931):34, 196–98.

1936: RED CLOUD

Although not technically an interview, this article contains references to personal conversation and some of the earliest first-hand information about Willa Cather from those who knew her while she was growing up. Although it has a number of inaccuracies, it is intriguing because it varies on a number of points from other popular and better-known stories. It is also interesting that although the University gave Cather an honorary degree in 1917, this appears to be the first substantial mention of their famous graduate in any alumni/ae publication.

Elsie Goth Marshall was born in Red Cloud in 1910. She attended the University of Nebraska–Lincoln (1931–36) and was visiting her family in Red Cloud when she made a "spur-of-the-moment" decision that, since Willa Cather was visiting at the same time, she would write this article. Although she says "not so very long ago," the interview occurred at least five years before publication. Willa Cather's last visit to Red Cloud was in the fall and winter of 1931–32, following her mother's death.

Mrs. Marshall now lives in Dayton, Ohio. ☞

STORY BY WILLA CATHER'S NEIGHBORS

as told to Elsie Goth

The most interesting stories about a famous person are those that do not usually find their way into print. They are the stories that only the people back home really know, that they reveal on special occasions, and that they treasure to tell again when old friends get together.

Those of you who have read only of Willa Cather's having been born in Virginia and having moved to Nebraska at an early age have missed the most telling facts in her life, for to most biographers the biography starts with the writing of her books. But her old neighbors know the story of the days when she deliberately refused to go to school, when she was planning to become a doctor or if not a doctor an undertaker, when she was one of America's first co-eds with bobbed hair, when by sheer will-power and perseverence she cured herself of lameness.

It is true that she and her family had lived in the hills of Winchester, Virginia where they were bound by folkways and customs of long years standing. Transplanted from the confines of their ancestral home to new, growing plains country, the impressionable nine-year-old daughter reveled in its newness. She sensed the freedom everywhere about. She visited continually as though the unfettered spirit of the country were elusive and to capture it she must keep constantly in touch with the people. To aid her pursuit she appointed herself postmistress for the community and rode twelve miles each day for the mail. On her rounds of delivery she stopped to chat with the Norwegian, French and Bohemian neighbors. Though only a few of their words were intelligible to her, her fancy could supply the rest of the story. She saw them through eyes made

Willa Cather's "Office" in Red Cloud,
from the *Nebraska Alumnus*, April 1936

discerning in contrasting her new home with her old. The daily lives of these people seemed as fairy tales to her, yet she kept her ardor and vivid imagination leveled to truth's foundation. She checked the account of one person against the same story as told by others and never forgot which way was right.

From one of these visits she brought away a strange illness which the doctor could not identify. In some way it affected the muscles of one leg so that she had to use a crutch to ease the strain on them. She feared the favored leg would wither from disuse so she discarded the crutch. For six months every step was a painful task; then the leg began to show signs of returning to health. Two years later it was completely normal again.

During this confined period her studies with her grandmother had been more intensive. They had studied the *Bible* and *Pilgrim's Progress*. Willa learned to repeat long sections of each. The story of *Pilgrim's Progress* became so real to her that she developed it into a game. She cut out pictures to illustrate the various adventures of Christian and arranged them on a big cardboard sheet, five feet long and three feet wide. Her brother, Roscoe, fashioned squared paths between the pictures. The whole family played the game with enthusiasm and they grieve now that it is lost. In the evenings the family listened to tales from Shakespeare, Dickens and a first edition of Louisa M. Alcott.

This was the total of Willa's "booklearning" until the family moved from Catherton Township to the little town of Red Cloud. There it was convenient for Willa to begin her formal education. It was convenient but not practical, for Willa's likes and dislikes were ever well defined and the teacher became one of her dislikes. Truant rules were unknown so Willa discontinued public school. She pursued knowledge with a greater fervor than those who did attend regularly. She would lock herself in her upstairs bedroom and read for hours. Her family allowed her to buy any books or magazines she desired and she chose wisely. A little cottonwood tree, just tall enough to brush against her window when the wind blew hard, kept her company as she read. She loved the incessant companionable whisper of its leaves and yet today is partial to cottonwood trees. The bold letters—O-f-f-i-c-e—printed on the closed door, the secure lock, and the quiet personality within barred would-be intruders. But these could not exclude the noise of young brothers across the hall. She felt she could not concentrate to the best of her ability there so she asked her father for an outside room of her own. In answer to her request he built a lean-to against the horse barn. This new "Office" was made eight feet wide, thirteen feet long, and seven and one-half feet high. The south and west sides each boasted a many paned window to admit the noon and evening light. On the east front a divided door opened inward. The upper third swung free from the lower section to allow for ventilation while the lower two-thirds was high enough to keep inquisitive children from peering over or climbing in. An old-fashioned heating stove sat behind the door and a low couch sat beside it, against the north wall. Even when the door was closed and the thinker within believed herself free from interruption, she would be disturbed by children coaxing her to come and play. They would often pry up a window to slip in a toad or a mouse. But she gave no heed to the intrusion nor to their coaxing and continued steadily with her studies. In a corner of the lean-to opposite the stove a low corner desk still stands on one sturdy leg. On the other side of the door, against the south wall, stands the old bookshelf. The tiny building has now been demoted to a position out in the country beside a garage. It is used as a catch-all for small farm tools and one would hardly imagine that it once protected periods of study and incubation of knowledge which have been translated into internationally read literature.

In addition to her constant association with books Miss Cather sought out the best learned men of the town and absorbed much of their knowledge. The proprietor of the clothing store, who was an Oxford graduate, taught her some Greek and Latin between customers. She discovered a Norwegian neighbor lady and her father who were talented in music. From them she learned the stories of the operas, the spoken drama, the fundamentals of harmony, rhythm and time. She would sit and listen by the hour to the music they played but she did not care to produce the sounds herself. The mechanics of production detracted from her enjoyment of the result. She became acquainted with a lawyer and had the ambition to become a lawyer, too. For several months she studied law diligently. Then she thought it would be better to become an undertaker. With the help of the only man in the town of that profession she bent her energies toward learning his trade. Again she had the desire to become a doctor. She worked in the doctor's drug store during Christmas rush and was repaid with enough wallpaper to line her "office." For similar services the following year the doctor gave her a magic lantern with hand-painted slides imported from Germany. She hung up a bed sheet and gave frequent shows for the neighborhood with her lamplit lantern. Later when occasion arose she gave anesthetics for the doctor. In between times she practiced his methods of surgery on chloroformed dogs. These amateur operations were always fatal to the victim but she continued her studies and experiments.

She came to know the county superintendent, Evangeline King, now Mrs. O. C. Case. Under the guidance of Miss King, Willa spent two years in high school at Red Cloud. Then she entered the University of Nebraska. Even there she wore her simple, easily-donned shirts, short skirts and shingled hair. (How the neighborhood buzzed when she had her hair clipped!) She still desired to become a doctor and signed her letters home "William Cather, M.D." Her folks addressed their replies in the same manner. When "William" went down to the post office to get "his" mail, the clerk answered the request with a curt, "Other side, please, for the gentlemen's mail." Her requirements for comfort and ease of dress did not falter even under such treatment.

She found a place on the University magazine "The Kiote." At one time the paper offered a prize for the best article submitted on football. Dorothy Canfield was attending the University. She and Willa Cather collaborated and sent in their composition. They received the ten dollars but a few years ago when the article was reprinted in a limited edition both termed it "probably the worst ever written." Miss Cather found her training a good basis for composition and rhetoric. She did so well that one of her manuscripts was among a group sent to C. H. Gere, then editor of the *Nebraska State Journal.* She attended a drama and wrote a report of it. Mr. Gere recognized her ability and gave her a place on his staff. After graduation she took a position with the Pittsburgh Leader as telegraph editor and dramatic critic. Then she became head of the English department in the Allegheny High School. Here she published "April Twilights" and "The Troll Garden." Later she secured a position with McClure, which she quit to have time for her writing.

When she is at work she writes three hours each day and spends the rest of the time in touch with music, books, nature, or friends. She writes down the general idea first then rewrites by sorting and pruning her first attempt. This process is repeated over and over until it is as perfect as she can make it. Miss Cather once said, "It is not the writing but the rewriting that counts."

From the usually acid pen of H. L. Mencken we have this praise of her work: "The whole enchantment is achieved by the simplest of all possible devices. . . Here a glimpse, there a turn of phrase, and suddenly the thing stands out, suddenly it is as real as real can be . . . and withal moving, arresting, beautiful, with a strange and charming beauty."

Miss Cather still has some very close friends in Red Cloud and maintains her membership in the Episcopalian church there. Not very long ago she was visiting in the town. At a tea given in her honor the talk turned to food. She thinks it an unforgivable sin for a woman not to know how to cook. She confessed being fond of good food and that one of her preferences is four strips of bacon every morning.

Another friend once volunteered, ''I have read your last book. And I . . .''
''Oh, I hope not,'' interrupted Miss Cather crisply.

Always the right word must go in the right place for her. Sometimes she moves a hand as she pauses to grasp the fitting word and when she voices it, it is never a foreign word, never a many-syllabled word but is always the just-right word. Little traits of phraseology which she remembered as characteristic of her old neighbors, she has put in her stories with hardly a word out of order. So perfectly has she reproduced them that the neighbors have been able to identify many of her characters. One man is proud to be the husband of ''My Ántonia''; a cousin of the famous author is Mrs. Alexander, the business lady in ''O, Pioneers''; and the ''Lost Lady'' is the wife of a former governor of Nebraska. And so her neighbors take their places in her work, while she holds a place in their memories.

The Nebraska Alumnus, April 1936.

1940: NEW YORK

Stephen Vincent Benét (1898–1943), had long been an admirer of Willa Cather and had reviewed a number of her books before he and his wife, Rosemary, conducted what was to be Willa Cather's last known interview, sometime in the waning months of 1940. The style implies that the interviewers had never met Cather. However, Benét's frequent reviews, Cather's early friendship with William Rose Benét, Stephen's older brother, and their mutual involvement with the Church of the Transfiguration on East 29th Street, ''The Little Church around the Corner,'' would suggest the possibility that they had some previous contact or acquaintance.

The interview includes a comprehensive summary of everything that Cather had done to this point in her life, including her recent novel, Sapphira and the Slave Girl. *The interviewers had no way of knowing that she would not complete another novel before her death.* ☞

WILLA CATHER: CIVILIZED AND VERY AMERICAN

by Stephen Vincent and Rosemary Benét

What makes the artist? From what creation does the creative gift itself spring? We must, as the Scotch proverb says, dree our weird . . . but is the pattern imposed from without, or is it self-chosen? Does fate pursue the artist or does the artist make his fate? A biographer can, if he likes, take an unequivocal stand and evolve a clear case for either heredity or environment. But the fact remains that one mind finds its richest and deepest material in a time and place that might be anathema to another and that no writer can ever tell in advance what sort of experience is going to be most valuable for him. And experience itself can be valueless, unless one has the eye to see and the tongue to tell.

Let us take the case of Miss Cather, for here we have a genuine artist. Like fine silver or porcelain, her product is unmistakable. We do not have to turn the piece to find the hallmark or the crown and crossed-swords imprint. We know by the look and the shape and the weight in hand. Miss Cather has written a great many very different books. Each is unmistakably her own—the work could not be done in that way by any of her contemporaries. The work is also entirely American . . . the feeling for the frontier, the look of the land and the light in Nebraska could not be captured by a stranger. Though the style has deep French roots, the flower is American. When we ask about early influence, she tells us of a remarkable teacher she had at the University of Nebraska, a Swede who was teaching French . . . not, at first glance, a very compatible combination. "He suggested that I read *Colomba*," she said, and then proceeded to remember, with great vividness and effect, the story of a Corsican vendetta, remarking on the line, the impact and the fact that the description of Corsica reminded her of Nebraska. "It seemed the best writing I'd ever read." There is no question that a spark was struck here, a spark that burned long and well. But think of the copies of *Colomba* that have been sold! Every student who has had two years or so of French knows the textbook edition with its picture of Prosper Mérimée in a black bowtie. There are dog-eared copies moldering in many attics—but few of the owners have produced first-flight novels as a result of this touchstone.

But before that particular catalyst did its work there were shifting experiences and deep memories. Willa Sibert Cather was born December 7, 1876, on a farm near Winchester, Va., the daughter of Charles Fectigue Cather and Virginia Sibert Boak. The Cathers were Irish; the Siberts, Alsatian, and her other ancestors were English. On both sides they had been Virginia farmers for three or four generations. When Willa Cather was eight years old, her father bought a ranch at Red Cloud, Neb., a town named for the famous Sioux warrior. The country was thinly settled; the people, for the most part, Swedes, Danes, Norwegians, Bohemians, and Germans, came to conquer a last frontier. Since she did not go to school at first, Willa Cather had a chance to get thoroughly acquainted with her new neighbors. A keen and observing mind had a new landscape and a whole new set of experiences to fit into the scheme of things. She herself has said of that period: "I grew fond of some of the immigrants, particularly the old women who used to tell me of their home country. . . . I have never found any intellectual excitement more intense than I used to feel when I spent a morning with one of these pioneer women at her baking or butter-making. I used to ride home in the most unreasonable state of excitement. . . . This was with me the initial impulse."

Later, she went to the high school at Red Cloud and graduated from the University of Nebraska at nineteen. (She now has five honorary Litt. D.'s.) The next few years she spent teaching at Pittsburgh and working at short stories. Through her first short stories she met S. S. McClure and, in 1906, joined the staff of *McClure's* magazine. Two years later she became the managing editor of *McClure's*, a position she held for four years. During the period of editorial work she wrote little. She still remembers how most of the magazine fiction she saw at that time fell into the conventional commercial pattern, an example she decided not to follow. Her first novel, *Alexander's Bridge*, showed something of Edith Wharton, something of Henry James, but, rather more than either, a knowledge of the sort of economical architecture that has made the short French novel. Even so there was a certain difference. *Alexander's Bridge* was not a good novel, but the hero did build bridges. In Henry James, he would have talked about building them. The huge, endlessly spinning, endlessly refining web of the Jamesian style never really suited Miss Cather. She wanted to get things clear.

She began to get them clear in her next three books, *O Pioneers!*, *The Song of the Lark*, and *My Ántonia*. "It takes a great deal of experience to become natural," as she herself has said. She returned to the places of her youth—to the West that had never been told about, the farm women, the pioneers and their children, the ambitious girls who heard the long whistle of the trains going East and hoped some day to go. And in *My Ántonia* she produced a complete and rounded classic—one of the few American novels to which the word classic may genuinely apply. It is as fresh today as the day it was published, and that was twenty-two years ago. The crystal globe of the imagination has held and contained a section of living earth.

So there we have the secret, of course, the youthful memories called back, set down and refined by the scrupulous artist. Do we? That might account for Thea Kronborg and for Ántonia. It hardly accounts for one of Miss Cather's finest books, *Death Comes for the Archbishop*. That is written not about Nebraska but about New Mexico in the '50s. Miss Cather went to New Mexico to visit her brother, an engineer with headquarters at Santa Fe. She liked the feel of the land and explored the back country in the days before the automobile had smoothed all paths into four-lane highways. She saw the Snake Dance and the pueblos before they became tourist attractions. She met a remarkable Catholic priest and saw the work he had done. She heard of some of his predecessors—of the cultivated and inspired missionary who built a fine Romanesque cathedral—the man whom she calls in her book Father Jean-Marie Latour. From that visiting and that knowledge came one of the finest books both on the region and on the spirit of the Catholic Church—though the author belonged to neither one and was neither a Southwesterner nor a Catholic. By intuition and the seeing eye she has managed to fix unforgettably a time, a place, and a spiritual force.

It would be valuable to discuss each book in its turn, but limits of space prevent. This particular department would like to put in a special word for *The Professor's House,* a book, perhaps, less appreciated by Miss Cather's wider public than by other writers and one that shows extraordinary shifts of color as you turn it under the light. *A Lost Lady,* perfect in scope and range, remains what it was, a small chapel very near the cathedral. *One of Ours* received the Pulitzer prize and, despite its sincerity of purpose, is the one real failure among Miss Cather's major novels. For once, with Claude Wheeler, the clear eye did not see and the architecture is confused. That happens, too, with good novelists.

The leading popular misconceptions about Miss Cather are (a) that she was born in the West and (b) that she is a Catholic. "I'm an Episcopalian and a good one, I hope!" Among the more scholarly but equally false surmises made about her work Miss Cather cited two. One student of the subconscious said that she had been strongly influenced by death at the time she wrote *Death Comes for the Archbishop.* The use of the word in the title and the beautiful passage at the end of the book showed that. As a matter of fact, as she points out, death did not closely touch her life until later on. Another amateur psychologist made much of the fact that she tended to use the letters of her own name in the names of her heroines—they had an *R* and ended in an *A* like hers. The fact that many Scandinavians and all Bohemian girls' names do end in *A*—an explanation that would have occurred to any Nebraska farmer—was something he had never heard of.

All experience has been grist to Miss Cather's slow, fine-grinding mill. Her new book, *Sapphira and the Slave Girl,* goes back to her earliest days in Winchester. It is as though she had looked back affectionately at her childhood and thought, "Why, there is something I have never used!" and recalled it with the clearness of morning air. So clear was this part of her life that the speech of the people, white and black, as she had heard it as a child, came back to her as if it had been stored on phonograph records in her brain. "When I went back to Winchester as a young woman to visit my aunt, I went down a road and found I knew what was coming next all the way along." *Sapphira and the Slave Girl* has the same sense of "knowing the road before it comes." Yet it was not easy. She started it as a complete history of the manners and customs of the valley — and then cut out all that background that was not essential to her story. "I weighed what I cut out — and it came to a good six pounds." She doesn't like what she calls "arid botanical knowledge" but she is tireless in assembling her facts. She never skimps; the work is there, but it mustn't show. To use her own excellent phrase, "It must all seem as easy as a fish slipping into water."

"Elegance of line" and "lack of useless ornamentation" in any form appeal to her. She notices it wherever she sees it, in a fine modern bank building in New Brunswick, in a tennis game, in the structure of a French novel, or in the stairway at Mount Vernon. (Mount Vernon was one of her early memories. She has always remembered the beautiful stairway, the maze, and the swallows nesting by Washington's tomb.) And that feeling for line is found in all her work.

"The ear is as important as the eye," she comments — the comment of a writer whose style has euphony as well as clarity, music as well as veracity. Conversation should be set down in the mind, she says, "just as a violinist remembers how another violinist played a piece of music ten years ago."

Miss Cather's life is very much her own. There is no ivory tower about it; she is too hearty for that. But she does not go in for personal appearances, speech making, banqueting, public autographing, and the like. She lives as she chooses, without fuss, whether it is in the West or a New York apartment in winter or New Brunswick in the summer where she has gone since she could no longer go abroad. She writes for two hours in the morning, using a pen. Of medium height, with clear blue eyes, she gives an impression of great intellectual vitality and serenity combined, calm strength and lively independence. Having a limited amount of time, she does not bother with things or people who are antipathetic or unsympathetic. "It's no use," she says philosophically. But she has great warmth and interest in what she does like, her friends, any phases of the arts, the country, good food, good wine. Though she fits perfectly in her New York environment, one cannot imagine her being entirely satisfied by metropolitan life. Her living room is quiet; the city rumble is far away. There is a large bust of Keats in the corner, a charming image of the Infant Jesus of Prague on the bookshelf, a portrait of George Sand over the mantel, and an orange tree near the open fireplace. It is a pleasant abode, but for permanent living, one feels sure, she would need more spacious earth. There is an unhurried feeling about her, in contrast to the brisk nervousness of the city, like a strong river in a deep channel.

As a person and as an artist she is both civilized and extremely American. She has always had a deep feeling for the frontier, for its freshness and strength, for the wild beauty of new land. At the same time she has liked to put a highly cultivated person against that setting. And that was not an artistic device—it belonged and belongs to the whole roll West from Jamestown. It was part of the frontier as daring and action were part of it. In her own life and work she suggests just that combination—strength, simplicity, and fortitude mixed with a high degree of civilization. It is the strong stalk that flowers, and with Willa Cather the strength and the flower are one.

New York Herald Tribune Books, 15 December 1940.

Speeches

1890–1933

From the time Willa Cather made her oration at the Sunday School program in the Baptist Church in Red Cloud in 1885, she was frequently tempted to speak publicly. Her commencement address in 1890 was reprinted in full in the local paper. During her years at the University of Nebraska she acted in a number of plays and gave several orations. After she achieved fame she was asked to give speeches, lectures, and talks to all kinds of groups and organizations. She consistently turned down such requests. Only on rare occasions did she give speeches.

Part of her reluctance is explained by an early experience that she had in Pittsburgh. A friend, Mrs. George Gerwig, had very quickly involved her in the club life of her new city and on one occasion had taken Cather to a tea given by the editor of the Dispatch. *The topic of the day happened to be Carlyle. When the young journalist was called upon to give an impromptu speech, her college essay on Carlyle came back to her in a flash and she stood up and recited the entire work with great fervor and enthusiasm. She felt it was a great dramatic performance and said that all the women thought it had been improvised and fell all over one another trying to shake her hand. Following that experience she had been called on repeatedly to make other speeches, a great distraction. She needed to put a stop to speechmaking at once before it made more interference with her work (ALS to Mariel Gere, 10 August 1896, NSHS). She admitted to her old friend Will Owen Jones that she was able to write more stories in Red Cloud because she was too involved in the society act in Pittsburgh. Since she had been received more warmly than most strangers in Pittsburgh her vanity compelled her to be involved, and she could in no way play the role of a hermit (ALS to Will Owen Jones, n.d., but probably the summer of 1896 or 1897, NSHS).*

Cather's years as a teacher and a new staff member at McClure's *curtailed her speaking engagements for a time, no doubt because her work kept her so busy during those years. After she had published her first two novels and left journalism, she returned to Pittsburgh to give a speech about some of the materials and experiences she had gathered in the intervening years. Although she refused many requests to speak in the East, she seemed more ready to respond to those from the places she had lived before New York. In 1921, in an unprecedented spate of oratory, Cather gave at least four public addresses in her home state of Nebraska. Although she taught at the Breadloaf conference in Vermont in 1922 (her only such engagement), she did not give speeches again until 1925, when she undertook another tour, speaking at Bowdoin College, the University of Chicago, and Cleveland. On all of these occasions, Cather spoke out boldly about a number of controversial and deeply felt issues.*

Her last major public address was a brief lecture carried by NBC *radio at the Princeton banquet held in New York City in 1933. Since Cather had been the first woman ever to receive an honorary degree from Princeton University, the speaking engagement was a form of repayment.*

Cather never considered herself a public speaker. Even though she received much recognition and appreciation for her speeches, her correspondence reveals that she never felt as much "in control" as she did when she was communicating in writing. The immediate response, while gratifying, threw her off—appealed to her baser motives. In a 1926 interview in Grand Central Station (see "Interview" section), Cather said that she thought the "greatest obstacle" for American writers was "the lecture bug." She went on to say that that lecturing was "especially destructive to writers, even so much worse than alcohol, takes their edge off." It destroyed the writer's higher sensitivities, made the writer feel "puffed-up" and self-important. Her final advice to the young writer who wanted to lecture was simple: "Don't!"

1890: RED CLOUD

Willa Cather graduated from the Red Cloud High School in June 1890. She was a member of a class of three, all of whom gave orations at the graduation exercises. Her two classmates were both male, and, typical of the times, they were both predicted as having a great and promising future by the reporter from the Red Cloud Chief. *Cather, as a female, was said to be "a great surprise" for her logic.*

Her speech is eloquent—and electrifying—when it is remembered that it came from the mouth of a sixteen-year-old girl with little formal education. ☞

SUPERSTITION VS. INVESTIGATION

by Willa Cather

All human history is a record of an emigration, an exodus from barbarism to civilization; from the very outset of this pilgrimage of humanity, superstition and investigation have been contending for mastery. Since investigation first led man forth on that great search for truth which has prompted all his progress, superstition, the stern Pharoah of his former bondage, has followed him, retarding every step of advancement.

Then began a conquest which will end only with time, for it is only the warfare between radicalism and conservatism, truth and error, which underlies every man's life and happiness. The Ancient orientals were highly civilized people but were dreamers and theorists who delved into the mystical and metaphysical, leaving the more practical questions remain unanswered, and were subjected to the evils of tyranny and priestcraft. Those sacred books of the east we today regard as half divine. We are not apt to think as we read those magnificent flights of metaphor that the masses of people who read and believed them knew nothing of figures. It is the confounding of the literal and the figurative that has made atheists and fanatics throughout the ages.

All races have worshipped nature, the ruder as the cause, the more enlightened as the effect of one grand cause. Worship as defined by Carlyle is unmeasured wonder, but there are two kinds of wonder, that born of fear and that of admiration; slavish fear is never reverence.

The Greeks, lacking the intense religious fervor of the Orient, entertained broader views. Their standard of manhood was one of practical worth. They allowed no superstition, religious, political, or social, to stand between them and the truth and suffered exile, imprisonment, and death for the right of opinion and investigation.

Perhaps the strongest conflict ever known between the superstitious and investigative forces of the world raged in the dark ages. Earth seemed to return to its original chaotic state, and there was no one to cry, *"Fiat lux."* The old classic creed fell crashing into the boundless path, and the new church was a scene of discord. All the great minds were crushed, for men were still ruled by the iron scepter of fear, and it was essential that they should remain ignorant.

Superstition has ever been the curse of the church, and until she can acknowledge that since her principles are true, no scientific truth can contradict them, she will never realize her full strength. There is another book of God than that of the scriptural revelation, a book written in chapters of creation upon the pages of the universe bound by mystery. When we are morbid enough to say that the world degenerates with its age we forget that the heroes and sages of history were the exceptions and not the rule; what age since the world's foundation can leave such a record upon the pages of time as the nineteenth century? What is it that characterizes our age and gives the present its supremacy? Not skill in handcraft, for the great masses of art lie sleeping among the tombs of Hellas and Italy; not in clearness or depth of thought, for our literary and philosophical lights are gleams from the fires of the past. In the Elizabethan age, a book was written asserting that nature is the only teacher, that no man's mind is broad enough to invent a theory to hold nature, for she is the universe. With the publication of the *Novum Organum* came a revolution in thought; scientists ceased theorizing and began experimenting. Thus we went painfully back to nature, weary and disgusted with our artificial knowledge, hungering for that which is meat, thirsting for that which is drink, longing for the things that are. She has given us the universe in answer.

It is the most sacred right of man to investigate; we paid dearly for it in Eden; we have been shedding our heart's blood for it ever since. It is ours; we have bought it with a price.

Scientific investigation is the hope of our age, as it must precede all progress; and yet upon every hand we hear the objections to its pursuit. The boy who spends his time among the stones and flowers is a trifler, and if he tries with bungling attempt to pierce the mystery of animal life he is cruel. Of course if he becomes a great anatomist or a brilliant naturalist, his cruelties are forgotten or forgiven him; the world is very cautious, but it is generally safe to admire a man who has succeeded. We do not with-hold from a few great scientists the right of the hospital, the post mortem, or experimenting with animal life, but we are prone to think the right of experimenting with life too sacred a thing to be placed in the hands of inexperienced persons. Nevertheless, if we bar our novices from advancement, whence shall come our experts?

But to test the question by comparison, would all the life destroyed in experimenting from the beginning of the world until today be as an atom to the life saved by that one grand discovery for which Harvey sacrificed his practice and his reputation, the circulation of the blood? There is no selfishness in this. It came from a higher motive than the desire for personal gain, for it too often brings destitution instead. Of this we have the grand example in the broken-down care-worn old man who has just returned from the heart of the Dark Continent. But perhaps you still say that I evade the question, has any one a right to destroy life for scientific purposes? Ah, why does life live upon death throughout the universe?

Investigators have styled fanatics those who seek to probe into the mysteries of the unknowable. This is unreasonable. The most aspiring philosopher never hoped to do more than state the problem; he never dreamed of solving it. Newton did not say how or why every particle of matter in the universe attracted every other particle of matter in the universe. He simply said it was so. We can only judge these abstract forces by their effect. Our intellectual swords may cut away a thousand petty spiderwebs woven by superstition across the mind of man, but before the veil of the *"Sanctum Sanctorum"* we stand confounded, our blades glance and turn and shatter upon the eternal adamant. Microscopic eyes have followed matter to the molecule and fallen blinded. Imagination has gone a step farther and grasped the atom. There, with a towering height above and yawning death below even this grows sick at soul. For over six thousand years we have shaken fact and fancy in the dice box together and breathlessly awaited the result. But the dice of God are always loaded, and there are two sides which never fall upward, the alpha and omega. Perhaps when we make our final cast with dark old death we may shape them better.

Red Cloud Chief, 13 June 1890.

1915: PITTSBURGH

While she was working on McClure's *magazine, Cather was first exposed to the famous and great. On assignment in the Boston area for the biography of Mary Baker G. Eddy, she met Sarah Orne Jewett and Mrs. James T. Fields. She was to draw upon the experience many times—both consciously and unconsciously—during her career.*

The speech she gave in Pittsburgh in 1915 was only the first of many recollections of the meeting that she was to make. Cather clipped the article about the speech from the Pittsburgh Dispatch *and sent it to her family, headed with the inked notation: "You might show this to Carrie Sherwood"* (WCPM *Collection*). ☞

BRILLIANT LITERARY LECTURE BEFORE CLUBWOMEN

by May Stranathan

Glimpses of the home of James T. Fields in Charles Street, Boston, which was for many years the innermost circle of the literary life of America, were given by Miss Willa Sibert Cather in her talk before the College Club of Pittsburg on Friday afternoon, when she took for her subject "The Art of Sarah Orne Jewett." The descriptions of the Fields residence was of more than usual interest, because of the fact that Mrs. Fields, who had lived there for sixty years, died last week, almost the last of the large circle of literary folk who were wont to meet there. Mr. Fields, who was the first American publisher for nearly all of the great English as well as American writers of his day, including Dickens, Thackeray, and Tennyson, besides being a publisher, was the personal friend of the men and women whose books he made known to the world, and many of them made the Charles Street residence their headquarters while in America. Here Thackeray wrote the chapters of *Henry Esmond,* and here, at the famous Sunday breakfasts given by the Fields, gathered the literati of the time.

Miss Cather told of the "long drawing room," where for many years Mrs. Fields received her guests, and which was filled with precious literary relics, including a lock of the hair of John Keats and first manuscripts of many famous writings. Many actors and actresses were as much at home in the Fields residence as were writers, though Ellen Terry was quoted as saying that she never felt quite at ease in the long drawing room, for fear she might break some of the sacred bones stored there.

For many years Mrs. Fields and Sarah Orne Jewett were close friends, and after the death of Mr. Fields, Miss Jewett spent a part of each year with Mrs. Fields, and it was here that Miss Cather, also a visitor at the Fields home, met her, and they became close friends. Miss Cather predicted for Miss Jewett lasting fame, since she wrote from the heart of life, depicting the New England character with truth and beauty. Her short stories were deemed better than her novels. Her work was said to bear a marked similarity to that of Turgenev, the Russian author, and Miss Cather told how William Dean Howells, when the books of Turgenev began to appear, gave Miss Jewett a volume, saying, "Here is an author who writes just like you do." Miss Cather quoted from a letter from Rudyard Kipling to Miss Jewett in which he told her there was more virility in one volume of her stories than in the entire work of many young authors who imagined they were writing virile literature, because they wrote of cowboys, horse-thieves, mining expeditions, and western fights. "Virility is power and poise, not noise," the letter said.

Miss Cather's story of the latter years of the life of Sarah Orne Jewett was pathetic. Following an accident in which she was thrown from a carriage, Miss Jewett found herself unable to continue her writing. She felt that she was being left behind and forgotten, but when Miss Cather visited England she found Miss Jewett's works regarded as classics there, and she met appreciation of them from many of the younger authors who had not known the author personally, as had so many of the literary men and women of former years. With much pleasure Miss Cather looked forward to bringing back this word to her friend, but before she returned she received the news of the death of Miss Jewett.

The Pittsburg[h] Dispatch, 10 January 1915.

1921: HASTINGS AND OMAHA

Cather's whirlwind speaking tour of the Midwest caught the eye of people beyond her homeland. Dr. Wilbur Cross wrote to her requesting a transcript of her remarks, but Cather replied that there existed no such thing. She said that not a single word of her speeches had been put on paper, and, consequently, she could not provide him with the required manuscript. Further, she noted, she would have prepared it much more carefully for print than for an informal lecture—because in the latter a person can quite easily modify extravagent statements (TLS to Wilbur Cross, 10 January 1922, BLYU).

Many Nebraska papers reported Cather's speeches, and her old classmate at the University of Nebraska, Harvey Newbranch (1875–1959), who was by that time editor of the Omaha World-Herald, *editorialized on her greatness—and her authentic voice for Nebraska.* ☞

WOMAN'S CLUB

Miss Willa Sibert Cather, the noted writer, who was the guest of honor at the opening meeting of the Hastings Woman's Club, held October 14, afforded the members a most pleasant and interesting half hour in a short talk on the native trees of the state.

The same simplicity of style, the same clearly drawn word-pictures are found in her speaking as in her stories—stories that are dear to the heart of every man and woman of Nebraska.

Miss Cather would quicken the love of her "home" people through a strong appeal to the women of the clubs of the state to protect the native trees, especially the giant cottonwoods.

These trees were planted and carefully nourished by the early pioneers, but today, they are neglected and often destroyed. She points out their strength, shown in the great branching limbs, and their beauty of late fall.

She brings home pictures from France, where she saw the cottonwood extensively cultivated, honored by being planted around some of the most historic spots in France and loved by everyone. The children call the cotton, which the trees shed in late summer, summer snow. They play in it, use it for making pillows, and in various other things.

She grants that cottonwood is not a good shade tree, but it relieves the level, monotonous plain with its tall uplifting branches of silver covered with golden leaves, ever rustling in the faintest breeze.

Andrea Zorn, the great artist, speaks in the most glowing terms of the great beauties of cottonwoods and the locust hedges. Etchers delight in their rare beauty of design.

It is known that a large number of people in America seriously object to these trees, that in some localities they are very objectionable owing to the cotton in the late summer.

The French say there can be no beauty without cost. Miss Cather urges new cottonwoods and hedges, planted east and west, north and south. She says if the hedges cause deep snow drifts in winter, use snow plows, as farmers do in New England; if they take up valuable ground, sacrifice a few bushels of wheat, but plant them for their beauty.

Hastings Daily Tribune, 22 October 1921.

WILLA CATHER RAPS LANGUAGE LAW AND ANTLES' BOXING REGULATIONS

"No nation has ever produced great art that has not made a high art of cookery, because art appeals primarily to the senses," declared Miss Willa Sibert Cather, who spoke Saturday afternoon before the Omaha Society of Fine Arts at the Fontenelle on the subject, "Standardization and Art."

Miss Cather told her audience that one of the things which retarded art in America was the indiscriminate Americanization work of overzealous patriots who implant into the foreign minds a distaste for all they have brought of value from their own country.

"The Americanization committee worker who persuades an old Bohemian housewife that it is better for her to feed her family out of tin cans instead of cooking them a steaming goose for dinner is committing a crime against art," declared Miss Cather, who kept her audience laughing and gasping at the daring but simple exposition she gave the meaning of art.

Laws which stifle personal liberty are forever a bar to the real development of art, Miss Cather insists.

"No Nebraska child now growing up will ever have a mastery of a foreign language," said Miss Cather, "because your legislature has made it a crime to teach a foreign language to a child in its formative years—the only period when it can really lay a foundation for a thorough understanding of a foreign tongue.

"Why," she added, "your laws are so rigid in Nebraska that a Nebraska farm boy can't stage a wrestling match in his barn unless he gives the state a minute description of himself and pays five dollars. One may receive a permit to travel all over France for $1.50, for a year, but a Nebraska farmboy has to pay five dollars to wrestle in his barn."

OW-H, 30 October 1921.

STATE LAWS ARE CRAMPING

Miss Willa Cather is expected to come to Lincoln Monday afternoon from Omaha where she has given several addresses. She will be a guest at the home of Mr. and Mrs. Max Westermann for a couple of days, leaving for New York, Wednesday. Miss Cather had much to say of Nebraska's "cramping laws" in her lecture at the Fontenelle hotel.

"Nebraska is particularly blessed with laws calculated to regulate the personal life of her citizens," said Miss Cather according to an Omaha report. "They are not laws that trample you underfoot and crush you but laws that just sort of cramp one. Laws that put the state on a plane between despotism and personal liberty.

"Why, it costs two farm boys five dollars and the filling out of a questionnaire as long as your arm if they want to go out in the barn loft and hold a wrestling match for the neighbors after the day's work is done. It costs them five dollars, and you can get a passport good for a year in France for $1.50."

Miss Cather denounced the language law vehemently, declaring that no child born in Nebraska can hope to gain a fluent speaking knowledge of a foreign language because the languages are barred from the schools under the eighth grade.

"Will it make a boy or a girl any less American to know one or two other languages?" she asked. "According to that sort of argument, your one hundred percent American would be a deaf mute."

"Art can find no place in such an atmosphere as these laws create," declared Miss Cather. "Art must have freedom. Some people seem afraid to say or do anything that is the least bit different from the things everyone else says and does. They think anything irregular is naughty. It was an irregular thing that Father Damien did when he went to the South Sea islands to devote his life to helping the poor lepers. That was just as irregular as any of the reported antics of James A. Stillman—more irregular, indeed, because it was so much rarer! Yet we don't censure Father Damien for his noble work."

Miss Cather added that "cookery is one of the fundamentals of true art," and declared that "any American housewife who teaches her good Bohemian or other foreign neighbor that it is as well for her to feed her family off a can of salmon as a roast goose is committing a crime against Americanism and art.

"Too many women are trying to take short cuts to everything," she said. "They take short cuts in their housework, short cuts in their reading—short cuts, short cuts. We have music by machines, we travel by machines—soon we will be having machines to do our thinking. There are no short cuts in art. Art has nothing to do with smartness. Times may change, inventions may alter a world, but birth, love, maternity, and death cannot be changed."

Lincoln Evening State Journal, 31 October 1921.

NEBRASKA SCORED FOR ITS MANY LAWS BY WILLA CATHER

by Myrtle Mason

Miss Willa Cather, noted authoress, spoke before the Omaha Society of Fine Arts Saturday afternoon at the Fontenelle hotel. The subject doesn't matter.

"I am not a public speaker," said Miss Cather, and perhaps she is not. That, too, does not matter.

What does matter very much is that she is a great woman, and one feels it when she speaks as one knows it when she writes.

She sounded all her "r's" speaking in a rich, incisive voice. She was gowned with the good taste any woman in a small Nebraska town might show, but with no suggestion of Fifth Avenue shops. Utter absence of superficiality was there in Willa Cather. As a true perceiver of the true art, did she impress her audience. Miss Cather calls Red Cloud, Nebraska, where her parents are, home, despite years of residence in New York and abroad.

"Nebraska is not as propitious" a place for an artist as it was twenty years ago, she declared, adding that the same is true of the entire country. Among the things she named as having "helped retard art" are: standardization, indiscriminate Americanism, false conventions of thought and expression, aversion to taking pains, and superficial culture.

Speaking of standardization, she said: "Nebraska is particularly blessed with legislation that restricts personal liberty." The law forbidding instruction in foreign languages below the eighth grade and the anti-wrestling law were cited. "Everybody is afraid of not being standard. There is no snobbishness so cowardly as that which thinks the only way to be correct is to be like everyone else.

"Art is made out of the love of old and intimate things. We always underestimate the common things."

One common thing for which she made a plea was the cottonwood tree, against which she charged there is social prejudice. "They are not smart," she said.

"Art cannot live in an atmosphere of manufactured cheer, much less can it be born," Miss Cather declared in a brief discussion of the "Sunny Jim" and "Pollyanna schools" of "grape nuts" optimism.

"Life is a struggle or a torpor. All art must be serious, and comedy is the most serious of all. Art and religion express the same thing in us, — that hunger for beauty that we, of all animals, have.

"It has been said, 'Genius is the capacity for taking pains,'" she quoted. "Art is taking the pains for the love of it; art is just taking pains. A man must be made for his art; he must work for it, and he must work intelligently. Art thrives best where the personal life is richest, fullest, and warmest, from the kitchen up."

Letters are a "dead form of love," she stated, in referring to the warm details of life we are omitting to save time. "Time for what?" she asked.

"The poorest approach to art yet discovered is by way of the encyclopedia," Miss Cather told her audience.

"The greatest love of art we have is among simple, earnest people who love the natural things."

Amid the "money madness, the movies, and machine-made music" we have today, Miss Cather has a hope born on Armistice day. "The war developed a new look in the faces of people," she concluded, "a look like the pioneers used to have when they were conquering the soil. A new color was over the land. I cannot name it," she said. "But it was the color of glory."

Omaha Bee, 30 and 31 October 1921.

"DON'T IMITATE" IS ADVICE OF NOVELIST

"Don't try to imitate New York," was the plea of Willa Sibert Cather, Nebraska author, at a dinner given in her honor by the Nebraska League of Women Voters at the Brandeis tea room last night.

"It seems to me as I travel out through the great middle west, the people are trying to imitate New York," said Miss Cather. Red Cloud and Hastings are trying to be like Omaha; Omaha and Chicago are trying to be like New York. One thing I like about New York is that there we wear the kind of hats we like, we wear the kind of clothes that please us."

Miss Cather urged that cities develop individuality. "I wish that I could see across the continent a string of cities having their own particular kind of life, as the cities of the old world," she declared. "Does Marseilles try to be like Paris? Does Bordeaux try to be like Paris? Do Venice and Naples try to be like Rome? The people of Bordeaux are proud of their own dinner hour. They are proud of their own cooking."

OW-H, 30 October 1921.

PEOPLE YOU KNOW

Miss Willa Cather was the guest of honor at a dinner given Saturday evening by the Omaha branch of the League of Women Voters at the Brandeis tea room at Omaha. About two hundred were present. Miss Cather was the principal speaker. She criticized western towns for trying to duplicate New York in dress and manners. She urged the women to be more independent and not follow Chicago or New York. They should be more original. . . .

At the afternoon meeting of the Omaha league, Miss Cather attacked the Nebraska boxing law, criticizing it severely, and also the language law, saying of the latter that in a short time the children of Nebraska would know no other language than English and be only partially educated. She said there were too many repressive laws in Nebraska.

NSJ, 30 October 1921.

EVERY MAN A KING

by Harvey Newbranch

Why shouldn't we imitate?

This question may well be asked in view of the advice given by Willa Sibert Cather, distinguished Nebraska author, in her lecture here.

"It seems to me as I travel out through the great middle west, the people are trying to imitate New York," Miss Cather said. Her observing eyes have seen the smaller cities aping the greater. And she pleads for development of individuality.

If New York is successful and truly great, would it not be proper to copy that city's industry, gaiety, seriousness, and sadness? Should we not even imitate a great personality?

Decidedly not. Imitations are never the original. And counterfeits are an abomination. Monkeys imitate; so do children until they grow up and learn to reason. Intelligence seeks the cause and tries to discover principles. Where there is complete agreement between an individual's standards and those of his community, it is proper for him to conform. But he cannot agree with custom that is opposed to his essential ideas of what is right without becoming an improper person.

The proper person seeks full expression of the essential qualities of his being. If a community or even the world does not give him room, he is apt to be called an improper person. But so long as he remains sincere and devoted to the standard of what he considers correct, he is proper to himself even if he is not to the community standard.

To men who are really proper, the race owes whatever progress it has made. The so-called "proper" person, who bows to conventional modes of conduct because it is considered right, regardless of whether it is, is among the host of imitators who contribute nothing to progress.

When the race, the community, or the individual becomes more interested in discovering principles that are eternal, many old customs will be reverenced more highly; many will be abandoned and viewed as moss-grown ruins of the medieval age.

The desire must be to discover the spirit that made men, cities, and nations great. And again, tradition must be challenged in the reputation it has given outstanding men. The individualist travels a rugged road. Perhaps it is best so. The imitator of others may travel a safer and easier road, but he is not entitled to wear the crown jewels.

Miss Cather, as Omaha had an opportunity to learn during her short visit, practices what she preaches. She had the courage to be simply and frankly herself. She proclaims the truth as she believes it, serenely indifferent whether her angle of vision be that of the multitude or not. She does not strive to make "a good impression" in the conventional sense. She would scorn to resort to protective coloration. Her passion is to express herself, to reveal, as she sees it, human life with its joys and sorrows, its frailties and beauty, its needs, its aspirations, its rights that dignify it, honestly and with candor.

It is this essential integrity of mind and soul that has made it possible for Willa Cather to do work worthwhile, work that will live. The world is surfeited with people who do not care to be themselves, who are afraid to trust their own minds, who let others do their thinking for them, and regulate their living for them, and form their flabby characters for them. Whether writers or what not, they count in the census figures and in doing the necessary humdrum work of the world—and that is about all that they count. Progress toward beauty and truth depends on those who know themselves and are themselves, who carry their hearts on their sleeves.

Nebraska may well be proud of Willa Cather. She is sprung from its soil. She was taught in its schools. Her soul was given texture and form on its sweeping plains, unde its clear skies, in contact with the hardy pioneers who subdued its frontiers. And her voice, at once brave and tender in its sympathy, is like a refreshing breeze from its illimitable spaces, carrying invigoration for every human life where cowardice and cant and hypocrisy have wrought their soul-destroying work.

O W-H, November 1921.

1925: BRUNSWICK, MAINE

In May 1925, Bowdoin College commemorated the centennial year of a class that included Henry Wadsworth Longfellow and Nathaniel Hawthorne with "An Institute of Modern Literature." Mrs. Helen Hartley Jenkins of New York City provided most of the necessary funds in memory of her daughter. The Soci-

The Program of
The Institute of Modern Literature

Monday, May 4, 8.15 P.M.

Robert Frost—"Vocal Imagination"

Tuesday, May 5, 1.15 P.M.

Edna St. Vincent Millay—Readings from her poems

Wednesday, May 6, 8.15 P.M.

Hatcher Hughes—"Modern Tendencies in the American Drama"

Thursday, May 7, 8.15 P.M.

Margaret Deland—"Some Ways of Writing Short Stories"

Friday, May 8, 8.15 P.M.

Carl Sandburg—"Romanticism and Realism in Modern Poetry"

Saturday, May 9, 8.15 P.M.

James Stephens—"Gaelic Literature"

Monday, May 11, 8.15 P.M.

Henry Seidel Canby—"Hawthorne"

Tuesday, May 12, 8.15 P.M.

Irving Babbitt—"The Primitivism of Wordsworth"

Wednesday, May 13, 8.15 P.M.

Willa Cather—"The Talk About Technique"

Thursday, May 14, 3.00 P.M.

Professor Edmond Estève—(Lecture in French)—"Longfellow in France"

Thursday, May 14, 8.15 P.M.

John Roderigo Dos Passos—"The Modern Drama"

Friday, May 15, 8.15 P.M.

Christopher Morley—"The Phantasy Aspect of Literature"

Round Table Conferences Were Conducted By Each Lecturer On
The Morning Following His Lecture Which Were
Open Only To Bowdoin Undergraduates

Willa Cather spoke at the Institute of
Modern Literature at Bowdoin College in 1926

ety of Bowdoin Women provided one of the lectures—Willa Cather's. The institute was an ambitious undertaking that ran from Monday evening, May 4, until Friday evening, May 15, and included a number of notable literary figures, among them Robert Frost, Edna St. Vincent Millay, Carl Sandburg, Henry Seidel Canby, Irving Babbitt, John Dos Passos, and Cather. The afternoon and evening lectures were open to the public; on the following morning, the lecturer held a discussion that was open only to Bowdoin students.

Cather's speech at 8:15 p.m. on Wednesday, 13 May, was reported by the Christian Science Monitor, *at considerable length and by the* Boston Globe *on the following day.* ☞

MENACE TO CULTURE IN CINEMA AND RADIO SEEN BY MISS CATHER

Brunswick, Me., May 14—Willa Cather, whom critics have accorded a rare place as technician and artist in the field of the novel, reluctantly discussed technique in the novel here last evening before the Institute of Modern Literature. Reluctantly because she is a novelist who believes that there has already been too much talk about technique, who says that the only place where she never hears any discussion of it, any suggestion that such a thing actually exists, is among writers, and that therefore she felt she might not bring to the subject such sympathy and knowledge as had been expected of her.

Professor Frederick Brown introduced Miss Cather, whose lecture was arranged by the generosity of the Society of Bowdoin Women. Professor Brown paid tribute to Miss Cather's unremitting effort in editing the Mayflower edition of the poems of Sarah Orne Jewett, upon whom Bowdoin College conferred an honorary degree, and identified Miss Jewett as Miss Cather's literary mentor. Professor Brown felt that the upholding of a sound and beautiful tradition in American letters had been in considerable measure due to Miss Cather.

Miss Cather did not proceed with her formal talk until she had paid tribute to Miss Jewett. "I want to confirm the saying of Professor Brown as to my purpose in coming here," she said. "Longfellow and Hawthorne, whose commencement anniversaries you celebrate, did not bring me here. After all, Longfellow and Hawthorne both undoubtedly had good credits, and, therefore, they had to graduate from Bowdoin College. But this institution did not have to confer a degree upon Sarah Orne Jewett, so fine an artist, among the foremost in this country. And by conferring the degree Bowdoin College placed itself irrevocably on the side of the highest tradition in American letters. I have come, therefore, to express my gratitude to Bowdoin College.''

There was a space of silence. Sarah Orne Jewett's friends were in the audience. Her sister was there. Maine knew and loved Miss Jewett, and the institute paid her thus its tribute of honor and grateful memory.

Miss Cather took up her subject:

The subject is so big that the best thing to do would be to wish you good-night and not speak at all. On the novel in general I have rather pessimistic views, I think. I sometimes think the modern novel, the cinema, and the radio form an equal menace to human culture. The novel has resolved into a human convenience to be bought and thrown away at the end of a journey. The cinema has had an almost devastating effect on the theater. Playwriting goes on about as well as usual, but the cheap and easy substitutes for art are the enemies of art. Illiteracy was never an enemy of art. In the old days all forms of literature appealed to the small select audiences. I tried to get Longfellow's *Golden Legend* in Portland this afternoon to send away to my niece. The bookseller said he didn't have it and would not sell it if he did. He said he was cutting out all his two dollar books because people wanted Zane Grey and such.

At its best the novel has warmth and nearness to us all. Perhaps the novel has become too democratic, too easy to write. The language of the novel is a common language, known to everyone. Among fifty friends there may be many who know they have not much culture in music or art, but if your friends are like mine every one of such a number believes himself a final authority on the novel and quite capable, if he had a minute, to sit down and write one.

Back in the beginning of art, when art was intertwined inseparably with religion, there had to be great preparation for its ceremonials. The creature who hoped for an uplifted moment often endured privation in preparation for that moment. I do not think we should sit at home, in the clothes in which we have been working all day, and turn on the radio to hear the Boston Symphony. I think something more than passivity should be expected of the recipient of any such bounty as Brahms.

There is much talk in the critical magazines and in colleges about the technique of the novel. I never hear the talk among writers. Sometimes I think it is something the critics invented for the sake of argument. Of course there are several things that do make up what people mean by ''technique,'' this thing about which young professors talk so much.

I suppose plot is a part of technique. There are two kinds of novel writing.

One affects the plot a lot, the other not at all. Critics and teachers, I think, do not realize that they often pull one kind over into the other. Shakespeare thought so little of plot that he never made one, but even in him there is always a spiritual plot inside the crude, coarse, often violent plot he borrowed from Plutarch or someone else. He never cared where he got his plots. Sometimes the spiritual and crude plots fuse beautifully, as in *Othello*. All the lovely writing in *A Winter's Tale,* on the contrary, is in the pastoral places. It is manifestly wrong to consider plot as an essential part of the novel, when the writer has obviously not considered it.

Then there is characterization. I have found chapters and chapters on characterization in text books intended to be read by young people who did not know how to discriminate between the uses of ''which'' and ''that,'' iniquitous chapters certain to destroy true skill. Characterization is not an adroit process. It is difficult because it is so simple. The characters we want most to present are the characters whose charm we have felt most strongly.

Hate is a fruitful emotion, but it has not produced great literature. Dante's *Inferno* and the whole *Commedia* is inverted evil, hatred of evil because of the love of good. The great characters in literature are born out of love, often out of some beautiful experience of the writer. There is clumsiness and adroitness in everything. But when I hear speakers telling how characterization was done I feel they are going afar.

Atmosphere was invaluable to the novel before it was called that or had a name. Atmosphere should be felt and not heard. It has been overdone by the method of exploitation. Thomas Hardy understood atmosphere as perhaps few writers have, but Hardy's atmosphere is never obtrusive. It is like the sea on your Maine shore — always there. It is not my intention, however, to abuse my fellow writers.

Another thing we do not hear as much about, but which is very important, is the writer's relation to his material. Not only his emotional, moral, and spiritual relation, but his physical relation to it. The writer of a novel must decide at the outset upon his viewpoint. It is as important as the engineer's deciding on the strain of a bridge. And his relation to it may not constantly change without serious faults of form and coherency. I think there is frequently a too facetious relationship to material. Almost no writer dares write except as if he had something to sell.

Ah, if only there were such a thing as technique. The violinist makes his language by his technique. The actor by his. Pavlowa practices technique each day when she is at sea. I have watched her. . . . But what can the writer do? Pot hooks? Hangers? There is nothing so valueless as good writing. If he wrote a good book two years ago he cannot go back and write it over. The novel must vary between excitement, which has its value, and that purer beauty which satisfies us like an old Grecian urn. But let us not talk overly about technique which will divest the novel of its best quality. The author who writes to please, not his publisher or the critics, but himself, first comes close, I believe, to what the novel should be. It is not a perfect way, but it is good.

Christian Science Monitor, 14 May 1925.

THREE MENACES TO HUMAN CULTURE
Willa Cather Names Them in Bowdoin Lecture

The modern novel, the motion picture, and the radio are a menace to human culture, declared Willa Cather, the author, in a lecture last evening on "The Talk About Technique" at the Bowdoin College Institute of Modern Literature.

Miss Cather was introduced by Prof. Frederic W. Brown, who said that she came to the institute as a tribute to Sarah Orne Jewett, for whom she had for many years had the greatest admiration, and who has been one of the few women to receive an honorary degree from Bowdoin. The lectureship for the evening was made possible by the society of Bowdoin women.

In opening her lecture Miss Cather said that it was good fortune rather than any special merit that made Bowdoin the Alma Mater of Longfellow and Hawthorne, but in the case of Sarah Orne Jewett it was a case of selection.

Regarding the novel in general, Miss Cather said that she had rather pessimistic feelings. The present-day novel was largely used as an aid to travelers, she said, to assist them in passing the time while riding from place to place.

"The novel, as we know it today, is the child of democracy, and is not a high form of art. A novel today partakes of all of our infirmities. The novel is too easy to write and too easy to read. You join a group of a dozen friends and you will find some one who cannot pass on music or a painting, but who does not hesitate to criticize a novel, and most of the group feel that they could write one.

"In critical magazines, at dinners, and at women's colleges one hears much talk about technique, but you never hear it mentioned or talked of by writers. Young critics and young professors usually have much to say about it to their classes.

"Atmosphere was just as effective before it had a name. It is only the writer's personal relation with the locality. It should be felt and not heard. The writer's relationship to his material is not only his emotional and moral relationship, but also his spiritual. Every thoughtful writer has to decide on his relationship as necessarily as the architect has to figure the strain on a bridge. It is really a technical matter in which the fine artist excels and the clumsy one remains clumsy.

"Technique, as it applies to a novel, is full of faults, as nearly all great novels have great blemishes from the standpoint of technique. Novels live by their plusses, not by their minuses. They live because of what they have, not because of what they lack. You cannot improve on the technique of a great writer, because his faults are necessary. Laboratory methods are best in science, but have not place in art."

In closing, she mentioned *Carmen,* which she characterized as one of the greatest love stories of all times.

Special Dispatch to the *Boston Evening Globe,* 14 May 1925.

The proceedings of the Bowdoin conference were finally recorded in book form in 1926. An Institute of Modern Literature *contained the full text of the introductory remarks made by the president of Bowdoin College, Kenneth C. M. Sills; an address on Hawthorne and Longfellow given by Bliss Perry of Harvard; an address on "The Class of 1825" by Edward Page Mitchell, class of 1871; and a series of articles by Arthur G. Staples on the various speeches, which appeared originally in the* Lewiston (Maine) Evening Journal. *These articles were introduced by "A Statement of Fact", which pointed out that such hurried writing against newspaper deadlines "assures nothing except freedom from guile and utmost candor." Apparently the book was prepared with the same velocity. The article about Cather's speech misspells her name in the title.*

Arthur G. Staples (1862–1940), Bowdoin, class of 1882, was editor of the Lewiston Evening Journal *for twenty-one years. He was employed by the paper for fifty-seven years. At the time of his death he was called "one of the best known newspaper men in the north-east"* (NYT, *3 April 1940, p. 23, col. 2). He was long active in the Republican party in Maine and served as a delegate to the Republican National Convention from 1904 to 1924.* ☞

WILLA CATHA—NOVELIST
What No One Knows about Technique.

by Arthur G. Staples

Willa Cather is substantial. She is a "Seventy-Four, Line of Battle," about which one may fancy the bumboats of the days of "Midshipman Easy" to be puttering, much as certain "best sellers" putter around the great artists today.

She spoke at the Bowdoin Institute at Brunswick, Wednesday evening, on the "Technique of the Novel," leaving the novel as she always does, "unfurnished" —just a place for a passion and a flame and an art that is artless.

Just to indicate what Maine thinks of Willa Cather, let us say that our patient folk gathered at Memorial Hall at Bowdoin College, hours before the opening of the lecture and half filled it as soon as the janitor had fumbled the key in the lock and turned on the lights. Here and there an industrious dame did her knitting or another did a crossword puzzle, or read a book. If Miss Cather were to come again and talk—even though it be on the most uninteresting of topics, "The Freudian Backlash of the Binomial Theorem," for instance, the old campus would be again filled with cars and the roads to her charming presence would be blocked.

These distinguished men and women may think it impertinent to describe them in print—but they must remember that they are as the coming of Barnum and Bailey to us after all. We have not heard so many lions roar in ages, up in Maine. Big and little lions of the race of the superlions. Some have piped in numbers; some have sung their ditties; all have desiccated art and left its disjected members as scraps for the housekeepers to take away, or serve as ordered.

But Miss Cather, without suggesting any discriminations or comparisons to the detriment of the most delightful and useful expositions of genius, which have preceded her, has left perhaps the most profound and enduring impression on this Institute. She has the gift of expression vocally, she has the poise of Womanliness, the modesty of self-negation and that indefinable thing called Charm.

"Why," said a young girl next to us, one seat behind, "I thought Willa Cather was a mere girl."

THAT is due to her name—"Willa" should never grow mature or substantial. "Willa" should always be girlish, dreamful, passionate and Edna Millayish. But instead, here is a woman of fifty, with a face of exquisite intellectuality and sensitiveness and a suggestion of capability, dignity, force, thought, culture and all those things that one finds in the faculties of SOME colleges. She looks as though she belonged in a home, head of a family and leading a "movement." Harriet Martineau, Mary A. Livermore—that sort.

And so natural and simple of method, and sweet of personality—well, one must be guarded in adjectives when one is rather carried off his feet.

A certain morning newspaper Thursday, opens its story of Miss Cather's address by saying, "Terming the modern novel as the commuter's convenience, Miss Cather denounced the novel, the cinema, and the radio as being menaces to human culture, all three being cheap and easy amusements to the degradation of æsthetic culture."

Surely Miss Cather "denounced" nothing. She never did at all. She does not find fault with sociological movements. She said these things casually, as one might say that the rain will spoil a new spring "bunnit;" but Miss Cather would not "denounce" the rain.

Her address, instead of "denouncing" the novel, ennobled it. She gave us the Novel Demeuble (there should be a couple of acute accents on that word Demeuble). She took away from the so-called modern novel, all of its plush furniture, its what-nots, its essential realisms (as for instance, why should one in telling of the love affairs of a butcher, relate the methods of killing beef-cattle and give recipes for making sausage?) and she left us the suggestion that the Art of the novel transcends that of any other form of expression in certain ways— chiefly as the theater for the play of emotions, or as she often said, instincts; not taken "straight," but flaring up like flames through the tale itself.

Miss Cather was introduced as speaking under the auspices of the Society of Bowdoin Women. Professor Brown, who has had much to do with the selection of speakers, said that perhaps even at that Miss Cather might not have come to Bowdoin, were she not the friend throughout life of Sarah Orne Jewett, an honorary alumnus of Bowdoin, and it was through affection towards this close friend that Miss Cather had been turned toward Maine.

The suggestions of Professor Brown were approved by Miss Cather as she came forward to the reading desk. She carried a silk bag in her hand, a "practical" bag, large enough to carry manuscript and other material which is none of our business. But we mention it because she took out a watch and laid it down and said, sotto voce, "A watch is the most essential part of a lecture." Miss Cather wore (being a man, I do not know about these things), but mother would have called it a "wrap" over a blouse of Persian orange silk or maybe it was not

Persian orange at all, and the wrap was trimmed with the same color and occas-
sionally slipped down over her shoulders, and Miss Cather would pull it back.
One person next in the settee along with me said it was a "Doctor's gown;" but
it was NOT. It was just what Miss Cather should have worn, and that shows how
far gone we are in adoration.

Miss Cather talked one hour and twenty-five minutes, and if you expect a
verbatim report of it or even a summary of it, you will have to go to some other
shop. I can not do it. Every sentence fitted into the next—even though Miss
Cather said it was desultory. And she said something all the while along lines
that she has said many times before in her writings and especially in her discussion of the Novel. These comments of hers on the novel are exactly on the same
basis of what an intelligent editor says of the newspaper.

It is much like what the Scotchman said of his third wife, recently wedded:
"She's a vairry good woman; but she's nae God's masterpiece." Miss Cather
is like an honest editor who worships the possibilities of the newspaper, yet
recognizes its shortcomings. And Miss Cather has been an editor; has grubbed
along the line of reporters and has known the gray of the morning when the
paper was closed and tight, as perhaps was the sporting editor.

In short, Miss Cather seeks to strip the Novel of its extra and inessential
furnishings and set it up as we have said—the four walls and place for plain
furnishings out of one's own intellectual, physical, spiritual stock.

Her lecture opened with a tribute to Sarah Orne Jewett, her friend. She said
it was an accident that Longfellow and Hawthorne were graduated from Bowdoin. They had to be graduated; their marks were all right. But Bowdoin chose
Sarah Orne Jewett to be an honorary alumnus and that is to Bowdoin's credit.
Here was selection.

Miss Cather began her theme of the Novel with reference to the belief of
some scientists who are pessimistic regarding endurance of human life on
earth, that the end will come by the ultimate domination of insect life—the bug
and the parasite will kill.

The analogy of this with the endurance of Art, especially æstheticisms, is
apparent. Art may be killed by the insect world of its own. The cinema is killing
the theater, i.e., the art of the actor; the radio is killing the lecture; the novel of a
certain sort may be killing the greater literature. The novel is the child of democracy. It is the commuter's convenience. But all search of true art and æsthetics
requires some preparation. One must get himself into a proper state of mind.
One does not sit down in his business suit or her kitchen dress to listen in at the

radio to hear a symphony concert by the Boston Symphony. It requires a certain mental house-cleaning and that is reached by regaining one's equanimity, or a change of garb, or a moment's reading or contemplation.

In old days, literature appealed to a small audience. Miss Cather had stopped at a bookseller's in Portland to buy Longfellow's *Golden Legend*—she used to read it and love it—but the bookseller said that he did not keep such books; as a matter of fact, he was about through selling anything over $2 books—all they want is Zane Grey—at which the undergraduates "wooded up" on the stage and Miss Cather turned and smiled with appreciation at the students—for she, too, has been a schoolmarm.

Machine labor has done old-fashioned thoroughness to the death. The man who made a perfect shoe or a perfect chair was an artist. He put self into it—and that is what makes the artist of the novel. Machine made shoes, machine made chairs, machine made art or machine made novels are not æsthetic. The expert craftsman had to be educated; had to have æsthetic education—even though he did not read or write.

Education is merely learning to do things well. It is better than a superficial education of the land. Old-fashioned people either did not read at all or they read the Bible and the Almanac. The modern novel is the child of the democracy; the old-fashioned novel dealt with courts and pageants; they were tales of another life, whereas the modern novel dealing with its subjects as it does, cannot be the highest form of Art. It can never satisfy the æsthetic longing as does Keats' *Ode to a Greek Urn*. The modern novel is a hybrid—a Castor and Pollux, half of the time in the stars and half in the grubby earth.

You see how far Miss Cather's lecture transcends the limits of any abstract or description. It was a constant reflection of intellectual consideration of many problems of society and literature. The novel manufactured to entertain great multitudes must be considered exactly as one considers other merchantable matters—soap or perfume or cheap furniture. Fine quality is a distinct disadvantage in articles made for great numbers of people to be sold to those who want change rather than a thing that wears.

After this and more of prelude, Miss Cather began on the stated subject of her lecture, "Technique." Really she knew nothing about it. Technique is an overlay. She had never heard a writer discuss it and she had been much among them. It is never mentioned. It is reserved for teachers of rhetoric and novel-writing among young professors in colleges and among critics. They use it. She seemingly had no objection—if they knew what it was. She wished them well.

There is technique in violin playing or in acting. Later on, in the address,

Miss Cather referred to this with some pathos and sadness. The violinist may arise after a bad night and yet play right on—that's technique; practice on a single theme and in a fixed manner.

The actor may have met a tragic hour, and his mind be far away; but he goes along because he has the technique. But the writer cannot. What he did yesterday counts nothing. He must not repeat. He must not even play his tunes or tell his tales in the same way. There is no technique, for him. His sole duty is to put *himself* on the paper, and yet he may be absent of mind or suffering of body.

The "Spiritual Plot"

Plot—that is heard much of among critics and is discussed by the book-makers on such subjects. They say "the plot shows poverty of invention." Great literature has no plot. There is no plot in Greek dramas. Shakespeare made no plots as such. He took a tale from Plutarch or Boccaccio or Chaucer and he added another plot to it. He had two plots, in fact, but they are not invention. The second was the spiritual plot. It is inside the rough plot of the tale. That was always a structure of his own. In some of his plays the two plots fuse into one— as in Othello. In others they do not fuse at all—as in Winter's Tale. We are not interested in the tale or the plot at all. We are interested in Perdita chiefly and that fair country. So it is wrong to consider plot where no plot is intended.

The Text-Book of Iniquities

There are text-books that are full of iniquities—awful things that deal with these matters. Miss Cather had recently picked up one that her niece had to use at public school. It required the child to name twelve instances where Silas Marner acted so and so and to state twelve more instances where Silas Marner suggests certain moral obliquities. We cannot remember these special twelve demands and have no need to remember them, but they amounted to a showing of the ridiculous sort of schoolmaster teaching that is going on. It made me think of Gerald Stanley Lee's old book, *The Lost Art of Reading,* in which the University of Chicago professor showed Keats how the *Ode to a Grecian Urn* should have been written. "If Shakespeare came to Chicago" he would be analyzed by some young chap who wanted to tell him how.

Characterization was similarly dealt with, as a matter of technique, and in speaking of this Miss Cather moved some more furniture—little of it real antique; most of it modern.

Nobody lays traps in writing a novel—nobody should. There is no technique of that sort. Characterization for instance is another word used by the critics. It is so simple; it is not adroit; it is not technique. What makes anyone want to present character? It is because it is interesting. Some unusual experience with someone makes one desire to present that character. It is primarily a matter of love. There is a literature of Hate—but Miss Cather passed it over, saying that it is minor and not productive, gives no pleasure, and all of the best examples such as Dante, are really negative love—hate depicted as a tribute to the paramountcy of love.

All great character depiction is born of love. There are no rules and no tricks about it. She spoke of a talk with a dear friend, George Arliss, the actor, regarding William Archer, a mutual friend, beloved by them. They talked about Archer and probably gave as fine a characterization of him as possible— no technique; just plain telling of reasons for loving him.

When her nephew comes to Miss Cather on the wharf as she comes from Europe, and tells her about the young lady to whom he has become engaged— her faults perhaps, her virtues surely, her charm, her loveliness, her winsomeness; he is doing characterization in a way to stump the novelist or technician.

What About Atmosphere?

Atmosphere. It was just as effective before it had a name. It may be said to be the personal relation of the artist with the country or the surroundings of which he is writing. Thomas Hardy had it—he knew how. Miss Cather spoke of another writer who tried to have it and did not get it. It is not a matter of notebooks. Local color is often a tight collar. People who are tone deaf as it were for the surroundings, should not attempt it. They dwell in the fog.

Then there is the most important thing—the novelist's own attitude— even his physical attitude; the point from which he proposes to look at his subject; for it looks different from different points of view.

This appertains also to spiritual and intellectual and moral viewpoints. There is much playing up of something to sell—much over joviality and sentimentalism on people who do not feel that way. It is enough to tell the tale simply. Nor is it well to write of instincts as if they were all. We do not care for these novels of nothing but amorous instincts. They are of value only when they flame up as volcanic fires through the crust. Miss Cather *did* give these a sound scoring. She mentioned a book wherein the amorous episodes of Anna Karenina were isolated and published—a flat, common love story of human weakness. But as it appears in Tolstoi's majestic tale, an incident growing out of environment tearing the upper crust of life—it is tragic.

Forget Technical Faults

Finally—for we must hurry on—technique is not the thing. All great novels are full of technical faults. Miss Cather mentioned them—*Les Miserables, Anna Karenina,* Turgenieff's works, *The Scarlet Letter*—full of them. Forget them. Read them for the depiction of the spiritual, mental, soulful life of the great genius that wrote them. Two books that she knew about were written by professors of colleges who had mastered technique. *You* have not read them. Nobody did.

Then to close up her thesis, Miss Cather told the story of Carmen, written without technique; carrying every fault that technicians would observe; yet undying. A love tale of immense tragic power. Not a kiss in it; not a love scene. So, too, she analyzed two forms of tales—Stevenson's *Kidnapped,* Conrad's *Nigger of the Narcissus,* and told how they violated all canons of technical art; but breathed the force and beauty of the artist.

Then Miss Cather looked at her watch and said, "O-o-o-h," and the audience broke into applause intended to encourage her to go on and on. She had been talking an hour and ten minutes.

She talked ten minutes more, about the finest things: Miss Jewett, Maine, the artist's technique of which we have spoken previously, such as the violinist's technique; Pavlowa's technique as contrasted with that of the writer and finally spoke of Marcelle Proust's great book that was majestic for three volumes and futility for the fourth and that yet would be immortal. She told of a talk with Joseph Hergesheimer about his recent book and closed all too soon with the tribute to Miss Jewett.

And then having moved all of the furniture of stuffiness out of the novel, she showed us the four walls, the theater of passion and of love, the playhouse of the personality of genius who shall make it noble if he himself is noble; despite plot or characterization, or atmosphere, or technique. It is just self projected into the æsthetic and artistic spectrum of human life.

An Institute of Modern Literature,
(Lewiston, Me: Lewiston Journal Co., 1926).

1925: CHICAGO

Following her speech at Bowdoin College in the late spring of 1925, Cather also accepted an invitation from Nathaniel Butler, assistant to the president of the University of Chicago, to give one of the William Vaughn Moody lectures there. She was quite nervous about the engagement and wrote to her old friend, Irene Miner Weisz, who lived in Chicago, asking her to make all the necessary arrangements for travel and lodging and to be with her at the lecture to hold her hand (ALS, Irene Miner Weisz, 4 November 1925, NLC).

The lecture was given on the evening of 17 November 1925 at Mandel Hall to what was called a capacity audience. She did not feel the speech went well and seemed to blame it upon the ugliness of the lecture hall. It made her feel wretched and caused her to stutter (ALS to Irene Miner Weisz, 20 November 1925, NLC). The lecture was reported by the Daily Maroon, *a university publication, and at greater length by the* Tribune.

Two days later, she left for Cleveland to fulfill another speaking engagement before the Cleveland Women's City Club (see Interviews, "1925: Cleveland"). That lecture went well, she felt, because the hall was lovely; the colors and soft lighting were relaxing, and the young, well-dressed audience—including several men—put her at ease (ALS to Irene Miner Weisz, 20 November 1925, NLC). ☞

"MACHINE-MADE" NOVEL DEPLORED

Prevalence of the "machine-made" novel was deplored by Willa Cather, noted writer, last night in a lecture on "The Tendencies of the Novel Today," before a capacity audience in Mandel Hall.

"A commuter's convenience" was one of the many terms which Miss Cather applied to the type of novel which she declared predominates today.

The beauty creating surge is not menaced so much by commercialism as by a "low form of itself," the authoress warned, condemning the importance attached to "plot" in the modern novel.

An optimistic outlook for the future of the novel was, however, expressed by Miss Cather.

Chicago Daily Maroon, 18 November 1925.

ART NOW ONLY RULE FOR WRITING NOVELS, WILLA CATHER SAYS

Willa Cather lectured this week at the University of Chicago on "The Tendency of the Modern Novel," and she said so many pertinent and important things that it seems only fair to share them with you who did not hear her. The novel— as an art form, as opposed to the machine-made novel—has changed, she said.

It has changed, for one thing, in the matter of length. It is as long now as the author believes it should be to express what he wishes to say, and it is, there- fore, either shorter than the old novel or longer, as the case demands. The rules of novel construction are not adhered to as they used to be.

She mentioned as an example *The Death of Ivan Ilych,* by Tolstoy, which begins with a funeral, proceeds to a vivid tale of Ivan's life, and ends with his death. According to all rules, such a technique is wrong. As art, it is right, she said. To have done that novel in any other way would have been as tragic and as silly as to have cut up a child and rearranged its members differently.

The novel is behind the other arts in that very matter, she said. A painter can see a pretty little clump of trees, and behind it the great cathedral, and, if the clump of trees allures him, he will paint his trees, sketch in the cathedral in its proper perspective, and go home pleased with himself. The novelist will see the clump of trees, but he is pressed to realize that behind them there is that great cathedral, and he is a rare artist who contents himself with his trees. The novel is like democracy, she said, with all of its virtues, but likewise all of its faults.

She spoke at length about the new freedom of subject matter. She voiced the belief that periods of the greatest freedom have never been periods of the greatest beauty in literary creation. The very fact that there are restrictions, things that one must not talk about, tends to make the art a richer one. That is also true of language, she said. There now are being used words which formerly were to be found only in patent medicine almanacs, and she bade her auditors beware of a language which had no bad words in it—and any word, by being generally used, ceases to be bad.

She said that the power to stir the reader erotically was the charge of dyna- mite which every great author had, but that, used to excess or even used without distinction, the charge lost every whit of its power.

"There is such a thing in life as nobility," she said, "and novels which celebrate it will always be the novels which are finally loved."

The novel of the future will be more experimental, she ventured. It will be more concerned with the emotional pattern of the characters than with the event pattern. Many happenings may be, as events, startingly important in a life, but they may leave a person almost cold emotionally. It is the true emotional pattern of his characters which the author will chart in the future. He will write about whatever makes an impact on his mind.

Chicago Daily Tribune, 21 November 1925.

1933: NEW YORK, NBC RADIO

The Pulitzer Prizes for 1932 were awarded at the dinner of the Friends of the Princeton Library at the Hotel Plaza in New York on 4 May 1933. Winners of the prizes in other years were asked to give brief addresses. Willa Cather was invited to represent fiction. She replied that she had not accepted an invitation to a public dinner for over three years but that she would be happy to attend the Princeton gala (ALS to Whitney Darrow, 24 January 1933, Darrow Collection, FLPU). As Herbert Putnam, librarian of Congress pointed out, the audience included "most of the crowned heads of literature" (NYT, 5 May 1933). Dr. William Lyon Phelps of Yale University was the toastmaster, and among the audience were Governor Wilbur Cross, Robert Frost, Hamlin Garland, Burton J. Hendrick, Ellen Glasgow, M. A. DeWolfe Howe, Morrie Ryskind, Walter Winchell, Ira Gershwin, and General John J. Pershing. Pershing, an instructor in mathematics and military science at the University of Nebraska during Cather's years there, had received a law degree the same year she graduated. He had been awarded the Pulitzer Prize for history in 1931. Stephen Vincent Benét, Edna Ferber, Zona Gale, Booth Tarkington, Thorton Wilder, E. A. Robinson, and George S. Kaufman were unable to attend (Whitney Darrow Collection, FLPU). Besides Cather, Elmer Rice represented drama; James Truslow Adams, history; Henry James, biography; and Robert Frost, poetry. The 1932 prizewinners were T. S. Stribling for fiction; Maxwell Anderson, drama; Allan Nevins, biography; Archibald MacLeish, poetry; and the late Frederick Jackson Turner, history.

The awards and the speeches were broadcast to a nationwide audience over the National Broadcasting Company. It was Cather's only radio speech and has never before been published. ☞

ON THE NOVEL

The novel, if it can be called a form of art, is a new arrival among the arts, and its most interesting developments are still to come. All the other arts are centuries older. Looking back over its short history, perhaps the most arresting thing one notices about the novel is its amazing elasticity and variety. Like the Tarnhelm which the Nibelungs made for Alberich, this lightly woven net of words has the power of transformation, can present a giant, a dragon, a mouse or a worm.

It is really astonishing what a long gallery of great books we must call novels for lack of a better word. *Anna Karenina* is a novel, and *Robinson Crusoe* is a novel. *Thais* is a novel, *The Pilgrim's Progress* and *Don Quixote* are novels. Because this is the most modern of literary forms, for the last three centuries the modern spirit has adopted it more often than any other. It gets, we say, nearer the people, great masses of people. It has a claim upon quick recognition, and suffers the penalty of speedy oblivion. The mediocre ones are soon forgotten, no matter what their momentary vogue may have been; and the very great ones, which survive, are seldom read; they are taken for granted.

Although this form of imaginative prose in its short history presents such a rich variety of subject matter, until very lately the American novelist has been confined, or has confined himself, to two themes; how the young man got his girl, whether by matrimony or otherwise, and how he succeeded in business. Whatever embellishments he brought into the fringes of his story, (dialect, local color, landscape gardening, historical padding), the real subject of his book must be one of these two themes; or, happily, both of them! The square-headed and determined young editor who declared that he would publish only stories of youth, love, and success, concisely announced a very general sentiment. Most people, and most editors, and most writers, sincerely believed that there were no other major motives in literature, and never had been. They believed that while architecture, painting, music, were concerned with so many aspects not only of human behavior but of human thought, and with all the mysterious experiences of the thing we call the soul, literature had been dedicated to the telling of these two stories over and over through the centuries. Of course only a people with very little background and very childish tastes could have any patience with such a shallow conception. How large a part do "youth, love, and success" play in the great Greek dramas? Or in the great epics? "Success" in our sense, never! In the Elizabethan drama these things have their place, certainly, along with all the other passions and motives and moods that govern the actions of men.

The great group of Russian novelists who flashed out in the north like a new constellation at about the middle of the last century did more for the future than they knew. They had no benumbing literary traditions behind them. They had a glorious language, new to literature, but old in human feeling and wisdom and suffering, and they were themselves men singularly direct and powerful, with sympathies as wide as humanity. They were all very big men, physically, (of rugged health, with the exception of Dostoevsky), and had no need to be continually defending their virility in print. Horse racing and dog racing and hunting are almost the best of Tolstoy. In Gogol, Turgenev, Lermontov, the earth speaks louder than the people.

That group of writers fixed the attention of every sensitive imagination the world over; the old icebergs began melting, the old forms began to break up. Joseph Conrad wrote *The Nigger of the Narcissus* without a woman in it, and no glory or promotions for anybody at the end of the voyage. Gradually our own writers began to look around them and see a few things in God's world. So long as their eyes were fixed on youth, love, and success they could see nothing whatever; they were like men being carried to the operating table; they were in a nervous chill because they knew they weren't always bubbling over with these three desirable things, and they wondered how long they could go on making the gesture. Constantly putting the accent in the same place is a terribly degrading habit for a writer. It makes his book a barrel organ tune, and him an organ grinder. Life isn't like that; it's so disconcertingly unexpected.

We have begun to look about us, but we have a long way to go. We cling to our old formulae; for the moment we stress the bad girl instead of the good, the rowdy who is kicked out of his great corporation instead of the smoothly polished young man who becomes its president. We won't face the fact that it's the formula itself which is pernicious, the frame-up.

When we learn to give our purpose the form that exactly clothes it and no more; when we make a form for every story instead of trying to crowd it into one of the stock moulds on the shelf, then we shall be on the right road, at least. We all start with something true, and then in the effort to make it bigger than it really is, we try to weld something false onto it; something delightful, usually, but that was not in the original impulse. . . .

The novel is the child of Democracy and of the coming years. There is a Latin inscription on the wall of the Luxembourg art gallery in Paris which expresses a sane and rational attitude toward Art. It reads something like this: "Because of the past, we have hope for the future." And we may say that for this latest and, not loveliest, child of the arts; From the past, from the Russian and the French and the English past, we may hope for the future.

Letters

1906-40

Willa Cather was a splendid letter writer. All the talent contained in her published works is evident in her personal correspondence as well. Yet she felt her letters to be quite different from the writing she did for publication. They were personal, not public, and often hurried and not revised. Following her feeling, her will absolutely restricts the publication of any of her correspondence. Cather's desire was that all of her correspondents destroy her letters after her death. Some did, but many others contributed the letters to various collections across the country. As a result, many of her letters are available to qualified scholars, but they may not be quoted directly. So they have often been paraphrased in an unavoidably slanted manner. Willa Cather always speaks in a clearer and more graceful style than anyone reporting on what she says.

An example of the strange results of the restriction placed on her letters is found in a curious footnote to an article in the March 1938 issue of American Literature *entitled "The Genius of Willa Cather." The author, Robert H. Footman, writes:*

> *Since I wrote these words, I have come across a relevant statement by Willa Cather, the source of which I am not at liberty to publish. She says: "In some books I have done more careful planning than in others, but al-*ways *the end was seen from the beginning, and in each case it was the end that I set out to reach—I mean, literally, the end of the story: not necessarily the scene, but the feeling of the end, the mood in which I should leave my characters and in which I myself should say good-by to them. But practically everything beside the central purpose or the central feeling comes spontaneously and unexpectedly, though they all grow out of the main theme and out of the feeling and experience that made me choose that theme. (138)*

Yehudi Menuhin quotes at length from two personal letters from Cather in his autobiography Unfinished Journey *(pp. 130 and 145). Others, while trying to respect her wishes, have come dangerously close to quotation, and some have paraphrased in a less than objective manner, at times distorting the actual content of the letters.*

However, Cather did write a number of letters intended for publication and allowed a few others to be published during her lifetime. Four of these were reprinted in On Writing. *Others have been reprinted on occasion in a variety of works.*

These letters, few though they are, frequently give new insights to Cather's theory of fiction and the art of writing. They whet the appetite in such a way that one can only hope her complete extant correspondence might be made available soon.

1906: PITTSBURGH

Willa Cather taught high school from 1901 to 1906. Her first position was at Central High School in Pittsburgh; two years later she transferred to Allegheny High School. Her students remembered her as a stimulating teacher, and one, Phyllis Martin Hutchinson, wrote: "She knew that the only way to learn to write was to write, and she set us to writing themes, one every class day, usually in the first ten or fifteen minutes of the period" ("Reminiscences of Willa Cather as a Teacher," Bulletin of the New York Public Library, *June 1956). During the summer vacations, at Christmastime, during the spring, and even after graduation, Cather entertained her students at tea in the McClung home. She was said to be interested always in what they were doing and if they liked it. One of her more famous students, Norman Foerster, the critic and teacher, said, "Her teaching seemed natural and human, but without contagious sparks." (Quoted in E. K. Brown,* Willa Cather: A Critical Biography, *p. 72).*

After S. S. McClure came to Pittsburgh to recruit Cather for his magazine she decided to leave teaching. At the end of the school year she wrote an open letter to her homeroom class that was printed in the Allegheny High School newspaper at the beginning of the next term. The letter was reprinted in Chrysalis: Willa Cather in Pittsburgh, 1896–1906, *by Kathleen D. Byrne and Richard C. Snyder (Pittsburgh: Historical Society of Western Pennsylvania, 1980).* ☞

FAREWELL TO STUDENTS

6 June 1906

Dear Boys and Girls:

Now that I find that I shall not return to the High School next fall, I have a word to say to you. A number of my pupils in various classes, and especially in my Reporting Class, asked me, when I came away, whether I should be with you next year. At that time I fully expected to be. The changes in my plans which will prevent my doing so have been sudden and unforeseen. I should hate to have you think that I had not answered you squarely when you were good enough to ask whether I should return, or to have you think that I put you off with an excuse.

I had made many plans for your Senior work next year and had hoped that we should enjoy that work together. I must now leave you to enjoy it alone. One always has to choose between good things it seems. So I turn to a work I love with very real regret that I must leave behind, for the time at least, a work I had come to love almost as well. But I much more regret having to take leave of so many students whom I feel are good friends of mine. As long as I stay in New York, I shall always be glad to see any of my students when they come to the city.

I wish you every success in your coming examinations and in your senior work next year.

Faithfully yours,
Willa Cather

Wah Hoo, September 1906.

1909: RED CLOUD

Although Cather's public school education was short and somewhat spotty, she always maintained a certain fondness for her days at the Red Cloud schools. Her respect for and friendship with Mr. and Mrs. A. K. Goudy was maintained for many years. Mrs. Goudy had been principal of the high school, and the two women corresponded for over forty years. Evangeline King was another long-time friend. Cather's short story, "The Best Years," employs Miss King as a model for Evangeline Knightly.

In 1909 Cather had made plans to visit Red Cloud and had agreed to make a few remarks at the high school commencement in May. S. S. McClure had other ideas and decided to send her to Europe to search out writers and manuscripts for his magazine. It was the first of many such trips she was to make for the publication.

Since she could not be present, she wrote a letter to Edwin James Overing, Jr., the president of the Board of Education, who had invited her to speak, asking that it be read at the ceremony in her stead. The complete letter was printed in the Red Cloud Chief *on 27 May 1909, and parts of the letter have been quoted in Bennett's* The World of Willa Cather *and Woodress's* Willa Cather: Her Life and Art. ☞

COMMENCEMENT PROGRAM CONTINUED FROM LAST WEEK

Mrs. Dora Kaley read the following letter from Miss Willa Cather which explains the reason for her inability to be in attendance here. Mrs. Kaley has a very pleasing manner of reading, and owing to her perfect articulation she could be easily heard in every part of the house.

April 30, 1909

My Dear Mr. Overing:

As I wrote you sometime ago, I had very much hoped to be present at the Red Cloud commencement exercises this year. I had made all my plans to go west about the first of May, and until a few days ago confidently expected to be at home by the time the school year closed.

Within the last two or three days, however, I have seen that instead of turning westward I must face in the opposite direction, and that very soon. I am sailing immediately for London to attend to some business matters there.

Since you asked me to go on the commencement program, I had expected to get something ready for you on my way west, but my hurried departure will not leave me time to prepare any sort of paper to send you. I would be glad to write something on the way over and send it back to you, but the time would be so short that in all probability anything mailed from England would not reach you before the 19th. Let me thank you for the invitation and ask you to express to the Board of Education my regret at being unable to accept it.

Since I cannot be present, therefore, I will ask you to let this letter represent me, if you see fit.

I have been interested in the Red Cloud schools for many years, and have kept in touch with them through so many brothers and sisters, that to think about them and wish them well has become a mental habit. I could not forget the schools if I tried; they play a part in many of my happiest memories, and some of my truest friends have been closely connected with them. If I had no other reason to love the schools of my own town—and I have many others—I should always love them because of Mr. and Mrs. A. K. Goudy and Mr. and Mrs. O. C. Case. When my father first moved into Red Cloud from his ranch, and I was taken to the old high school building to be entered as a pupil in the Red Cloud schools, Mrs. Case—then Miss King—was principal, and she was the first person who interviewed the new county pupil. She had a talk with me up in the old bell room. I remember her well as a stalwart young woman with a great deal of mirth in her eyes and a very sympathetic, kind voice.

I was placed in a class in Miss Gertrude Sherer's room. I do not remember much about what went on during my first day in school, but that afternoon I brought away three distinct impressions: that Trix Mizer was the prettiest little girl I had ever seen, that Margie Miner was so jolly I wanted awfully to know her, and that Eddie Emigh never looked at his book because he was always looking at Trix.

The next year Miss King was made principal of the South Ward School, and I was a pupil in her *A* grade. I am very sure that Miss King was the first person whom I ever cared a great deal for outside of my own family. I had been in her class only a few weeks when I wanted more than anything else in the world to please her. During the rest of that year, when I succeeded in pleasing her I was quite happy; when I failed to please her there was only one thing I cared about, and that was to try again and make her forget my mistakes. I have always looked back on that year as one of the happiest I ever spent.

After I left Miss King's room she became County Superintendent. As I went on through the high school she always helped and advised me; she even tried very hard to teach me algebra at night, but not even Miss King—who could do almost anything—could do that.

After I went away to the State University there came a year or two when I was so taken up with new things and people, and so much excited about my work in Lincoln, that I saw comparatively little of my old friends. Just before I went away to school Miss King had married Mr. Case, and when I began to see a good deal of my old friends again, I learned to care for Mr. Case almost as much as for his wife.

I believe I am not the only graduate of the Red Cloud schools whose courage Mr. and Mrs. Case revived time and again. I believe that all the boys and girls whom they helped will agree with me that one of the things best worthwhile in life is to keep faith with those two friends of ours who gave us their confidence. In the long summer evenings Mr. Case and his wife used to sit on the front porch behind the vines and the little maple trees and plan out useful and honorable futures for the Red Cloud boys and girls. There is nothing for us to do now but to try to realize those generous dreams of theirs.

I can scarcely realize that it has been nineteen years since I stood on the stage in the Red Cloud opera house with two little boys—if I remember rightly we all three looked like little boys—and made my Commencement speech. Let me warn the graduates of 1909 that the next nineteen years will go so quickly that they won't have time to turn around in them.

The thing I best remember about my own graduation is the class tree. It was a little crook-backed honey locust that Alec Bentley and John Tulleys dug out of a row of locusts on my Grandmother Cather's land. I don't know why I was more interested in the tree than in any thing else about graduating, but I was. My brothers and I carried water from the High School pump and watered it ever so many times that summer. The tree wilted and peaked and pined and languished all summer. But look out for what it would do next summer, we thought. But next summer it was no better, nor yet the next. The thing simply would not grow. For years it seemed to stand still. For the matter of that we all stood still; John didn't grow, and Alec didn't grow, and I didn't grow. But the tree, at least, was getting ready to grow. I went home one summer to find that after having been a crooked bush for years and years it had really shot up to a considerable height. The tree stands in the south-east corner of the High School yard, and I hope the Red Cloud boys and girls will be good to it.

I hope none of your graduates tonight are as much frightened as I was when I got up to deliver my important oration. When Mr. Goudy read my name and I rose and went to the front of the platform, the room looked as if it were full of smoke, and the people seemed to have run together. I looked at this blur and made out three faces looking intently at me: Mr. Henry Cook in the front part of the house, and further back, Mr. William Ducker and Mrs. Case. These three friendly faces gave me courage, and I am sure they always will.

With a world of good wishes for your graduates, Mr. Overing, and greetings to my old schoolmates, I am,

Faithfully,
Willa Cather   *Red Cloud Chief*, 27 May 1909.

1922: ST. PAUL

Thomas Alexander Boyd (1898–1935) was a journalist, editor, biographer, and novelist. Following service in World War I, he became a reporter for a St. Paul, Minnesota, newspaper and later became literary editor of the St. Paul Daily News, *where his weekly column, "The Literary Punchbowl," produced a lively exchange of ideas. On 12 February 1922, the literary page of the* Daily News *ran a large picture of Willa Cather next to Boyd's editorial, "A Revaluation." In that editorial, Boyd called for a redefinition of the term* novel. *He claimed that satire, romance, extravaganzas, tracts, and picturesque stories were all being called novels, and that such sweeping inclusion was misleading. The true novelist was not, in Boyd's opinion, to have any underlying motive in his fiction writing: "To be a novelist the writer must make of himself the sounding-board of life. Complete objectivity should be his aim and to his work he must bring boundless observation. Willa Cather once said that the effect produced by the sight of an orange lying on a green table cover was sufficiently striking. A number eleven shoe set beside the orange would be incongruous" (p. 6). Boyd went on to say that the novelist should not make use of actual experiences; that would make it peculiar to one person and not pertinent to a larger audience. "To be a true novelist—the sounding-board—the novelist must be content with a certain self-effacement." Objectivity would lead to humility.*

He concluded the column with the definitions of a novel as found in the Encyclopedia Britannica *and* Webster's Standard Dictionary.

Whether Cather was a regular reader of the St. Paul Daily News *is not known. Perhaps it was her picture on the page and the reference to her in the column that caused the article to be called to her attention. She responded to the ideas presented by Boyd in a letter that was printed in "The Literary Punchbowl" on 5 March 1922.* ☞

ON LITERALNESS

In your editorial "A Revaluation" all that you say is true, and yet I do not think you make it clear why it is true. Of course a writer of imaginative literature must not be literal; he must be *able* to be literal; he must know everything he touches well enough for that. But if he is an artist he will not be literal, because no artist can be. If he has the proper equipment to be a writer of fiction at all, he will never have to puzzle as to how far he should be literal; he has a selective machine in his brain that decides all that for him. If he has not such an instrument, he had better choose another profession.

An artist uses any particular scene or incident not to show how much he knows about it, or because it is in itself interesting. He uses it because of a certain effect of color or emotion that will contribute to his story as a whole, because it is in the mood of the story, or helps to make the mood. Therefore, in writing this scene, he will use as much detail as will convey his impression, no more. . . . The writer does not 'efface' himself, as you say; he loses himself in the amplitude of his impressions, and in the exciting business of finding all his memories, long-forgotten scenes and faces, running off his pen, as if they were in the ink, and not in his brain at all.

St. Paul Daily News, 5 March 1922.

1925: LONDON

Although Willa Cather's first published book was a collection of poetry, April Twilights, *in 1903, that was not the genre for which she became famous. She had begun writing poetry for publication in 1892. Bernice Slote has outlined her career as a poet in considerable detail in her introduction to* April Twilights (1903), Revised Edition *(Lincoln: University of Nebraska Press, 1968). Cather selected and revised poems from the first collection to be included in her 1923* April Twilights and Other Poems *and again in the 1937 version in her collected works. But as Slote points out,* "April Twilights *of 1903 marks the virtual end of Cather's writing of poetry." Her letter to Alice Hunt Bartlett makes it clear that poetry was of little interest to her creative energies by 1925.*

Alice Hunt Bartlett (1869–1949) was the American editor of the Poetry Review *of London for nearly thirty years, having become interested in poetry after the death of her husband, Dr. William Allen Bartlett, in 1921. In 1924 she received the gold medal of the Poetry Society of Great Britain. She was a vice president of the Poetry Society of London and was involved in numerous literary societies in England and the United States. The American poetry section of the* Review *was her creation, and the eleventh segment included Emily Dickinson and Robert Hillyer, besides Cather. Mrs. Bartlett's historical drama,* Washington Pre-eminent, *was chosen as the basis for the pageant held in the nation's capital celebrating the bicentennial of the birth of George Washington in 1932.*

The introductory material is quite familiar, even though the chronology of certain portions of Cather's life is somewhat telescoped. The complete article also reprinted "In Rose Time," portions of "A Likeness," "A Silver Cup," "Going Home," "Macon Prairie," and the entirety of "Spanish Johnny" and "L'Envoi." ☞

THE DYNAMICS OF AMERICAN POETRY — XI

by Alice Hunt Bartlett

Willa Sibert Cather gives us from her own knowledge of American life, and we may depend on her pictures, in which we find a Virginia background and a father who exhibited pioneer blood and crossed the Alleghennies and the Mississippi Valley to settle in the West, and on a ranch in Nebraska, when Miss Cather was but nine. From such neighbours as the little girl found in the sparsely settled country, Scandinavians, Russians and Bohemian farmers, she must have made her first world contacts.

The nearest school was at Red Cloud, and there she received her only schooling until she entered the State University and graduated at nineteen, going at once to Pittsburgh, where she was employed on the *Pittsburgh Leader* as telegraph editor and dramatic critic. On this paper she had her first experience in writing, and shortly after published her first book of verse, *April Twilights* (Badger, Boston, 1903), a slim book of poetry filled with her woods in winter, white birches, evening songs and laments, legends and taverns and hawthorne trees, the night express and rose time. . . .

Miss Cather writes me:

"I am afraid you will have a hard time proving that I have been an 'effective force in American poetry.' I do not take myself seriously as a poet. However, since you ask me which ones of my poems I prefer, I will tell you some of them. 'A Likeness,' 'A Silver Cup,' 'Going Home,' and 'Macon Prairie,' I think are the best ones. I believe 'Spanish Johnny' is most popular."

The Poetry Review 16 (1925).

1927: LINCOLN

Willa Cather, as she recalls here, was first published in the Nebraska State Journal. *Her introduction to the craft of journalism and her first real employment came from the* Journal. *She always remembered that paper with a certain fondness and esteem.*

Cather had become friends with the Gere family soon after entering the university. She was devoted to Charles Gere (1838–1904), the publisher of the Journal, *and was greatly saddened by his sudden death. One of her later characters, Godfrey St. Peter, in* The Professor's House, *undoubtedly owes his fine hands to Cather's memory of Mr. Gere. She was also a close friend and correspondent of Mrs. Gere and her three daughters—Mariel, Frances, and Ellen—throughout her life.*

Will Owen Jones (1862–1928) was another long-time friend and correspondent. Jones had graduated from the University of Nebraska in 1886, becoming the city editor of the Journal *shortly thereafter. He was promoted to managing editor in 1892, just before Cather began working for the paper, and held that position for the rest of his life. He and his wife had one daughter, named Mariel in honor of the eldest Gere daughter.*

Little did Cather realize that this would be one of the last of her many letters to W. O. Jones. Early in 1928, on Sunday morning, January 19, he died while attending services at First Plymouth Congregational Church in Lincoln. ☞

CONGRATULATIONS FROM WILLA CATHER

June 2, 1927

Dear Mr. Jones,

Certainly I wish to send my congratulations to the *Journal* on its sixtieth birthday. I have many pleasant memories connected with it, with the *Journal,* I mean, not with its birthday. You see I still write as badly as ever.

The first time I was ever confronted by myself in print was one Sunday morning (please don't append an editorial note here, stating just how many years ago it was) when I opened the Sunday *Journal* and saw, stretching out through a column or two, an essay on "Some Personal Characteristics of Thomas Carlyle," which Professor Hunt had given you to publish, quite without my knowledge. That was the beginning of many troubles for me. Up to that time I had planned to specialize in science; I thought I would like to study medicine. But what youthful vanity can be unaffected by the sight of itself in print! It had a kind of hypnotic effect. I still vaguely remember that essay, and it was a splendid example of the kind of writing I most dislike; very florid and full of high-flown figures of speech, and, if I recall aright, not a single "personal characteristic" of the gentleman was mentioned! I wrote that title at the top of the page, because it was the assigned subject, and then poured out, as best I could the feeling that a fervid reading of *The French Revolution* and *Sartor Resartus* had stirred up in me. Come to think of it, that flowery effusion had one merit— it was honest. Florid as it was, it didn't overcolor the pleasure and delightful bitterness that Carlyle can arouse in a very young person. It makes one feel so grown up to be bitter!

A few years after this, I began to write regularly for the Sunday *Journal,* you remember, and I was paid one dollar a column—which was certainly quite all my high-stepping rhetoric was worth. Those out-pourings were pretty dreadful, but I feel indebted to the managing editor of that time that he let me step as high as I wished. It was rather hard on his readers, perhaps, but it was good for me, because it enabled me to riot in fine writing until I got to hate it, and began slowly to recover. I remember that sometimes a bright twinkle in Mr. Gere's fine eyes used to make me feel a little distrustful of my rhetorical magnificence. He never corrected me, he was much too wise for that; he knew that you can't hurry nature. But I think his kindness, his easy wit, the ease and charm of his personality, helped me all the time. When he was listening, with such lively sympathy and understanding, to one's youthful troubles, he would sometimes sit stroking his dark beard with his hand. No one who ever saw Mr. Gere's hands could ever forget them, surely. Even in those days, when I was sitting in his library, it more than once came over me that if one could ever write anything that was like Mr. Gere's hands in character it would be the greatest happiness that could befall one. They were dark and sinewy and so much alive; in a whole worldfull of hands I've not seen any others that seemed to me to have such a singular elegance. None in the least like them, indeed. You see, even very stupid young people addicted to cheap rhetoric are yet capable of perceiving fineness, of feeling it very poignantly. I was very fortunate in my first editor. He let me alone, knowing that I must work out my own salvation; and he was himself all that I was not and that I most admired. Isn't it too bad that after we are much older, and a little wiser, we cannot go back to those few vivid persons of our early youth and tell them how they have always remained with us, how much pleasure their fine personalities gave us, and give us to this very day. But, after all, it's a good fortune to have Mr. Gere alive in one's memory—not one but a thousand characteristic pictures of him, and I congratulate the *Nebraska State*

Journal and myself that we both had such an editor in our early activities.

You told me in your letter, dear editor, that you did not wish me to make yourself the subject of my letter, but I am sure you will have no objection to my recalling Mr. Gere to the many friends who felt his quality as much or more than I.

With pleasant memories of the past and good wishes for the future of the *Nebraska State Journal,* I am most cordially yours,

    Willa Cather   *NSJ,* 24 July 1927.

1927: RED CLOUD

The Brodstone Memorial Hospital in Superior was built in 1927 by Lady Vestey, the former Evelyn Brodstone, in memory of her mother, Matilda Emelia Larson Brodstone. She donated much of her hometown during her remarkable lifetime (see Interviews, ''1928: Superior'').

   Cather's childhood friends, the Miner girls, had introduced her to the Brodstone family, and when the hospital cornerstone was to be laid, the request for Cather to write the inscription was channeled by Mary Miner Creighton.

   The style and form of the letter make it obvious that Cather never intended for it to be read at the ceremonies — let alone published in the local newspaper. However, the personal tone and genuinely affectionate remarks make it a highly revealing insight into the author's personal relations. ☞

MISS CATHER WRITES INSCRIPTION FOR STONE

The corner stone of the new Brodstone memorial hospital at Superior was laid last Sunday with appropriate exercises. The event was of interest to Red Cloud people for two reasons. The Brodstone family are known by a number here, and the inscription on the corner stone was designed by Miss Willa Cather.

During the exercises the following letter, written by Miss Cather to Mrs. E. A. Creighton of Red Cloud, was read by Mr. Frank Stubbs of Superior:

Jaffrey, N. H.
Sept. 17, 1927

My Dear Mary:

    Why surely, I'll be glad to do it, for you, for Evelyn, and most of all, for

Mrs. Brodstone. But I wonder what kind of inscription is wanted? There are so many kinds! I should think it ought to tell something true about Mrs. Brodstone, something that was like her—that we remember her by. Can't you give me some hints, tell me some of the things that, in talking it over, you and Carrie have said ought to be mentioned?

I got your letter only yesterday, and just at a first flash I put down some lines that seemed like the memory of Mrs. Brodstone that came by in my mind. An inscription really has to be a little stiff to have dignity—can't be flowery, or very wordy. I suppose the first part of the tablet, the first lines, will be a statement of gift, and the name of the hospital, will they not? I mean something like this:—

> The Brodstone Memorial Hospital
> Given to the City of Superior by
> Evelyn, Lady Vesty, in loving
> memory of her mother,
> —— —— Brodstone,
> who was born in (——) 18—,
> and died in Superior, Nov. 19—.

What I mean, Mary, is that this formal part would be arranged by Evelyn, or her secretary, or the Board, wouldn't it? And you want me to come in with a personal note, just after. Am I right?

Well, the lines that flash into my mind as being really like Mrs. Brodstone, as I knew her, are something like this:

> She brought across the seas
> a high courage,
> a warm heart,
> a rich relish of life,
>
> and a hand skilled and untiring in those domestic arts that
> give richness and beauty and reality to daily living.
>
> In later life she travelled far,
> but her heart was here, and all her
> journeys brought her home.

The second paragraph, "In later life, etc.," seems to hint of the later years of her life which were so different from the earlier part of it and which never changed her in the least, except to make her sounder and more seasoned than ever. Of course Mrs. Brodstone was many things not mentioned above; she was, when I first knew her, so eminently sound and seasoned; but an inscription ought to hint at the most characteristic qualities, and to me the fine thing about Mrs. Brodstone was the way she could make flowers grow and gardens grow, and the way she could cook gorgeous food and do things with her hands, and the hearty way in which she accepted life.

Now maybe some special sort of inscription is wanted, laying stress on certain things. If so, you'll have to give me the requisite information, and I'll do the best I can.

With love always,
Willa   *Red Cloud Chief,* 20 October 1927.

1929: OMAHA

Harvey E. Newbranch (1875–1959) had been a friend of Willa Cather's since her days at the University of Nebraska. He, too, was an alumnus, having graduated in 1896. Iowa-born, he worked briefly on the weekly Arbor State *in Wymore, Nebraska, before entering the university. He joined the staff of the* Omaha World-Herald *in 1898 as a reporter and went on to be a political writer, the telegraph editor, and the night editor; in 1905, he was made associate editor with responsibility for the editorial page. In 1910 he became editor and in 1944 editor-in-chief. His editorial, "The Law and the Jungle," written in 1919 following the Omaha Courthouse Riots, won him a Pulitzer Prize for that year. Another editorial, "God Hates a Coward" (1949), received a special Freedoms Foundation Award.*

Newbranch followed Cather's career with interest (see Speeches, "1921: Nebraska"). The following letter by Cather was published in the Diamond Jubilee edition of the World-Herald *on 27 October 1929 and was reprinted in the* Red Cloud Chief *and William M. Curtin's* The World and the Parish. ☞

"WILLA CATHER MOURNS OLD OPERA HOUSE"

Dear Mr. Newbranch: It's a newspaper's business, is it not, to insist that everything is much better than it used to be? All the same, we never gain anything without losing something — not even in Nebraska. When I go about among little Nebraska towns (and the little towns, not the big cities, are the people), the thing I miss most is the opera house. No number of filling stations or moving picture theatres can console me for the loss of the opera house. To be sure, the opera house was dark for most of the year, but that made its events only the more exciting. Half a dozen times during each winter—in the larger towns much oftener—a traveling stock company settled down at the local hotel and thrilled and entertained us for a week.

That was a wonderful week for the children. The excitement began when the advance man came to town and posted the bills on the side of a barn, on the lumberyard fence, in the "plate glass" windows of drug stores and grocery stores. My playmates and I used to stand for an hour after school, studying every word of those posters: the names of the plays and the nights on which each would be given. After we had decided which were the most necessary to us, then there was always the question of how far we could prevail upon our parents. Would they let us go every other night, or only on the opening and closing nights? None of us ever got to go every night, unless we had a father who owned stock in the opera house itself.

If the company arrived on the night train, when we were not at school, my chums and I always walked a good half mile to the depot (I believe you call it "station" now) to see that train come in. Sometimes we pulled younger brothers or sisters along on a sled. We found it delightful to watch a theatrical company alight, pace the platform while their baggage was being sorted, and then drive off—the men in the hotel bus, the women in the "hack." If by any chance one of the show ladies carried a little dog with a blanket on, that simply doubled our pleasure. Our next concern was to invent some plausible pretext, some errand that would take us to the hotel. Several of my dearest playmates had perpetual entry to the hotel because they were favorites of the very unusual and interesting woman who owned it. But I, alas, had no such useful connection; so I never saw the leading lady breakfasting languidly at nine. Indeed, I never dared go near the hotel while the theatrical people were there—I suppose because I wanted to go so much.

How good some of those old traveling companies were, and how honestly they did their work and tried to put on a creditable performance. There was the Andrews Opera Company, for example; they usually had a good voice or two among them, a small orchestra and a painstaking conductor, who was also the pianist. What good luck for a country child to hear those tuneful old operas sung by people who were doing their best: *The Bohemian Girl, The Chimes of Normandy, Martha, The Mikado*. Nothing takes hold of a child like living people.

We got the old plays in the same day [way?], done by living people, and often by people who were quite in earnest. *My Partner, The Corsican Brothers, Ingomar, Damon and Pythias, The Count of Monte Cristo.*

I know that today I would rather hear James O'Neill, or even Frank Lindon, play *The Count of Monte Cristo* than see any moving picture, except three or four in which Charlie Chaplin is the whole thing. My preference would have been the same, though even stronger, when I was a child. Moving pictures may be very entertaining and amusing, and they may be, as they often claim to be, instructive; but what child ever cried at the movies, as we used to at *East Lynne* or *The Two Orphans?*

That is the heart of the matter; only living people can make us feel. Pictures of them, no matter how dazzling, do not make us feel anything more than interest or curiosity or astonishment. The "pity and terror" which the drama, even it its crudest form, can awaken in young people, is not to be found in the movies. Only a living human being, in some sort of rapport with us, speaking the lines, can make us forget who we are and where we are, can make us (especially children) actually live in the story that is going on before us, can make the dangers of that heroine and the desperation of that hero much more important to us, for the time much dearer to us, than our own lives.

That, after all, was the old glory of the drama in its great days; that is why its power was more searching than that of printed books or paintings because a story of human experience was given to us alive, given to us, not only by voice and attitude, but by all those unnamed ways in which an animal of any species makes known its terror or misery to other animals of its kind. And all the old-fashioned actors, even the poor ones, did "enter into the spirit" of their parts; it was the pleasure they got from this illusion that made them wish to be actors, despite the hardships of that profession. The extent to which they could enter into this illusion, much more than any physical attributes, measured their goodness or badness as actors. We hear the drama termed a thing in three dimensions; but it is really a thing in four dimensions, since it has two imaginative fires behind it, the playwright's and the actor's.

I am not lamenting the advent of the "screen drama" (there is a great deal to be said in its favor), but I do regret that it has put an end to the old-fashioned road companies which used to tour about in country towns and "cities of the second class." The "movie" and the play are two very different things; one is a play, and the other is a picture of a play. A movie, well done, may be very good indeed, may even appeal to what is called the artistic sense; but to the emotions, the deep feelings, never!

Never, that is, excepting Charlie Chaplin at his best—and his best—I have noticed, really gets through to very few people. Not to his enormous audience, but to actors and to people of great experience in the real drama. They admire and marvel.

I go to the picture shows in the little towns I know, and I watch the audience, especially the children. I see easy, careless attention, amusement, occasionally a curiosity that amounts to mild excitement; but never that breathless, rapt attention and deep feeling that the old barnstorming companies were able to command. It was not only the "sob stuff" that we took hard; it was everything. When old Frank Lindon in a frilled shirt and a velvet coat blazing with diamonds, stood in the drawing room of Mme. Danglars' and revealed his identity to Mme. de Morcerf, his faithless Mercedes, when she cowered and made excuses, and he took out a jeweled snuff box with a much powdered hand, raised his eyebrows, permitted his lip to curl, and said softly and bitterly, "A fidelity of six months!" then we children were not in the opera house in Red Cloud we were in Mme. Danglars' salon in Paris, in the middle of lives so very different from our own. Living people were making us feel things, and it is through the feelings, not at all through the eye, that one's imagination is fired.

Pictures of plots, unattended by the voice from the machine (which seems to me much worse than no voice), a rapid flow of scene and pageant, make a fine kind of "entertainment" and are an ideal diversion for the tired business man. But I am sorry that the old opera houses in the prairie towns are dark, because they really did give a deeper thrill, at least to children. It did us good to weep at *East Lynne,* even if the actress was fairly bad and the play absurd. Children have about a hundred years of unlived life wound up in them, and they want to be living some of it. Only real people speaking the lines can give us that feeling of living along with them, of participating in their existence. The poorest of the old road companies were at least made up of people who wanted to be actors and tried to be—that alone goes a long way. The very poorest of all were the *Uncle Tom's Cabin* companies, but even they had living bloodhounds. How the barking of these dogs behind the scenes used to make us catch our breath! That alone was worth the price of admission, as the star used to say, when he came before the curtain.

Very cordially yours,
Willa Cather

OW-H, 27 October 1929.

1935: HASTINGS

One of the Cather family's oldest and dearest friends was the Right Reverend George Allen Beecher (1868–1951), the second (and last) Bishop of Western Nebraska from 1910 to 1943. He had met and become friends with the family shortly after his consecration and confirmed Cather's brother, James, and his wife, Ethel, in 1920. In December 1922, Bishop Beecher served as master of ceremonies at the celebration of her parents' Golden Wedding Anniversary, and on December 27 of that year he confirmed Cather and her parents into the Episcopal Church. She corresponded with him regularly and always invited him to dine with her when he was in New York City (see George Allen Beecher Collection, NSHS).

When Beecher observed the Silver Anniversary of his consecration, Carrie Miner Sherwood wrote Cather asking her to send a letter of congratulations, since she could not be present. The letter that follows was the formal response to that request, sent to the Dean of St. Mark's Pro-Cathedral, the Very Reverend Francis R. Lee, and later printed in the Hastings Daily Tribune. *Cather also wrote a personal letter to Carrie telling her that the formal letter did not say it all. She wished to be able to write the bishop a personal note to express her admiration. She knew that Carrie and Elsie both knew how much she loved him and how proud she was of him. She said she had met a great many bishops in her day, but none of them looked the part and filled the part as her own Bishop Beecher. She wished that Carrie or Elsie would tell him exactly how she felt, for she was always rather shy about communicating her admiration to those people she admired (ALS to Carrie Miner Sherwood, 25 November 1935, WCPM).*

Six years later, when Bishop Beecher's new cathedral was consecrated in Hastings, Cather was again unable to be present. She wrote the bishop of her extreme regret. She said that she wished she could be in Hastings in the lovely new cathedral on St. Andrew's Day to join in the service and to kneel in joyful thanksgiving to heaven for her own bishop. She would give thanks for all that the bishop meant to her and both her parents and so many of her friends (ALS to George A. Beecher, 25 November 1941, NSHS).

Until her death Cather was to remain a loyal friend and regular correspondent with Bishop Beecher. The last letter she wrote to him was less than five weeks before her death. On All Soul's Day, 2 November 1947, Bishop Beecher conducted the memorial service for Willa Cather at Grace Church in Red Cloud. ☞

MISS CATHER WRITES

Among the many messages received by the committee in charge of the observance of Bishop George Allen Beecher's twenty-fifth year in the Episcopate was one from Miss Willa Cather, the author.

Miss Cather and Bishop Beecher have been friends for many years. Her letter in full:

In response to your kind invitation, may I send through you my greetings and grateful remembrances to the bishop and Mrs. Beecher on the twenty-fifth anniversary of his consecration as bishop? I wish with all my heart that I could be in Hastings on the thirtieth of November.

I know that some of my friends from Red Cloud will be there on that day, for our bishop is greatly beloved in my home town. He has shared so many joys and sorrows with us there that he has become a part of the life of the town, quite as if he lived there always.

When I reflect that he certainly means as much to all the congregations in his diocese, then I think what a glorious thing it is to touch the lives of so many people. I can remember many scenes at which Bishop Beecher was present, and to every one of them, ecclesiastical or social, he added vitality and warmth and distinction.

He has the power of making one feel that the present service, the present moment, is rich and precious; that life is full of splendid realizations which have nothing to do with material gains or losses. I have never spent an hour in his company without feeling the happier for it, and these meetings, sometimes years apart, have left such vivid pictures in my memory that I often turn to them.

Again and again I have seen Bishop Beecher make the simplest church service a memorable occasion. That is why I am so sorry to miss the anniversary services in Hastings on the thirtieth; I know that I am missing a ceremony which would give me deep satisfaction. On that day my thoughts will be with the Bishop and Mrs. Beecher and with the friends from Red Cloud who will be enjoying the anniversary services in my stead.

Willa Cather

Hastings Daily Tribune, 2 December 1935.

1939–40: SCHENECTADY

The College English Association was formed in 1939 and soon thereafter began publishing a newsletter, entitled at various times the CEA *Critic, and, more simply, the* News Letter *of the* CEA. *In one of the very early issues, Henry Seidel Canby, a longtime friend of Willa Cather, was prevailed upon to write a short essay about the place of contemporary fiction in the teaching of literature. Following Canby's contribution, Cather was also asked to respond to the general topic. Her first reply was printed in the December 1939 issue. The discussion generated so much correspondence and controversy that the following year she was asked to reply again. Her response was to allow a portion of a letter to "a friend" be reprinted. Those four paragraphs, concerning the structure of* The Professor's House, *were reprinted in* On Writing, *but without the preceding letter or any contextual explanation. Incidentally the Mesa Verde was discovered by Richard and Al Wetherill in 1882. Cather misspells the name on other occasions.*

At its inception the News Letter *was published at Union College in Schenectady, New York. In 1970, the publication split into the* CEA *Critic and the* CEA *Forum.* ☞

CONTEMPORARY LIT. AGAIN

My dear Editor:

Like Mr. Canby, I do not believe in courses in contemporary literature, and for just the reasons which he advances, namely:

> I think that the material is still too untested for satisfactory teaching, and that the very large majority of teachers are not sufficiently in the atmosphere of the writing world to interpret and discriminate in any definite way.

But I am afraid you will not think me very obliging if I merely quote Mr. Canby—you will think I am taking a very easy way of replying to your question.

I have also other reasons. In the first place, most American boys are hurried into active life so early, that even the few who have the possibility of developing literary taste have scarcely time to do so. Unless they read the great English classics in high school and in college, they never find time to read them. And that means that in their maturity they have no background. By "classics" I certainly do not mean rather special things like the works of Sir Thomas Browne or De Quincy, but the great books that still influence the life and thought and standards of the English speaking peoples. Within the last five years, for example, an amazing number of quotations from Shakespeare's plays and sonnets have been pertinently used in the editorial columns of the New York *Times* and the New York *Herald-Tribune*. In each case the editor used them not to exhibit his knowledge, but to drive home his point. I think we should all, in our school days, be given a chance at Shakespeare, Milton, Fielding, Jane Austen—coming down as late as Thackeray, George Eliot, George Meredith, and Thomas Hardy. I don't mean that *Macbeth* or *The Egoist* or *Henry Esmond* can be "taught" at all. I mean that the students can be "exposed," so to speak, to the classics. If the germ "takes," even in very few, it will develop, and give them a great deal of pleasure in life. And those who do not catch the infection will certainly not be at all harmed.

As regards contemporary literature, the work of living authors, I think young people should be allowed to discover for themselves what they like. For young people, half the pleasure of reading new books is in finding them out for themselves. If a boy goes quite wild about a very silly new book, his teacher can never convince him that it is not good. If he finds a really good one out for himself, it counts with him for a great deal more than if he had been told he must read it. No book can be called a "classic" until it is a hundred years old, surely. How many so-called "classics" have you seen die in your own lifetime, Mr. Johnson? A fine taste for literature is largely a matter of the ear, and is as rare as absolute pitch in music. But a great many boys and girls can enjoy a great play like *Julius Caesar* because of its relation to life, and they do get *something* out of the power and beauty of the lines.

While I do not believe that English literature can be "taught" in the sense that Latin can be taught, I know from experience that an instructor who is really steeped in his subject, who loves both literature and life, can, by merely expressing his own honest enthusiasms, or his honest objections, have a great influence on young people. If the English teacher is vain and opinionated, and wishes to astonish his classes by a lot of diagrams and formulae which are supposed to explain to them how *Julius Caesar* was written, and why *Far From the Madding Crowd* is a fine novel, he will prejudice his better students against the subject he teaches, and will immensely reinforce the self-satisfaction of the shallow and conceited ones.

Willa Cather   *News Letter of the CEA*, December 1939.

LITERARY EXPERIMENTATION

(Members of the CEA will recall the discussion started by Mr. Henry Canby and carried on in these columns over the desirability of English courses exclusively devoted to contemporary literature. In the course of that argument it was pointed out that much writing of the moment is experimental, and that the author himself is testing devices and techniques which later may be abandoned.

Miss Willa Cather who has been overburdened by letters from strangers, especially teachers and students, asking her judgment on literary matters, may have had her burden made heavier as a result of her contribution to this argument in last December's "News Letter." Yet she graciously permits us to reprint the following paragraphs from a letter to a friend which will serve to illustrate her own experimental attitude in one of her books. —Ed.)

Let me try to answer your question. When I wrote *The Professor's House,* I wished to try two experiments in form. The first is the device often used by the early French and Spanish novelists; that of inserting the *Nouvelle* into the *Roman.* "Tom Outland's Story" has been published in French and Polish and Dutch, as a short narrative for school children studying English.

But the experiment which interested me was something a little more vague, and was very much akin to the arrangement followed in sonatas in which the academic sonata form was handled somewhat freely. Just before I began the book I had seen, in Paris, an exhibition of old and modern Dutch paintings. In many of them, the scene presented was a living room warmly furnished, or a kitchen full of food and coppers. But in most of the interiors, whether drawing-room or kitchen, there was a square window, open, through which one saw the masts of ships or a stretch of gray sea. The feeling of the sea that one got through those square windows was remarkable, and gave me a sense of the fleets of Dutch ships that ply quietly on all the waters of the globe—to Java, etc.

In my book I tried to make Professor St. Peter's house rather overcrowded and stuffy with new things; American proprieties, clothes, furs, petty ambitions, quivering jealousies—until one got rather stifled. Then I wanted to open the square window and let in the fresh air that blew off the Blue Mesa, and the fine disregard of trivialities which was in Tom Outland's face and in his behaviour.

The above concerned me as a writer only, but the Blue Mesa (the Mesa

Verde) actually was discovered by a young cowpuncher in just this way. The great explorer Nordenkjöld, wrote a scientific book about this discovery, and I myself had the good fortune to her the story of it from a very old man, brother to Dick Wetherell. Dick Wetherell as a young boy forded Mancos River and rode into the Mesa after lost cattle. I followed the real story very closely in Tom Outland's narrative.

Willa Cather   *News Letter of the CEA*, October 1940.

Index